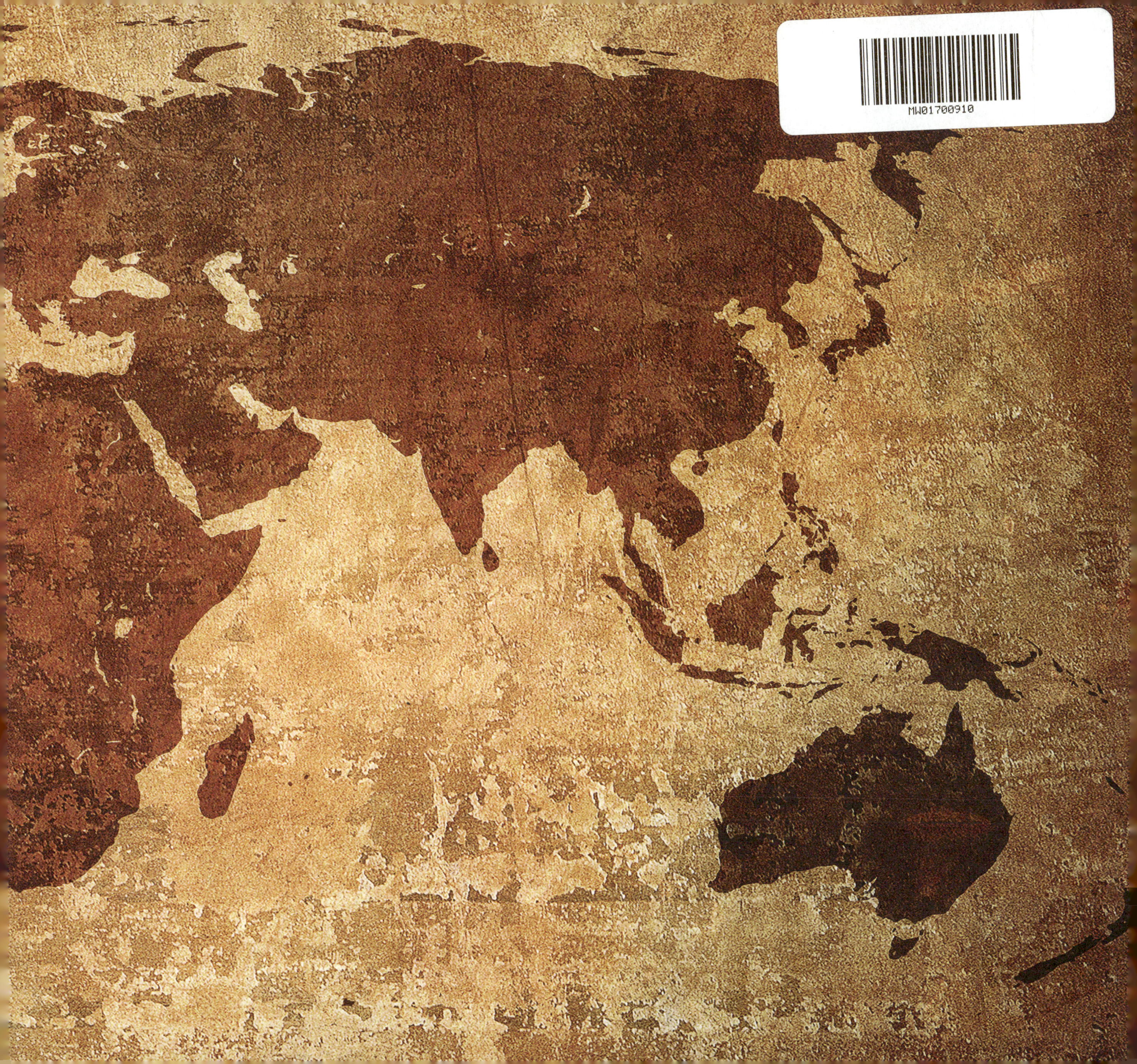

May you remain always

Wild in Spirit!

Michael Powers

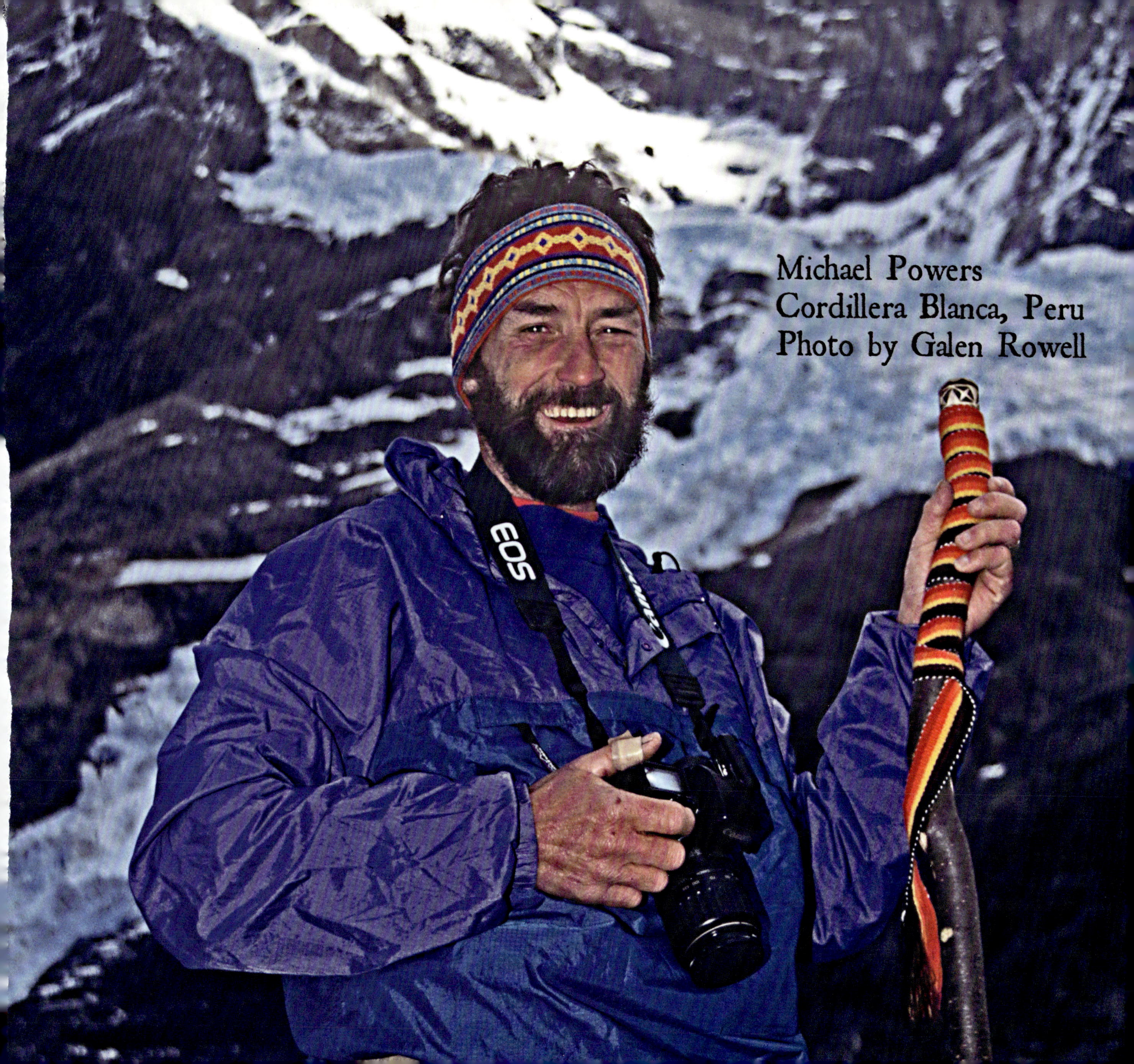

Michael Powers
Cordillera Blanca, Peru
Photo by Galen Rowell

Wild in Spirit

MICHAEL POWERS * OCEAN STUDIO

Photographs and text by Michael Powers
except where otherwise noted

www.oceanstudios.net

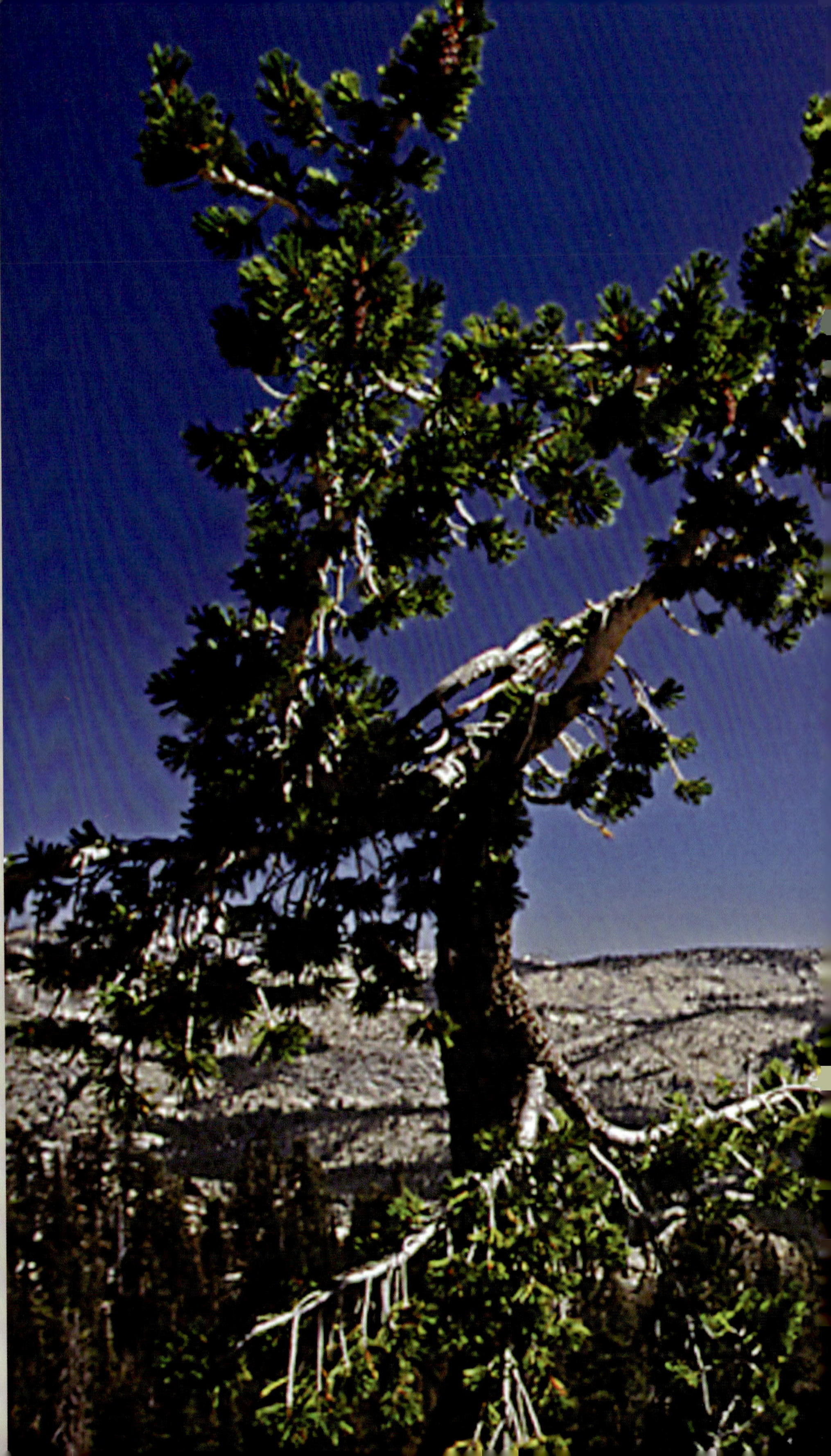

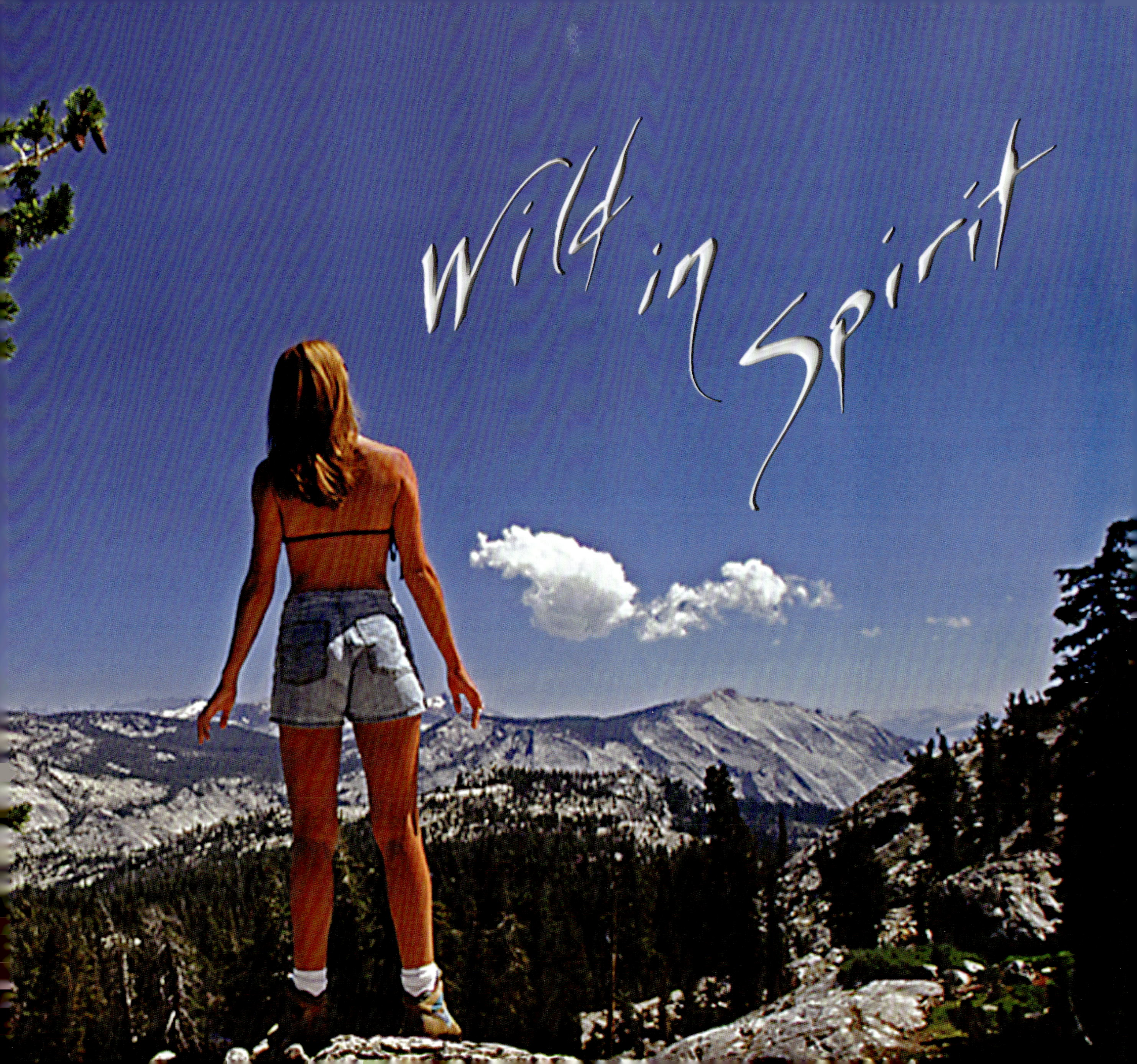
Wild in Spirit

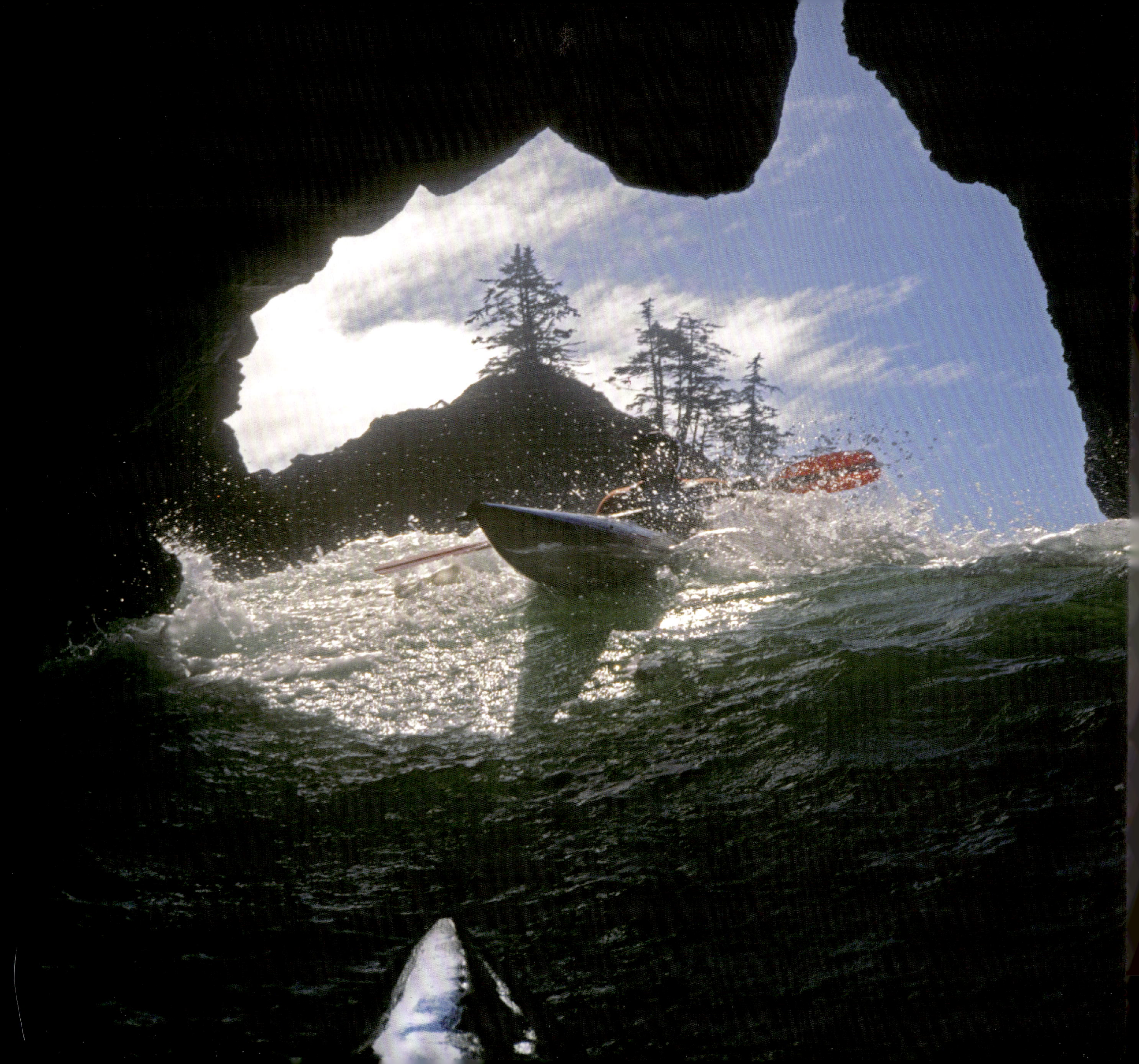

PHOTOGRAPHS AND WORDS OF REDEMPTION FOR THE NATURAL WORLD

Venturing beyond this page could be like taking that final, powerful stroke with a kayak paddle that propels you deep within a mysterious and beautiful sea cave, or those final arduous steps high on a mountainside that lead to the rooftop of the world and vistas never before seen.

Many extraordinary adventures over many years produced the wide spectrum of photography presented in *Wild In Sprit.* Yet it soon became apparent that images alone told only part of the story. Thus began the seeking out and careful listening to expressions of social consequence from many cultures and centuries of time. The inspired utterances of poets, prophets, world leaders, celebrities, visionaries and passionate proponents of mother earth began to accumulate and coalesce into a common theme. Eureka moments began to occur with increasing frequency, each time a quotation and a pinnacle photographic image were joined together and magically became more lucid and persuasive than either one standing alone - what the ancients revered as *conjunctivo*, or sacred marriage. Thus the weaving together of epiphanies and jewels of transcendent wisdom with our most cherished and evocative photographs progressed, and ultimately became a trusted method of retelling the time-tested, universal stories in compelling new ways.

Wild In Spirit bears special homage to the *cantadoras*, the keepers of the old stories, who have kept alive the essential traditions and survival skills for all the centuries of humankind's existence, simply by continuing to pass them down among their people. Another rich source of natural wisdom has been modern day wilderness and adventure travel guides, who by leading urban folks back into intimate communion with the natural world and indigenous cultures have become *de facto* custodians and teachers of ancient beliefs and knowledge that otherwise might be lost forever.

The heartfelt intention of this first major book from Ocean Studio is to fan into flame the spirit of *wildness* still smoldering deep within us all - and thereby nurture in the hearts and minds of readers, a greater understanding and empathy for the natural world. At its best, *Wild In Spirit* will serve as a portal through which we may pass at will to face the challenges, perils, and rewards of living life outdoors, courageously and with great purpose - a state of mind, body and spirit that the Vikings knew as *friluftsliv*, life outside in the free air, beneath the open sky.

— Michael Powers and the Ocean Studio Alliance

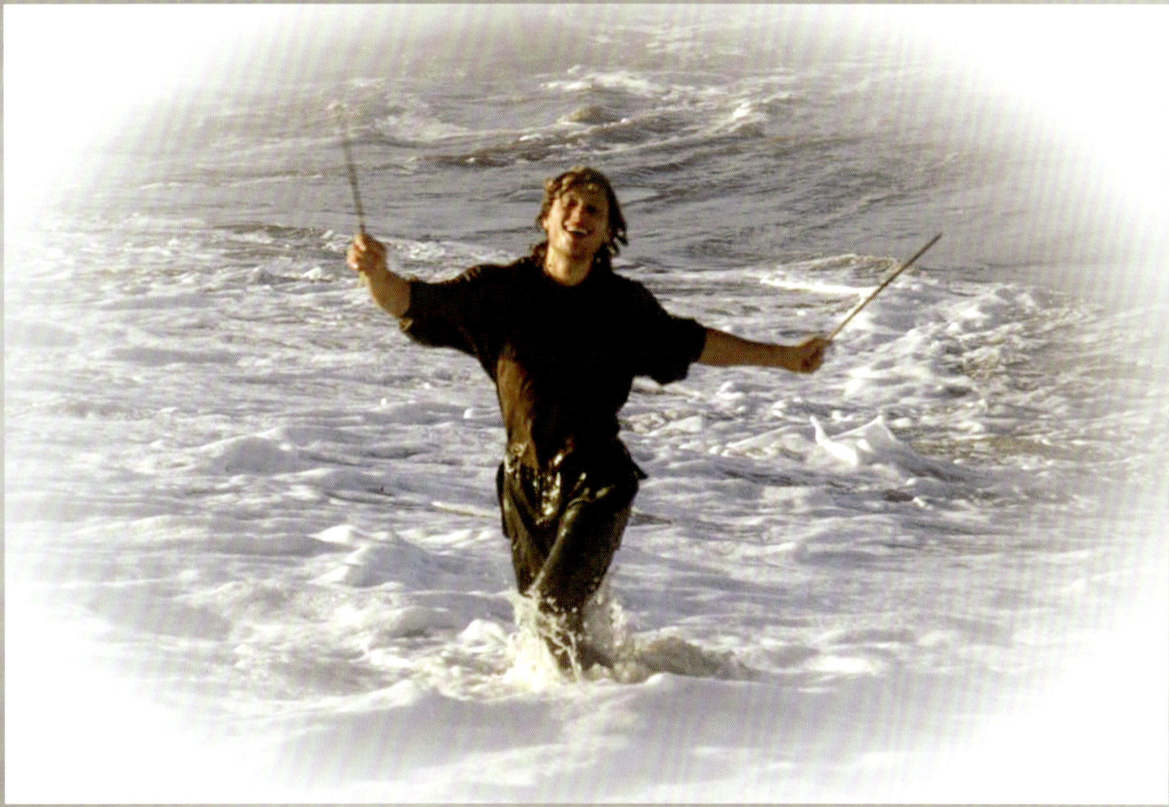

Dedicated to
Misha Dynnikov, Eric Soares and Galen Rowell,
great adventurers all, who have gone ahead to show us the way.

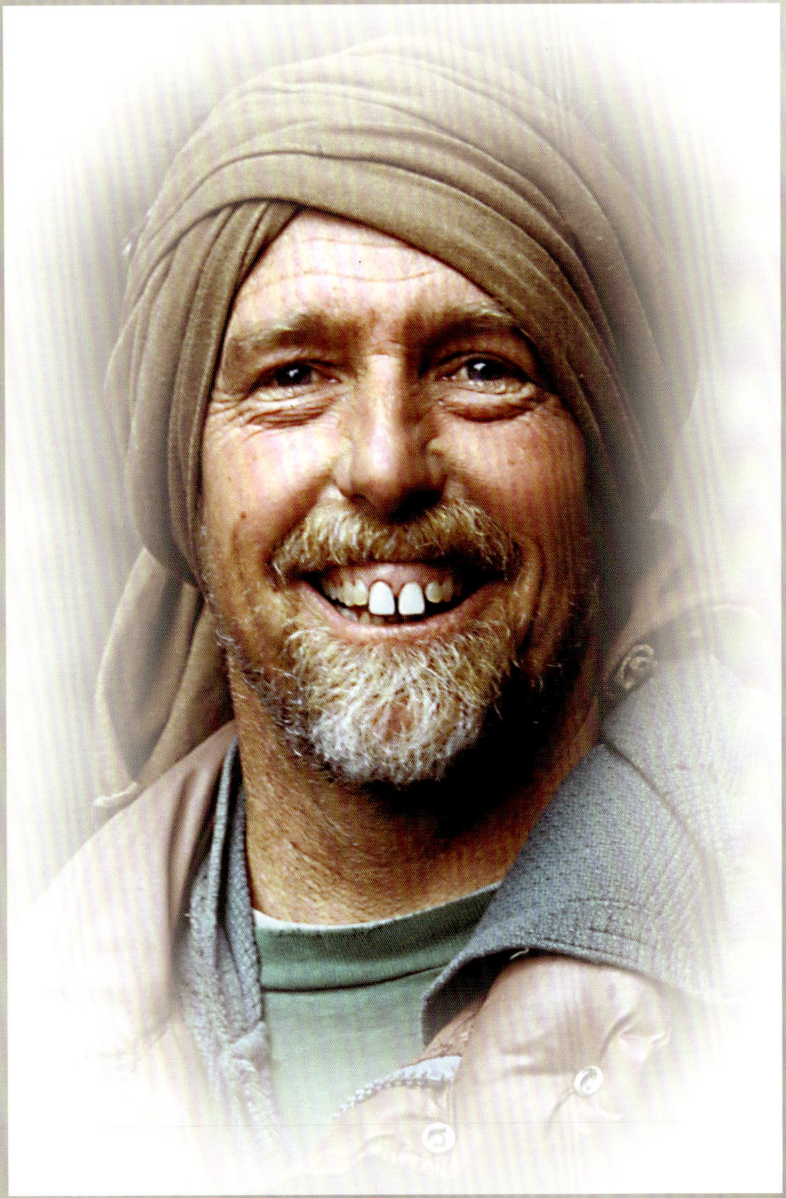
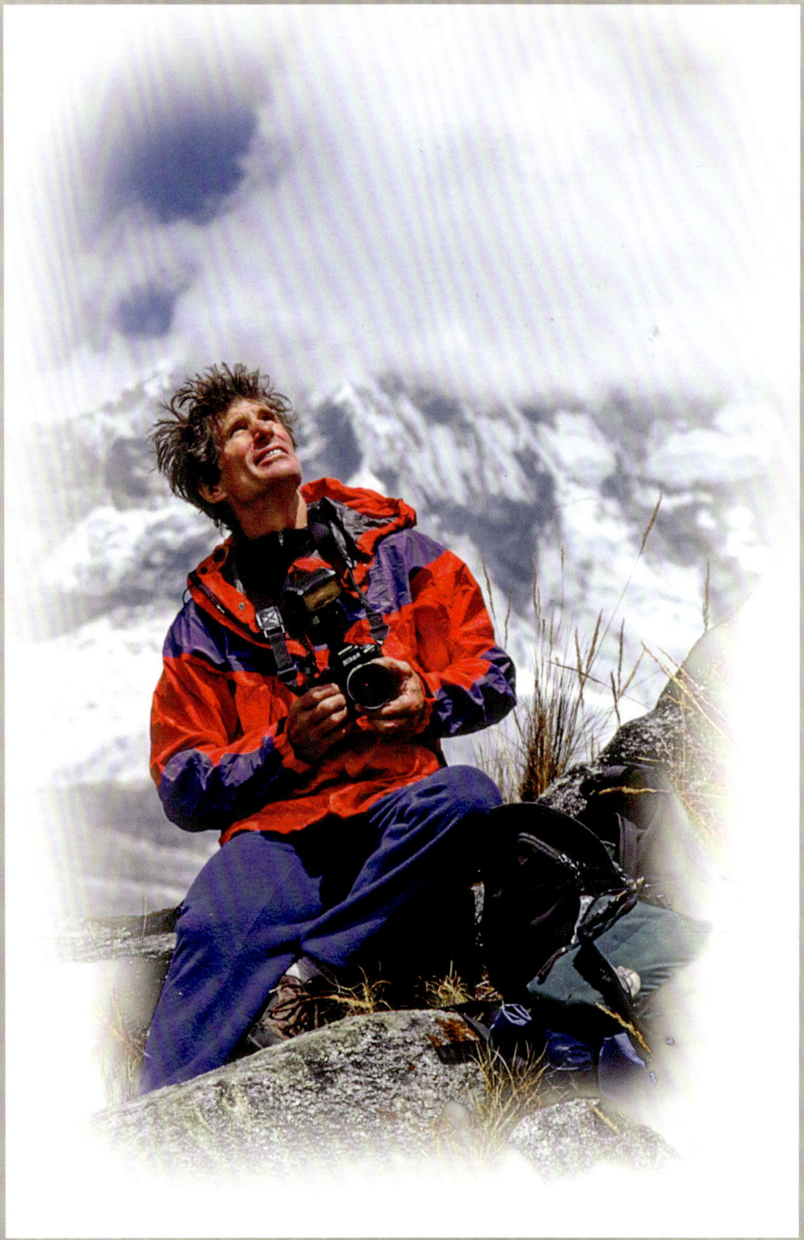

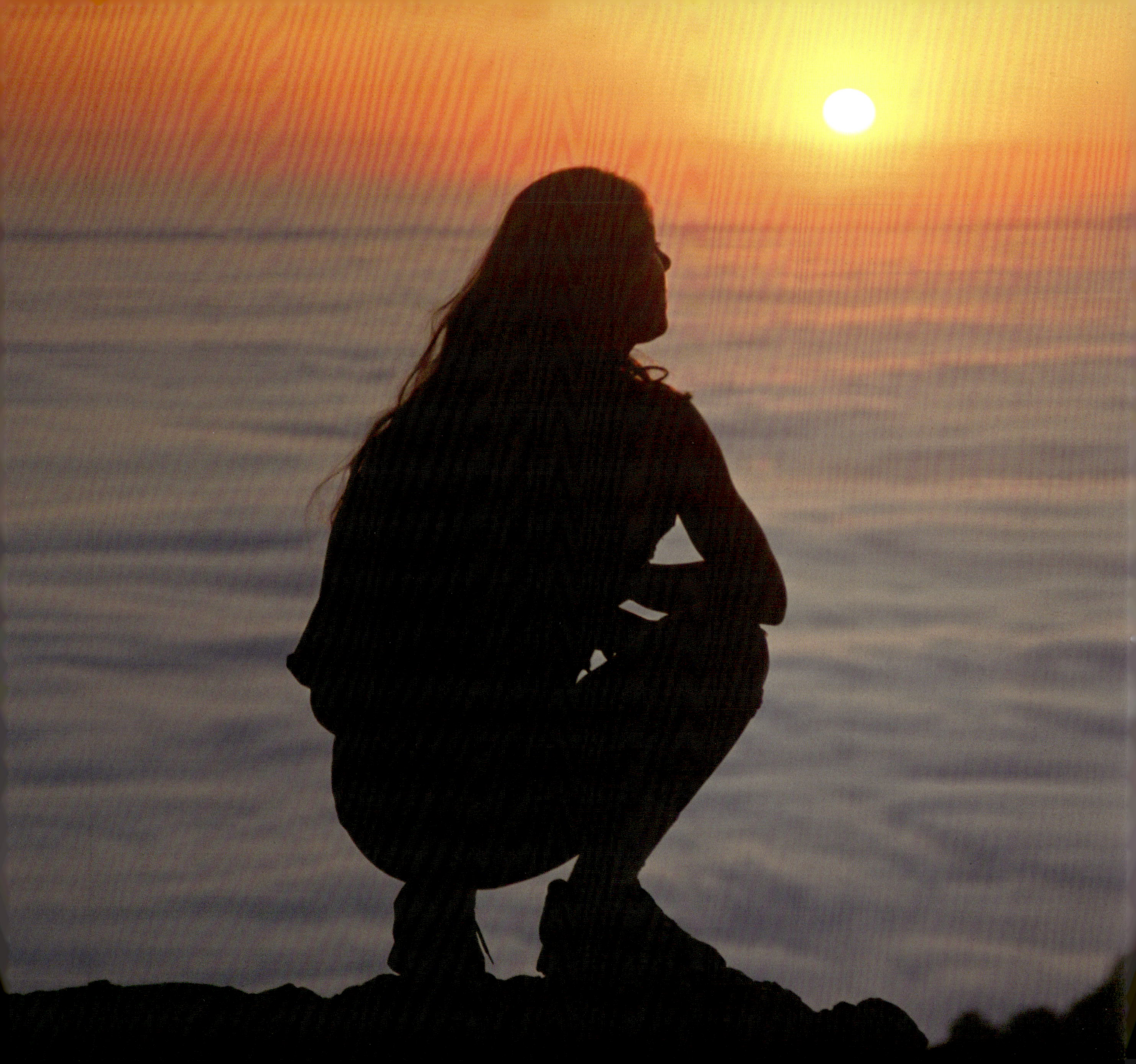

We would like to live as we once did, but history will not permit it.

- John Fitzgerald Kennedy

2

Just as the Coastal Miwok might have done when they gathered at dusk on outlook on the western slope of Mount Tamalpais centuries ago, Nani Venegas sits transfixed by the magic of the sun setting over a cloud-shrouded sea. Nani came to America from Chile with her young son Ivan when she was 22 in search of a new life.

Mt. Tamalpais was a sacred place to the Miwok Indians, although they believed an evil spirit dwelled on the summit and never ventured there.

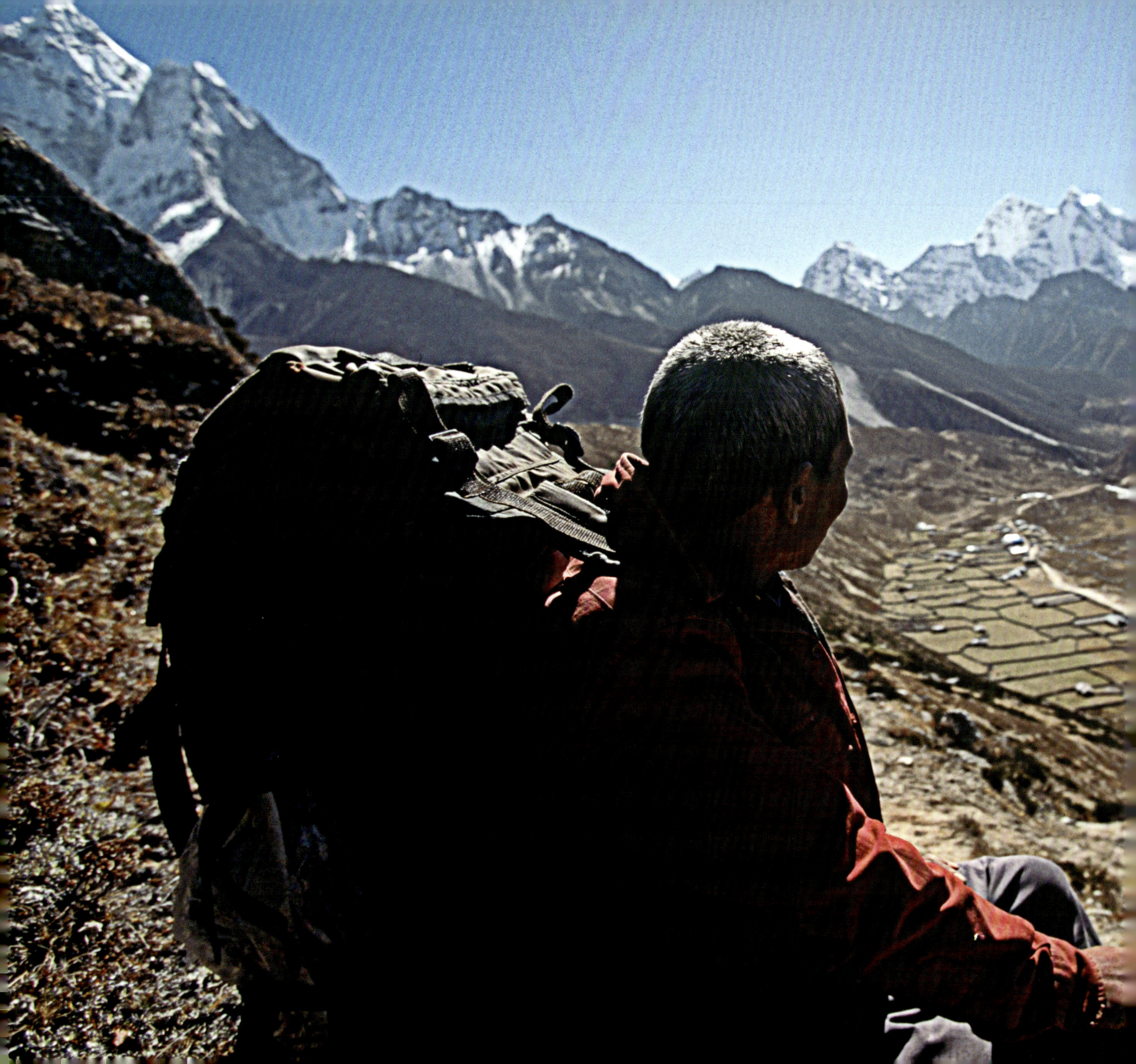

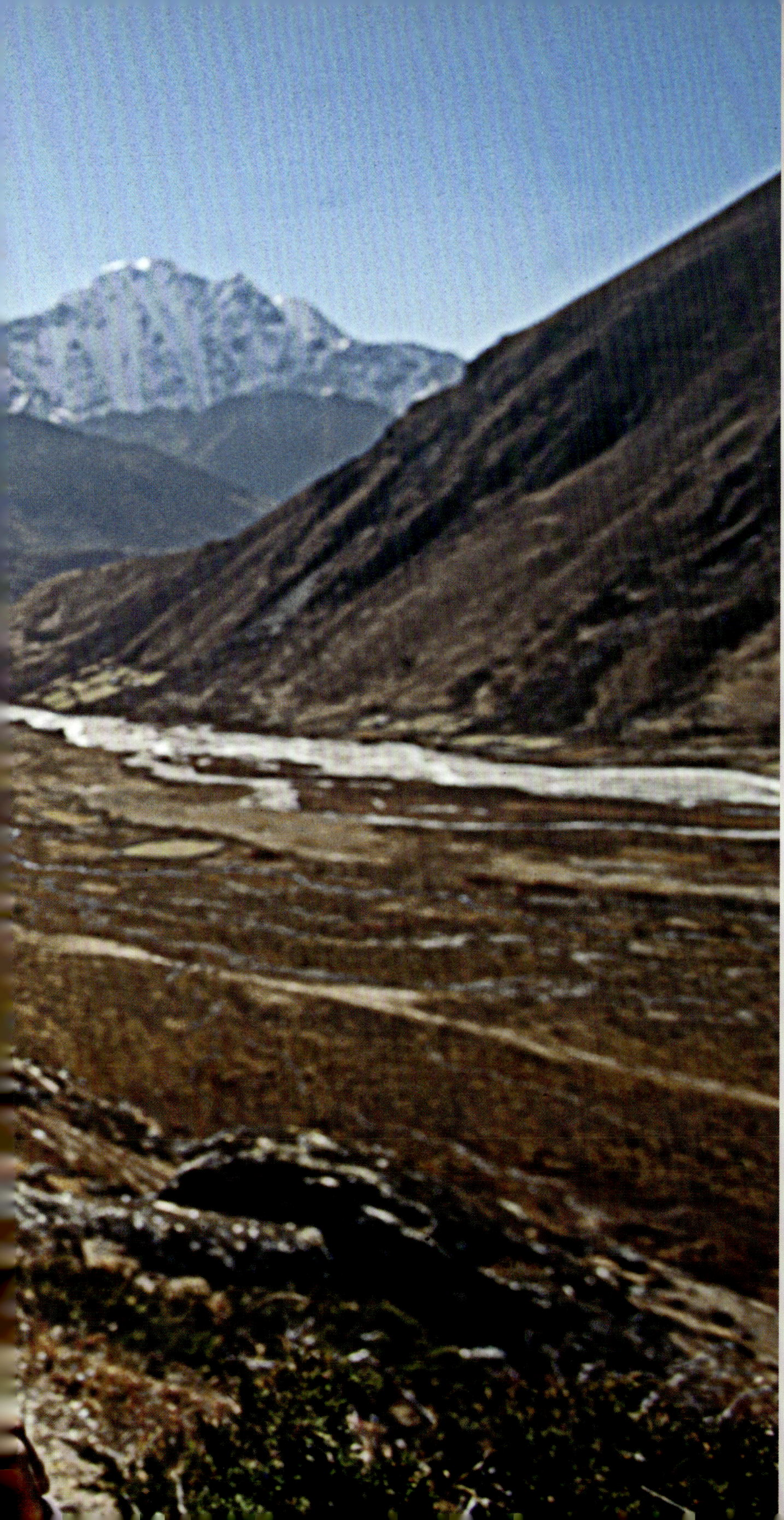

The rains of God's mercy cannot gather on mountaintops of pride, but flow easily into into valleys of humbleness.

- Paramahansa Yogananda

4

Phurtemba was one of the Sherpas guiding a party of trekkers through the Khumbu region of Nepal towards Mt. Everest. He was older than the others and rarely spoke, and when he did his words were few and carefully chosen. Phurtemba seemed to possess a saintly quality. Yet from the offset it was obvious from the beginning that he and the other Sherpas were not a servile people. They worked tirelessly to provide everything necessary for the trekkers' comfort and safety. Even as the group reached higher altitude and the temperature grew bitter cold at night, they greeted their charges cheerfully when they arrived at their tents each morning with hot tea or coffee. The Westerners grew to feel that the Sherpas would risk their lives to save them if an emergency arose. Yet they could also clearly see that the Sherpas were a proud, free people and would never be their servants.

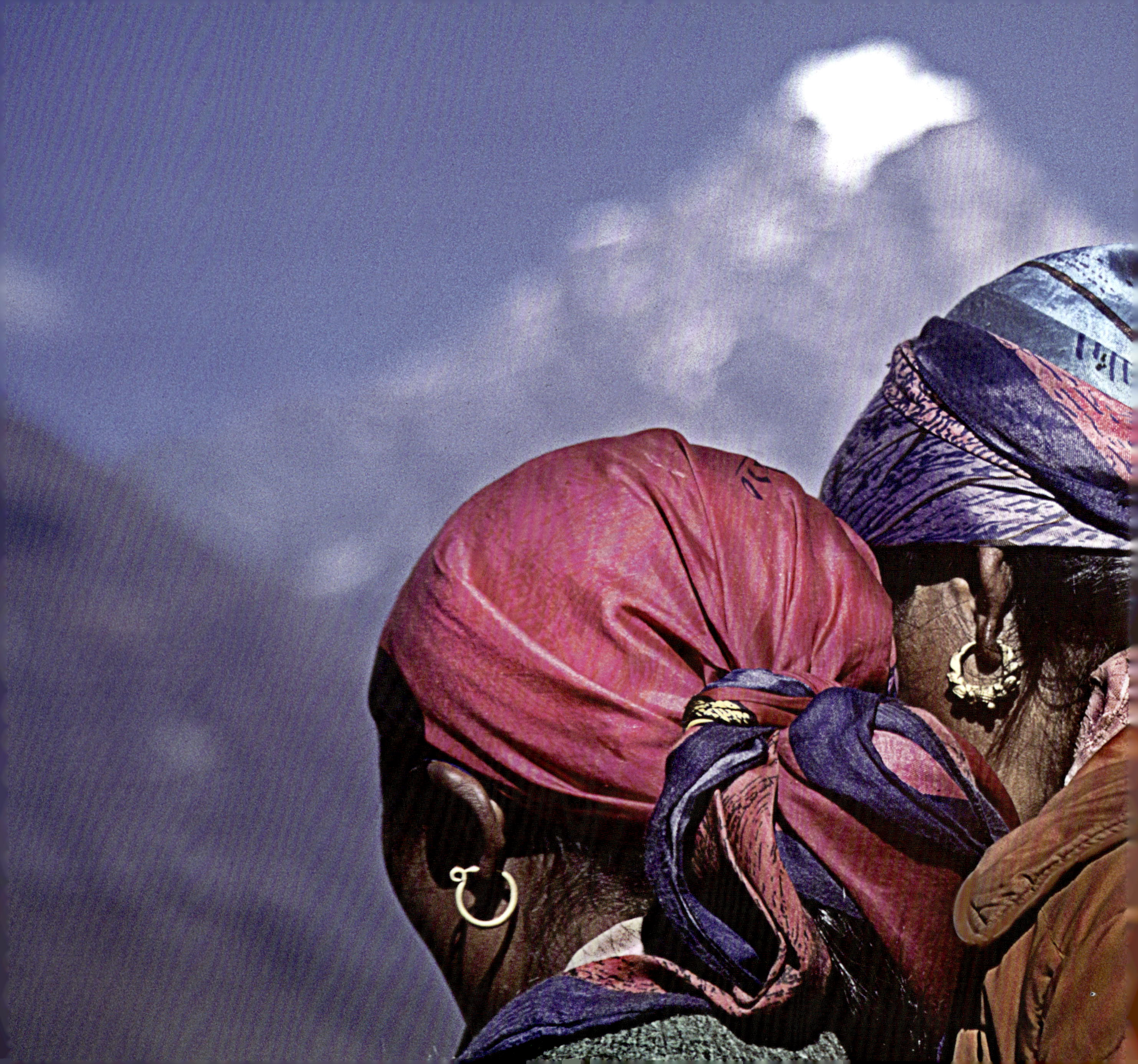

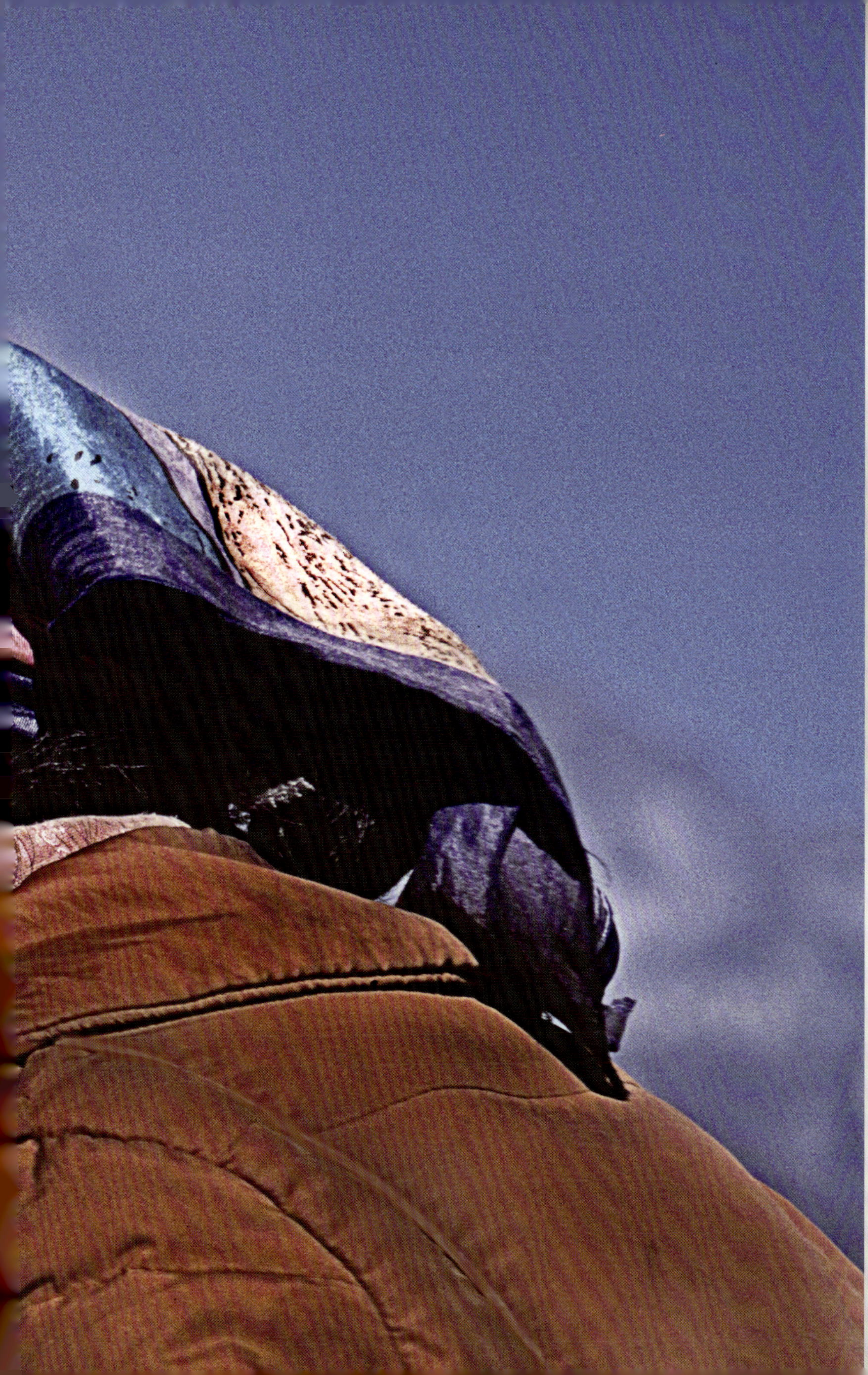

It is my contention that those wisdoms... about learning to live with the landscape, and learning to survive with the landscape are applicable, not just to adventuring, but to our whole way of life.

- author & explorer Jon Turk

Two Sherpa women meet on the trail above Tengboche Monastery in the Khumbu region of eastern Nepal to exchange cordialities. Just like their male counterparts, the Sherpa women are renowned for their skills and endurance at high altitude. Pasang Lhama, the first Sherpa woman to summit Mt. Everest, is a national heroine to the Nepalese people. Along with others in her climbing party, she perished a short time after summiting Everest when a violent storm caught them still high on the mountain.

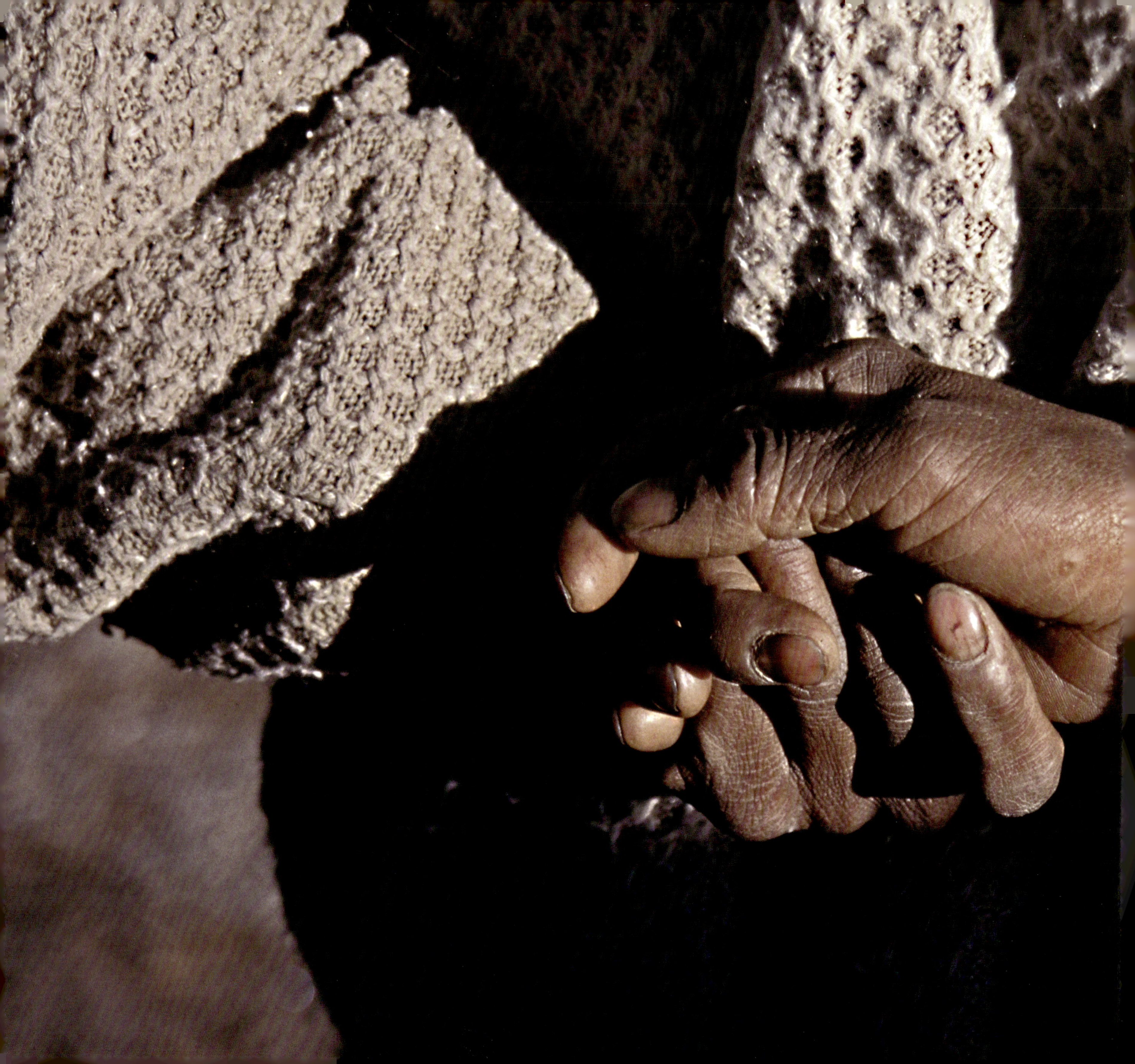

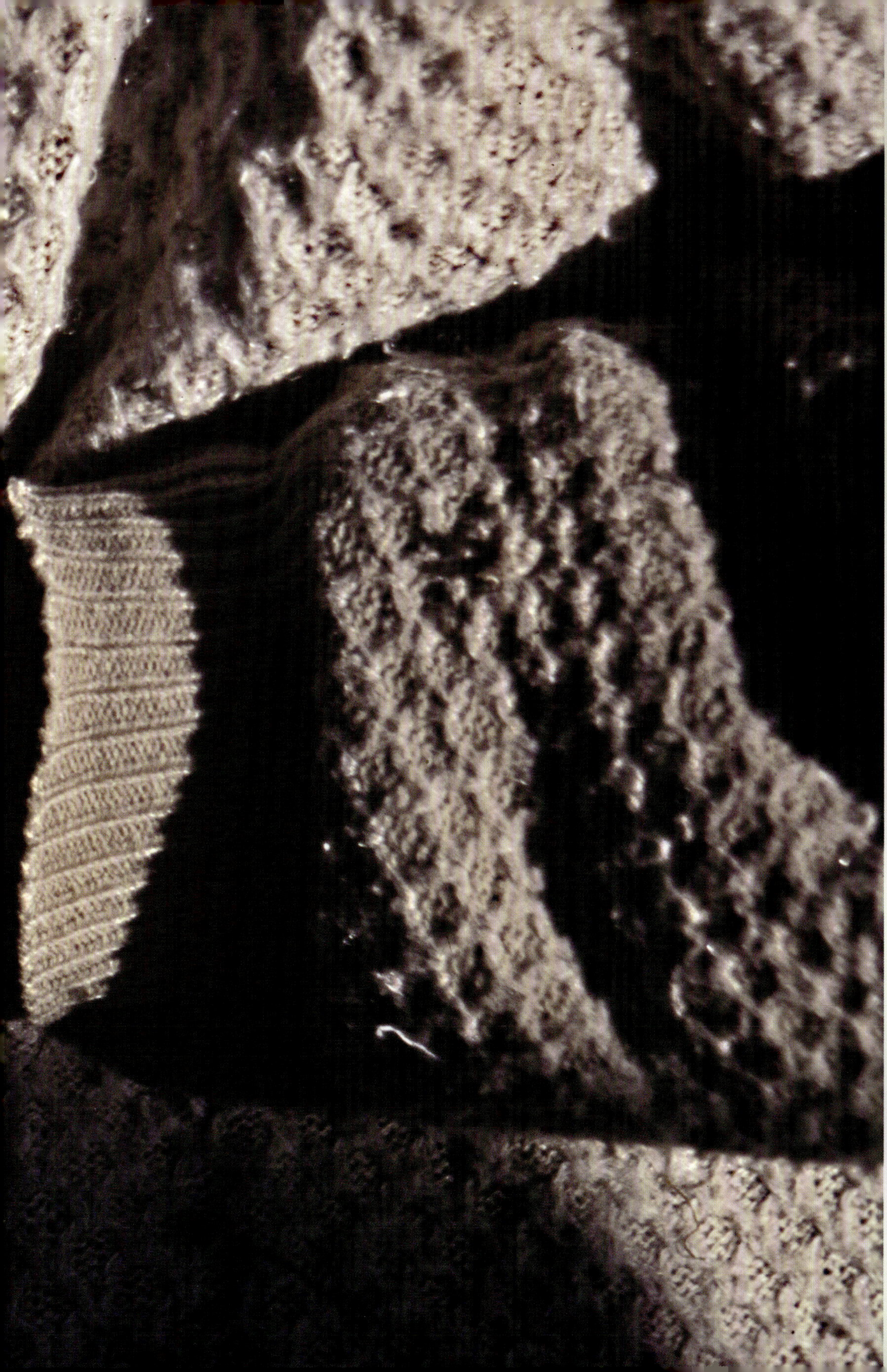

The game is not about becoming somebody, its about becoming nobody.

-Baba Ram Dass

At a Sherpa village high in the precipitous Khumbu region of eastern Nepal, a woman patiently awaits her yak to be loaded for the week-long journey to the ancient marketplace in 11,286' Namche Bazaar.

Of life's two great prizes, beauty and truth, I have found the first in a loving heart and the second in a laborer's hand.

- Kahil Gibran

9

Since time immemorial Tibetan traders have endured perilous crossings over snow-bound Himalayan passes to reach the centuries-old marketplace of Namche Bazaar. The weathered hands of an ancient craftmen tell a poignant story of a lifetime of harsh existence in this high-altitude world. He offers for sale to passing trekkers a little charm box of traditional design that he fashioned from silver and gems gathered from mines in his native Tibet.

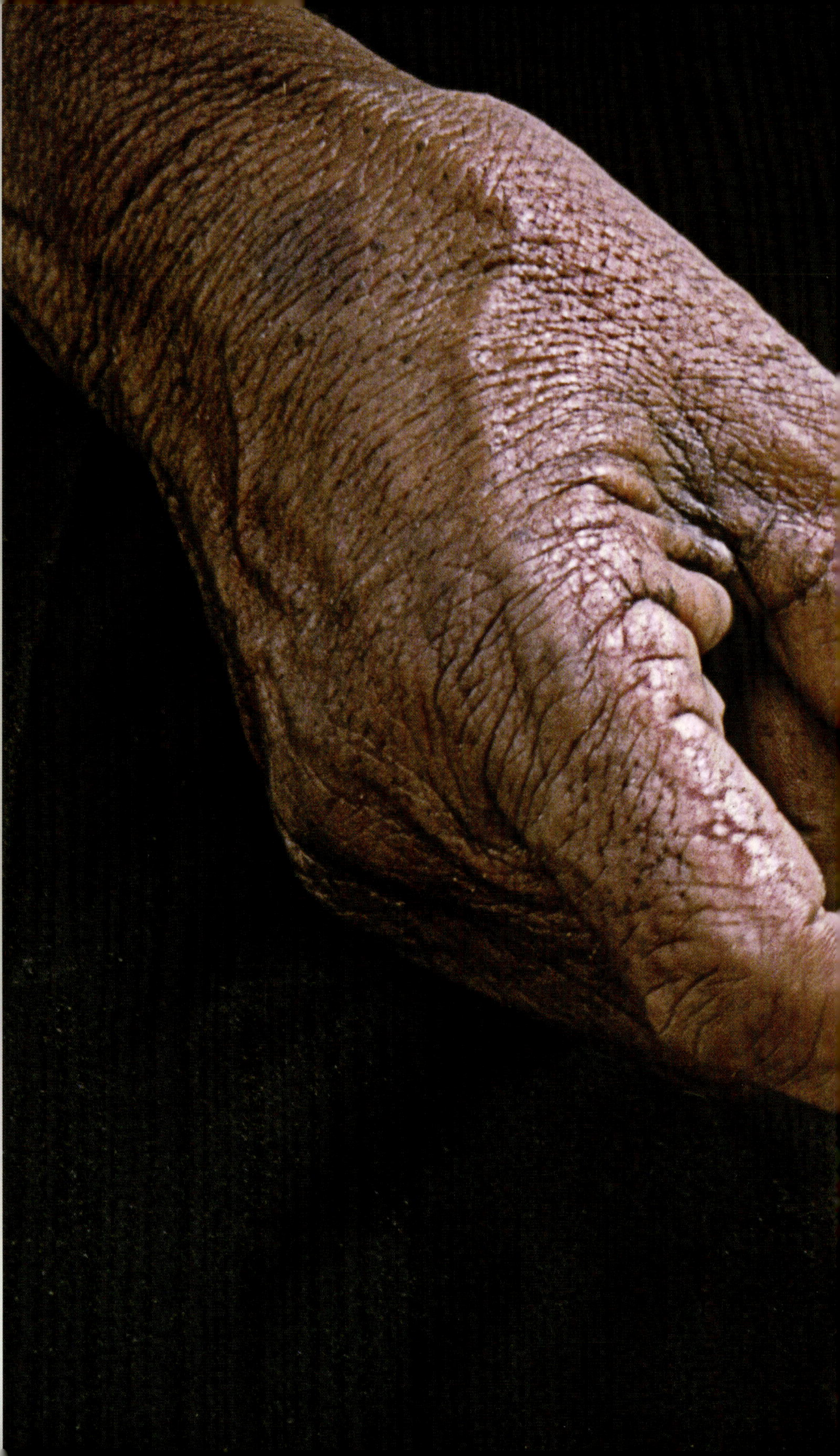

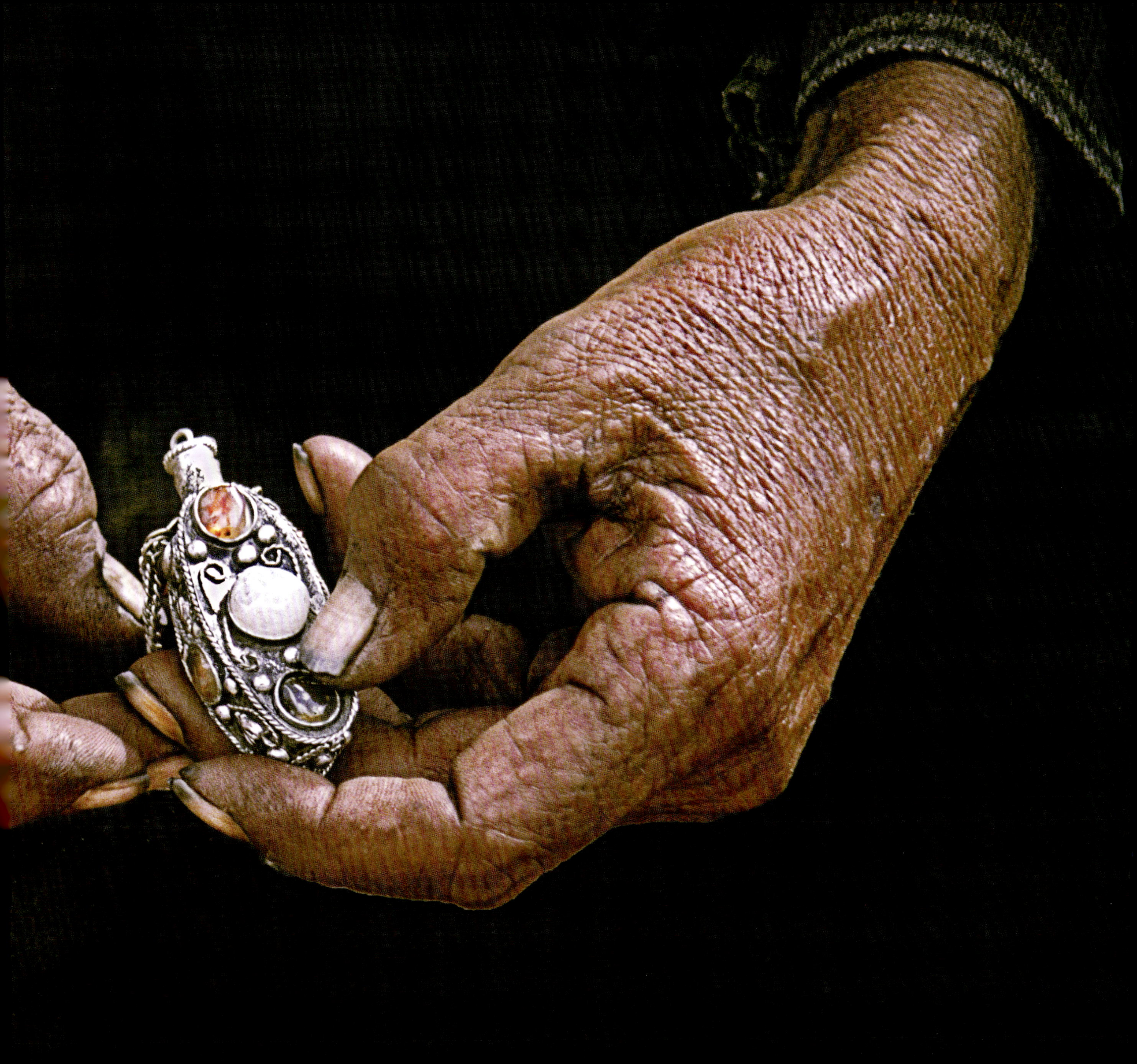

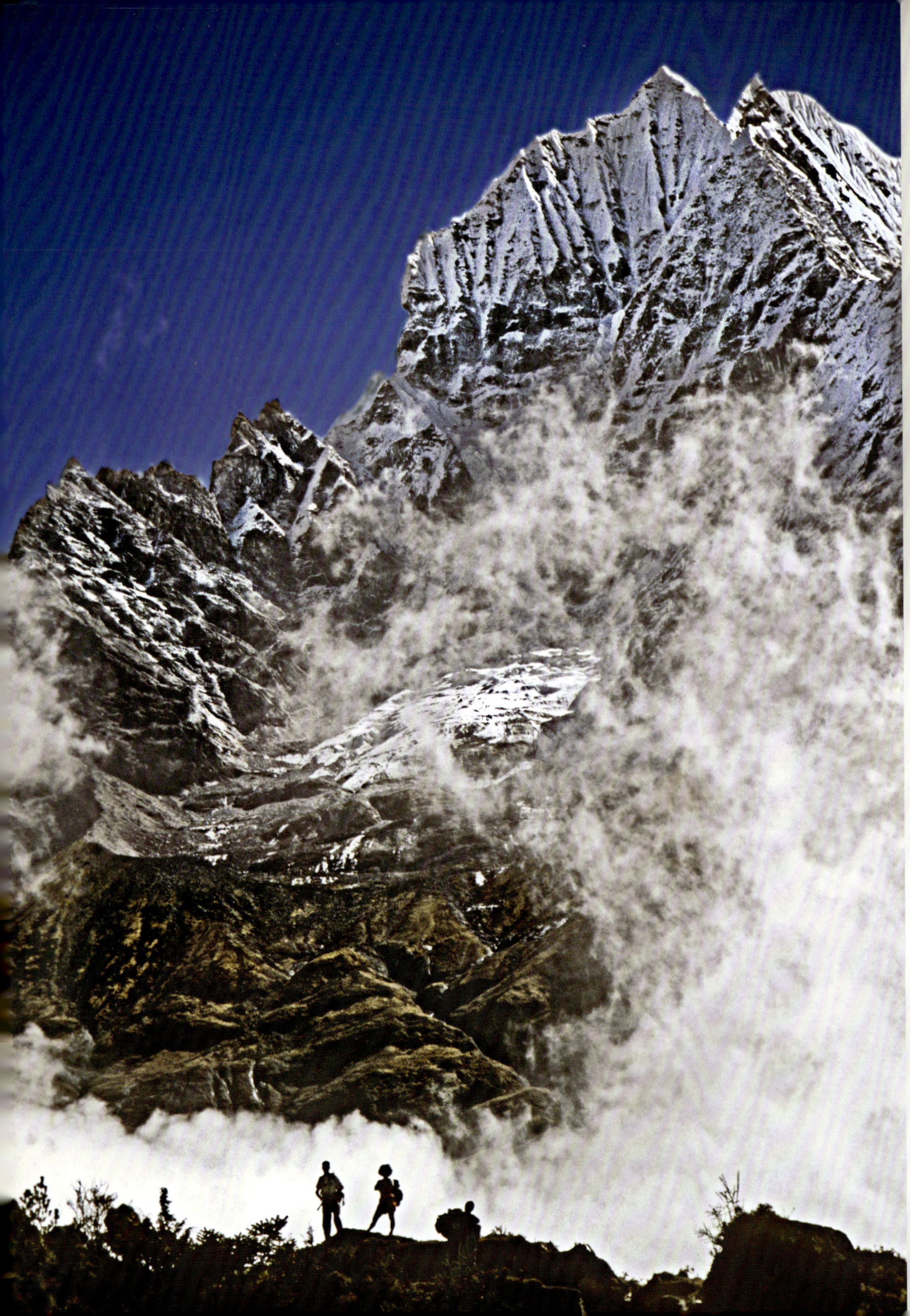

The smaller we come to feel ourselves compared to the mountain, the closer we come to participating in its greatness. I do not know why this is so.

- Arne Ness, Norwegian deep ecologist

Two trekkers and a Sherpa porter pause along an ancient trading route leading through the Himalayas towads Mt. Everest on the border with Tibet in eastern Nepal. From about 11,000', they gaze up at a great peak rising still more thousands of feet above their heads.

The spectacular granite spires of Torres de Paine National Park rise to create a dramatic finale at the southern terminus of the great Andean mountain range in Chilean Patagonia. The region was designated a World Biosphere Reserve by Unesco in 1978.

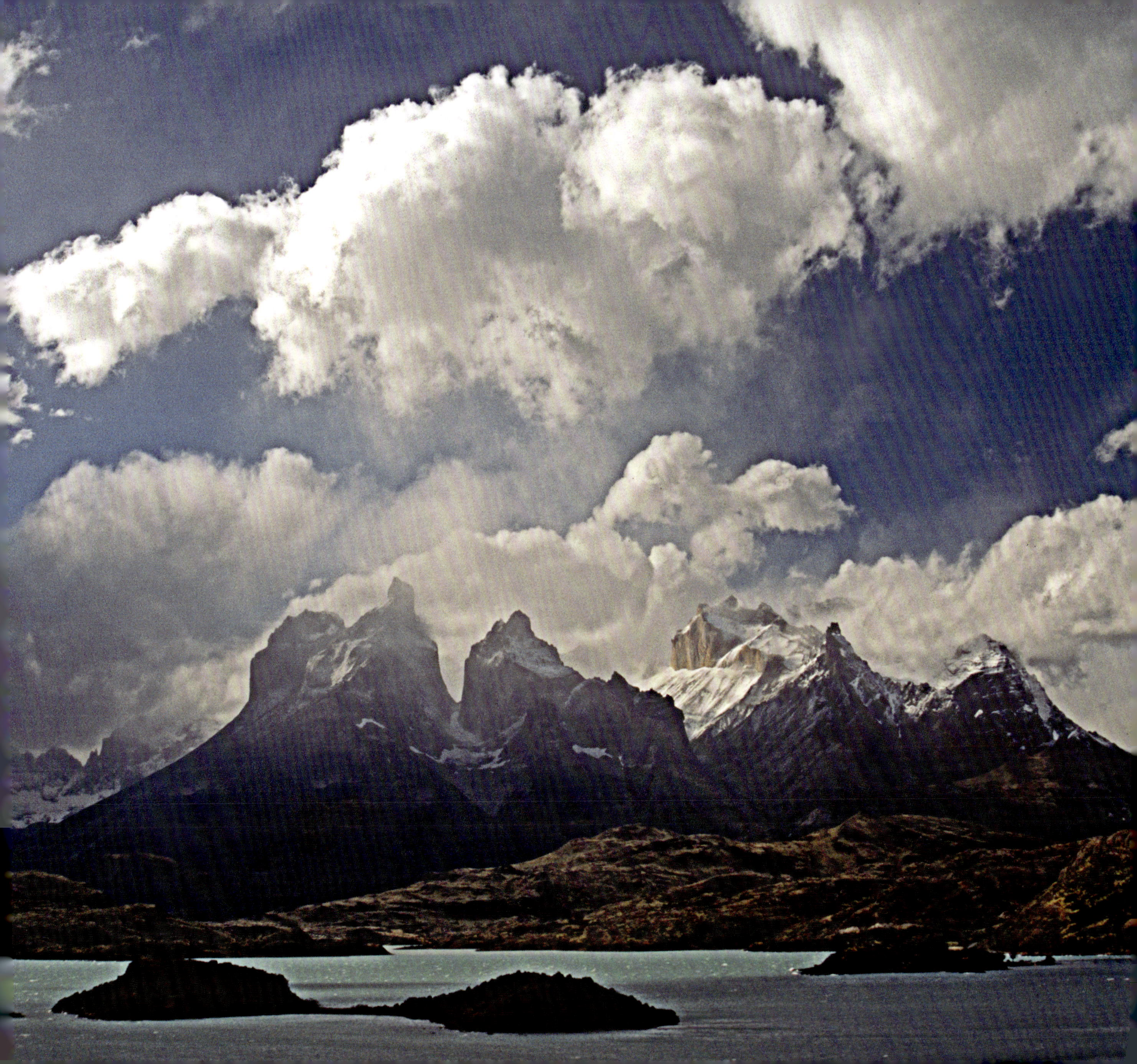

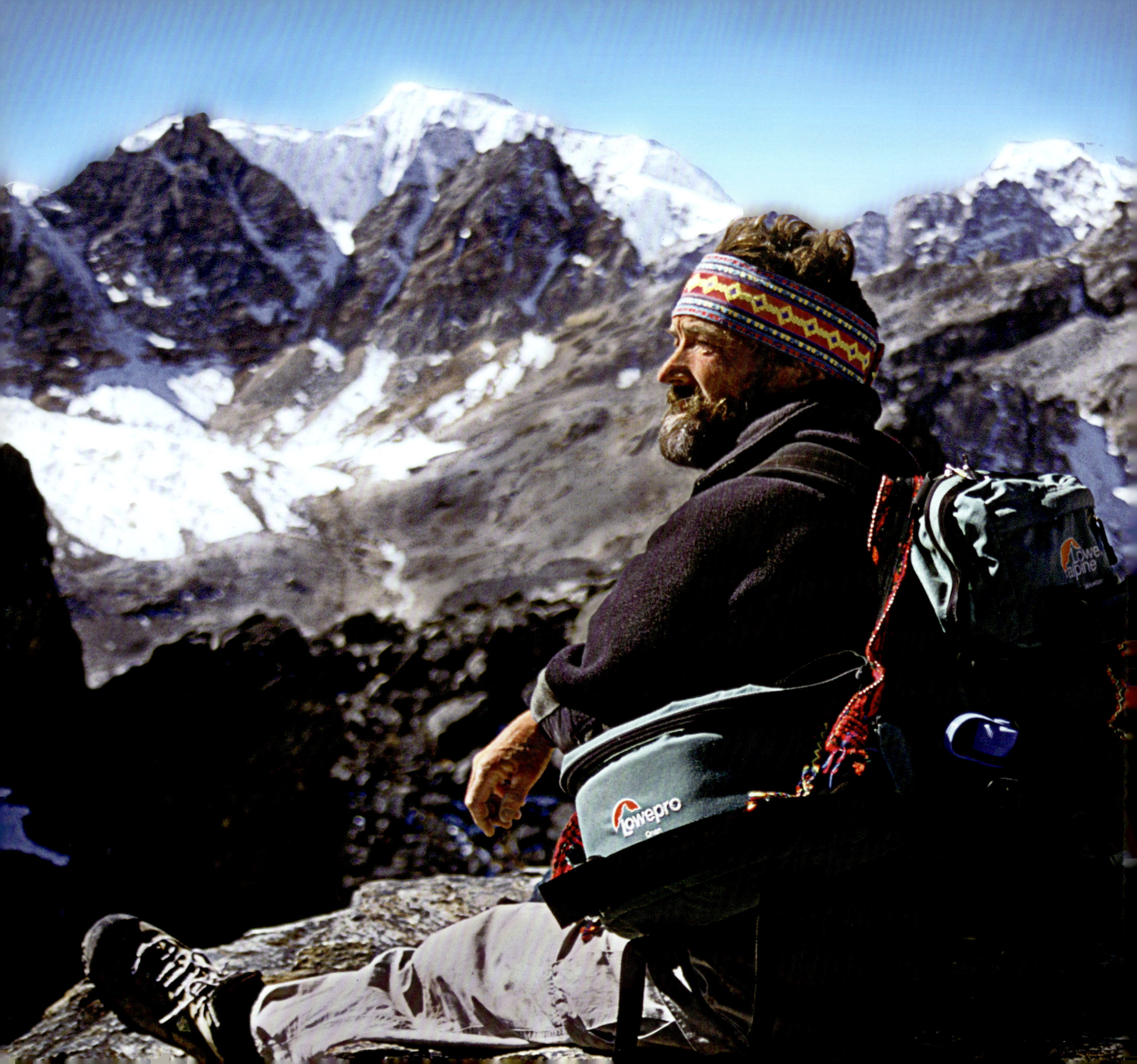
Lowepro

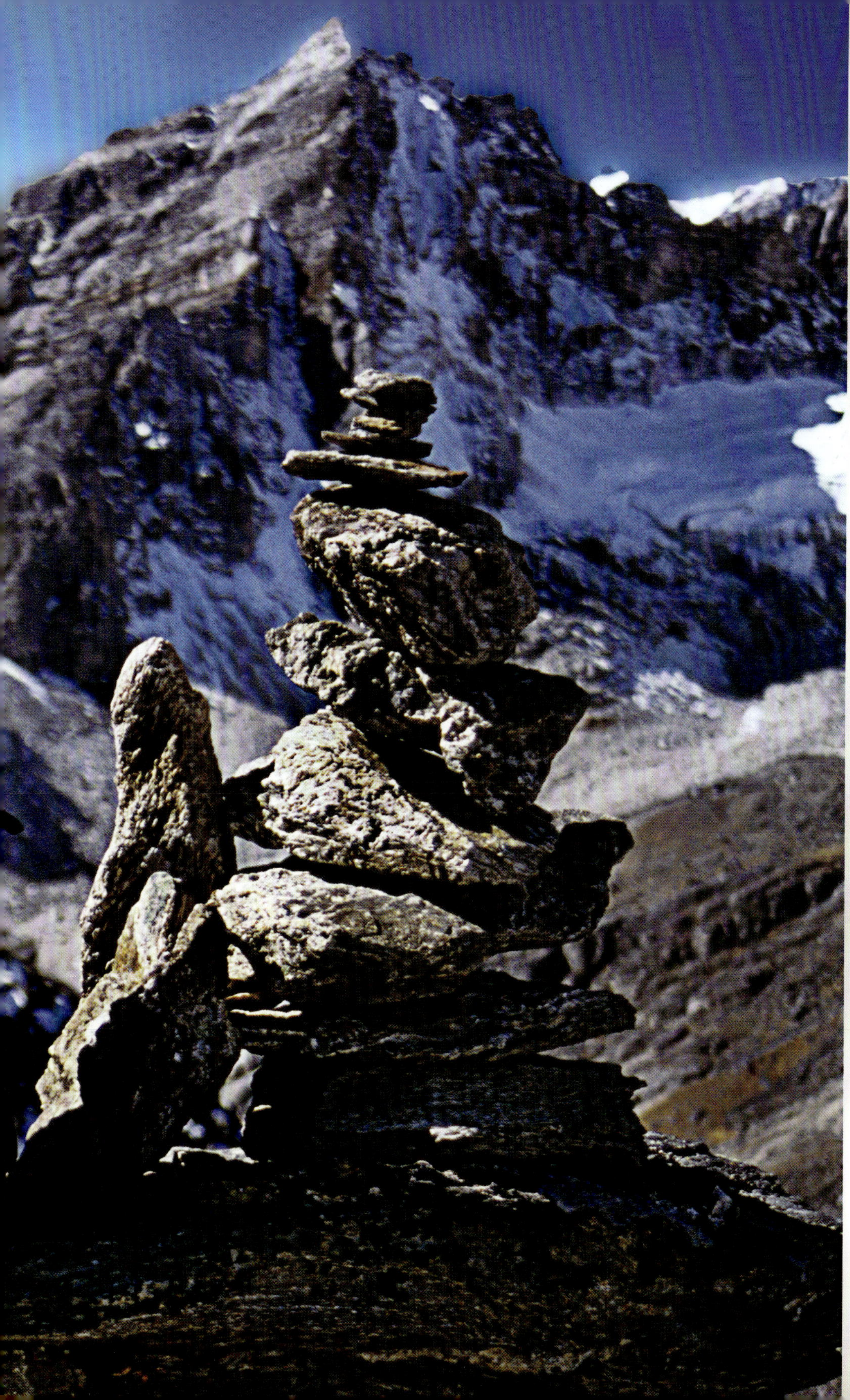

For small creatures such as we, the vastness is bearable only through love.

- Dr. Carl Sagan

In about a half day, a well-acclimated trekker can climb from the small glacier-fed lake at it's base to the 15,700' summit of Gokyo peak in the Khumbu region of eastern Nepal. From here on a clear day the vistas in all directions are literally breathtaking of some of the Himalaya's greatest peaks, including Mt. Everest.

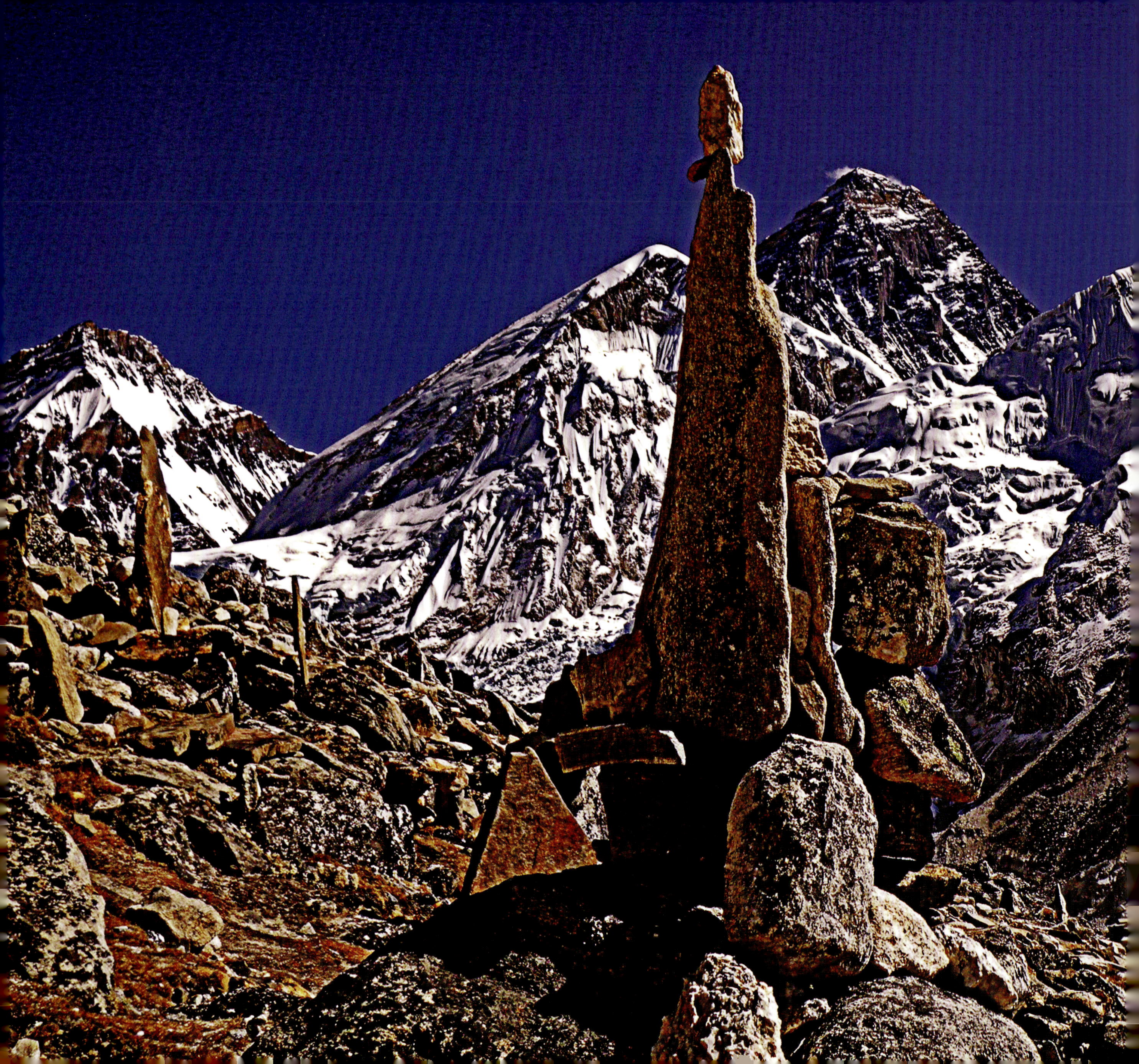

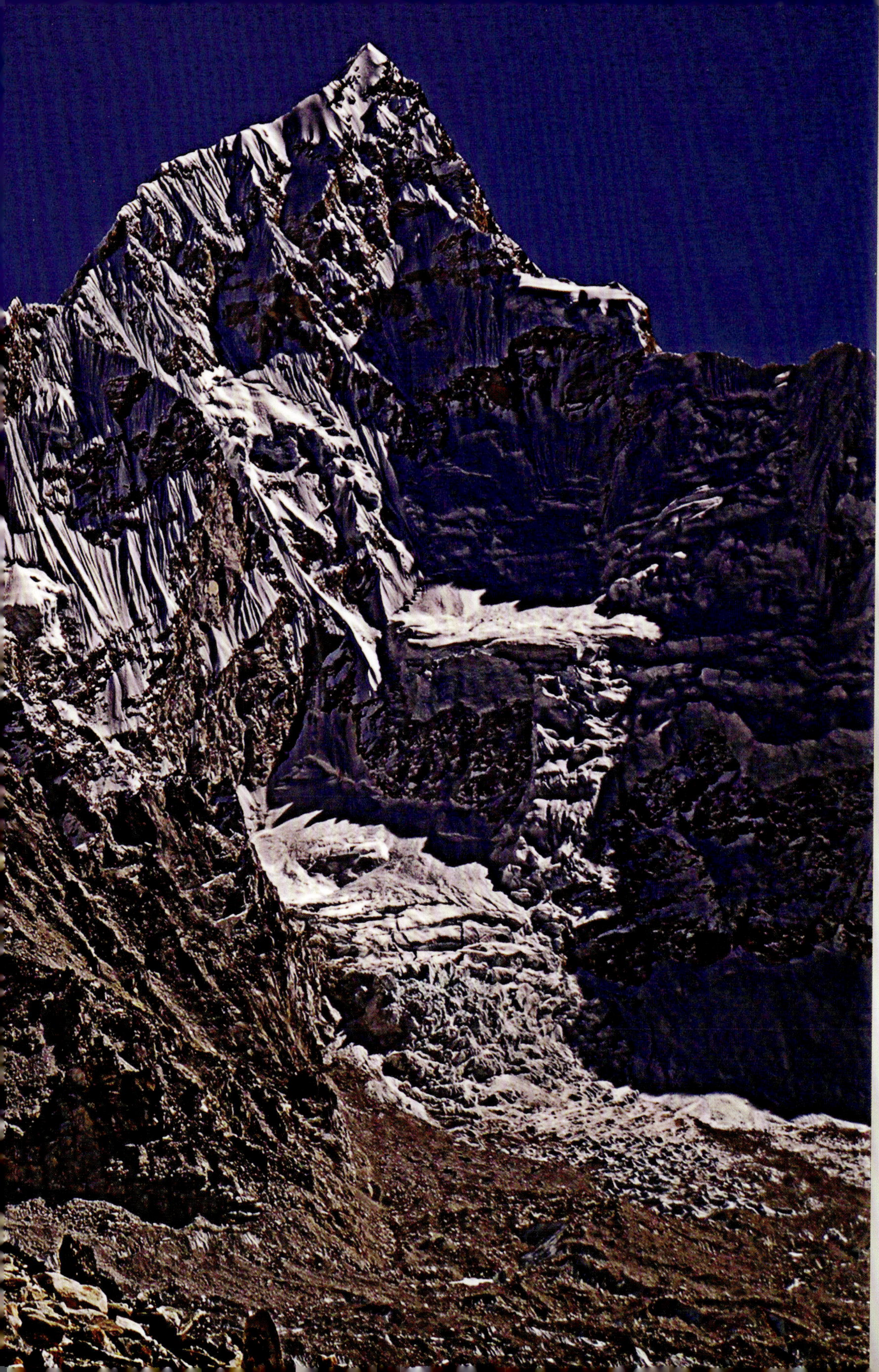

Truth is a pathless land.

- Krisnamurti

16

A legion of stone *stupas* greet trekkers as they approach the 18,200' summit of Kala Patthar and its dramatic closeup views of Mt. Everest. Stupas associated with different spiritual traditions have been erected on mountain peaks and vista points along high-altitude trails throughout the world as long as man has ventured up high. They are enduring symbols of the wonder and reverence that nature's alpine cathedrals of stone and sky naturally inspire.

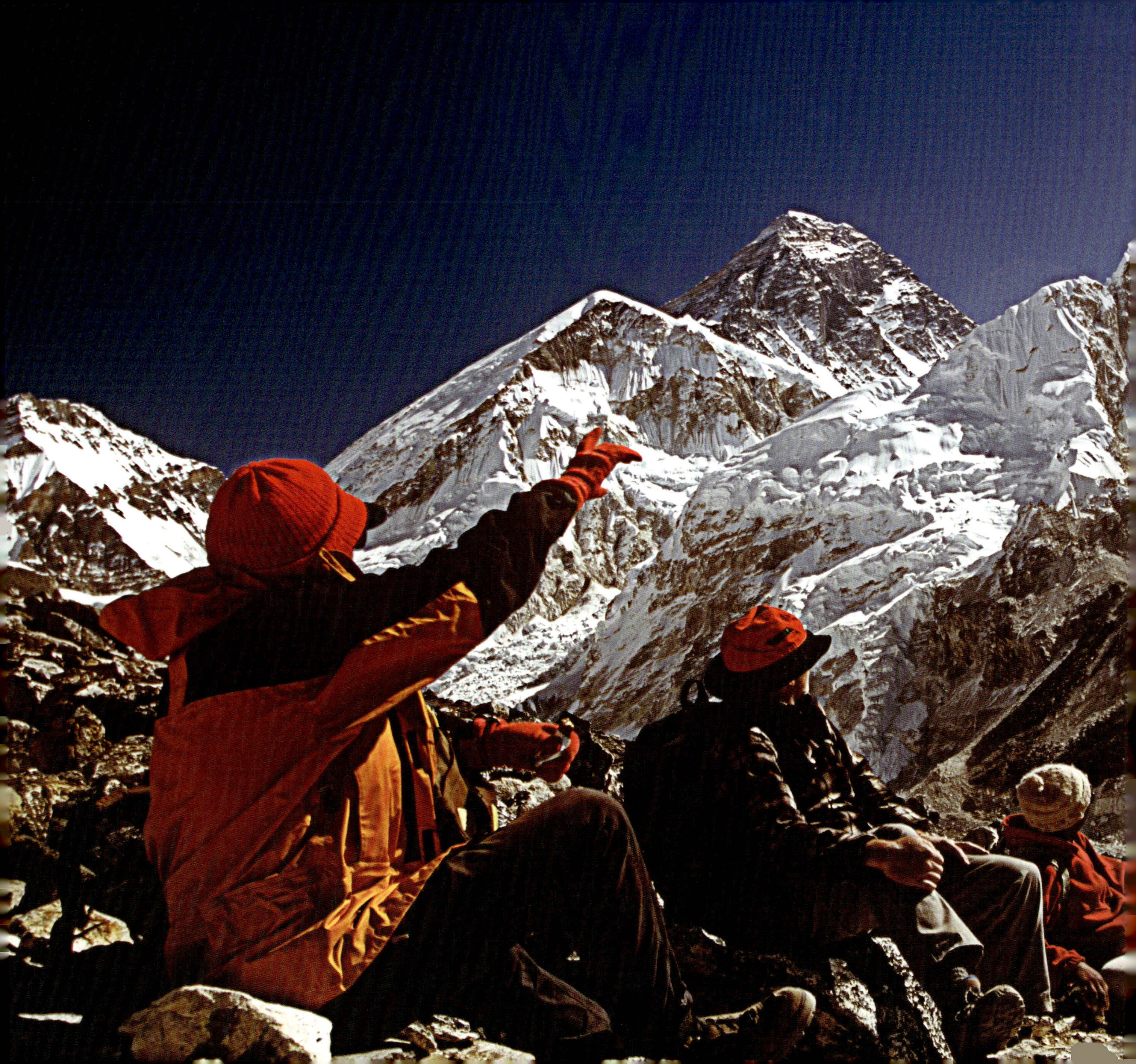

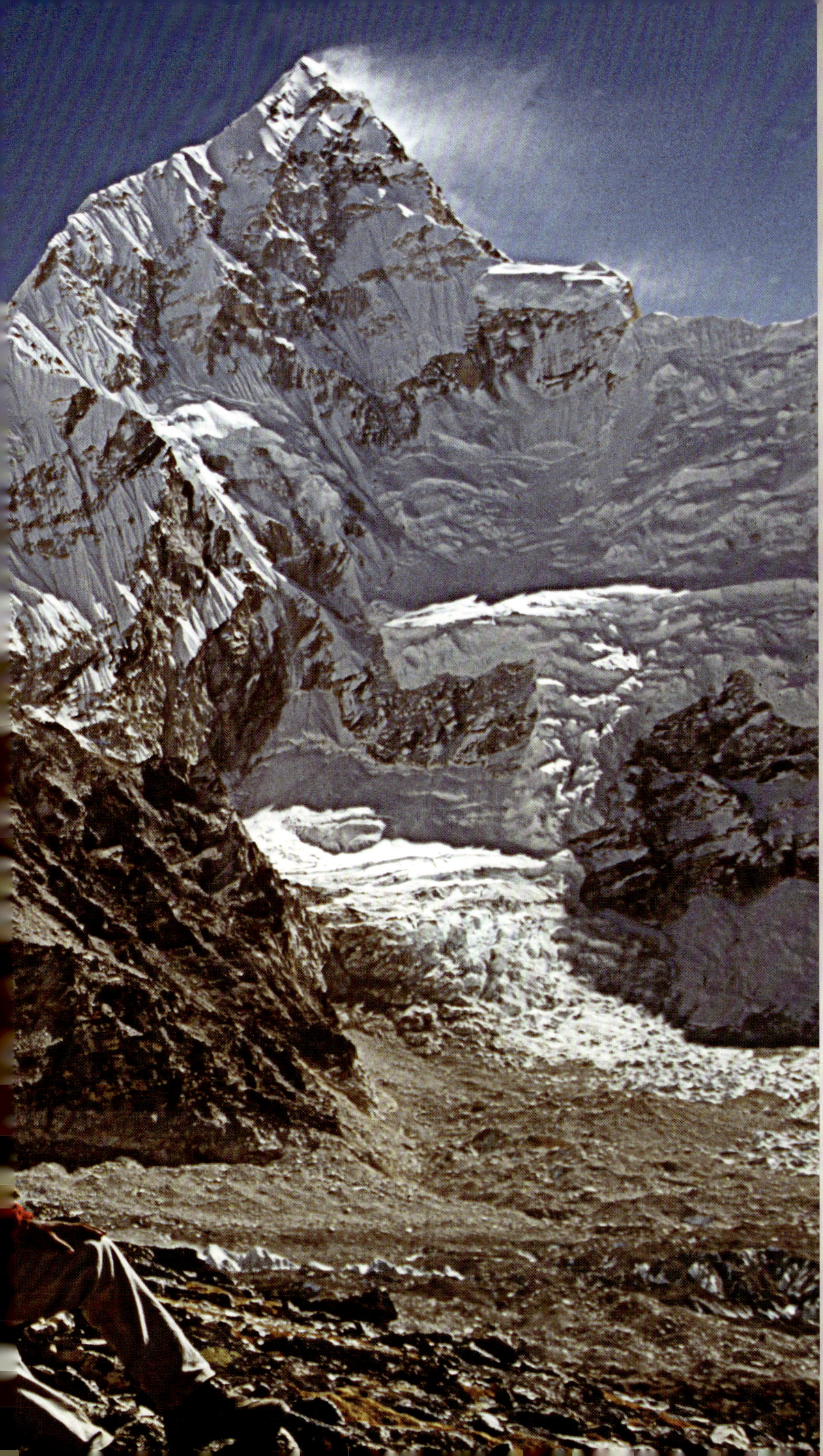

Mountains are not
fair or unfair,
they are just dangerous.

- Reinhold Messner

Ten days of trekking through the magestic Himalaya of eastern Nepal at ever-increasing altitudes and a final push to the 18,519' summit of Kala Patar brings breathless adventurers face to face with Mt. Everest. Mountain guide Richard Munroe points to where 100-mph jet stream winds can be clearly seen blowing tons of ice and snow off the summit of 27,790' Nuptse. Rising behind Nuptse, nearly five and a half miles above sea level up on the border with Tibet is the world's highest mountain - "*Chomolungma*, Mother Goddess of the Sky" to the Nepalese.

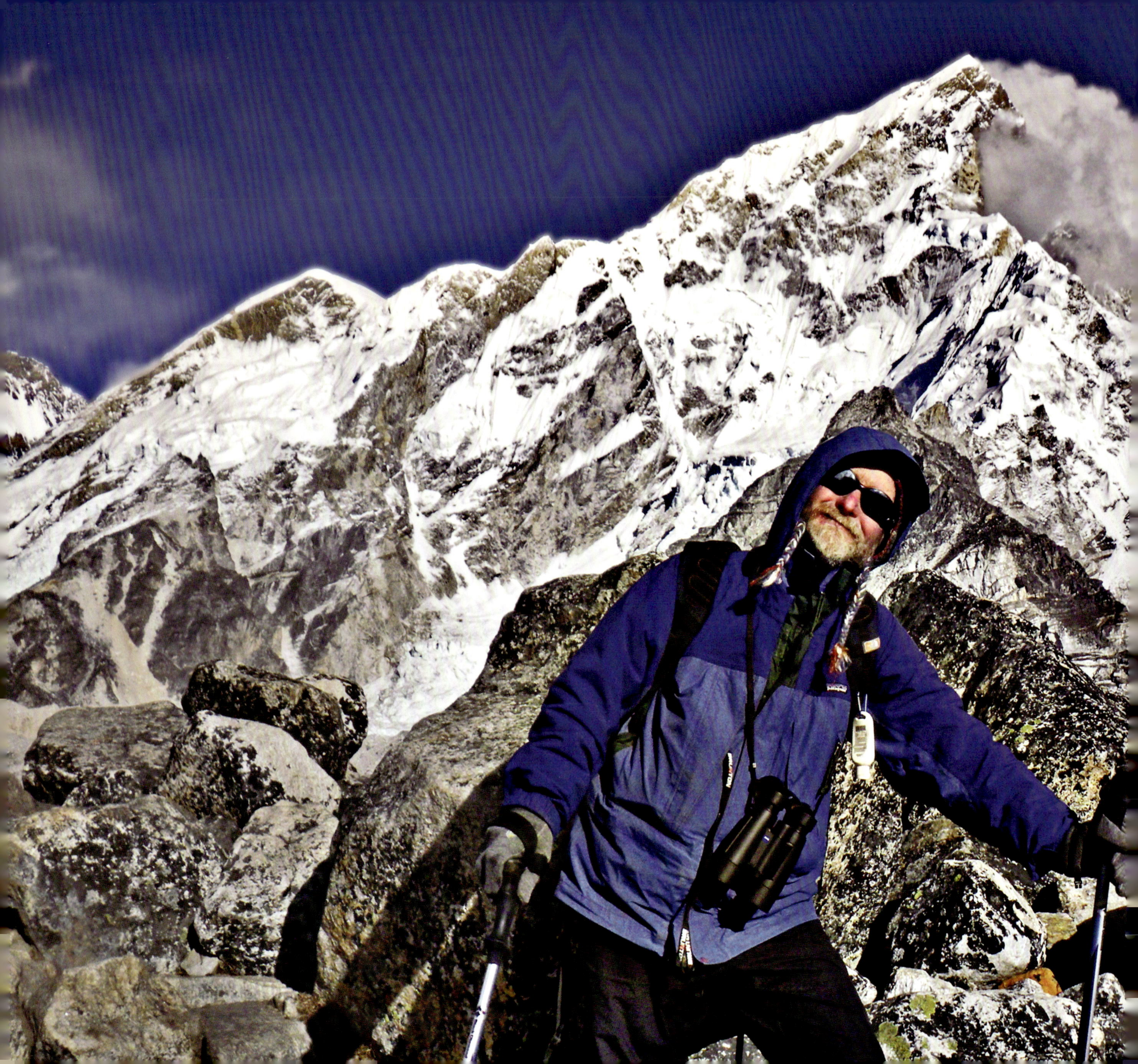

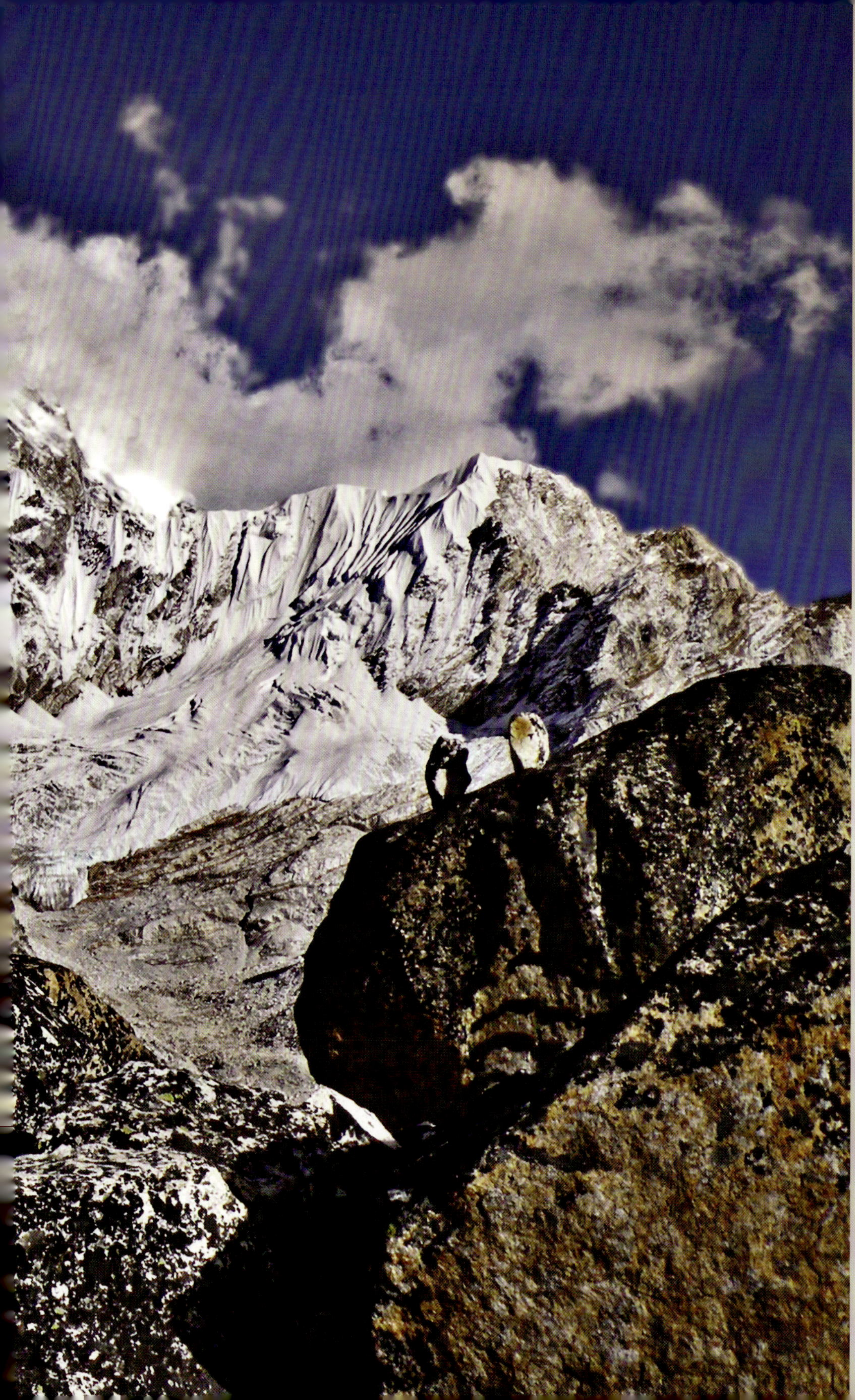

Live the life you have imagined.

- Henry David Thoreau

Ten days of trekking to ever-increasing altitudes in eastern Nepal leads naturalist/adventurer Tim Sullivan to the 19,200' summit of Kala Patthar. Rising nearly two more miles in elevation behind Tim on the left is 29,029' Mt. Everest. The sheer scale of everything in the Himalayas tends to boggle the minds of visitors. From the top of Kala Patthar, even the world's highest mountain appears somewhat eclipsed by a lesser but much closer peak - the magnificant south face of 25,790' Nuptse.

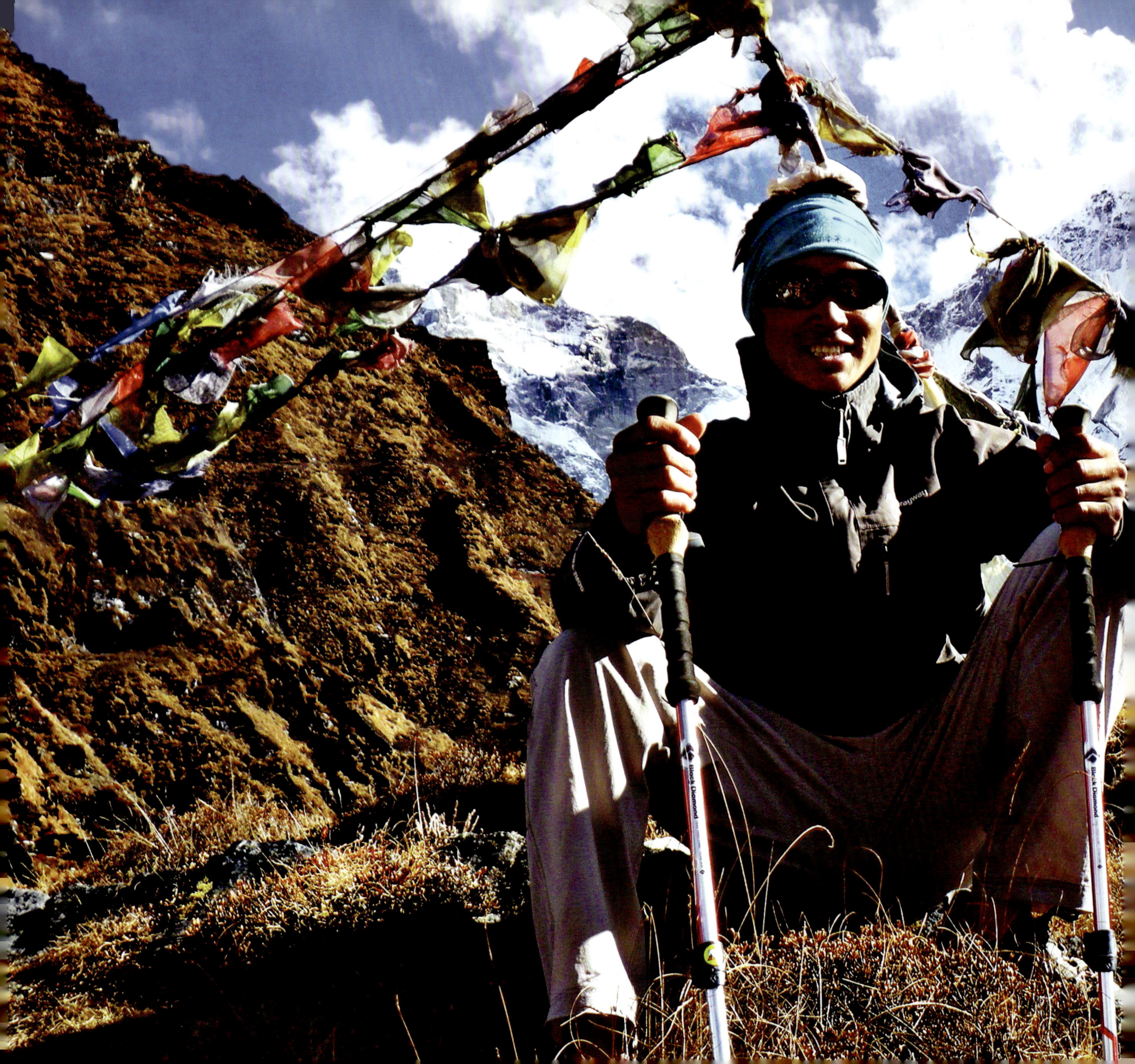
Black Diamond
Black Diamond

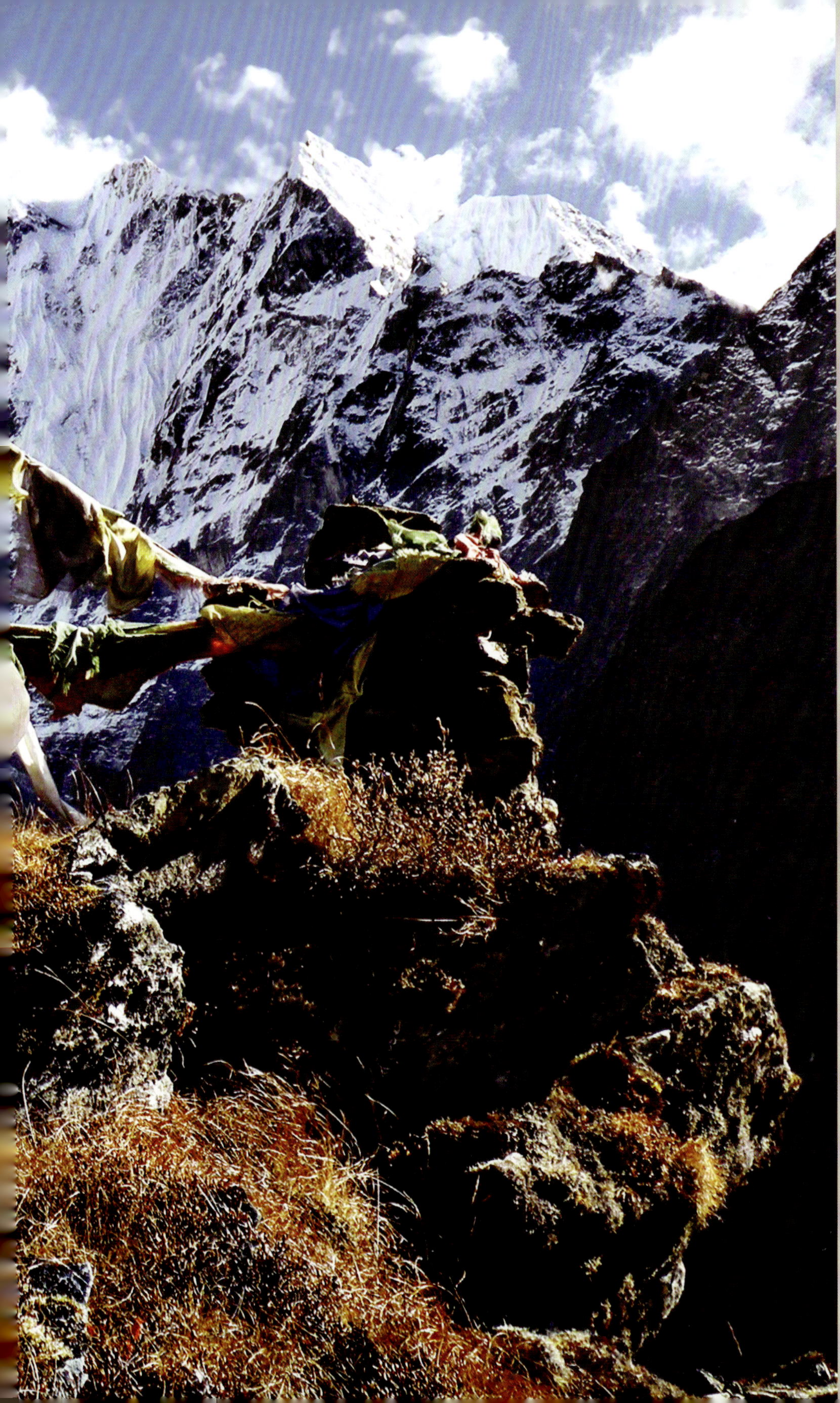

I do not wish to take a cabin passage, but rather to stand before the mast on the deck of the world from where I can best see the moonlight on the mountains.

- Mark Twain

Pemba Sherpa patiently waits on a 17,000' pass for his lowlander clients to catch up as they trek through his *Khumba* region homeland in eastern Nepal. Pemba is just 24 years old, but has already helped Westerners reach the summit of Mt. Everest twice. The renown of Sherpas as high-altitude mountain guides is legendary. So it was not surprising when Edmund Hillary chose a young Sherpa, Tenzing Norgay, as his climbing partner for the first successful ascent of 29,028' Everest in 1953.

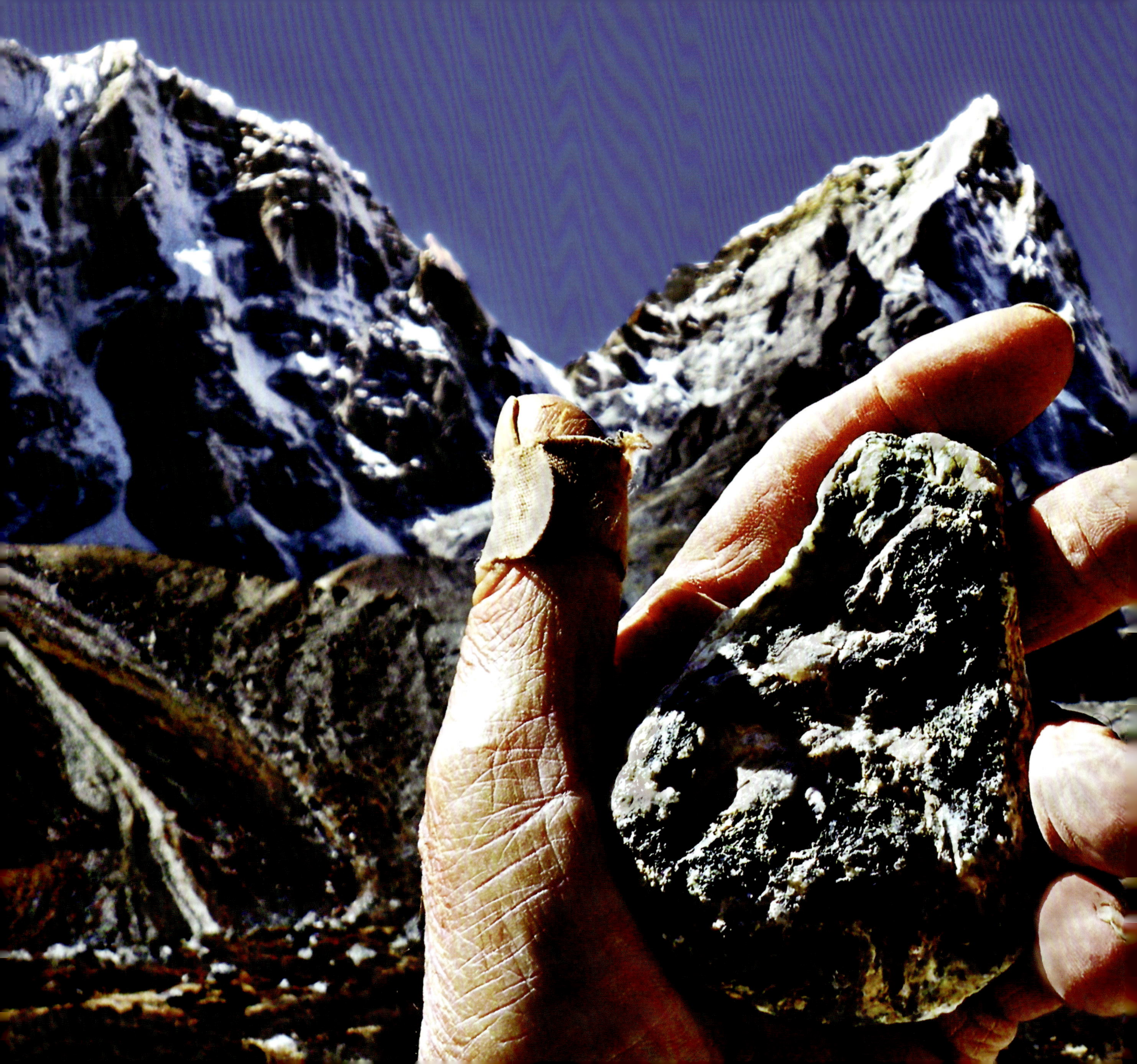

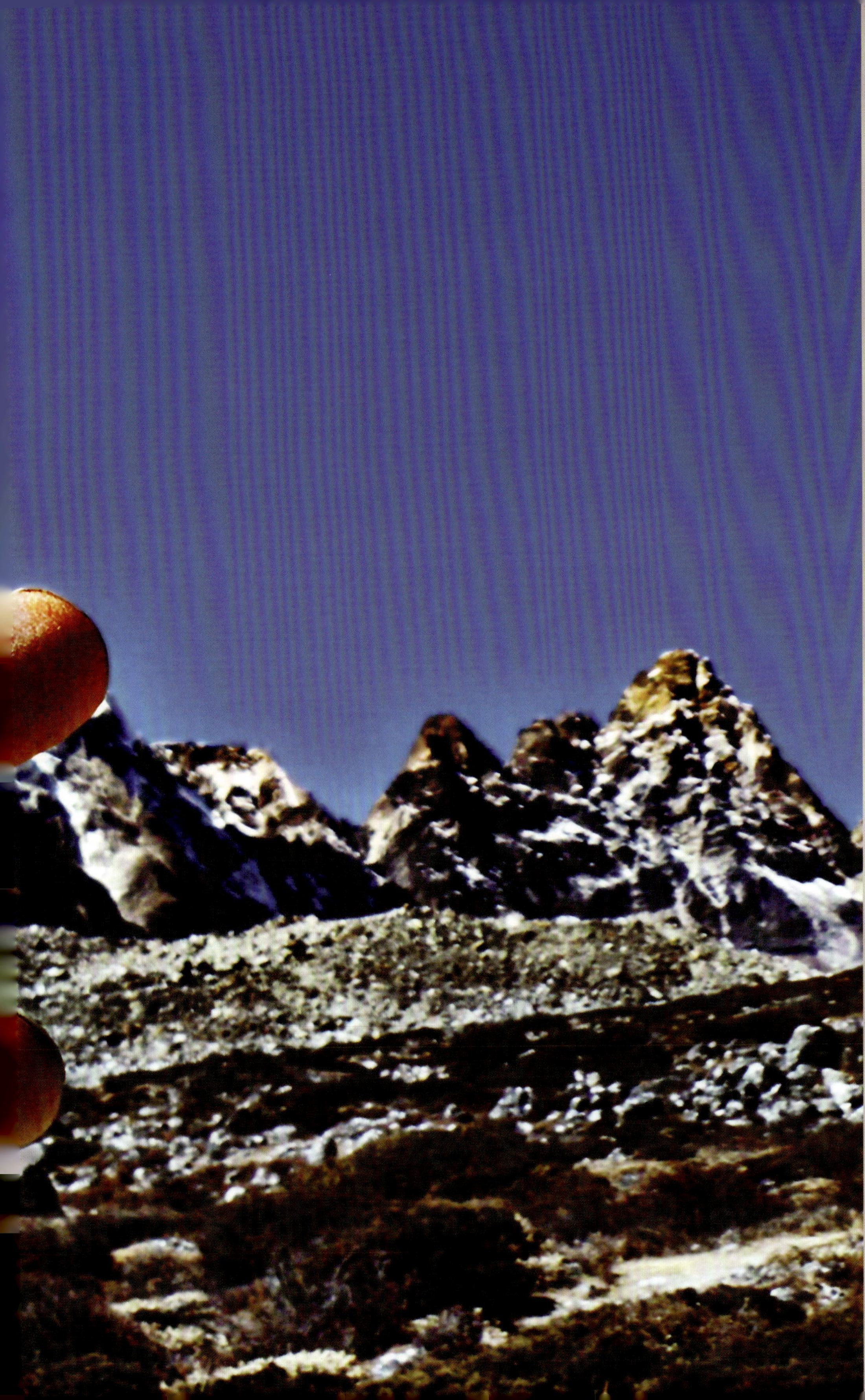

What amazing things you find when you search for them.

- Sacagawea, Lemhi Shoshoni woman who accompanied the 1804-06 Lewis and Clark expedition as a guide and interpreter.

A stone picked up along the trail to Mt. Everest in eastern Nepal appears to replicate the form of the Himalayan peaks above. Vestiges from a vast spectrum of geological history and even shells from ancient seabeds are commonly found at high elevations in the Himalayas, evidence of a colossal upheaval still occurring as the vast tectonic plate beneath the Indian Ocean continues to plow northward on a collision course with the soft underbelly of mainland Asia. Scientists estimate that the resulting upthrust of the Himlaya range has caused Everest to gain over nine kilometers of altitude in the past fifty million years.

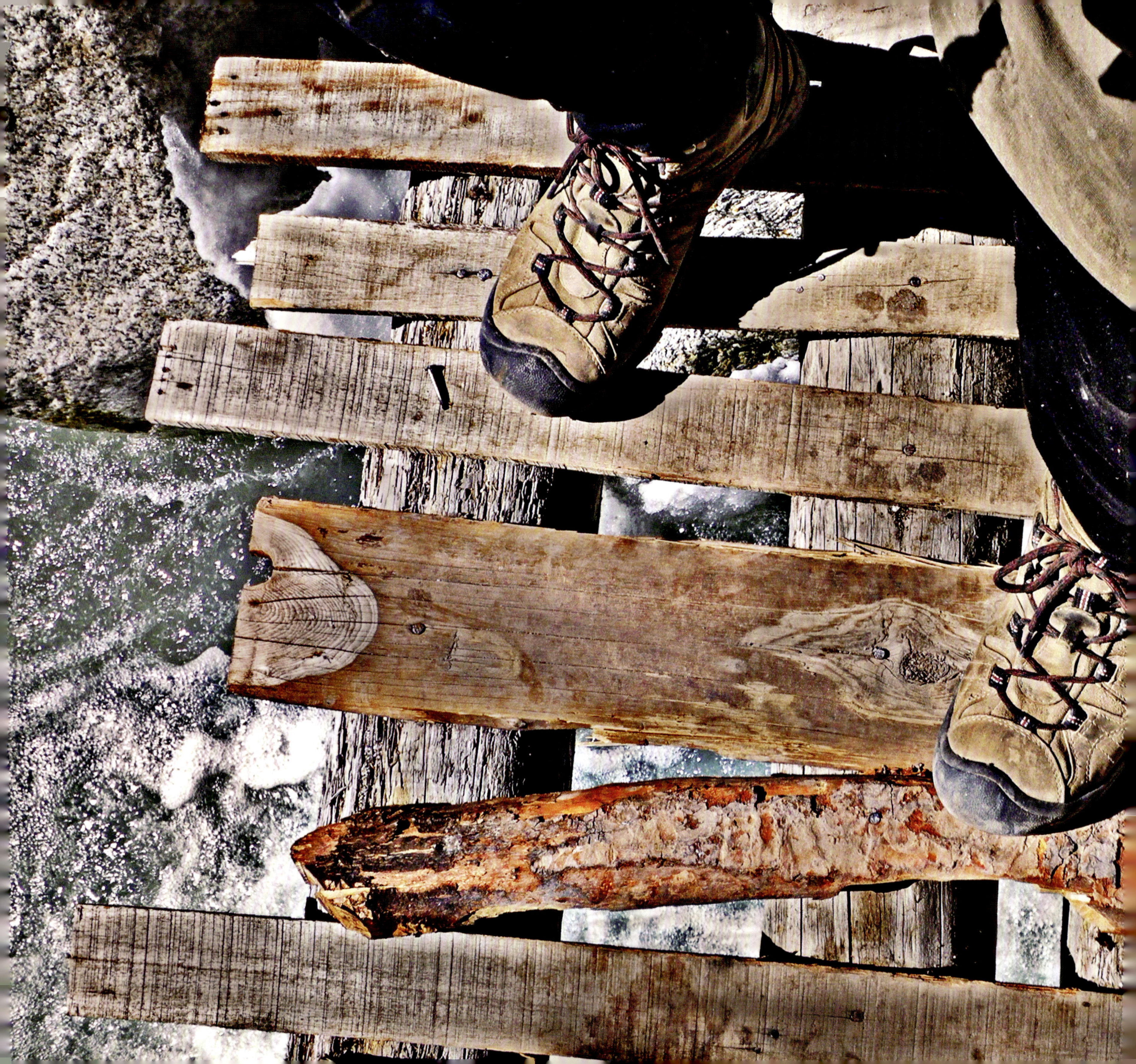

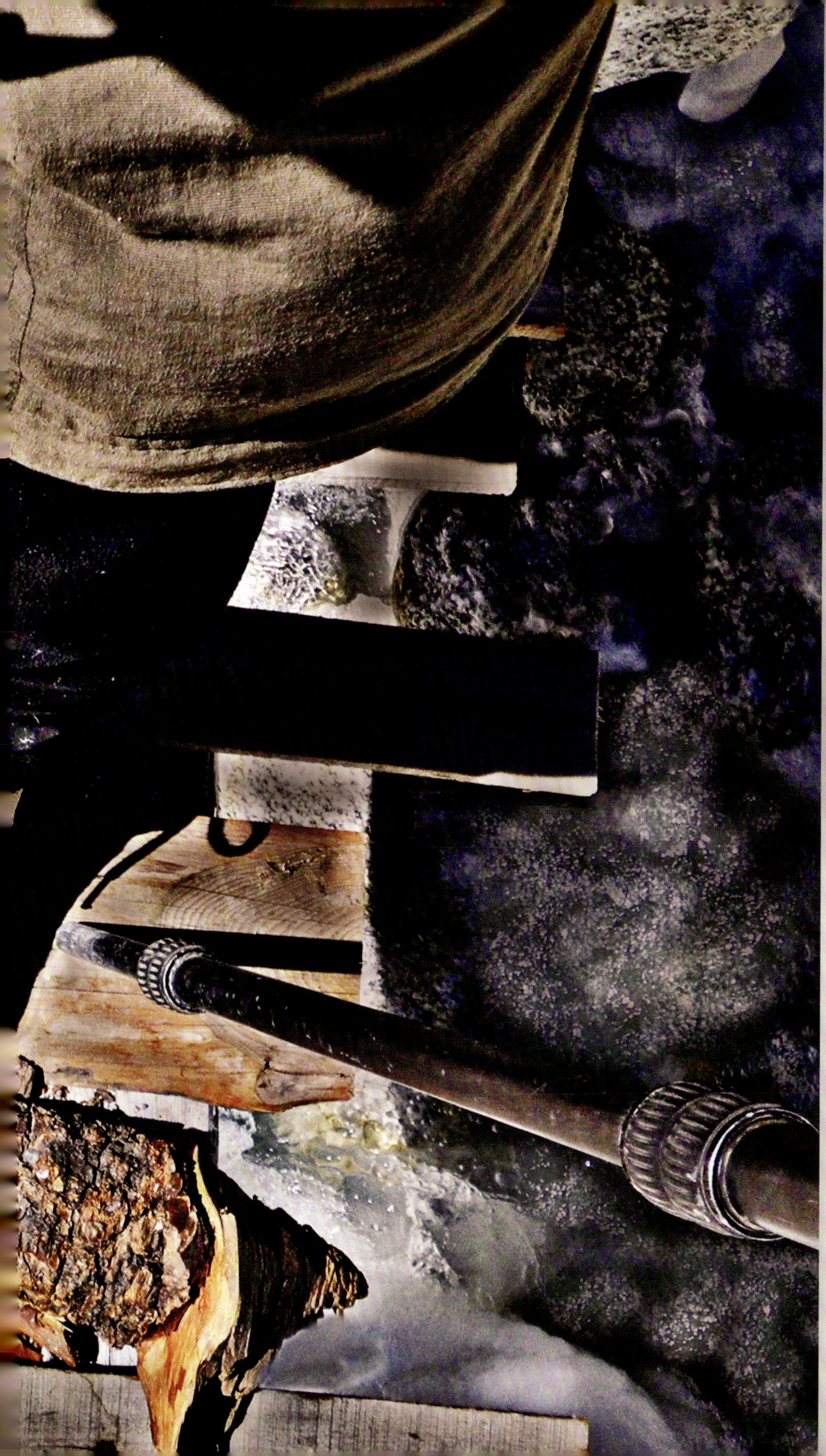

You are permitted in time of great danger to walk with the devil until you have crossed the bridge.

- old Bulgarian proverb

Adventuresome trekkers exploring an especially remote and little-traveled trail in a remote corner the *Khumbu* region of eastern Nepal had to choose between trusting a rustic Sherpa's bridge or fording the whitewater stream below. After a few anxious moments most chose to trust the bridge, which trembled and swayed a bit - but held up just fine as they crossed one at a time.

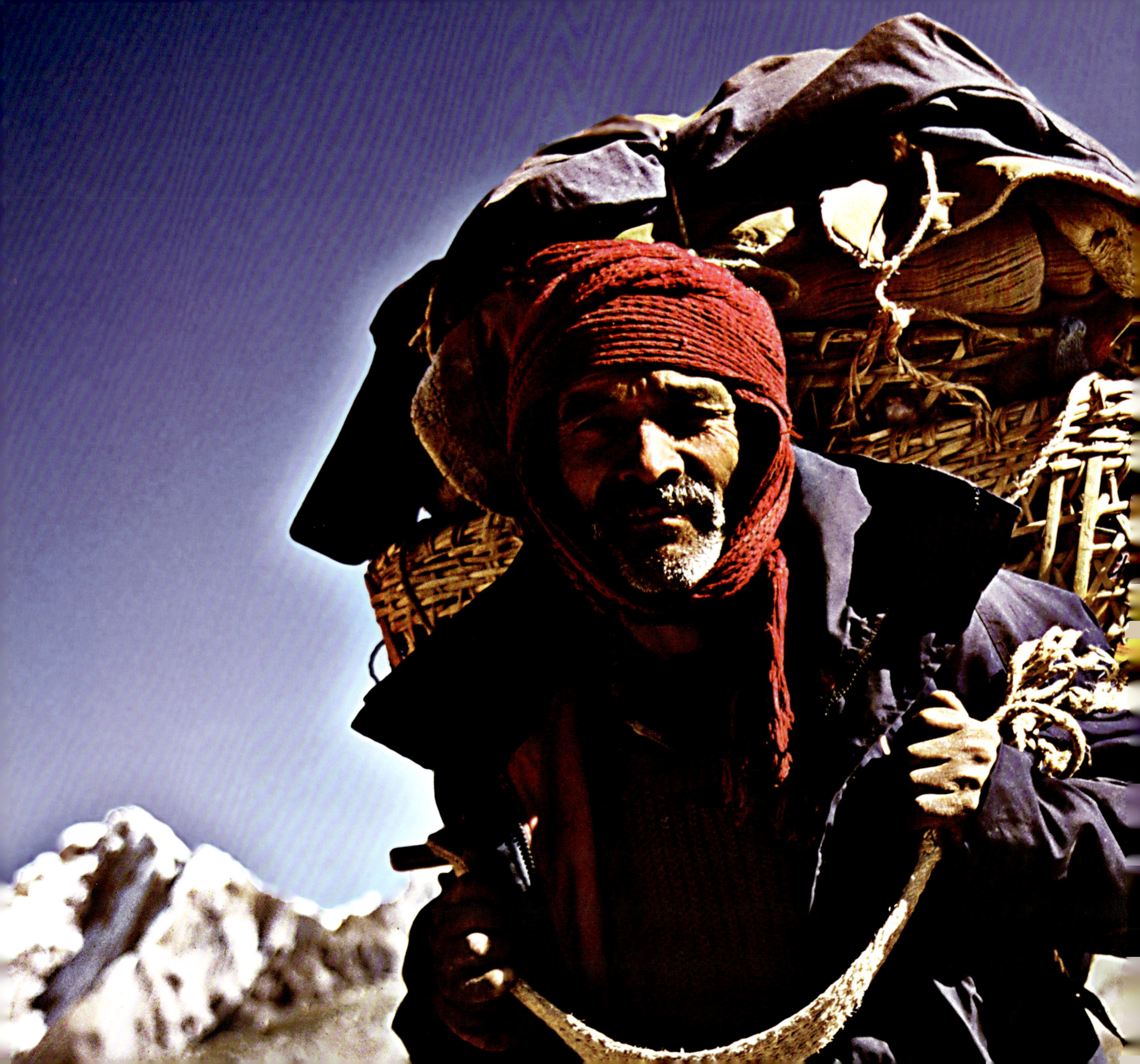

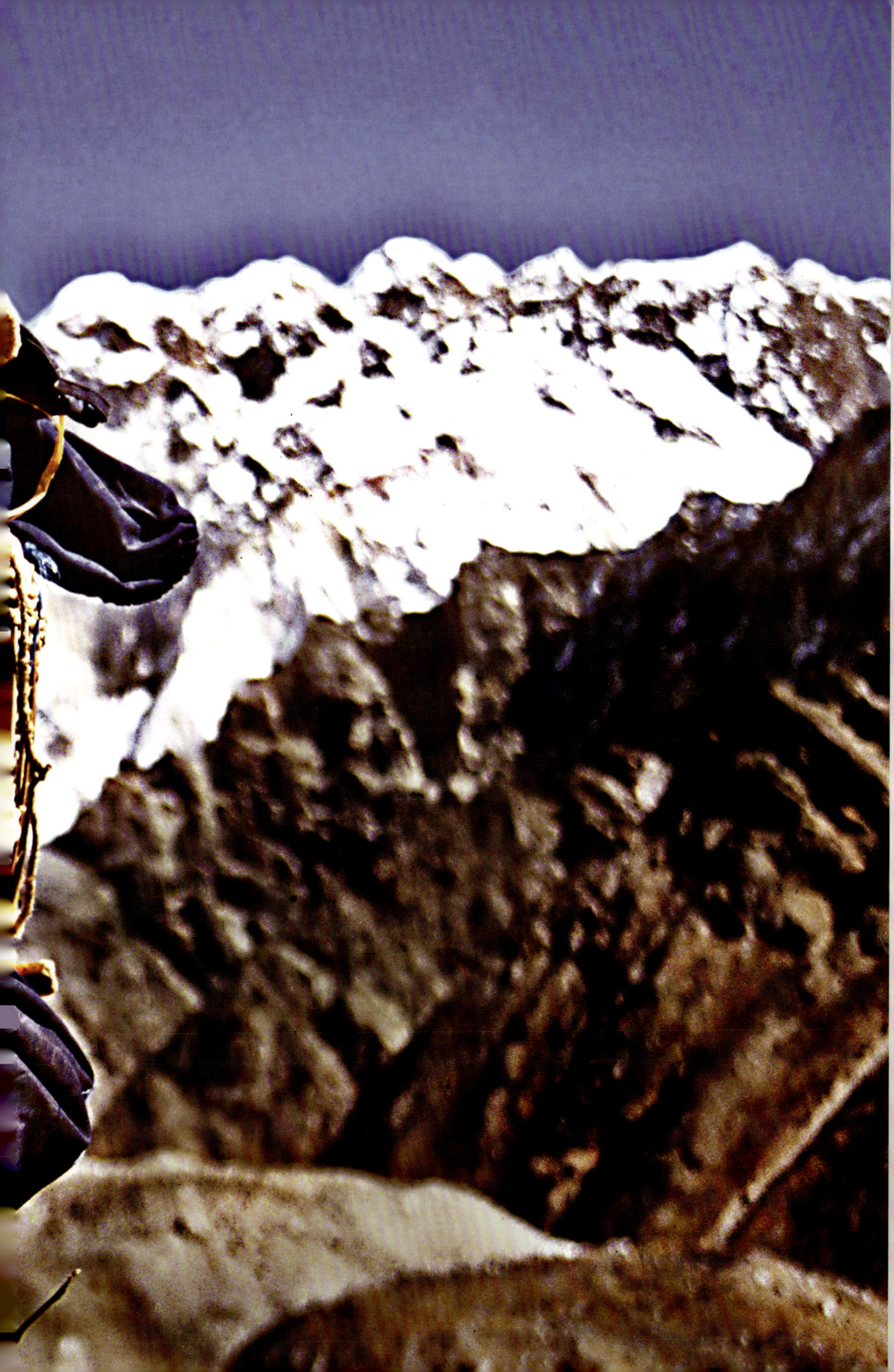

Having the fewest wants I am nearest to the gods.

- Socrates

28

Soundless as a raven in the wind, the porter's weathered face appeared unexpectedly behind us on a 15.000' pass deep in the mystical Khumbu region of the Himalayas. His striking demeanor bore a resemblance to an ancient Omar Sarif, or perhaps Anthony Quinn. While many high-altitude porters in eastern Nepal had Mongol features that signified their Tibetan origins, the man's acquiline face revealed his Indo-Nepalese ancestry. After remaining along us for a few timeless moments gazing out over the stunning vistas, he continued his journey without ever uttering a word.

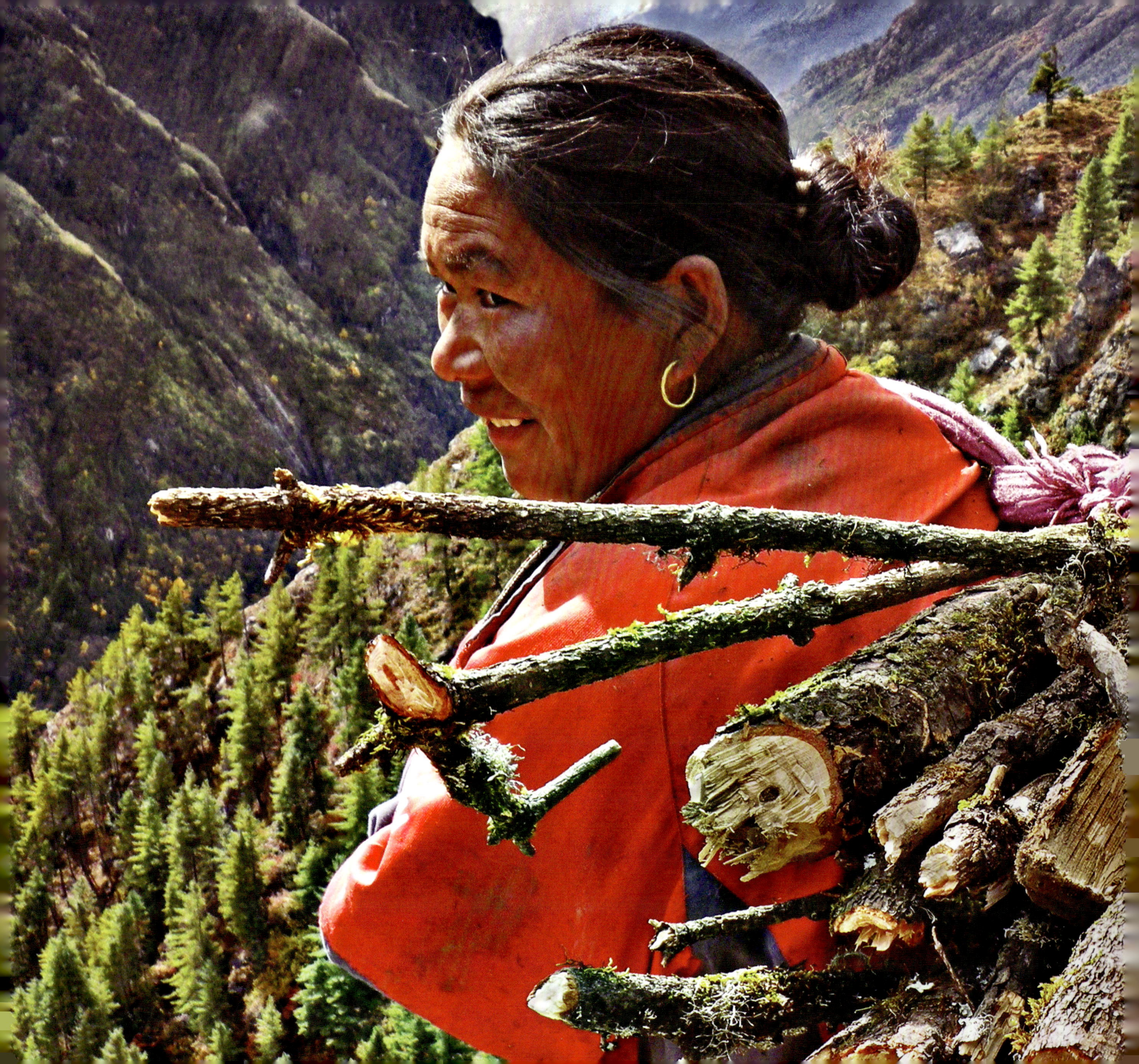

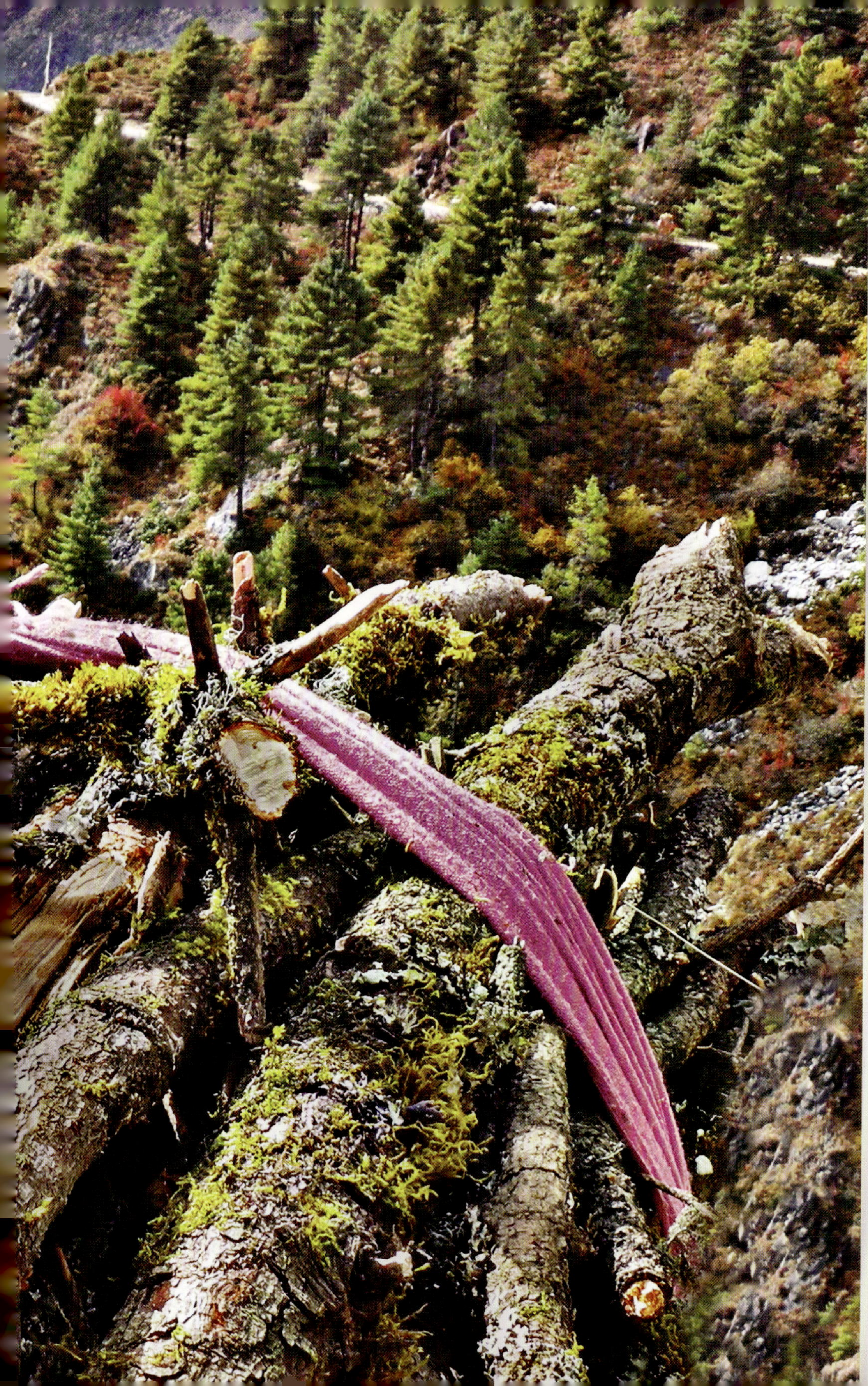

My soul is a dark forest.
My known self will never
be more than a little clearing
in the forest. Gods, strange
gods, come forth from the
forest into the clearing of
my known self, then go back.
I must have the courage
to let them come and go.

- D. H. Lawrence

Like her ancestors who crossed the high Himalaya passes to reach eastern Nepal from Tibet some 600 years ago might have done, a Sherpa woman carries her night's supply of firewood back to her summer hut. The steep, treacherous terrain of the Himalayas has always made the use of wheeled transportation impractical. For untold centuries, virtually everything necessary for human existence in the high country has been carried on the backs of yaks and people. Thus the endurance and ability of the Sherpas to perform strenuous tasks at high altitude have long amazed outsiders.

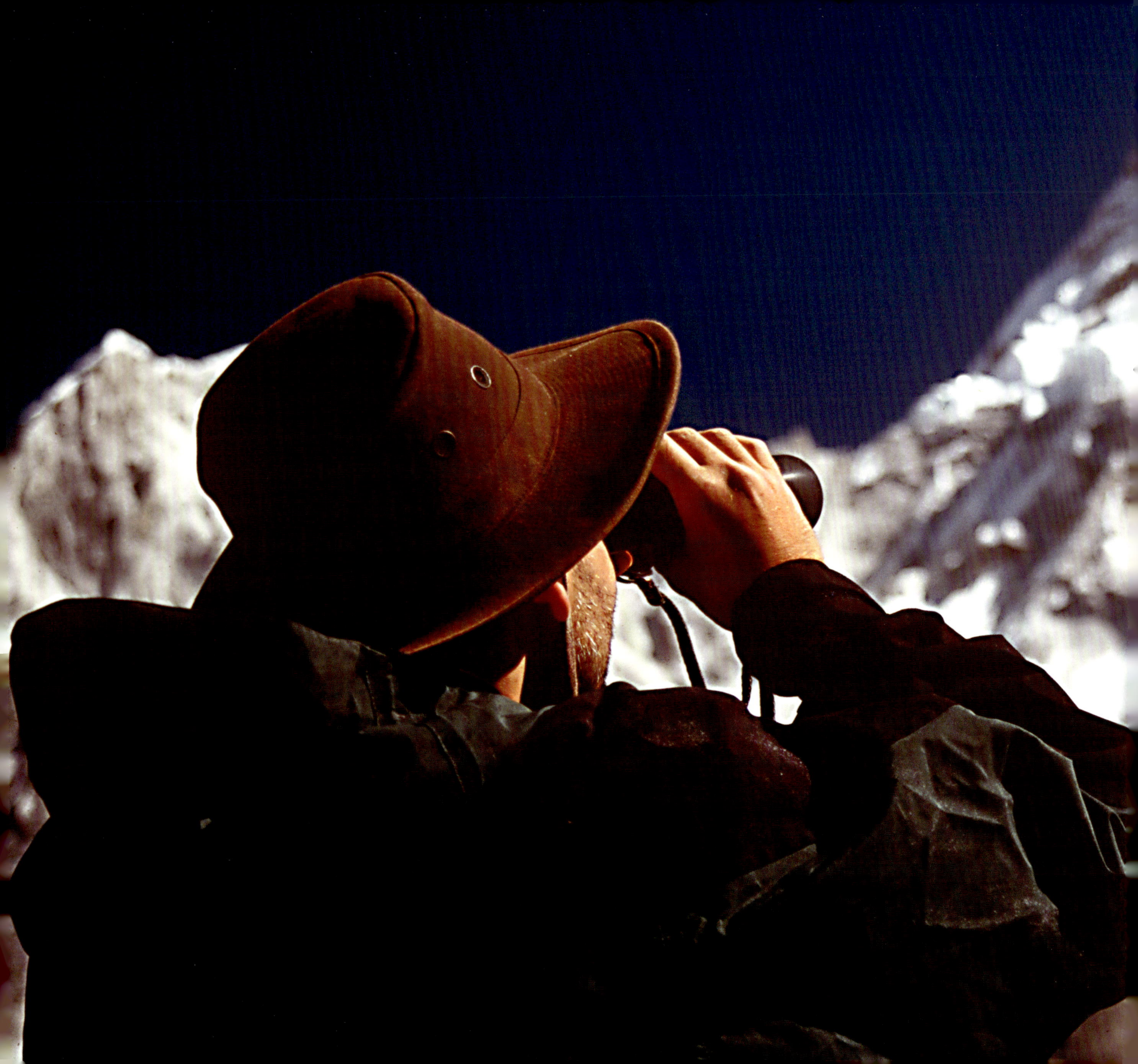

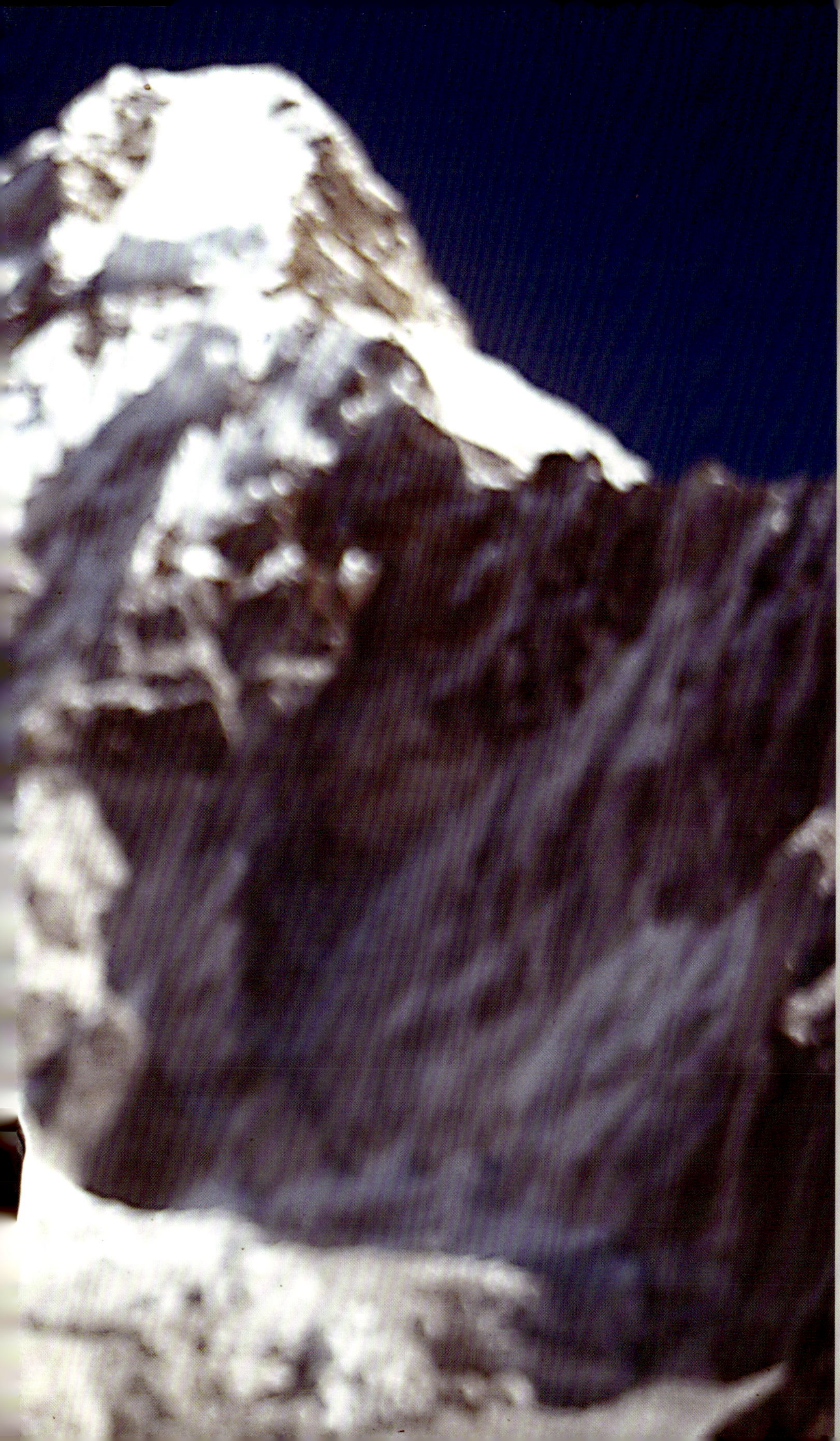

In nature's infinite book of secrets, a little I can read.

- William Shakespeare,
Anthony and Cleopatra

Ama Dablam dominates the sky for several days as trekkers advance through the Khumbu region in eastern Nepal towards Mt. Everest. '*Ama*' means mother in Nepalese, and a '*dablam*' is a special pendant or charmbox worn by Sherpa women to carry precious keepsakes or images of the gods. A massive hanging glacier flowing down the north face of Ama Dablam is thought to represent a dablam, and two ridges extending out from the summit resemble a mother's arms. Hillary once considered the 22,494' peak "unclimbable". The mountain's soaring ridges and steep faces earned it the name "Matterhorn of the Himalayas." Ama Dablam is regarded by many trekkers as one of the most beautiful mountains in the world.

The most interesting information comes from children, because they tell all they know and then stop.

- Mark Twain

Two young boys along a trail in the Khumbu region of Nepal became excited when they spotted two American trekkers emerging from a village kiosk with a freshly purchased bar of English chocolate. The prospect of a bite of that chocolate was obviously foremost in their minds. But when one of the foreigners expressed interest in first photographing the boys and their pet chicken, they seemed to grow uneasy. They became instantly cooperative, however, when the Sherpa guide accompanying the trekkers smiled and announced firmly in Nepali, "No photos... no chocolate!"

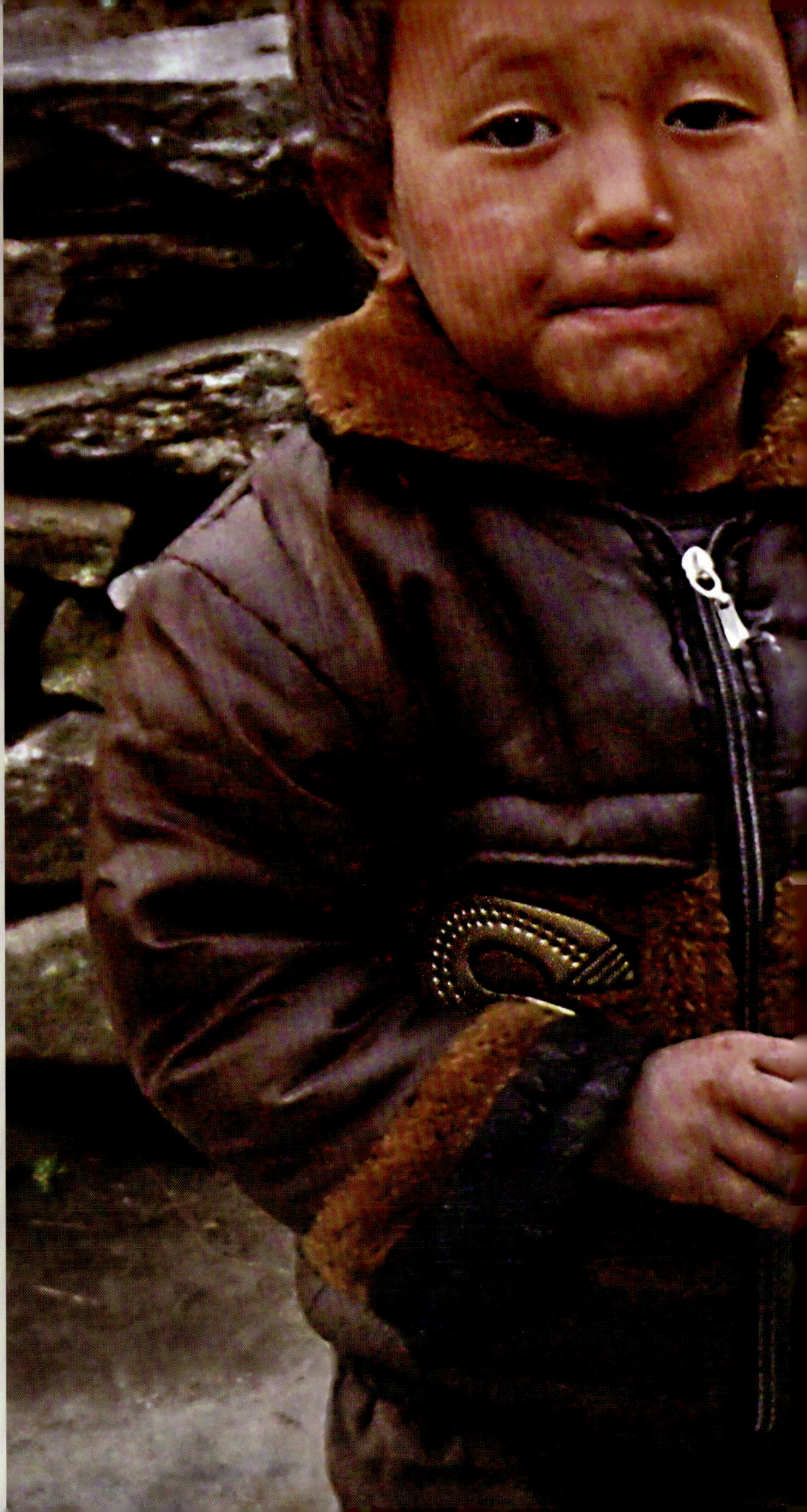

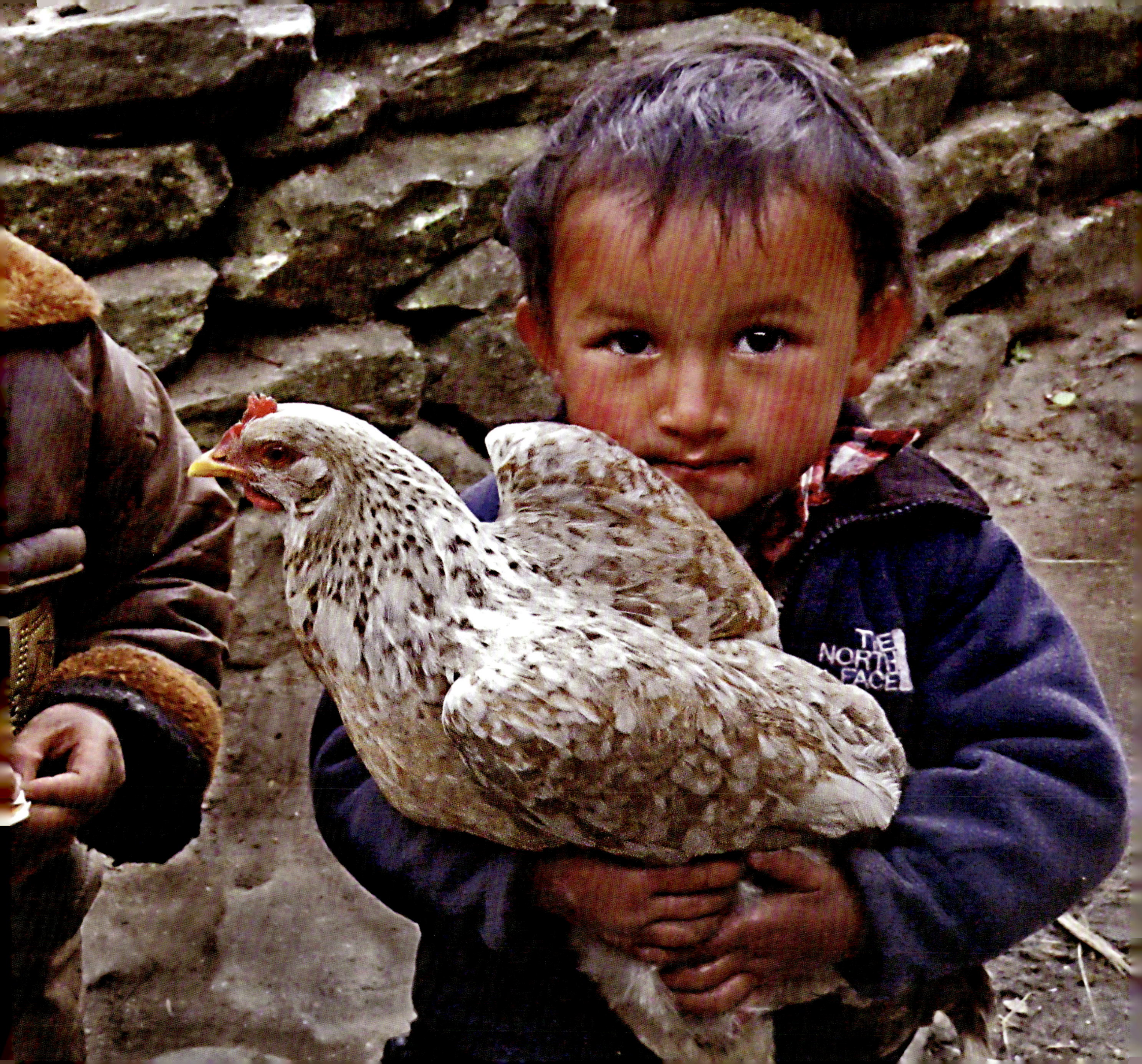
THE NORTH FACE

The mountains are calling and I must go.

- John Muir

35

The climax of many a grand trekking adventure in the *Kumbu* region of Nepal comes nearly four miles above sea level on the 18,513' summit of *Kala Pattar*. From here the highest point of land on earth, great Mt. Everest, *Sagarmatha* to the Nepalese, "the mother of the sky", rises nearly two additional miles in altitude overhead. Yet the Himalaya is indisputedly the most colossal mountain range in the world, and perhaps even more extraordinary vistas await the adventuresome who press on beyond *Kala Pattar*. Another arduous day of hiking up the ancient trading route winding across vast *Ngozumpa* Glacier through the clouds leads ultimately to 17,783' *Cho La Pass*. Breathless in the rarified air and surrounded on all sides by ice-crowned peaks, it is easy to imagine that one has entered at last into *Shangri-La*, legendary realm of the mountain gods.

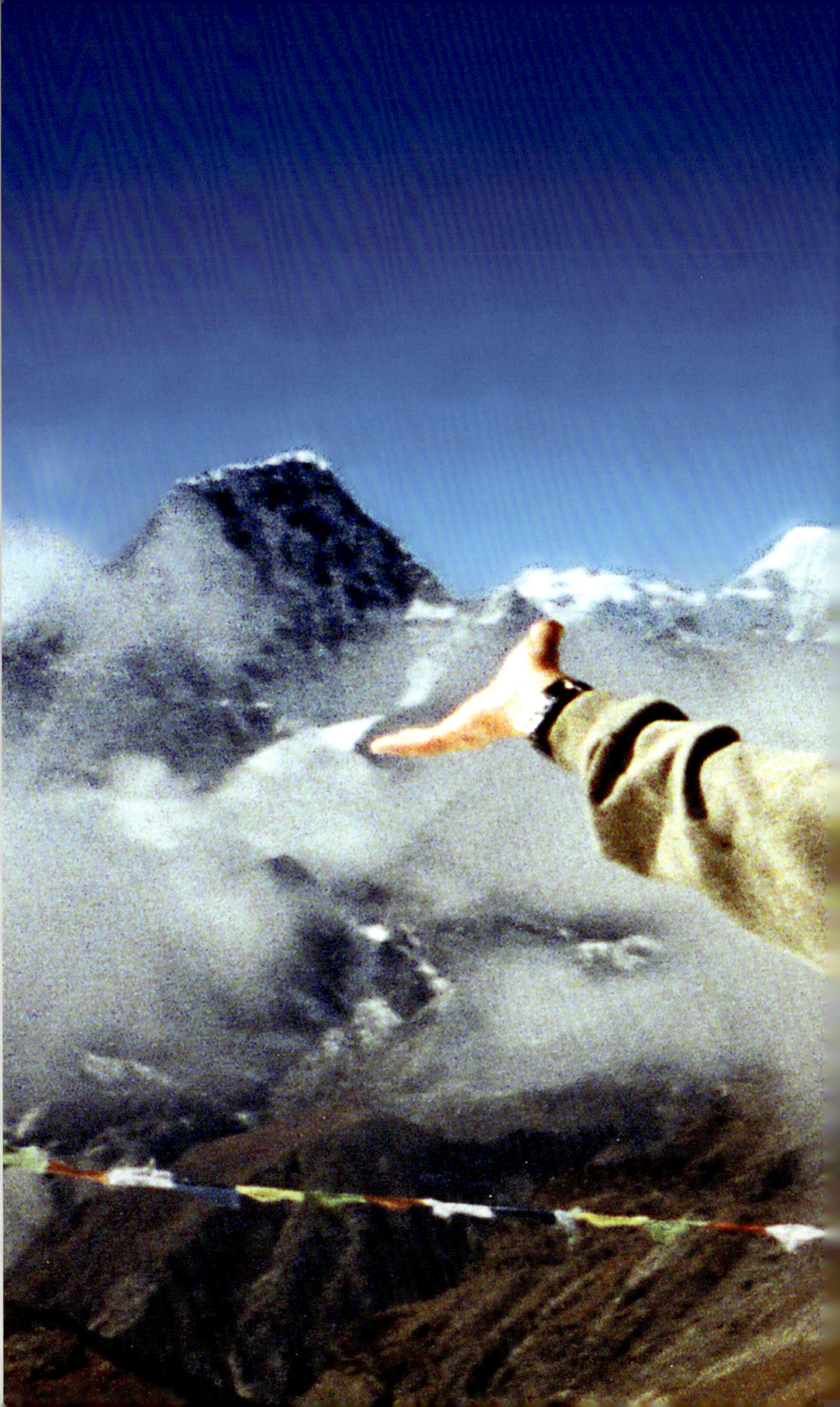

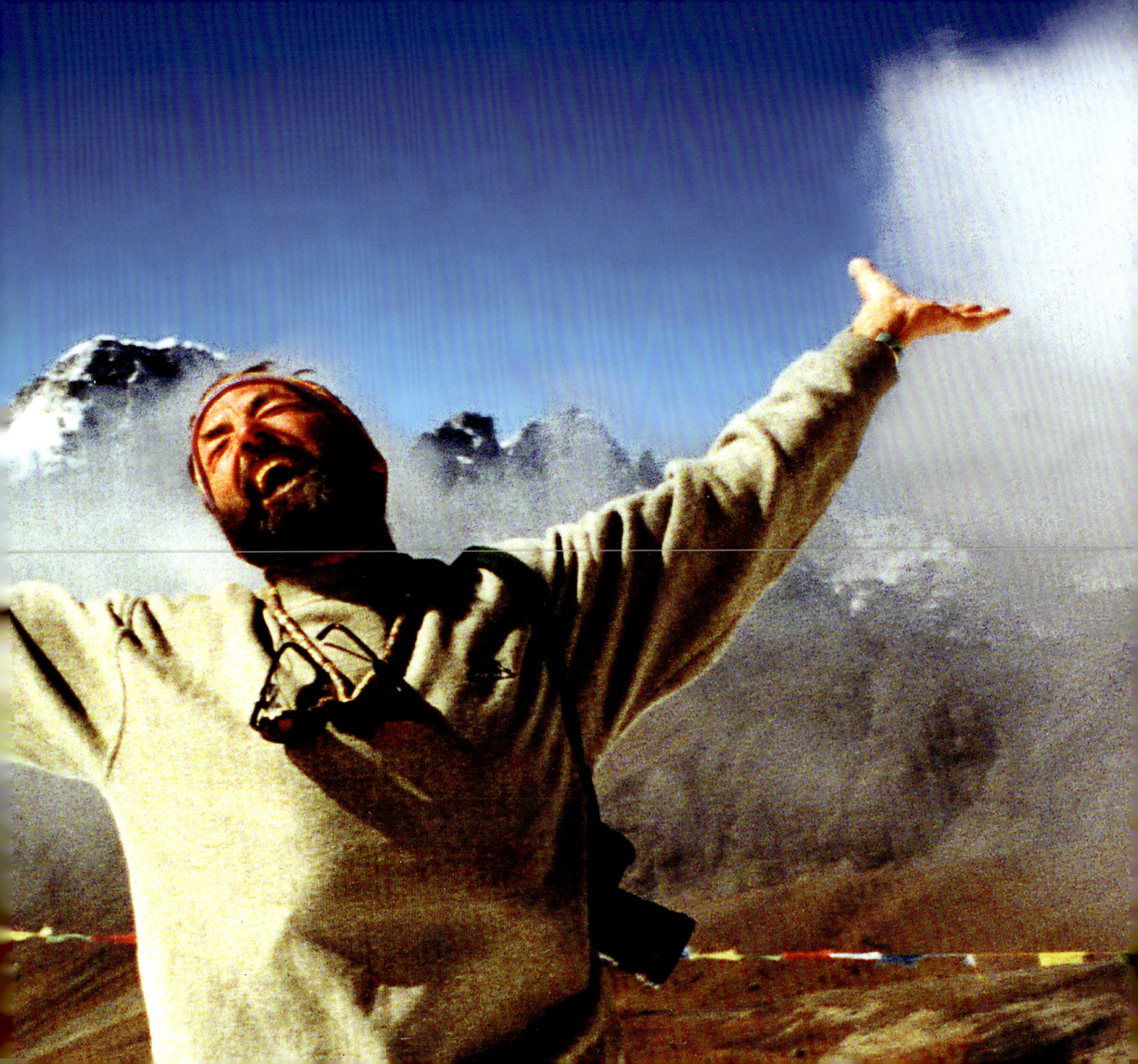

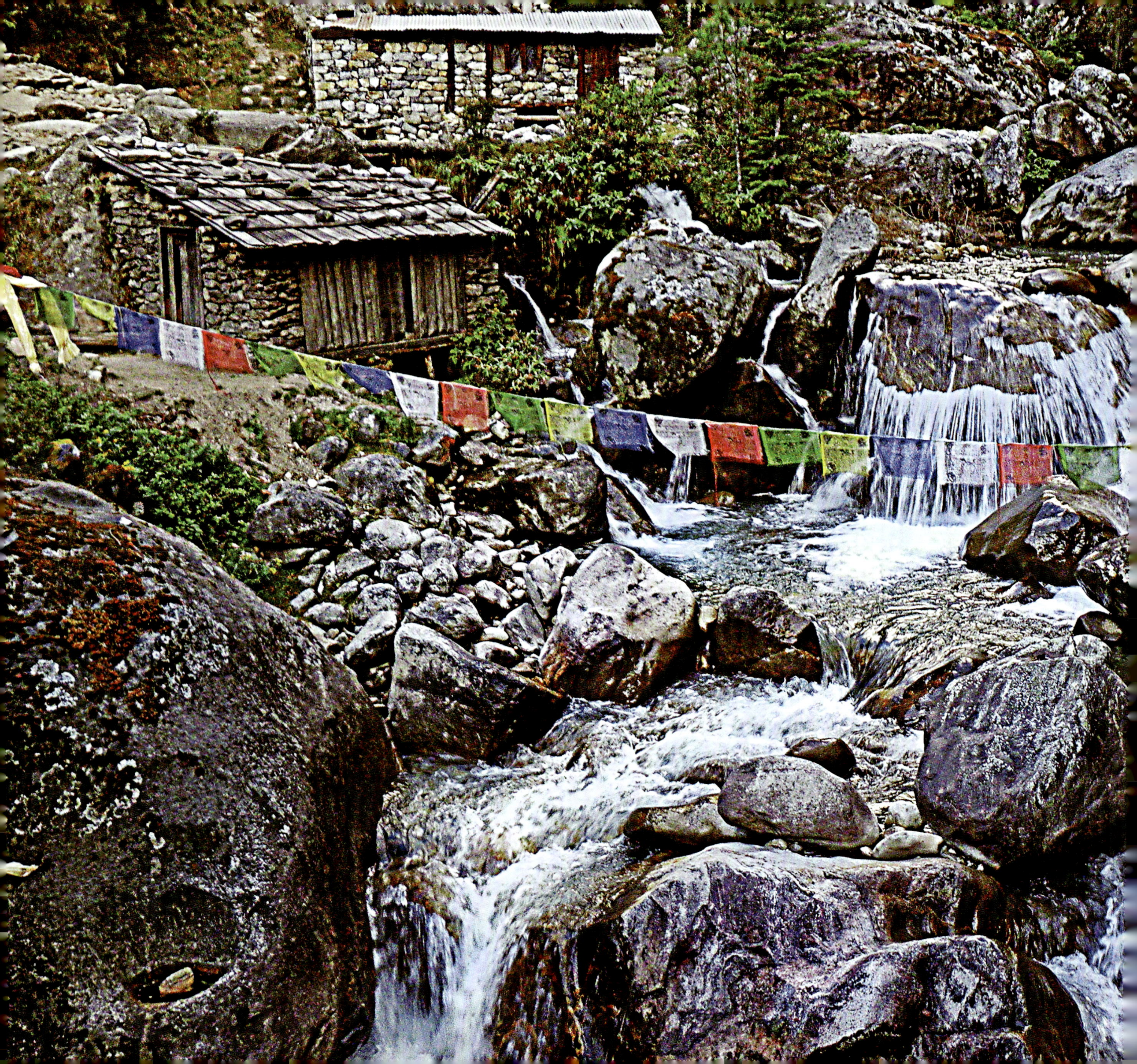

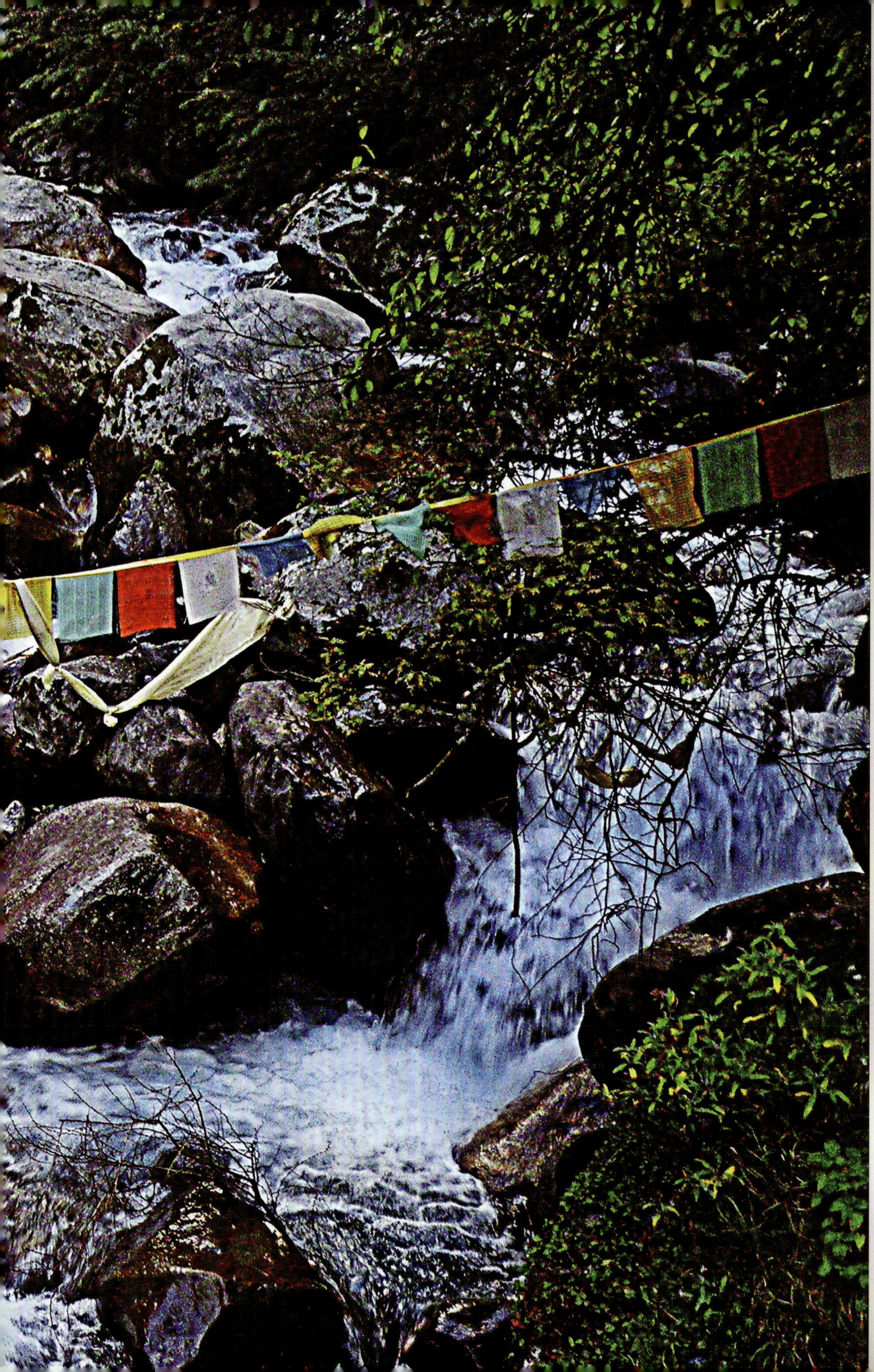

All the rivers run to the sea
yet the sea never overflows;
Back to the place where
the streams began, they
return to run again.

- Ecclesiastes 1:7

Rivers and streams running through the mountains have always been focal points of human spirituality. This is especially evident in eastern Nepal along the trails that countless trekkers, climbers and pilgrims walk each year to approach Mt. Everest. Buddhists monks believe that the prayer wheels they place along rivers, then kept in perpetual motion by water running down from the mystical heights, are sending out prayers for world peace.

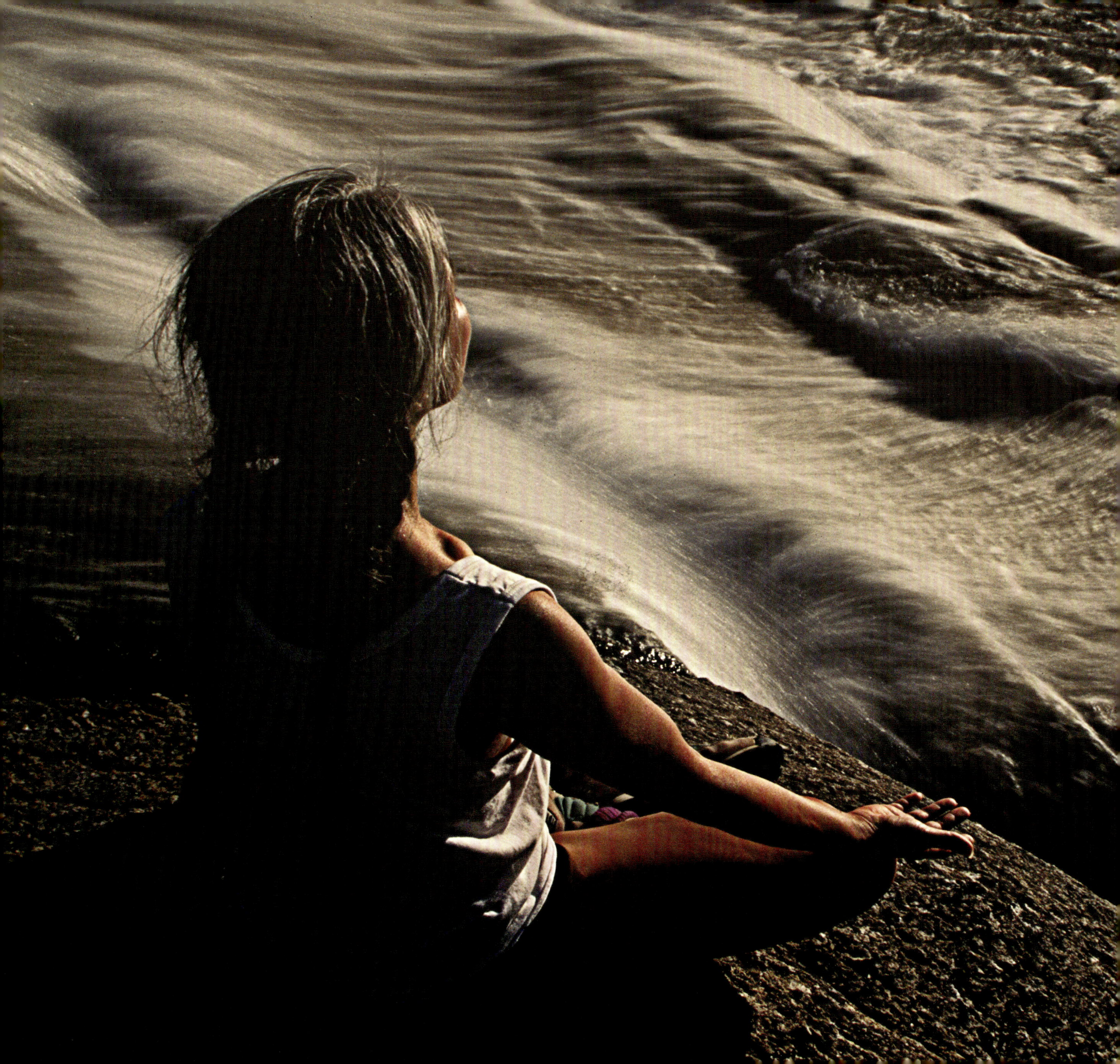

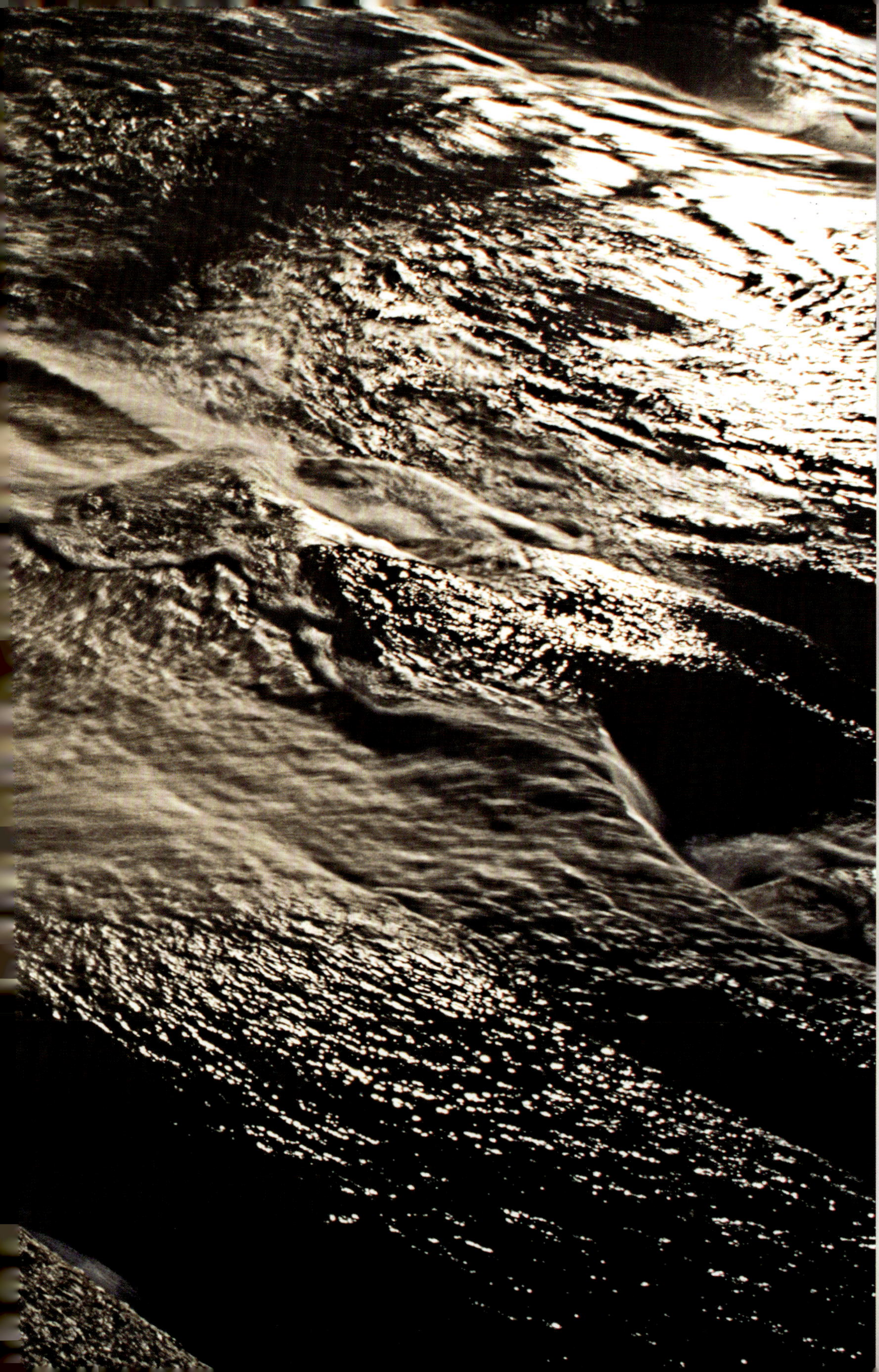

Rivers know this;
there is no hurry, we
will get there someday.

- Winnie the Pooh

40

On a leisurely multi-day backpacking trip through the magical Yosemite high country, Nani pauses in the warmth of the afternoon sun to listen to the song a swift-moving mountain stream and contemplate for a timeless time, the simple wonders of nature.

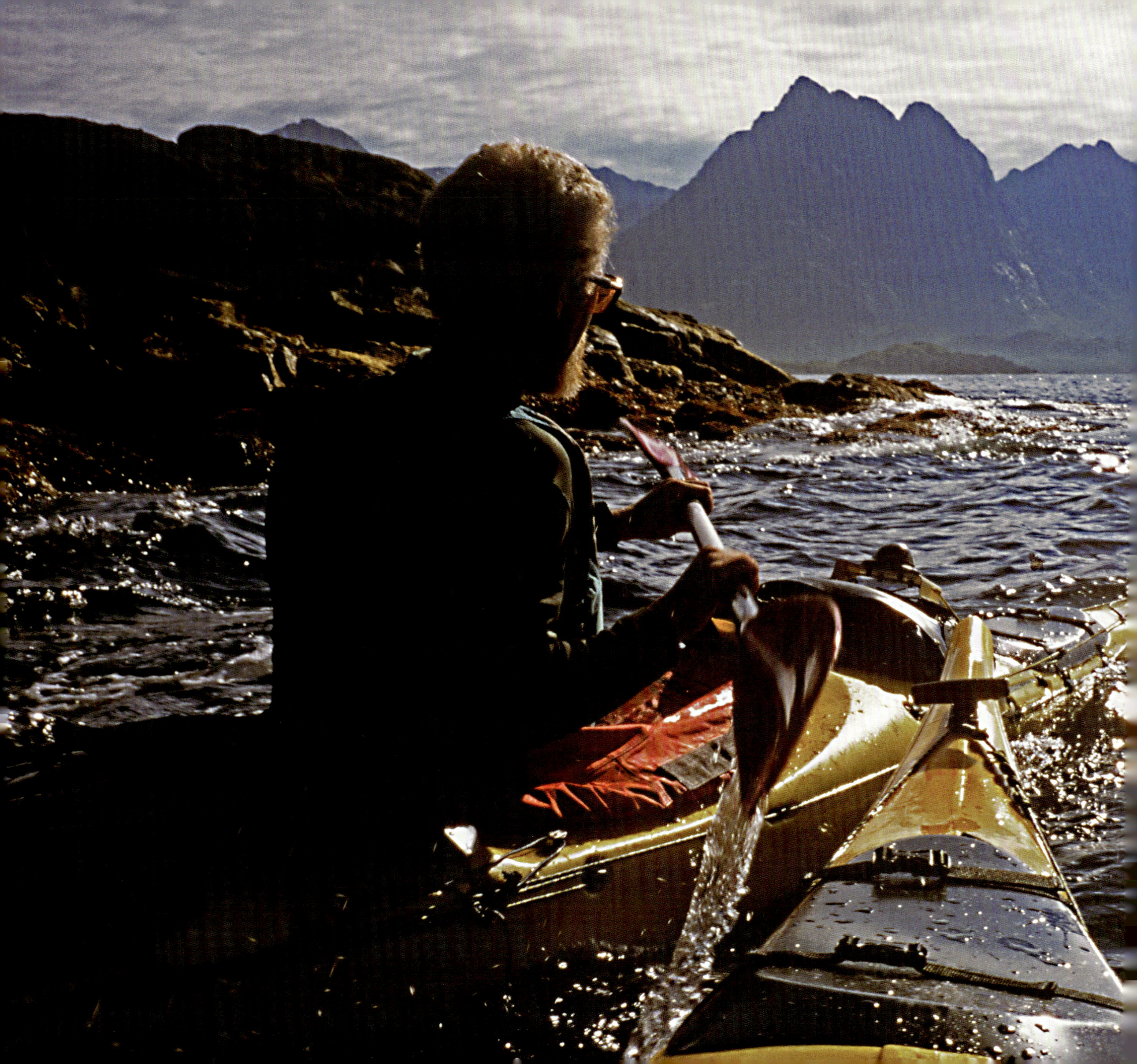

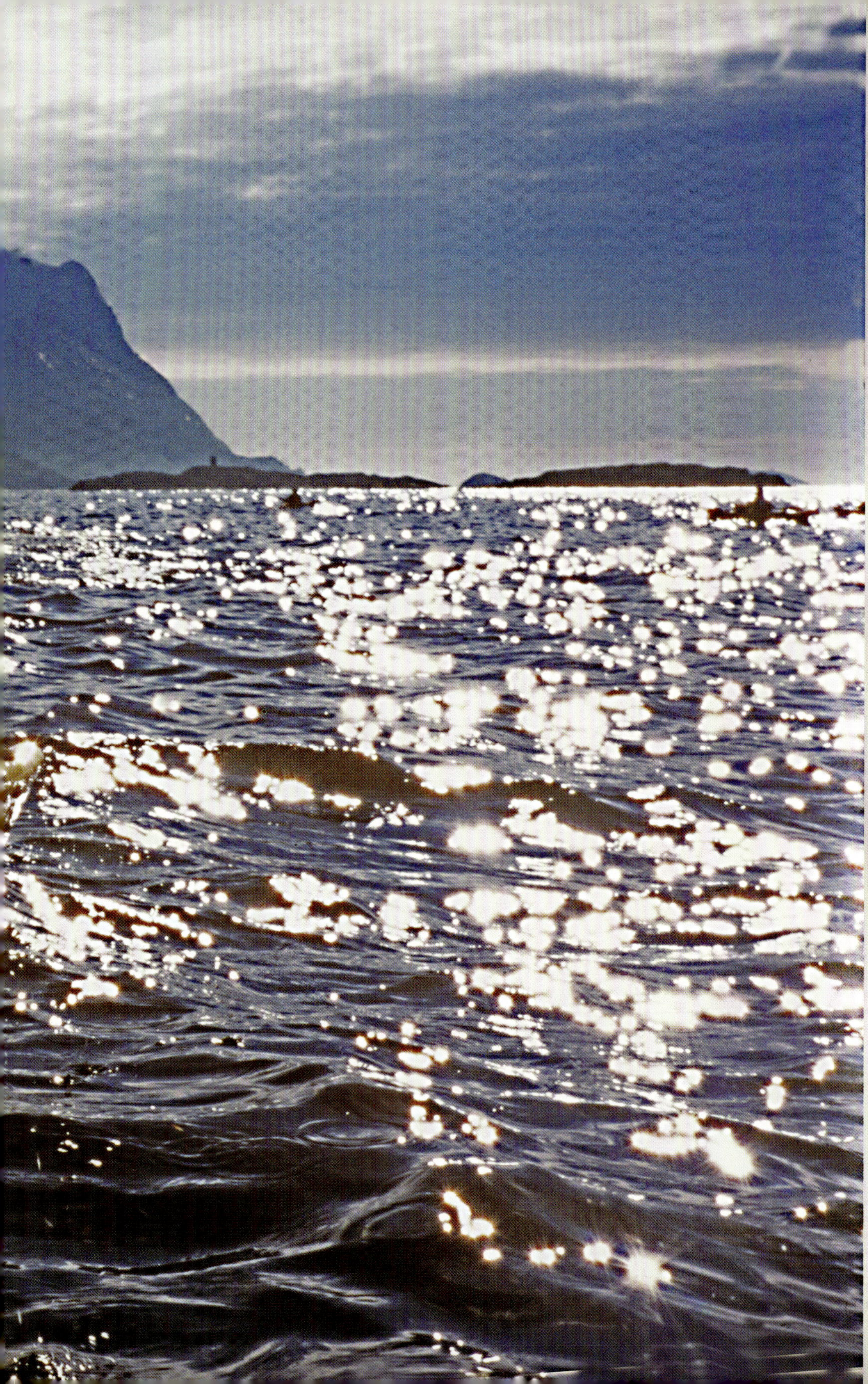

Not all who wander are lost.

- Tolkien

42

"Weather is everything here." a local fishermen once observed about his homeland of northern Norway. This becomes especially dear up beyond the Arctic Circle, where the craggy Lofoten and Vesterålan archipelagos thrust imprudently out into the often tempestuous Norwegian Sea. Its as if the old Viking gods were still battling over never-settled disputes out there. For this is where warm Gulf Stream currents collide with fierce polar storms, sometimes with explosive results. Yet some adventuresome modern-day sea kayakers find it hard to resist these mysterious islands - and in *midtsommer* when the sun never sets and the tropical waters flowing up from the Gulf of Mexico drive the Arctic chill away, the far north becomes a paddling paradise.

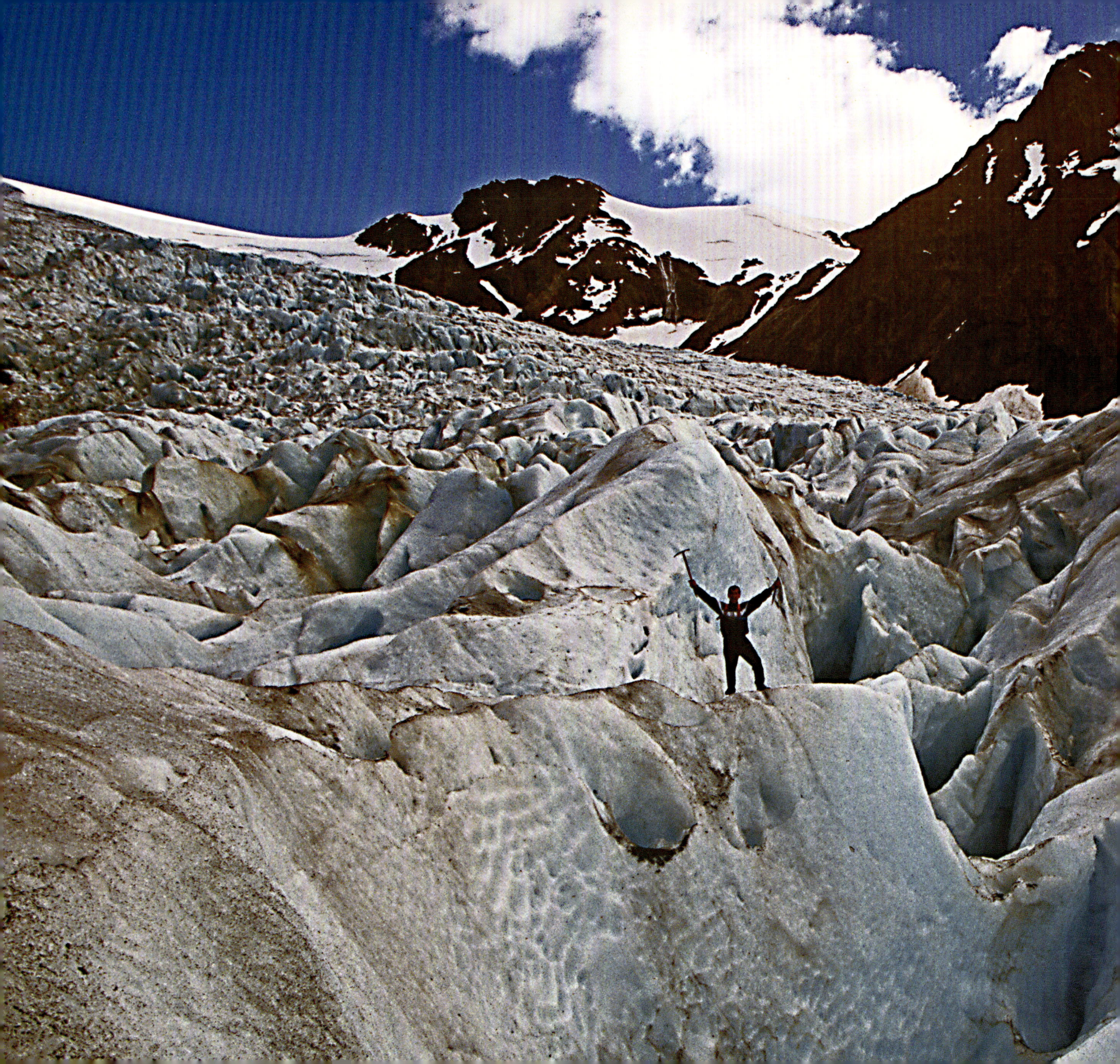

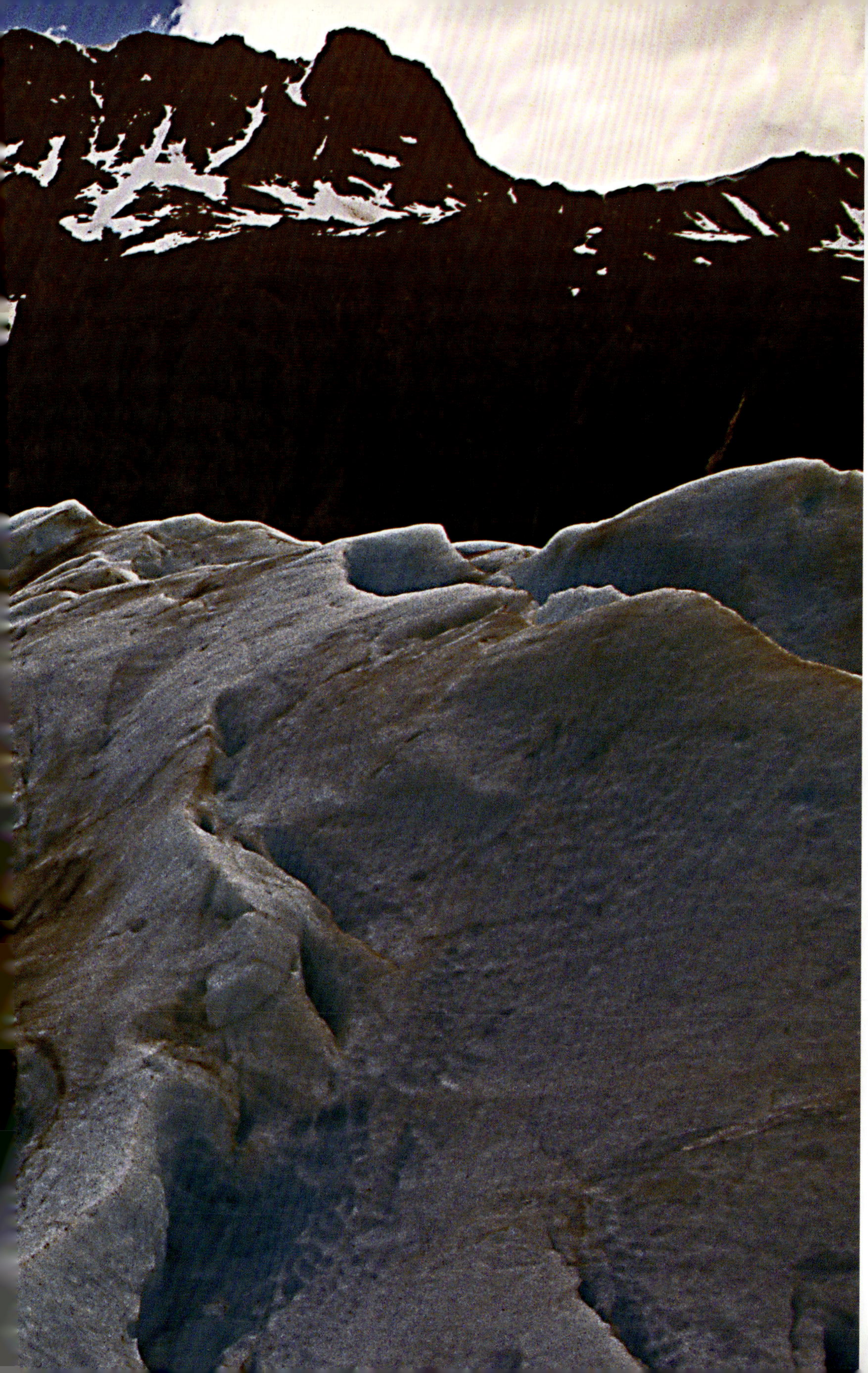

You risk tears when you let yourself be tamed.

- Antoine de Saint Exupéry,
The Little Prince

When Stienar Johansen is not busy tending the farm owned by his family for five generations, he loves shepherding ice climbers up into his beloved Svartisen Glacier nearby. Situated just north of the Arctic Circle along the rugged coast of northern Norway, Svartisen is the lowest elevation glacier in all of Europe. It presently reaches within a mile of the sea. Stienar recalls that when he was a young boy, long before the advent of global warming, the glacier flowed all the way down past the farm and spilled into the sea.

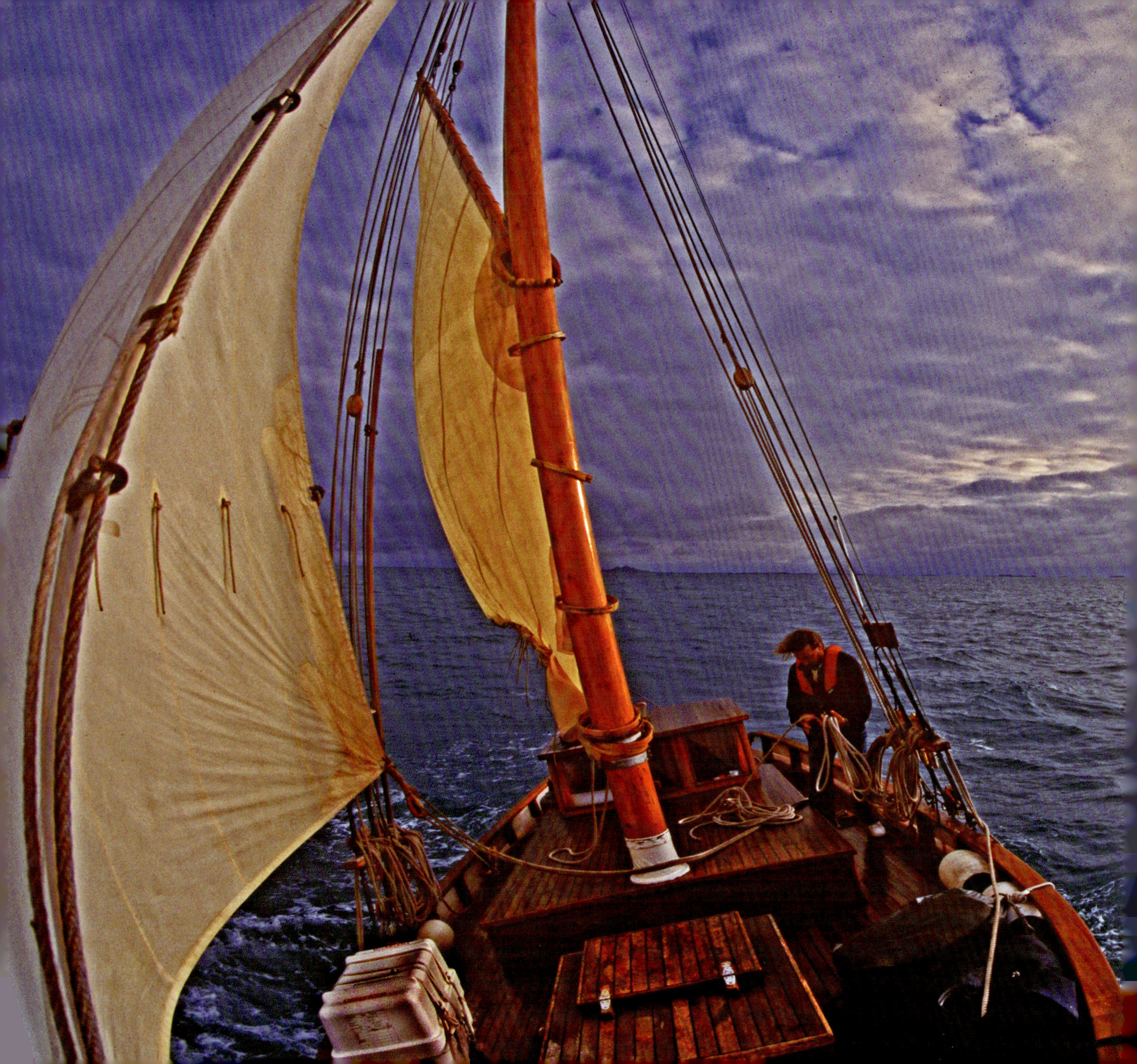

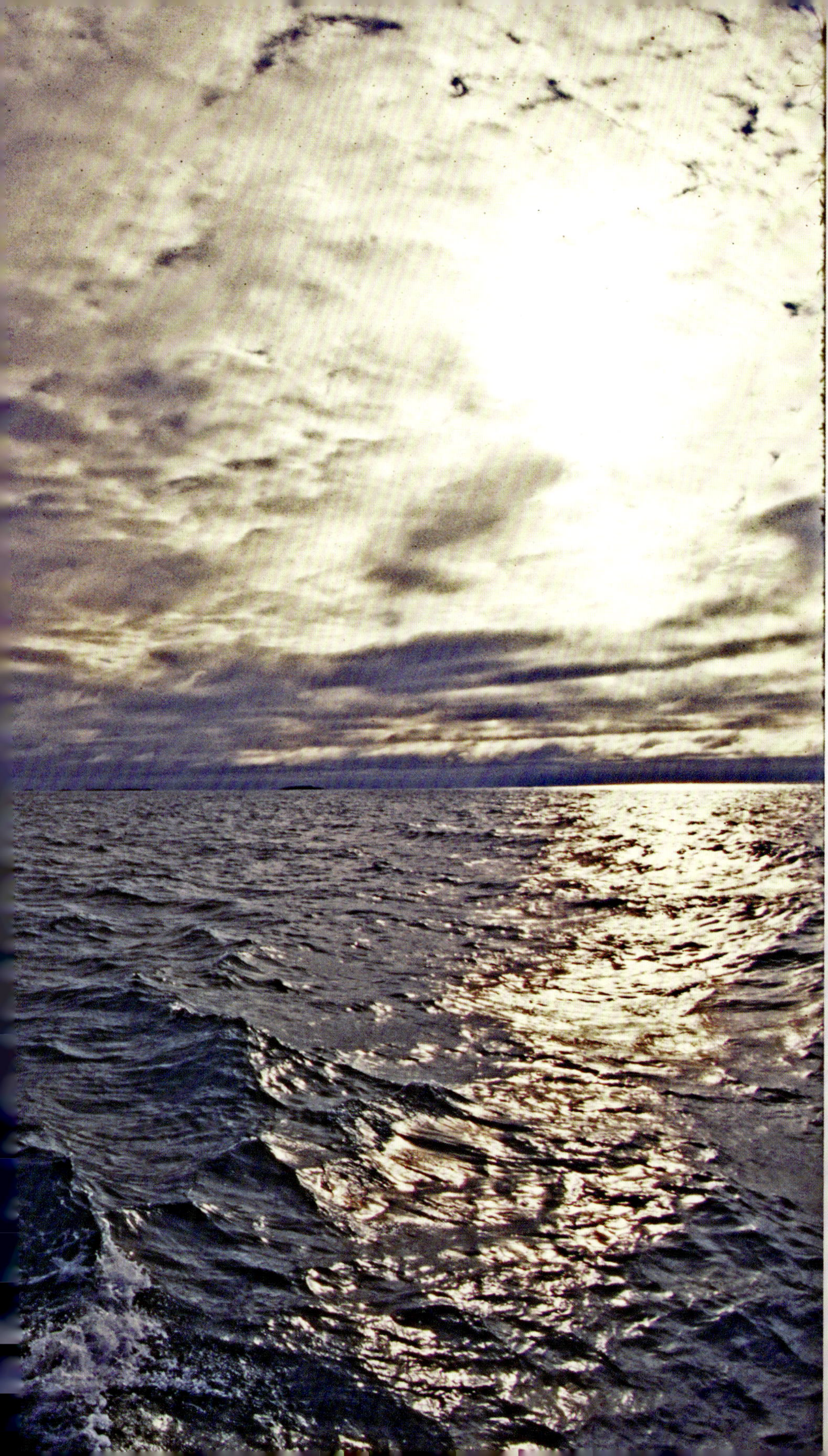

When we go back to the sea,
whether to sail or to watch,
we are going back from
whence we came.

- John Fitzgerald Kennedy

Helge is an old-school mariner who has faithfully followed the tradition of his Viking ancestors by building his classic wooden sailboat by hand with timbers hewn from great oak trees felled in the forests of his Norwegian homeland. Today he sails along the rugged, fjord-lined coast he knows so well, returning home to the old stone lighthouse located on a small rocky *øy*, or island, where he and his family live close by the blustery northern sea.

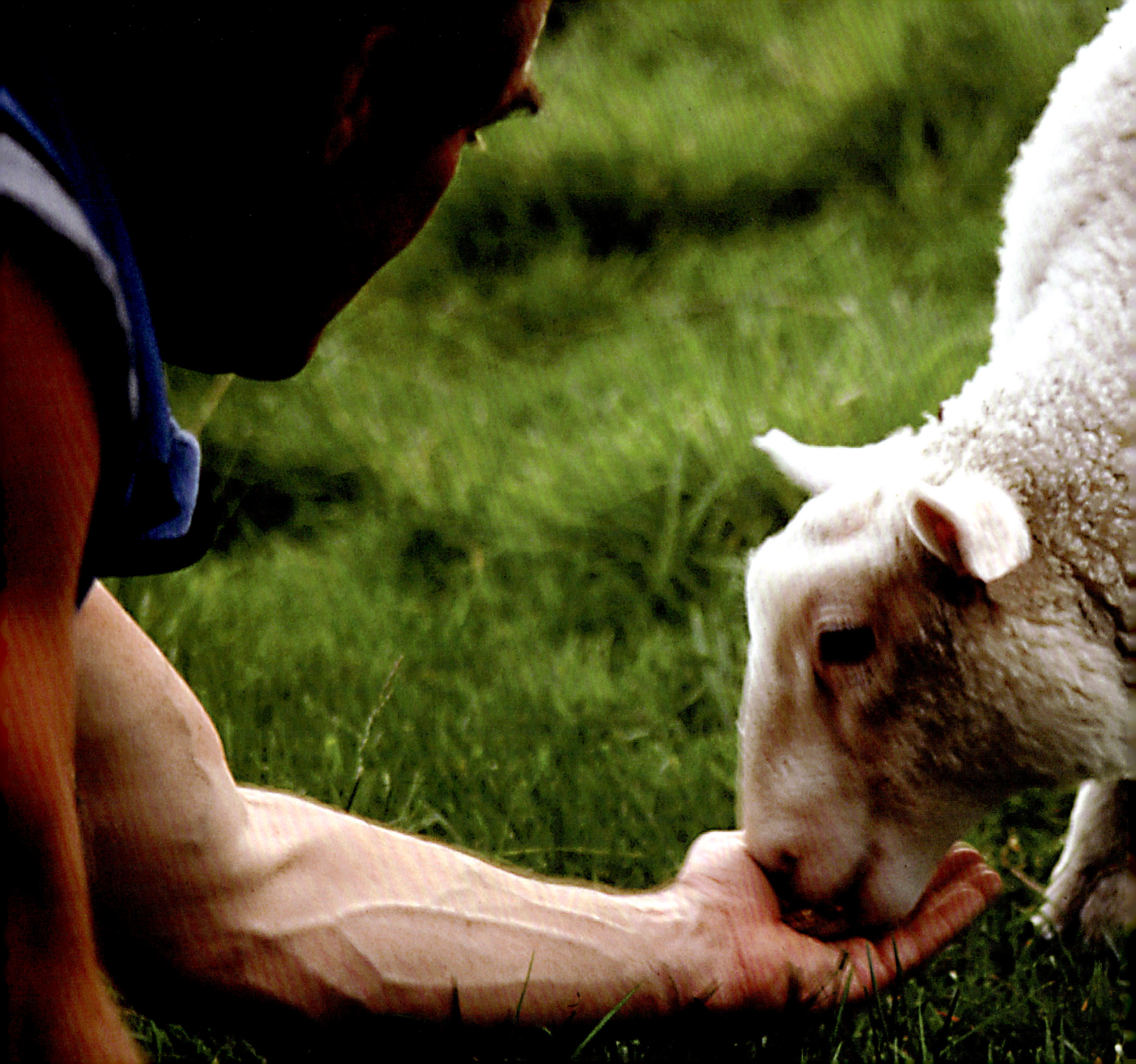

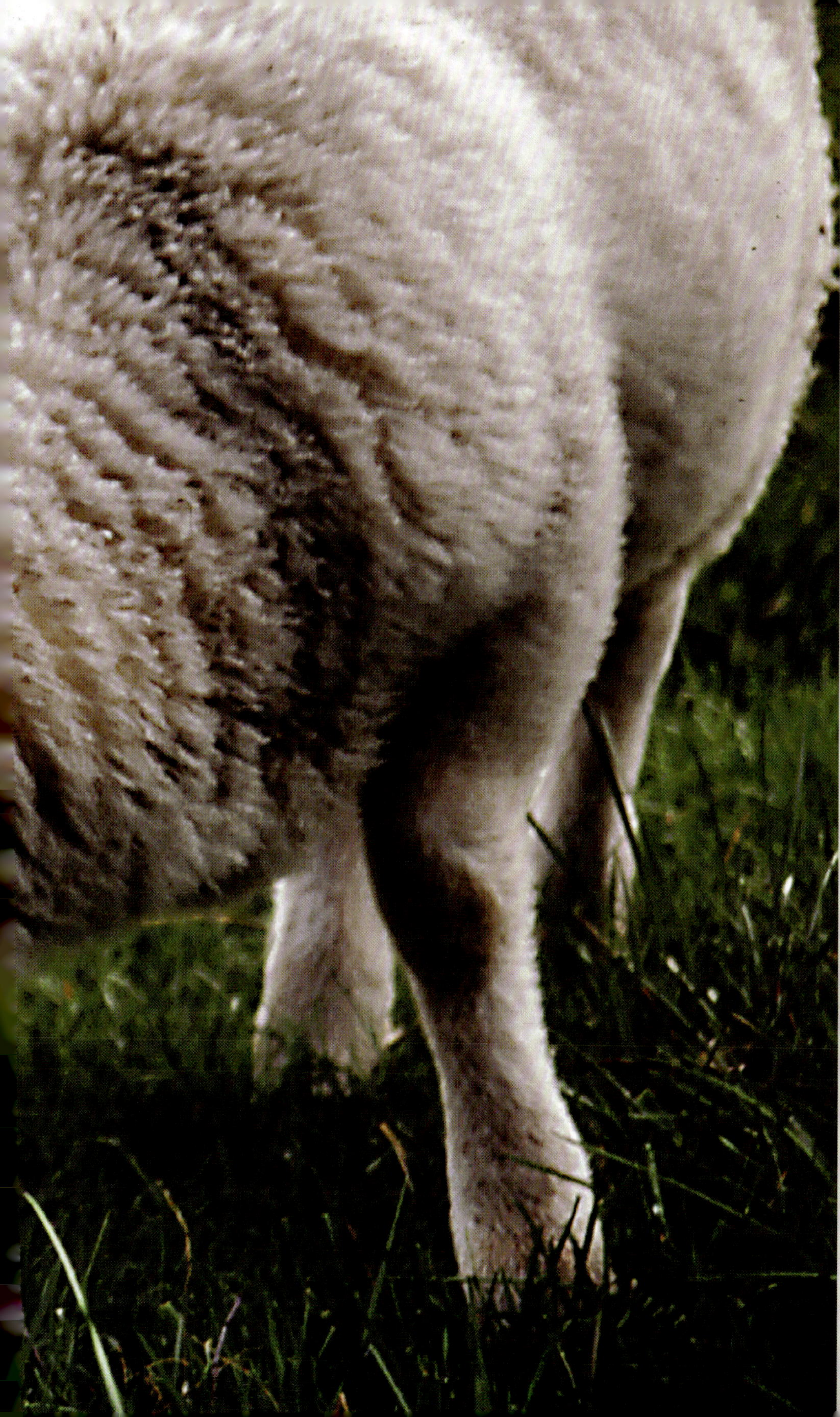

You are responsible forever
for what you have tamed.

- The fox, in The Little Prince

Each spring as they have done for untolde generations, Norwegian shepherds herd their flocks of sheep up to lush alpine pastures in the Jotunheimen Mountains. On a journey of self-discovery back to his ancestors' homeland, photographer Patrick Powers senses within himself the Viking blood that has always run through his veins.

The mind is an ocean.
The surface functions actively
while the deeper layers lie
eternally silent.

- Maharisha Mahesh Yogi

In the light of the midnight sun, the sleek bow of a sea kayak knifes silently through waters steeped in Viking history. Image captured with a waterproof camera in the midst a multi-day paddling adventure through the brooding and mysterious Vesterålen archipelago, off the coast of northern Norway above the Arctic Circle.

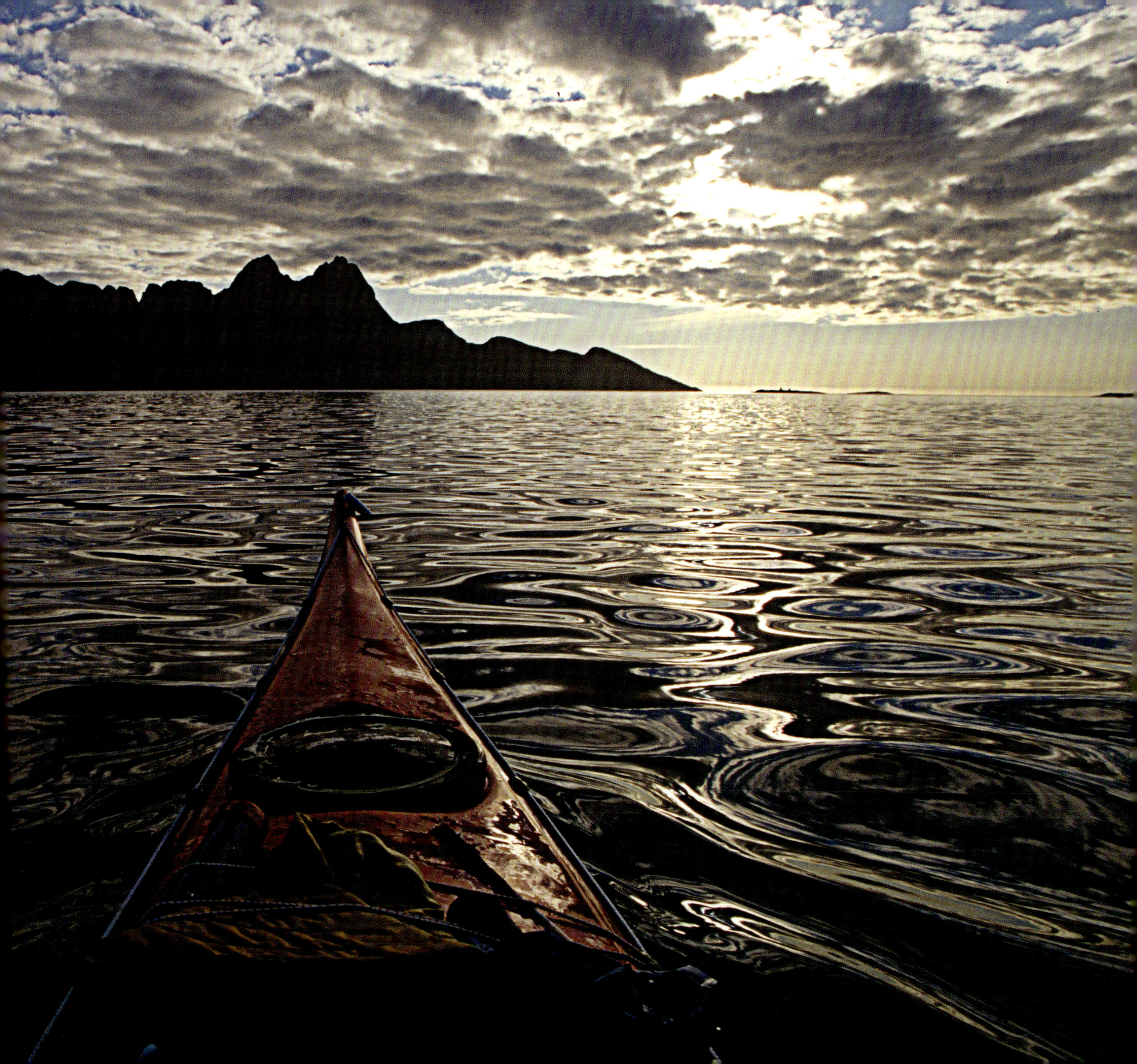

It is our task in our time and in our generation to hand down undiminished to those who come after us... the natural wealth and beauty which surrounds us.

- John Fitzgerald Kennedy

Residents and visitors to the San Francisco Bay Area are fortunate that the mountainous terrain surrounding many of the burgeoning flatland cities has limited urban sprawl to a greater degree than in many other parts of the country. Miraculously, some large tracts of forested land in northern California have survived to present times. Recognizing the preciousness of this imperiled natural treasure, non-profit land conservation agencies like the Peninsula Open Space Trust and the Midpeninsula Regional Open Space District have become dedicated to achieving protected status for as much of the region's remaining unspoiled lands as possible. For these last pristine wilderness corridors to remain intact is not just of enormous benefit to humankind - but essential also, for the survival of bay area wildlife.

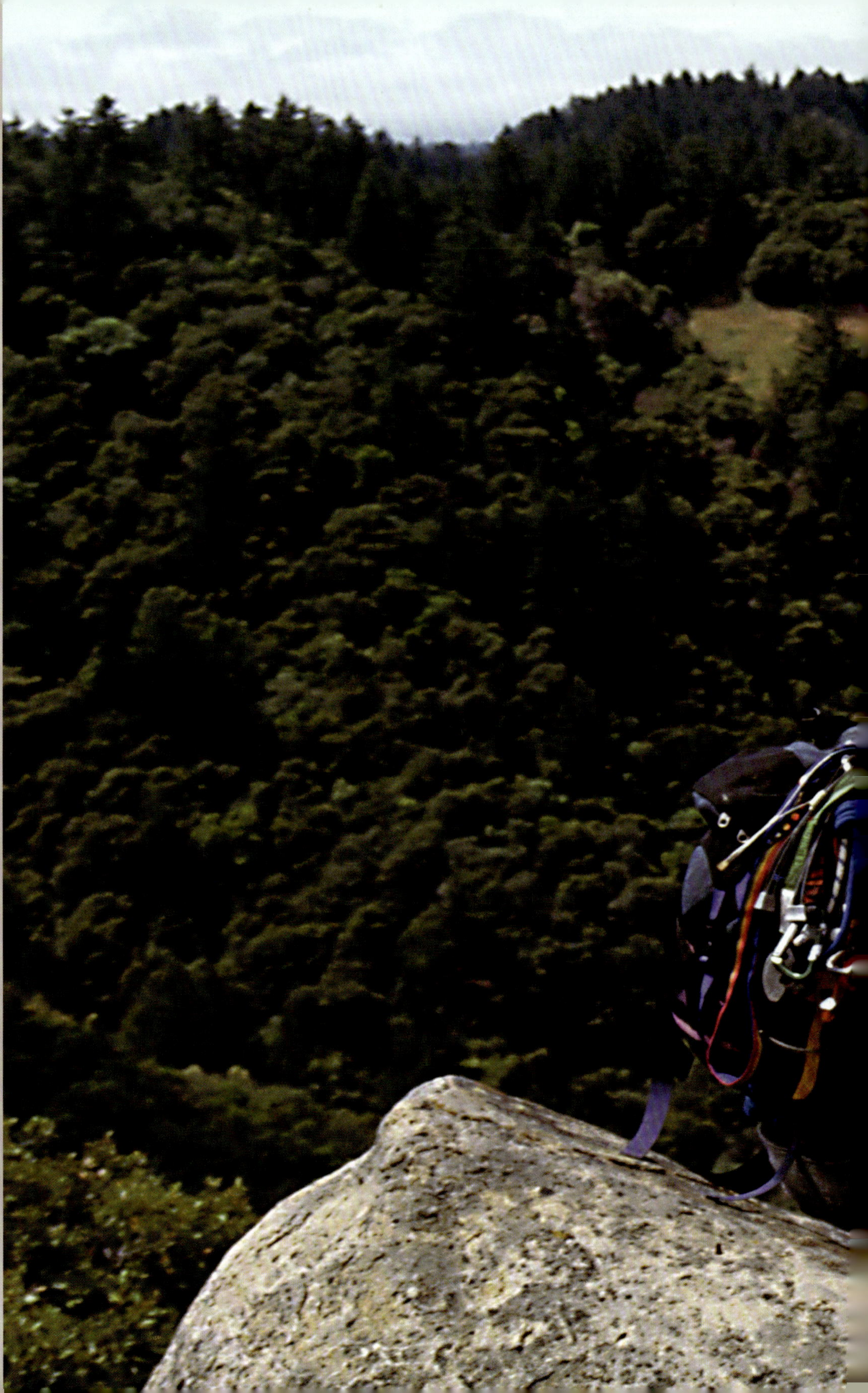

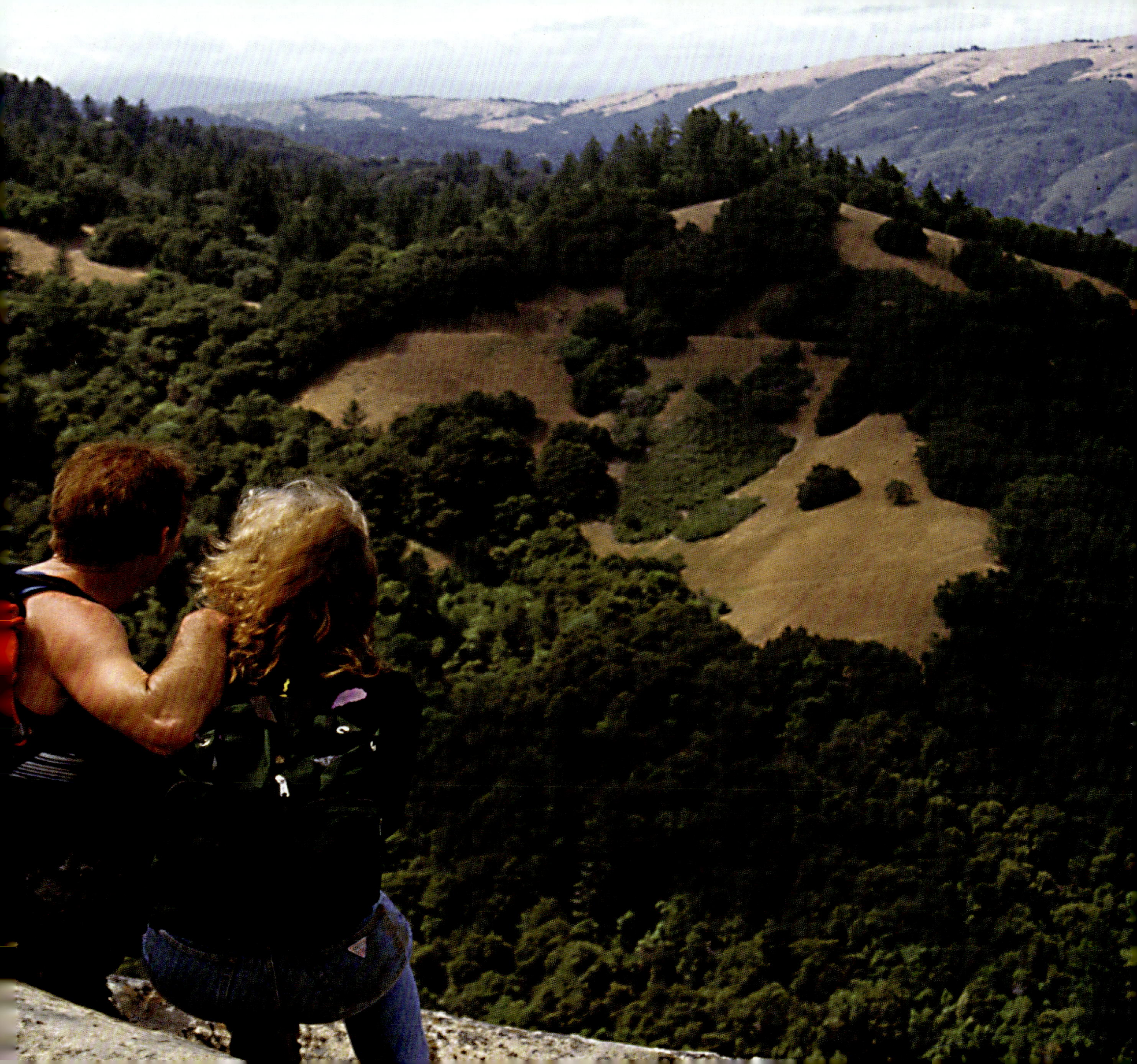

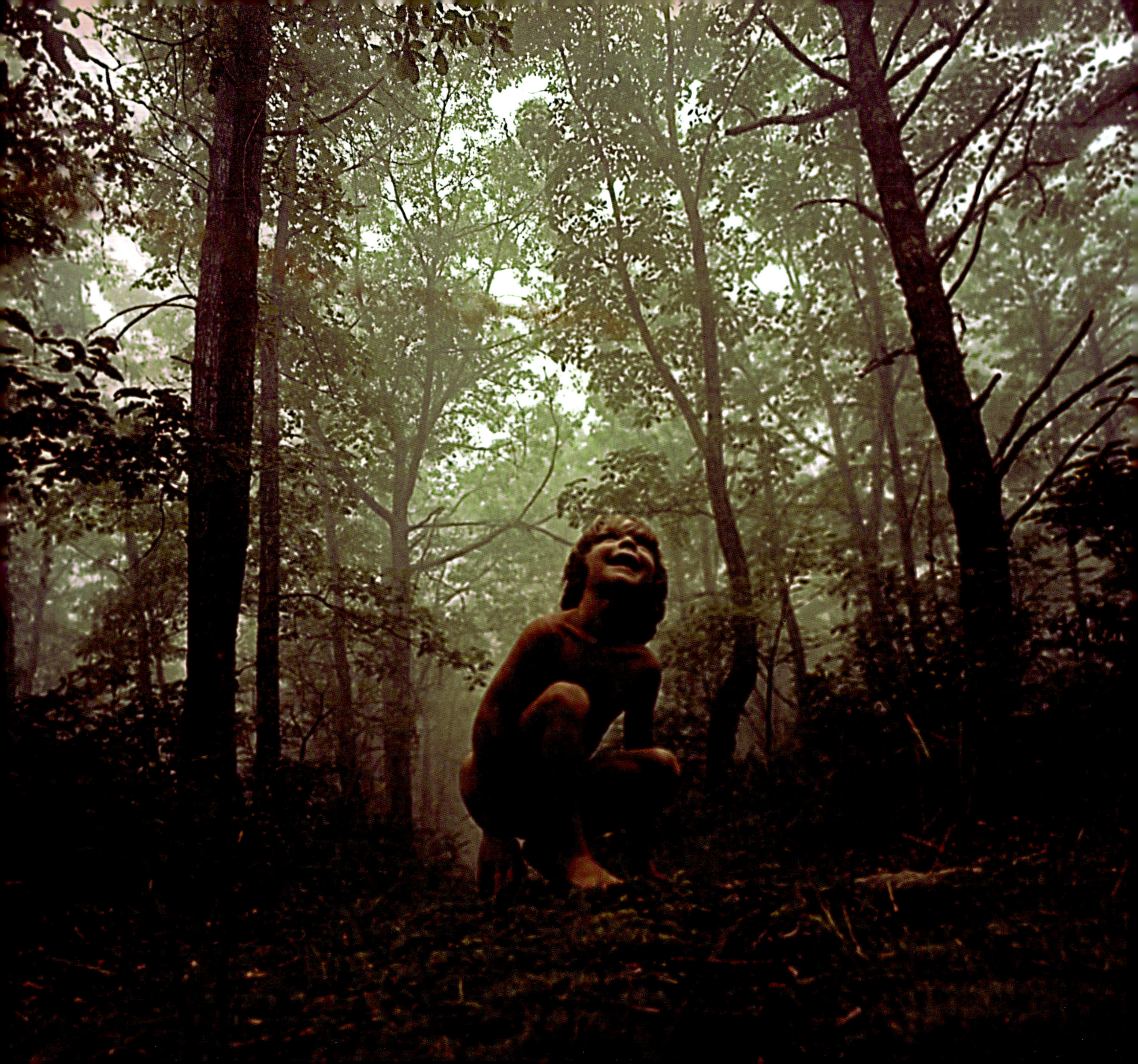

Out here we are free, my son.

- Billy, an ancient
Newfoundland Eskimo

On a road trip back east with his dad, five year-old Marc Powers awakened one morning among the wonder of a New England forest where they had stopped to camp for the night.

Eighteen year-old Marc and his horse Dusty cool down after a long springtime ride through the green hills above the family farm in central Oregon.

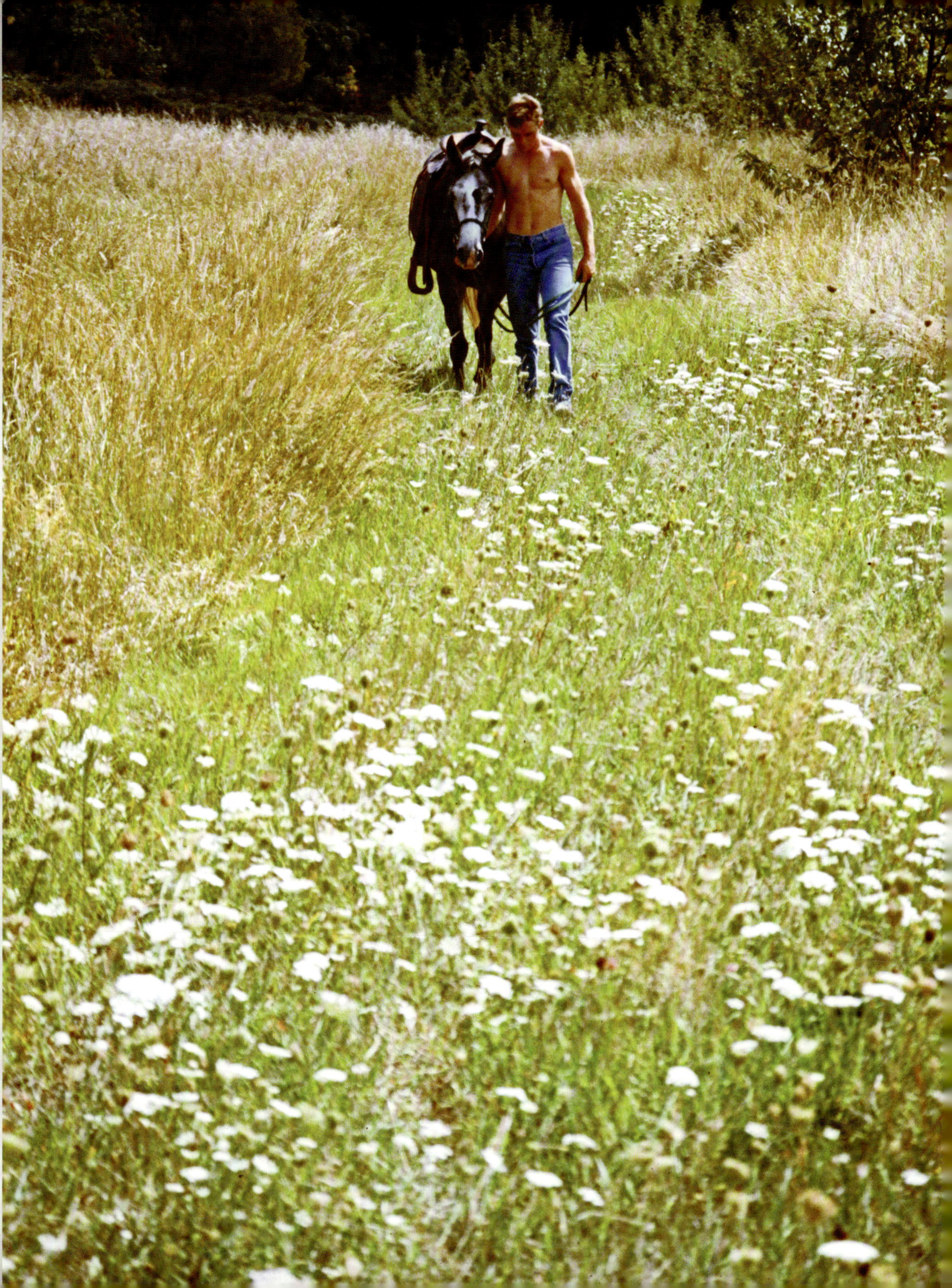

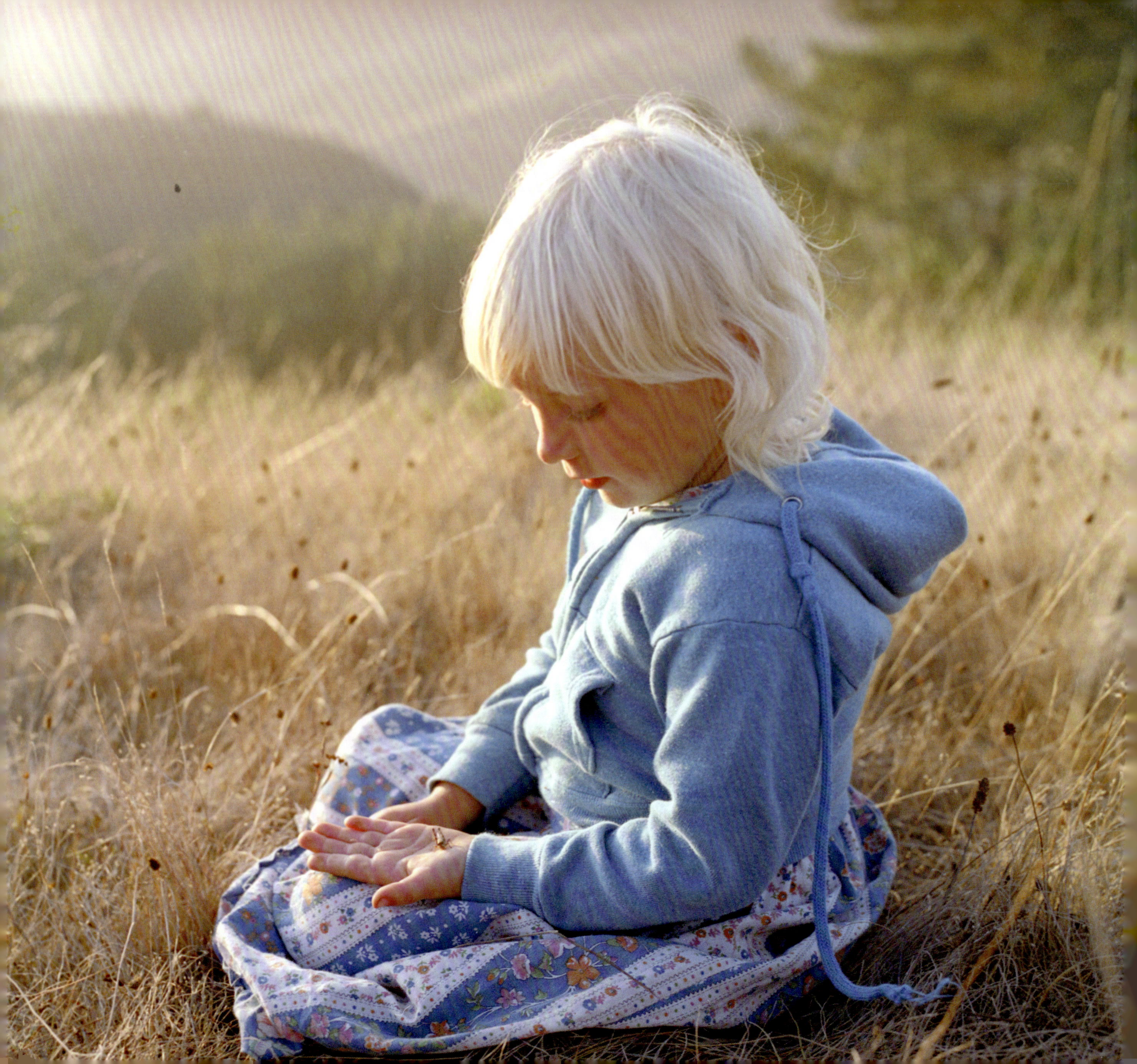

Think of all the beauty left around you and be happy.

- Anne Frank,
found in her diary

On a summer day in the coastal hills above her home in northern California, three year-old Chloe Pate contemplates the simple beauty of a grasshopper.

The wonders of nature have lost none of their magic for sixteen year-old Chloe as she stands at the foot of 70' Berry Creek Falls in the Santa Cruz Mountains.

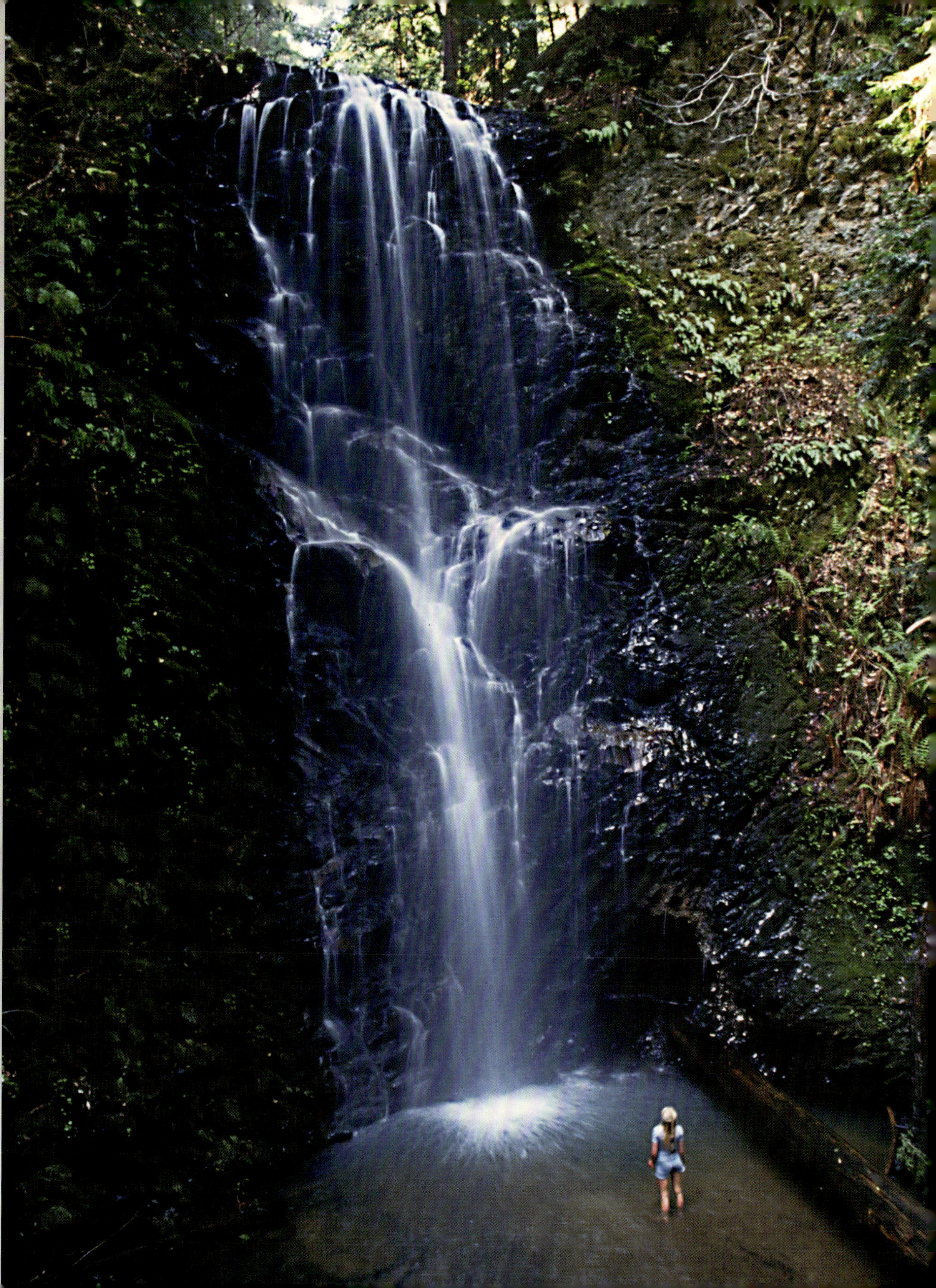

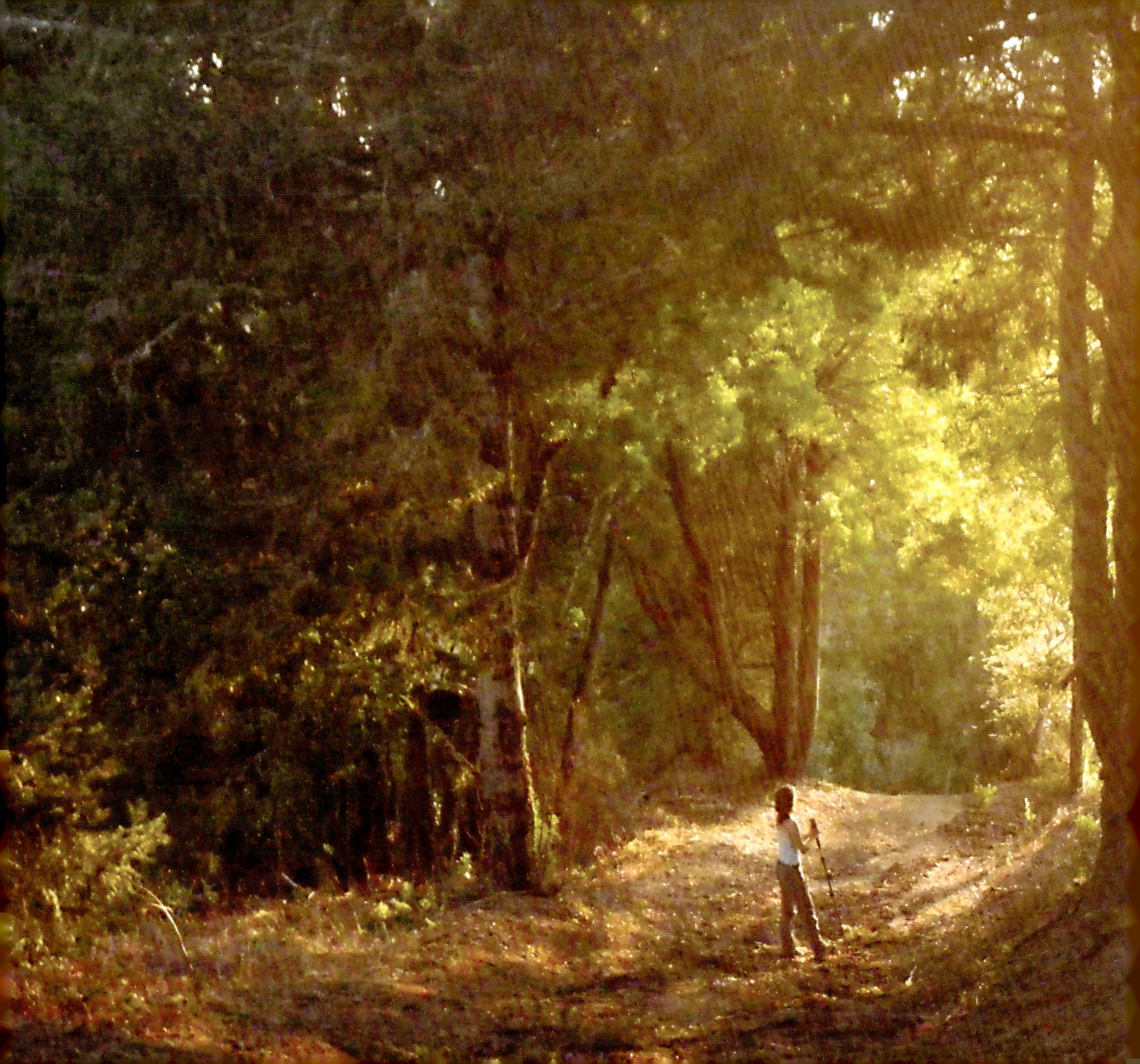

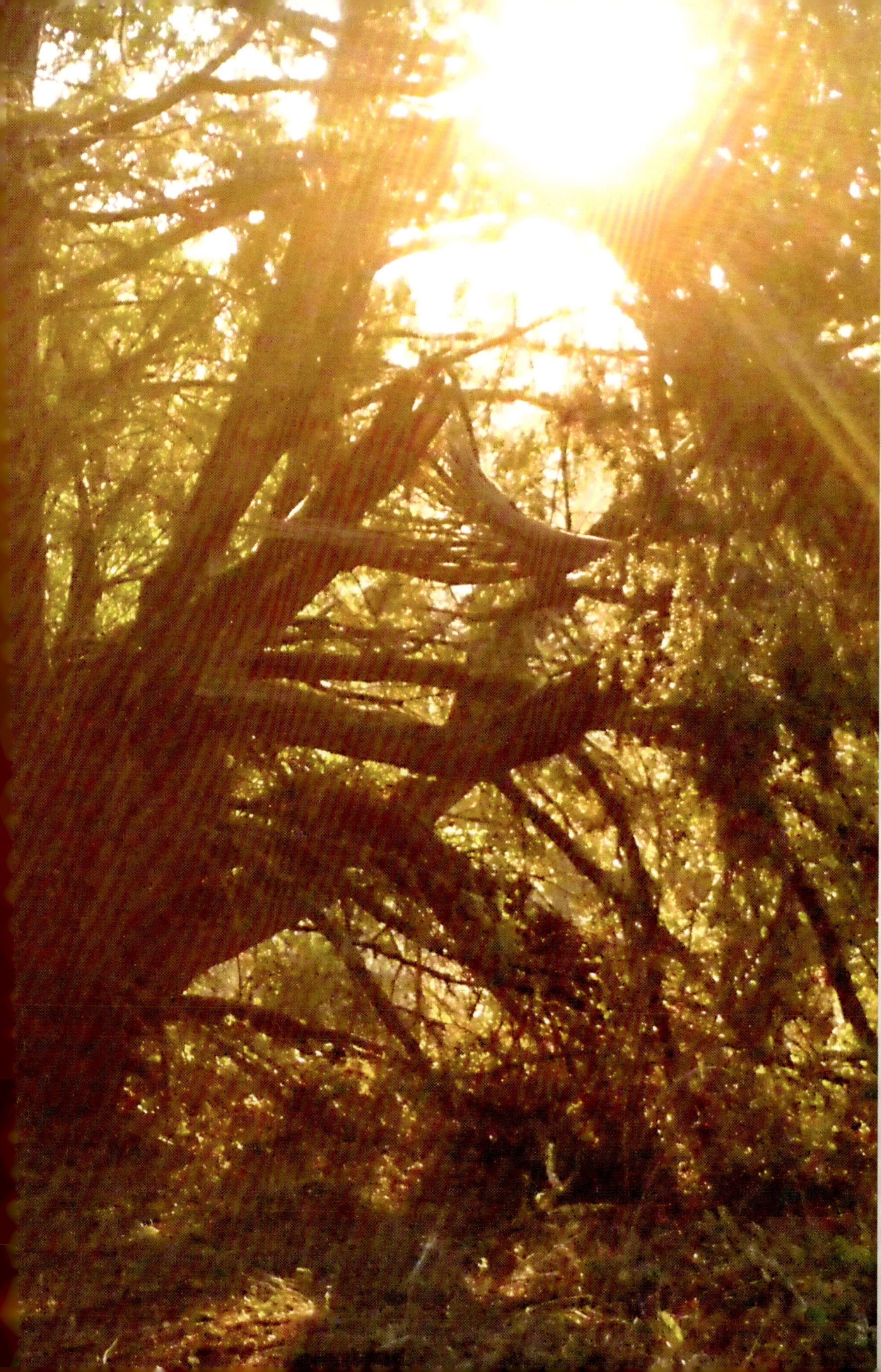

Walking is the great adventure, the first meditation, a practice of heart and soul primary to mankind. Walking is the exact balance of spirit and humility.

- Gary Snyder

A crescendo of autumn color resounds through the coastal mountains of northern California, inspiring a solitary hiker to pause for a moment and bask in the splendor unfolding around her. Marika has chosen spectacular but challenging Harkins Ridge trail for her hike this day. From deep in the ancient redwood groves of Purisma Canyon the trail climbs steeply into a very different world of deciduous hardwood trees, turning gold now in the warm afternoon sun. Lushly forested hills stretch out in all directions, and from the western horizon comes the glint of a distant sea. Fortunately this land still exists in its pristine state about an hour's drive from San Francisco - protected by the Midpeninsula Regional Open Space District, one of those commendable conservancy organizations dedicated to keeping some of the wilderness remaining around San Francisco Bay in its natural state forever.

Be yourself; everyone else is already taken.

– Oscar Wilde

In our crowded twenty-first century world, Tom Ferenz still finds room to breathe in the coastal mountains above his home a few miles south of San Francisco. Fortunately for Tom and other hikers and nature lovers, this still pristine land is now protected by the Midpeninsula Regional Open Space District, one of the commendable conservancy organizations dedicated to protecting forever, what is left of the wilderness around the San Francisco Bay.

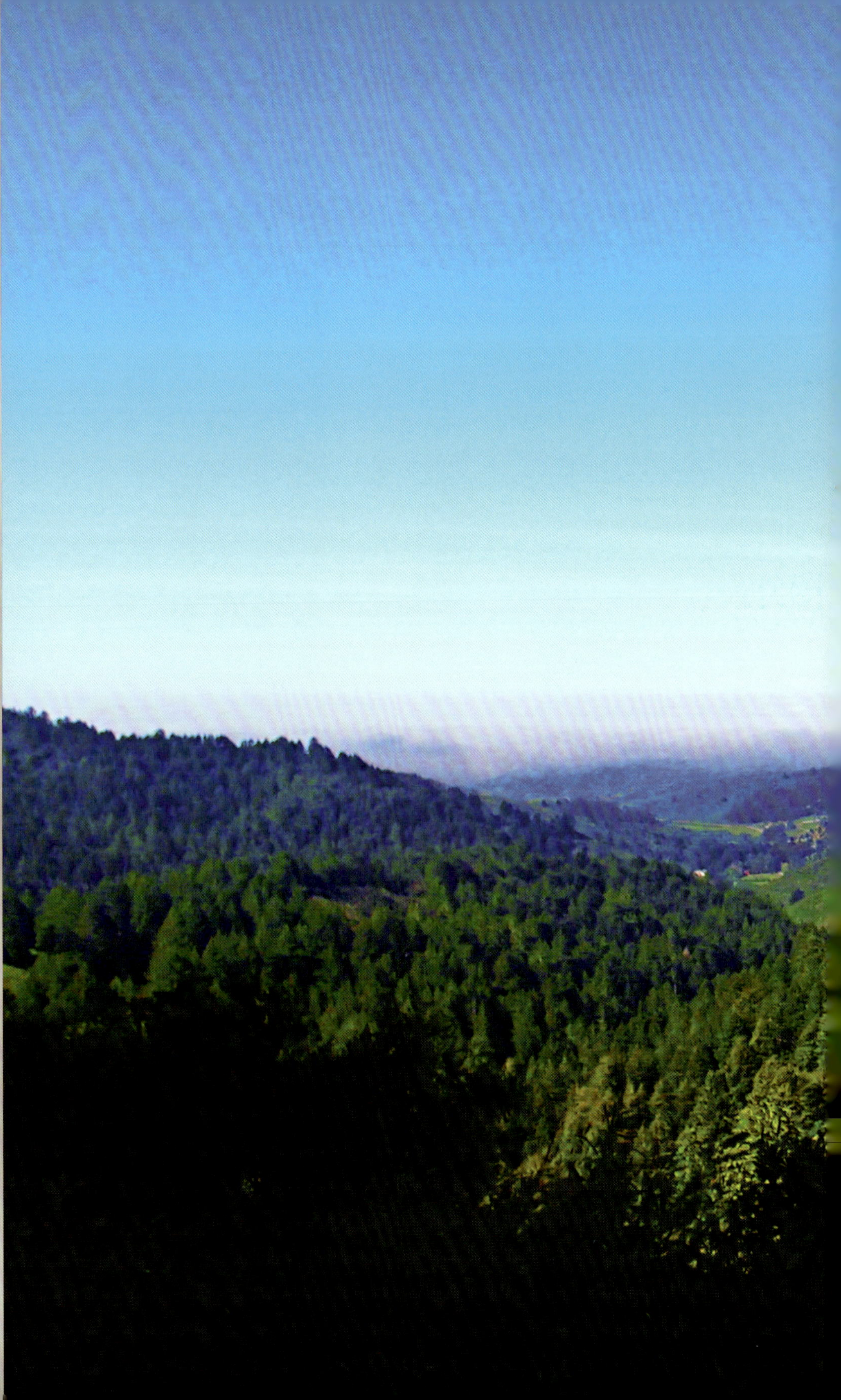

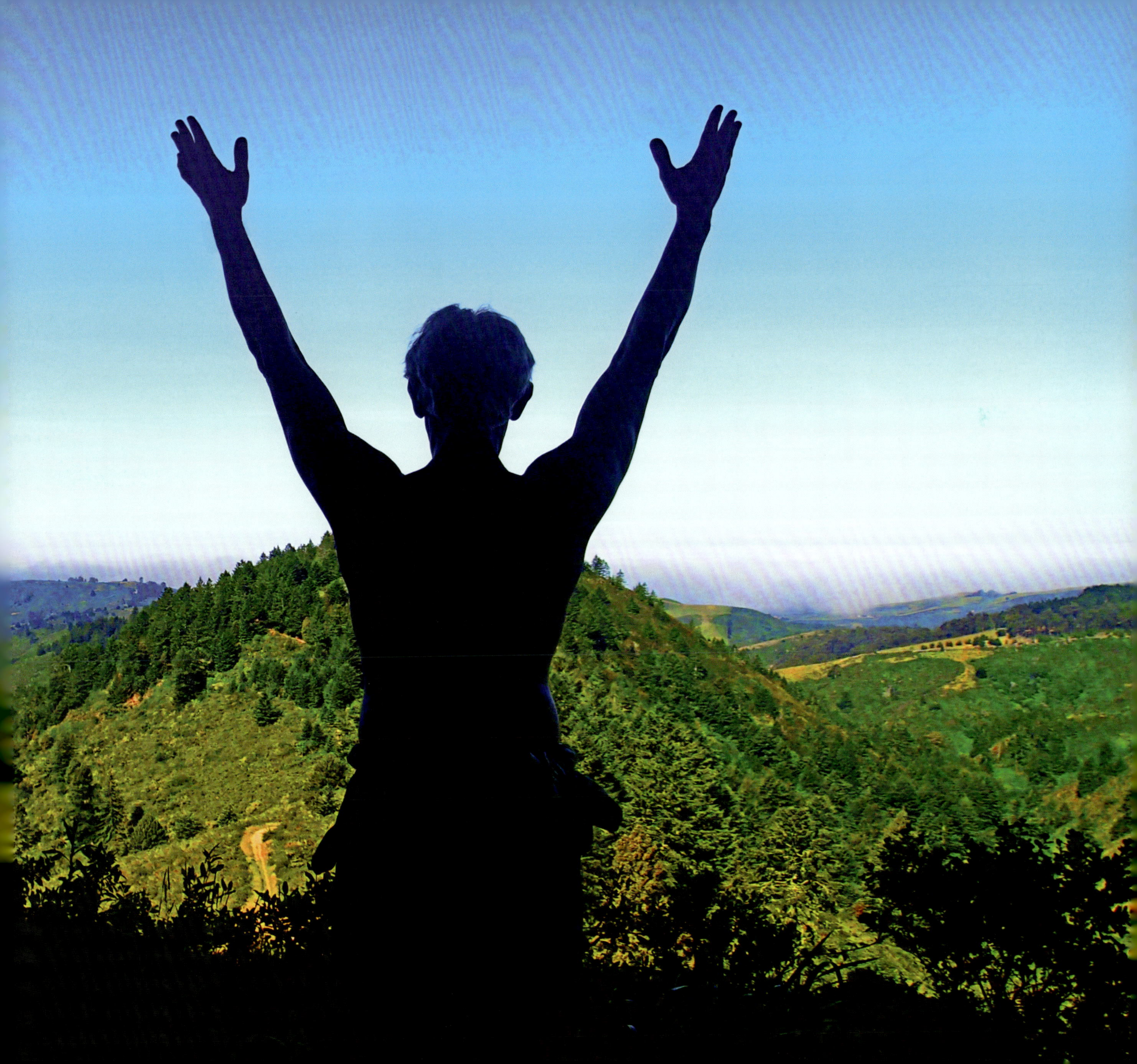

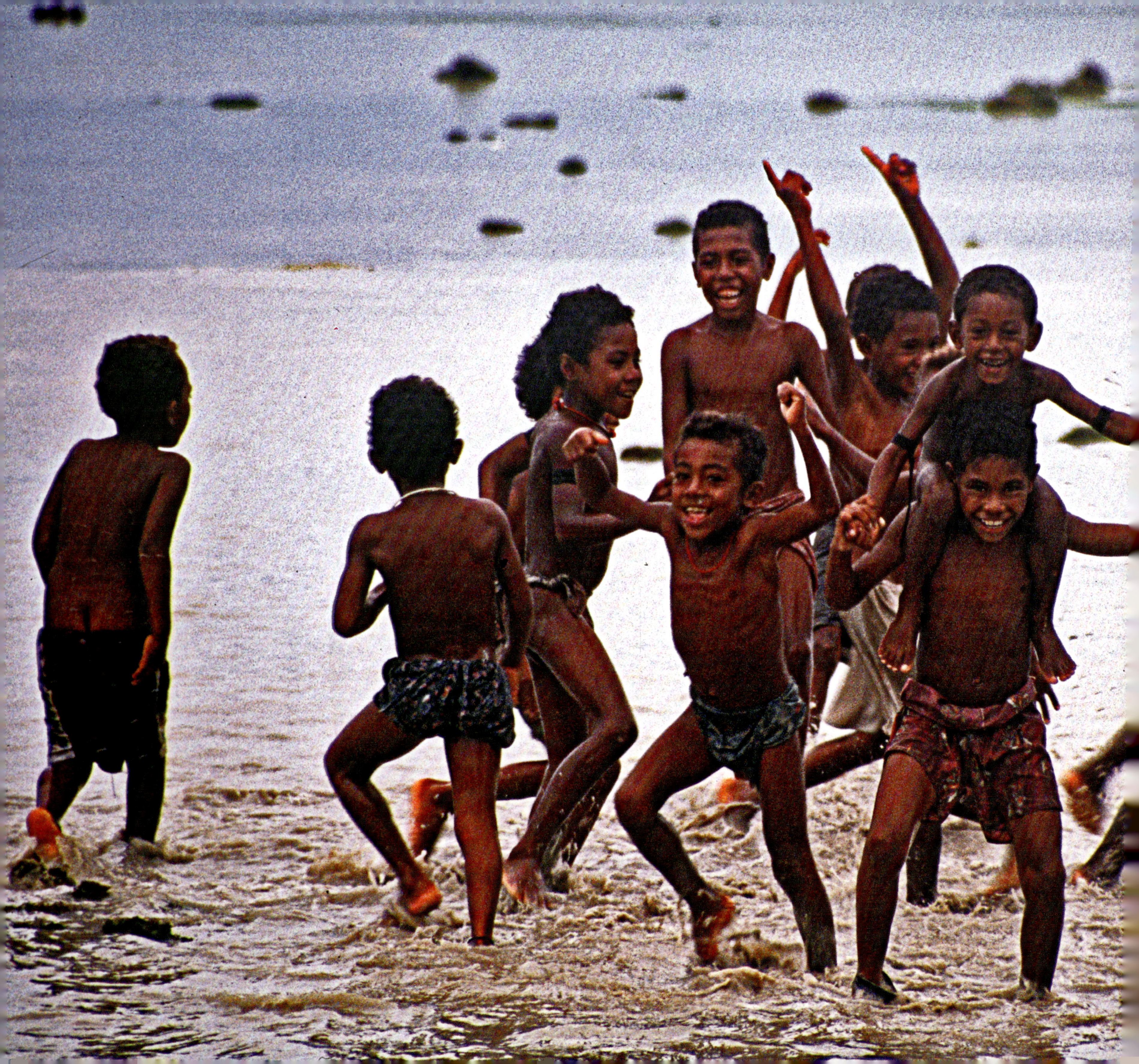

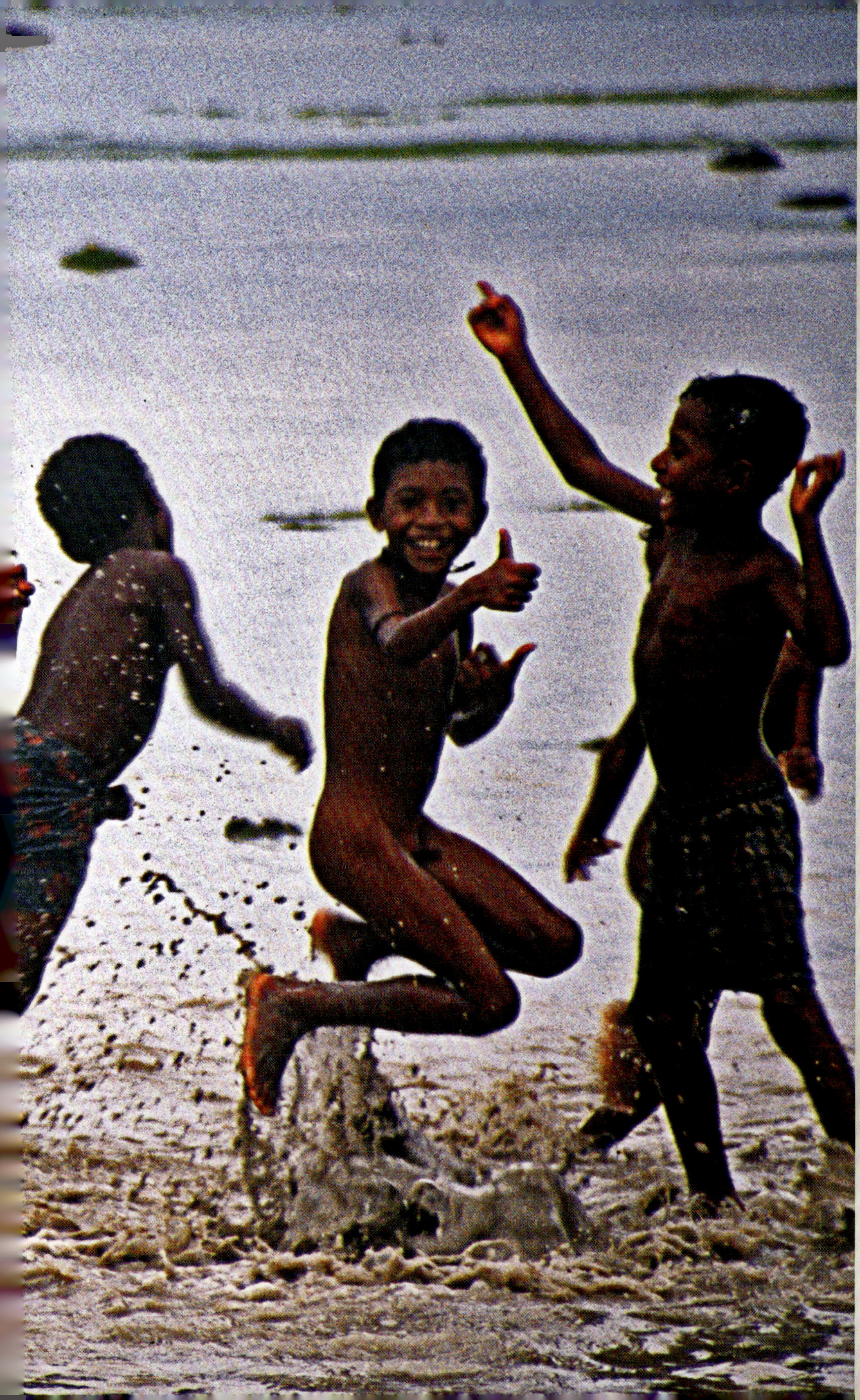

Clothes make the man.
Naked people have little
or no influence on society.

- Mark Twain

The unexpected arrival of light-skinned foreigners paddling modern sea kayaks to the beach in front of their village along the remote eastern coast of Papua New Guinea was sufficient reason for the local kids to go ballistic.

I know where you come from... the land where the green meets the blue.

- Papua New Guinea highlander speaking to a foreigner

Word that foreigners were approaching a remote village along the eastern Papua New Guinea coast had mysteriously preceeded them. So when Jessica and her fellow Americans landed their sea kayaks on the beach, they discovered the villagers already dressed in their ceremonial attire, waiting to greet them.

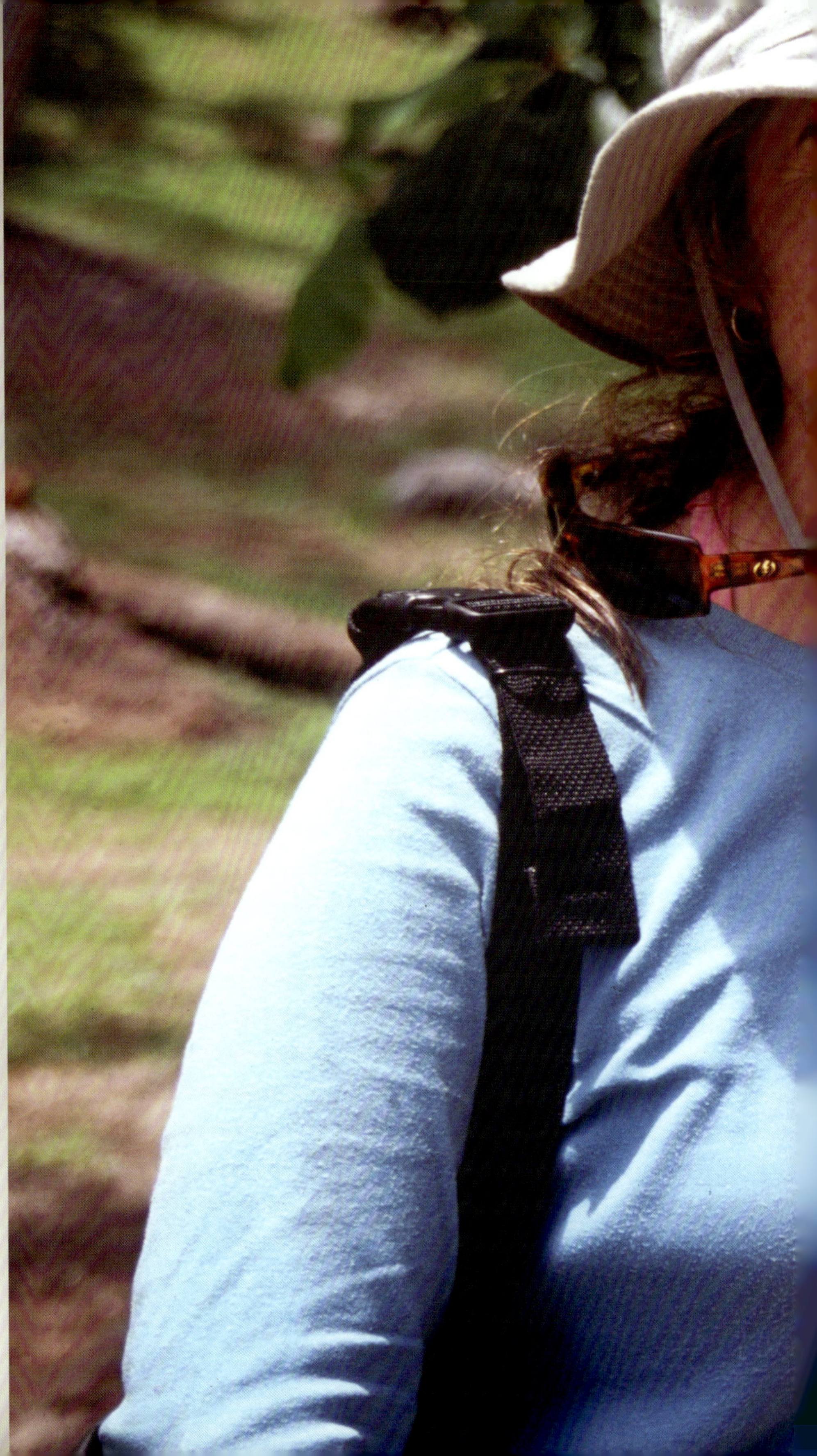

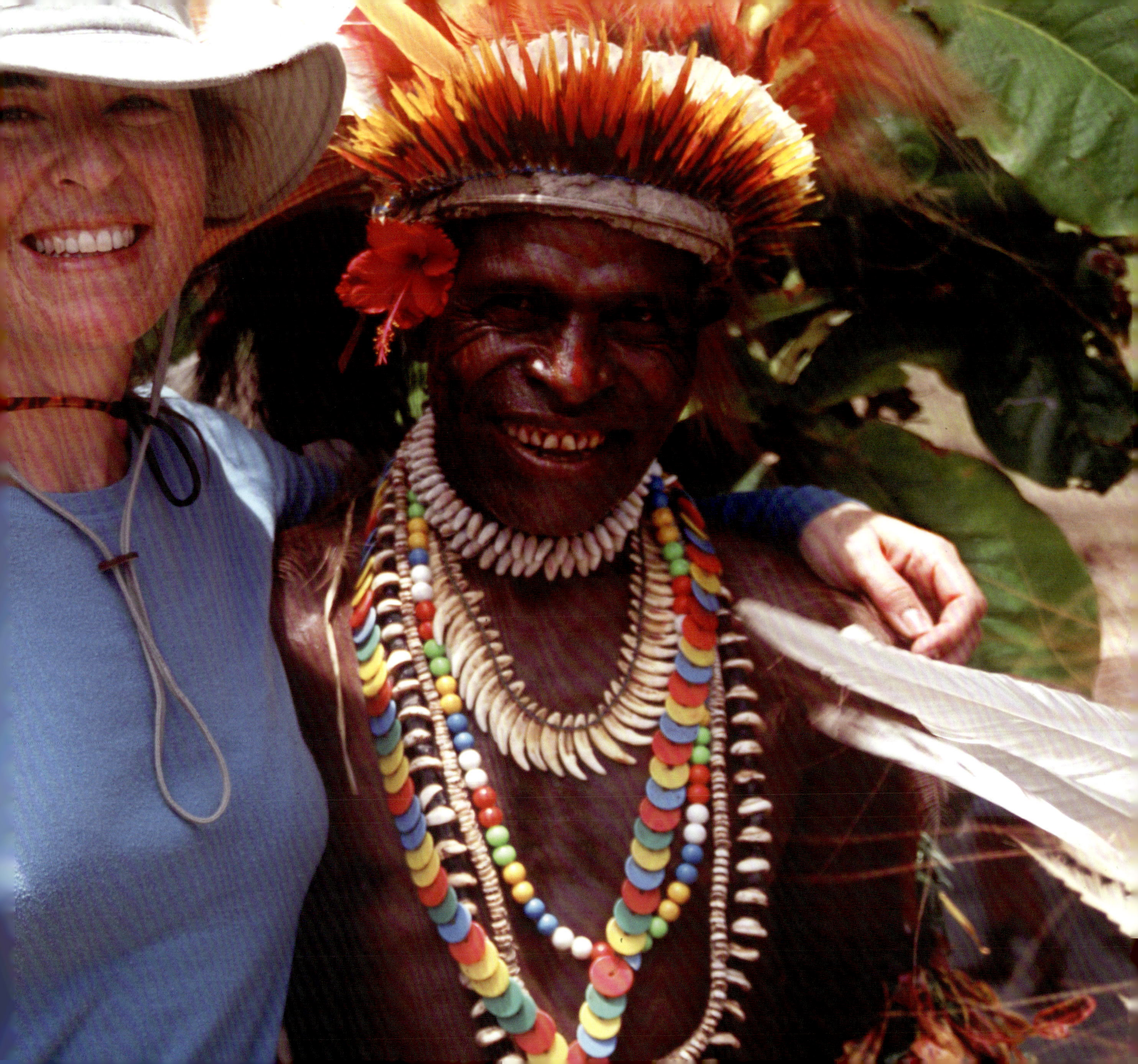

If you talk to a man in a language he understands it goes to his head. If you talk to a man in his language, it goes to his heart.

- Nelson Mandela

Like a scene from the stone age, a band of nomadic fishermen appear from the open sea and land their fleet of ocean-going outriggers on an uninhabited island in the Trobriand archipelago off the east coast of Papua New Guinea. Some of them immediately set to work smoking the fish they have caught that day. Others move into the rainforest to gather highly-prized betal nuts from which they will brew the mildly intoxicating drink they will consume in copius throughout the night. Also from the same forest a craftsmman selects a special type of tropical hardwood to carve into new paddles for their flotilla of outriggers.

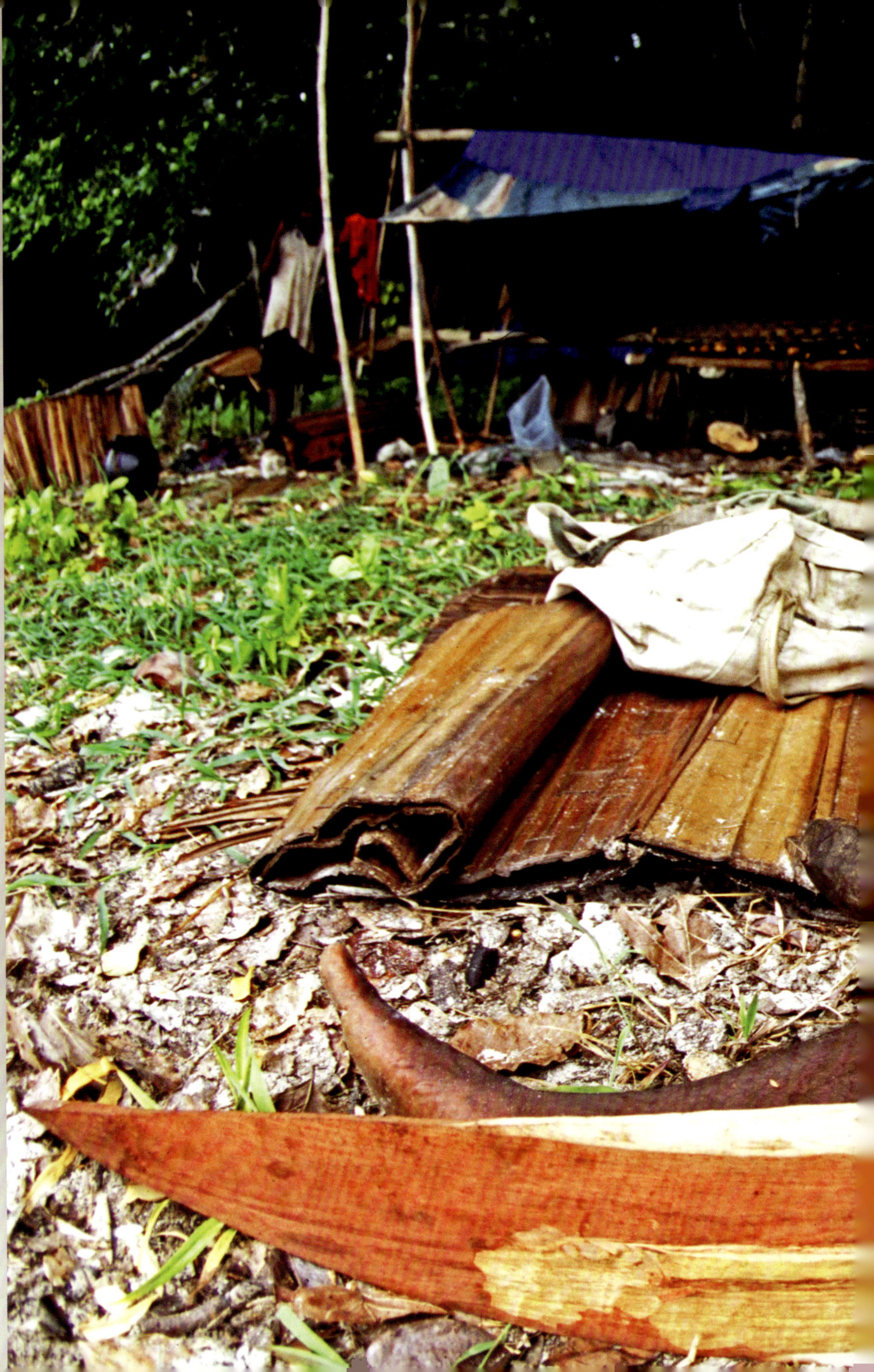

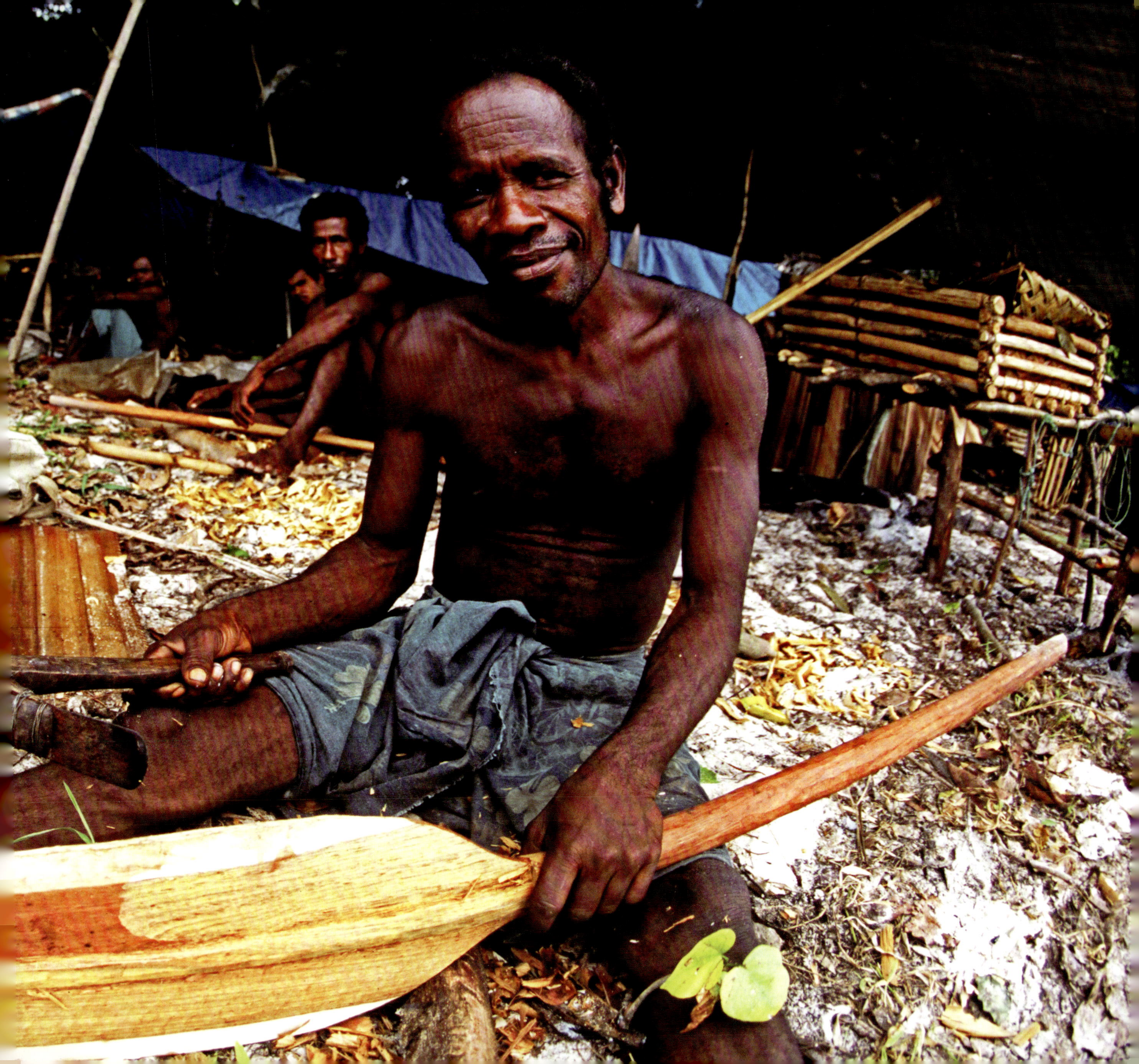

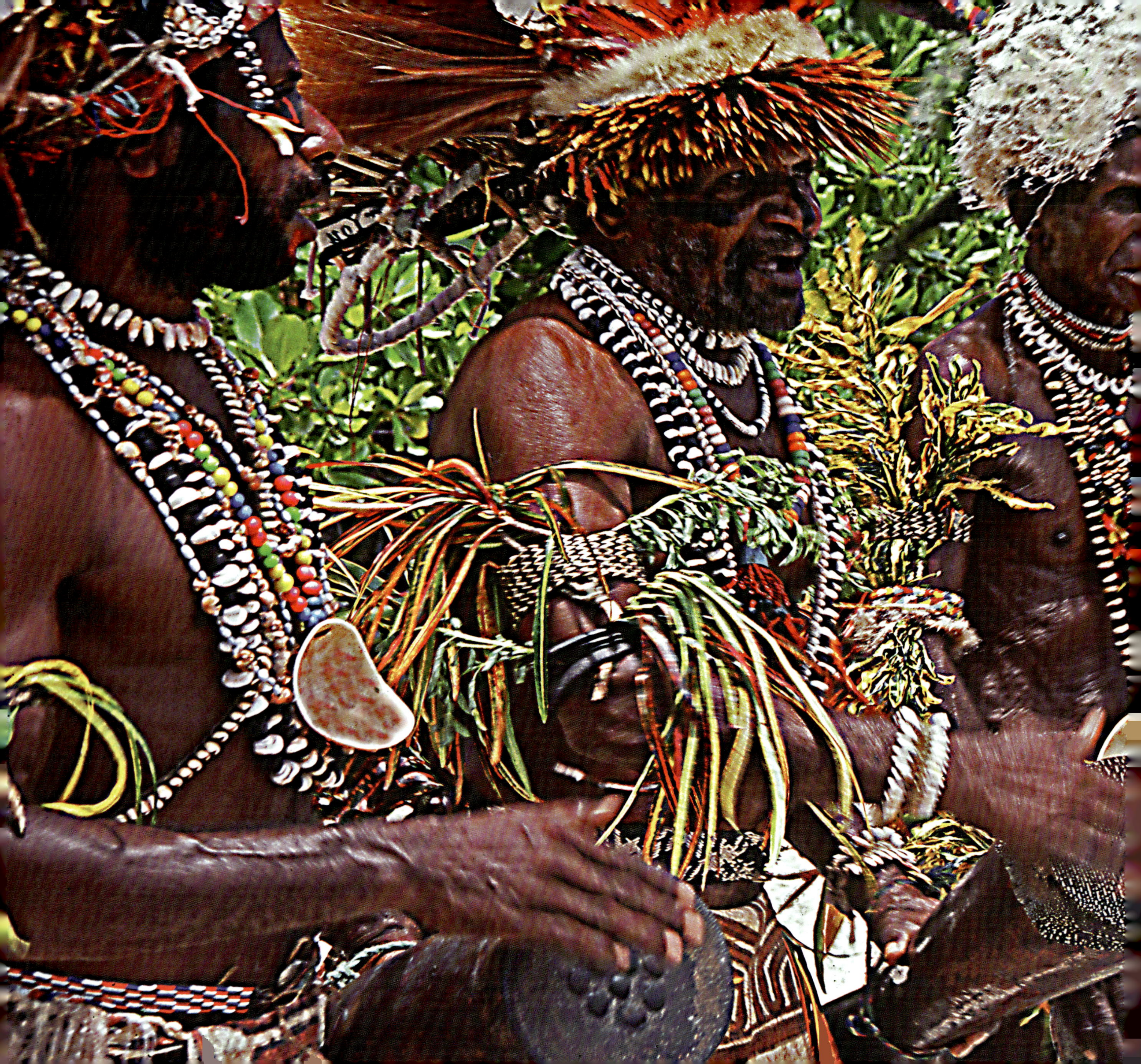

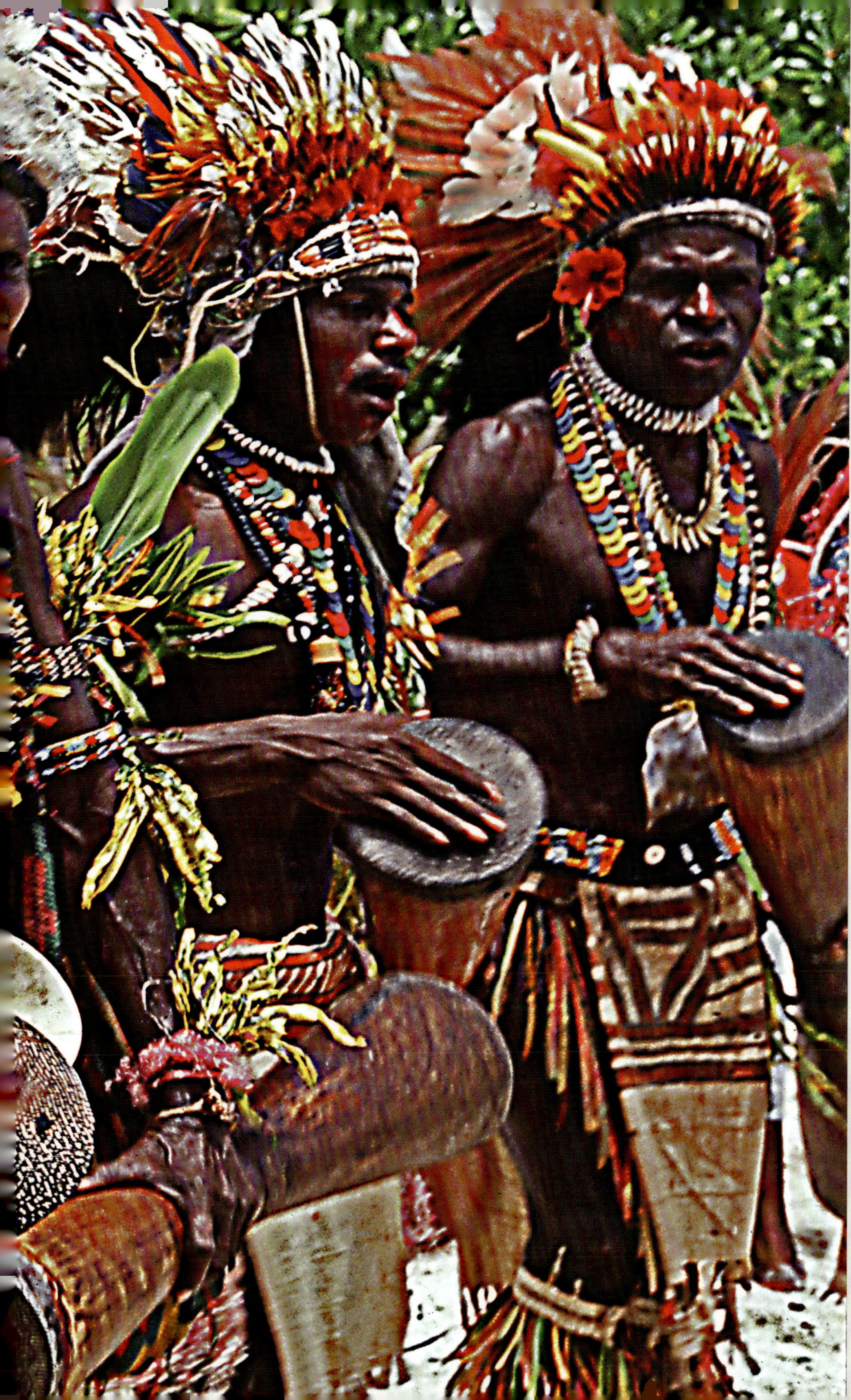

You white people go to church and talk about God. We dance and become God.

- Wade Davis, words of a Haitain elder from The Serpent And The Rainbow

The rugged interior of Papua New Guinea has changed very little in thousands of years. The highlanders, a third of the country's five million inhabitants, dwell mostly in isolated mountain areas, speak more than 800 local languages and countless minor dialects, and live scarcely emerged from the stone age. By contrast, the appeal to foreigners of diving and sea kayaking in the the lush tropical waters of Papua New Guinea has brought much more contact with the outside world to the coastal communities.

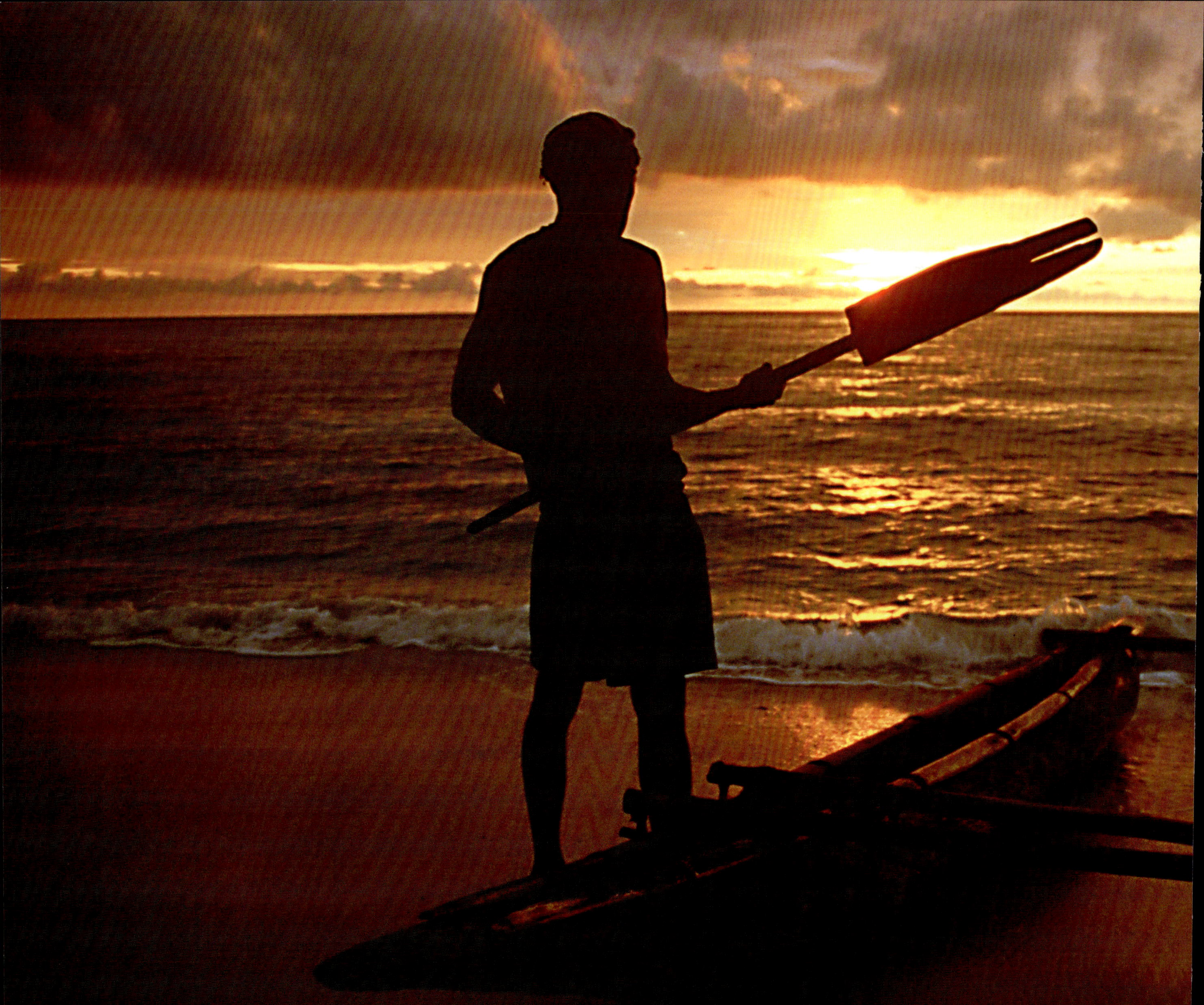

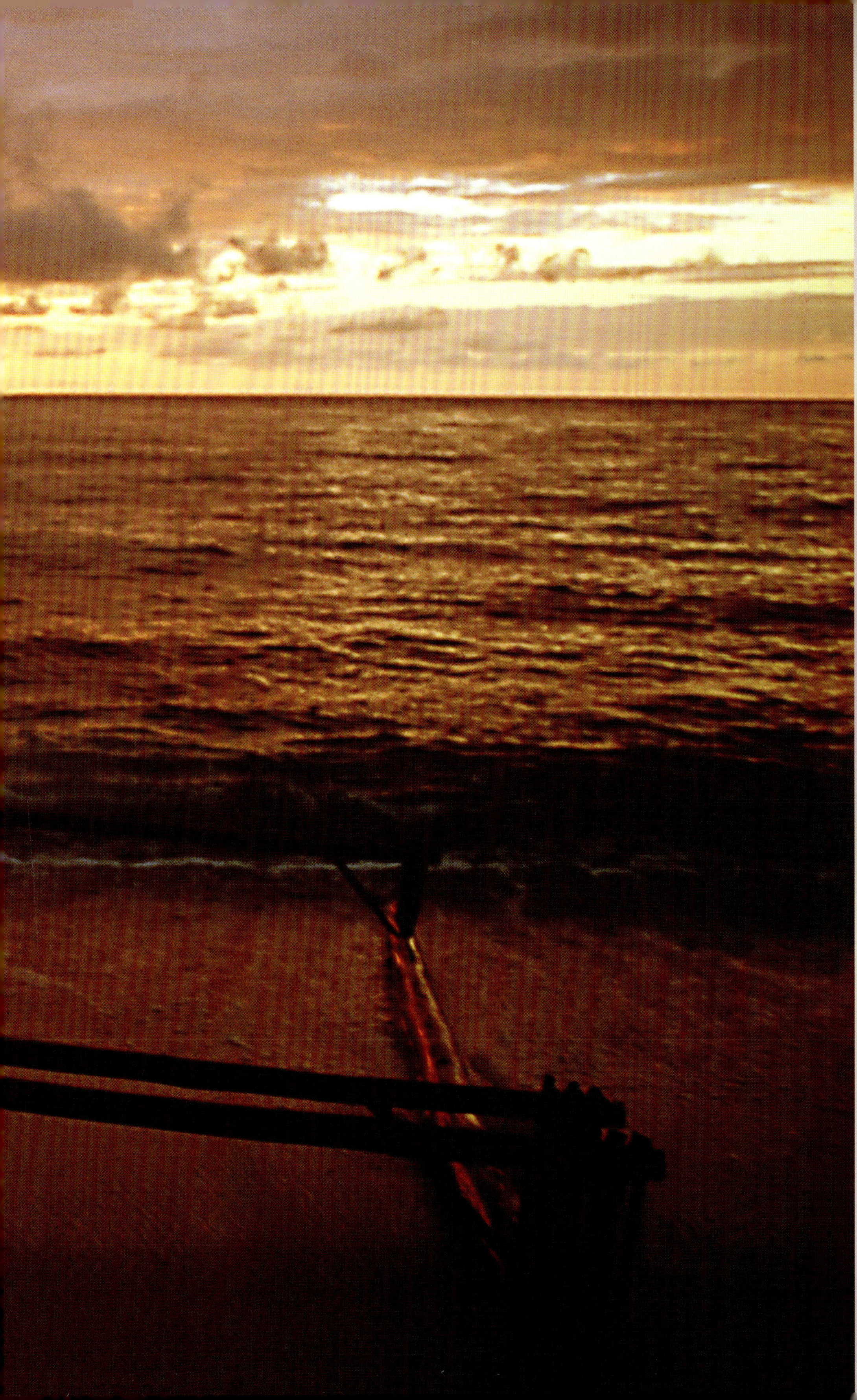

Both the wind and the people who live close to nature have much to teach us which we cannot learn within university walls.

- Thor Heyerdahl

Papua New Guinea is a island nation in Oceana with most of the rural population still living in small traditional villages and surviving by fishing and subsistence-based agriculture. Sailes was born and grew up in a little village along the remote eastern coast of the main island of the country. He carved the outrigger canoe that is his chief form of transportation around the nearly roadless region from a tropical hardwood tree cut down in the rainforest behind his village.

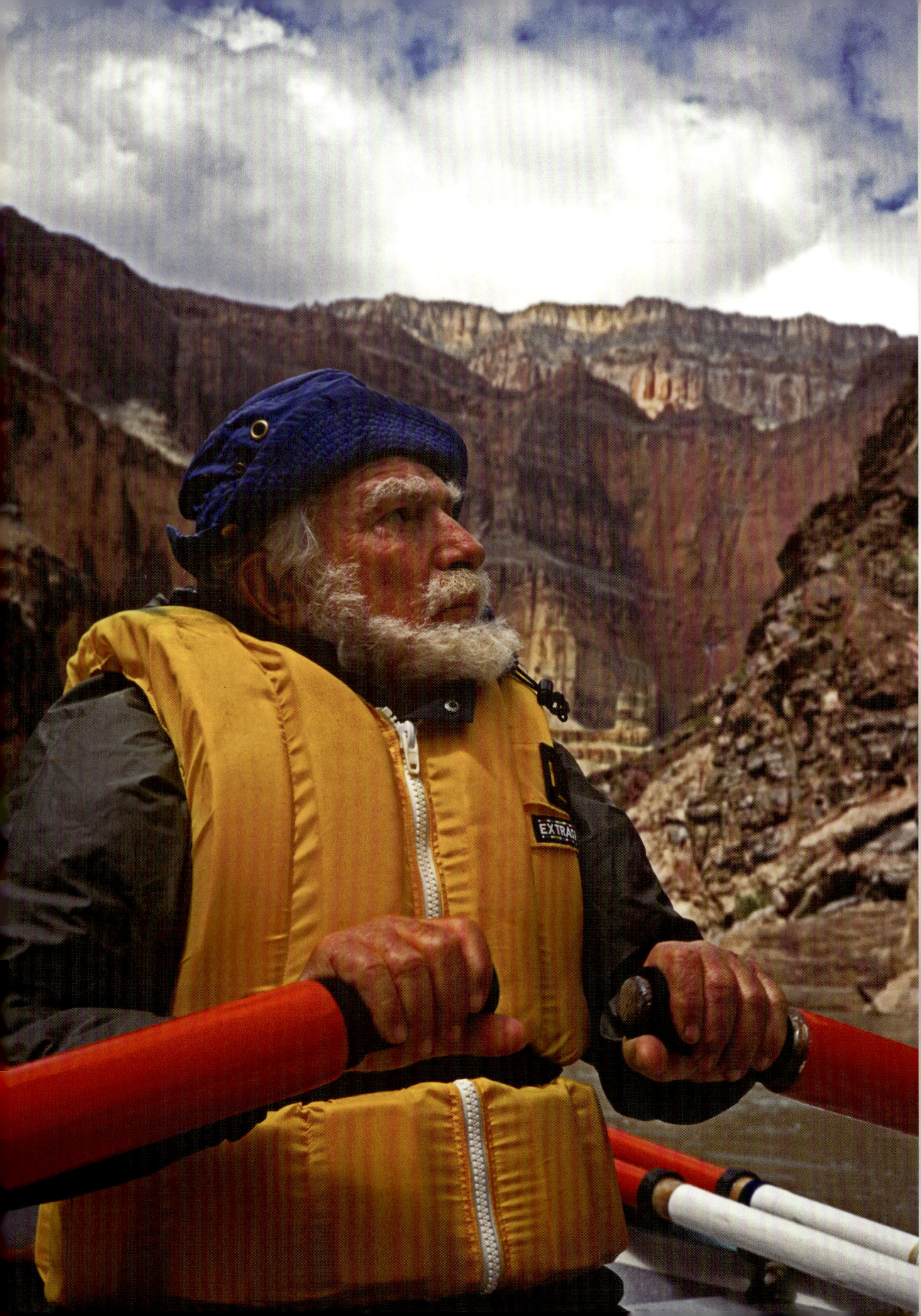

Saving it was an act of creation.

- Martin Litton

River consevationist *extraordinaire* and arch-druid of the Grand Canyon Martin Litton waxes contemplative as he rows his dory through a quiet section the Colorado River. Litton, like the native Americans who preceded him there, recognized the canyon as a holy place and battled fiercely to prevent it from becoming dammed and flooded.

Today the iconic Grand Canyon attracts a diverse multitude of people from all over the world. River folks come to feel the primal power of the mighty Colorado and others to hike, backpack, and even race the canyon's trail trail system that evolved from centuries of indigenous habitation. Pioneer National Geographic Society filmmaker Andy Cominos photographed these runners acending the North Kaibad trail during a "R2R2R" event. This challenging marathon demands contestants race down one side of the canyon from the rim to the river and back up to the opposite rim, then back down and up again to where they began - all in one grueling day. The average time for the run is about 20 hours.

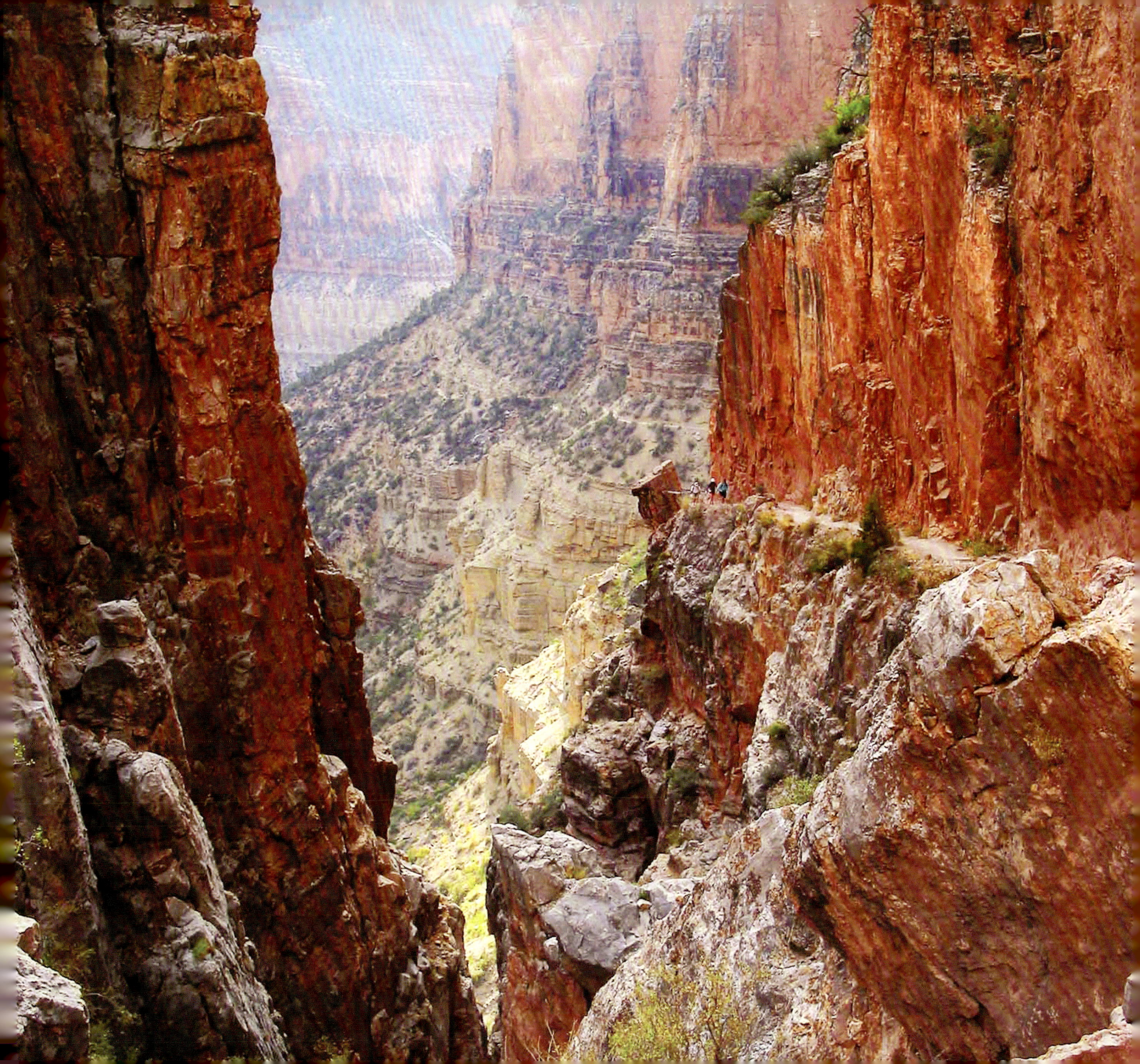

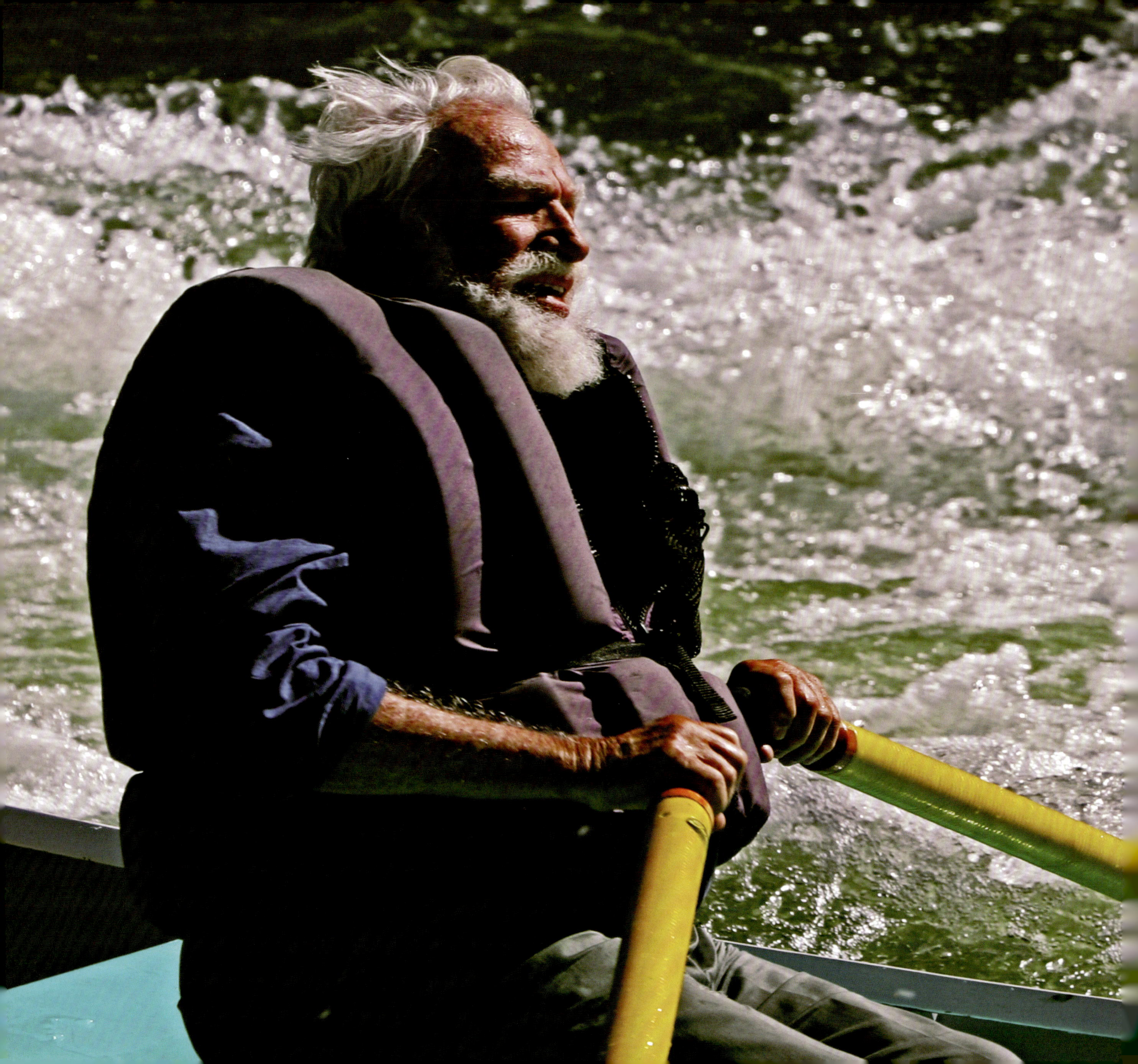

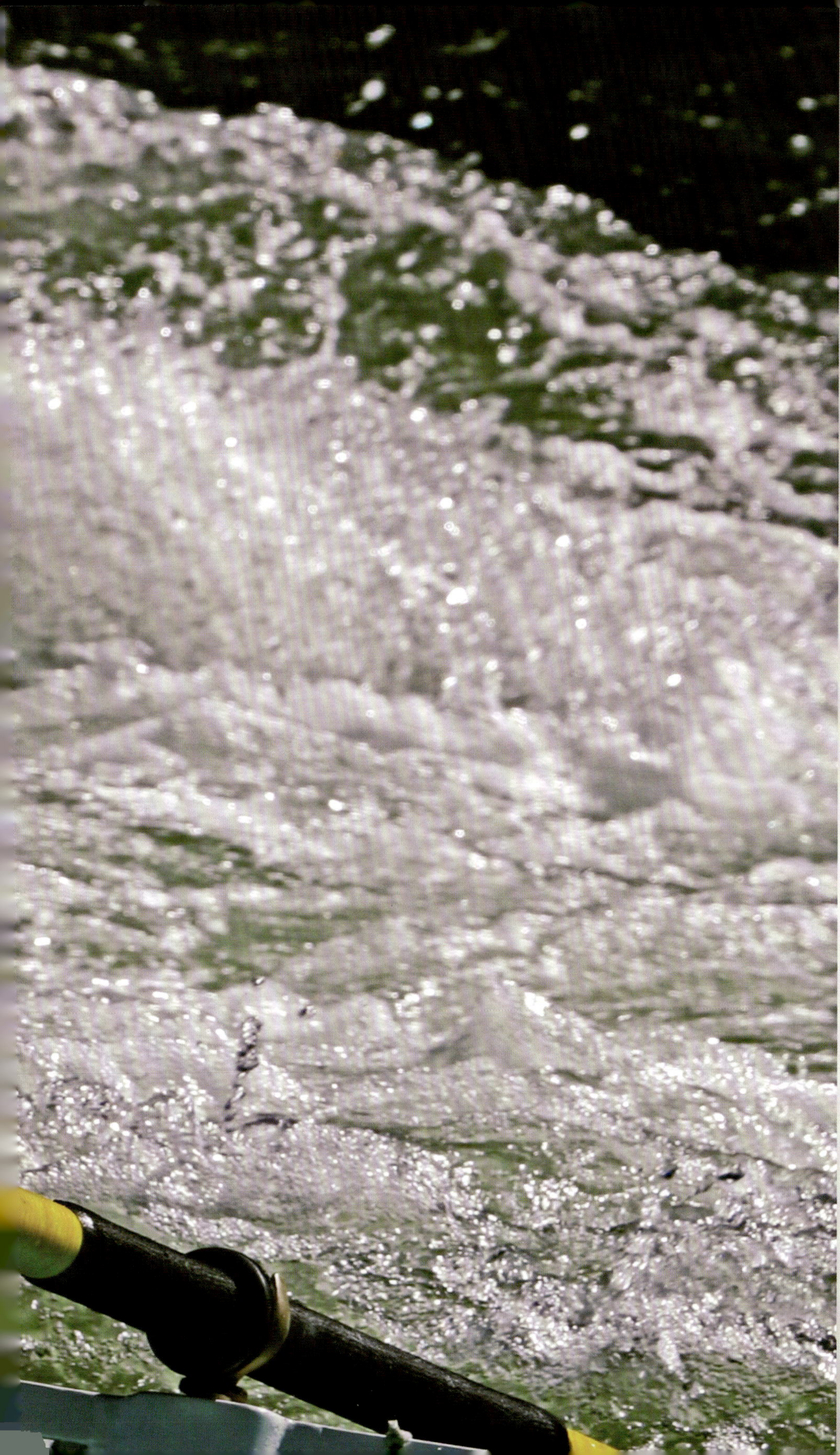

A dory is a shape that belongs on a river; it started on the ocean, conquered the waves of the sea and now conquers the waves of crashing water on almost any river. The dory says to you, "I belong on big waves; I'm stable, I'm sturdy, I'm wanting to go, and I respond to the oars beautifully."

-Martin Litton

74

In 2005 the pioneer river-running company OARS invited a select group of white-water guides and long-time friends and admirers of Martin Litton to join a commemorative river trip with him on the historic Main Salmon River in Idaho. To rendezvous with the group, Litton and two filmmakers left California in his classic Cessna 195 airplane, but the plane developed engine trouble after landing to refuel in Nevada. So the trio purchased a used car at a dealership and *drove* the rest of the way to Idaho, arriving in the remote little mountain town of Stanley just in time to begin the river trip. Once on the river, 87 year-old Litton rowed all the big whitewater himself - like the Class IV rapid shown here in Impassable Canyon. The filmmakers completed their film, The Good Fight, documenting Litton's life-long battle to save America's rivers and forestlands - which premiered at Telluride Mountainfilm where it won a major award, and went on to broadcast on the PBS television series *Natural Heroes.*

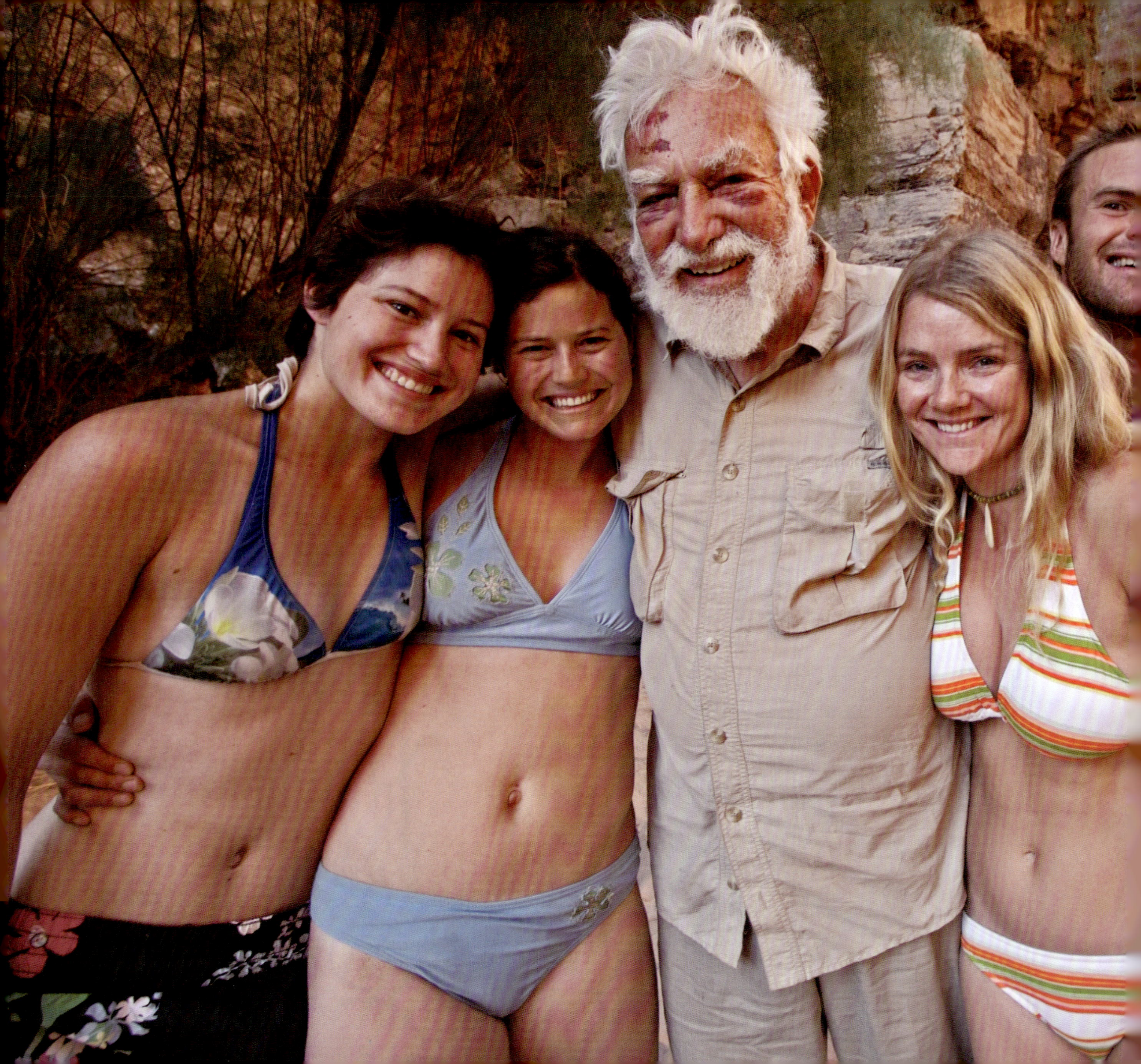

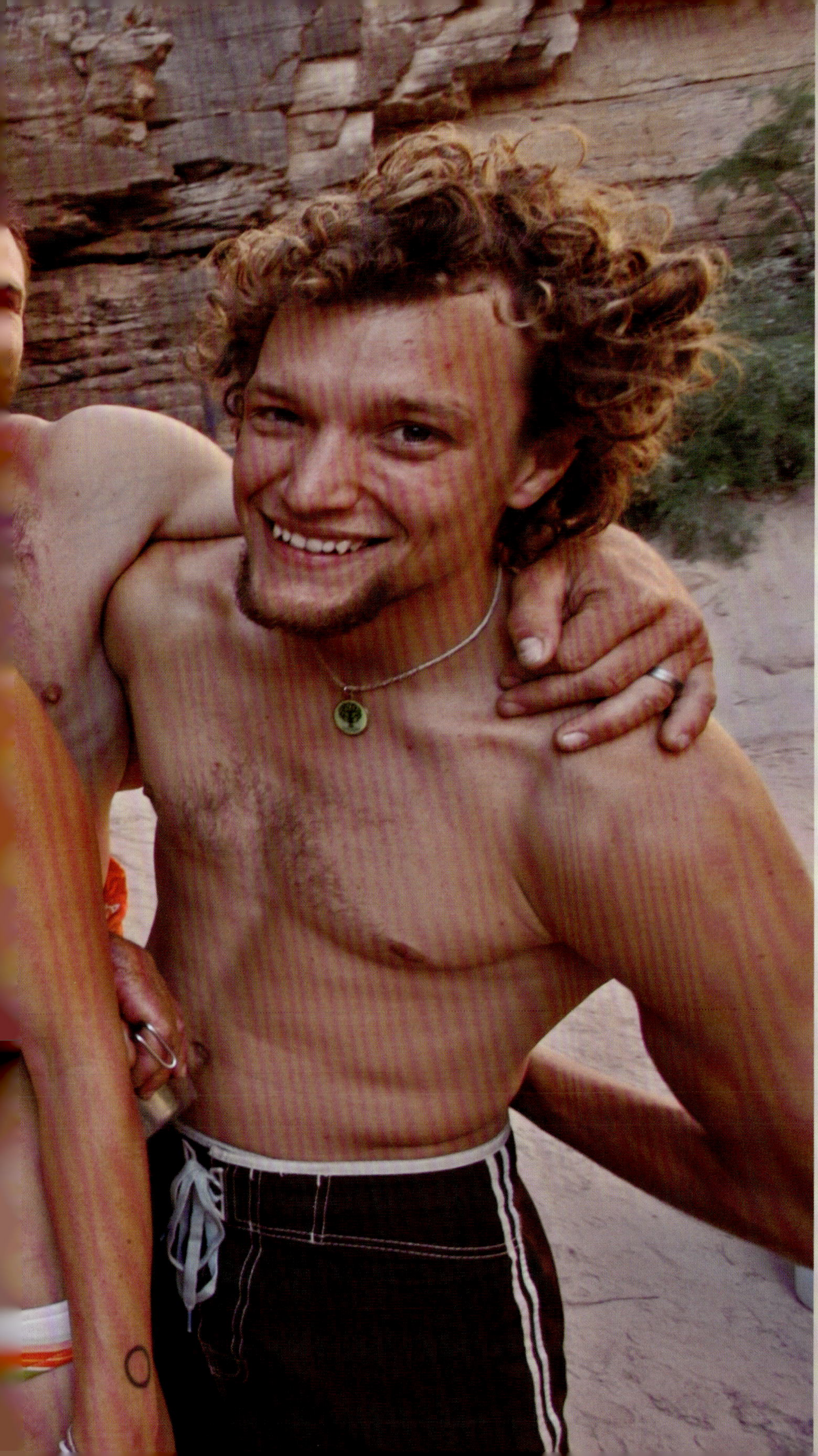

Unlike many of today's younger environmentalists, Martin Litton is not flawed with earnestness.

- John Balzar, Los Angeles Times

At an age when most sensible rivermen had long-since hung up their oars, 90 year-old Martin Litton could not pass up the opportunity to row a dory down his cherished Colorado River one more time. With a little help from sons John and Donald, he ran the entire 296 miles from Lee's Ferry to Lake Mead. Along with fellow conservationist and life-long friend David Brower, Litton is credited with stopping two planned dams from being built on the Colorado River that would have flooded the Grand Canyon and turned this great national treasure into a gigantic, silt-filled reservoir. So when Martin returned there once again in 2007, word spread quickly up and down the river and admirers of all ages started dropping by his camp to pay homage to the canyon's much-loved savior.

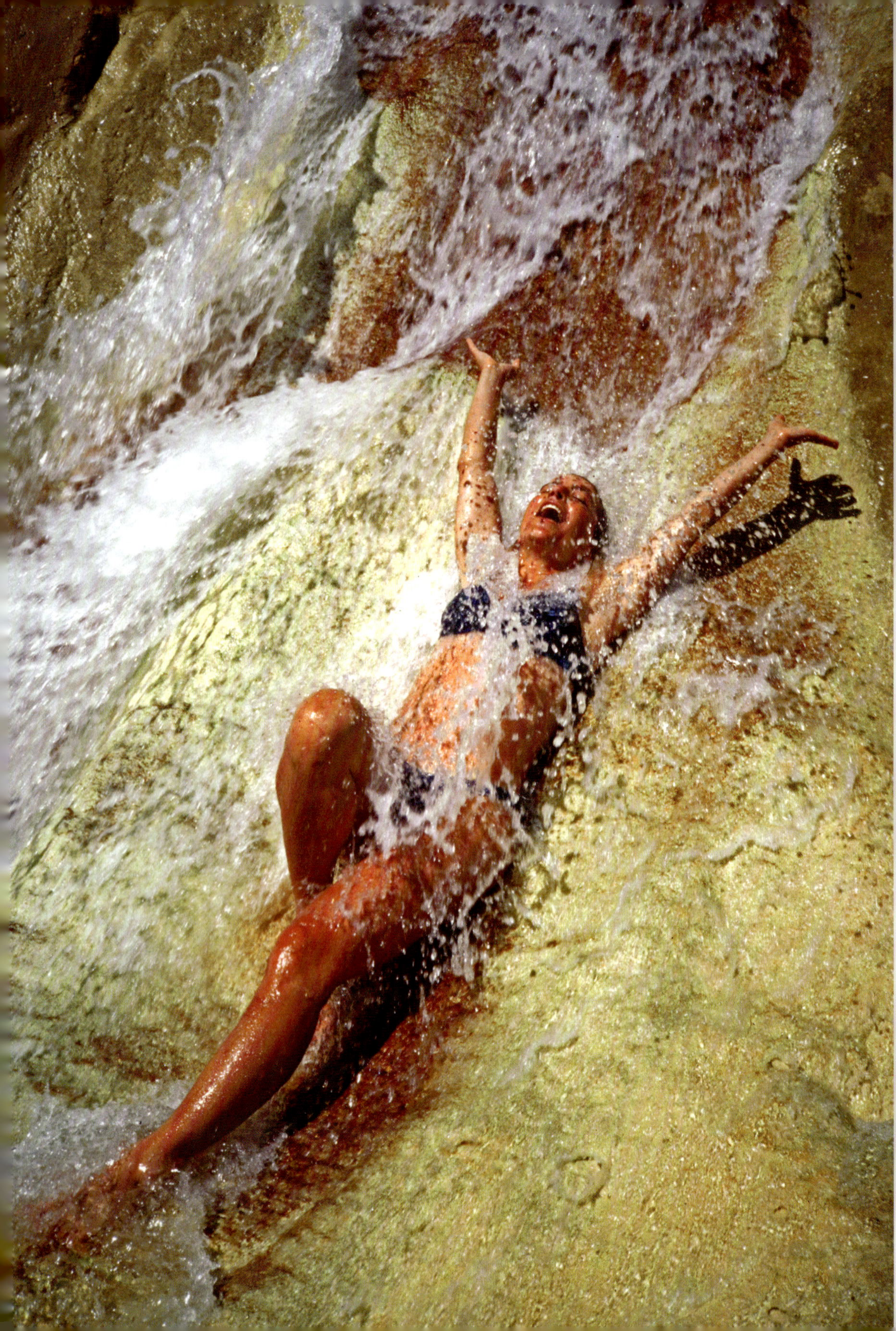

Humans are amphibians - half spirit and half animal. As spirits they belong to the eternal world, but as animals they inherit time.

- C. S. Lewis

Multi-award winning filmmaker Lili Schad finds immersion in a side canyon stream to be a welcome diversion during the making of a documentary about Martin Litton in the Grand Canyon. Litton, a legendary figure in the river conservation world, was being honored for his key role in helping save the Colorado River running through the canyon from the dam builders.

Following an age-old routine essential to their survival, a *campesino* family in the Andean highlands of Peru shepherds their animals back down from the high mountain pastures to the safety of the village compound for the night.

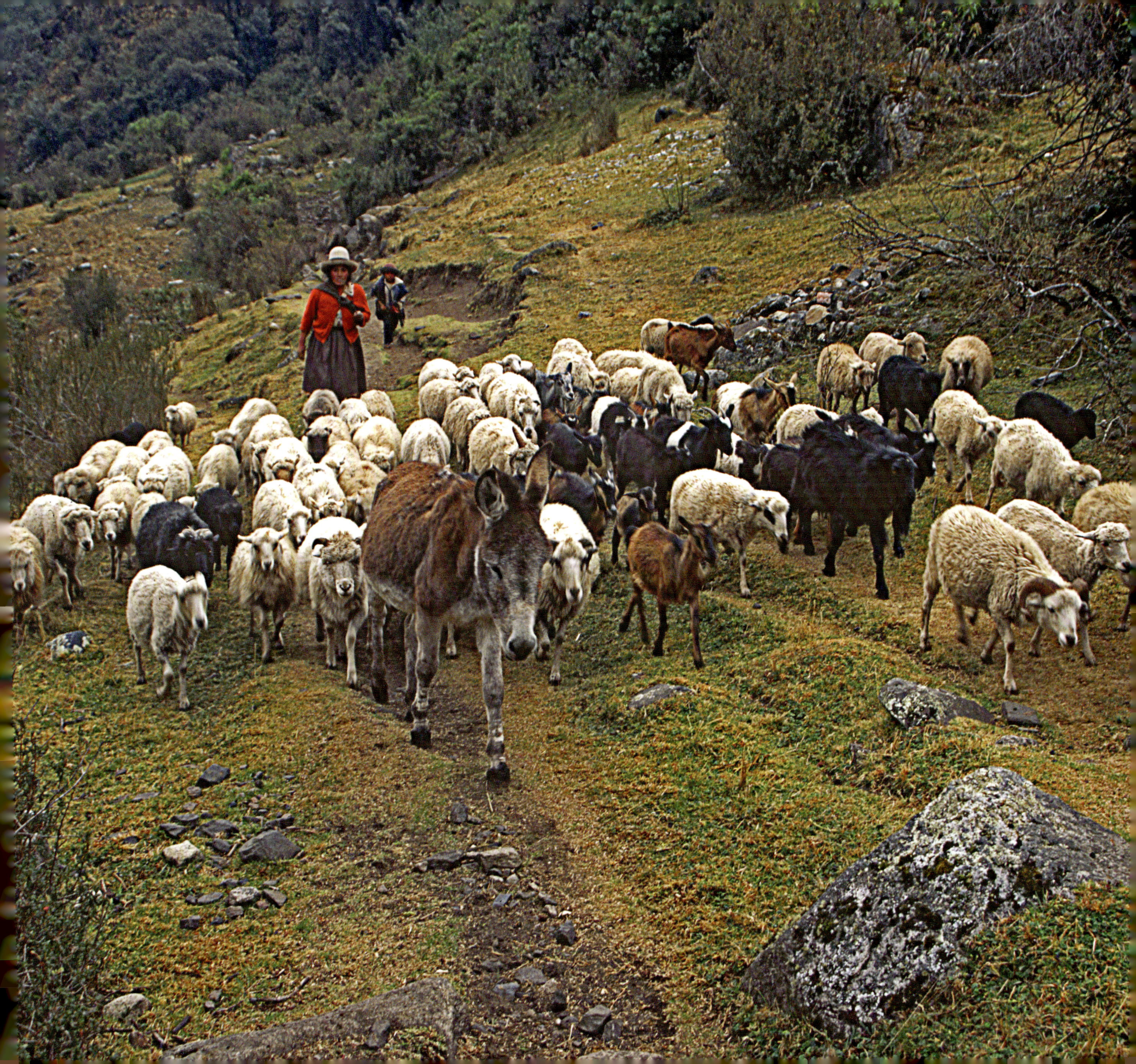

Let the beauty we love be what we do. There are hundreds of ways to kneel and kiss the ground.

- Rumi, 13th century Persian poet

A day of free climbing in the Santa Cruz Mountains soon becomes for adventure filmmaker Lili Schad, an exquisite dance of communion with the eternal rock and the sky. It matters little that the high-tech world of Silicon Valley is visible on the distant horizon. This is the domain of seldom-seen mountain lions and condors, who continue to roam here undisturbed. Fortunately for us too, this wilderness land is protected in perpetuity by the Peninsula Open Space Trust, a conservancy organization dedicated to acquiring and preserving pristine tracts of land around the San Francisco Bay area.

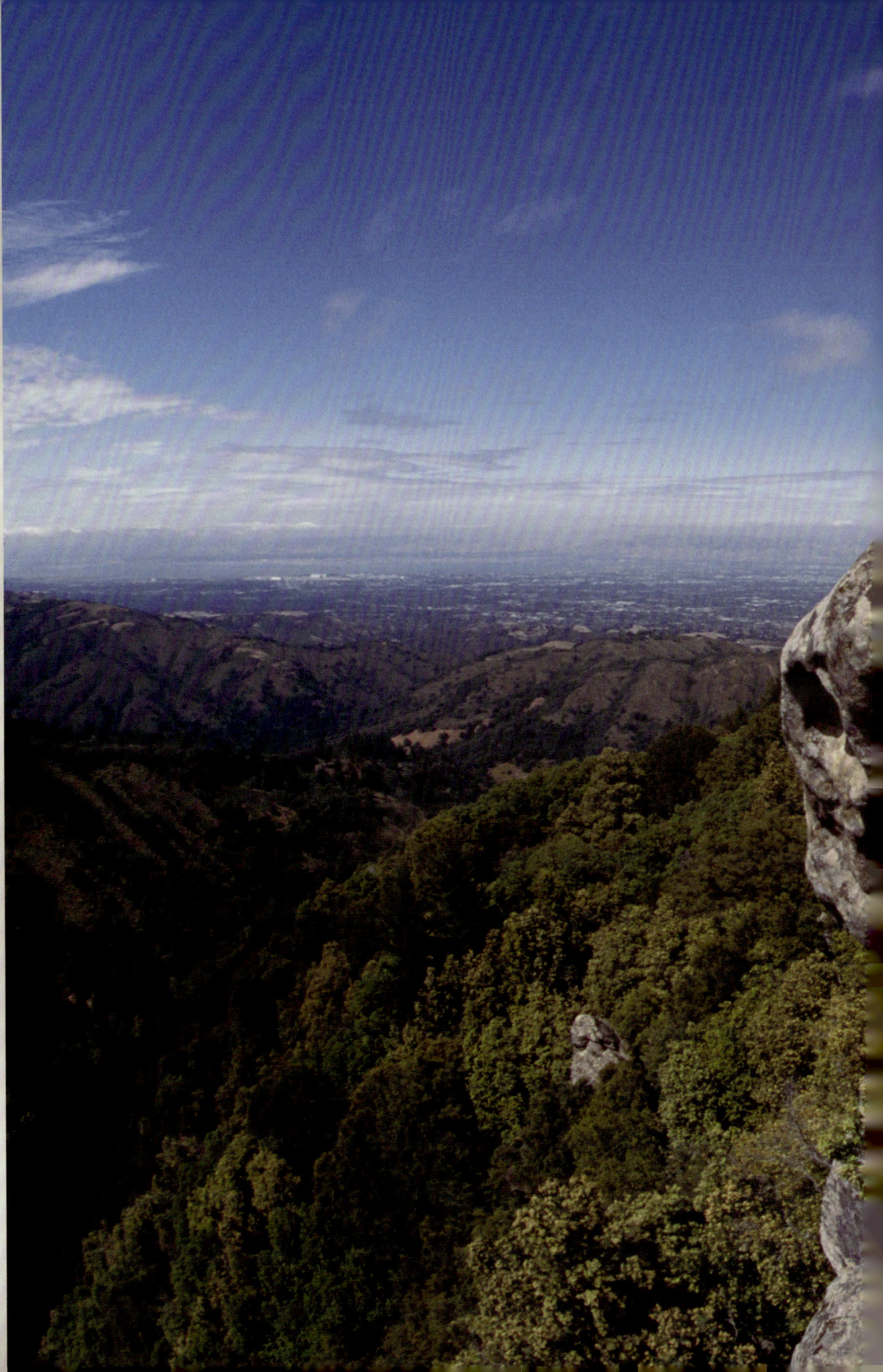

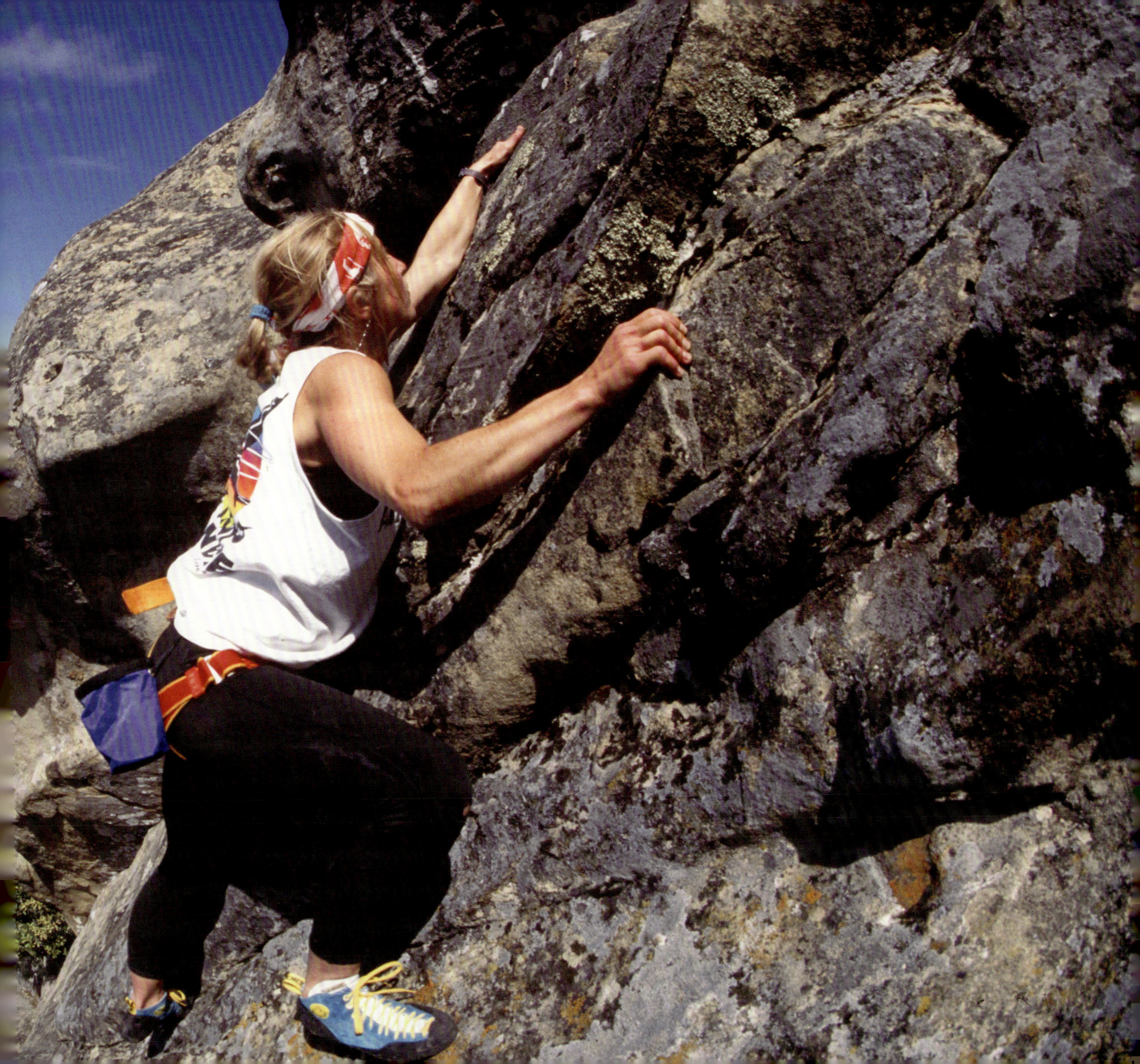

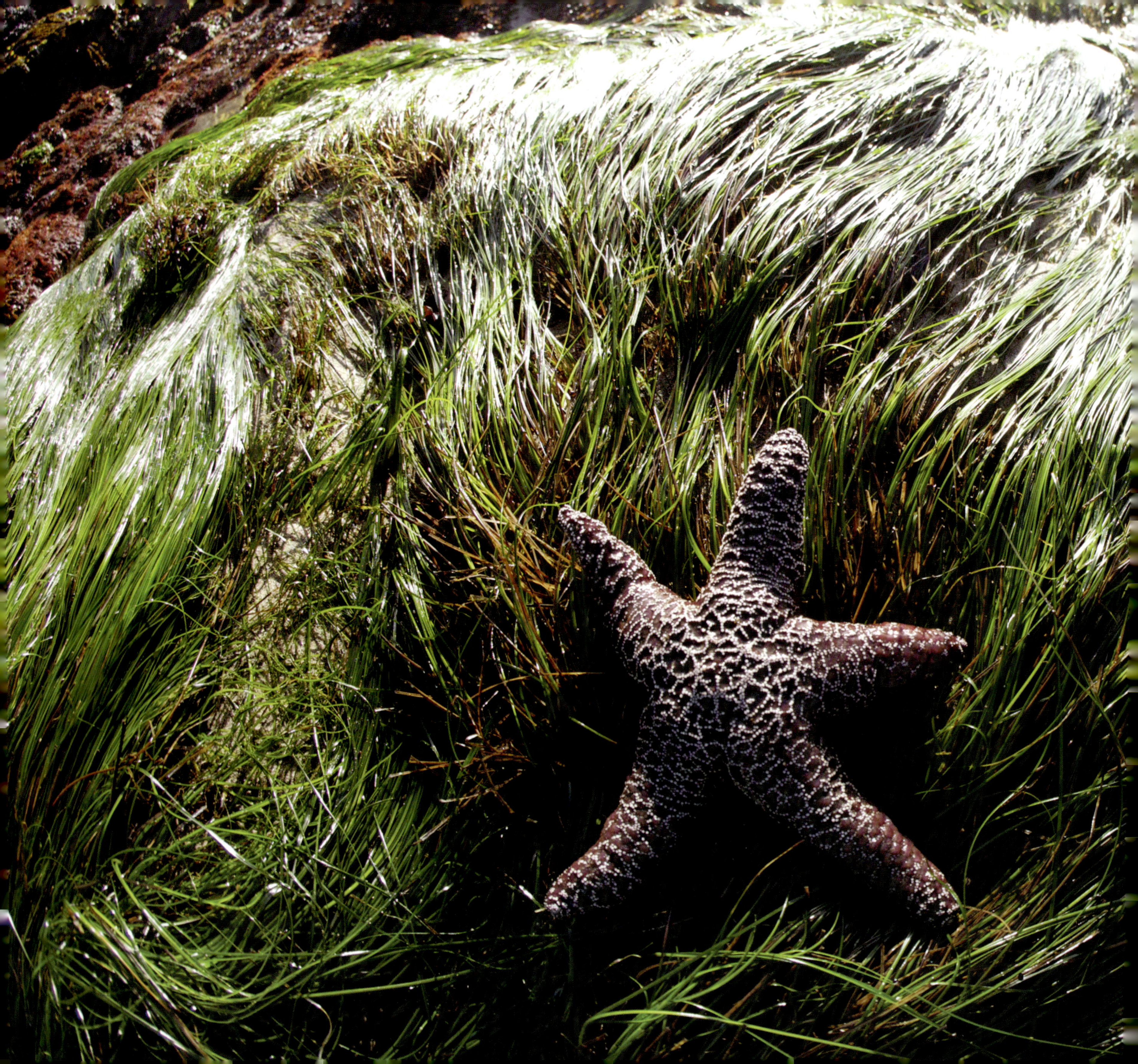

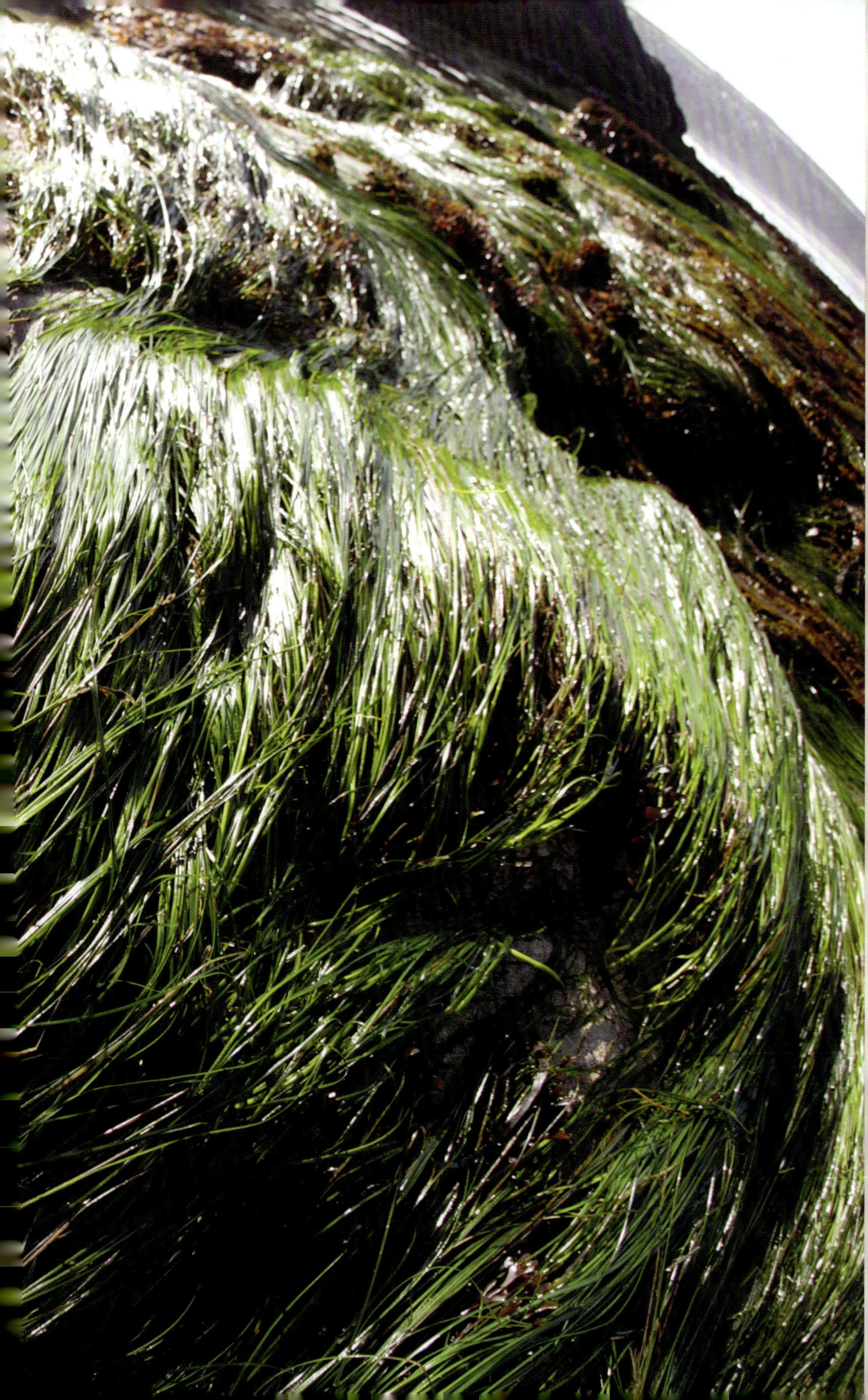

Look deep into nature and you will understand everything.

- Albert Einstein

Twice each month, the earth, the moon and the sun move into near perfect alignment and the immense mass of these heavenly bodies begins to to work together in unison to exert the maximum gravitational effect on all the oceans of our water planet. Shorelines everywhere alternately become flooded and exposed by the radically changing tide levels. The other-worldly treasures thus revealed by the extreme minus tides has always held powerful allure for human beachcombers and foraging shorebirds and alike.

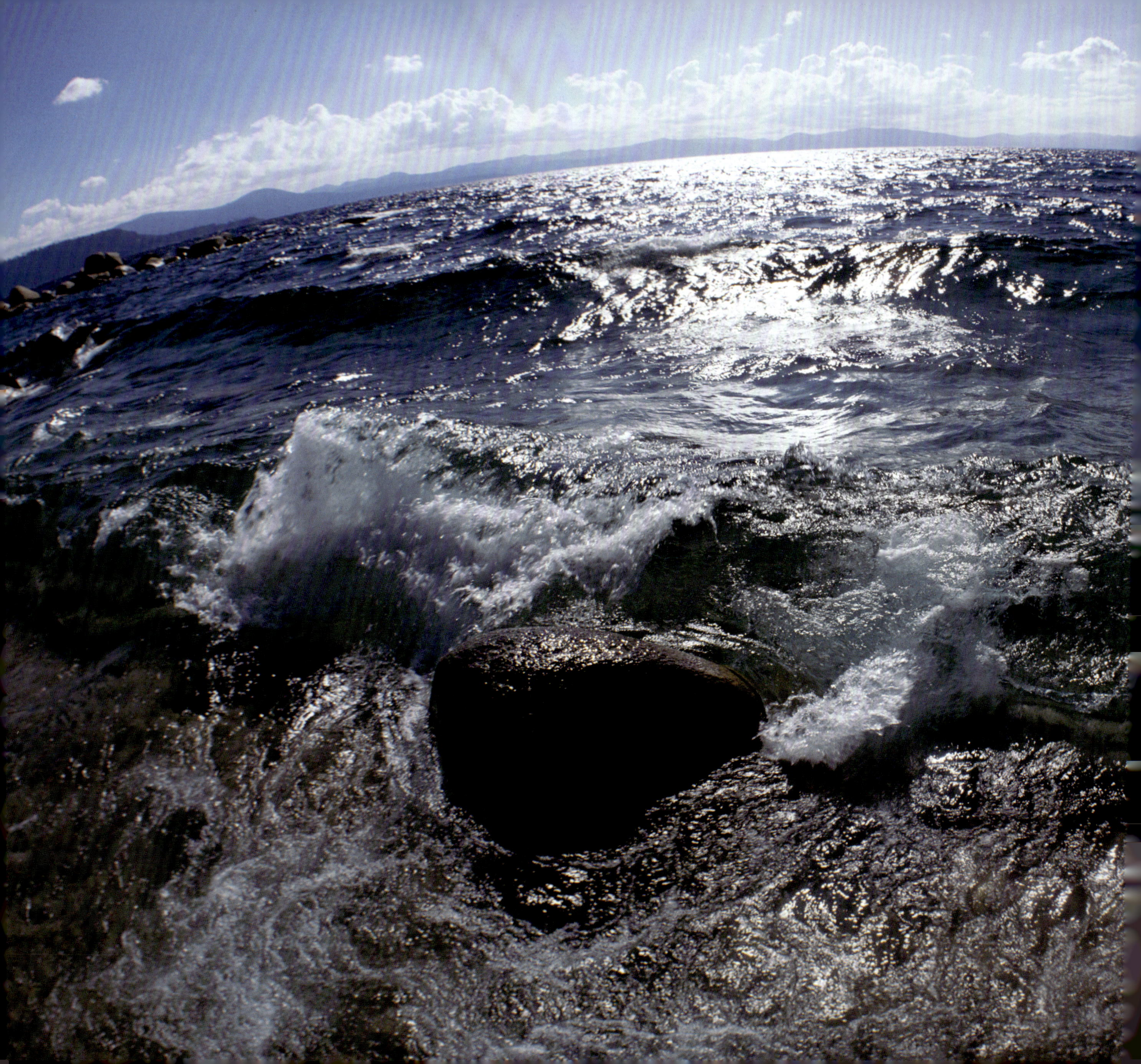

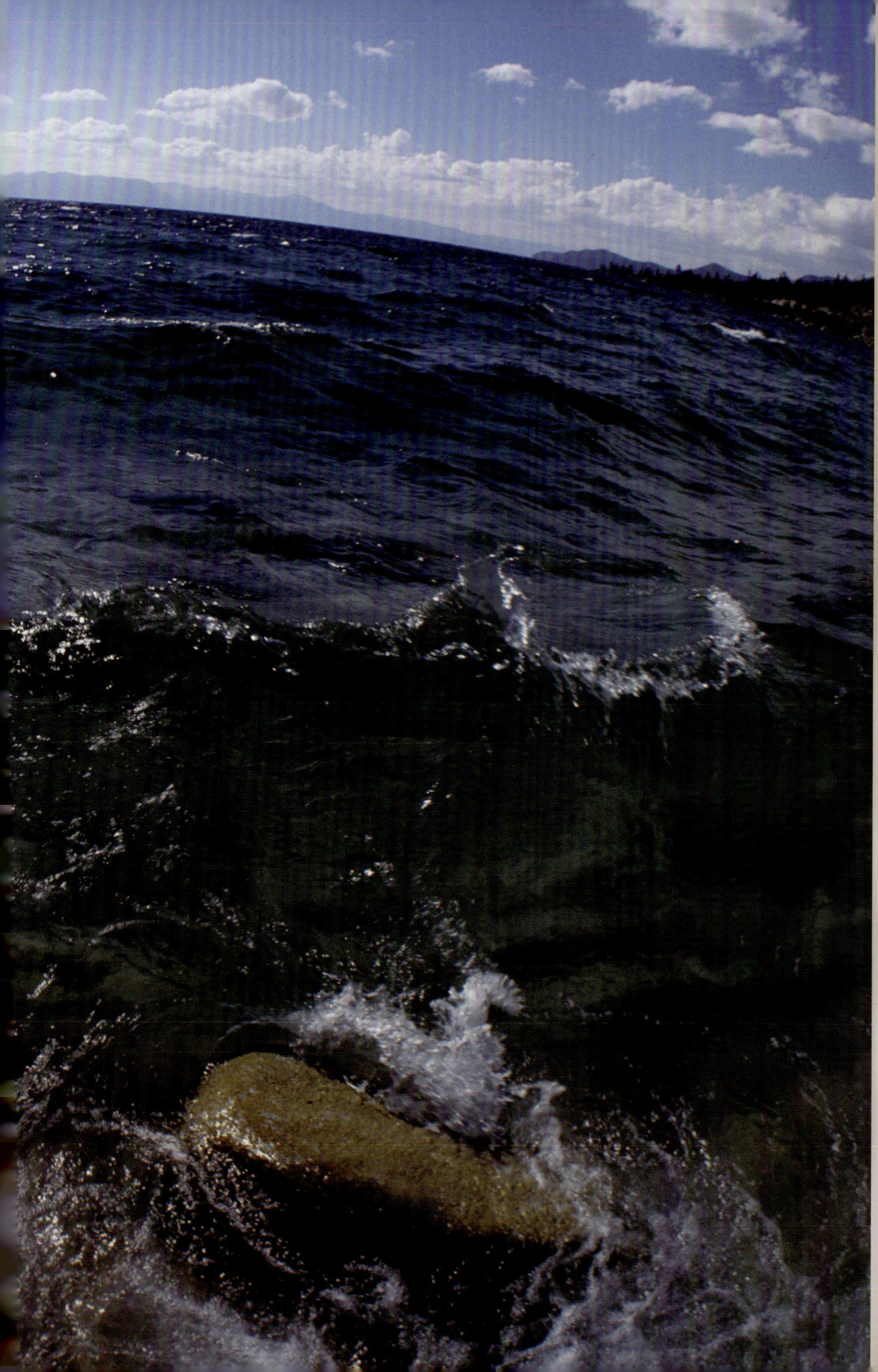

The sky is round and I have heard that the earth is round too. The wind in its greatest power whirls. Birds make their nests in circles and the mother's womb is round. Even the seasons form a great circle in their changing, and always return back from whence they came.

- Black Elk, Oglala Sioux holy man

Storm-polished stones lie scattered everywhere along the rugged shoreline of Big Sur, mute testimony of the continual wearing away of the westernmost flanks of the Santa Lucia Mountains by an all-powerful sea.

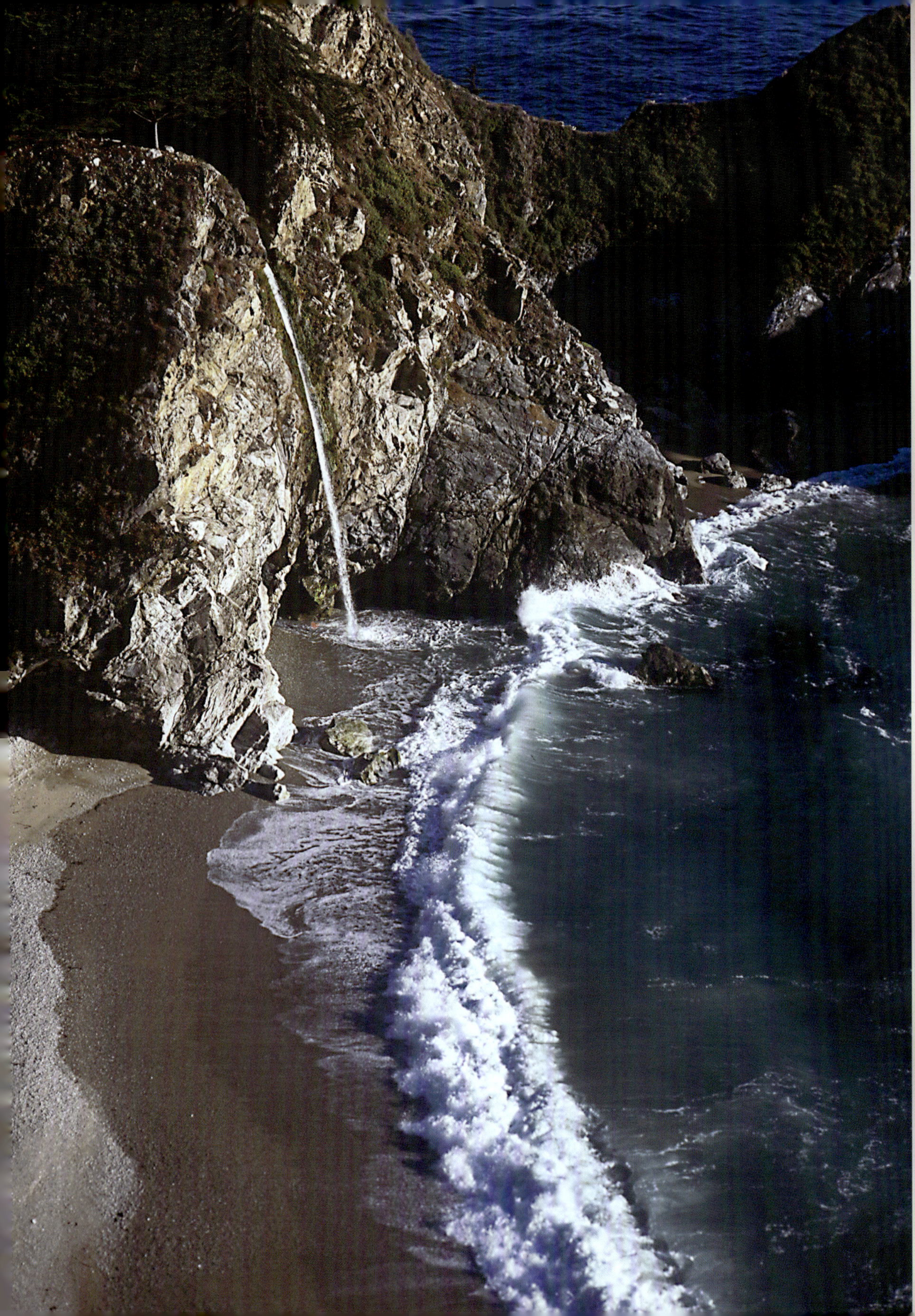

In a dream I walked with god through the deep places of creation; until all around me was an infinity into which we all flowed together and lived anew.

- Dag Hammarskjold, Swedish former United Nations Secretary General and Nobel Laureate

85

The massive stone cliffs rising from the sea along the coast of Big Sur only appear eternal to impatient human eyes. But here on the western edge of the Santa Lucia Mountains, the land is slowly but surely crumbling into a hungry sea. Powerful storm surf and tumbling streams never cease their tireless work of wearing away the rocky shoreline. A graphic example is oft-photographed McWay Falls, the iconic crown jewel of Julia Pheiffer Burns State Park.

Two kayakers exploring the shoreline of Big Sur landing where 84' McWay Falls thunders down to the sea. The unstable cliffs surrounding the cataract make land access to the little beach by hikers and climbers dangerous and strictly prohibited. Photograph by filmmaker Gordon Brown.

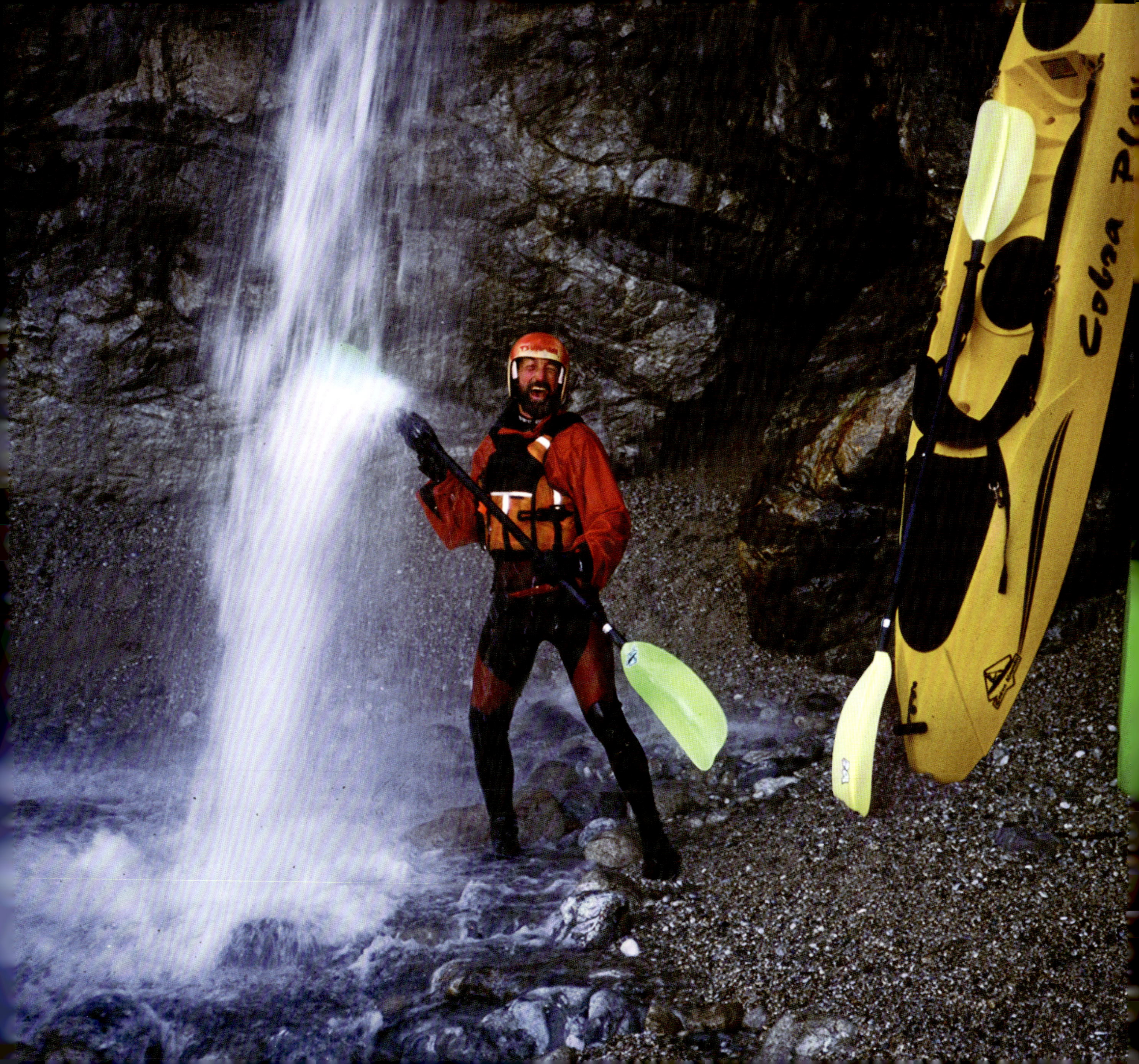
Cobra

Someday after we have mastered the wind, the waves and gravity, we shall harvest the energies of love. Then for the second time in history, men will have discovered fire.

- Teilhard de Chardin

Arrival at the edge of a swirling sea before dawn at Rocky Point on the Big Sur coast brings photographer Lars Howlett a deeply thoughtful moment. The siren's call of the brooding, mystical Sur has long proven irresistible to artists, poets and dreamers.

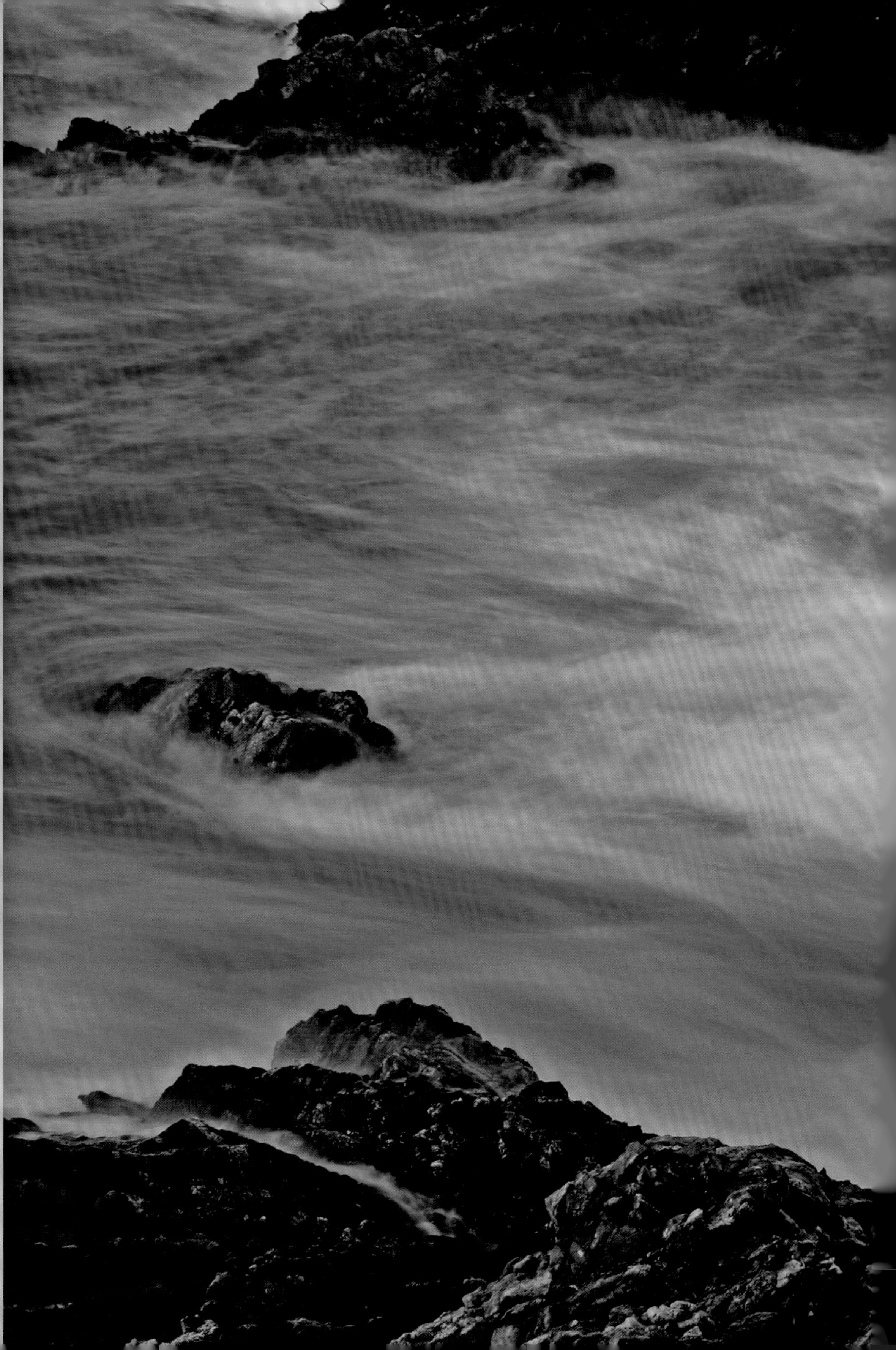

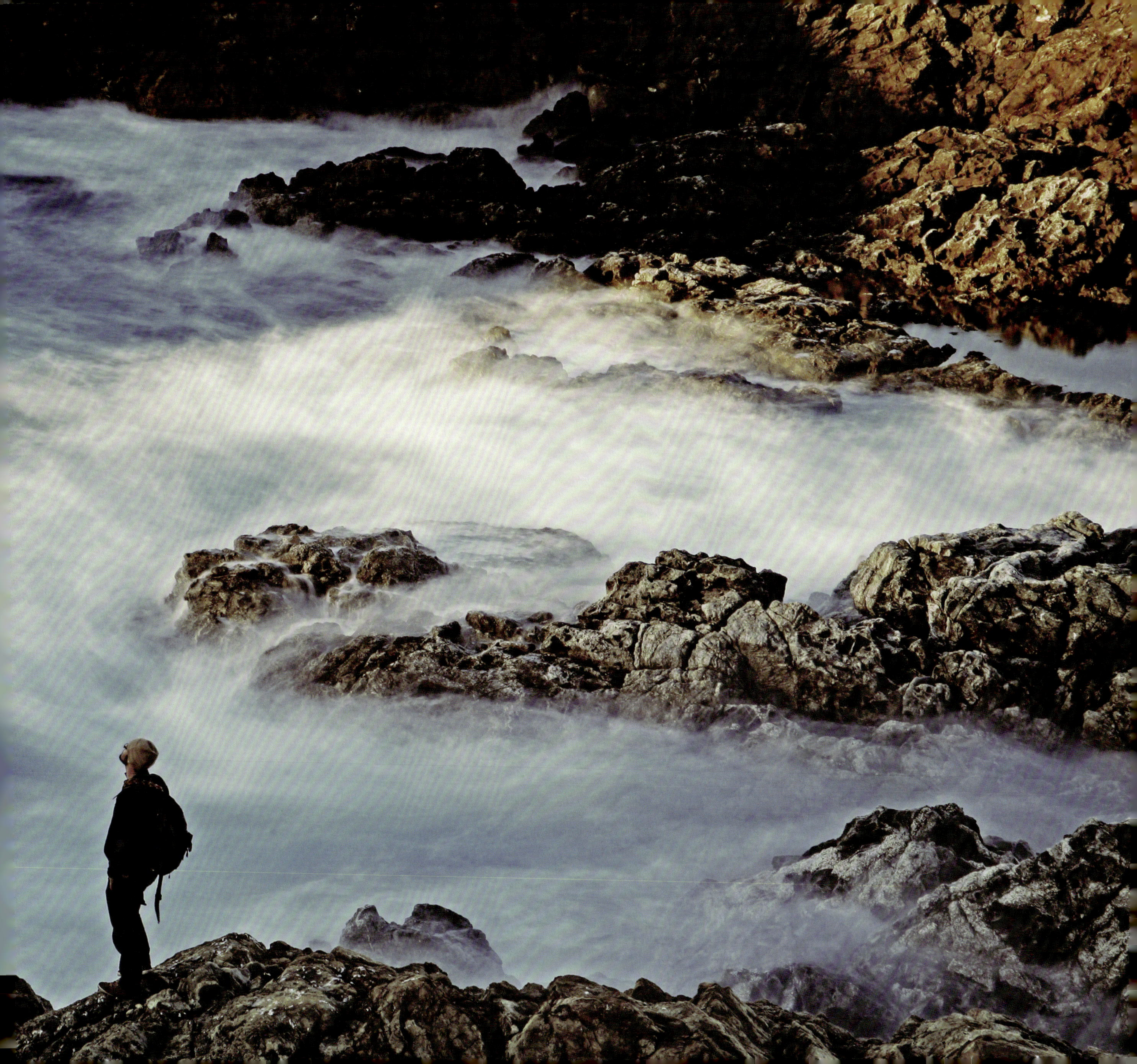

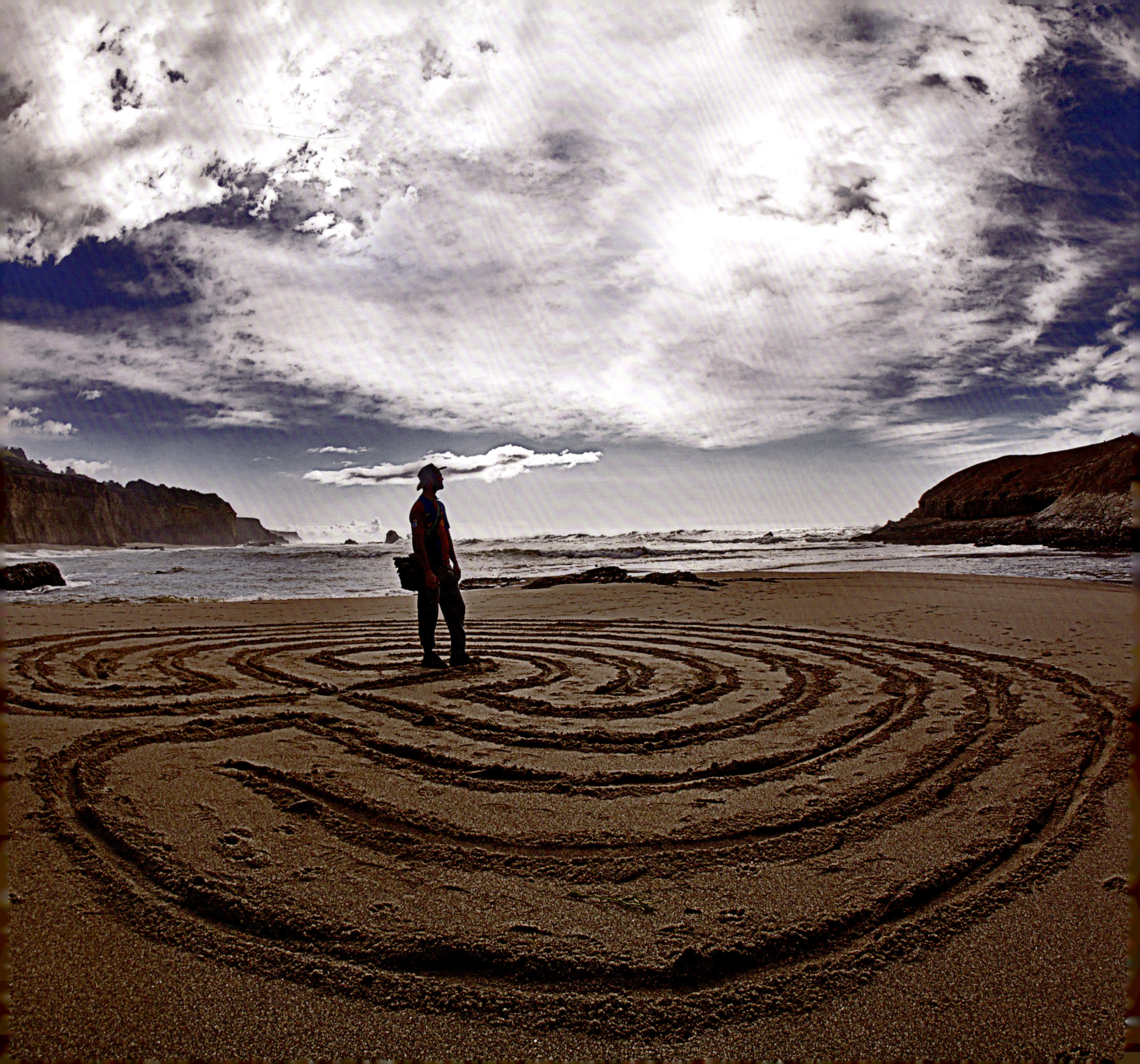

We have little to risk the adventure alone, for the heroes of all time have gone before us. The labyrinth is fully known.

\- Joseph Campbell

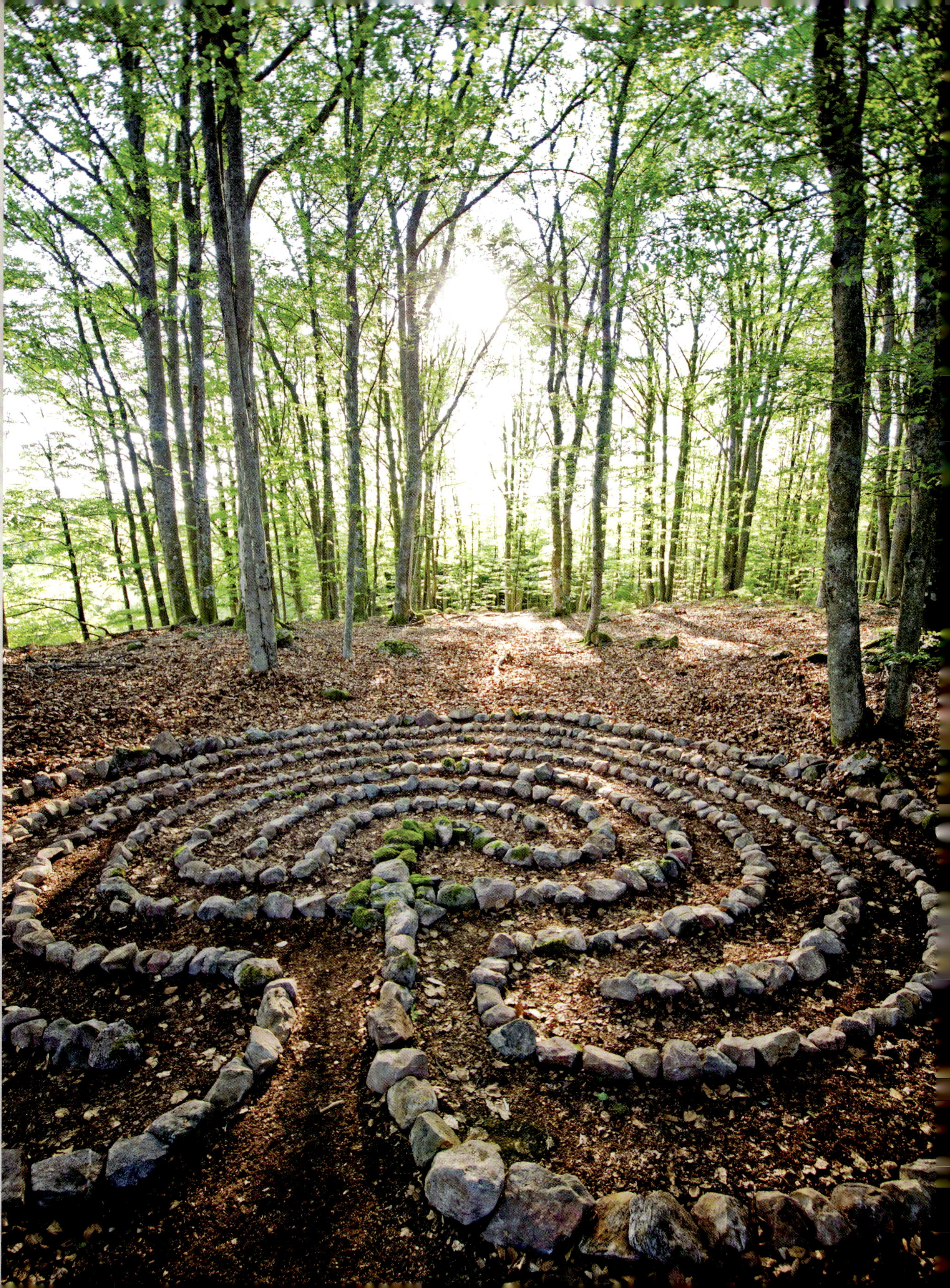

Lars Howlett enjoys a timeless moment within a labyrinth he drew in the sand at Greyhound Rock Beach, north of Santa Cruz on the northern California coast.

On his family's ancestoral land in Sweden, Howlett constructed a labyrinth from gathered stones. Then he returned at dawn the next morning to photograph his creation in the ethereal light of the rising sun.

Death is no more than passing from one room into another. But there is a difference for me. For in the other room, I shall be able to see.

- Helen Keller

With all the measured power and eloquence of a Tchaikovsky symphony, another summer day comes to a glorious conclusion at Miramar Beach on the northern California coast. A solitary surfer pauses to turn seaward and more fully absorb the mystery and drama unfolding all around him.

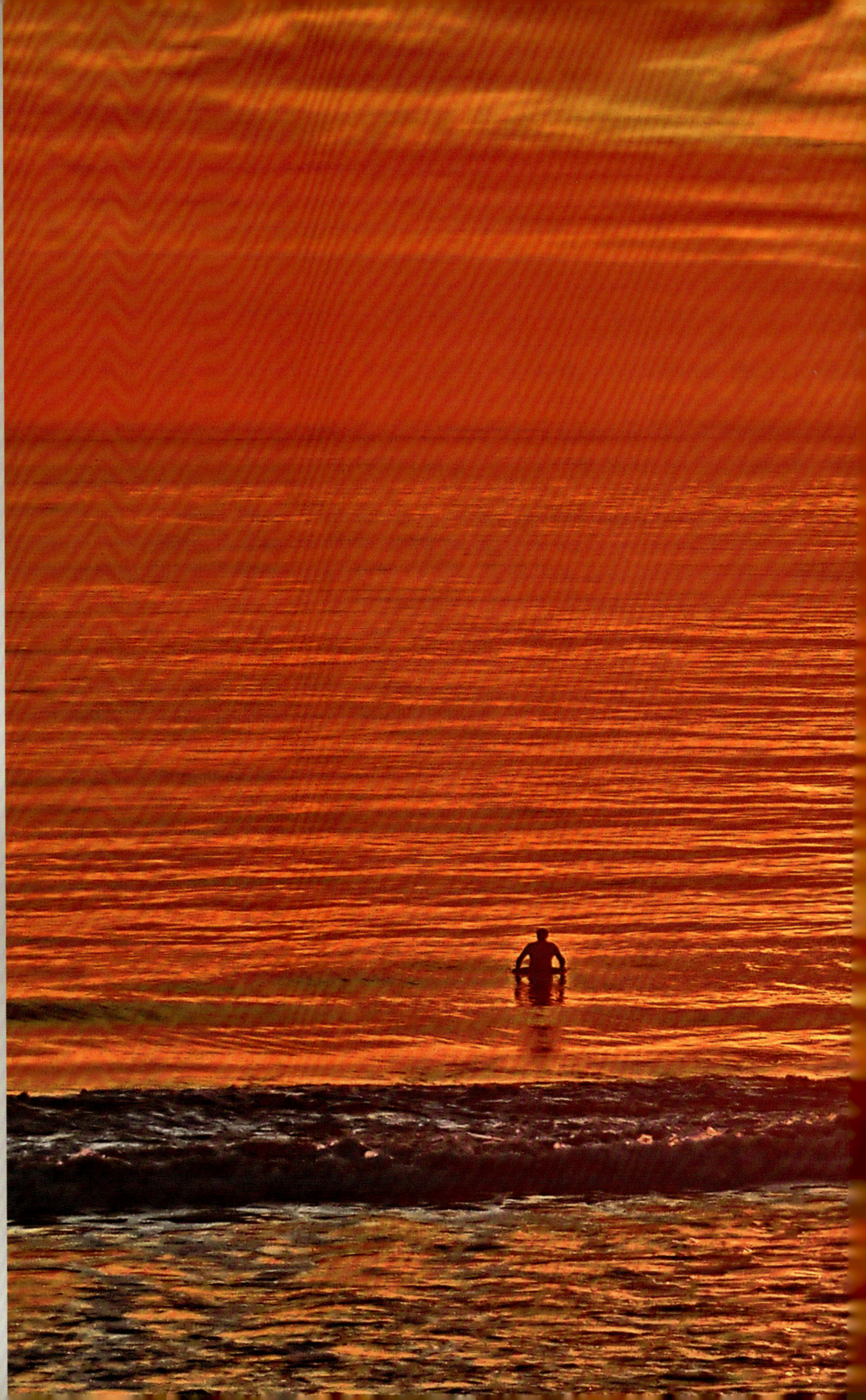

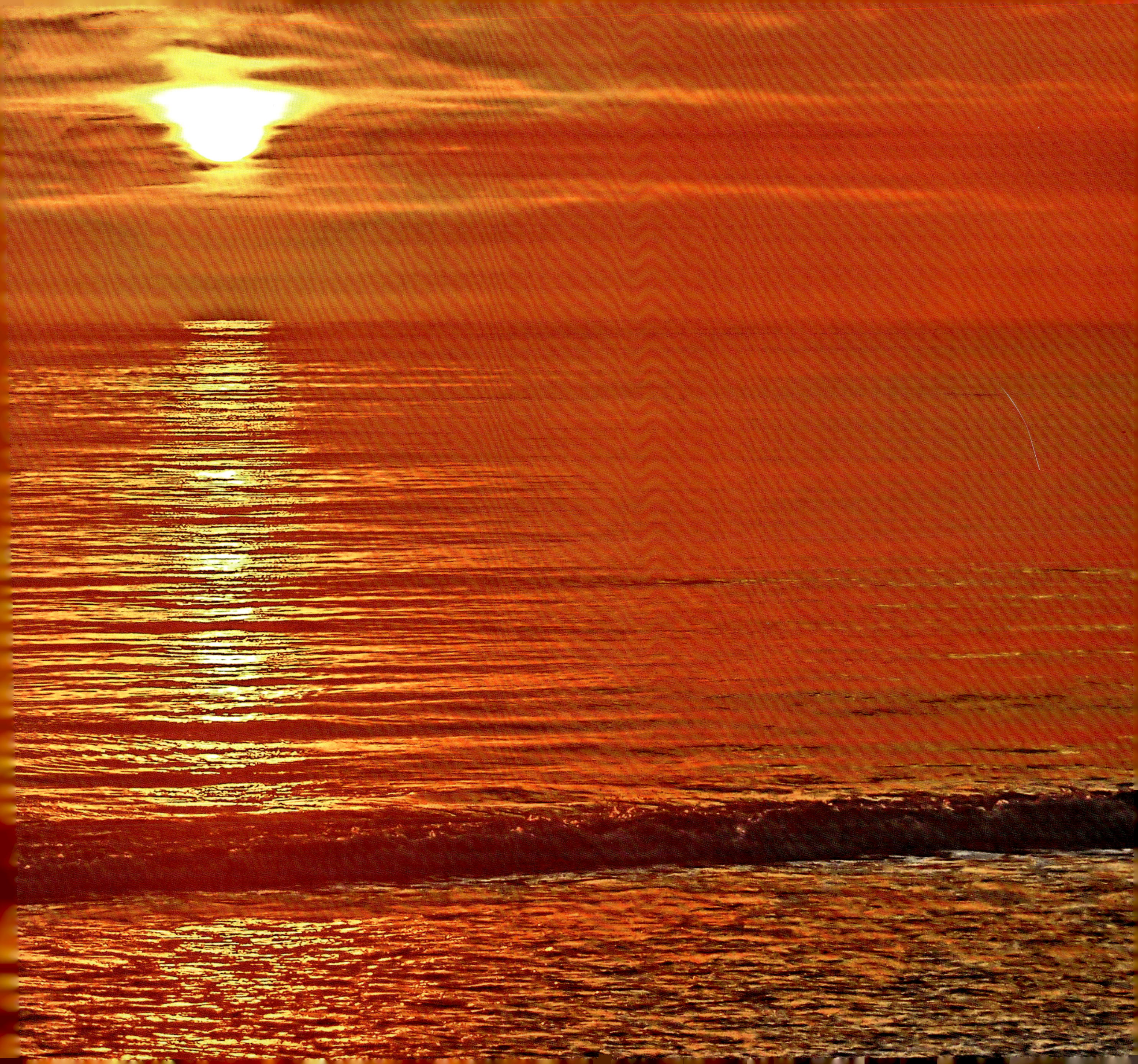

The crow that mimics a cormortant gets drowned.

- old Japanese fisherman's saying

93

The swell was small at Mavericks that day on the northern California coast, making it safe for two sea kayakers to paddle their double boat out and explore the rocky labyrinth at Pillar Point. The sea stack they approach was named Sail Rock by early settlers because in the old days it stood over a hundred feet high. Years of ceaseless wave and violent storms have now worn it down to a fraction of its original height. Off-shore rock formations like this, surrounded by surging whitewater and secure from land-based predators, provide crucially important refuge for marine birds and animals. This is especially true for diving birds like pelicans and cormorants, for whom it is essential to be able to dry their feathers and regain body heat between their dives into the sea in pursuit of fish.

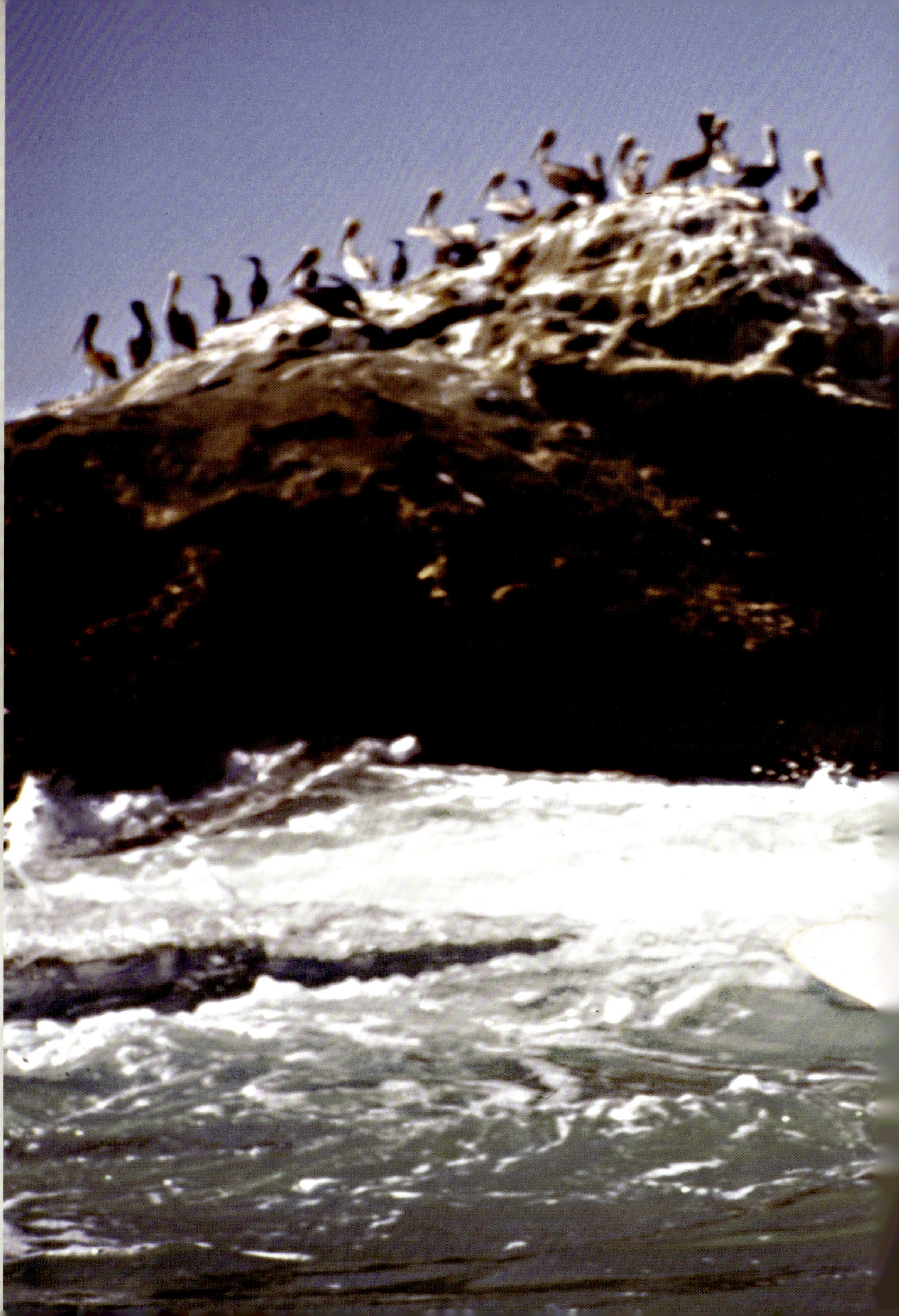

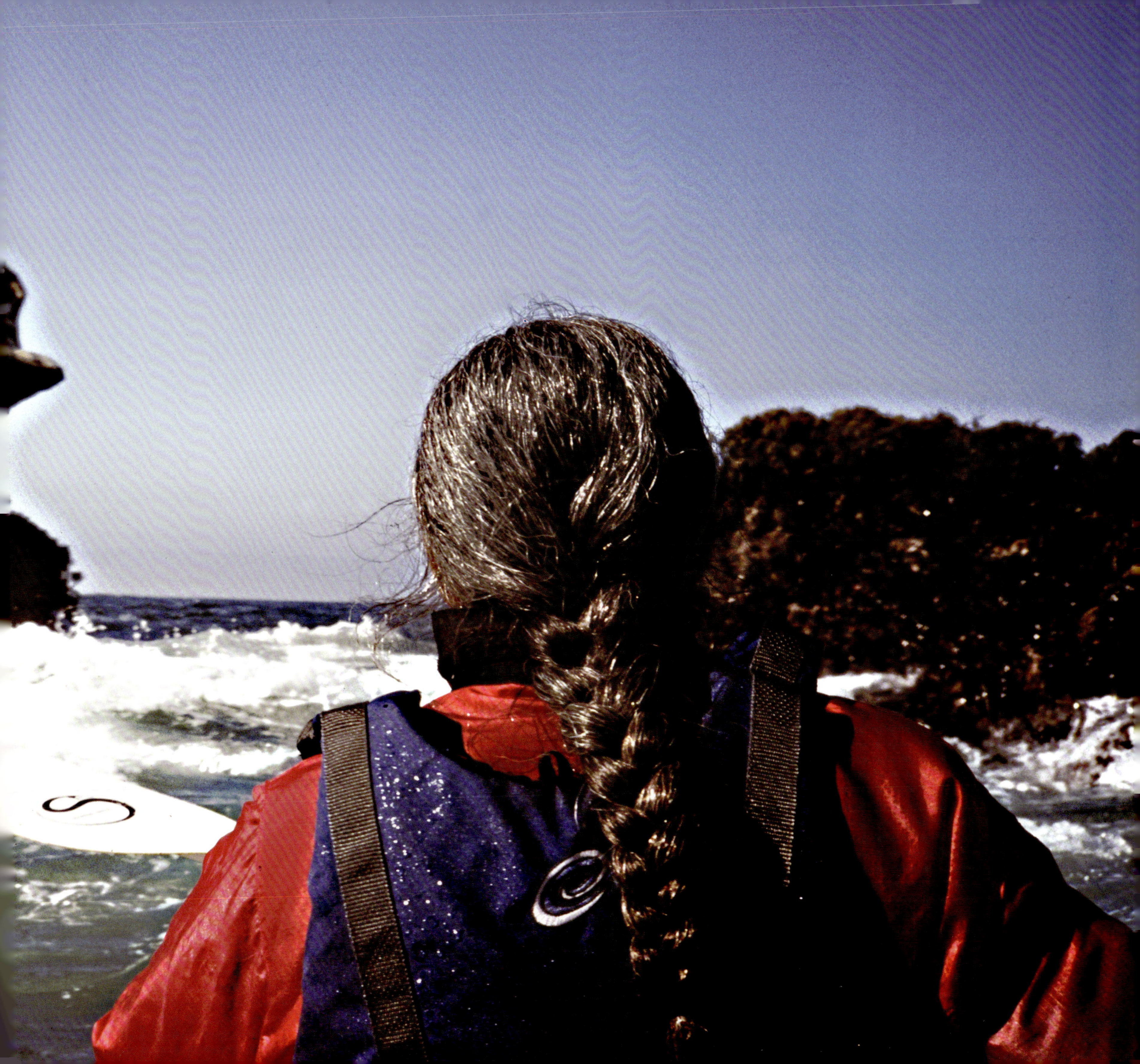

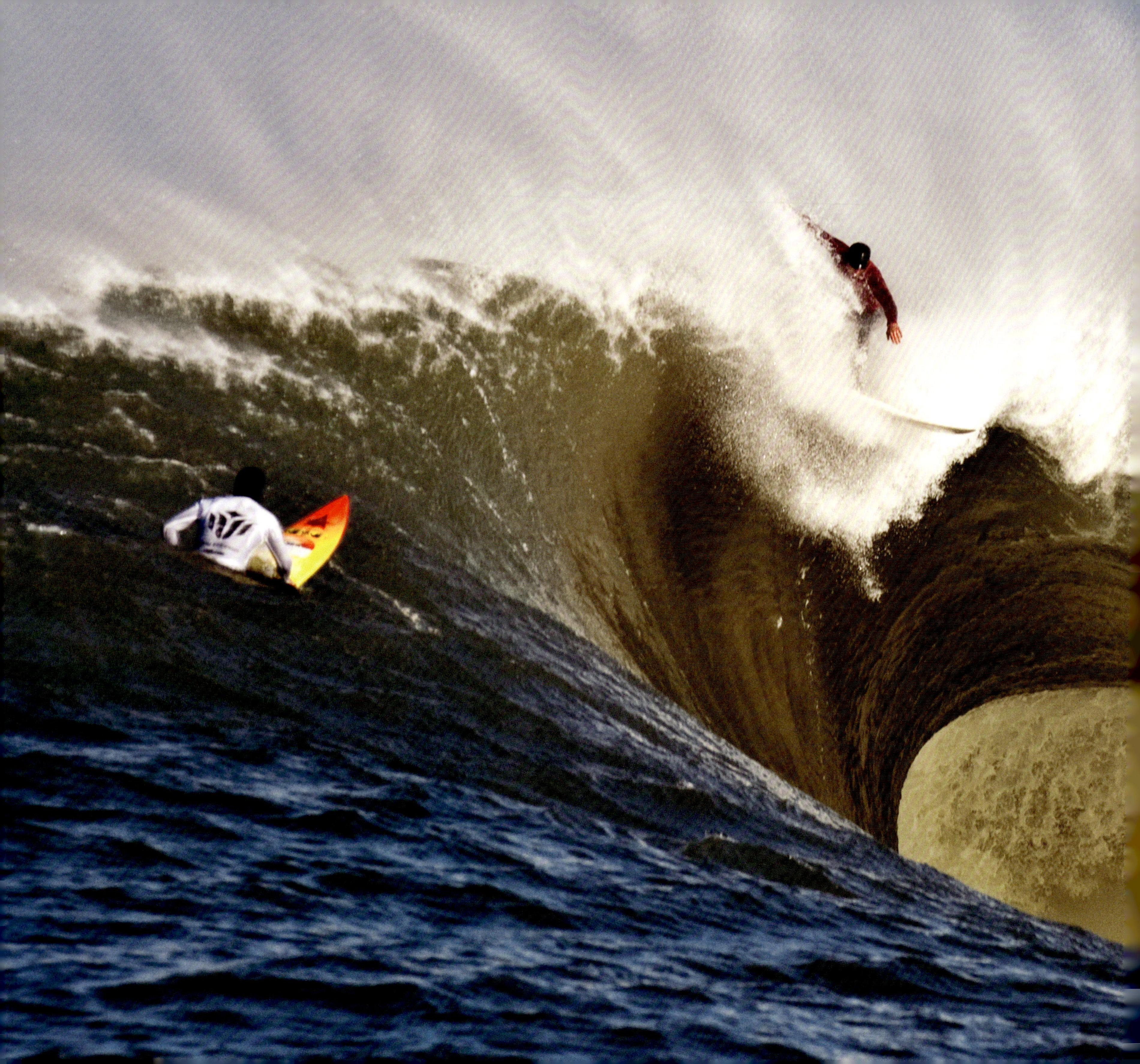

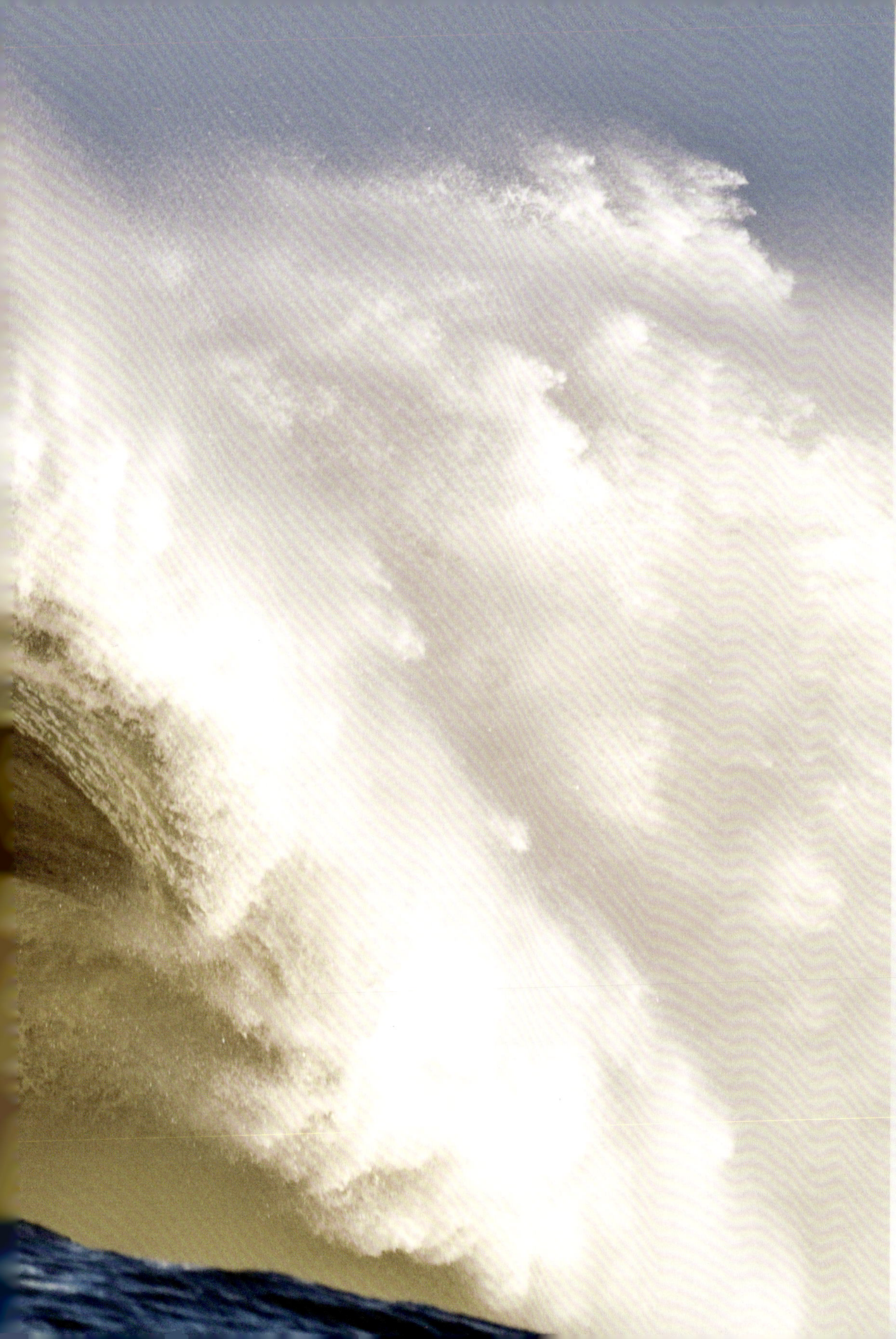

It's all about being there.

- Grant Washburn,
Mavericks big wave surfer

Evan Slater, one of the all-time greats of the big wave riding scene, poises at the edge of the abyss a split-second before wiping out at infamous Mavericks on the northern California coast. A 3-time winner of the annual Mavericks contest, Daryl 'Flea' Virostko, observes the impending carnage from his relatively safe vantage point. Arguably because the dangers are so great and the rewards so ephemeral, few recreational surfers ever make the transition to serious big wave surfing. Those who do, like base jumpers and 8000 meter mountain peak climbers, become a breed apart - regarded as lunatics by outsiders but rising to celebrity status within their own special worlds. Mavericks is a unique deep water point break, directly exposed to mega- swells charging down from the northern Pacific during the winter storm season. Once each year when exceptionally big surf is predicted, word goes out and contestants quickly gather from around the world to compete in the Mavericks Big Wave Invitational. The photograph was taken from a media boat at the 2011 contest by Lars Howlett.

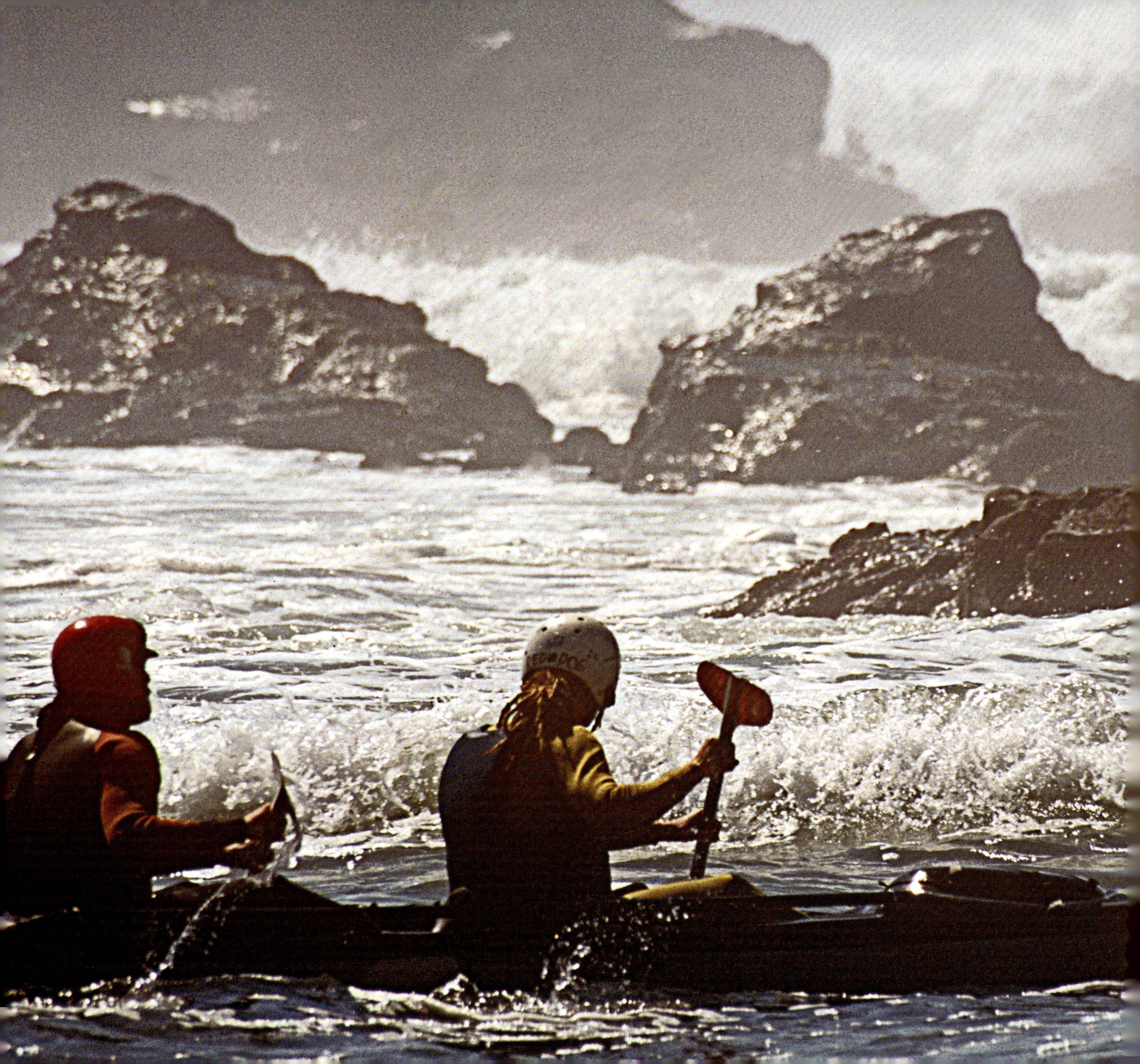

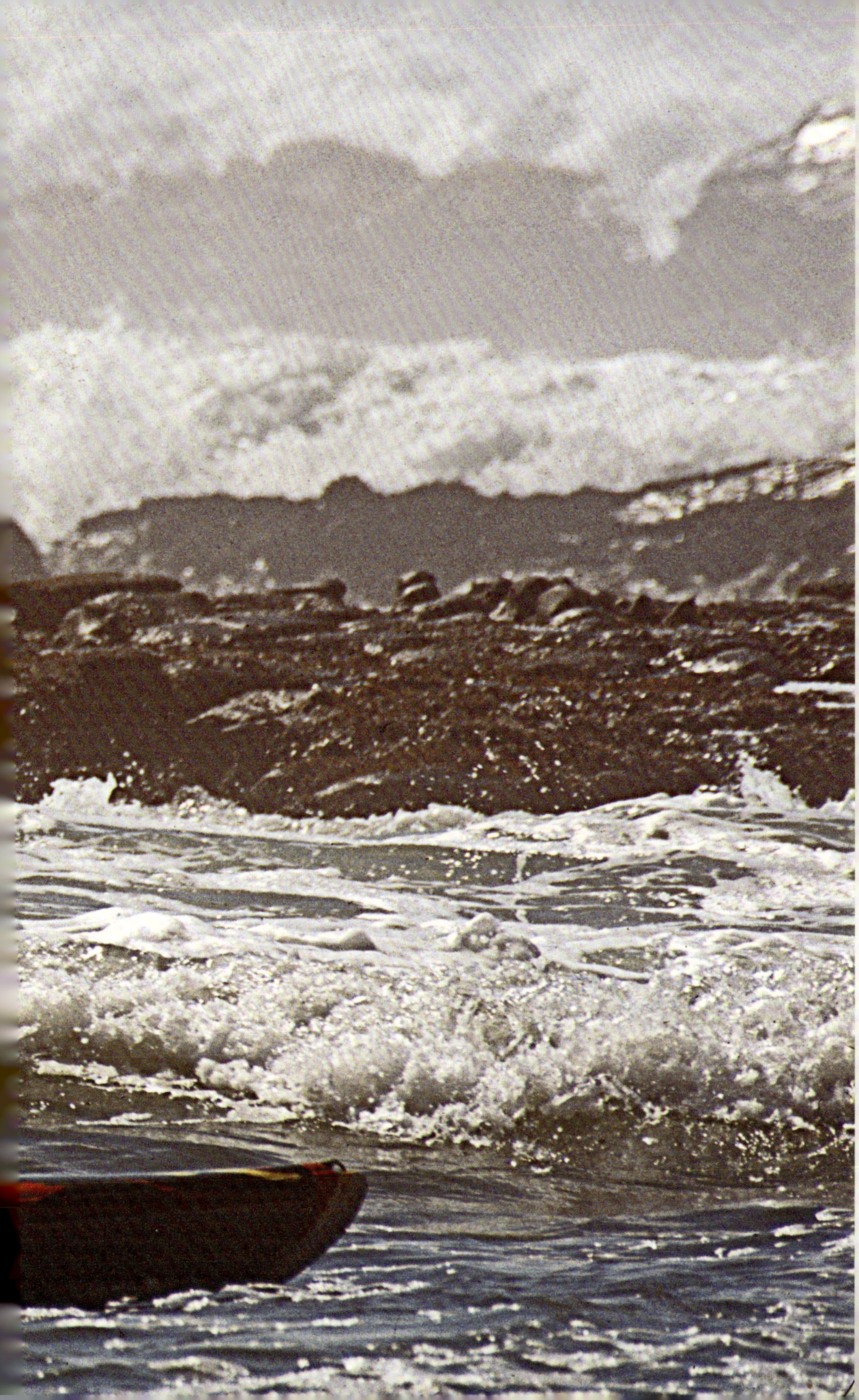

A storm at sea seems to arise from the beginnings of time, before the continents rose from the ocean depths.

- Jon Turk, author and modern day Arctic explorer

Eric Soares, aka Erikur or Red Dog, a commander of the Tsunami Rangers, shepherds an anxious newby out into the throat of the dragon at fabled Mavericks. The Rangers consider storm surf paddling at an exposed point break like Mavericks during the winter storm season an ultimate rite of passage for initiates to 'extreme condition' sea kayaking.

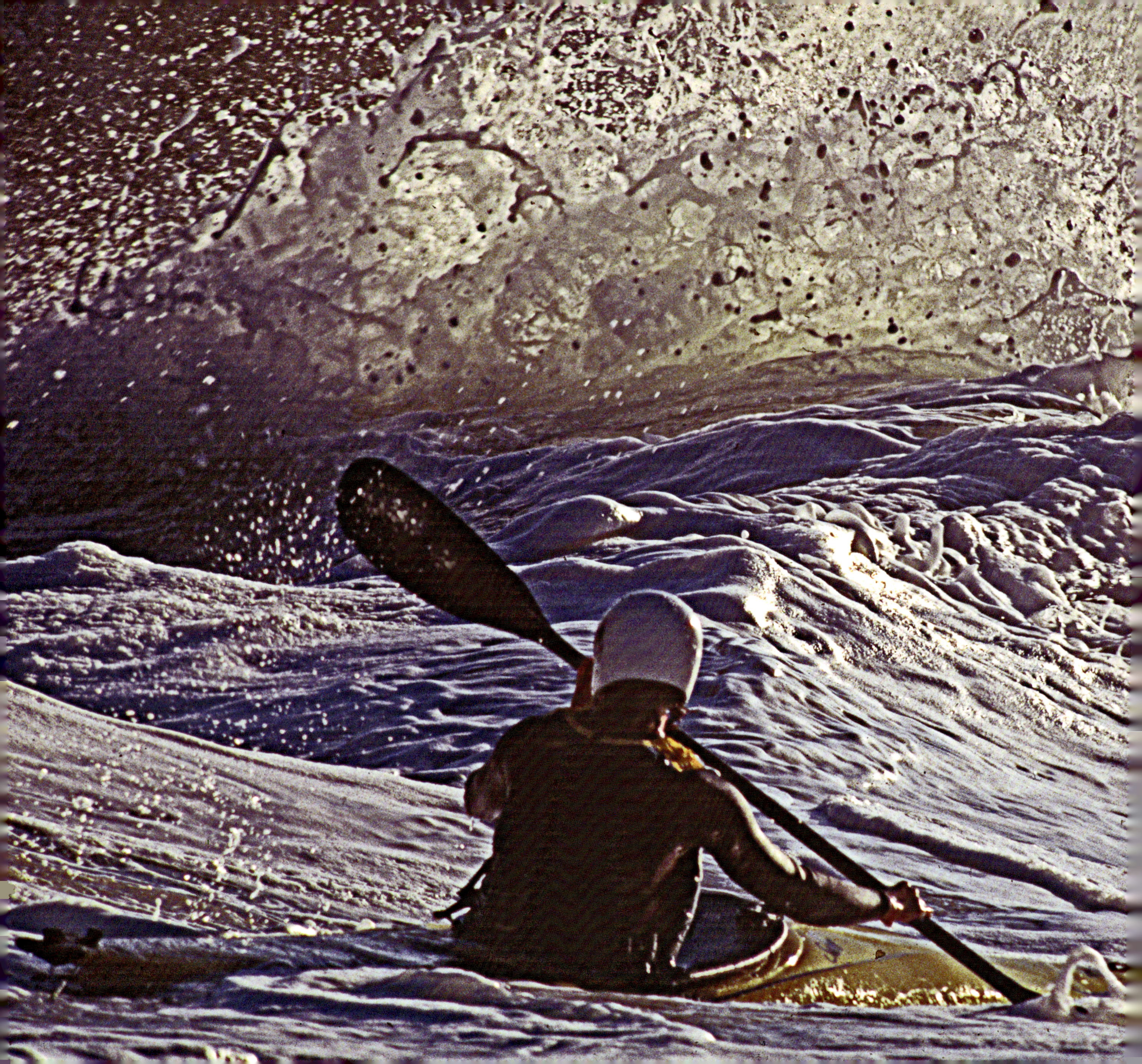

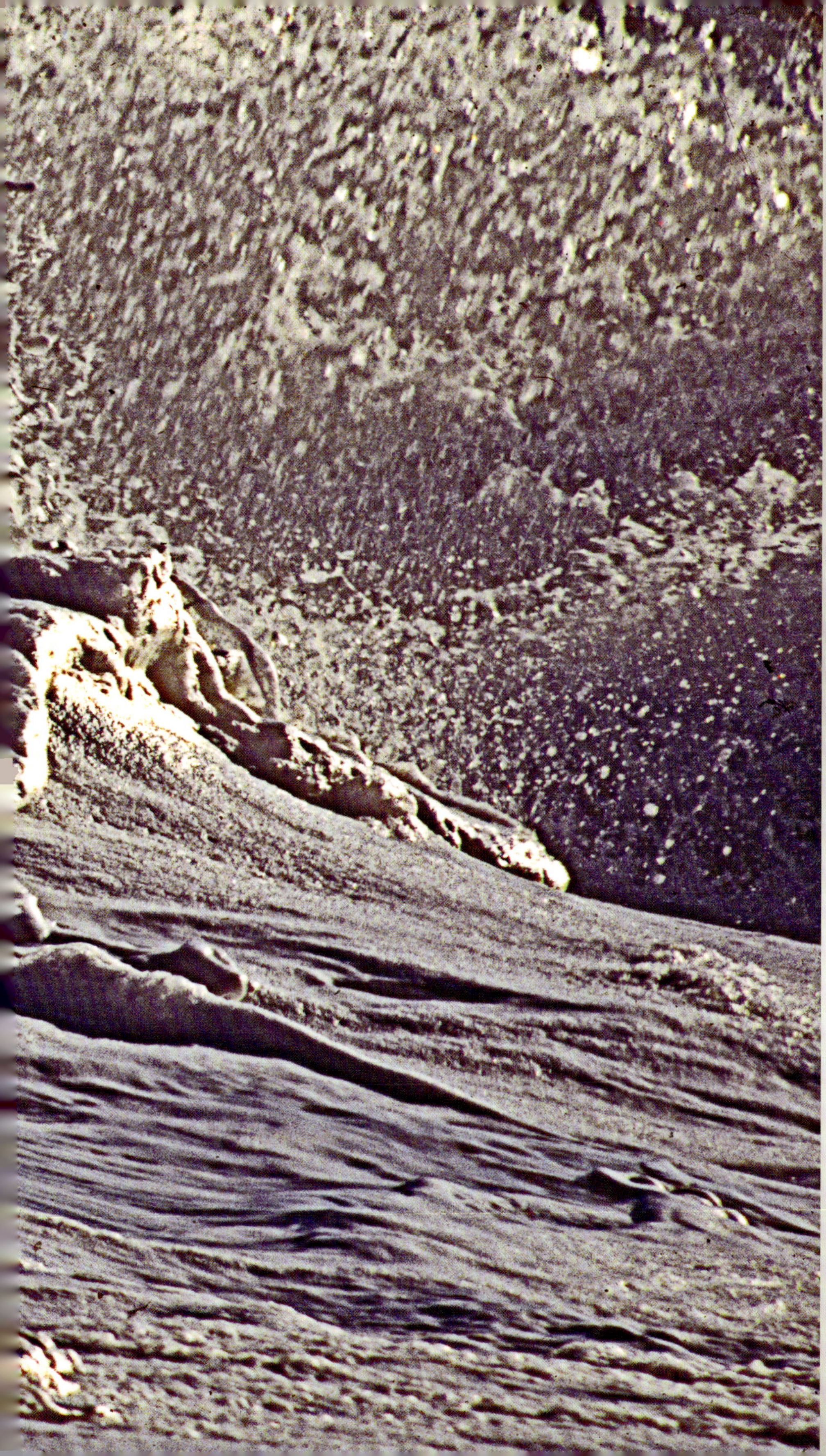

I am not afraid,
I was born to do this.

- St. Joan of Arc

Beth Borgeson's utter fearlessness while kayaking in big surf so impressed the Tsunami Rangers that finally they invited her to take the all-day, on-the-water test required for acceptance into the Rangers. In 1999 at the height of the winter storm season near her home at Davenport on the northern California coast, her test began. Beth's Viking spirit fully emerged that day, as she paddled out into the surf with the Rangers repeatedly in near gale force conditions and ultimately completed her test successfully. As a result she was duly awarded the honor of becoming the first woman ever officialy accepted into the Tsunami Ranger's elite "extreme condition" sea kayaking team.

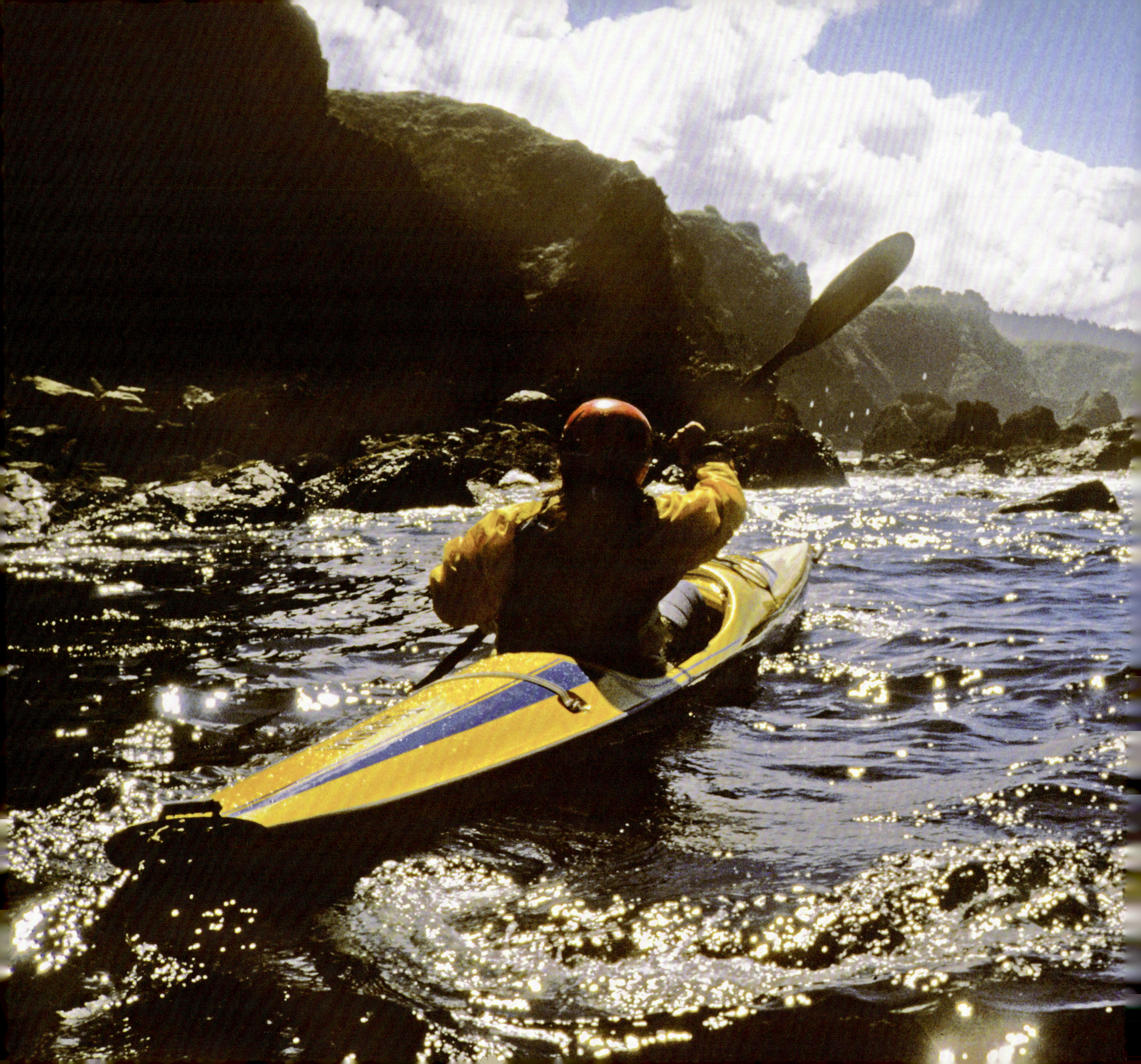

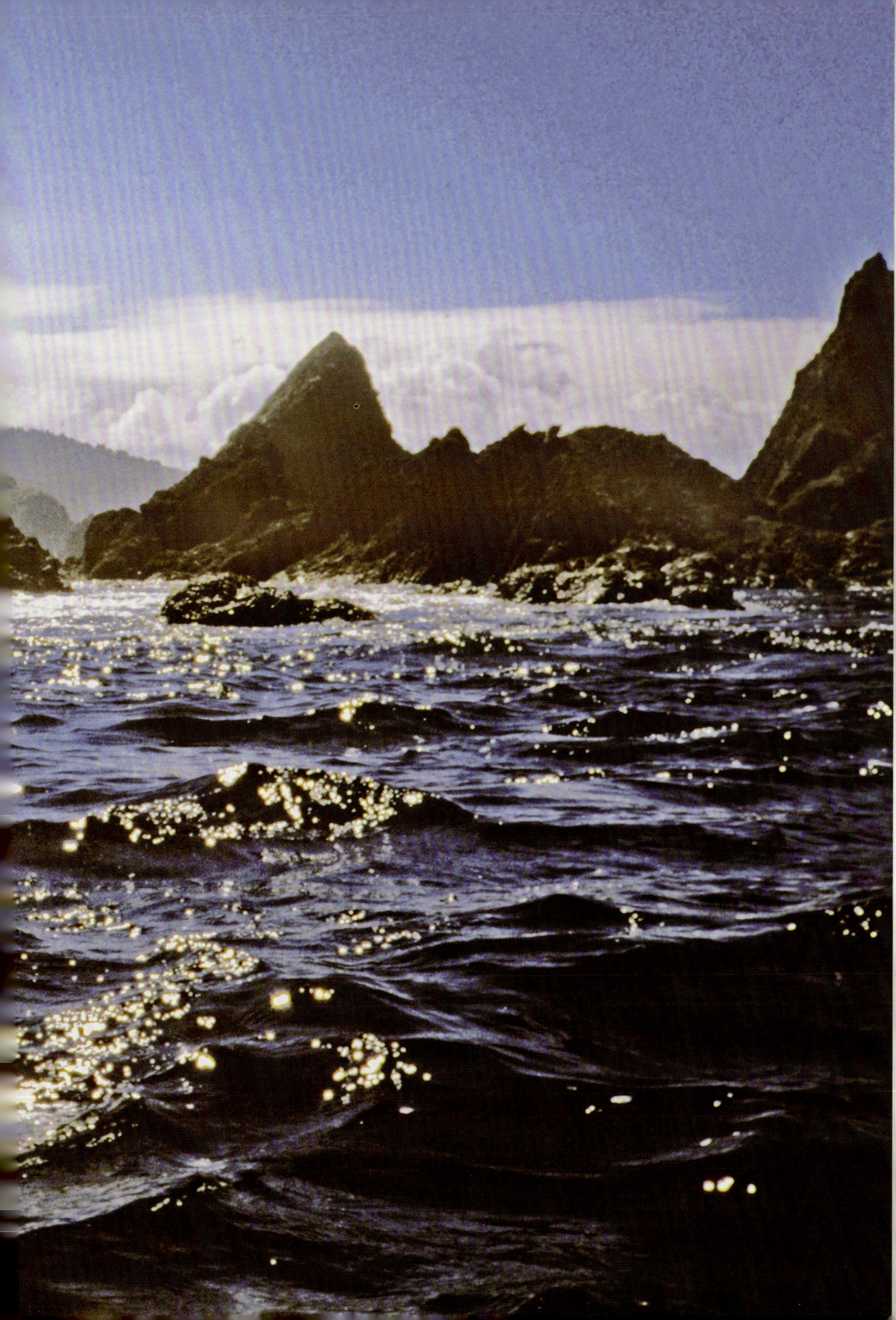

One should act in consonance with the way of heaven and earth, which is enduring and eternal.

- I Ching

Wherever mountainous terrain spills down directly into the ocean, the shoreline is sure to be rugged, cliff-lined and potentially perilous for sea kayaking. The spectacular Mendocino coast of northern California is a classic example, a place where only well-equipped, seasoned paddlers should venture. Bonnie Brill, on a multi-day exploratory mission there with the Tsunami Rangers, takes a turn leading the wolf pack through a watery minefield. She has wisely chosen a relatively protected route on the lee side of the off-shore reefs, affording her and the others some protection from the ten-foot swells charging shoreward from the open sea. But all hands still remain on high alert for that monster set that could arrive at any moment and fill the inner reef area where they paddle with big breaking waves.

A small group of thoughtful people could change the world. Indeed, it is the only thing that has.

- Margaret Mead

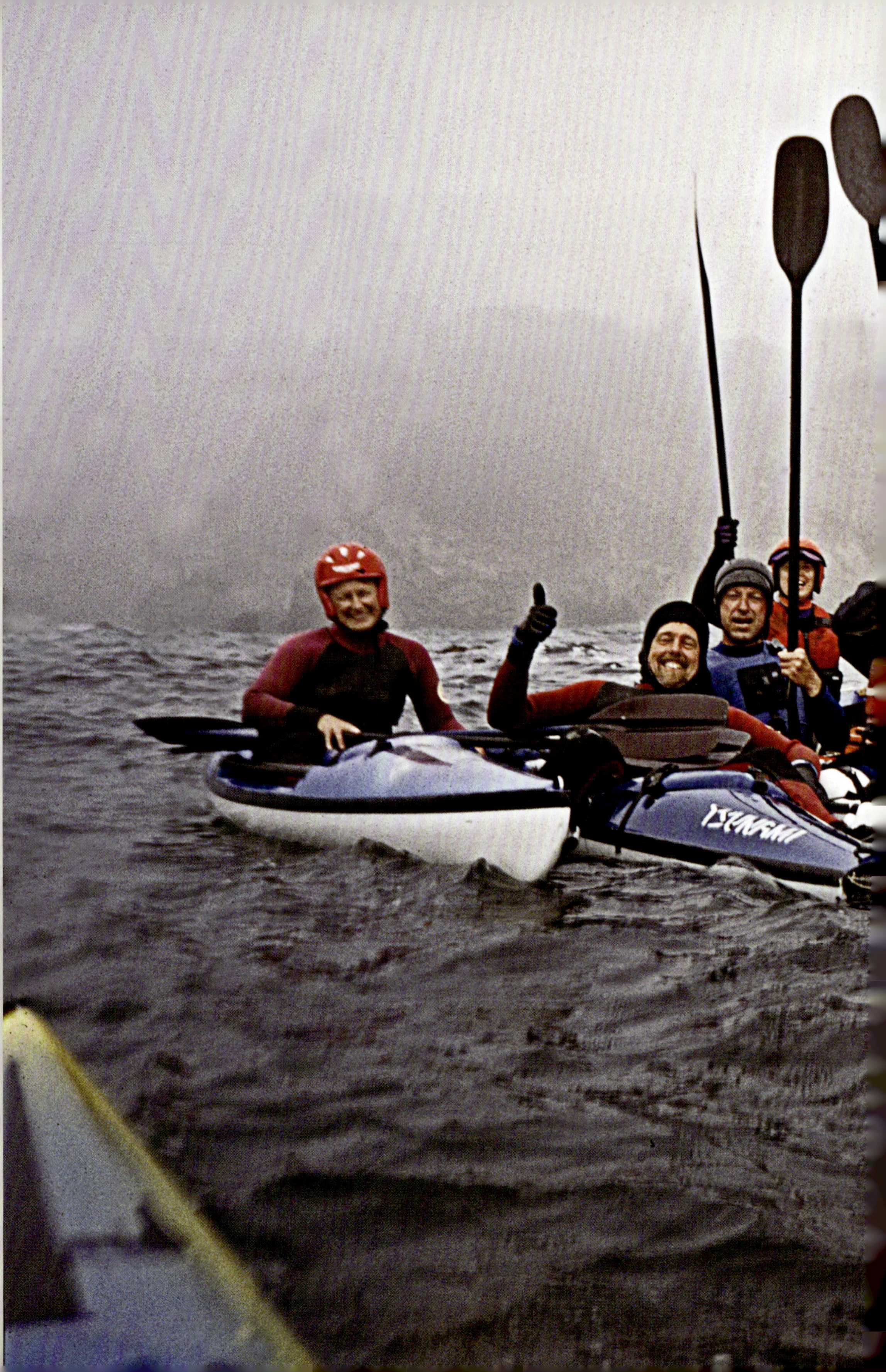

Paddling along the Pacific shoreline of southern Oregon, a Tsunami Ranger's team rafts up to reconnoiter and savor a few moments of warm-blooded tribal communion. Exploring a wild, exposed shoreline by sea kayak is one of life's sublime adventures and a resonably sane endeavor - when undertaken by experienced and properly equipped paddlers capable of launching and landing their crafts through breaking surf and rocks. The Rangers have discovered that it is generally safer, and more fun too, to paddle with others than alone.

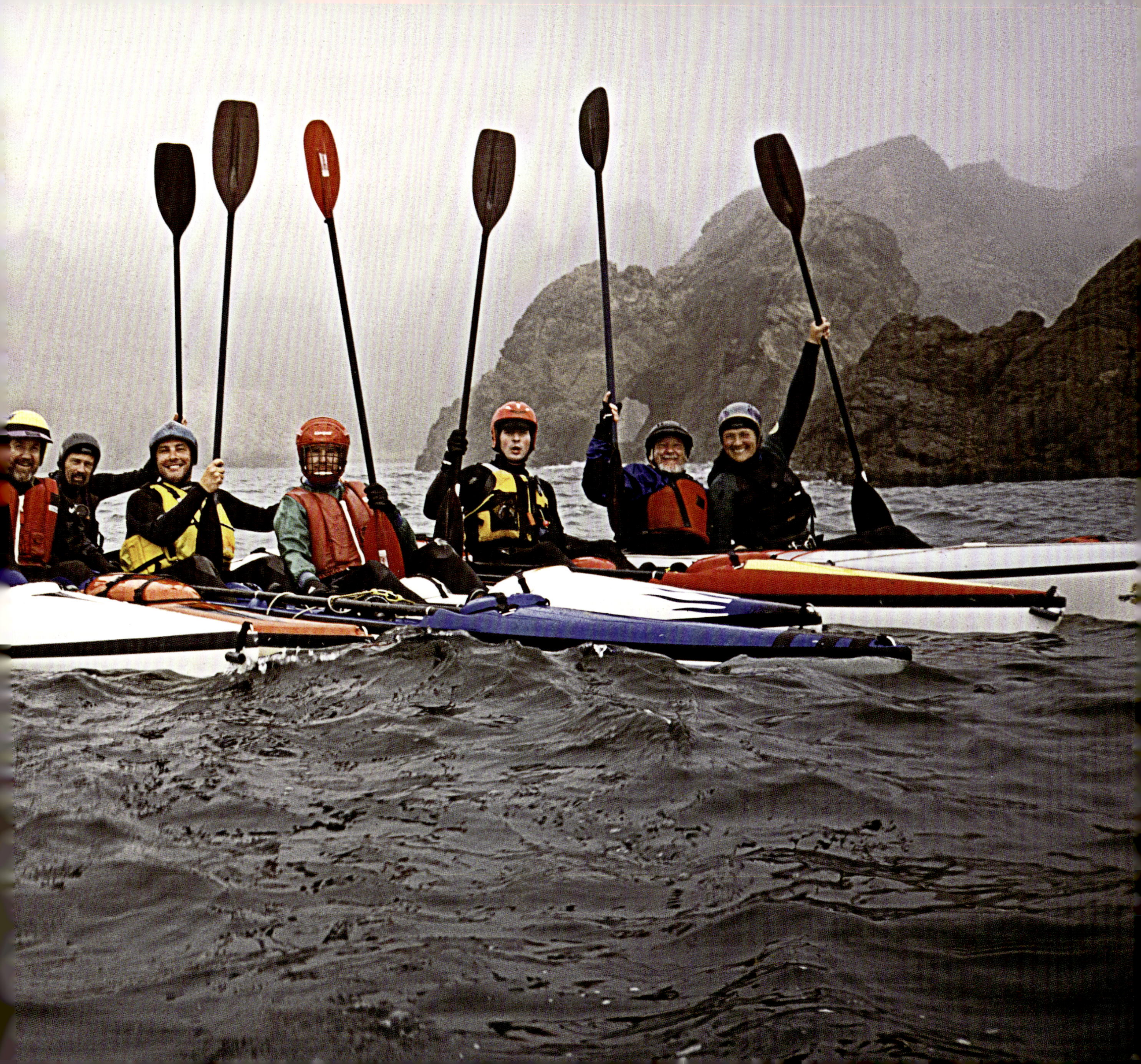

Dance when you are broken open
Dance in the middle of battle
Dance in your blood
Dance when you are perfectly free

- Rumi, 13th century Persian poet

105

The Tsunami Rangers were growing concerned as the sun began to near the western horizon. They had been kayaking for hours along an unfamiliar stretch of the Oregon coastline, and failed so far to find a suitable place to land and make camp for the night. Then in the last moments before sunset, the lead paddler raised his paddle to signify that he had spotted a glint of sand at the back of a cove. Everyone turned to race shoreward through the breaking surf and rocks. Stepping ashore, Captain Jim Kakuk christened the little beach *El Salvador* (the savior). Shedding their wetsuits, the Rangers spontaneously began to dance. Like warrior cultures everywhere and since time immemorial, they instinctually returned to ritual to express their gratitude for once again, having been delivered into safe refuge. Years of exploring wild, potentially dangerous coastlines around the world had shown the sometimes irreverent Rangers, the importance of pausing at special times to pay tribute to the Divine.

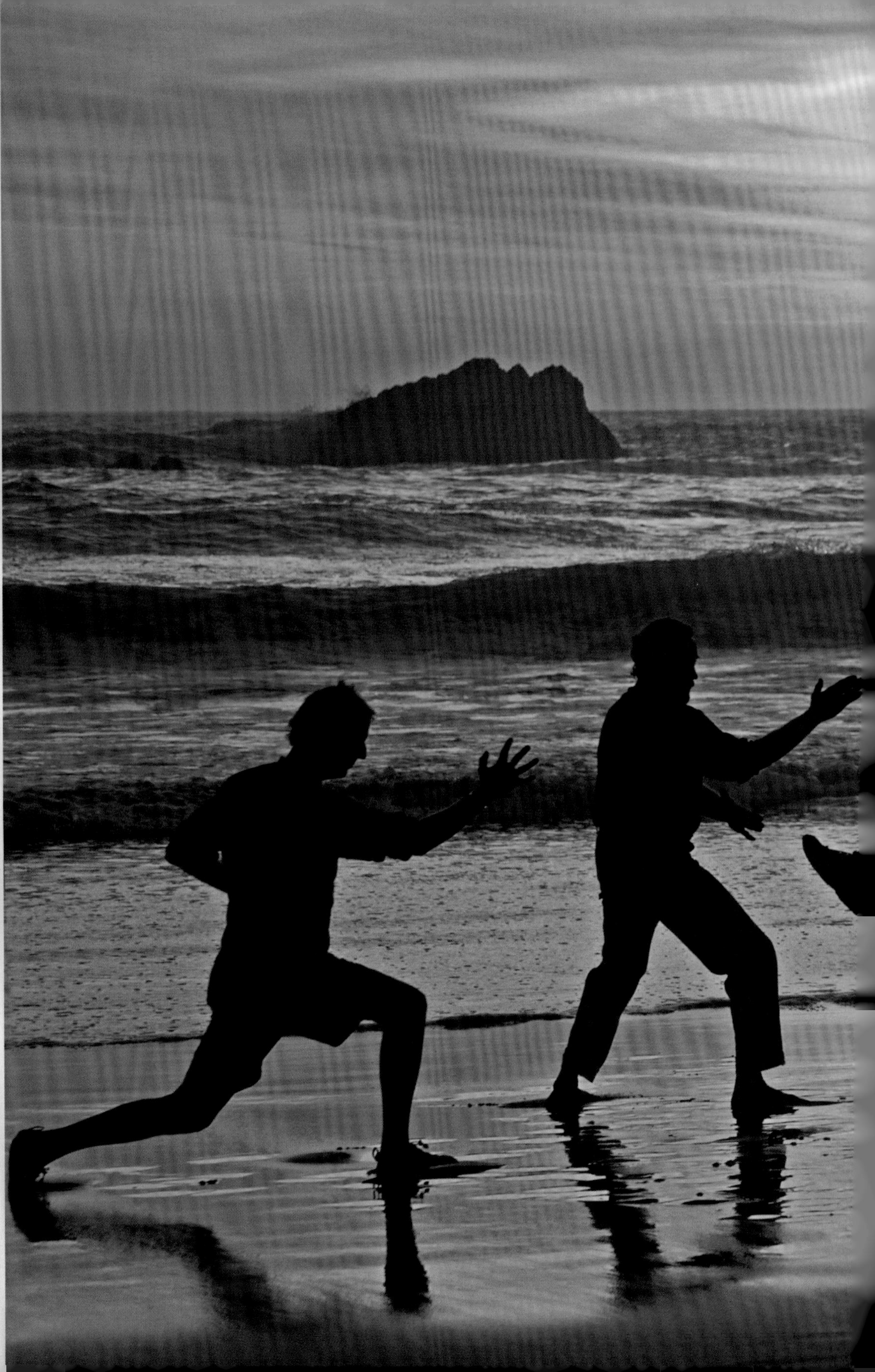

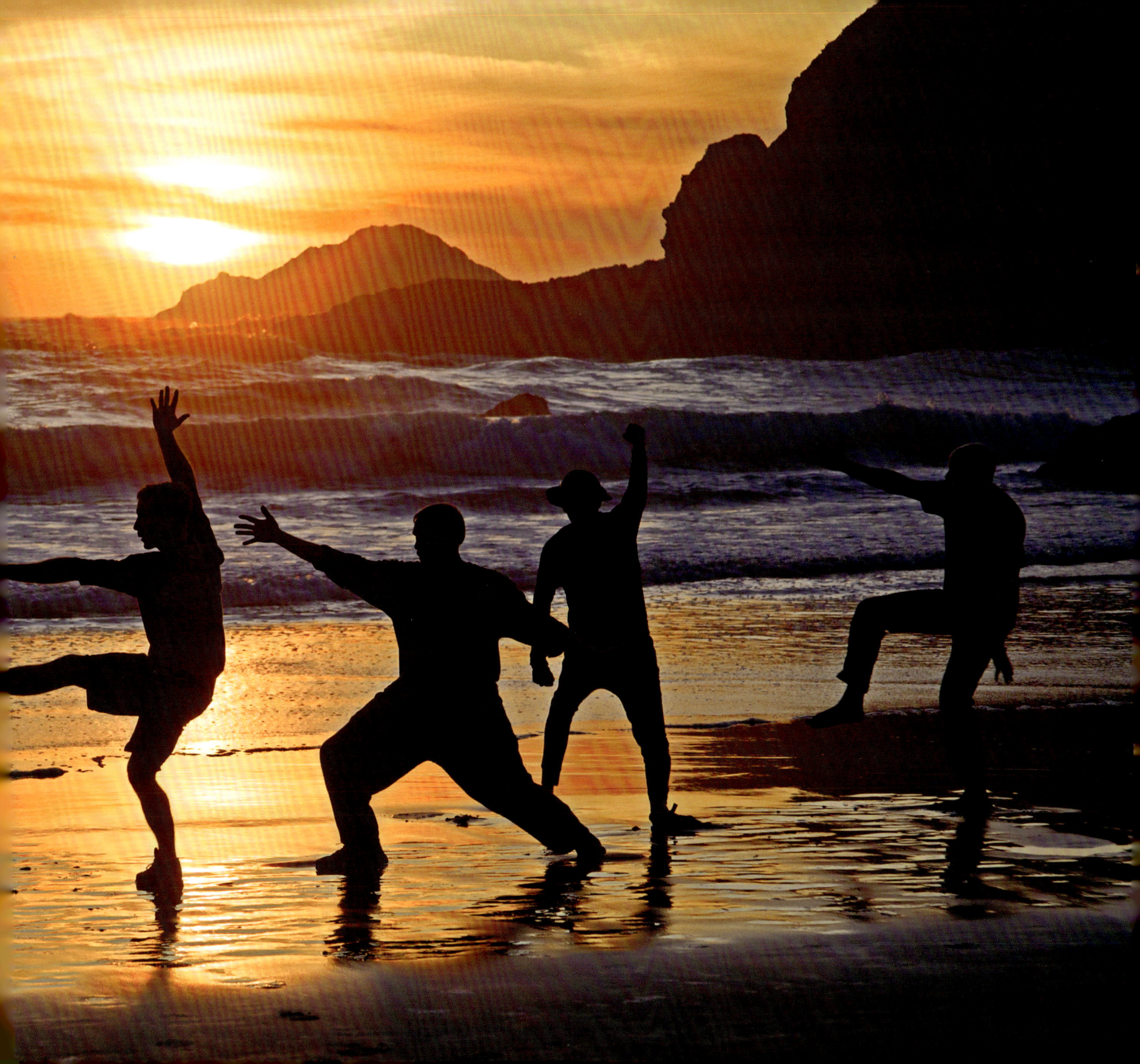

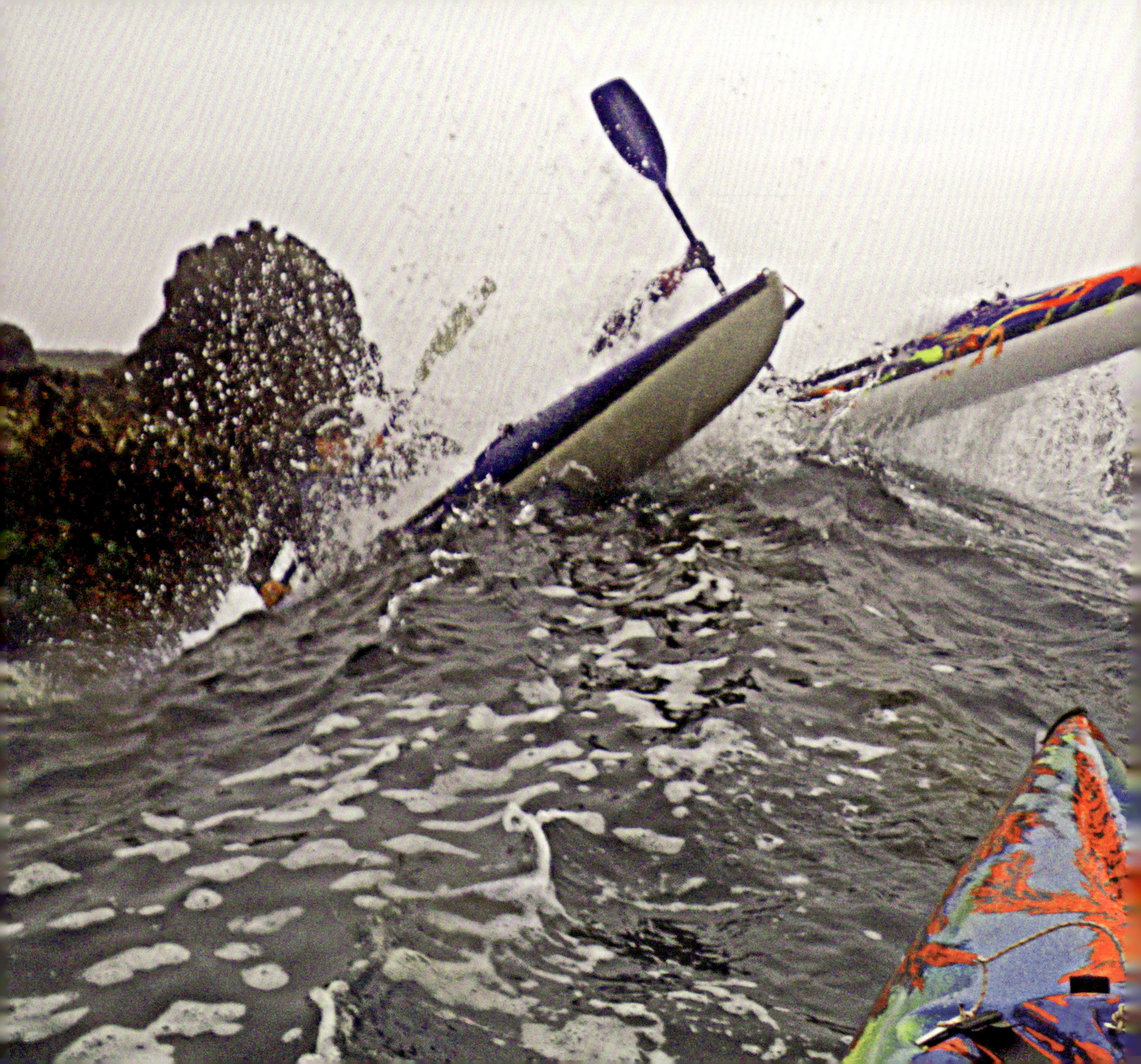

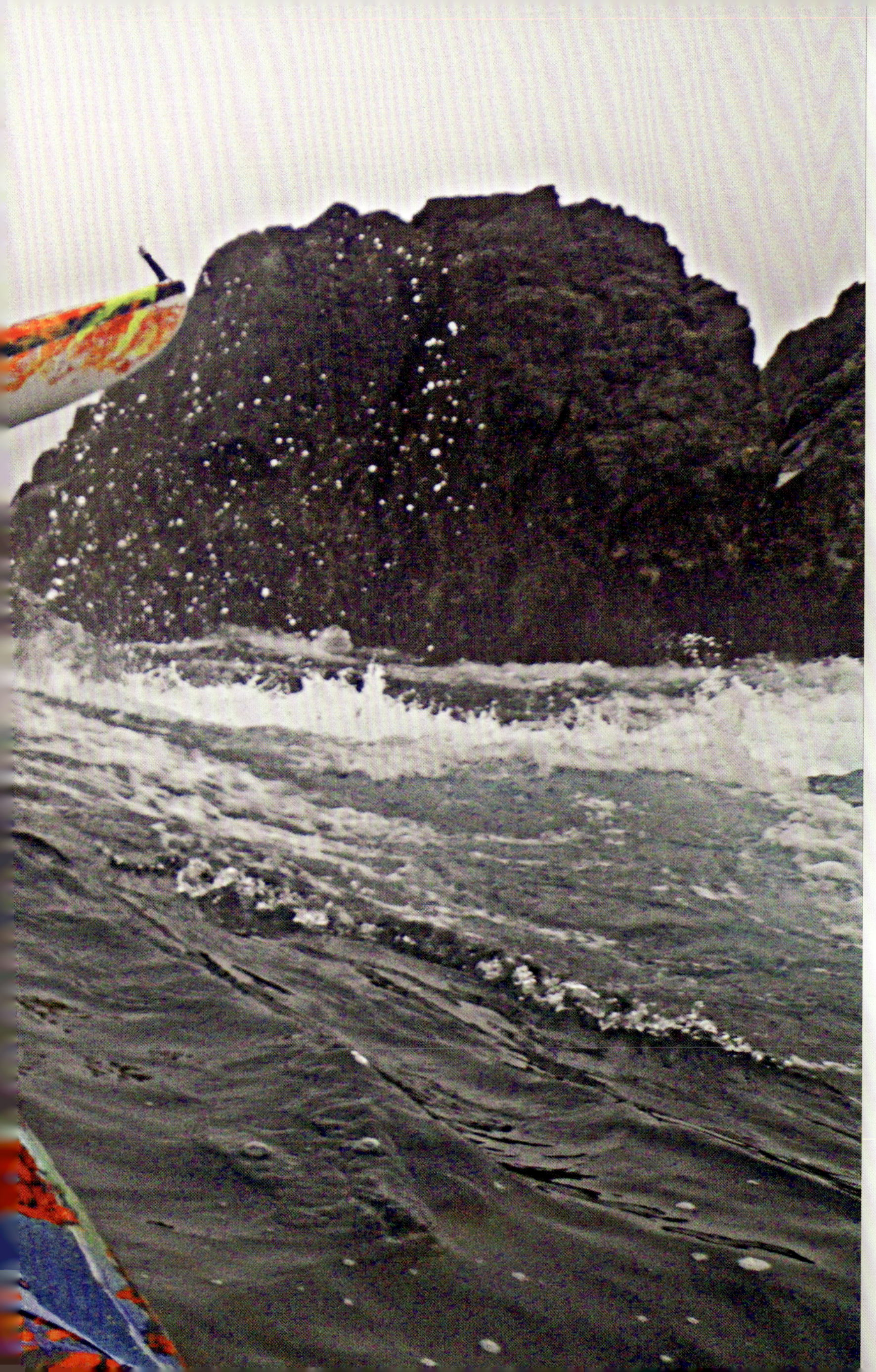

Only those who fail greatly can ever achieve greatly.

- Robert Kennedy, Sr.

Any exposed coastline where ocean swells roll in from the open sea and break over shallow reefs and rocks is bound to become hazardous for sea kayakers at times. But it is also an opportunity to hone paddling skills and have some great fun - like when Tsunami Rangers Eric Soares and Steven King were crossing an open sea reef in Big Sur just as a big set of swells showed up and their calm, peaceful world got totally exciting for a few moments.

No, we don't know where it will all lead. We just know there is something much bigger than any of us here.

- Steve Jobs

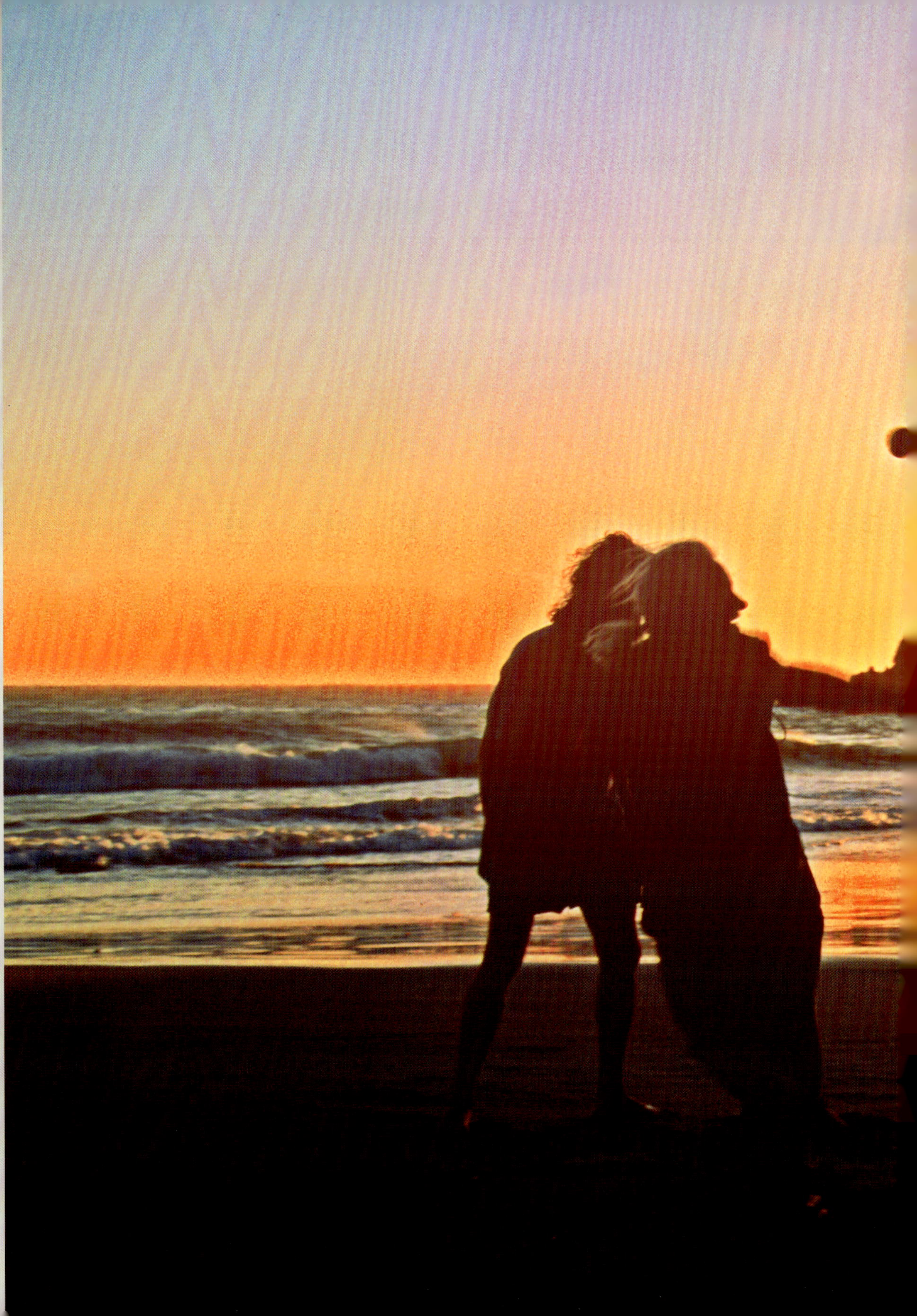

After an adrenaline-filled day of paddling the wild and exposed northern California shoreline, a spirited game of hacky sack in the last golden light of the setting sun is a fine way to wind things down for the Tsunami Rangers.

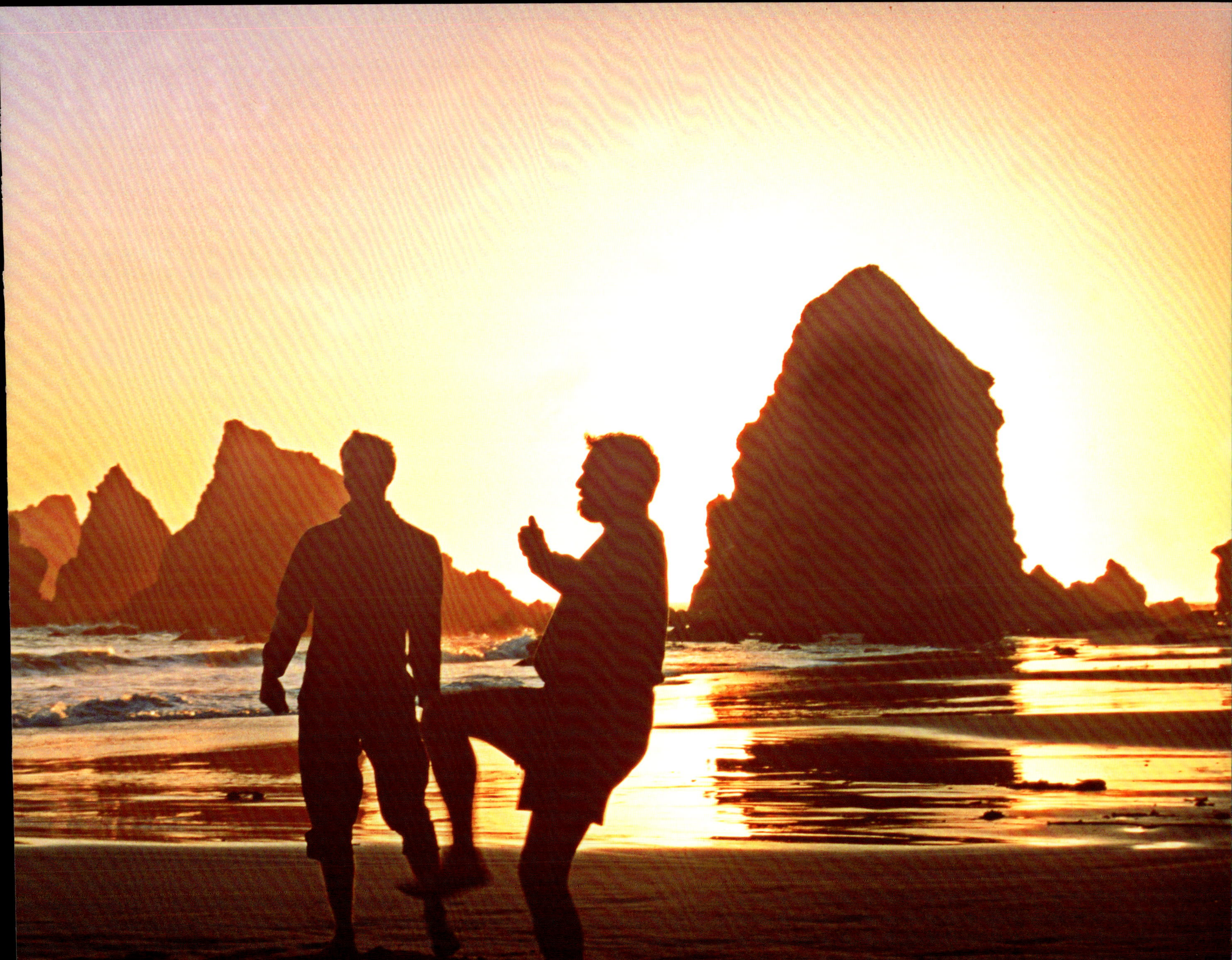

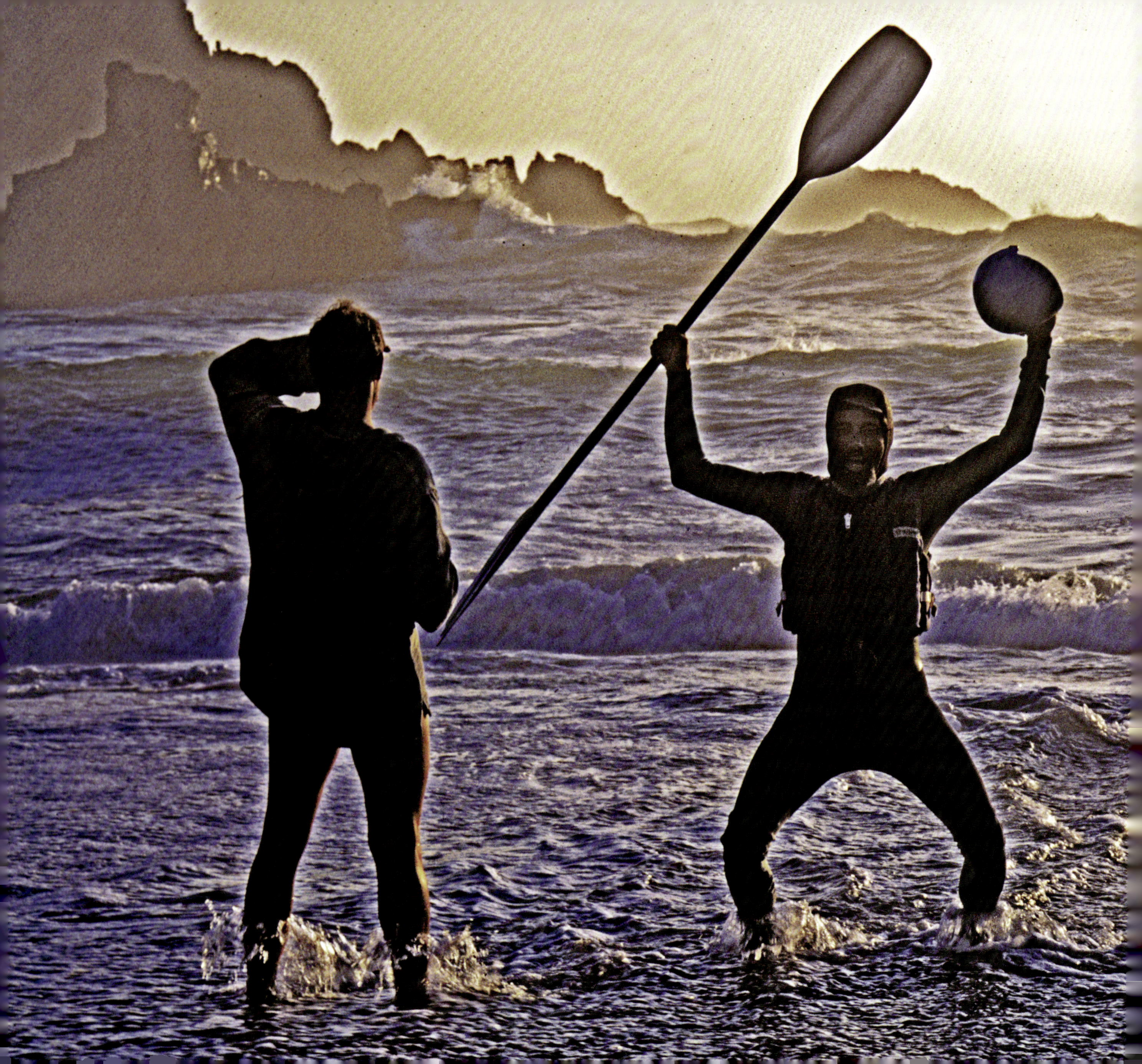

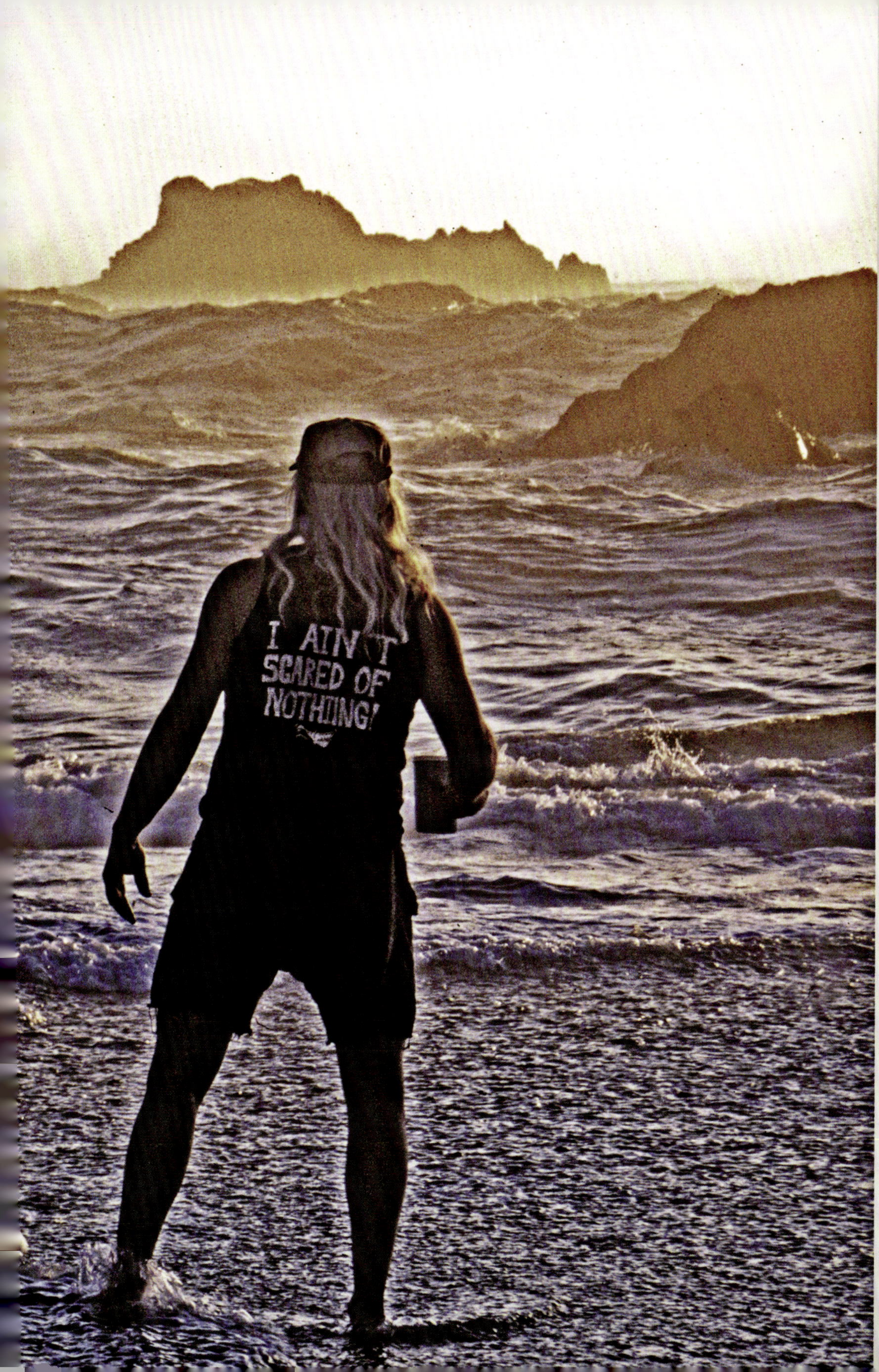

Man suffers only because he takes seriously what the gods made for fun.

- Alan Watts

A frolicsome trilogy of Tsunami Rangers make light of a tempestuous sea, now that they are safely ashore for the night somewhere along the the southern Oregon coast. It was a rip-roaring day out there kayaking today, with monster swells charging through from that Mexican hurricane down south - and by the looks of the ocean now, tomorrow promises to be even more exciting.

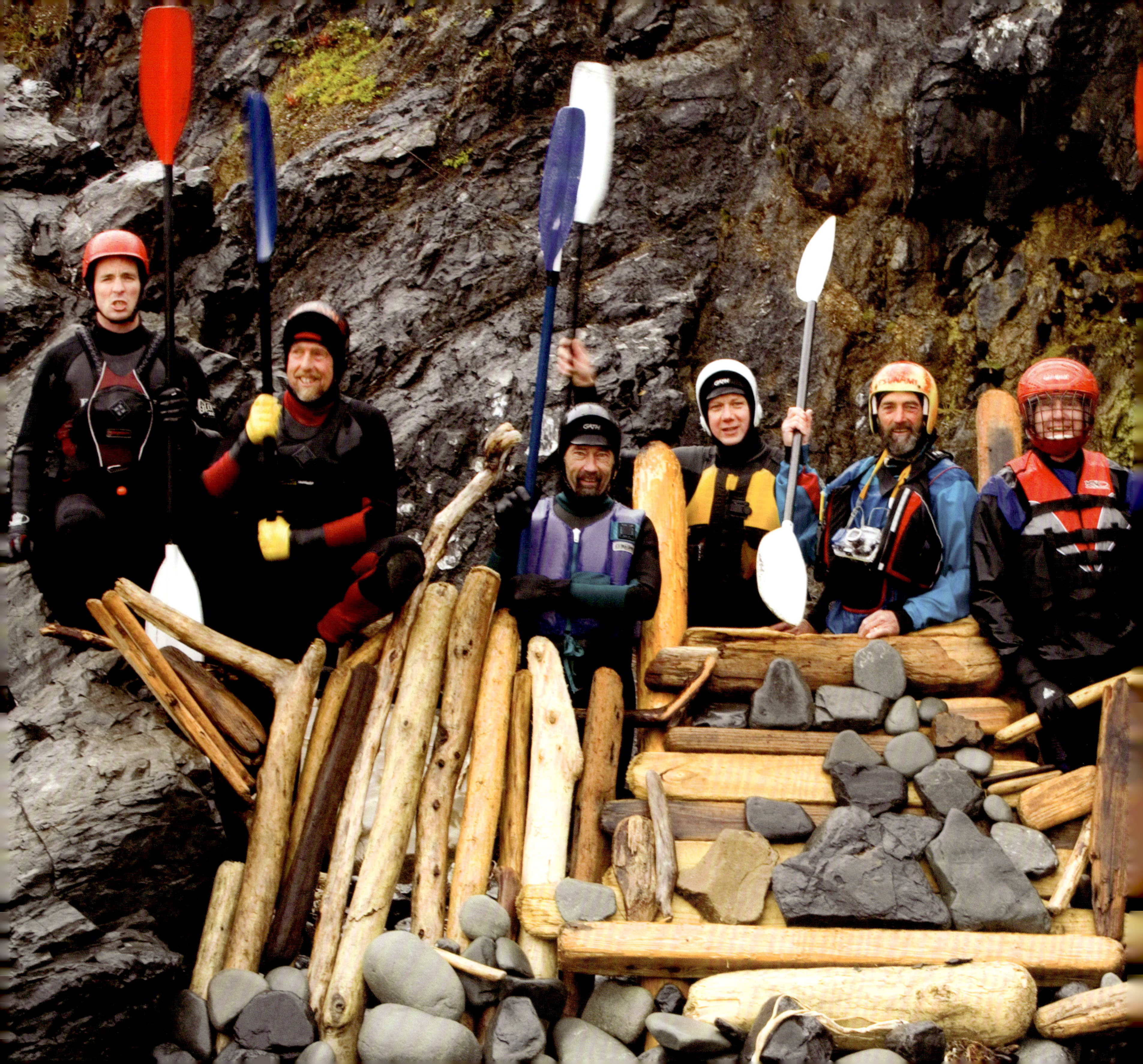

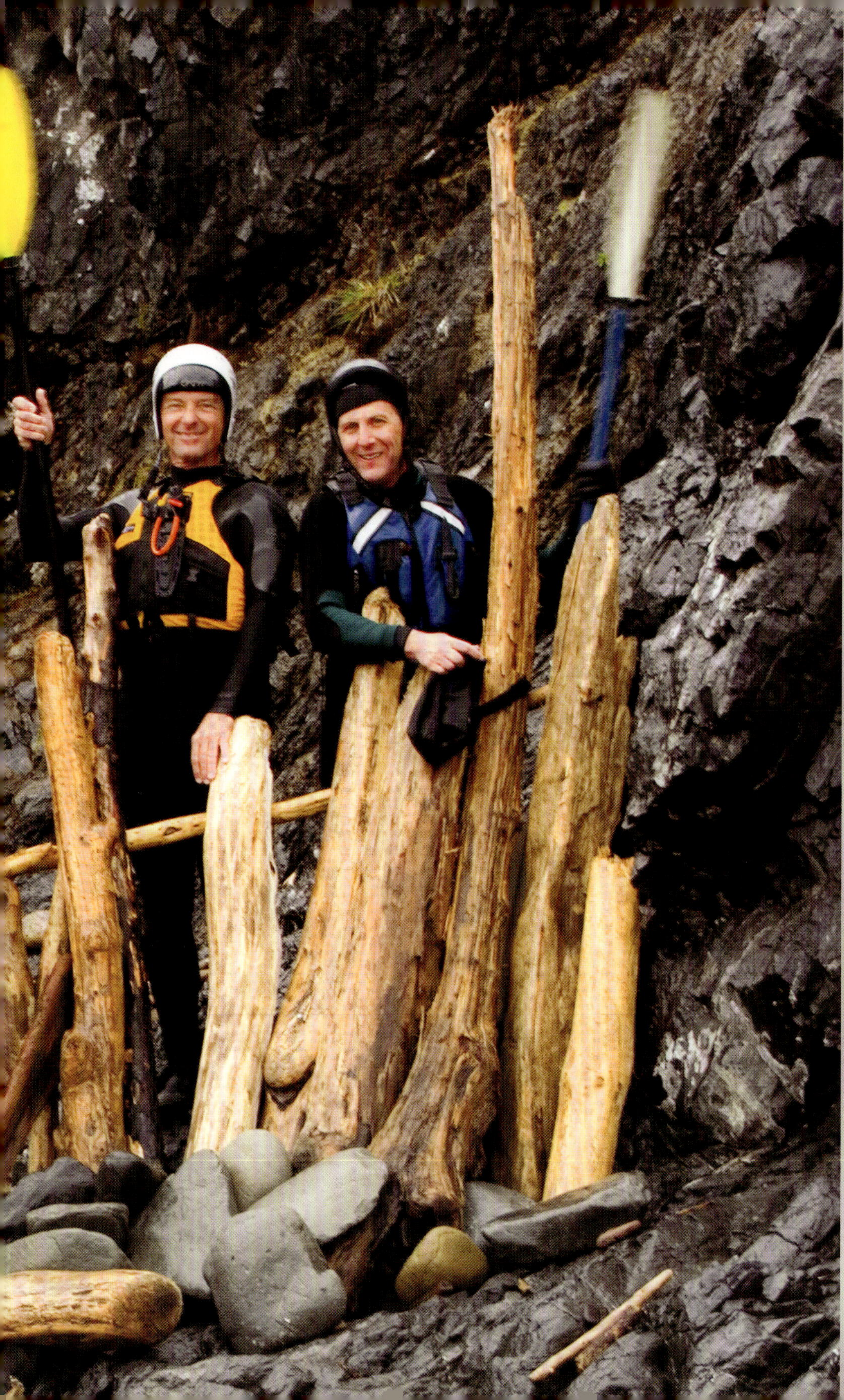

As you get older it is harder to have heroes, but it is sort of necessary.
- Earnest Hemingway

Emerging from a stormy northern California sea, the Tsunami Rangers landed their kayaks and gathered in a driftwood shelter left behind by beachcombers. Their mission that day was a serious one - the all-day, on-the-water testing of two new candidates, Steven King and Scott Beckland, for acceptance into the Rangers' 'extreme condition' sea kayaking team. Ultimately, both men passed the test and were duly initiated with great ceremony into the Rangers. Photograph by Bob Stender.

Only as a warrior
can one withstand
the path of knowledge.

- Carlos Casteneda

During the height of the 1993 winter storm season, award-winning adventure filmmaker Gordon Brown shot and directed a special for National Geographic Television about the Tsunami Rangers and the storm surf kayaking for which they had become well known in the paddling world. Seven years later on the southern Oregon coast, Brown himself underwent the all-day, on-the-water testing required for acceptance into the Rangers. Near the conclusion of his test Brown was directeded by the senior Ranger officers to paddle his kayak through a sea arch where big waves were breaking. Gordon responded without hesitation and went on to pass his test successfully.

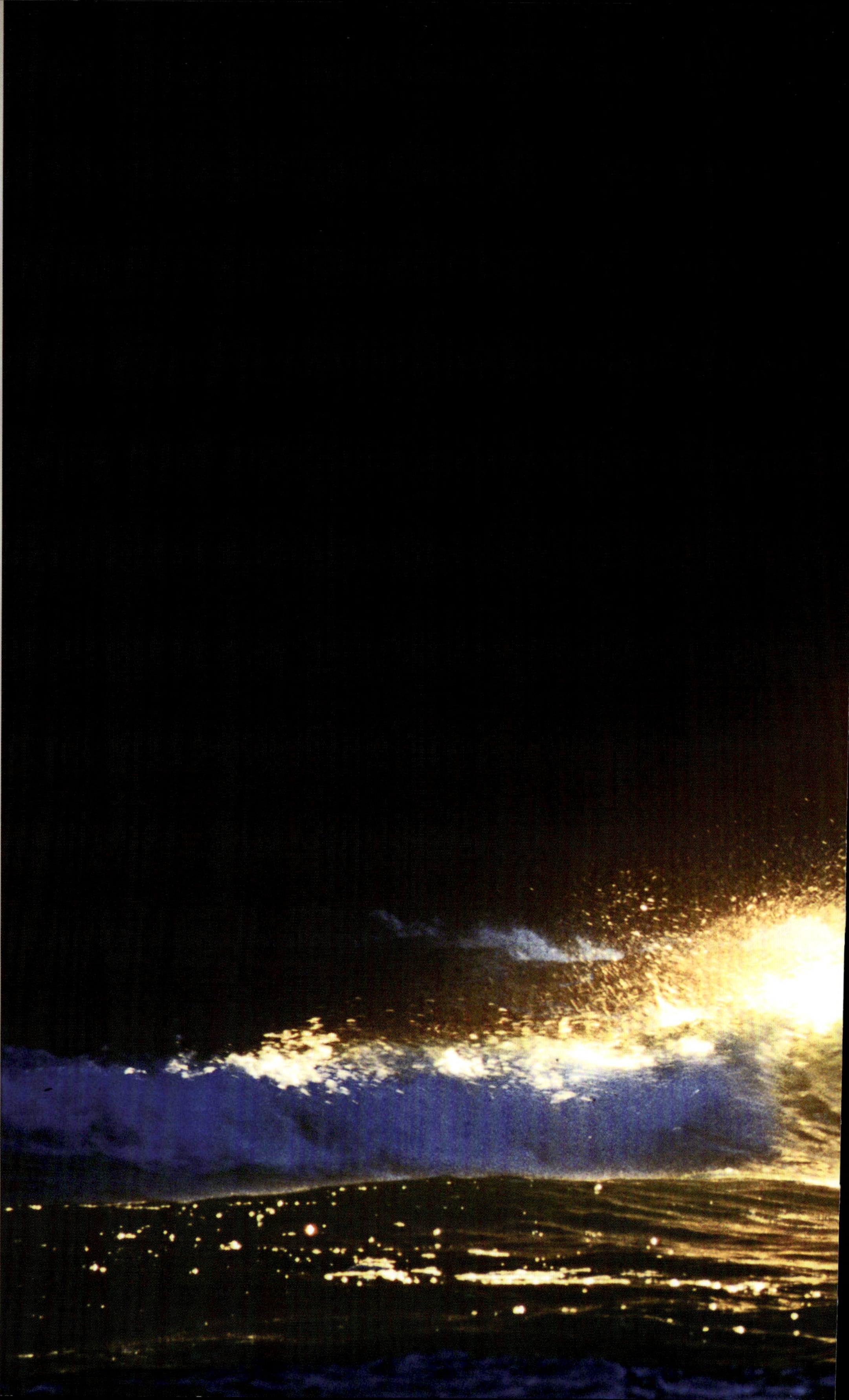

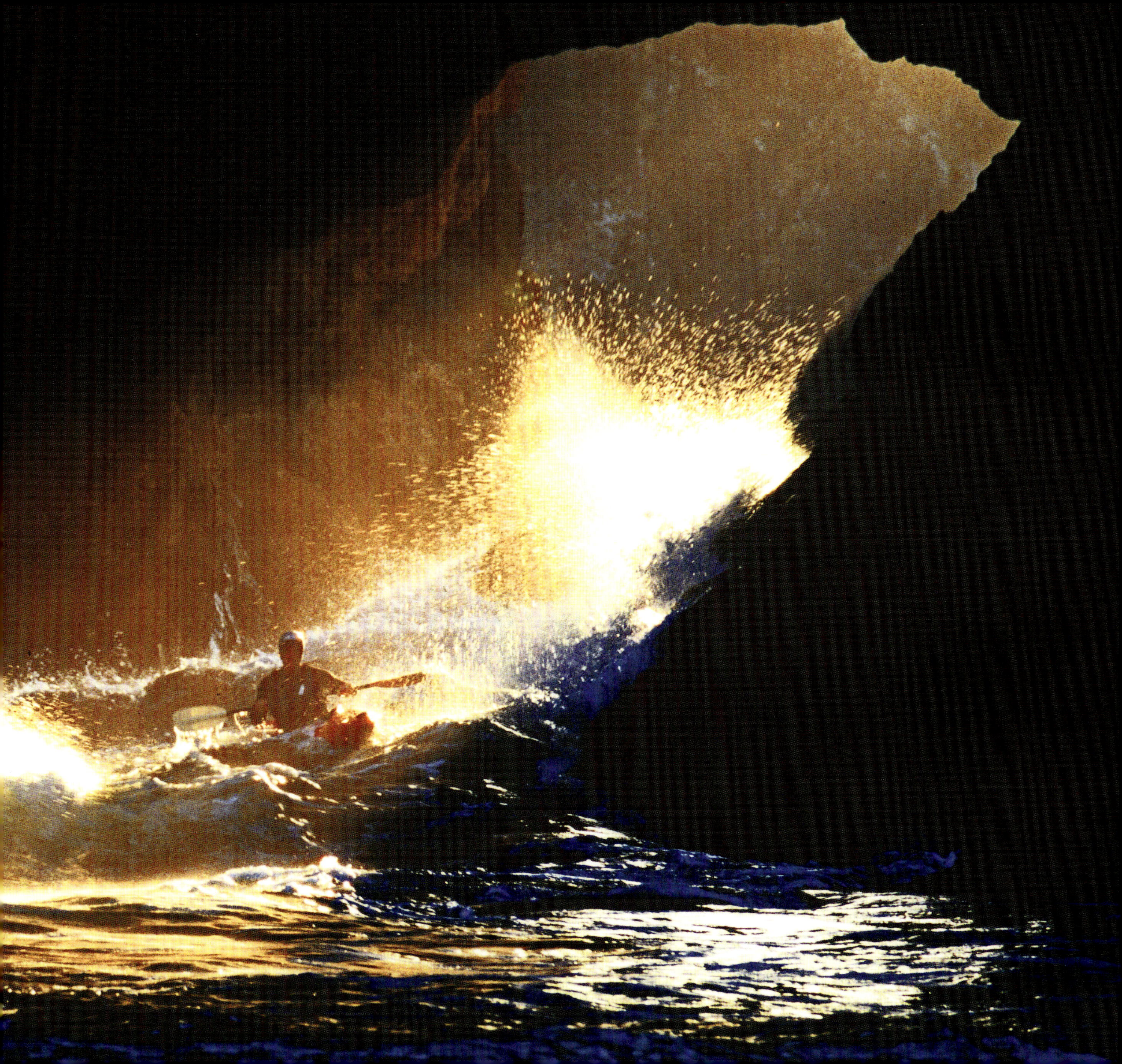

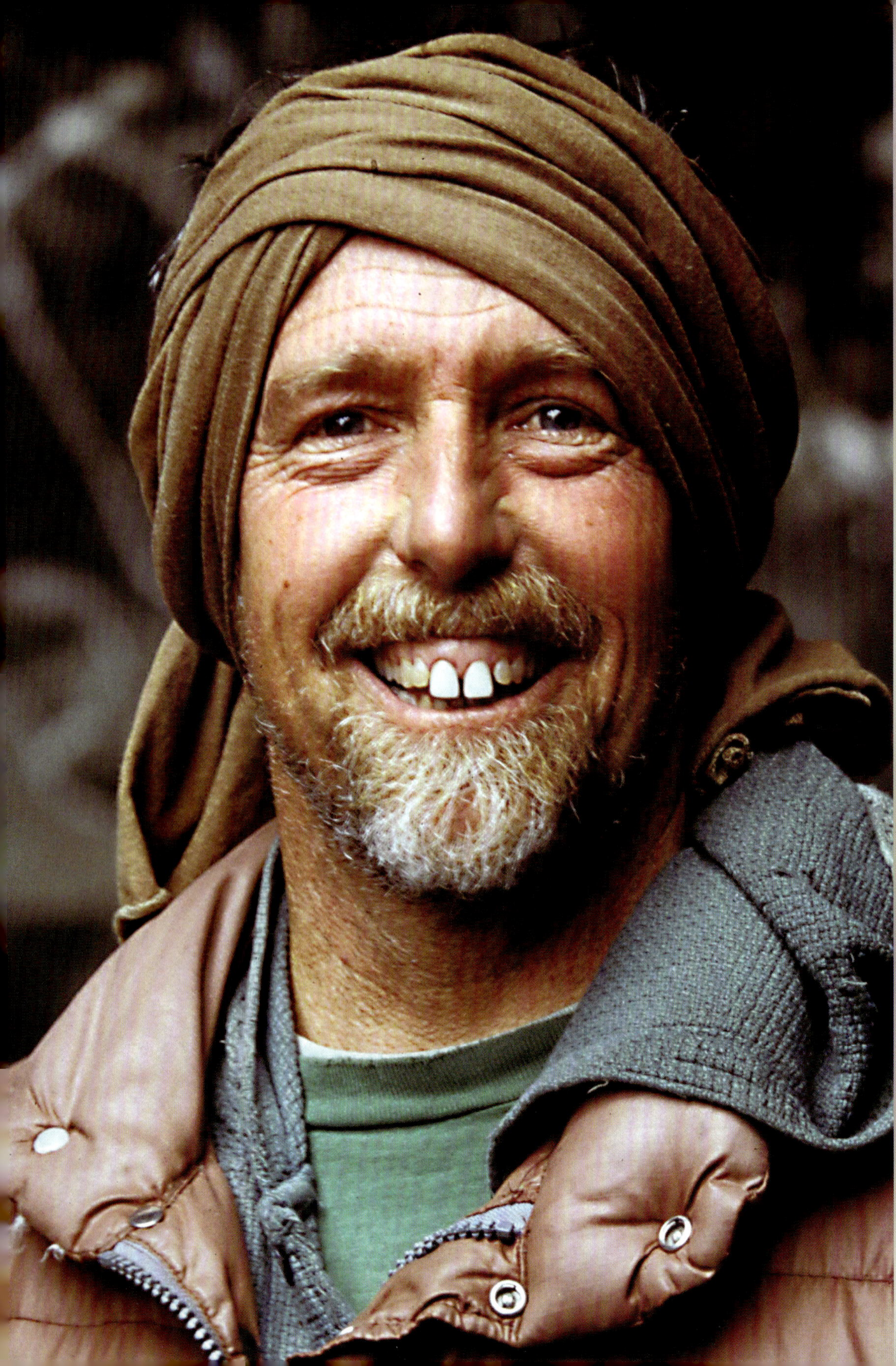

The sea has no king but God.

- Eric Soares, a Commander of the Tsunami Rangers

117

The rugged, boldly vertiginous southern Oregon coast has long been a favorite haunt of the Tsunami Rangers. Cathedral Cove, so named by the Rangers because of the god rays that stream down through a sea arch there around sunset, can only be reached by negotiating a challenging gauntlet of waves breaking over rocks. A well-hidden micro-beach at the back of the cove, whose exact location the Rangers have always kept secret, remains one of their most cherished camp sites. Just offshore from Cathedral Cove lies a rocky islet the Rangers call Dreamer Island. Steep cliffs rise around the perimeter of Dreamer and the only way to land a kayak there is by riding the crest of a wave as it breaks against the sheer flanks of the island and quickly disembarking onto a slippery ledge - a difficult and dangerous manuever known as a 'seal landing'.

After Ranger Commander Eric Soares death following a skiing accident in 2012, eleven Tsunami Rangers, including Soares' wife Nancy, returned to Cathedral Cove. The next day they all paddled out to land on Dreamer Island and climbed to its thickly forested summit. With great ceremony they scattered Eric's ashes there - just as he had requested.

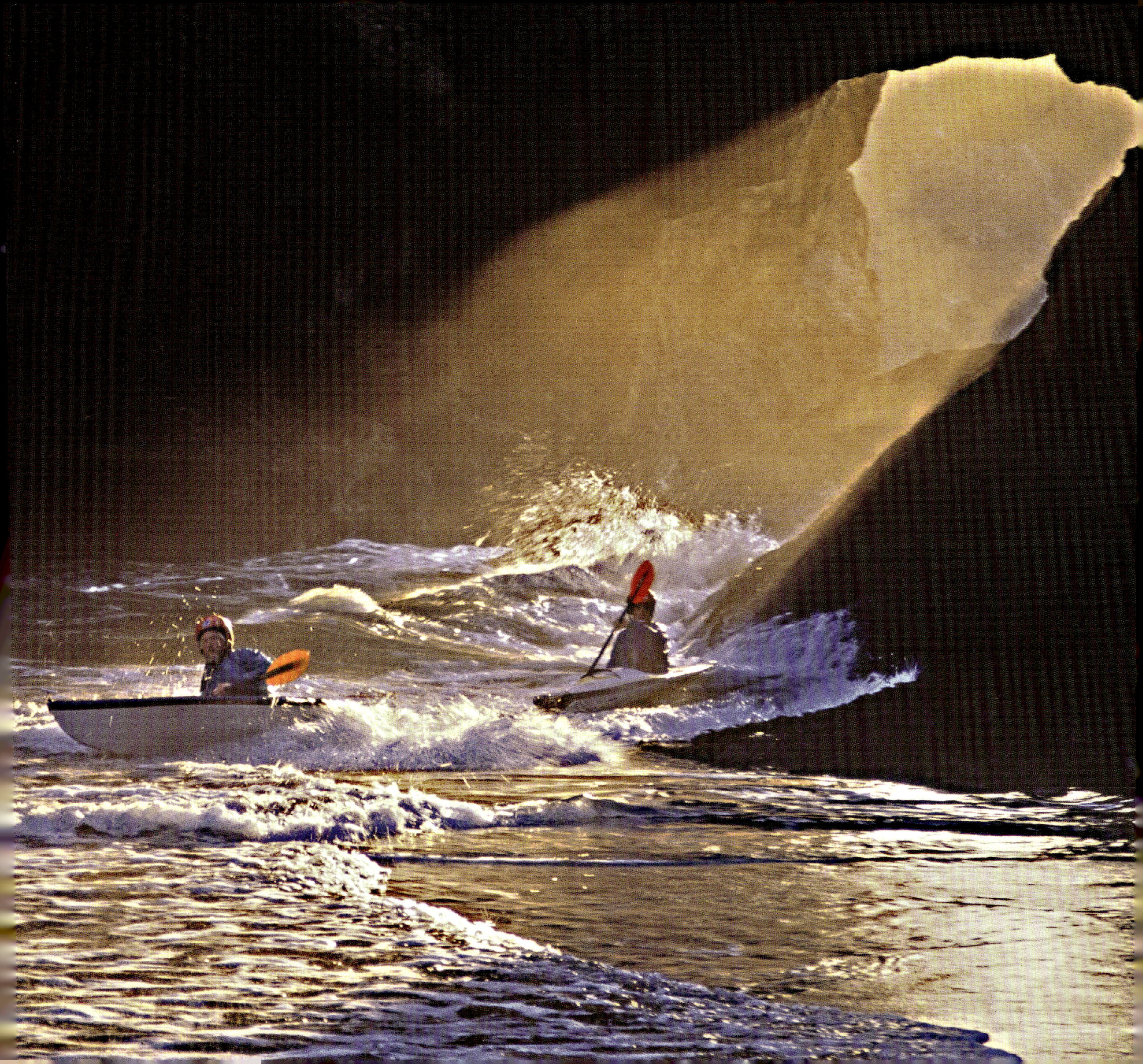

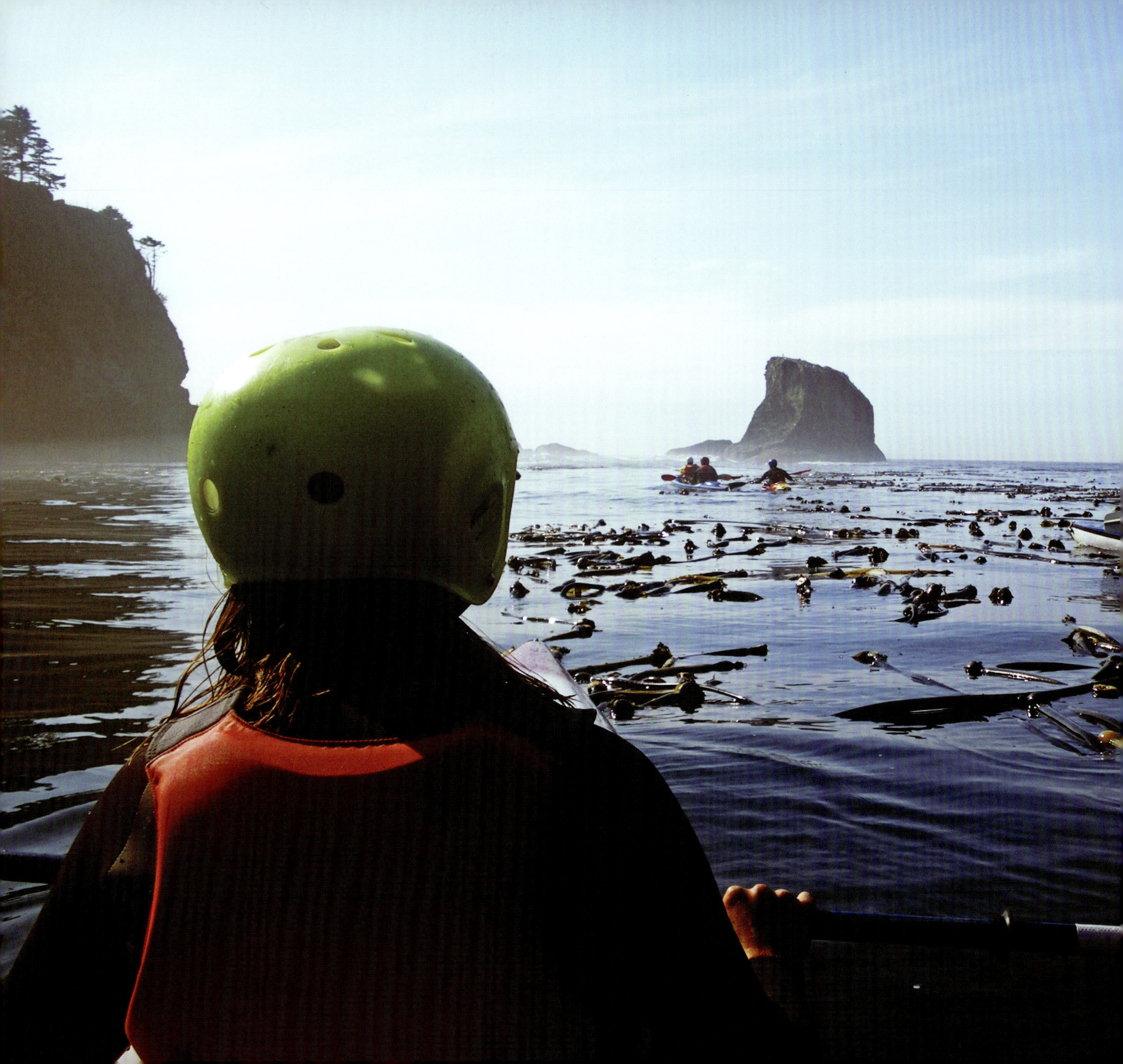

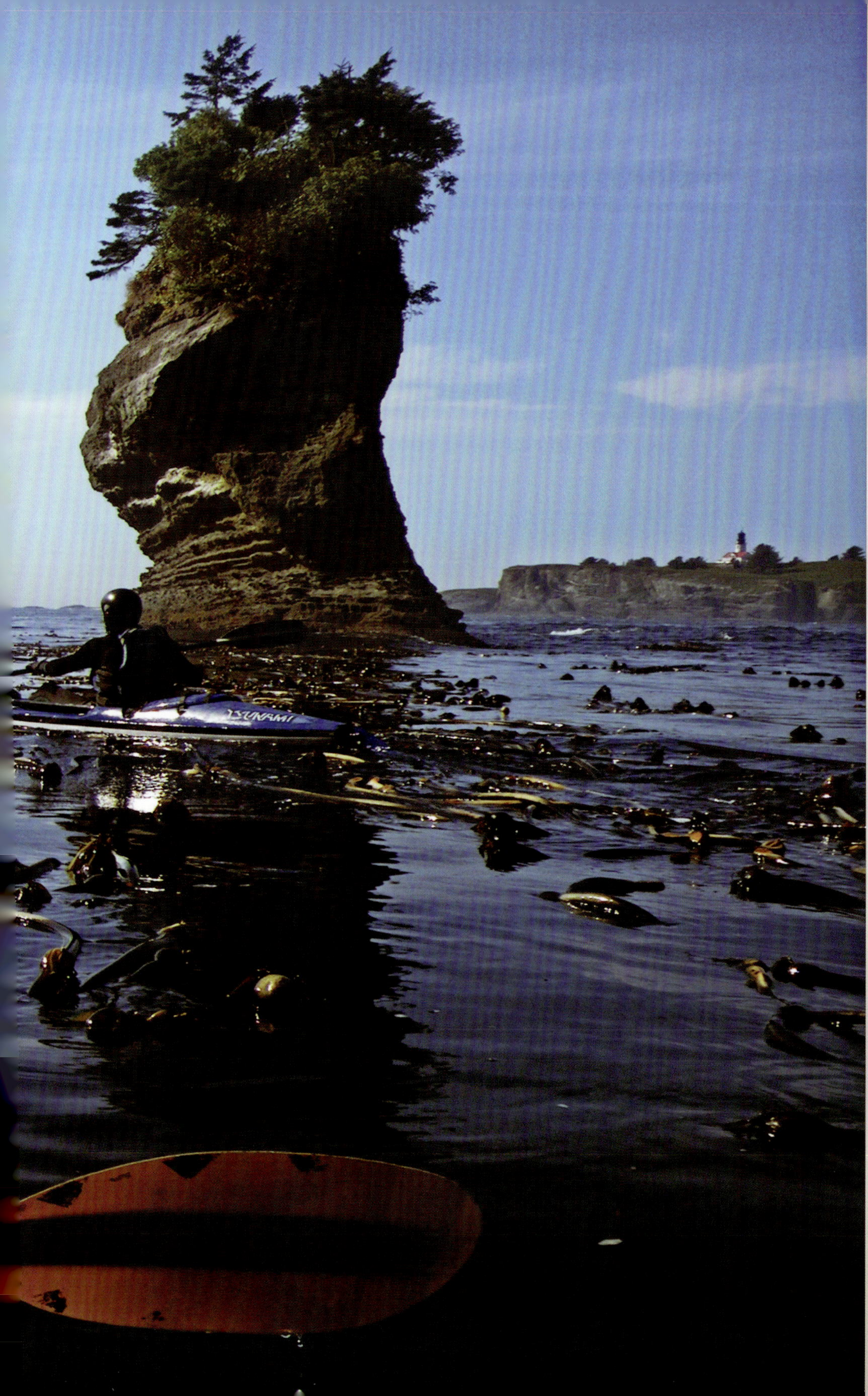

The places of the sea and the land change. There is no place on earth always land nor always sea.

- El Mas´ude,
Arabic geographer AD 950

From the front cockpit of her double kayak, Australian-born Sasha Joura basks in the serenity of the Strait of Juan de Fuca in rare form. Professional kayak guides Sasha and her partner Mark have traveled all the way from the North Island of New Zealand to join the Tsunami Rangers on a multi-day paddling exploratory. Everyone is pleasantly surprised to find the usually tumultuous waters surging up the strait between Washington State and British Columbia settled temporatrily into mirror-like smoothness. Yet in spite of the Rangers' penchant for storm surf paddling, they were pleased to find the notorious strait in such a tranquil mood. As they paddled west towards historic Cape Flattery, the unusual absence of wind and waves allowed them to savor other forms of adventure along the rocky shoreline - like getting up close and personal with the maze of sea caves, arches, sea stacks and other surreal geologic features they encountered.

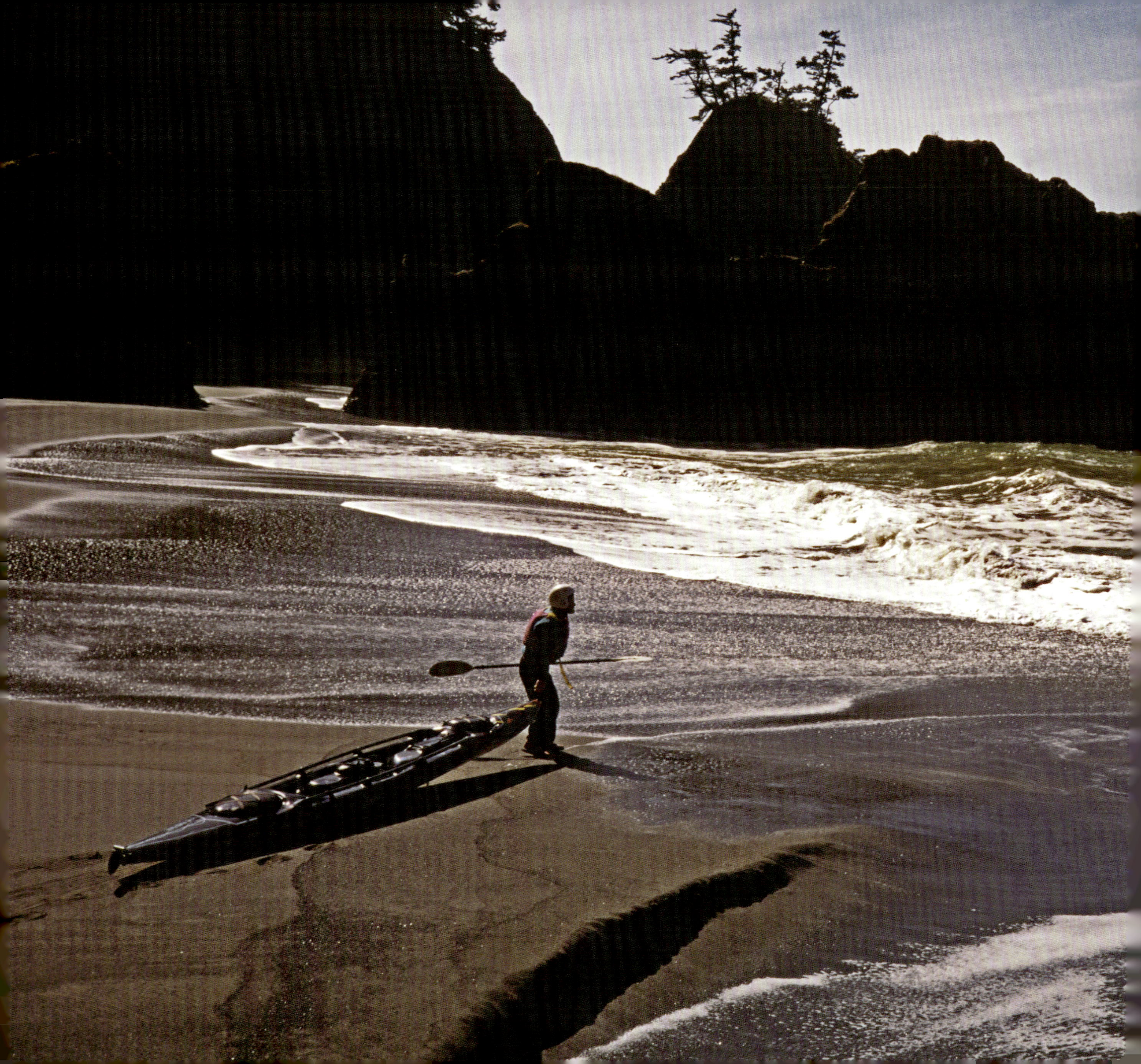

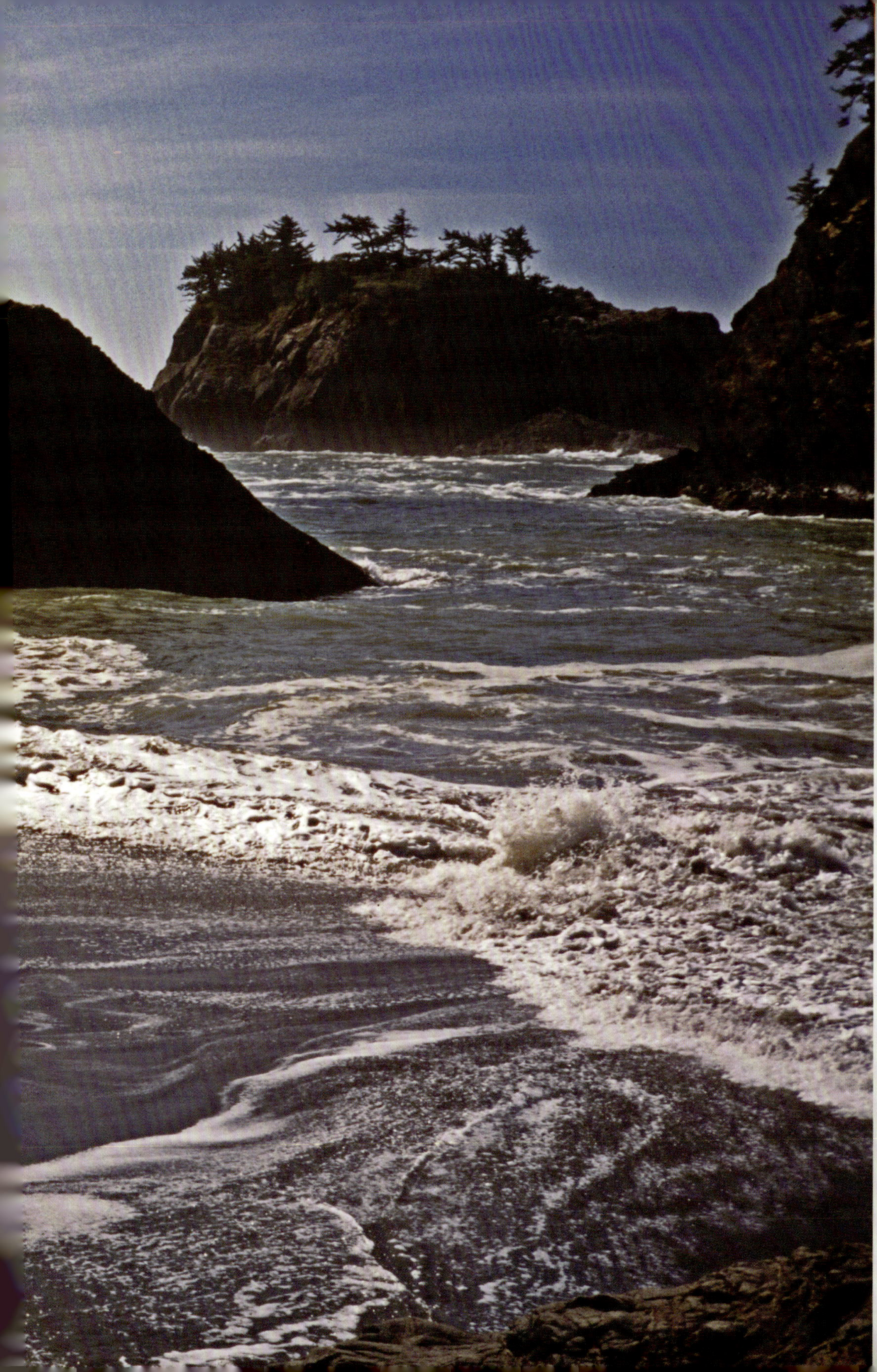

I must go down to the sea again, to the lonely sea and the sky.

- John Masefield,
British poet laureate

For experienced, properly equipped sea kayakers, the spectacular wilderness coastline of southern Oregon is a beautiful and reasonably safe place to paddle in the usually tranquil summer months. During the wintertime, however, powerful storm systems develop regularly in the Gulf of Alaska, generating strong winds and massive swells that can quickly transform the shallow waters along the rugged Oregon coast into a deadly maelstrom of huge waves breaking and rebounding among rocky cliffs - extreme paddling conditions that even the most skillful sea kayakers wisely avoid.

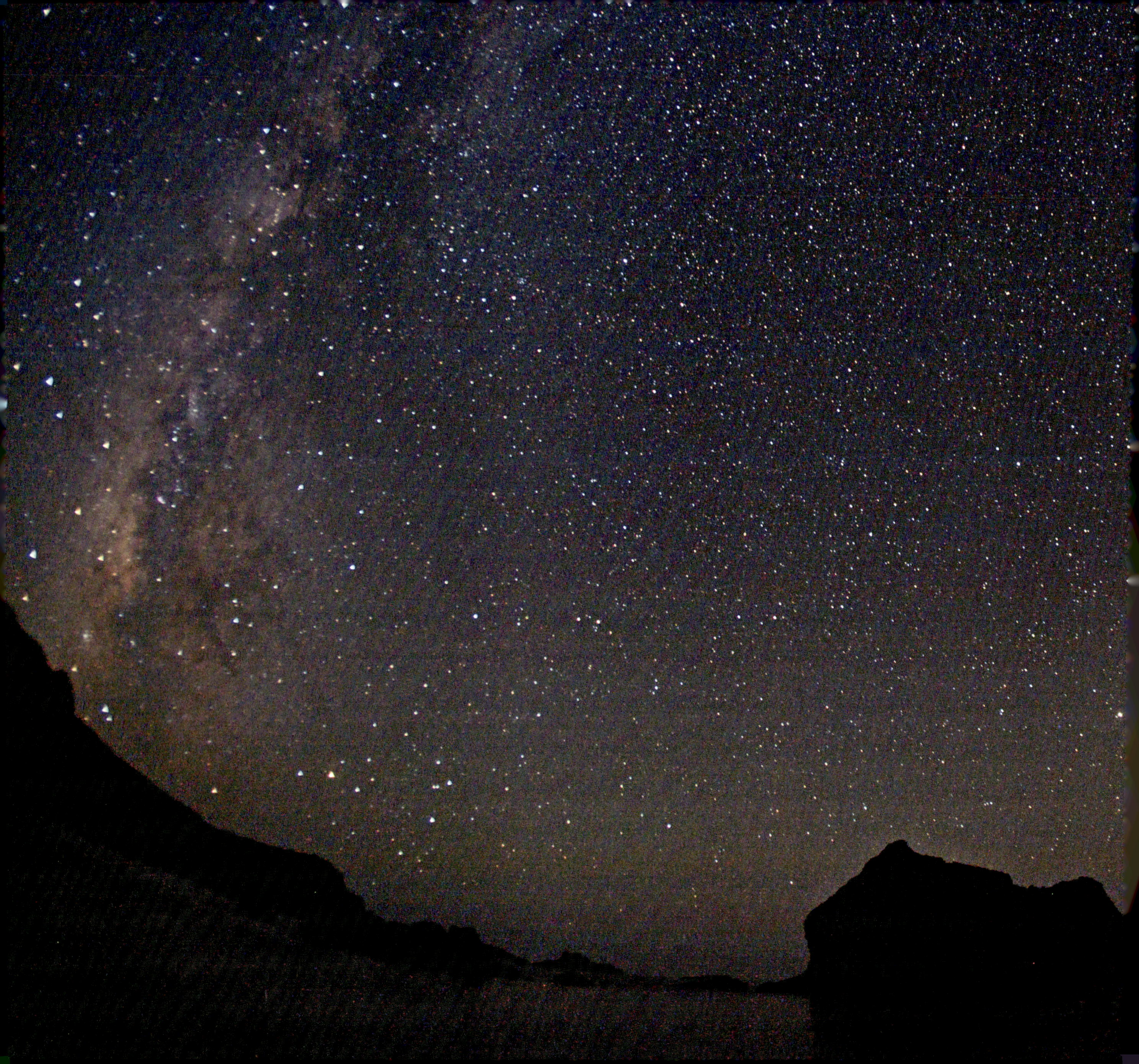

Perhaps they are not stars at all, but rather openings in heaven where the love of our lost ones shines down upon us to let us know they are happy.

- old Eskimo saying

It was autumn in California, when the night skies sometimes became exceptionally crisp and clear. The Tsunami Rangers, paddling along a remote and mountainous stretch of the northern coast, landed their kayaks to make camp for the night. They were far from the light-polluting effects of urban centers, and a passing cold front had further clarified the usually misty coastal sky, allowing the stars to shine that night with exceptional brilliance.

I would rather be a superb meteor, every atom of me in magnificent glow, than a sleepy and permanent planet.

- Jack London

125

Mt. Whitney, at 14,505' the highest summit in the contiguous United States, provides a magnificent backdrop for a Geminid meteor falling through a moonlit sky in California's eastern Sierra. This timelapse photograph was craftted by award-winning astrophotographer Tony Rowell. In his own unique style Tony follows in the footsteps of his father the late Galen Rowell, a pioneer of big wall climbing in Yosemite in the 60s who went on to become arguably the world's most famous adventure photograper of modern times.

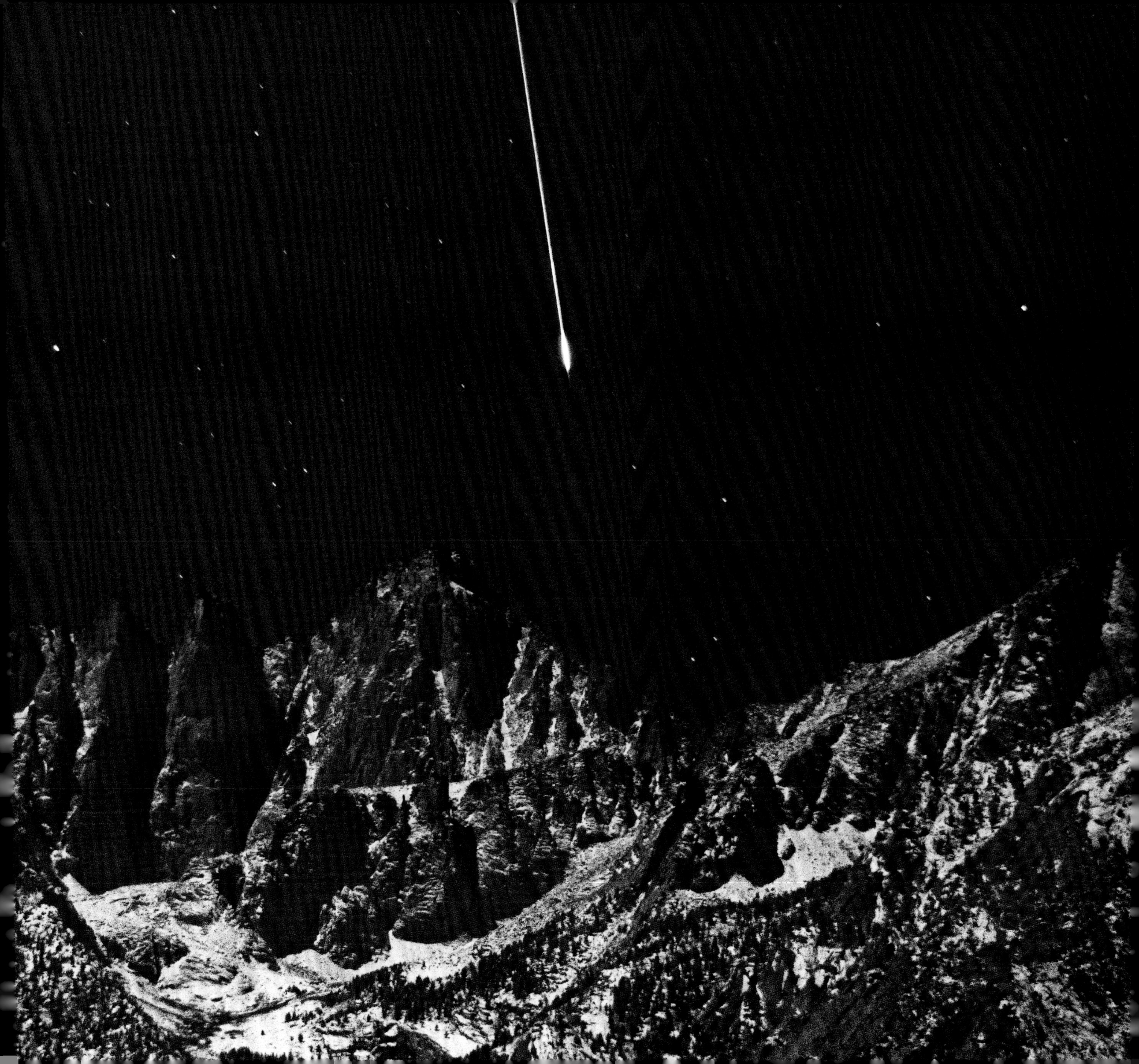

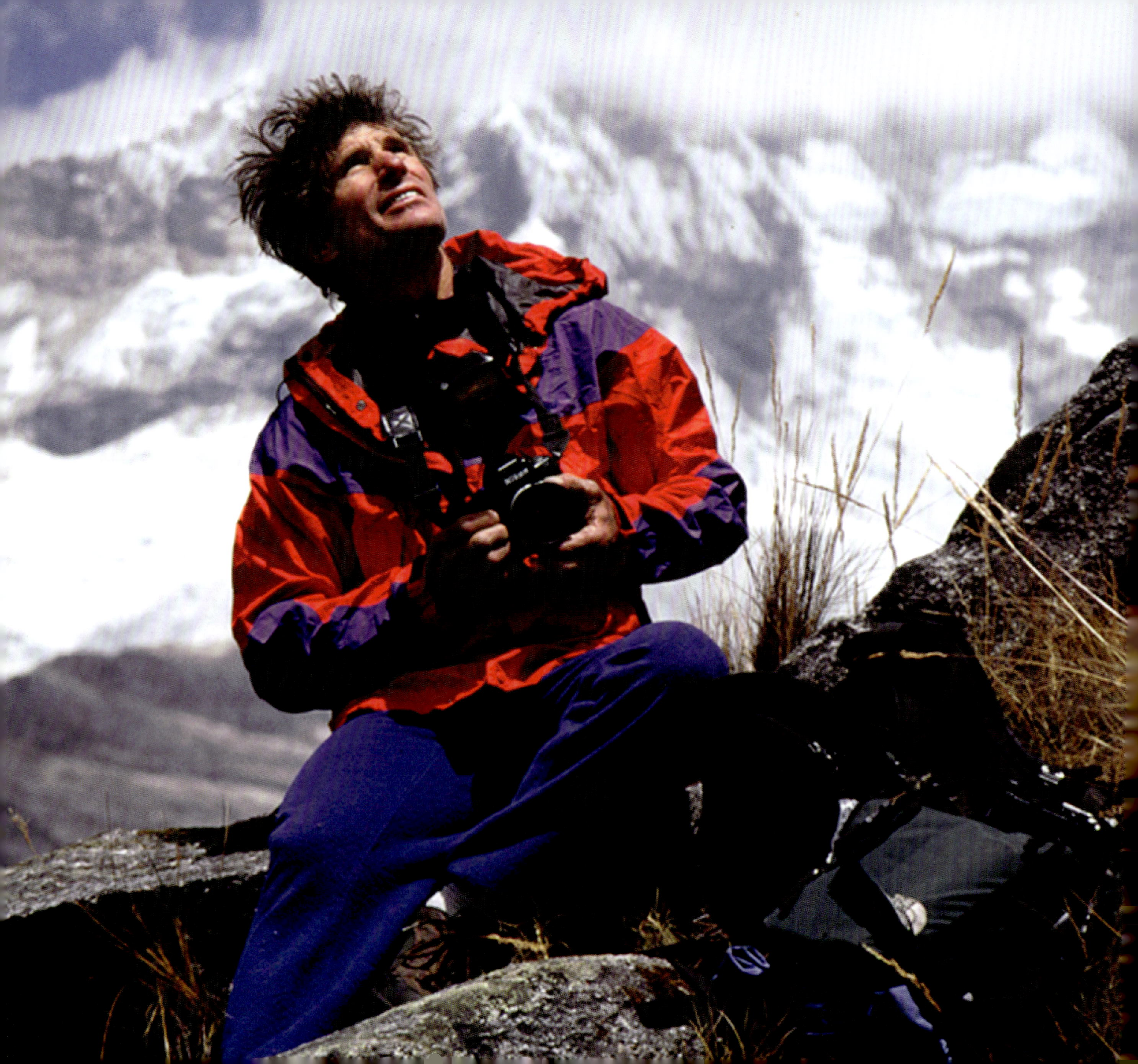

Mankind mastered the world by passing information from generation to generation.

- Galen Rowell

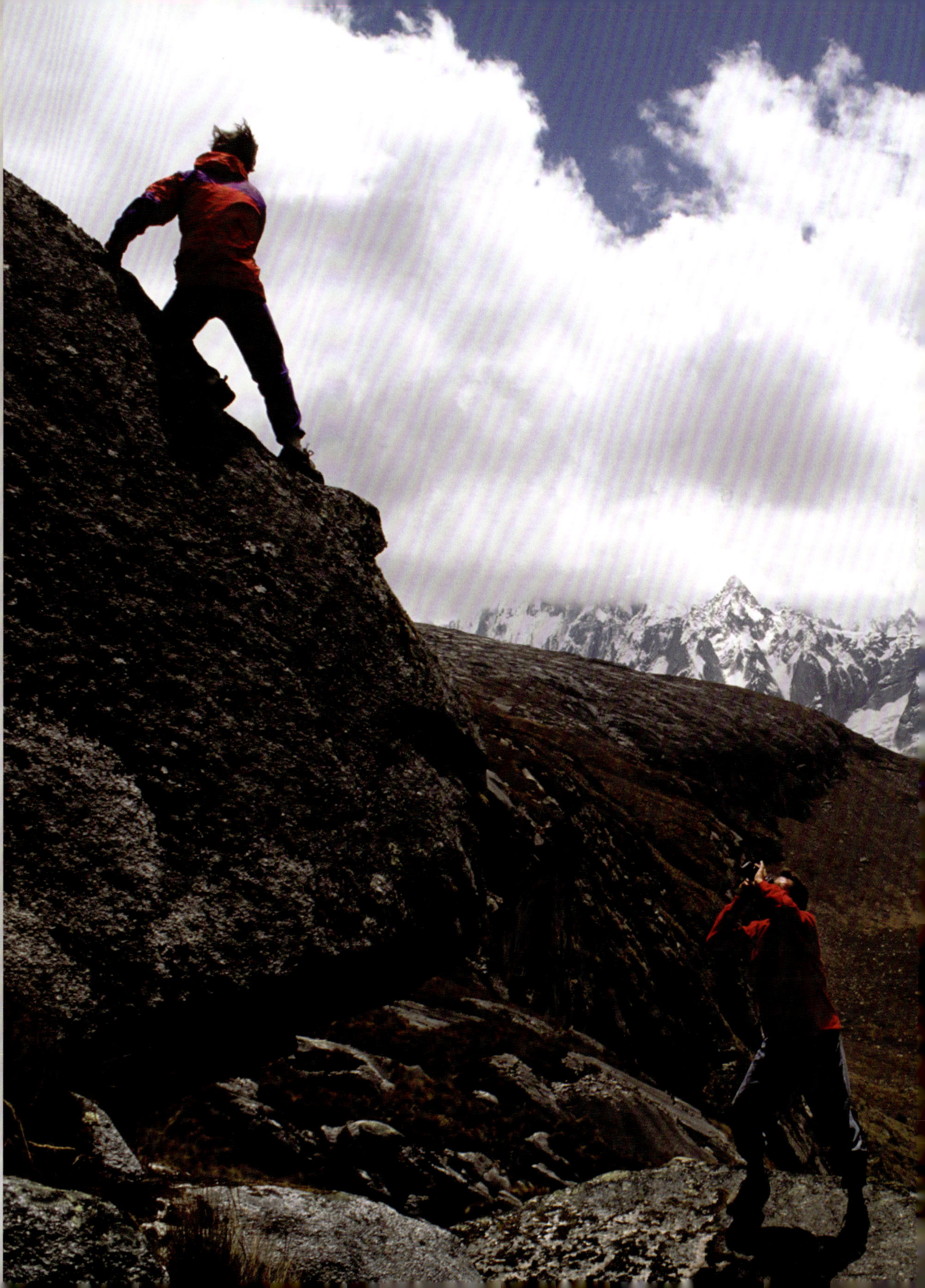

Master adventure photographer, author and mountaineer Galen Rowel becomes the subject himself of a cameraman's attention while leading a photo safari through the spectacular Cordillera Blanca range in Peru. Rowell's creative and physical prowess were legendary. Sometimes on the Cordillera trip when his group had reached camp, exhausted from trekking all day at high altitude, Galen would spot alpen glow glistening on a distant peak and race off in pursuit of a few more pinnacle images. At times like this he seemed larger than life, nearly immortal. Yet a few years later in August of 2002 as Rowell and his wife Barbara were returning from leading a photo workshop in the Russian Arctic, they perished in a small plane crash near their home in Bishop, California. Photo of Michael Powers photographing Rowell by long-time Peru guide Peter Frost.

You must look at the skies,
you must sing and dance,
write poems and suffer,
for all that is life.

- J. Krishnamurti

129

Galen Rowell took this photograph of his friend and climbing partner, Norwegian-born Lief Patterson, in the Karakoram Range in northern Pakistan. They were on their way down from an extended period at extreme altitude after a failed attempt to summit K-2, the world's second-highest mountain. The image captured Patterson's joyful first encounter with green grass in many months. Tragically, Lief was destined to perish among far less formidable mountains far away, a short time after Rowell took this picture. He had returned home to British Columbia, and to celebrate his homecoming he set off on skiis with his son on a Sunday afternoon. They died together without warning, when an avalanche suddenly engulfed them.

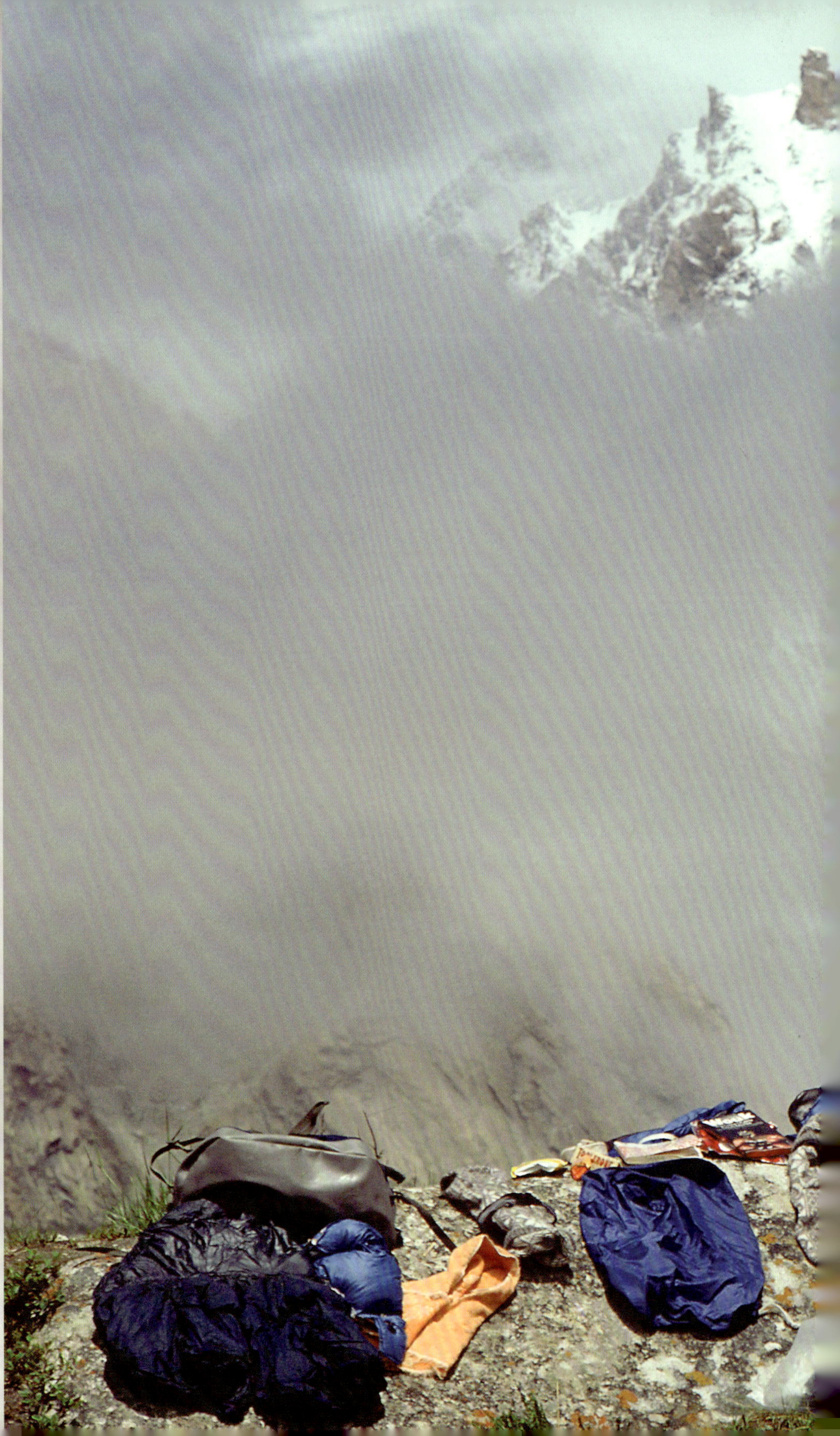

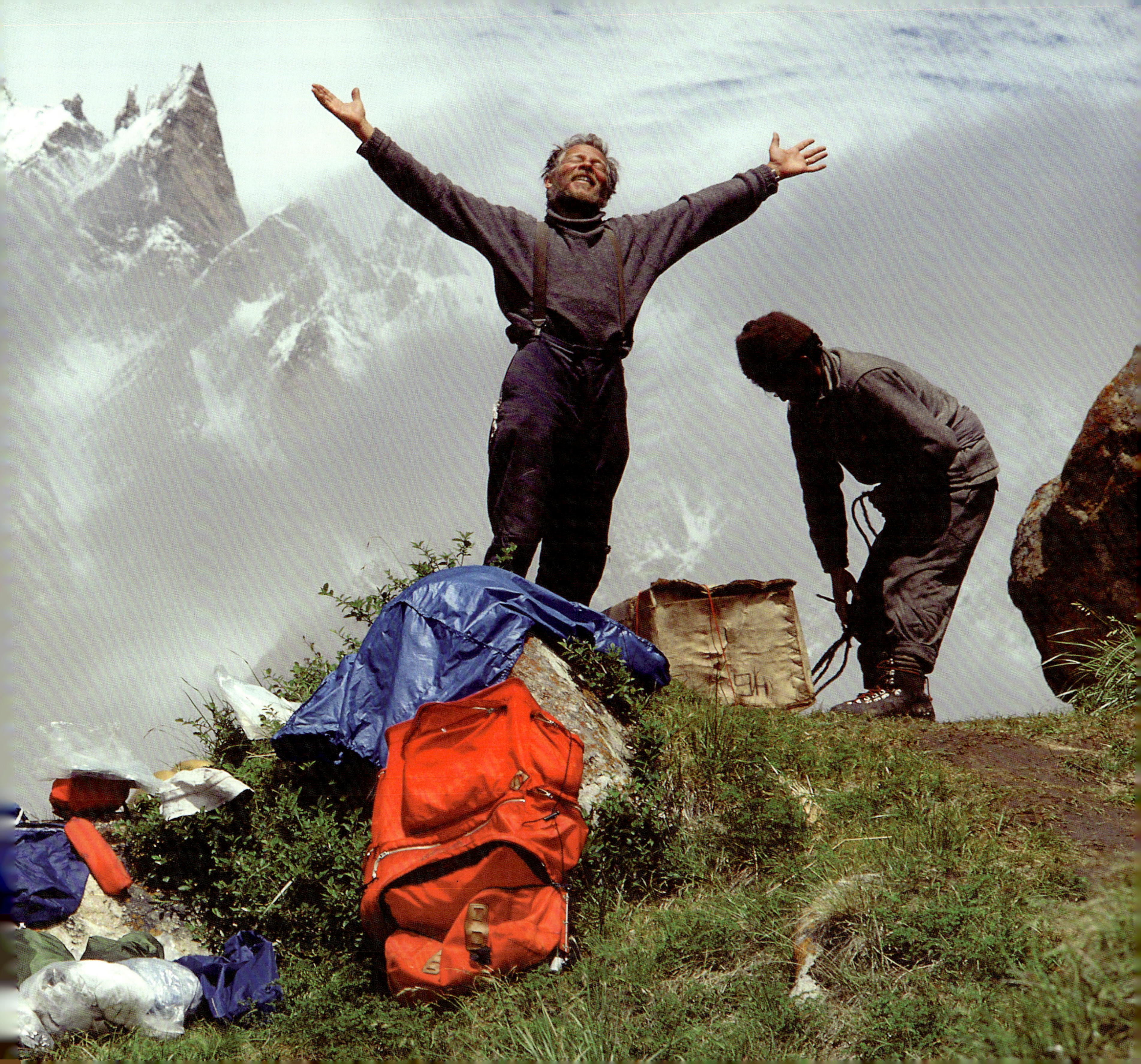

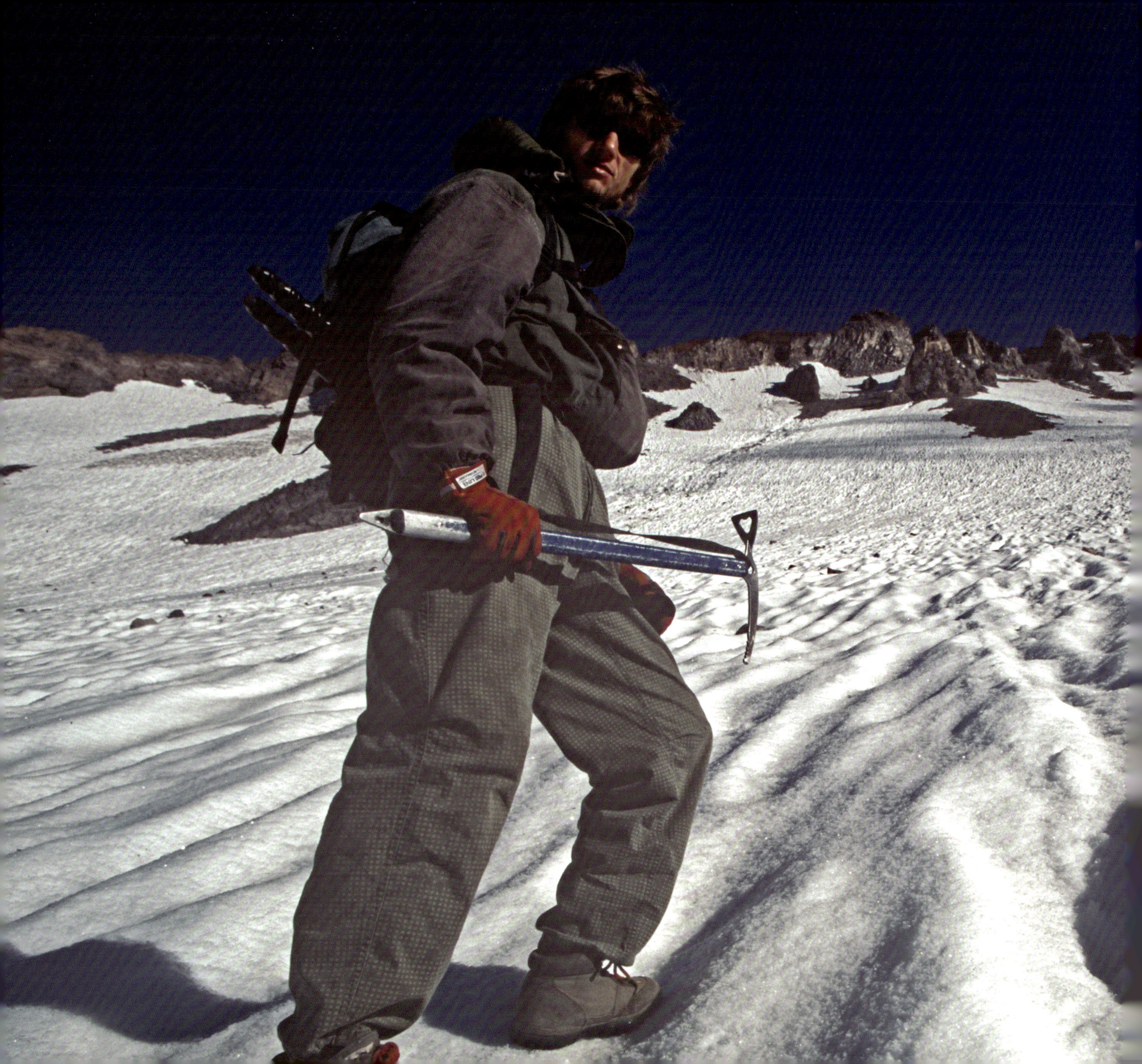

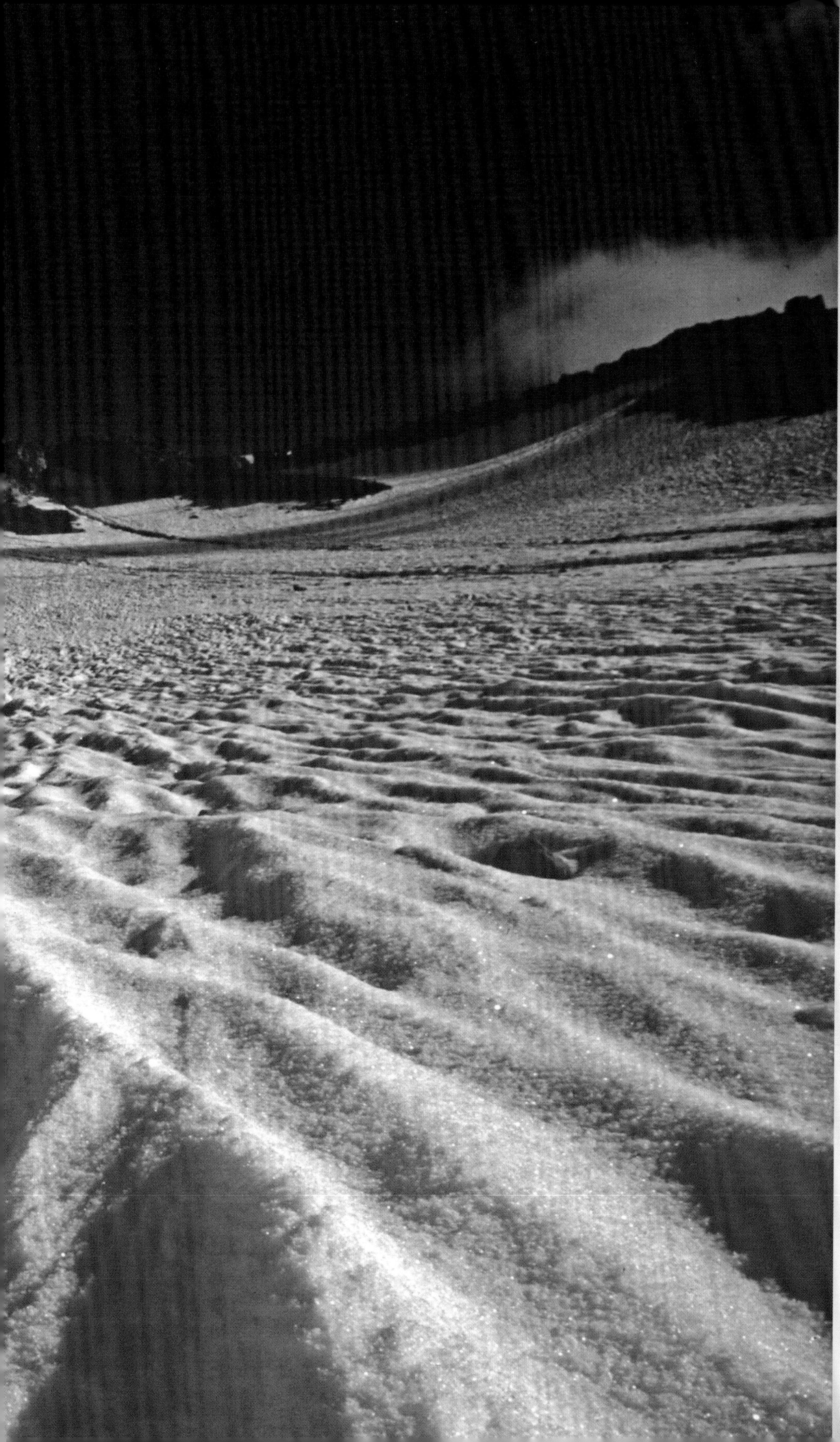

Many call me an adventurer and that I am, only of a different sort - one who risks his skin to prove his platitudes.

- Ernesto "Che" Guevara

It is mid-morning and Russian-born Misha Dynnikov is two miles above sea level on the western flank of Mt. Shasta and beginning the long slog up Avalanch Gulch. His plan is to reach the 14,179' summit and return back down before the afternoon sun begins to loosen the rocks in Red Banks above and allow them to begin hurtling down the Gulch. Falling rock is a leading cause of death and serious injury among climbers on Shasta. Another not-so-serious hazard is the hidden fumaroles high on the the mountain that sometimes release noxious fumes. The last full-scale volcanic eruption occurred on Mt. Shasta in 1786.

Fearlessness is better than a faint heart for any man who puts his nose out of doors. The length of my life and the day of my death were fated long ago.

- old Norse myth

Misha Dynnikov was a wild young spirit who came to America and embraced the dangers and challenges of extreme outdoor adventure with great joy and passion. He was a natural fit with the Tsunami Rangers and brought them bold new blood. Whether climbing fast and high in the mountains or paddling his battered kayak through a storm-lashed sea, he always seemed fearless and invincible - until at 38 years of age while diving alone off the big island of Hawaii, a perhaps too courageous young Misha vanished without a trace into the sea.

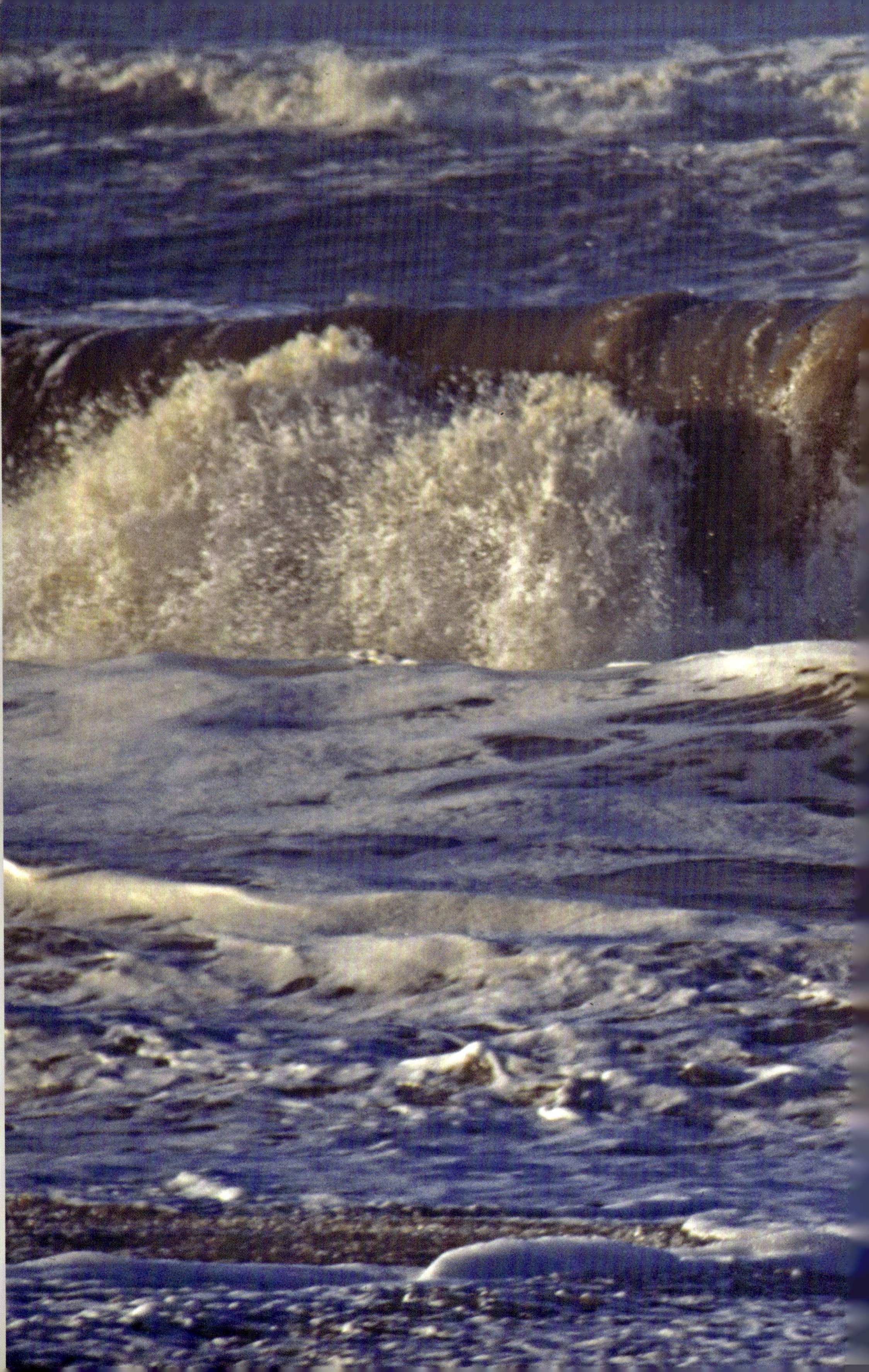

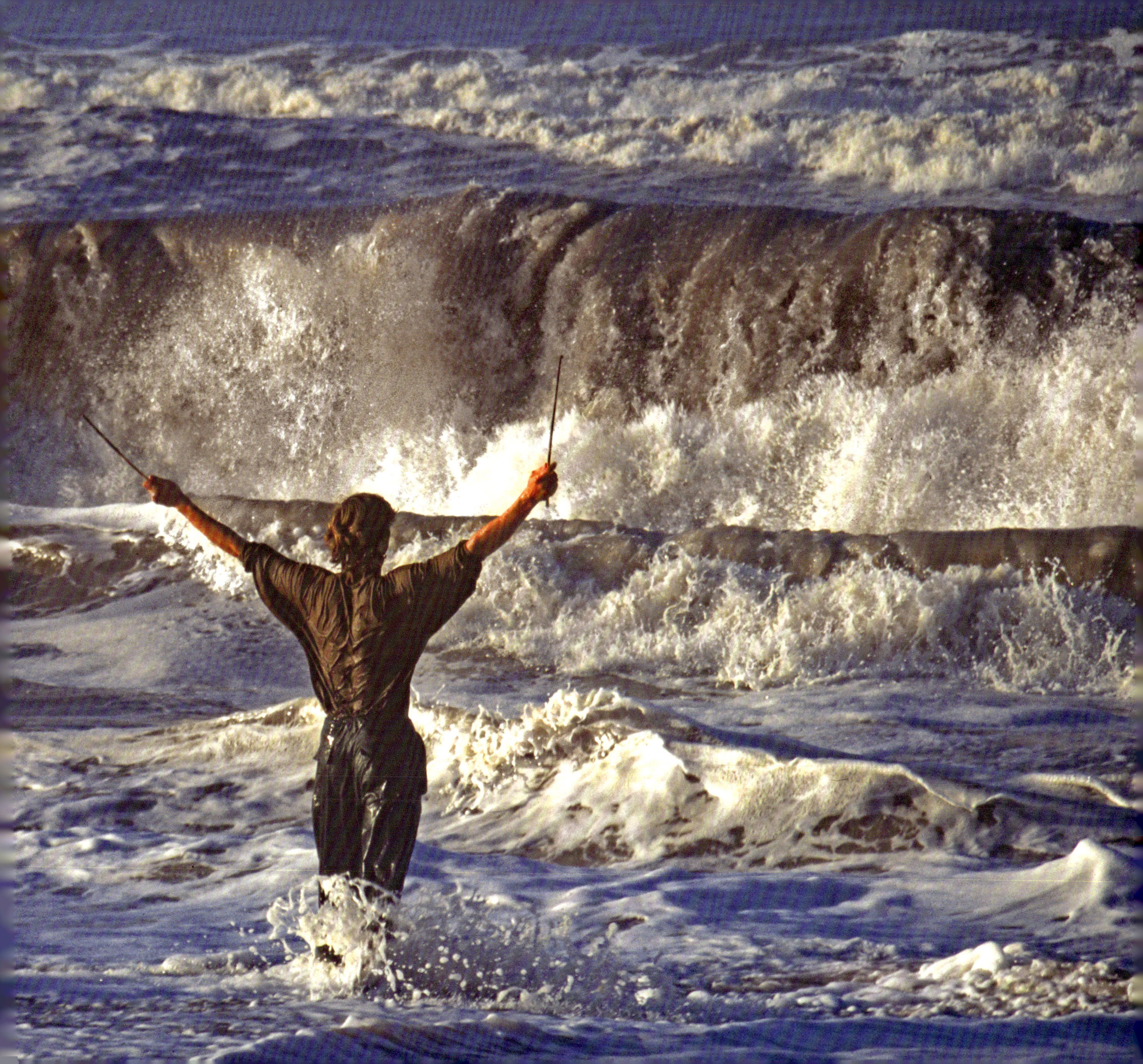

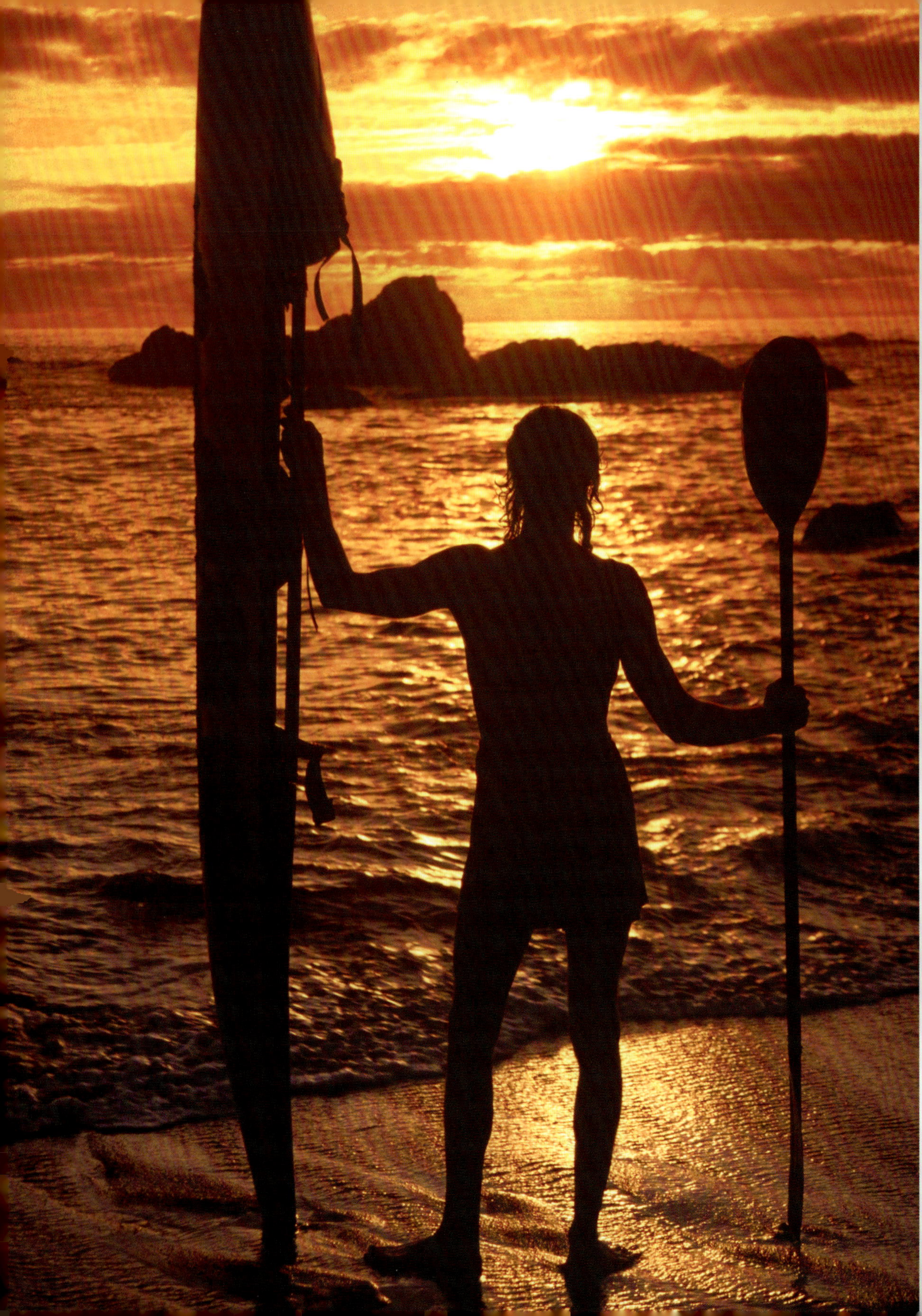

It is sometimes better to abandon oneself to destiny.

- Napoleon Bonaparte

135

Misha may be gone, but he will never be forgotten by those who climbed in the mountains or kayaked wild seas with him. Like a falling star that burned ever so brightly as it fell through the sky, he lived life too fully to last for a very long time.

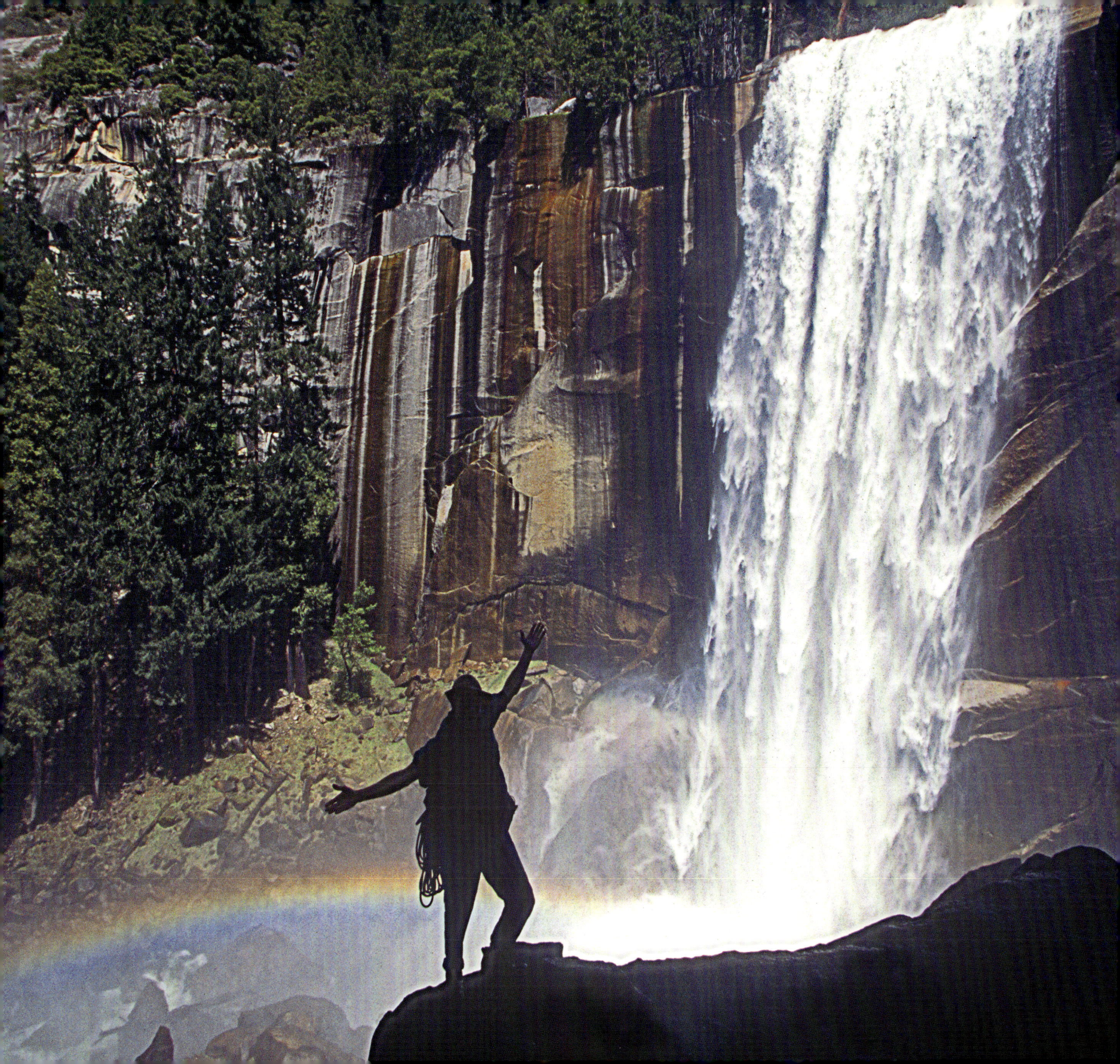

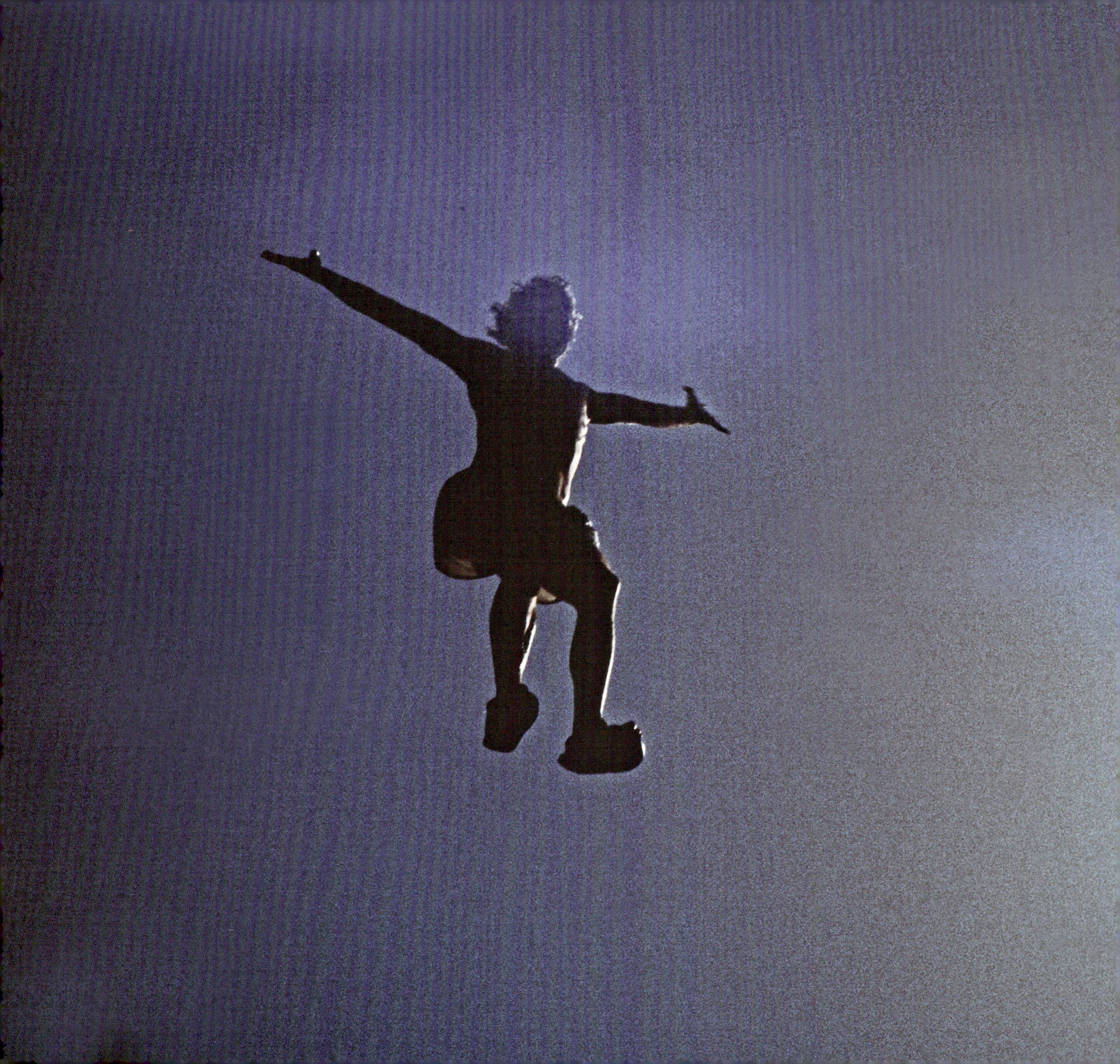

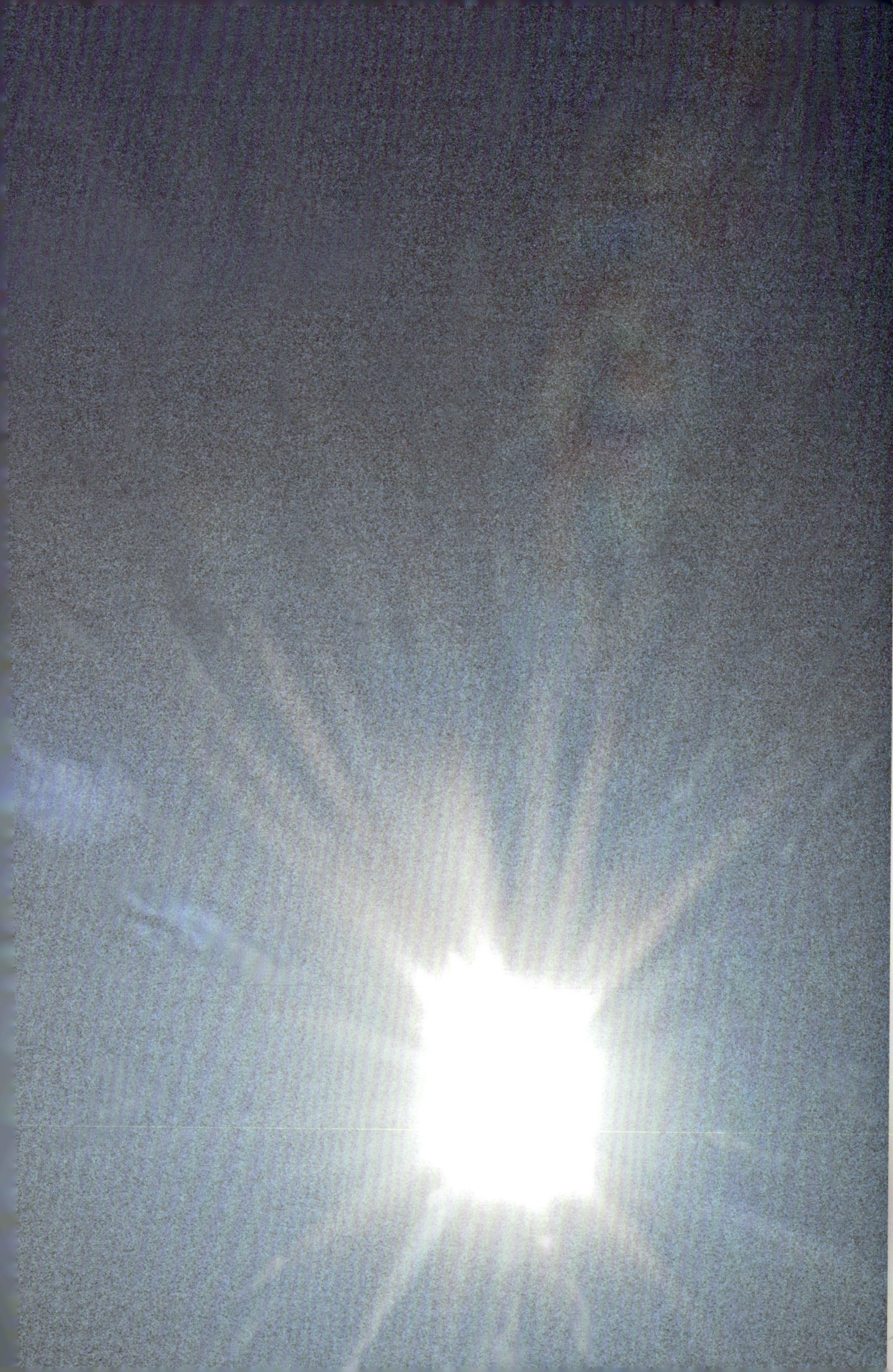

Death is a natural part of life. Rejoice for those around you who have transformed into the Force.

- Yoda,
from Star Wars III

A band of kayakers running the class II-III whitewater rapids of the South Fork of the American River in northern California came upon a quiet stretch of the river where other boaters had pulled out to dive off a big boulder into a deep pool. The photographer paddled his kayak into an eddy behind the boulder and waited until a young man made the jump to capture this image with his waterproof camera.

The most difficult thing
is the decision to act.
The fears are paper tigers.
You can do anything
you decide to do.

- Amelia Earhart

During the volatile sixties Mexico was a magical place for a young photographer with *poco dinero* and dreams of a life of adventure. For just a few *pesos* one could hire the *muchachos bravos* who hung around the *Torre de Buscadores* in Mazatlán to dive the 70 feet from the top of the tower into the sea.

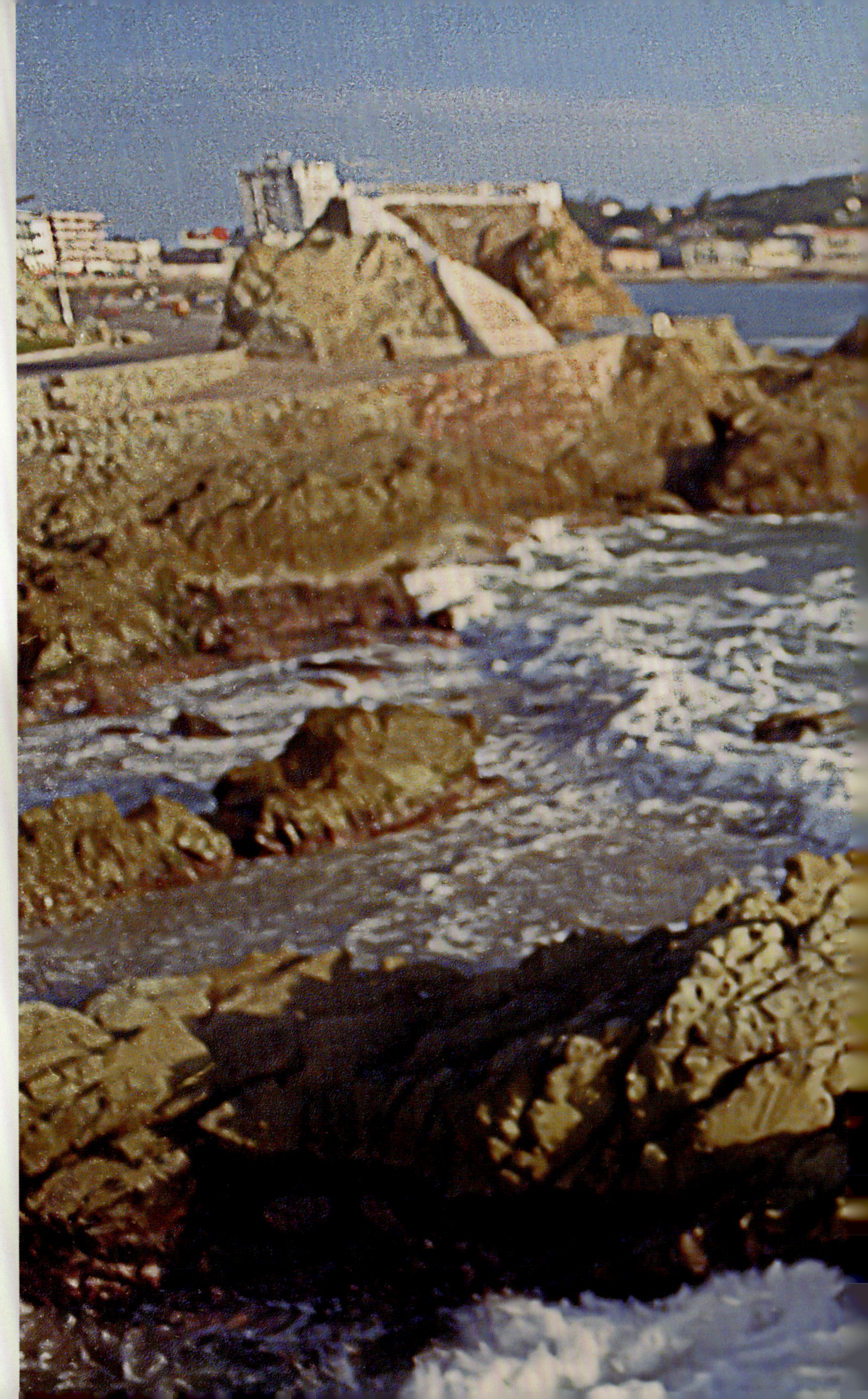

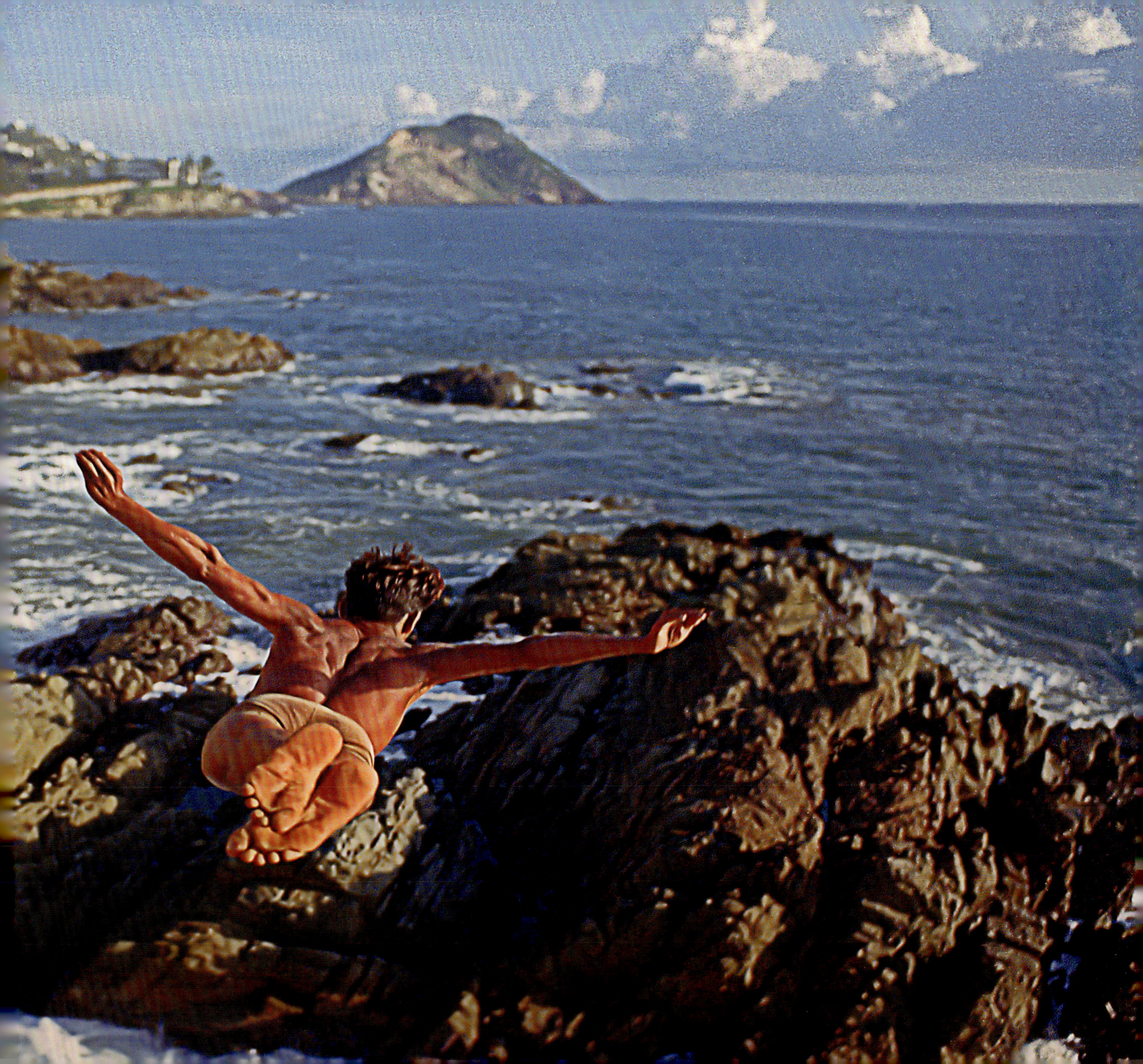

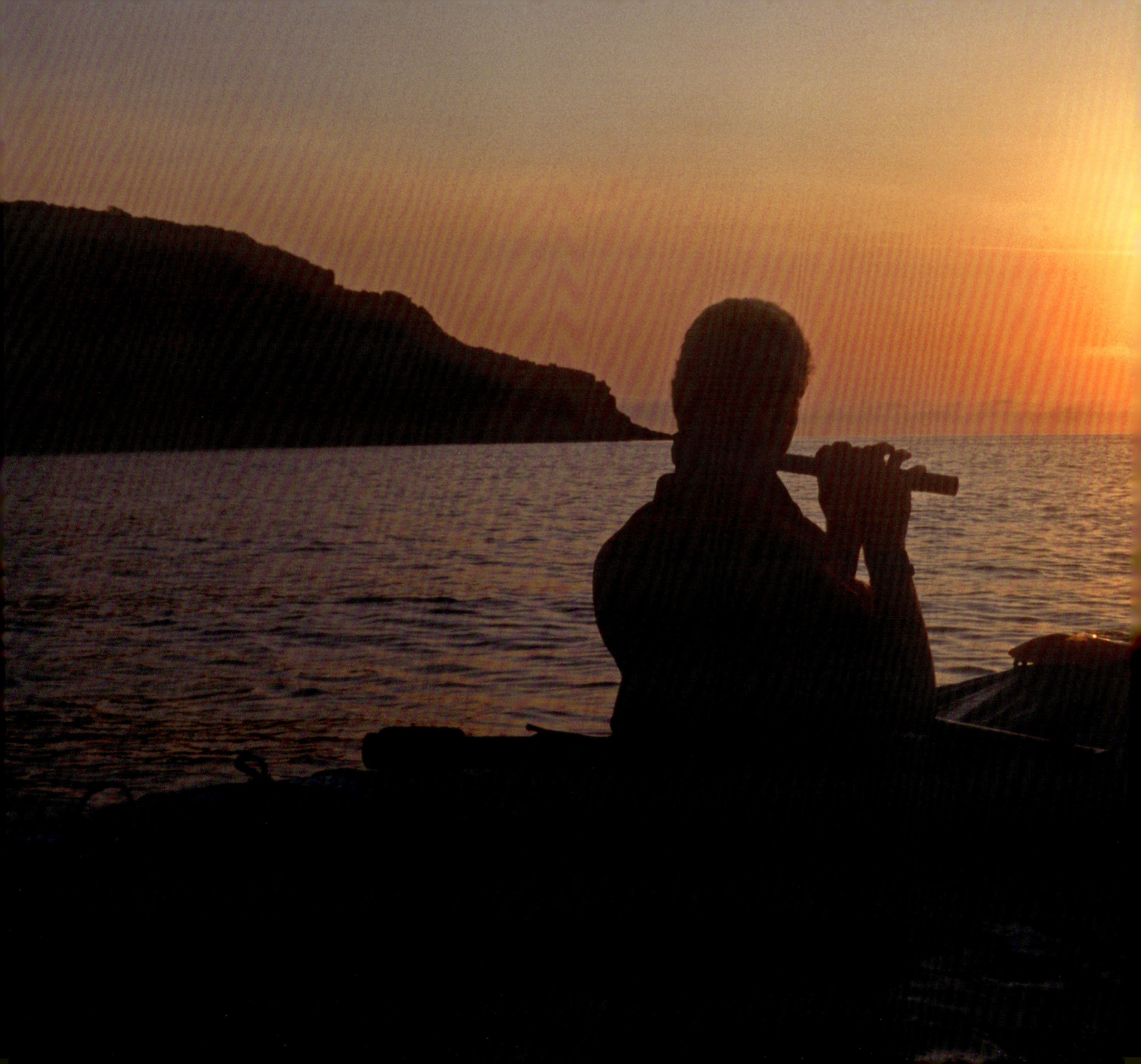

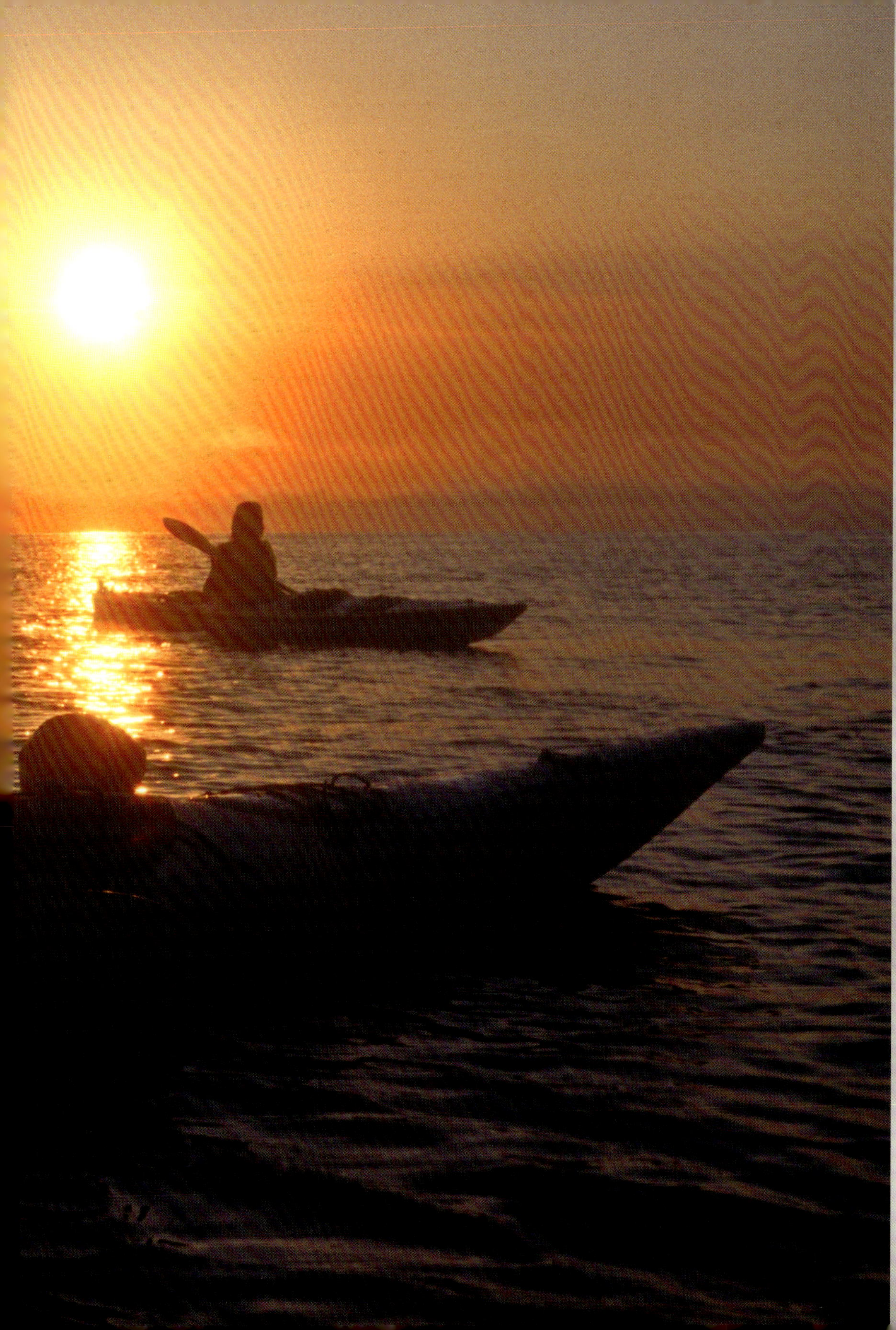

Once you have rowed past the Sirens, the choice of the route is yours. I cannot advise you which way to go or lead you through - you must decide for yourself.

- Homer,
from the Odyssey

A symphony of golden light heralds another desert sunrise on the mythical Sea of Cortez in Baja, Mexico. Two kayakers have slipped away from their sleeping camp for a close personal encounter with the magic of dawn.

From birth we carry the weight of gravity on our shoulders. But we only have to sink beneath the surface to be free.

- Jacques Costeau

A shadow passing over a multi-hued coral tapestry the photographer was exploring caused him to glance quickly upward. A golden form suspended overhead caused him to turn his dive camera towards the sky and shoot reflexively. Catherine was a young Brazilian girl working as a crew member on the *Galaxie*, a French-made sailboat upon which the group was cruising through the Fiji Islands.

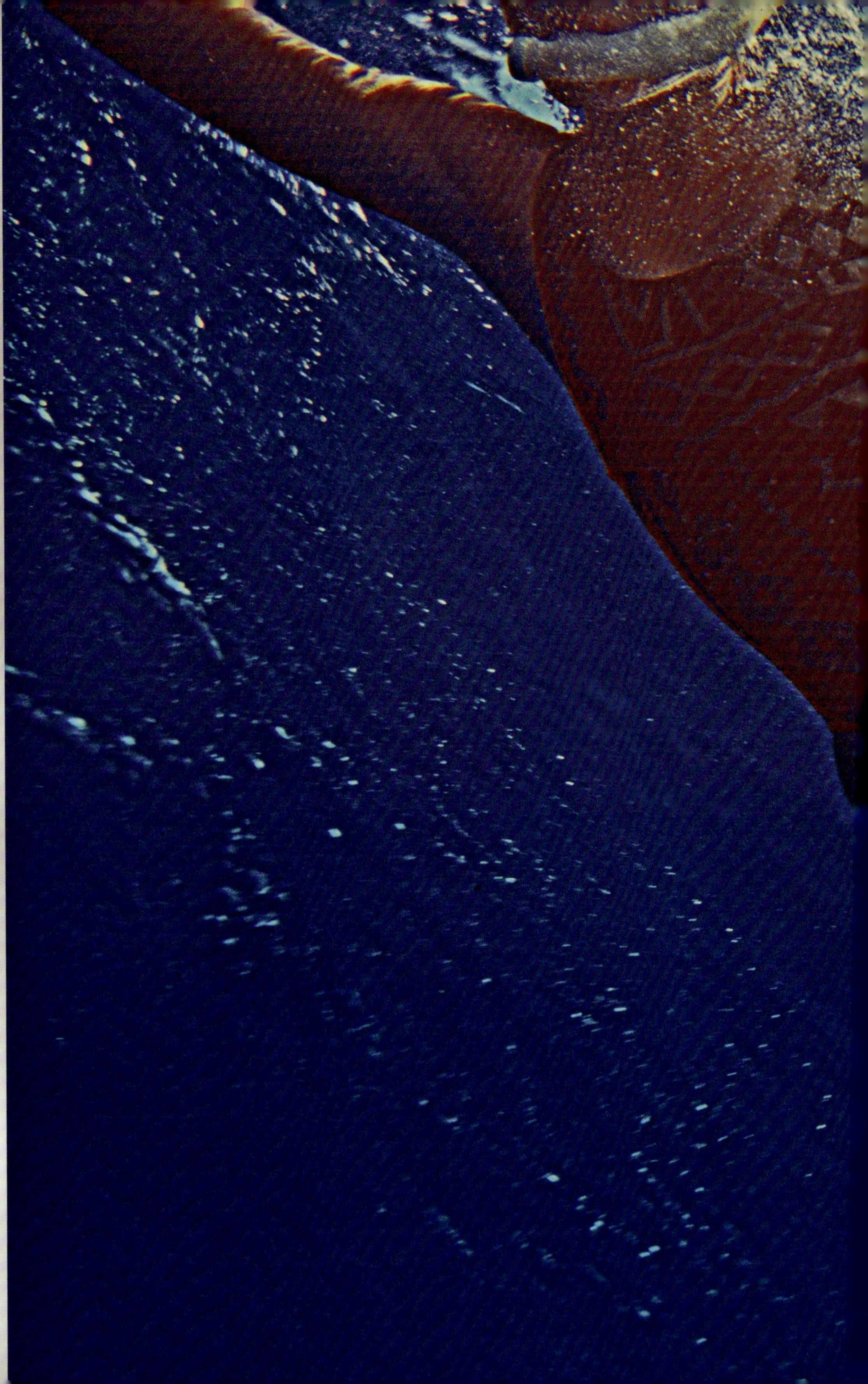

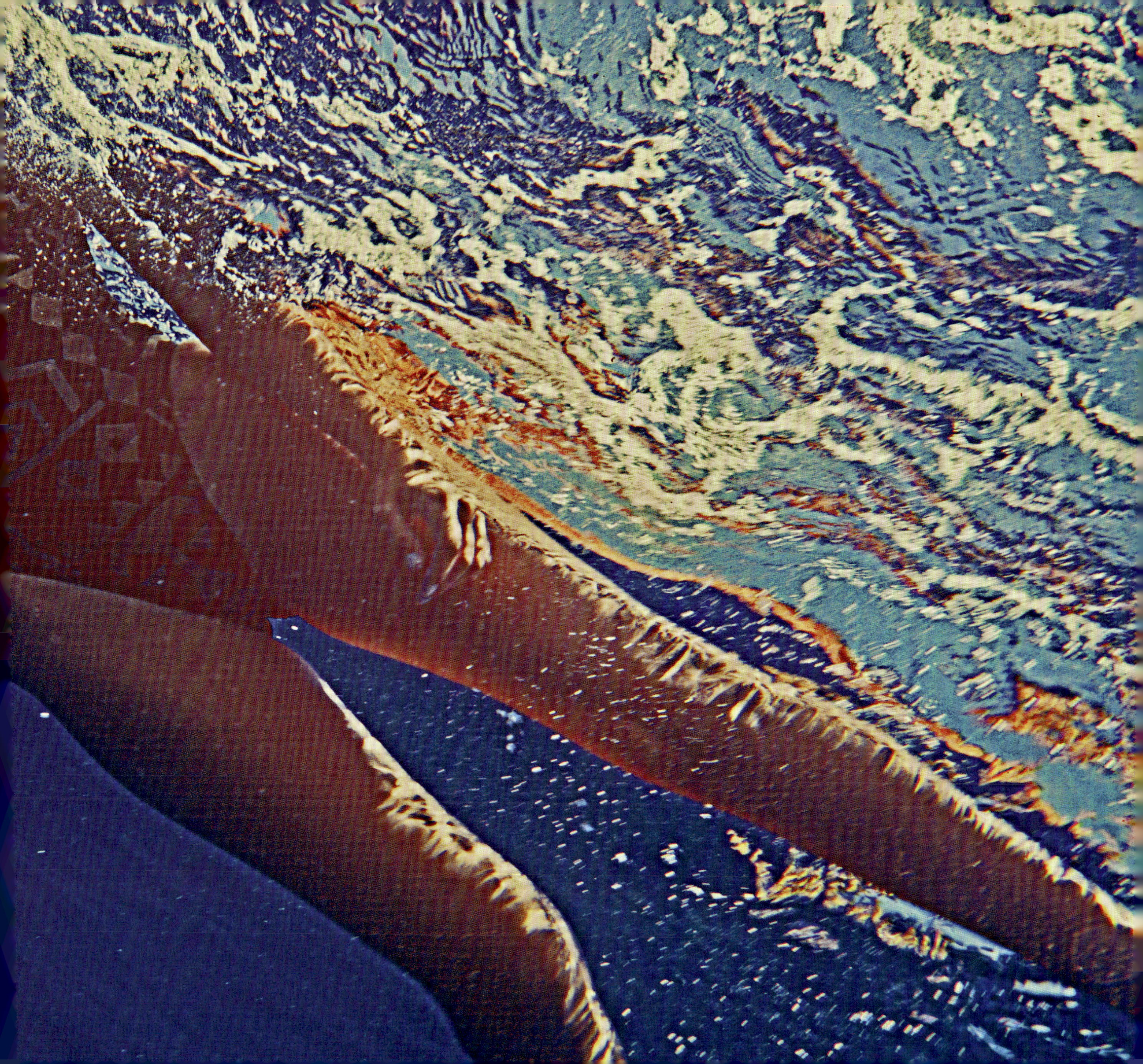

In the long history of humankind, those who learned to collaborate and improvise have always prevailed.

- Charles Darwin

145

The passengers and crew of a sailboat cruising through the Fijian archipelago disembarked one morning at a small native village. From the beach they spotted a tiny craft in big breaking seas, out beyond the coral reefs encircling the island. When the little boat returned across the inner lagoon and drew near the village, the travelers were amazed to see that its occupants were just two young boys and the contraption they had been paddling out in the open sea with such skill and confidence was a native-style kayak, fashioned entirely from scraps of old roofing tin. The visitors realized that like all tropical island folks, the Fijians were natural water people. Also like islanders everywhere, they were naturally resourceful and managed to get by quite well with whatever building materials happened to be at hand.

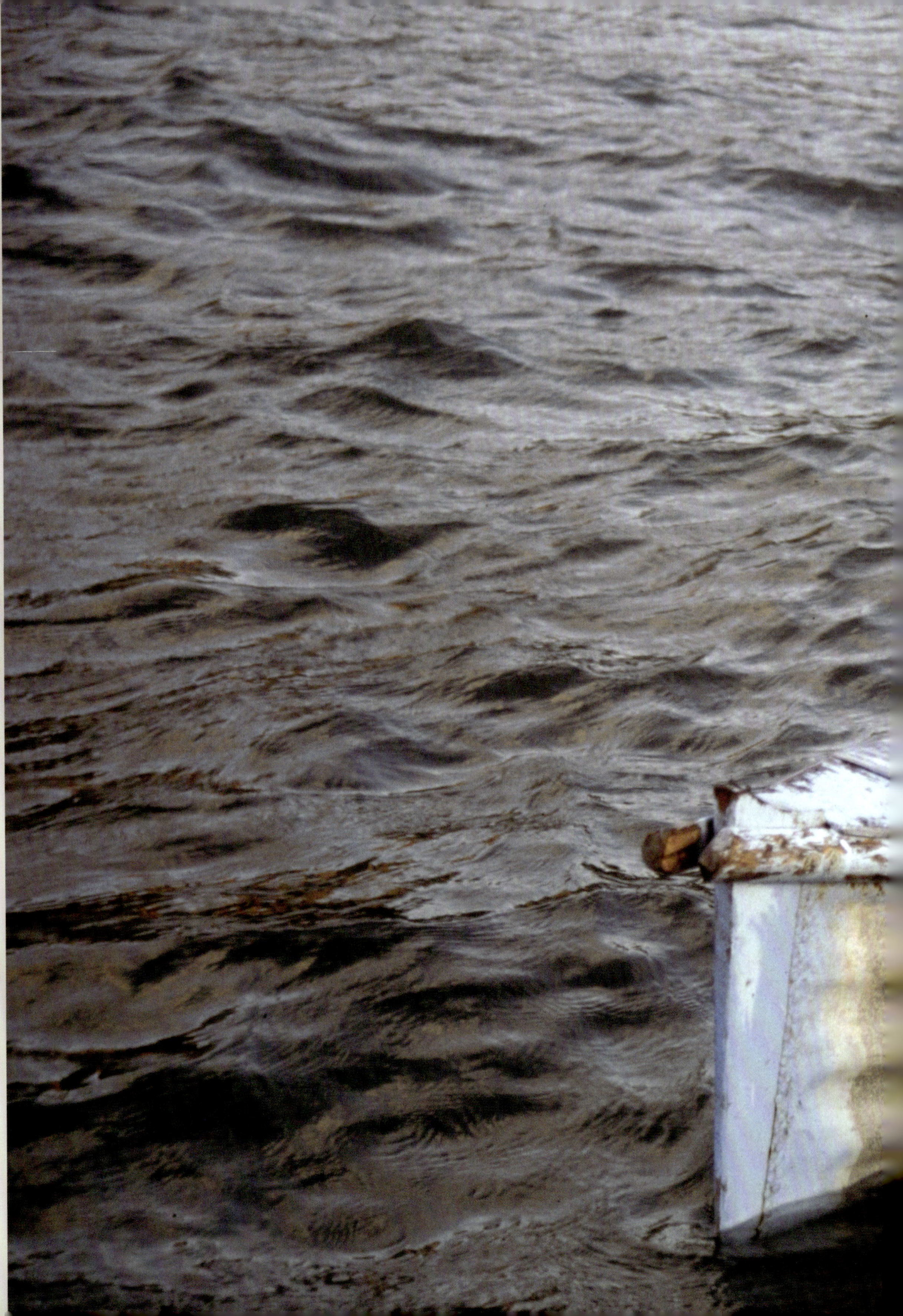

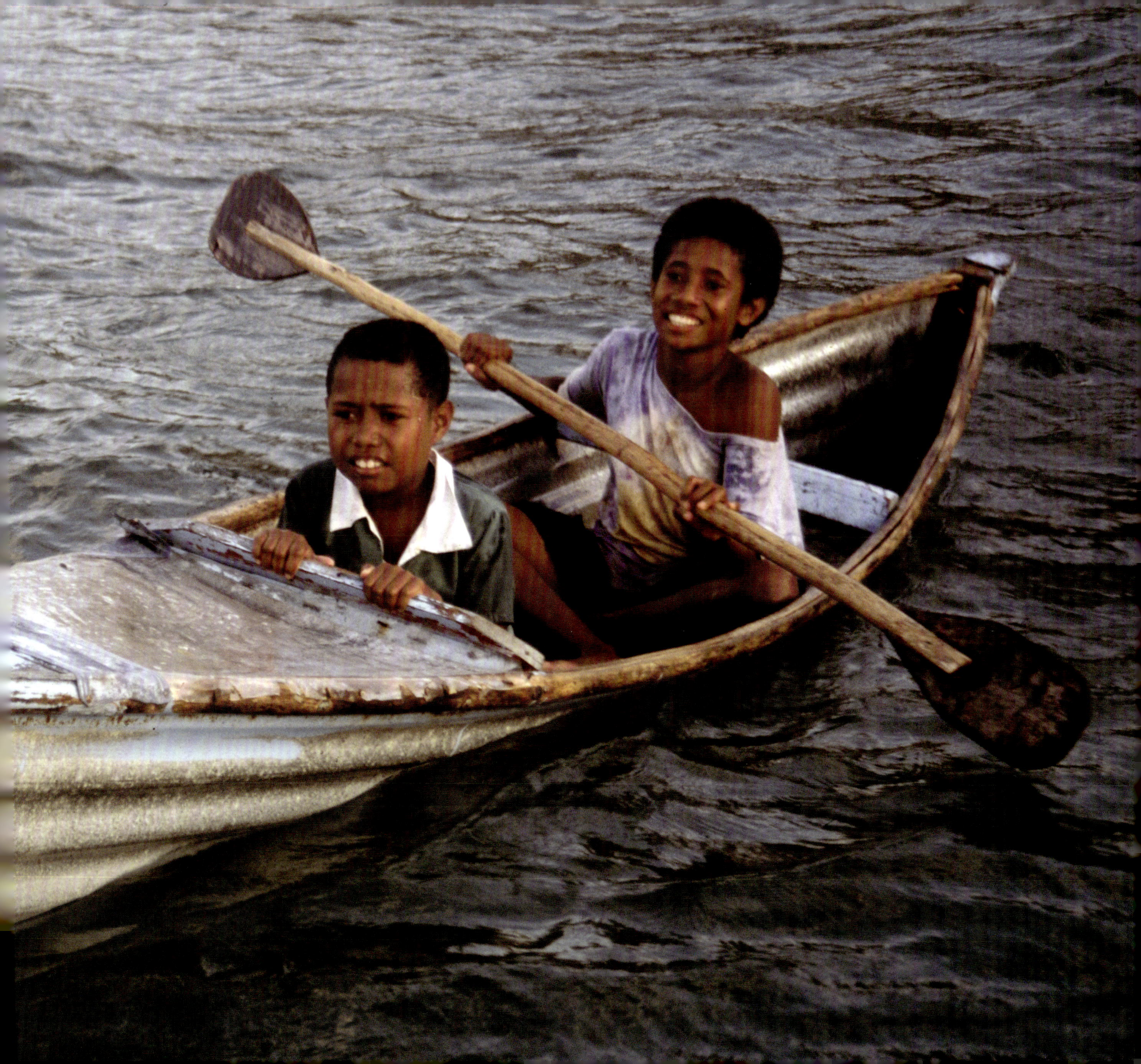

A ministering angel shall my sister be.

- William Shakespeare

El dia de mercado, the traditional market day, comes one day each week to many remote *pueblos* in the highlands of Guatemala. Some Indian families rise long before dawn and walk for miles down mounatin trails in the darkness to reach town early for this important event. Busy trading and selling what they have grown on their tiny plots of cleared land in the rainforest, parents often entrust the care of their younger children to their older siblings. This young cherub rests contentedly in her sister's *rebozo,* appearing in stark contrast to the haunting face of her *hermana major* - already old enough, perhaps, to have witnessed the suffering of her people in a world filled with strange and powerful forces. Photograph by Bob Stender.

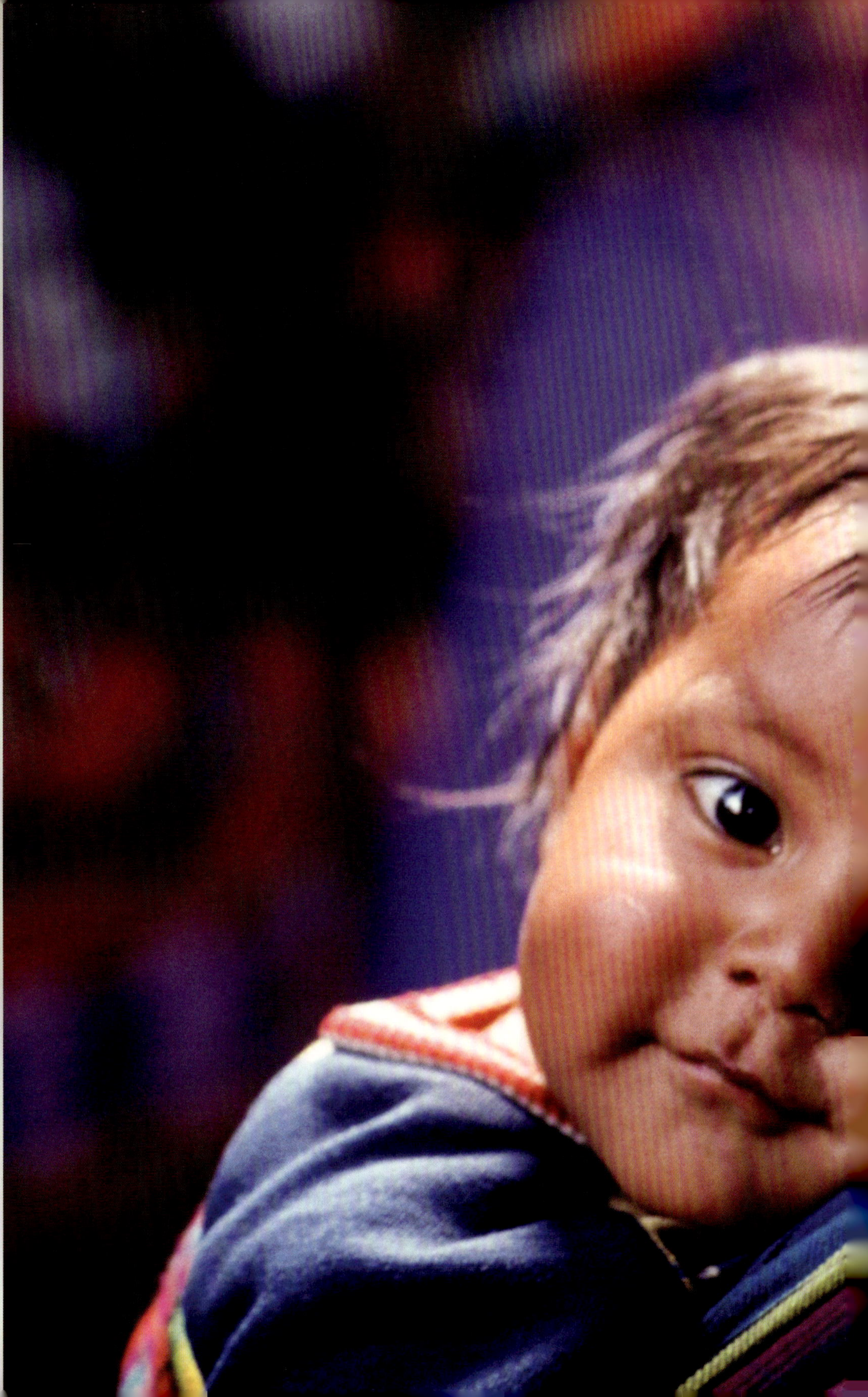

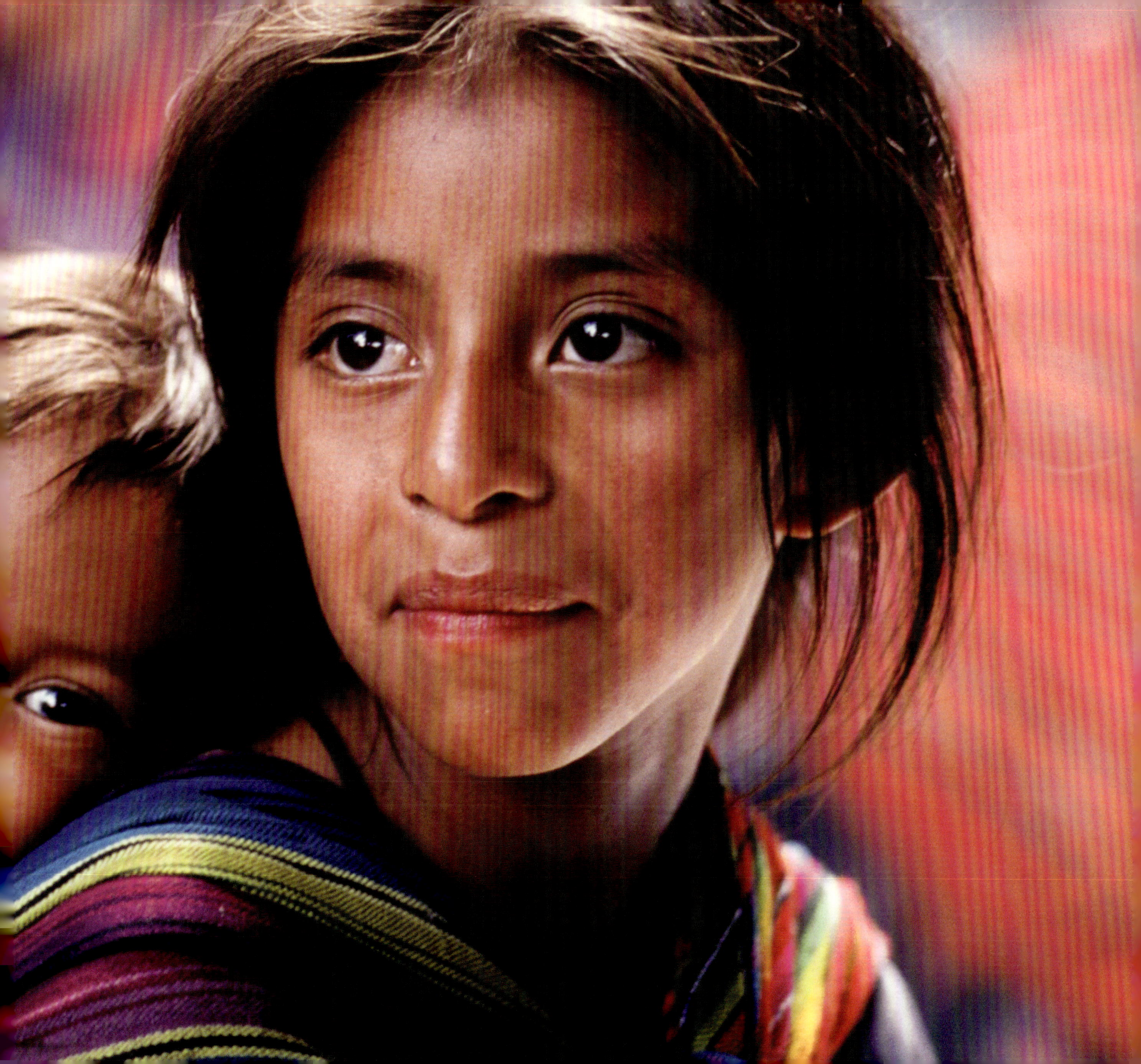

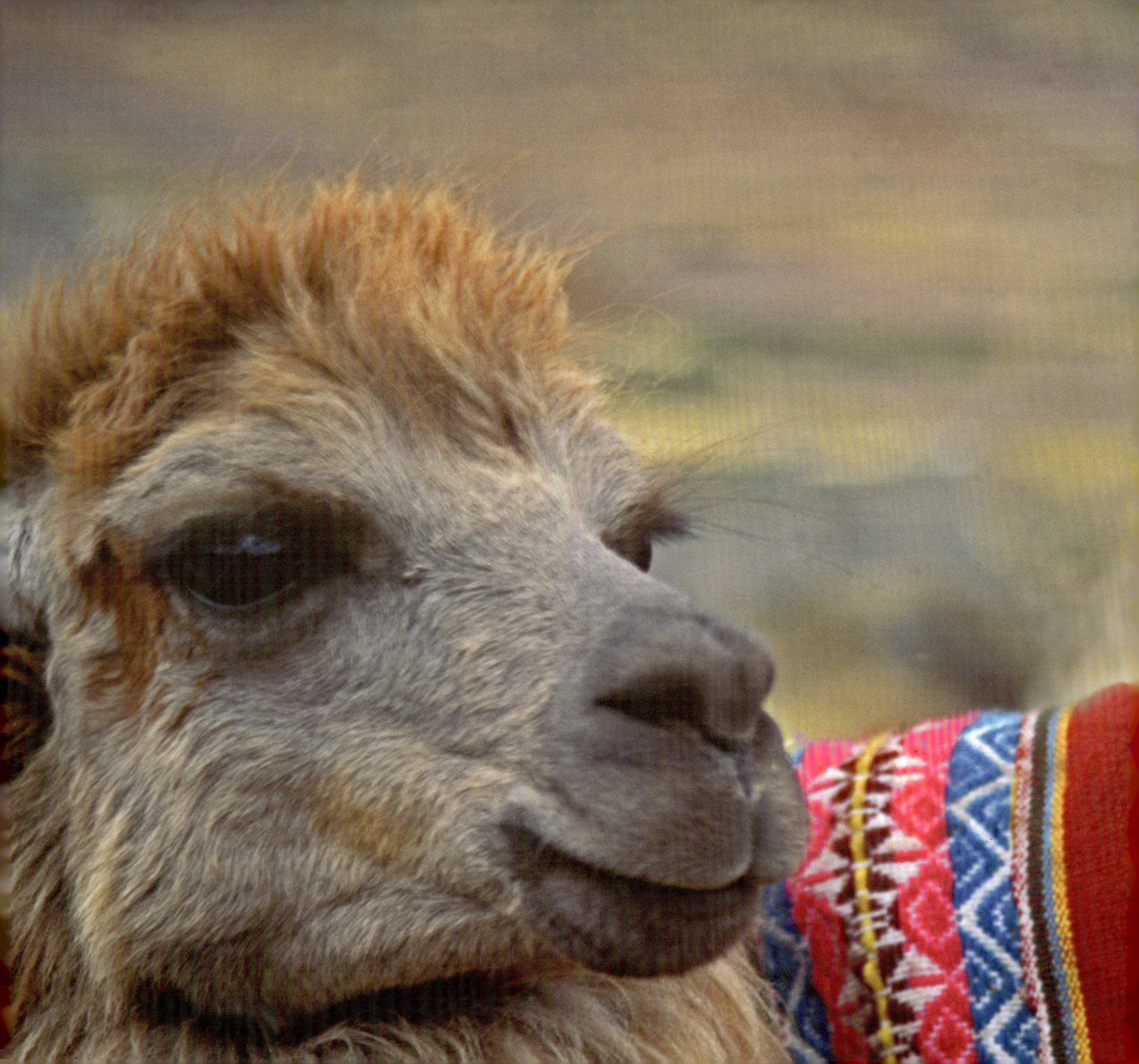

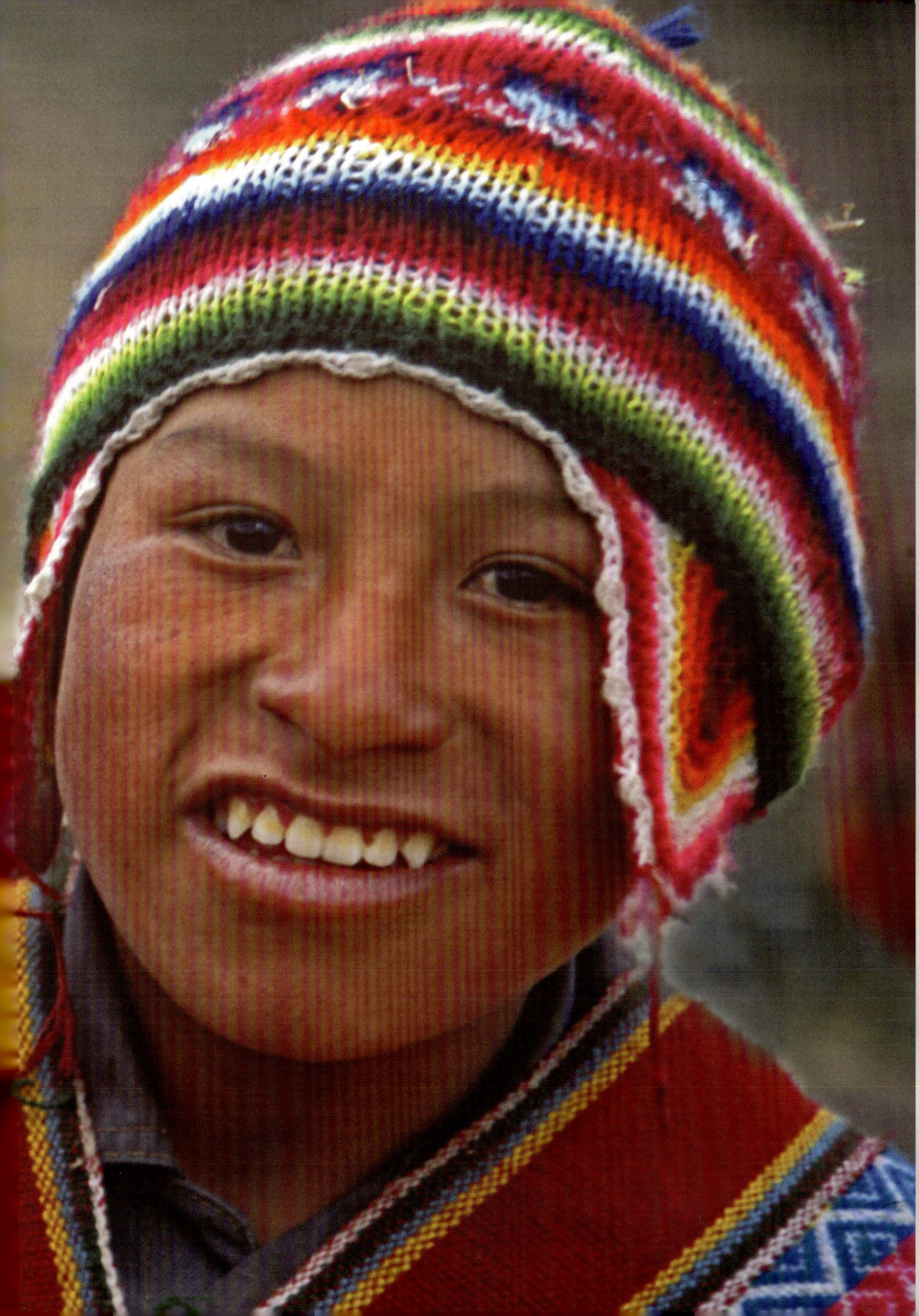

The best way to know God is to love many things.

- Vincent Van Gogh

A sight unchanged from pre-columbian times greeted trekkers as they approached the end of their 5-day trek through the Andian highlands on the Inca Trail in Peru. They were arriving at *Intipunko,* the Inca Gate of the Sun, which has stood for guard centuries on the crest of a mountain ridge above the long-lost ruins of Machu Picchu. A young Quechua Indian boy and his llama stood there, waiting silently.

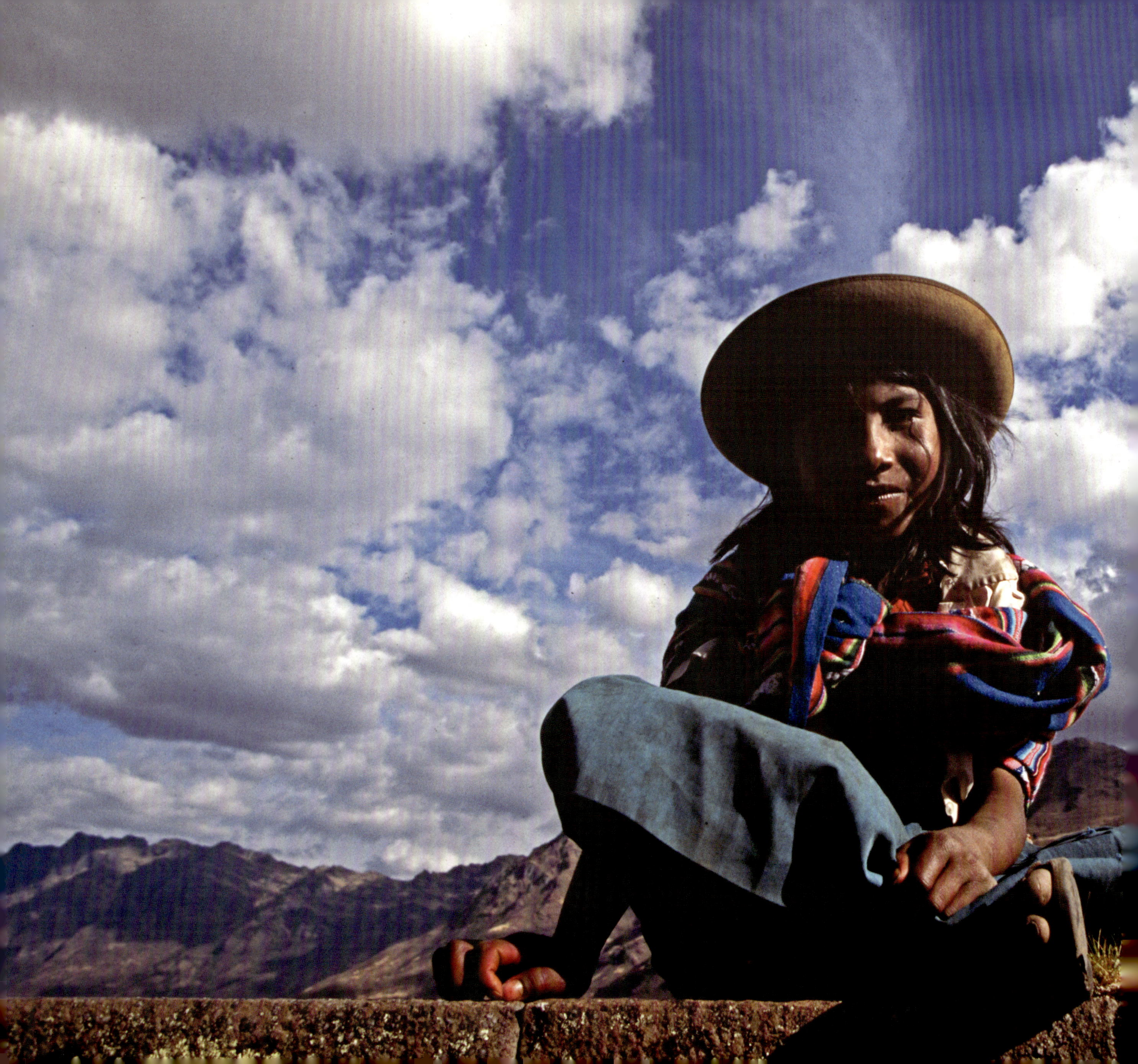

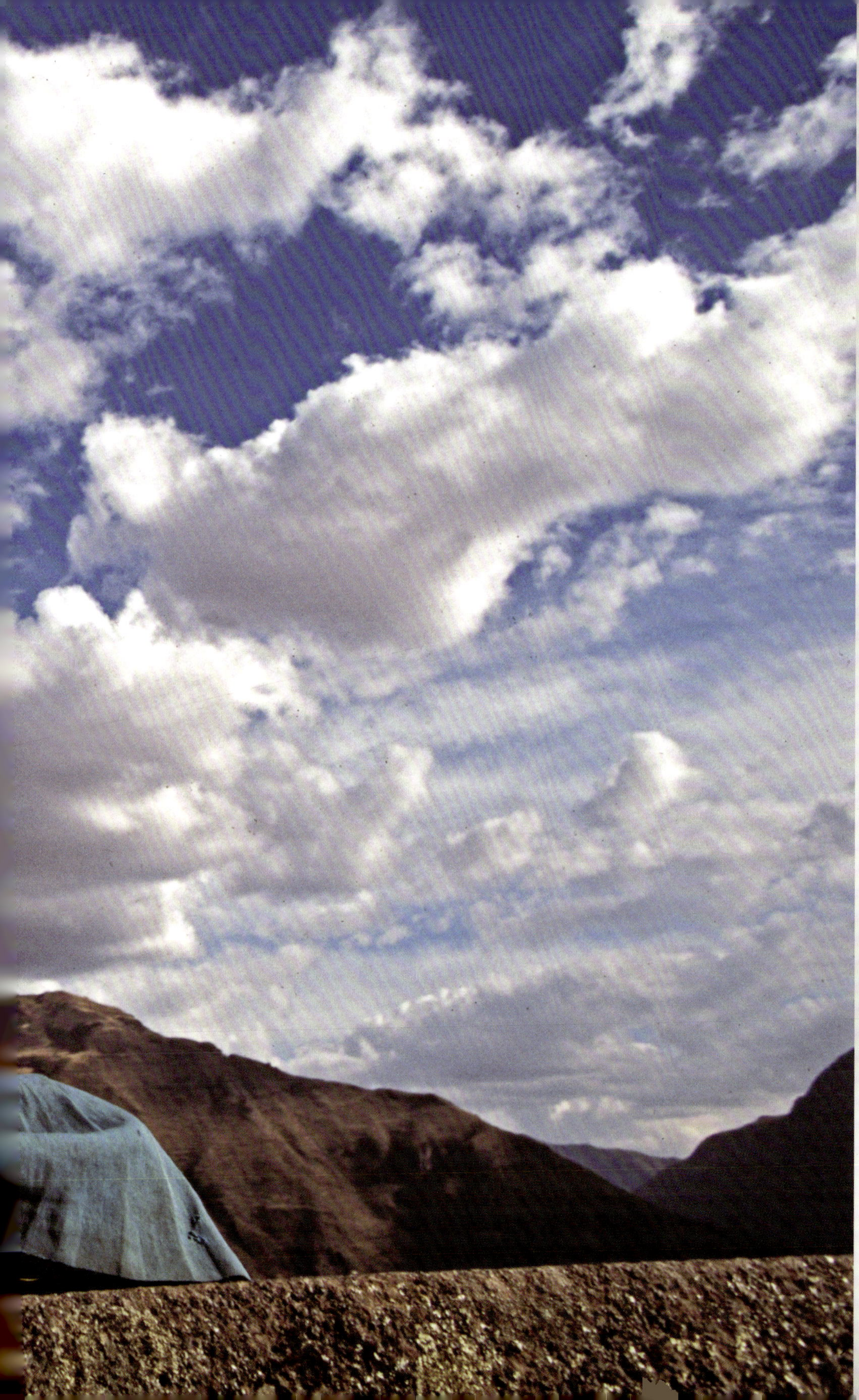

The quieter you become, the more you hear.

- Ram Dass

An aura of quiet power and mystery seemed to emanate from a young Quechua girl encountered sitting silently on an ancient Inca wall. The ruins surrounding her on the mountainside above the Indian *pueblo* of Pisac in the highlands of Peru were built by her ancestors centuries ago.

Whoever imagines himself a judge of truth and knowledge is bound to be shipwrecked by the laughter of the gods.

- Albert Einstein

The Pacific Ocean bordering the 3000 mile coast of western Chile is made both nutrients-rich and tempestuous by the Humbolt Current that sweeps up from Antarctica. Yet the great storms are soon forgotten when fair weather returns. An eager *pescador* awaits the incoming tide that will set his *lancha* free so he may return once again to the bountiful sea in pursuit of its rich harvest.

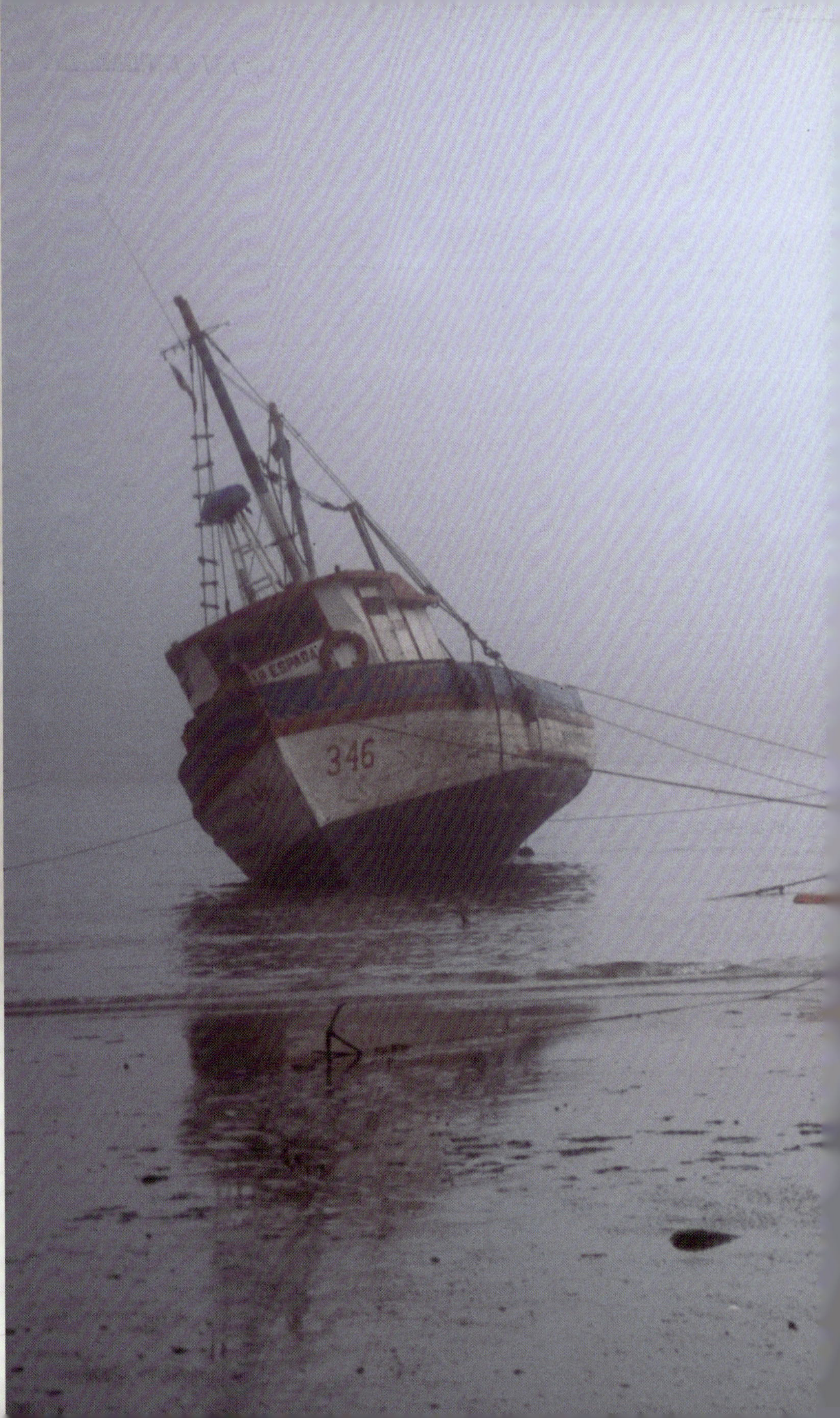

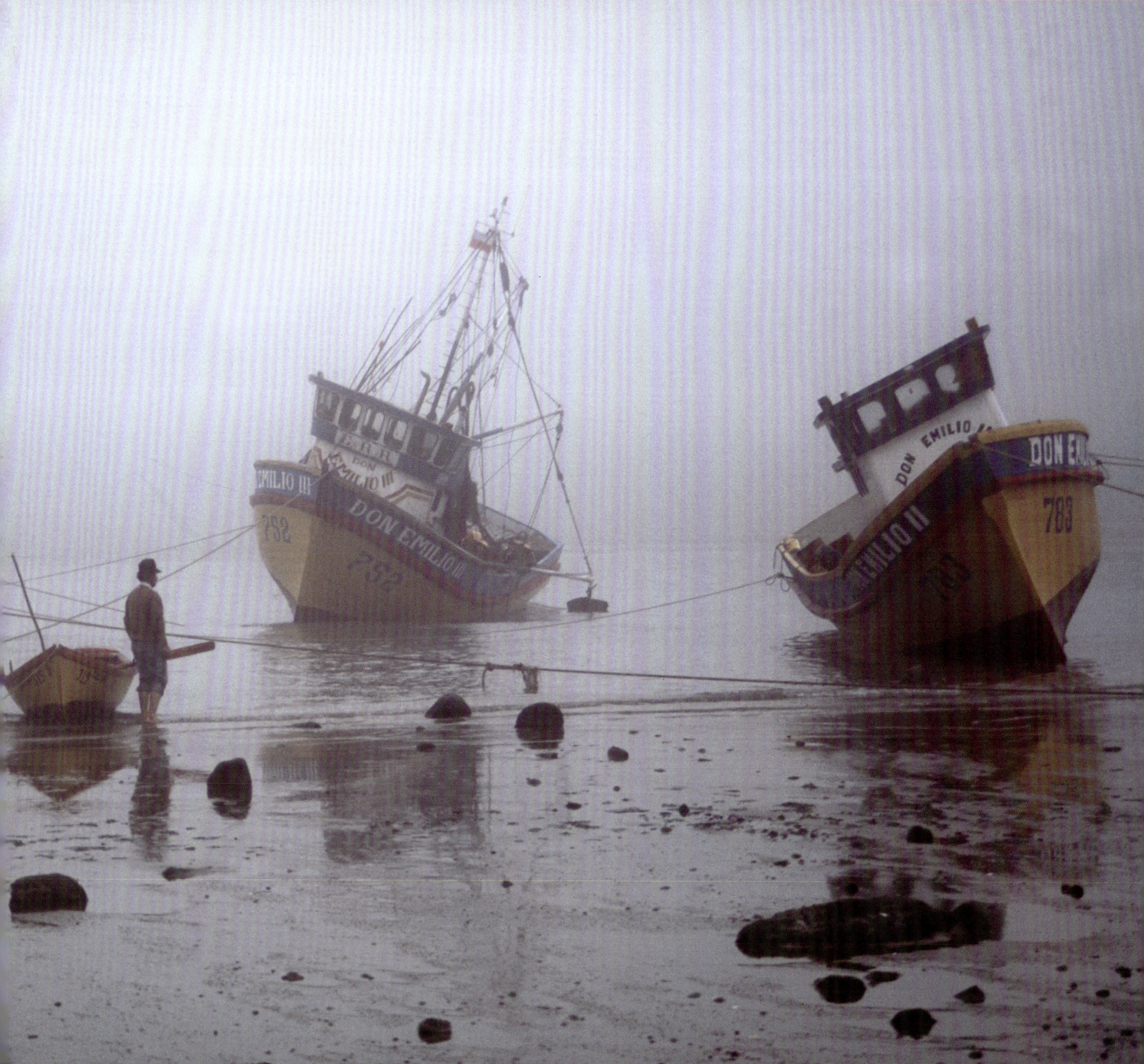
EMILIO III
DON EMILIO III
782
DON EMILIO II
DON EMIL
783
EMILIO II

You call them wild, but they aren't really wild, they are free. Animals aren't wild, they are just free.

- Native American saying

155

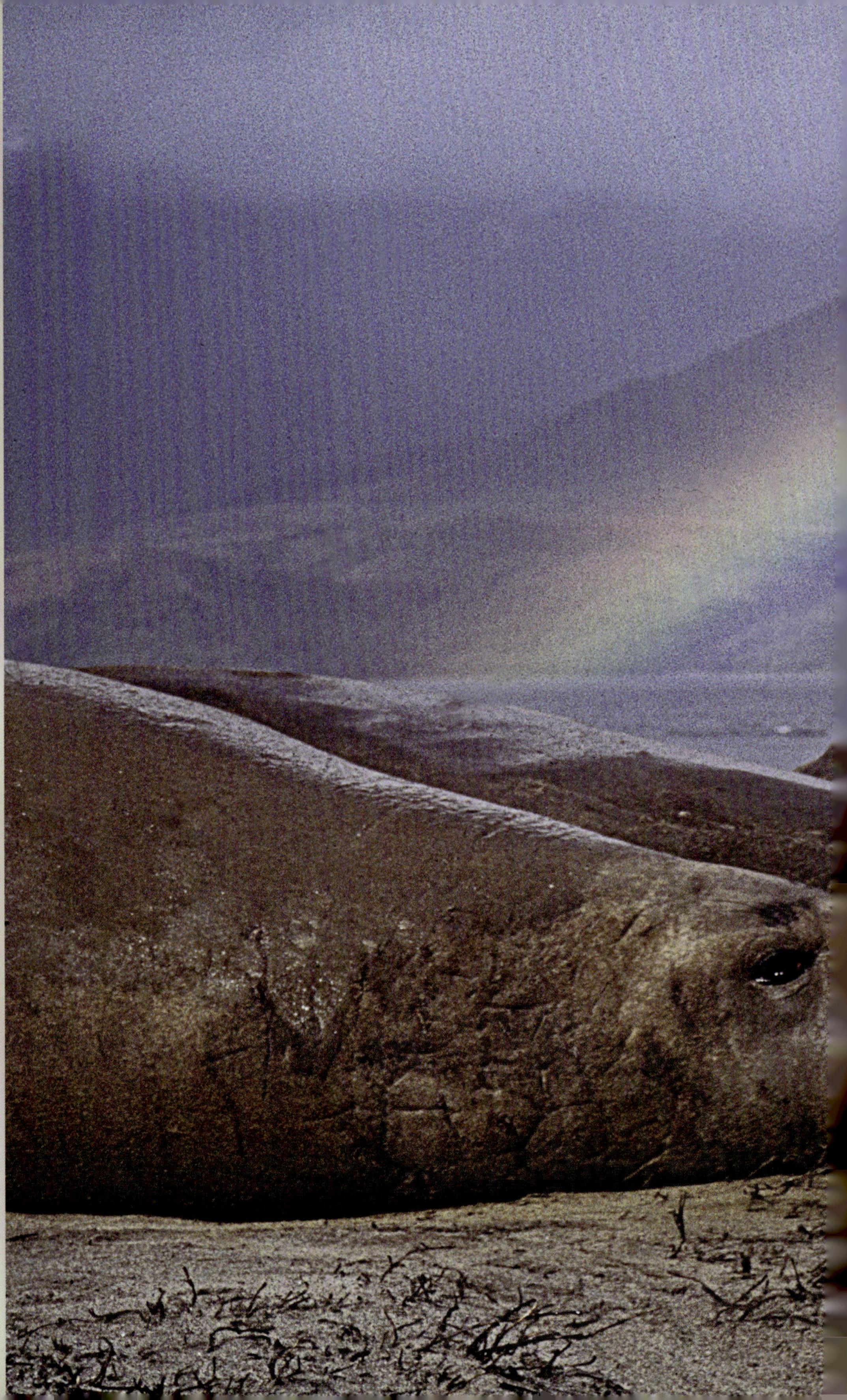

Tierra del Fuego archipelago, one large island and many smalller ones, collectively appear like a bent-over spear tip at the far southern end of South America. Magellan christened the region the "Land Of Fire" in 1520 when the Spanish explorer sailed by at night and spotted the Indians' fires burning on the islands at night. Sadly the indigenous human population has almost entirly disappeared, but the marine life is still abundant. Southern elephant seals are the most massive of all the land-based animals, with mature bulls weighing as much as 11,000 pounds. They may appear rather indolent when ashore soaking up precious warmth from the low-latitude sun - but once back in the sea they demonstrate extraordinary athletic abiliities, diving as deep as 5,000' and remaining submerged for up to two hours in pursuit of squid and fish. They are protected now, and consequently are fairly easy to approach by sea kayak there in the remote, seldom-visited fiords.

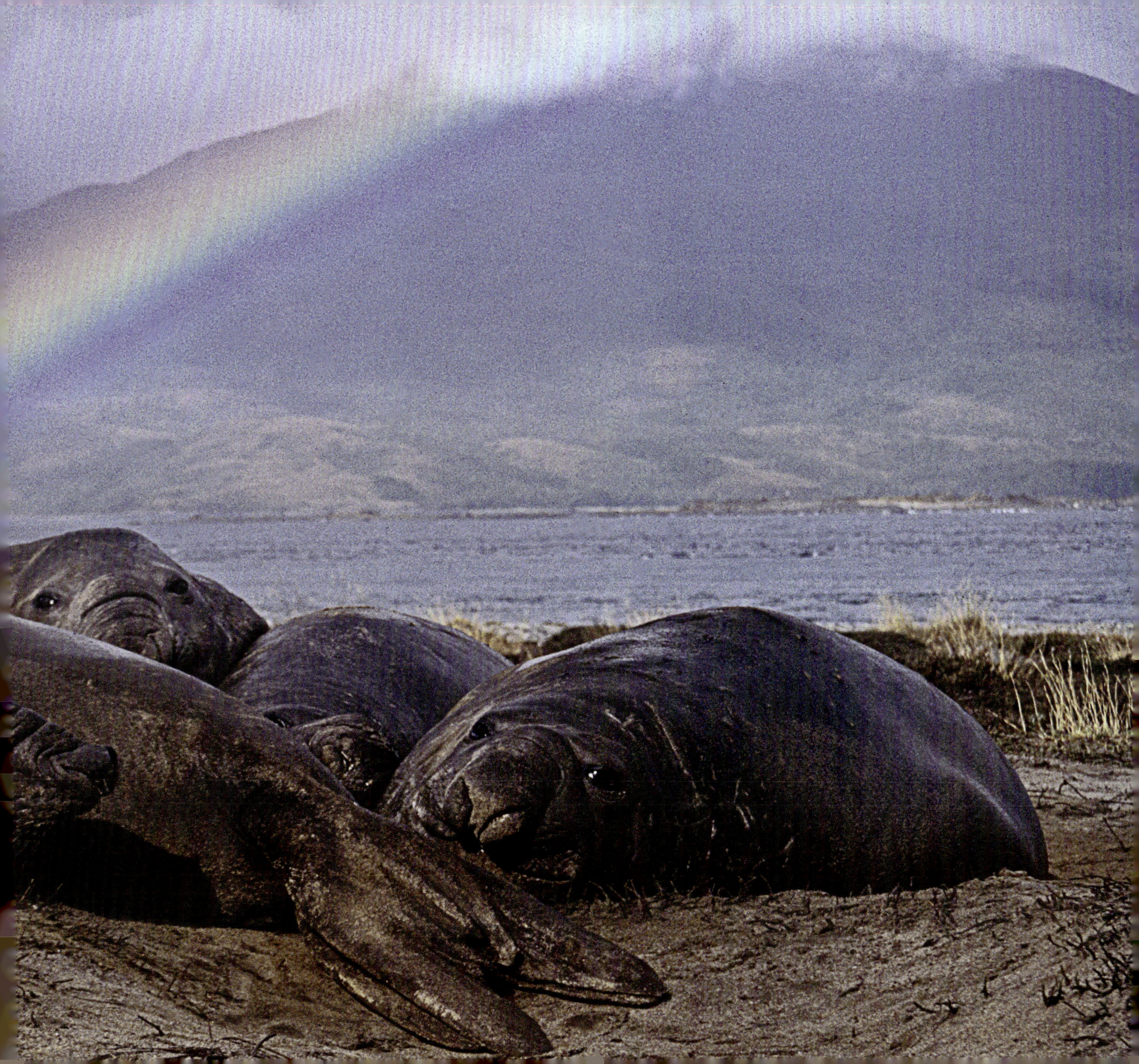

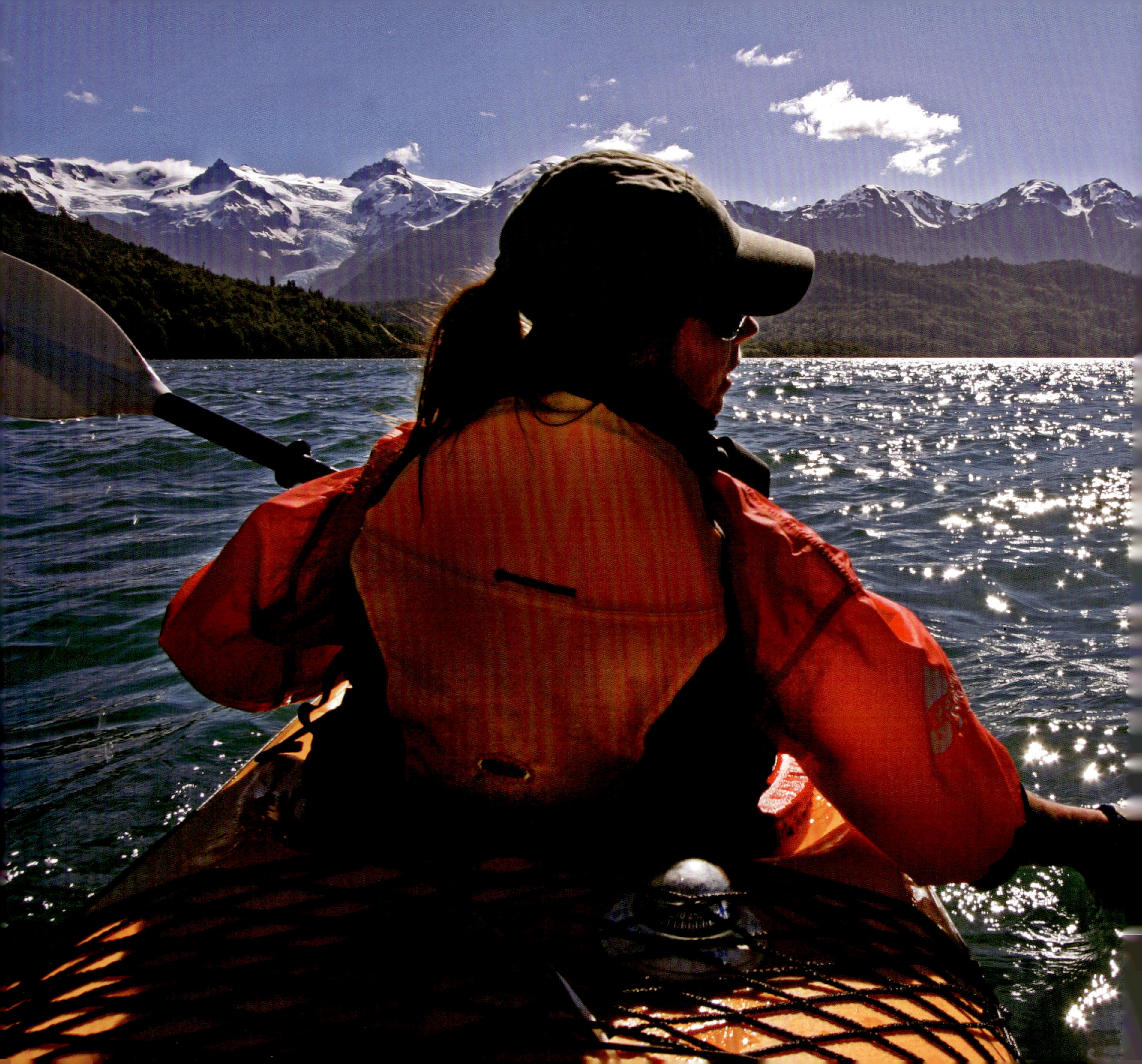

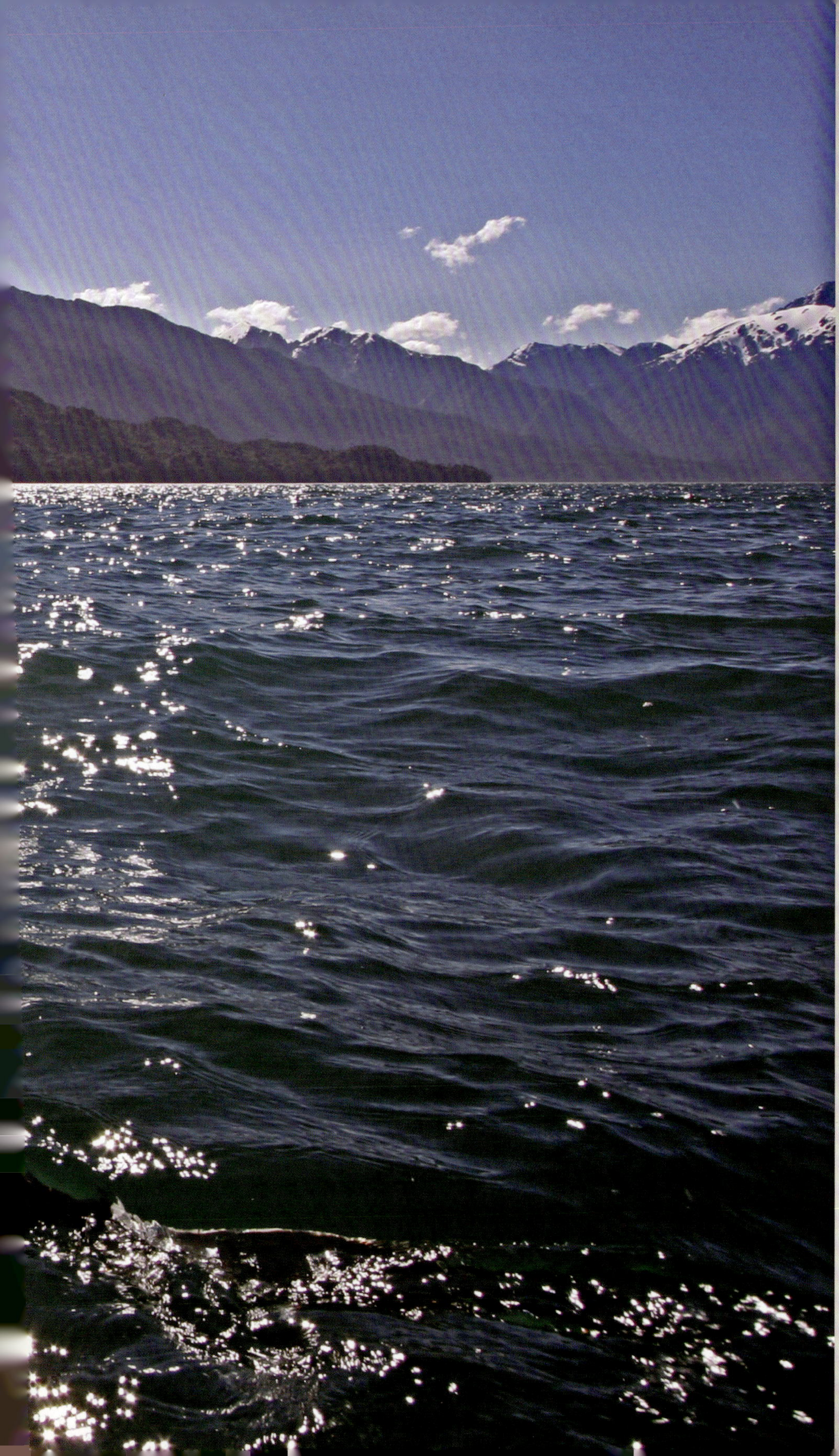

I don't want to be cute anymore... I want to be tough and brave.

- spoken by Marika Powers,
when she was three years old

Dedicated to focusing world attention on the Patagonian wilderness and the pressing need to protect it from dam building and mining interests, an inspired group of gringo and Chilean *expedicionistas* set out in 2007 to accomplish the first-ever 'multi-sport' crossing of the South American continent. They began by paddling sea kayaks northward along the Atlantic coast of Argentina. Turning west at about 42º S latitude, they traveled overland across the pampas to reach the westward-flowing headwaters of the *Rio Futaleufu* high in the Andes. There they resumed paddling their sea kayaks again to reach the frontier with Chile. But just a few kilometers beyond the border the great *Rio Futa* began a thunderous class IV-V descent through a seies of steep, narrow canyons. Undeterred, the team rode safely through the rapids in whitewater rafts. Once they reached lower elevation they switched modes of transportation once again and began riding sure-footed Chilean *corralero* horses. The rainforests through which they passed were so so dense they had terrified the *conquistadors*, who considered them impenetrable. When the canyons widened and the powerful *Futaleufu* reached vast *Lago Yelcho*, they returned to kayaks and continued to paddle westward. After 18 continuous days of travel, they reached the Pacific Ocean and the end of their epic adventure. Hopefully their efforts will help to encourage the preservation of the precious Patagonian wilderness.

Nothing has brought me closer to enlightenment than landscapes.

- Reinhold Messner

Patagonia today remains an untamed and sparcely populated world of snow-capped mountain peaks, flowing glaciers and powerful whitewater rivers - a place where condors and pumas still rein unchallenged. Vast temperate rainforests, that the horse-bound *conquistadores* considered impassable, still fill roadless Andean valleys. It is a landscape so formidible that even the mighty Andes forming the spine of South America for thousands of miles, seem to waver here and veer westward until they crumble and disappear into the sea. Photograph taken in the Futaleufu Valley by Crossing Patagonia Expedition member Jonathan Levine in 2007.

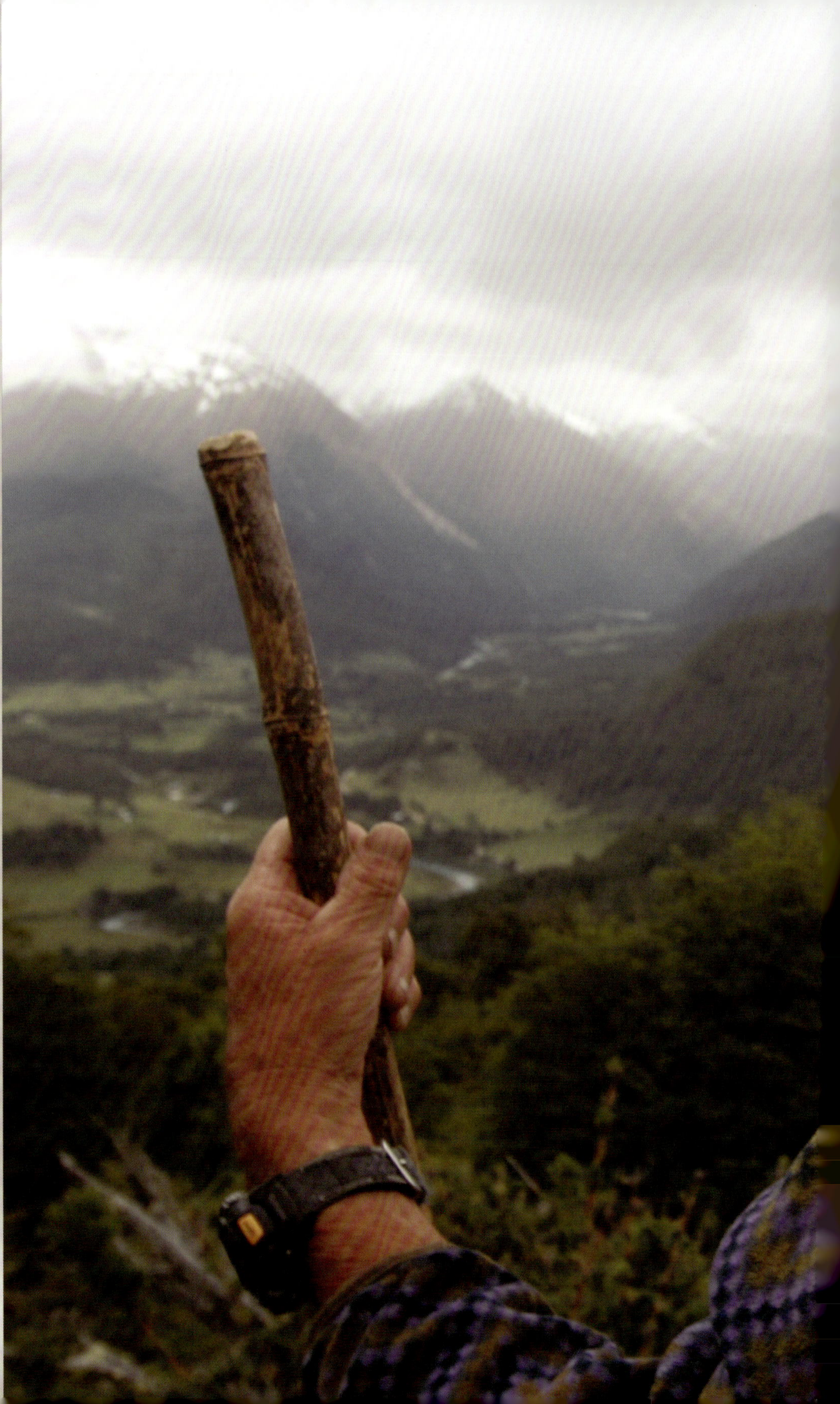

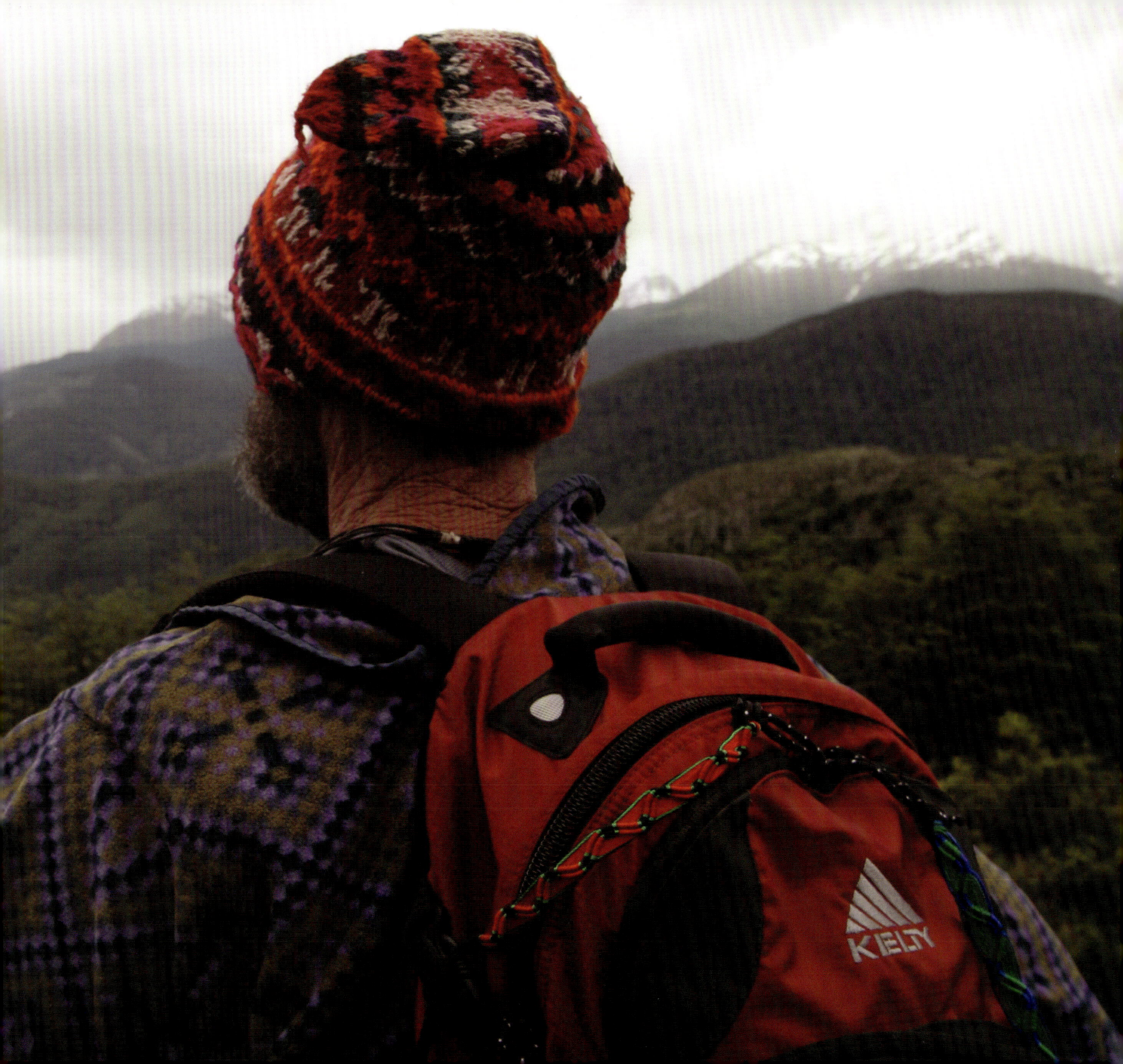
KELTY

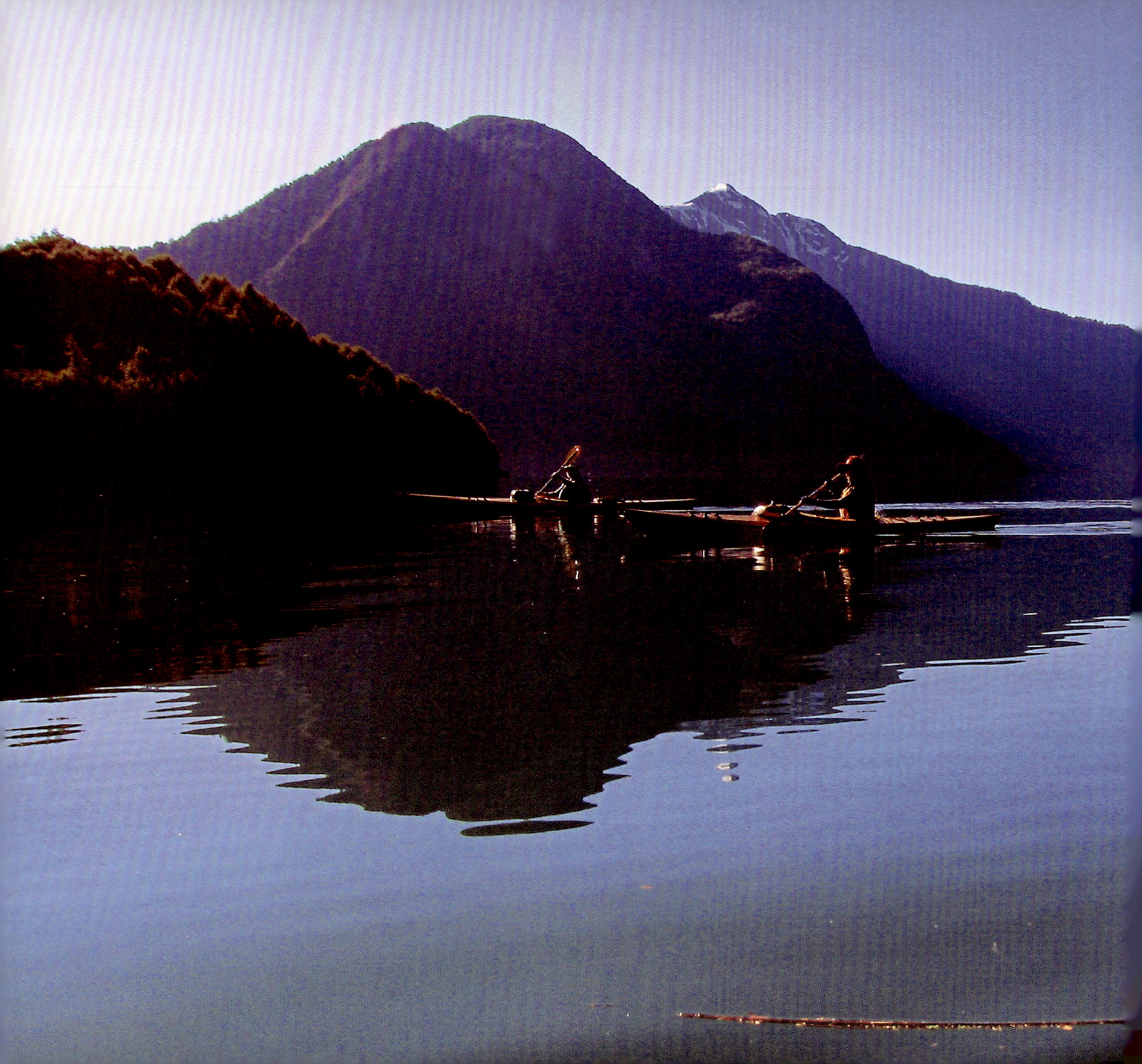

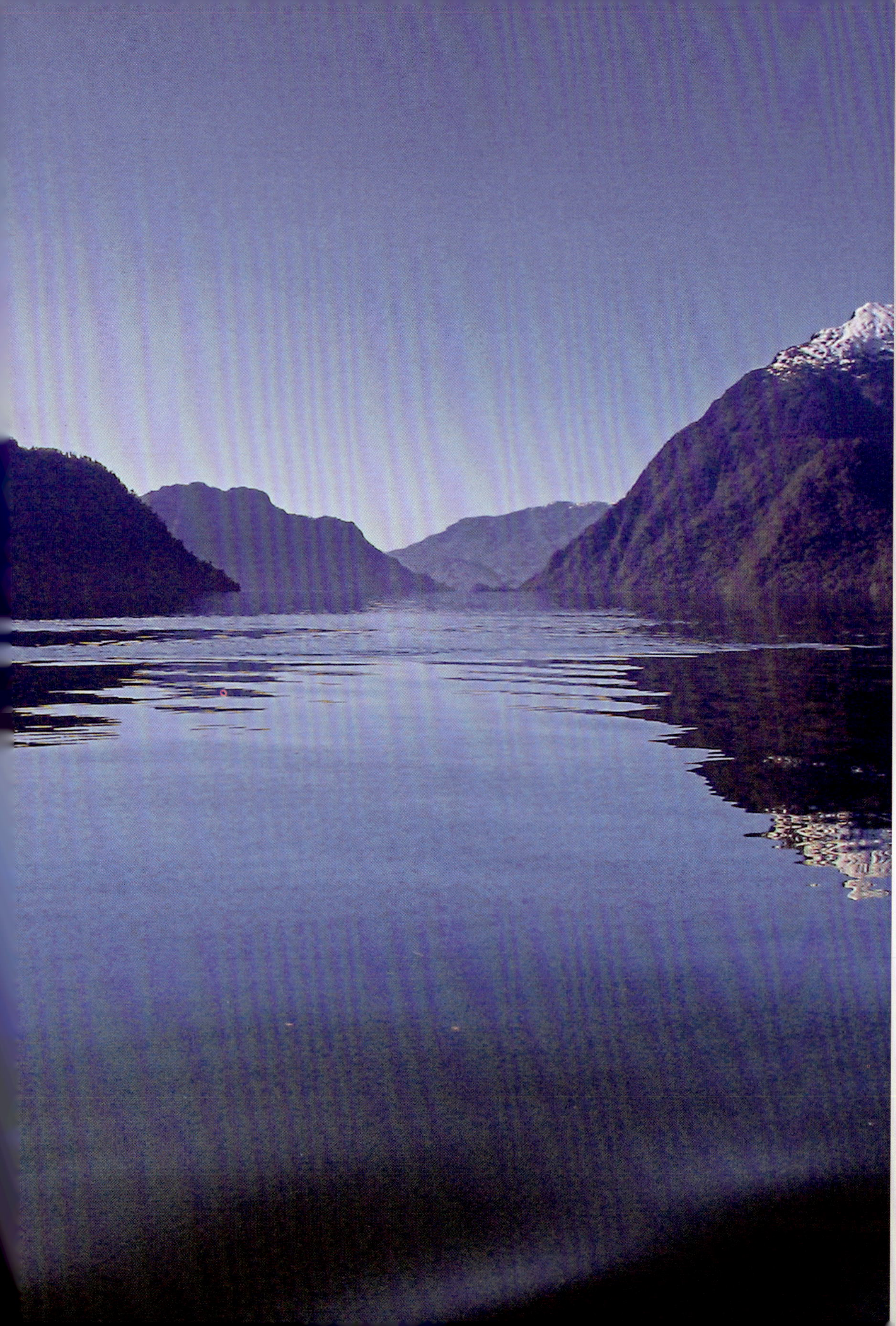

Glorious it is when wandering time has come.

- old Eskimo song

John Lockwood and Anne Kang approach the conclusion of a long paddle across the 75 km expanse of *Lago Yelcho* in southern Chile. Their international team ultimately accomplished the first 'multi-sport' traverse of Patagonia from the Atlantic to the Pacific. The purpose of their expedition was to focus world attention on the spectacular, still pristine Patagonia wilderness - and hopefully encourage its preservation for future generations.

But under it all they were men, penetrating the land of desolation and mockery and silence, puny adventurers bent on colossal adventure, pitting themselves against the might of a world as remote and alien as the abysses of space.

- Jack London

For the adventuresome of spirit, Torres del Paine remains a fairy tale world of vertigineous geography thrusting up between the Magellanic subpolar forests and the lonely Patagonian steppes far in the south of Chile. Awestruck newcomers might easily imagine this mystical realm was once a playground of the gods - who departed suddenly long ago, leaving all their playthings - craggy mountain peaks, thundering cascades, vast ice fields and flower-filled valleys, scattered everywhere.

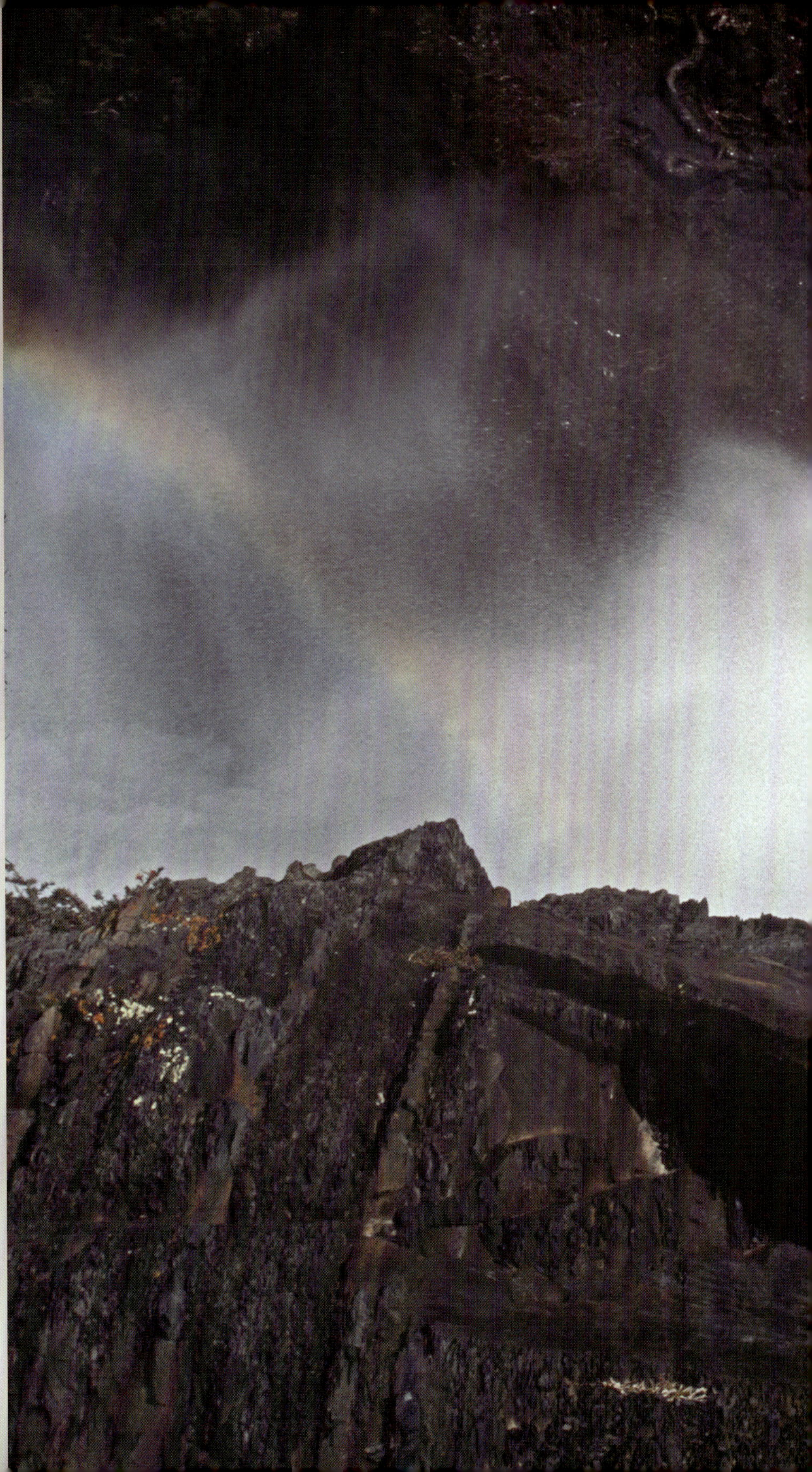

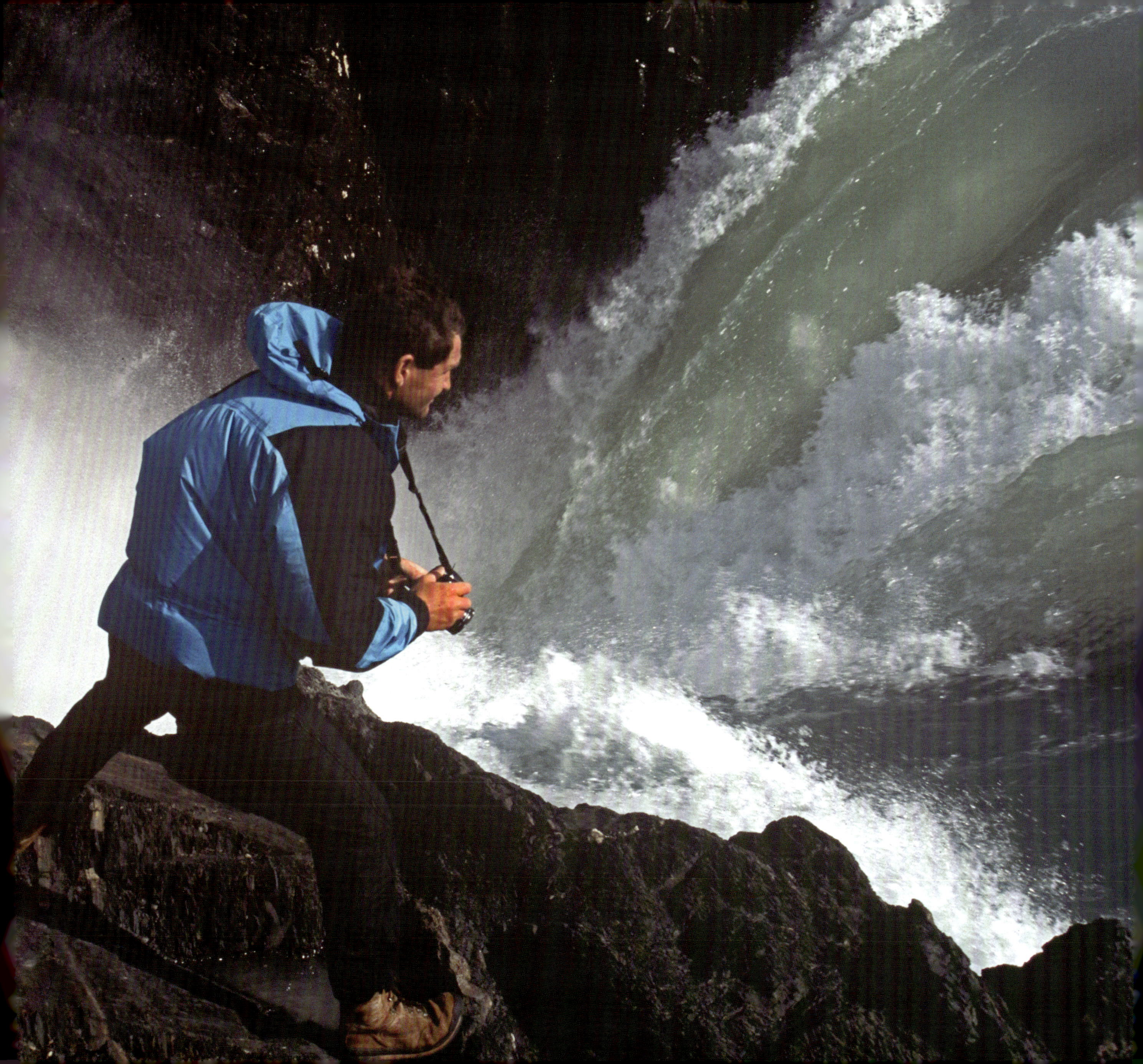

I hope to be capable of finding new dreams forever.

- Reinhold Messner

A lone hiker stands surrounded by the quiet splendor of *Parque Nacional Torres del Paine* in southern Chile. The *Cordillera Paine* massif rises some 2800 meters above the Patagonian steppes, its spectacular centerpiece. The 181,000 hectare park was recently designated a Unesco Biosphere Reserve.

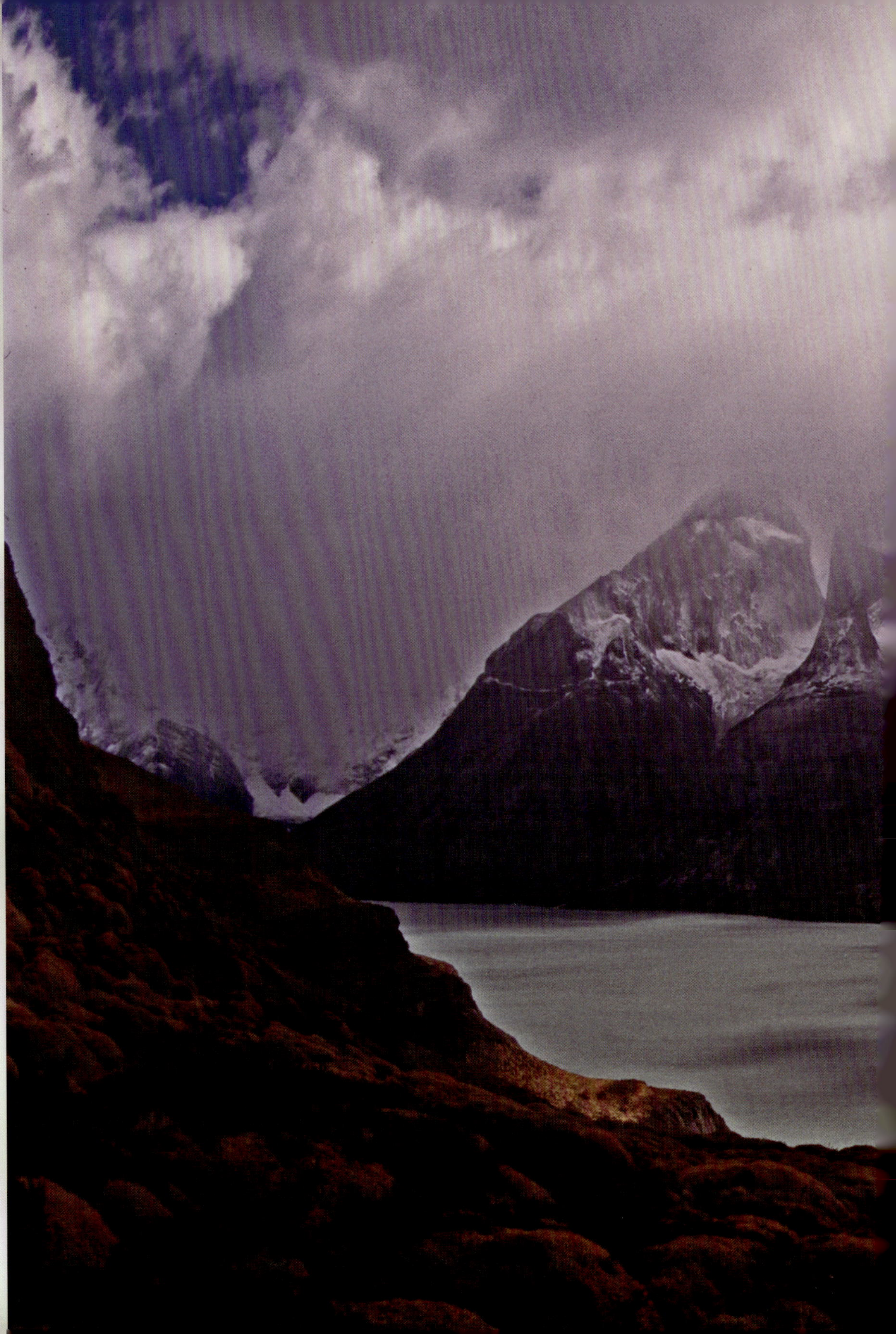

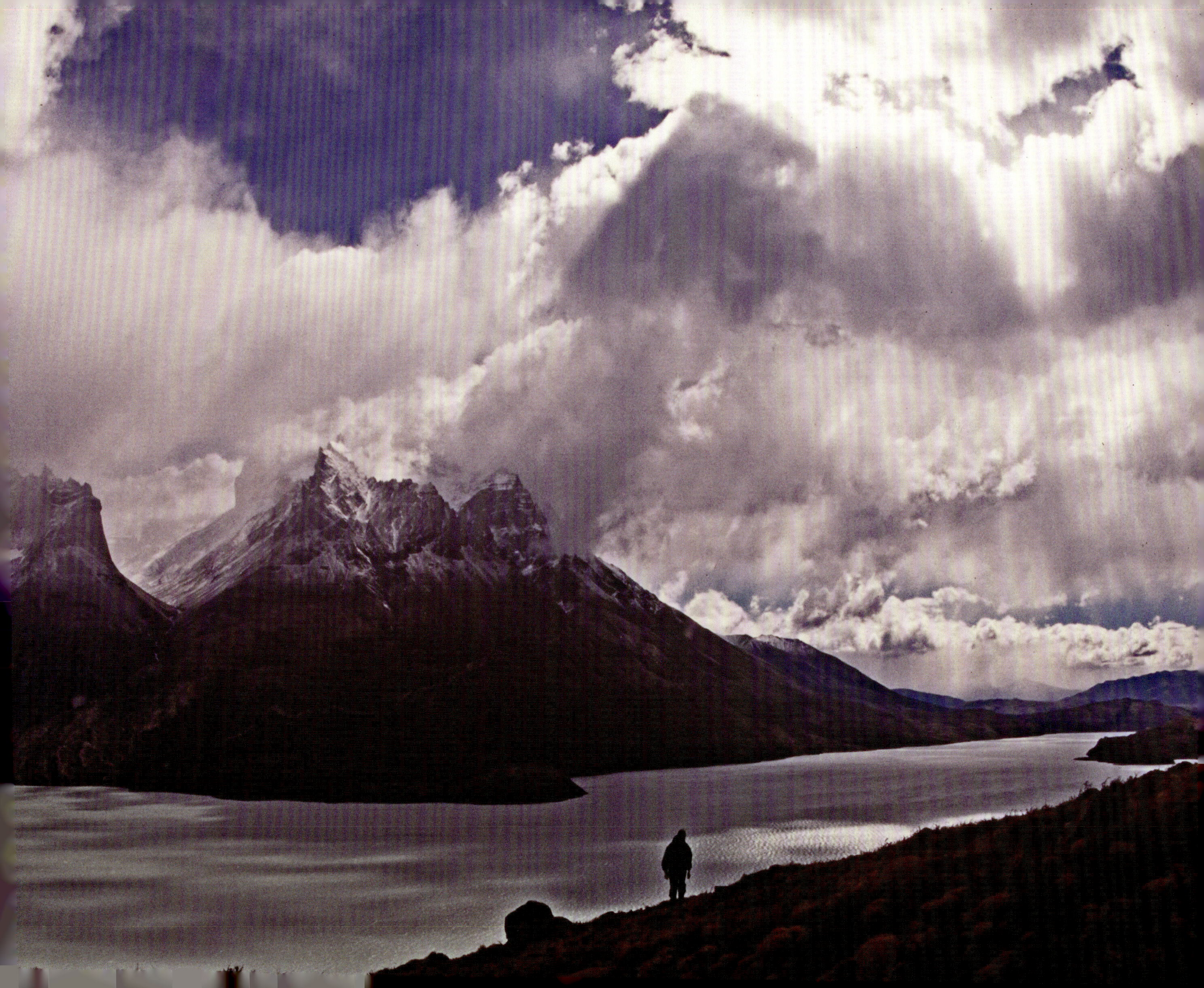

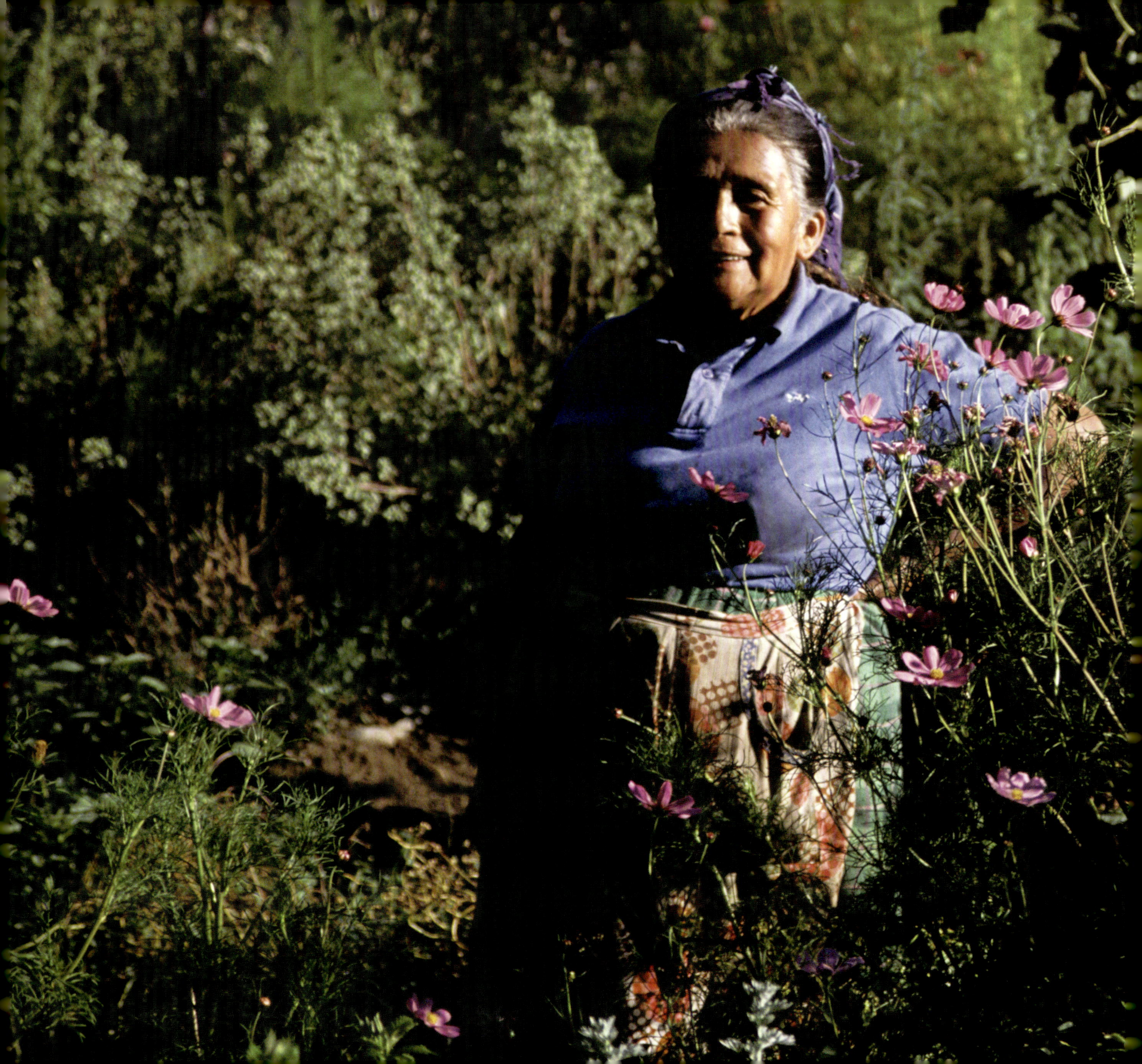

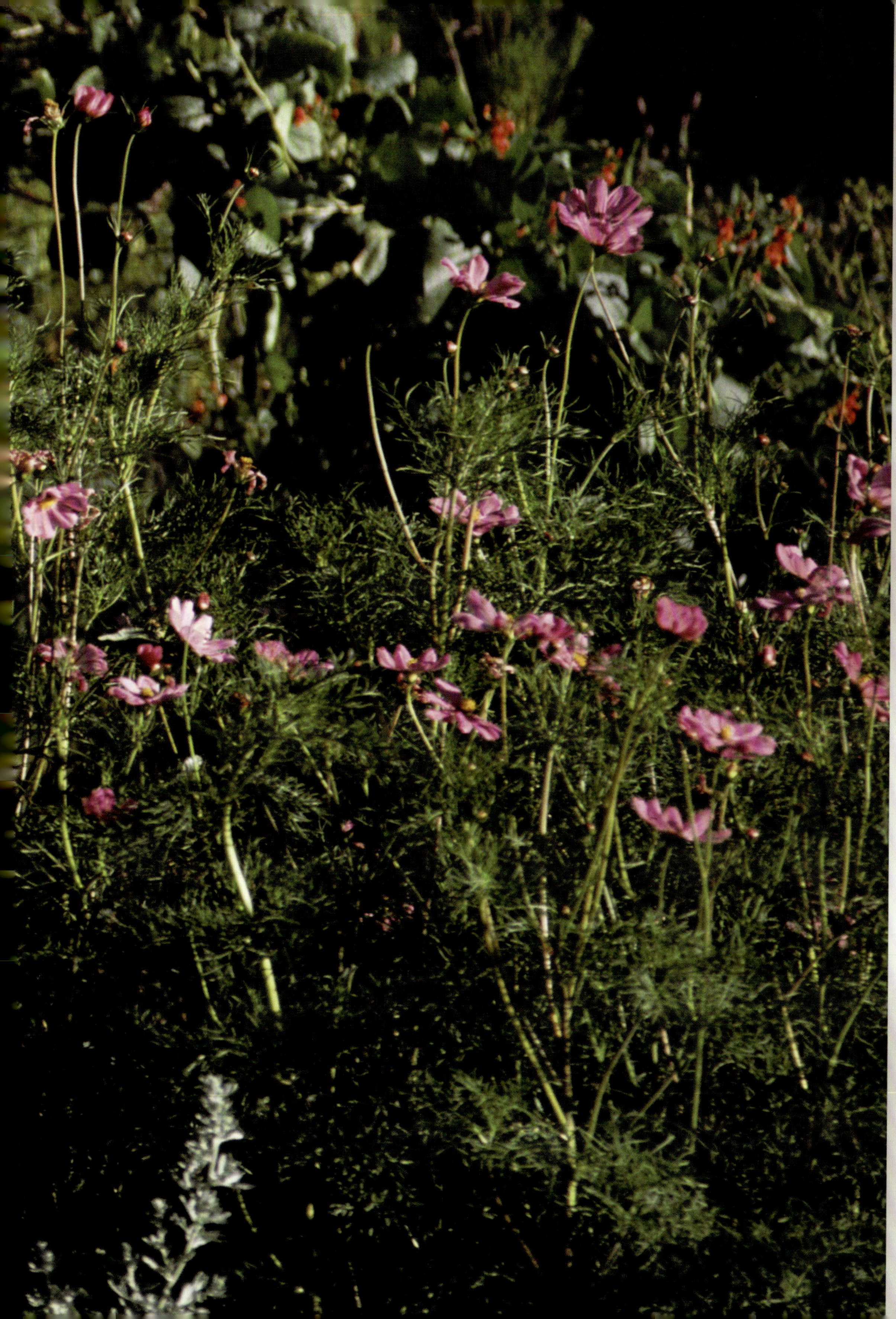

In three words I can sum up everything I have learned about life. It goes on.

- Robert Frost

168

A few years back, deep in the *Cañon de Bio Bio* in the south of Chile, a Puenche Indian woman named Maria could be found happily at work in her garden close by the great *Rio Bio Bio.* Sadly, and in spite of valiant efforts by conservationists and river runners from around the world, two dams were ultimately constructed on the venerable river. Maria's flower-filled garden and much of the other fertile bottom lands in the *Cañon,* the ancestoral domain of the Puenches where they had existed happily for centuries, as well as some of the world's greatest whitewater, have now disappeared forever.

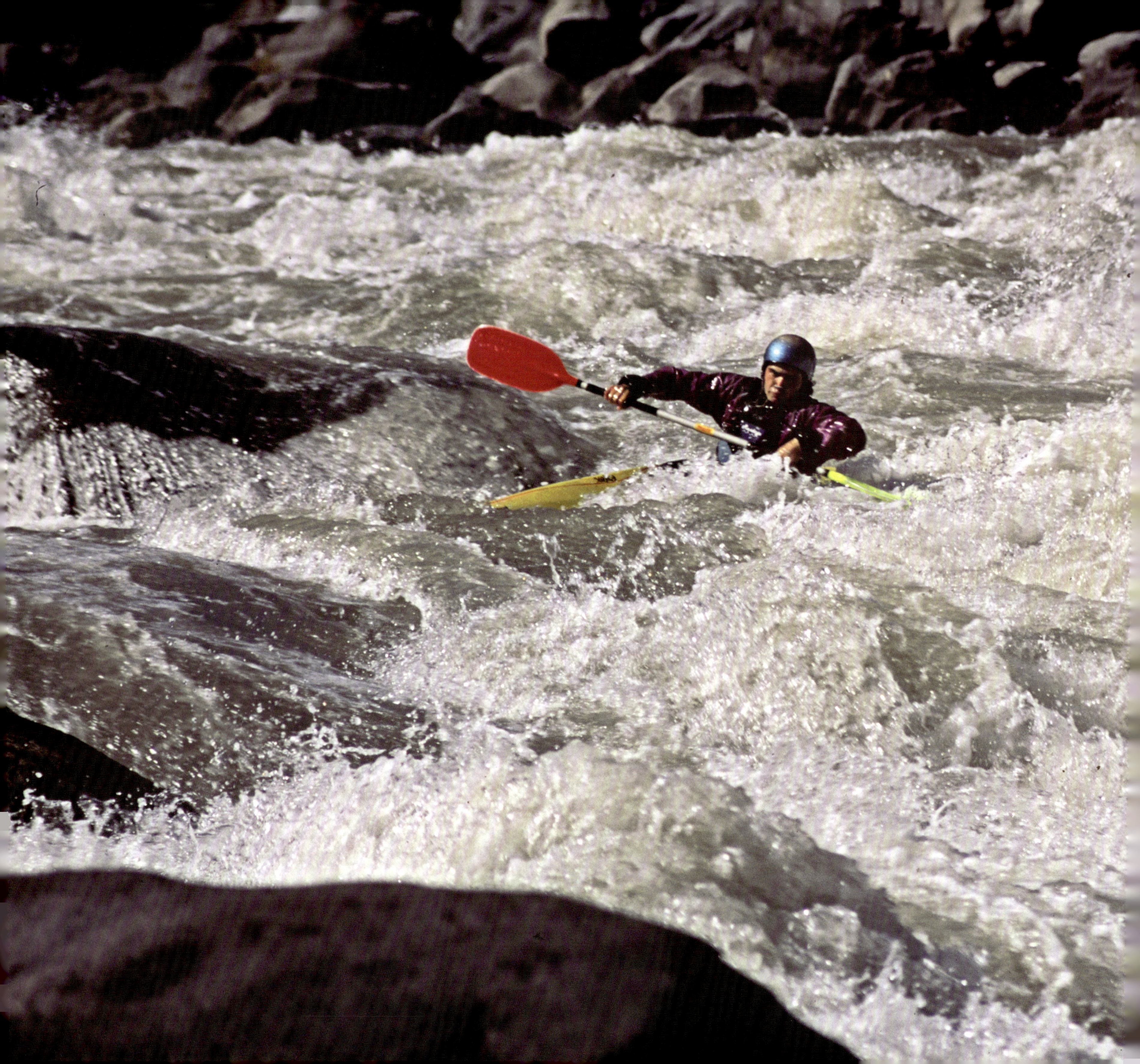

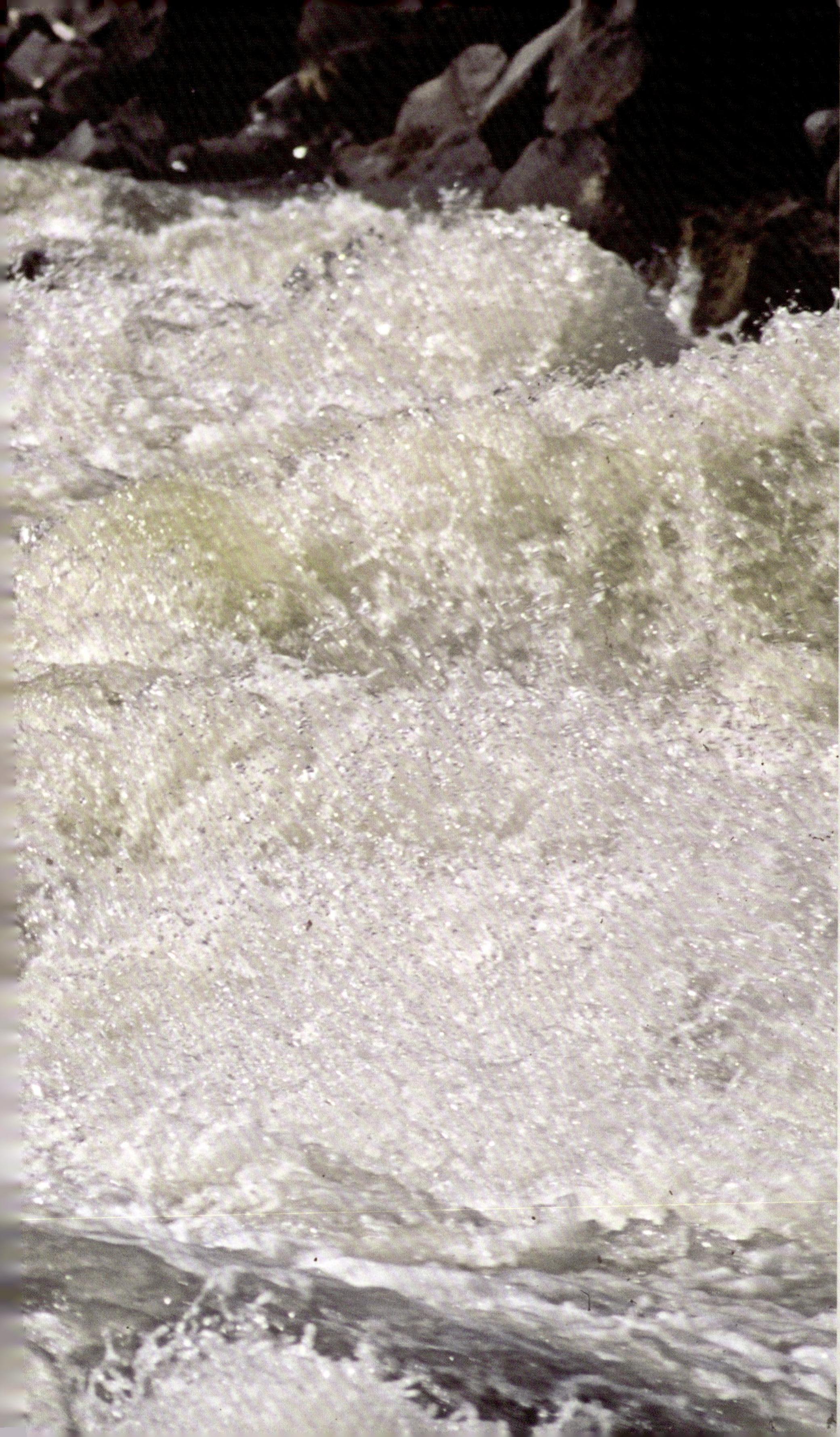

The moment you drop into a big rapid, your concentration is absolute. Any fear you might have had is gone - there is no room for it.

- Bob McDougall, in the film *Paucartambo, The Rest Of The River* by John Armstrong

Former whitewater champion of Chile Jaime Prado drops into legendary class IV rapid Lava South on the *Rio Bio Bio.* 20 year-old Jaime was serving as a safty boater for a group of Americans and Chileans, including Bobby, Michael and Max Kennedy, (three sons nof RFK), who were rafting down the river. Conservationists from the two countries had united to stand in solidarity with the Pehuenche Indians in opposition to two dams a foreign utility company was planning to build on the river. But in spite of valiant efforts by the river community and many others, the beautiful, once free *Bio Bio* has now been dammed and lands the Pehuenches occupied for thousands of years are now flooded and gone forever.

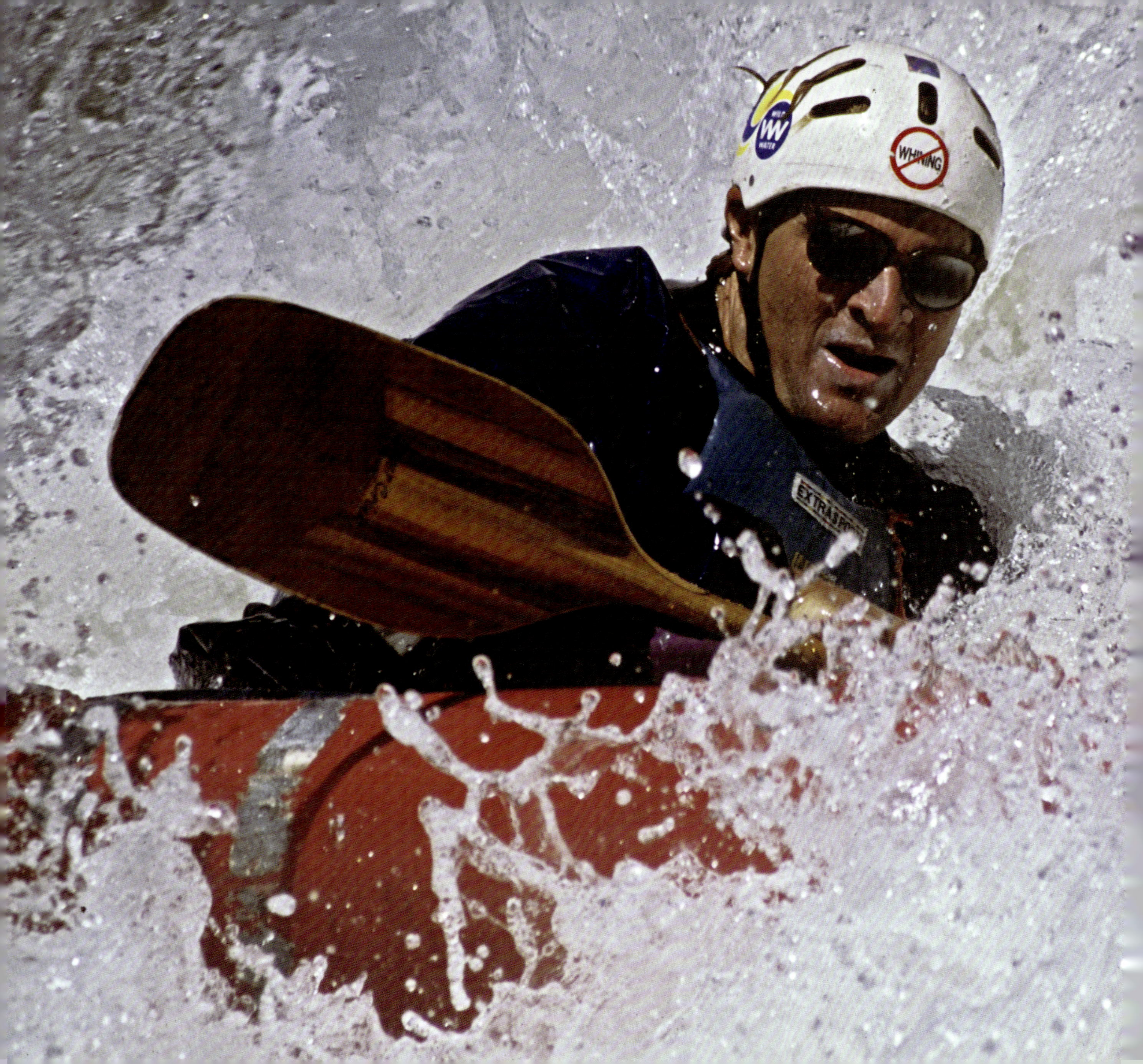
WHINING

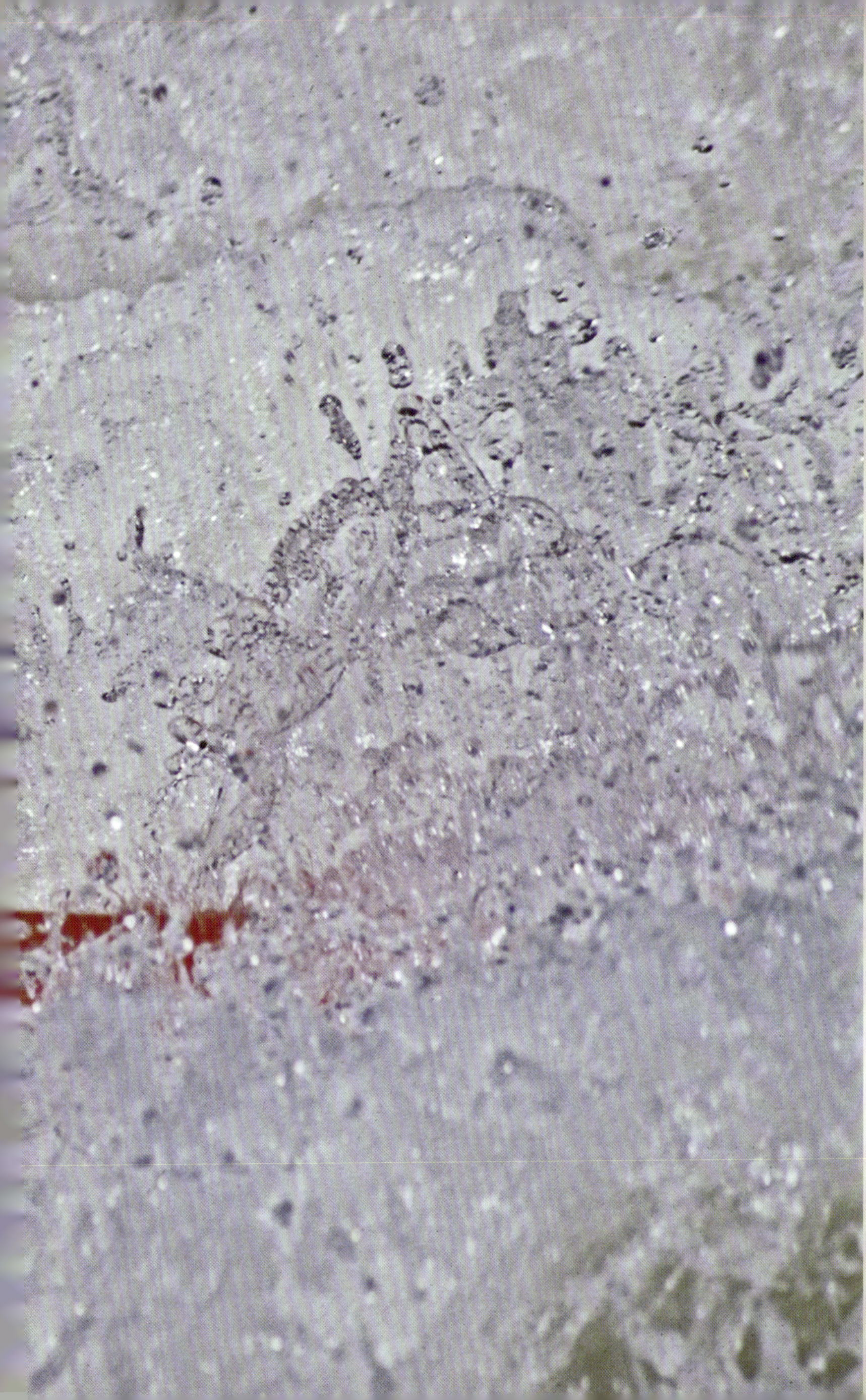

Boldness has genius and power in it.

- Johann von Goethe

172

Former Olympian kayaker Chris Spelius was among the first to challenge the colossal whitewater coursing down from the Andes in the south of Chile. Word soon spread of a treasureland of wildwater in the southern hemisphere - and it was only natural for "Spe" to begin shepherding other sufficiently skilled kayakers down the rivers he had discovered. Rafters followed and by the 1980s the Rios *Futaleufu, Bio Bio* and many others had become world renowned river running destinations. Yet in spite of desperate efforts by Spelius and many others, the first of two dams was built on the *Bio Bio* in 1993. Sadly, like free-flowing rivers all around our fast-developing world, those in Chile continue to be prime targets for dam building by international business interests. Fortuntely and due in part to fervent local oppostion, the *Rio Futaleufu* and the Baker further south in Chile still flow free today.

Courage is the price life exacts for granting us peace.

- Amelia Earhart

173

In the early 90s, international utility giant Endesa, the Chilean government and the World Bank conspired to dam the great *Rio Bio-Bio* in southern Chile. Consevationists and river runners from around the world rallied in defense of the much-cherished river, but to no avail. The ancestoral homelands of the Pehuenche Indians have now vanished beneath rising water from the dams, and some awesome world class whitewater, like fearsome *El Diente* (the Fang) rapid, run here by Michael Powers and photographed by Bruno Confortino, is now lost forever.

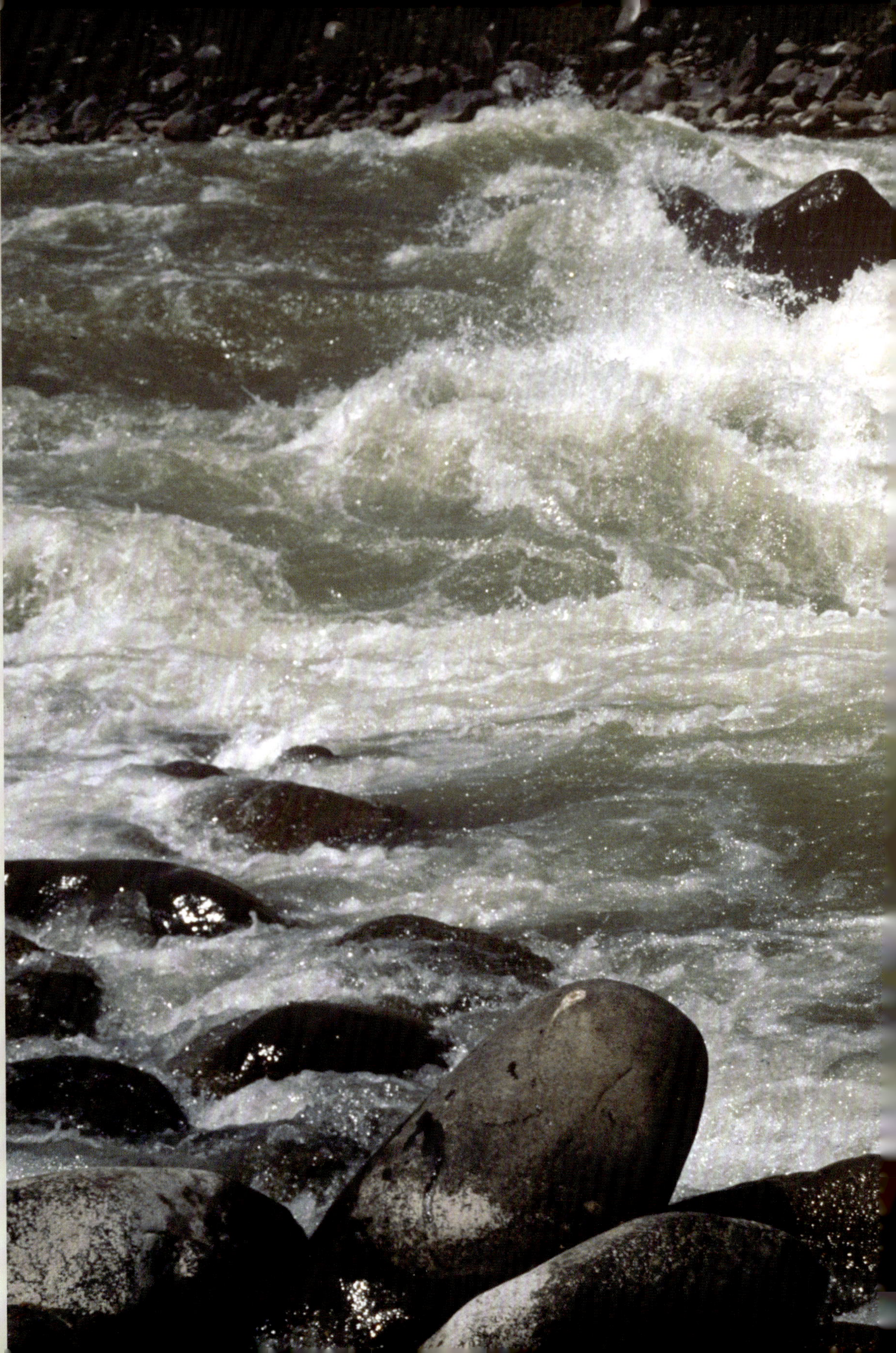

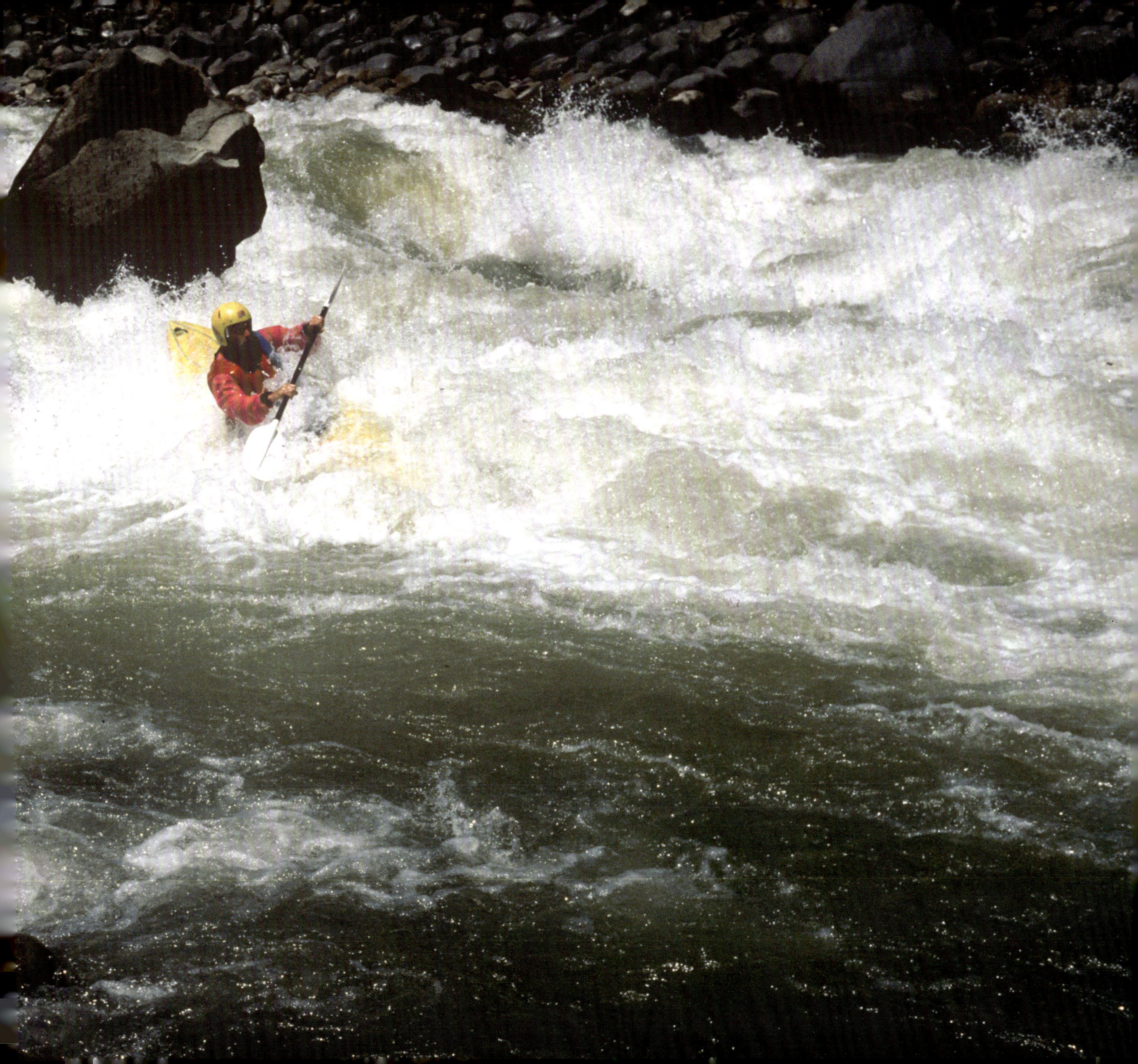

I think over my small adventures, my fears... those small ones that seemed so big and all the things I had to do. Yet there is only one thing - one great thing. To live to see the new light that dawns and fills the world.

- old Inuit song

Somewhere along the rugged wilderness coast of southern Chile, professional kayak guide Jaime Prado returns to the sea for a final exploratory paddle before sunset. Prado and two North American *amigos* were kayaking along the sparsely populated and sometimes roadless coast, searching for ocean front land to purchase for an outdoor adventure and education center they dreamed of building. Their quest for just the right property still continues today.

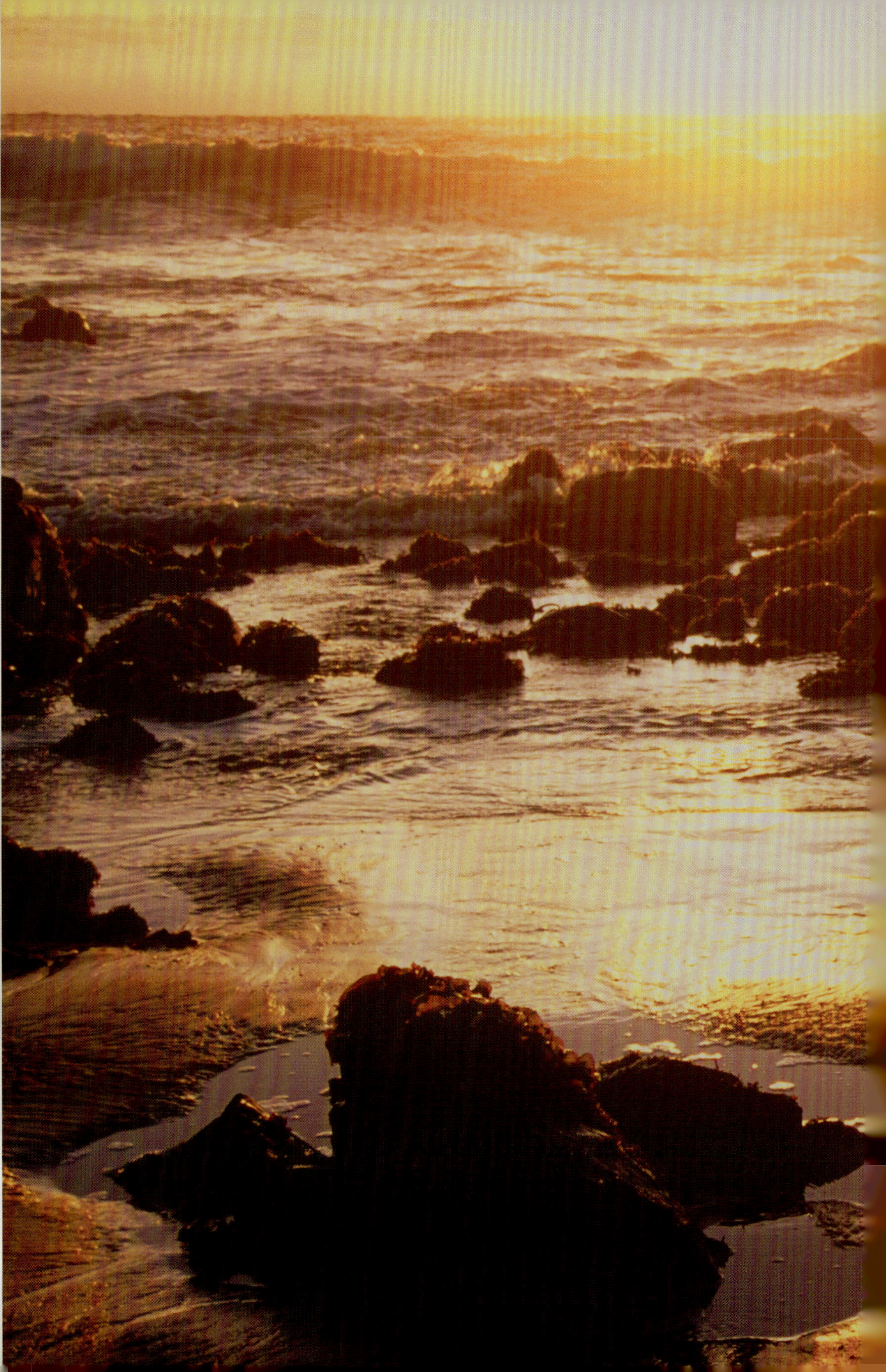

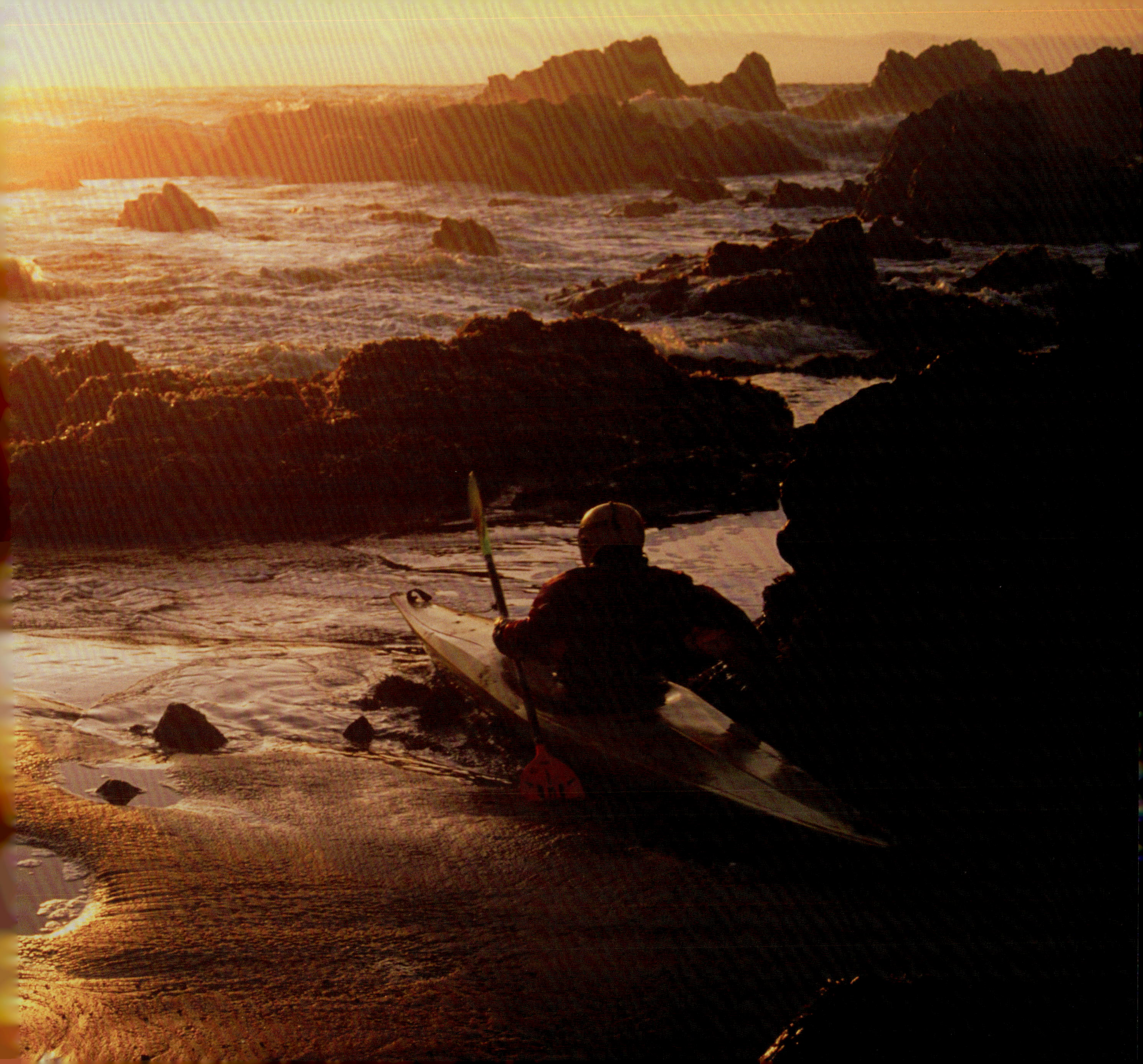

Life is either a daring adventure or nothing.

- Helen Keller

Total concentration is demanded of skilled kayaker Jaime Prado as he paddles through breaking seas and jagged rock along a typically rugged stretch of the Patagonia coast in southern Chile on a stormy day. The frigid waters of the Humbolt Current flowing from Antarctica generate weather consistently more volitile here than at equivalent latitudes in North America.

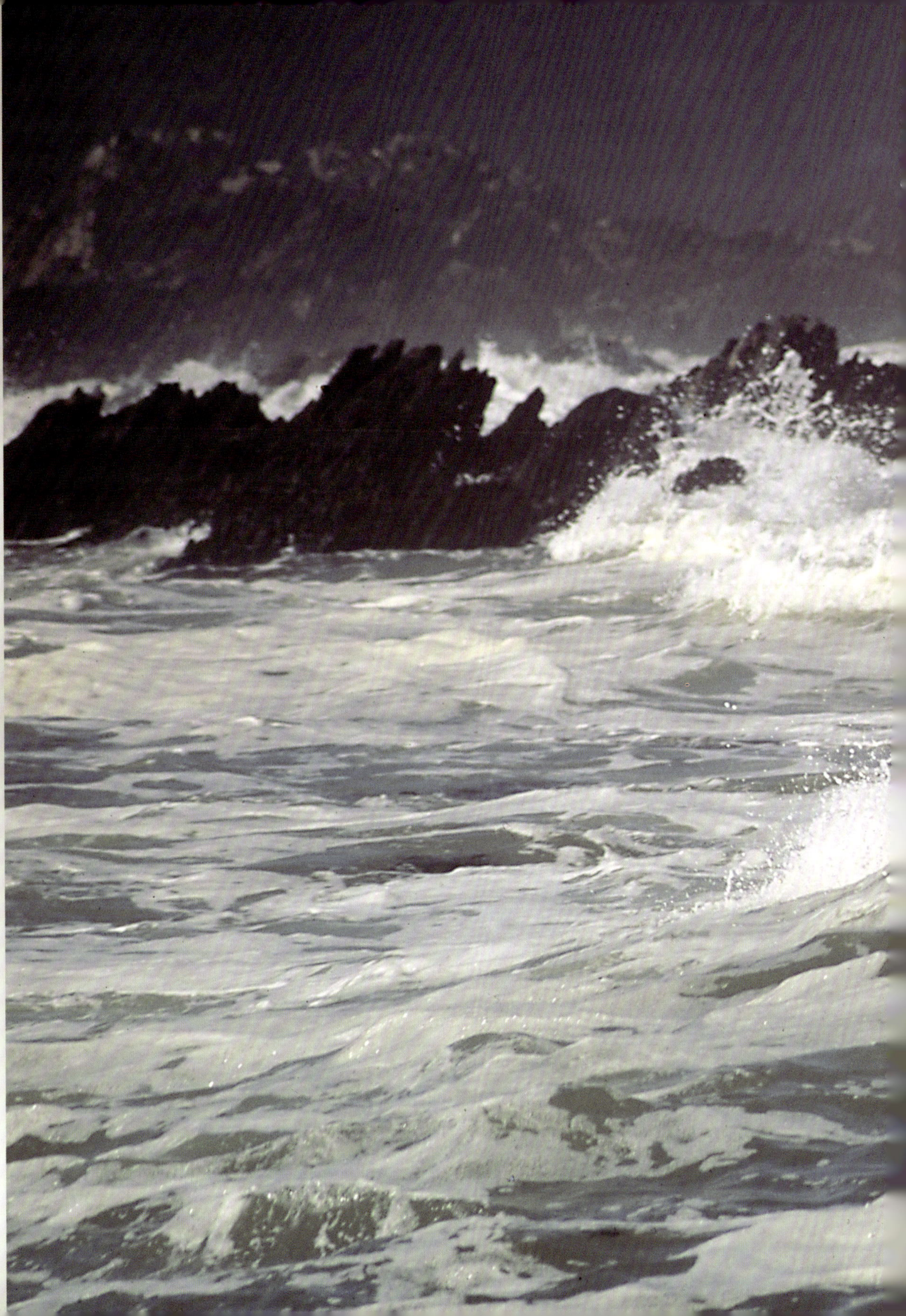

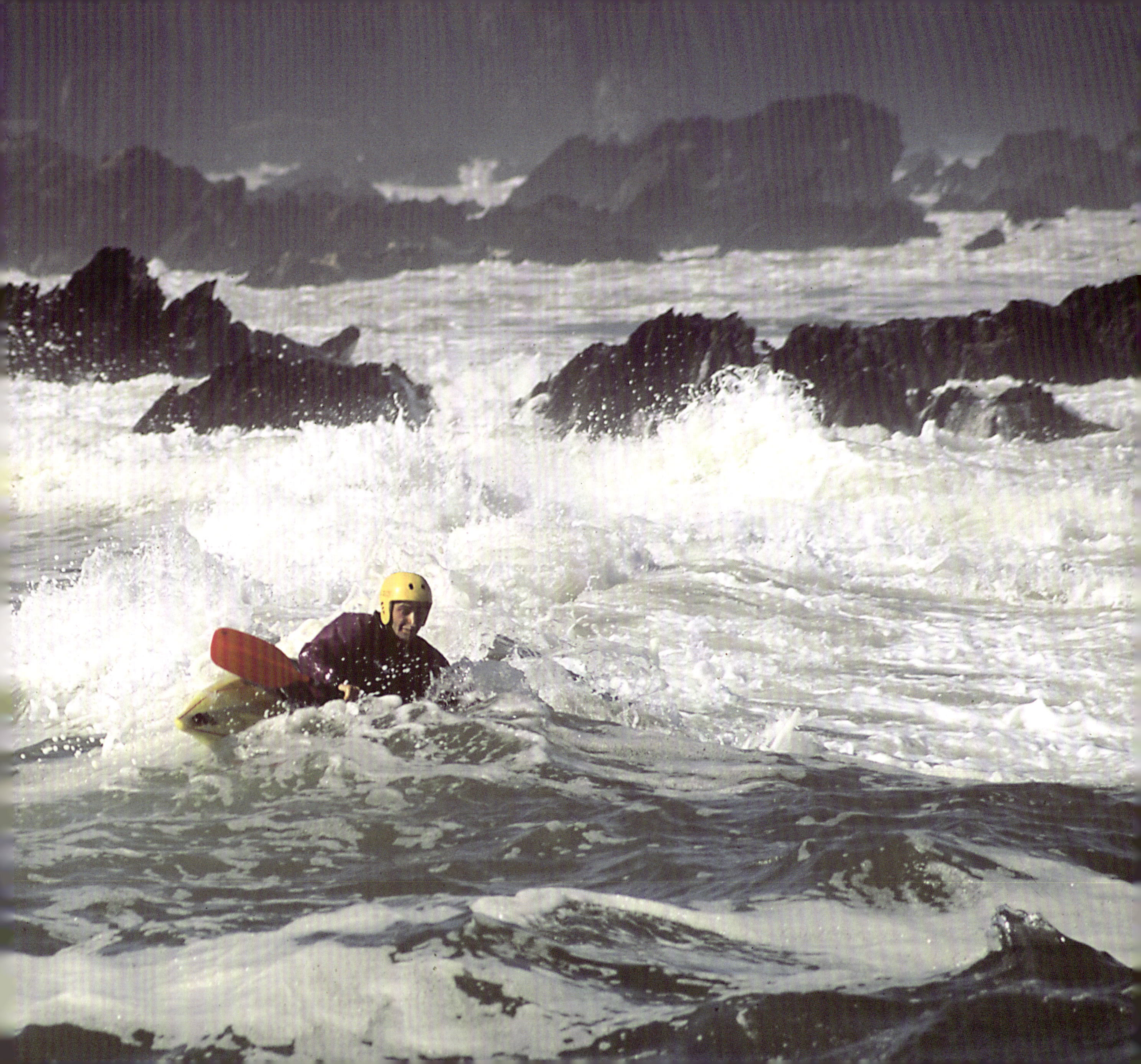

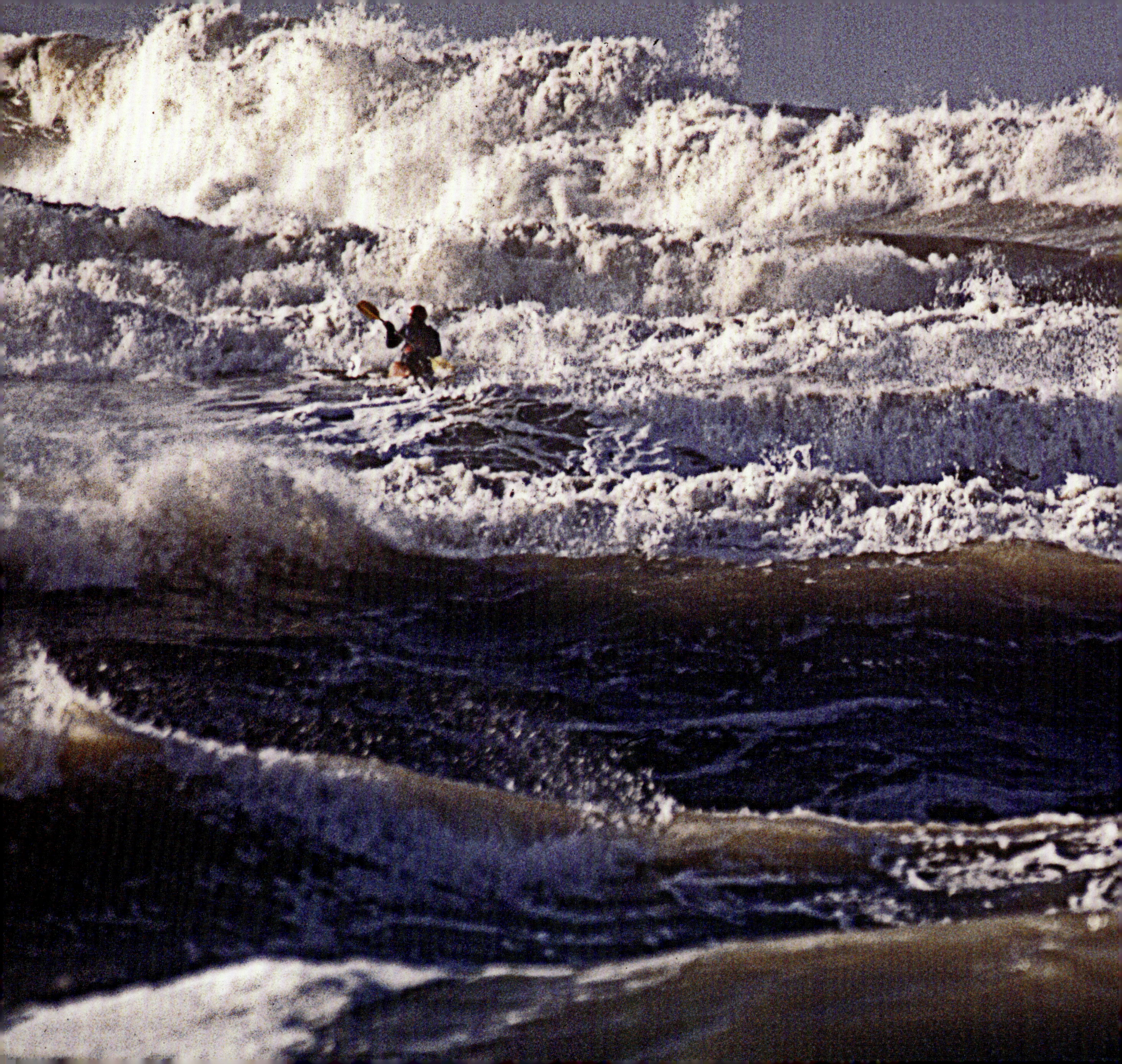

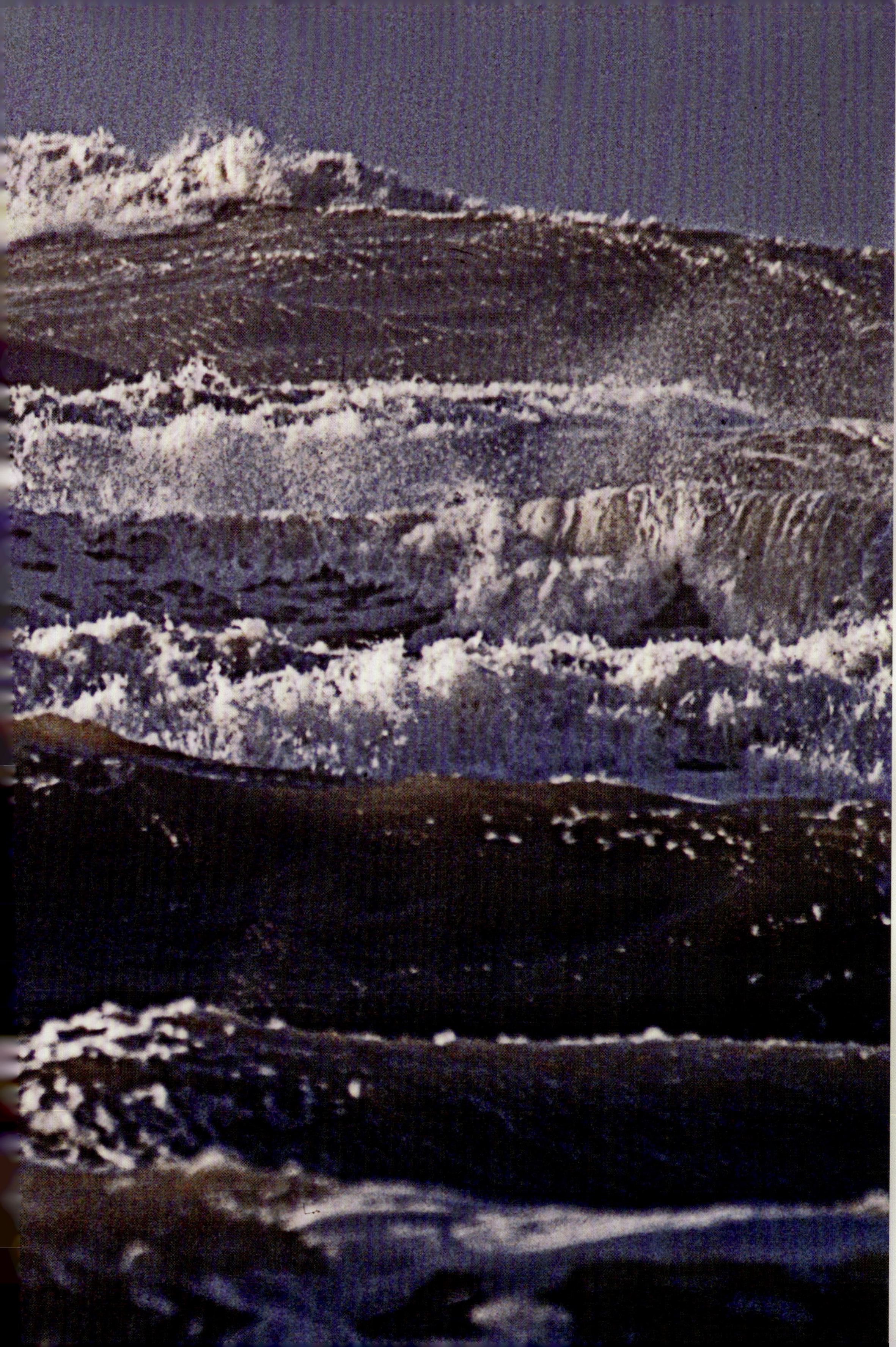

I have known the sea
too long to believe
in its decency.

- Joseph Conrad

An expert, properly equipped sea kayaker with a bombproof Eskimo roll in a skirted kayak (or open-deck Tsunami type boat with a seat belt) is arguably more capable of enduring extreme storm surf conditions in the open sea than any other form of ocean traveler - except perhaps crewmembers of a highly specialized Coast Guard surf rescue boat.

It is remarkable too, how the development and use of kayaks evolved through an evolutionary process that may have taken thousands of years, in the frigid Arctic regions of North America. Stone age hunter-gatherers, eager to gain access to the abundant marine wildlife they could see from shore, learned to fashion the first kayaks from materials at hand - basically, driftwood and animal skins. Later the Russian fur traders arrived and discovered the Aleut's proficiency at hunting sea otters from their tiny boats, or *baidarkas*, (skin boats) as the Russians called them. The ruthless traders promptly enslaved the Native Americans and forced them to hunt otters for them, which soon decimated the once prolific sea otter population along the Pacific coast all the way to Baja, Mexico.

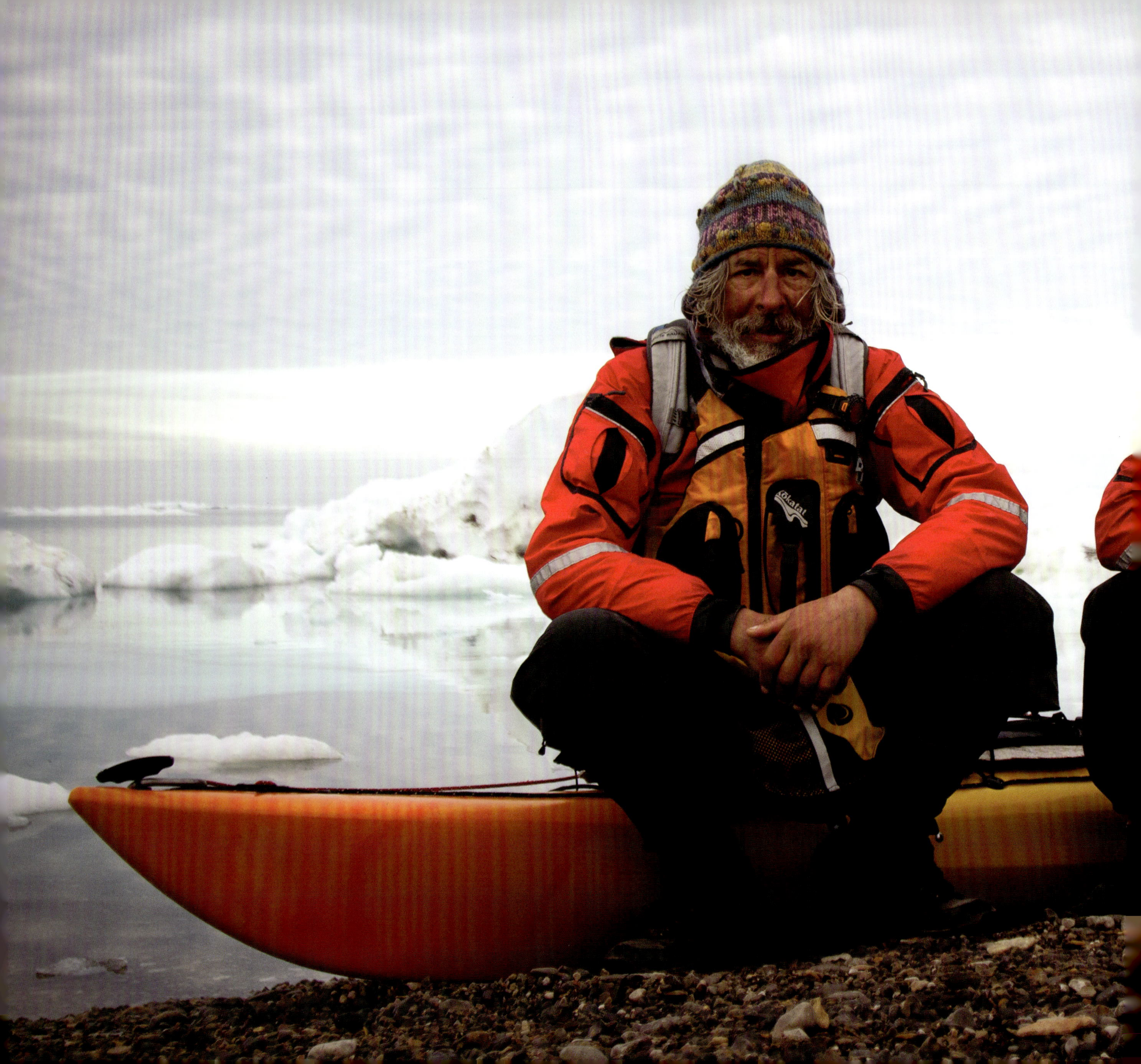

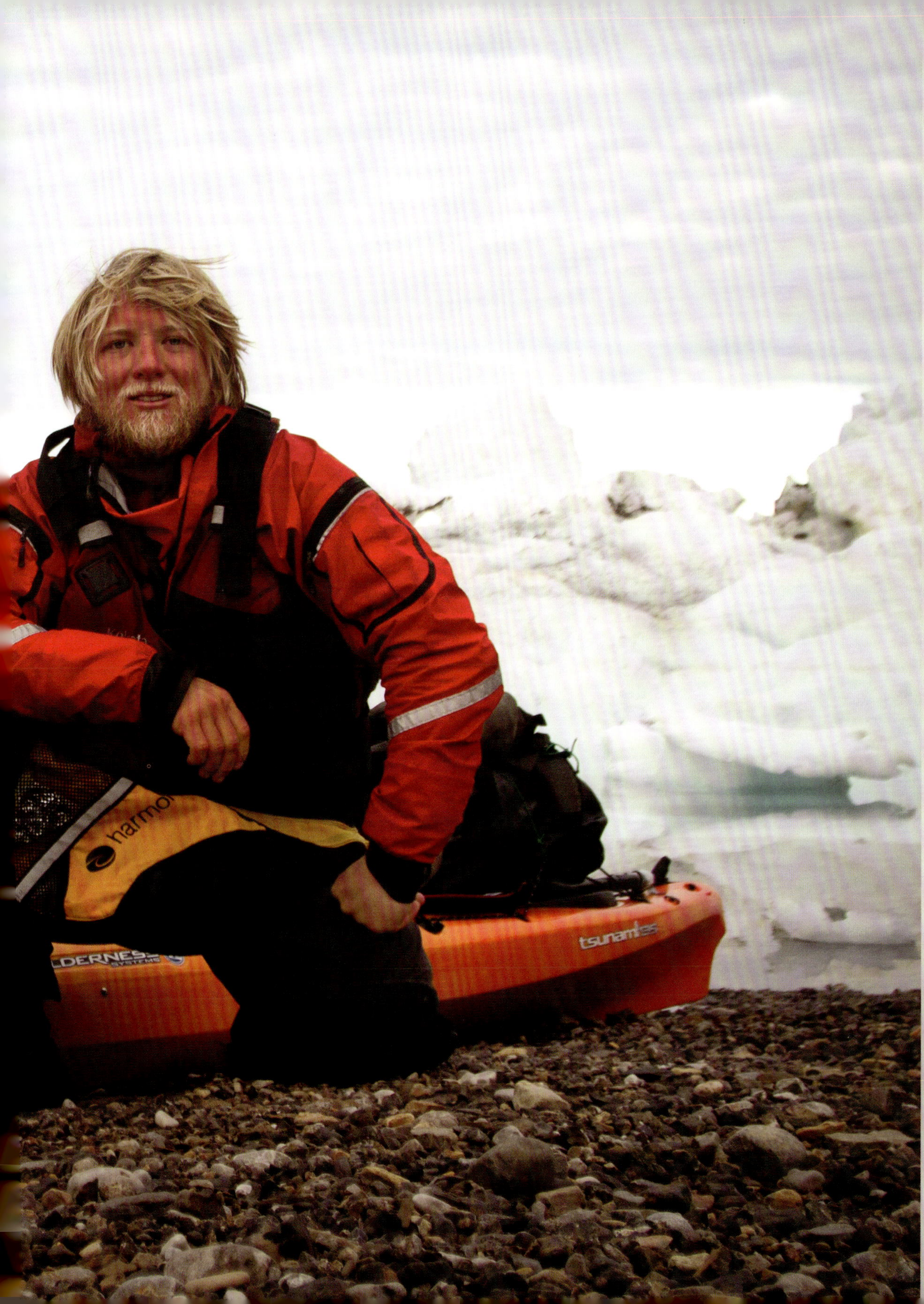

Pain is evanescent, but the richness of a great experience lasts forever.

-Jon Turk, author & Arctic explorer

Jon Turk and Erik Boomer rest for a moment in the midst of their daring, highly acclaimed 1,486 mile human-powered circumnavigation of Ellesmere Island in 2010. High in the Canadian Arctic and closer to the North Pole than any other land mass, Ellesmere is the 10th largest island in the world. Because it is totally encased by a frozen sea most of the year, Turk and Boomer knew they could never paddle around the island in the few brief weeks of mid-summer when the shoreline might beome at least partially ice-free. So they set off in May on skis, dragging their heavily- loaded kayaks behind them over the ice. After traveling 800 grueling miles in this way, the sea finally thawed enough to allow them to commence paddling. But in their sea kayaks the dangers continued - constantly shifting ice packs threatened to crush them, huge tusked and territorial walruses surfaced unexpectedly in front of their boats, and hungry polar bears sometimes stalked them. Photograph by Erik Boomer.

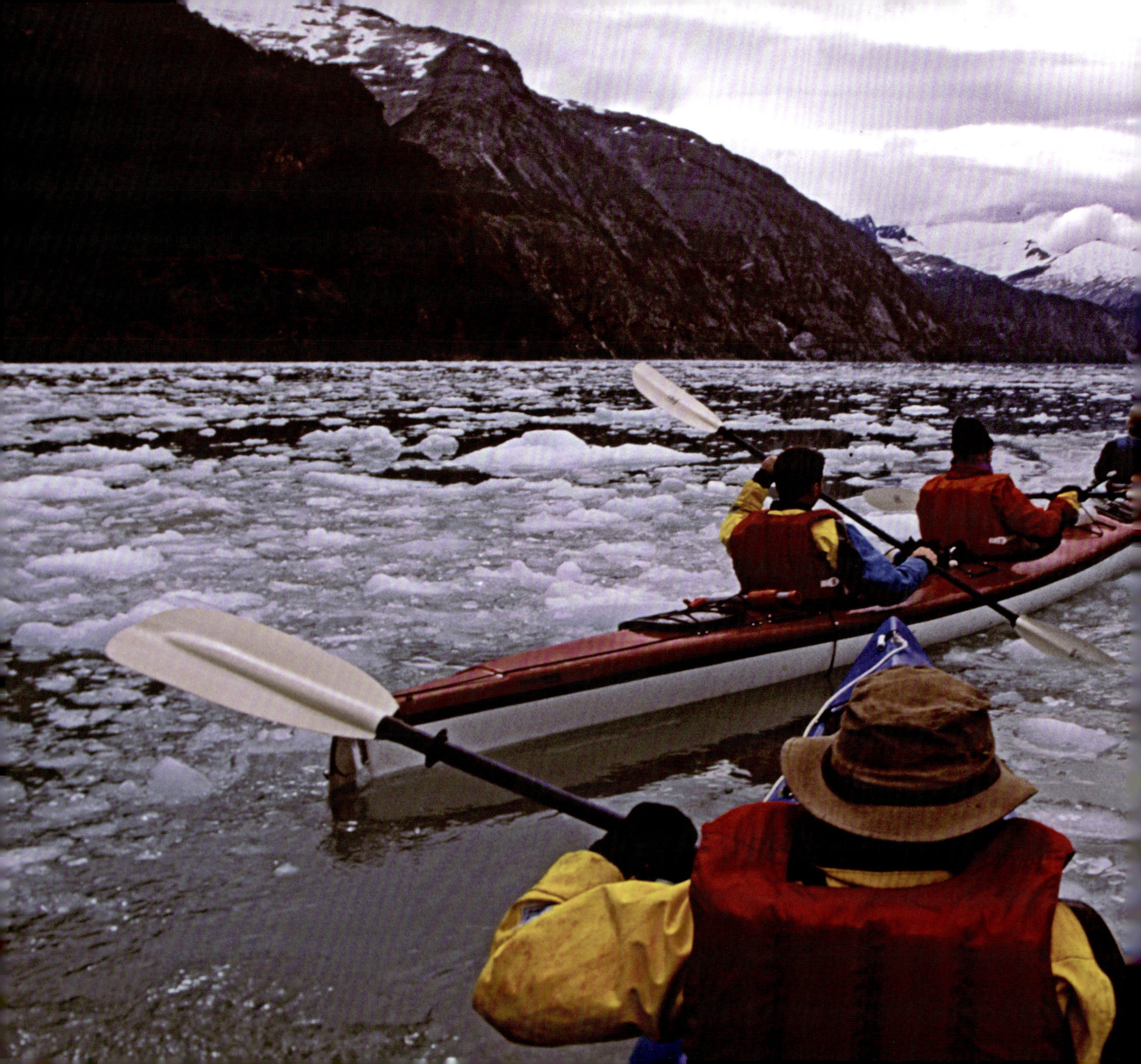

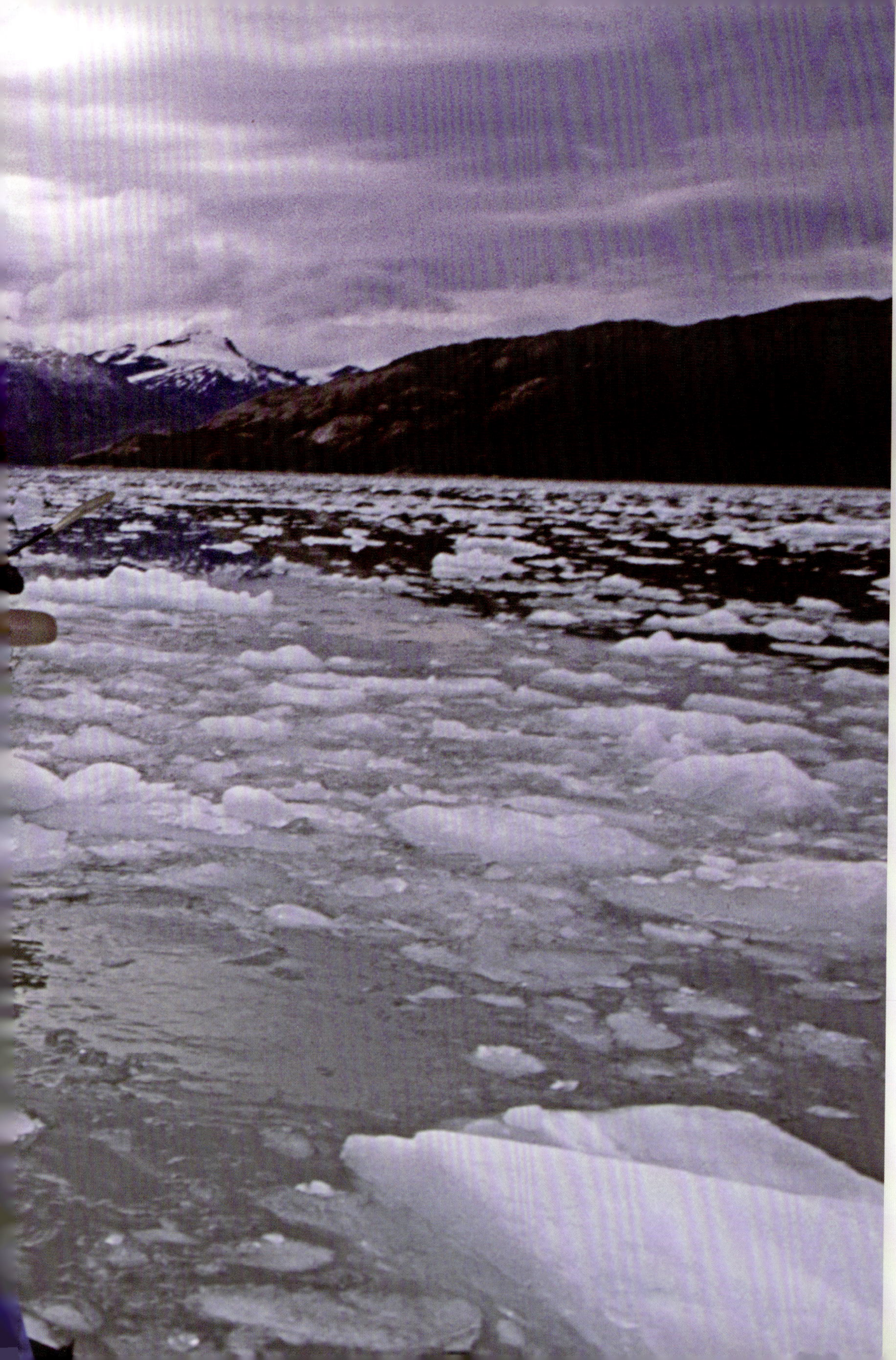

We must always remember with gratitude and admiration, the first sailors who steered their vessels through storms and mists and increased our knowledge of the lands of ice in the south.

- Roald Amundsen, Norgegian explorer who led the first expedition to the South Pole

At the southern tip of South America the Charles Darwin massif rises 8000' to form the craggy backbone of Tierra Del Fuego. Narrow fiords cut back deeply into the glacier-capped mountains. To explore the seldom-seen upper reaches of Fiord Marinelli, a sea kayaking team paddles a slalom course through a maze of brash ice. At the head of the fiord even more dramatic circumstances awaits them. An immense glacier of blue ice flows down from the heights and is continuously calving into the fiord a safe distance from where they paddle, sometimes with great violence and a sound like thunder.

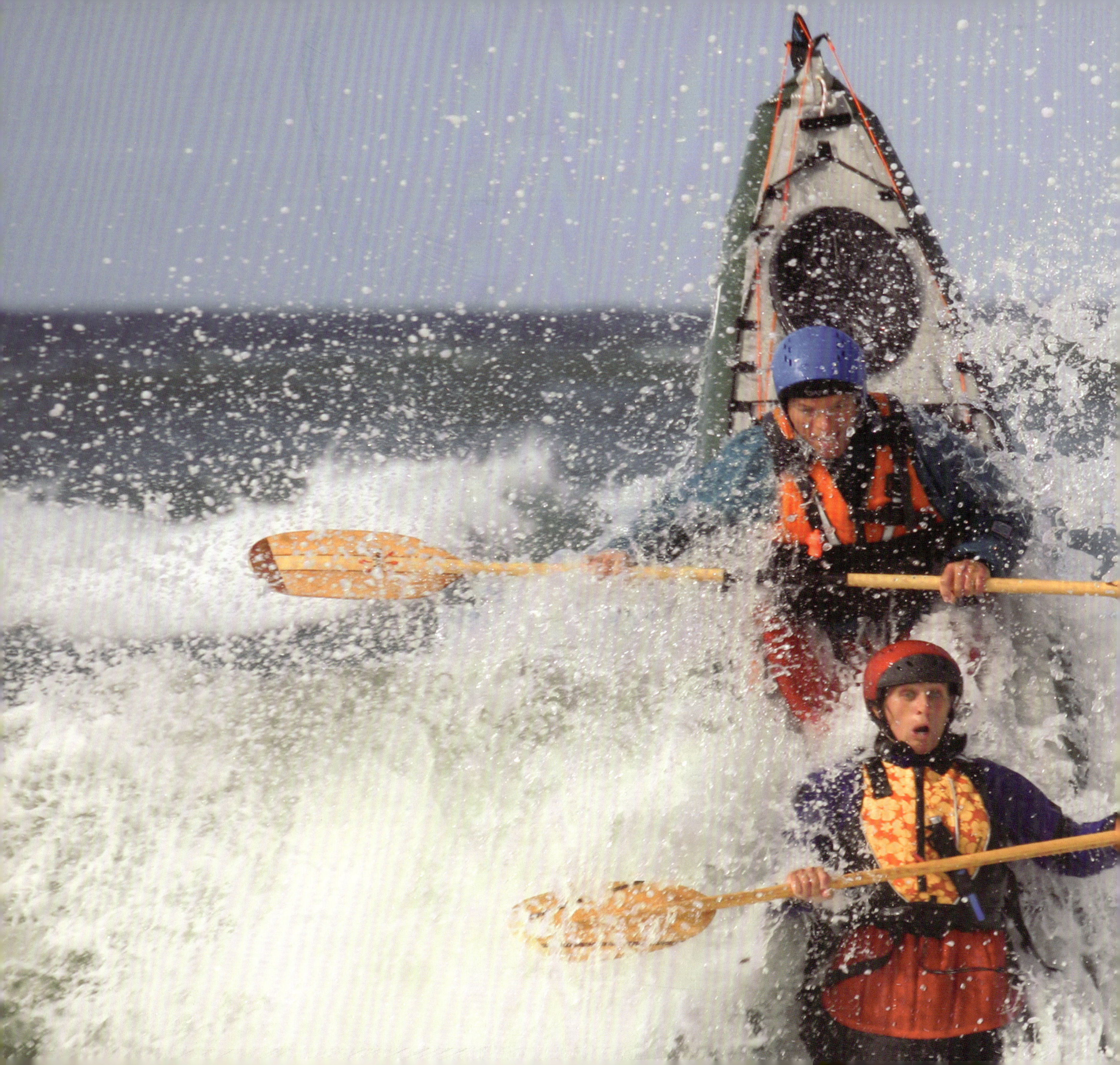

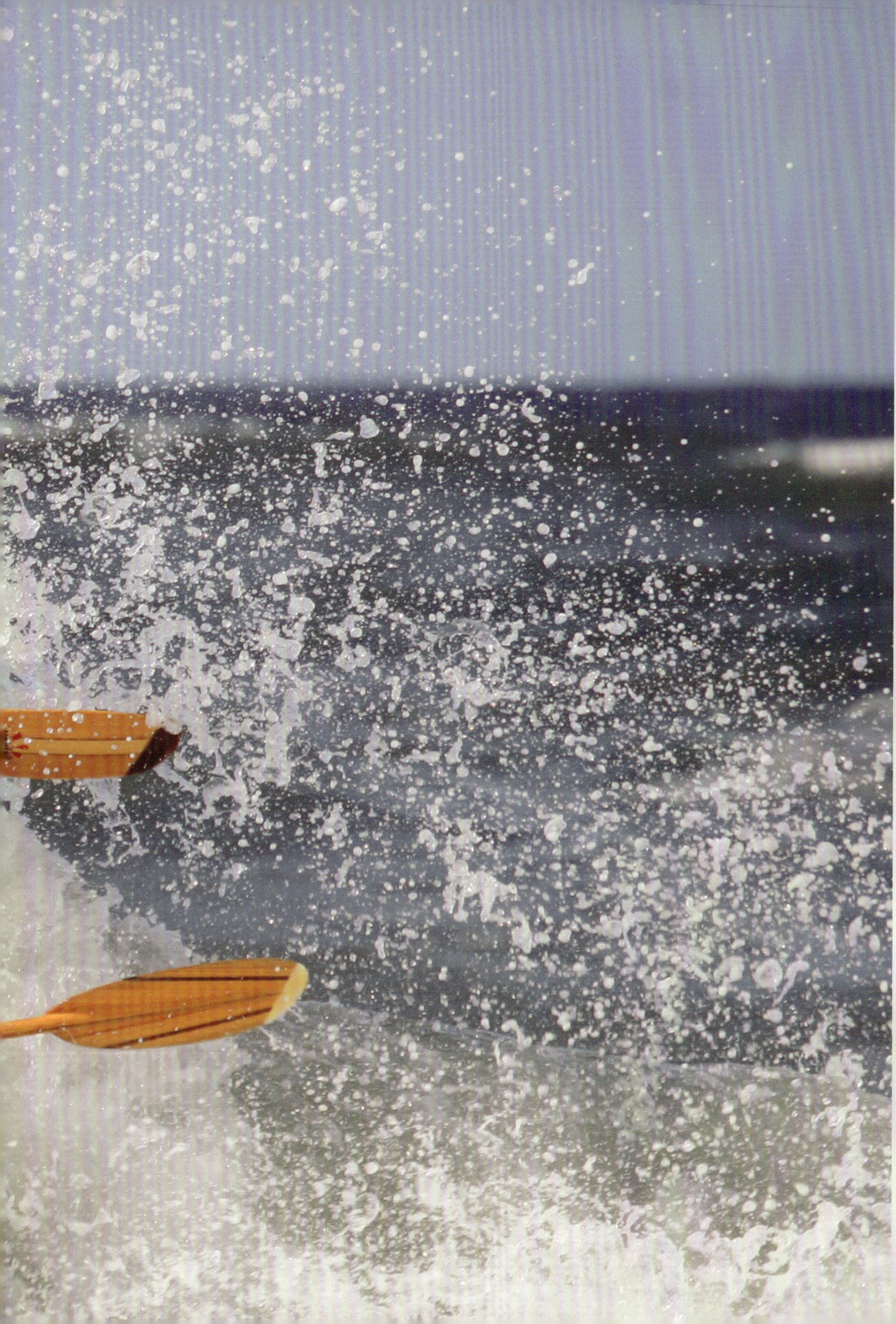

I've developed a
new philosophy...
I only dread
one day at a time.

- Charlie Brown

A first-time paddler gets more than she bargains for when she goes out for a surfing lesson with veteran sea kayak guide Gregory Berman. At Moss Beach a few miles south of San Francisco the sea floor drops off steeply a few feet from shore, allowing waves to nearly reach the beach before breaking. This enabled Berman to surf their inflatable tandem kayak right up to the shore before executing a dramatic 'nose stand' maneuver, much to the surprise of his unsuspecting passenger.

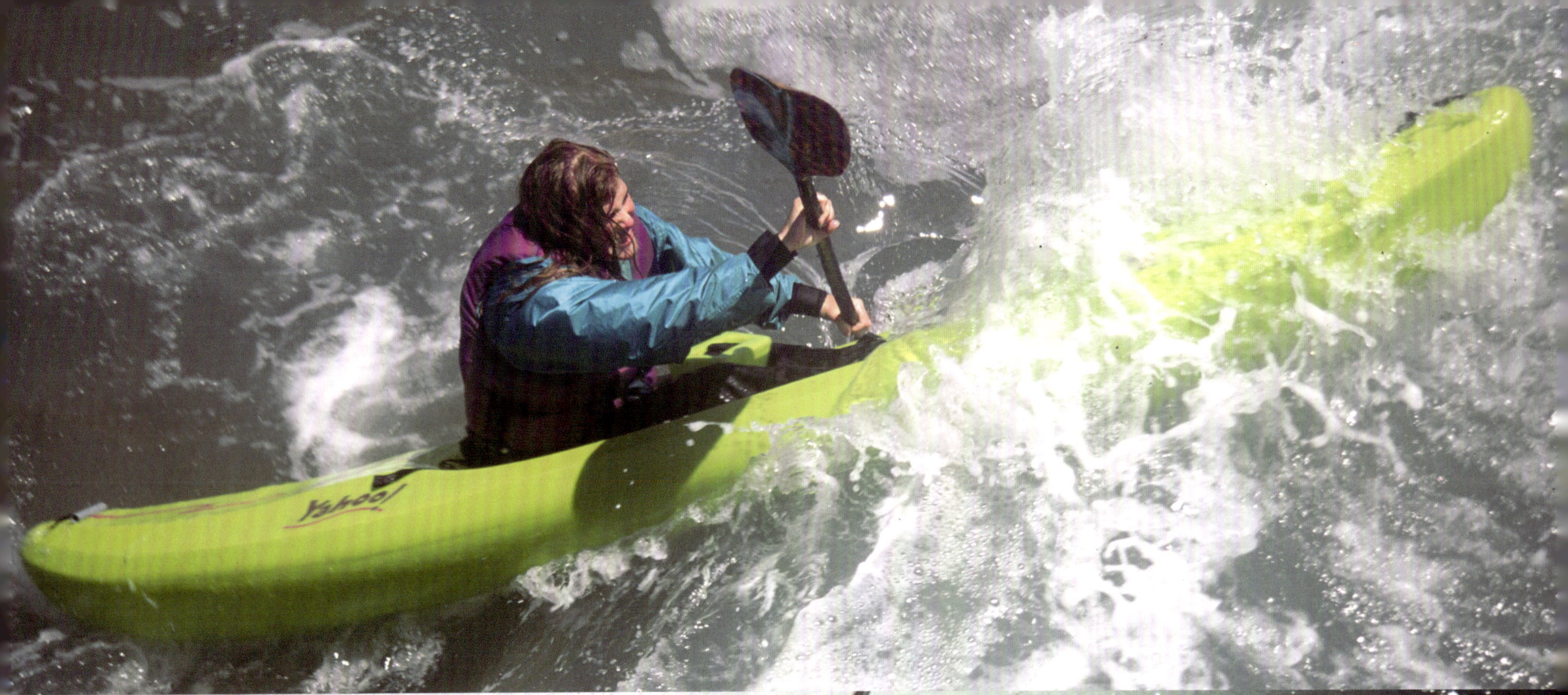

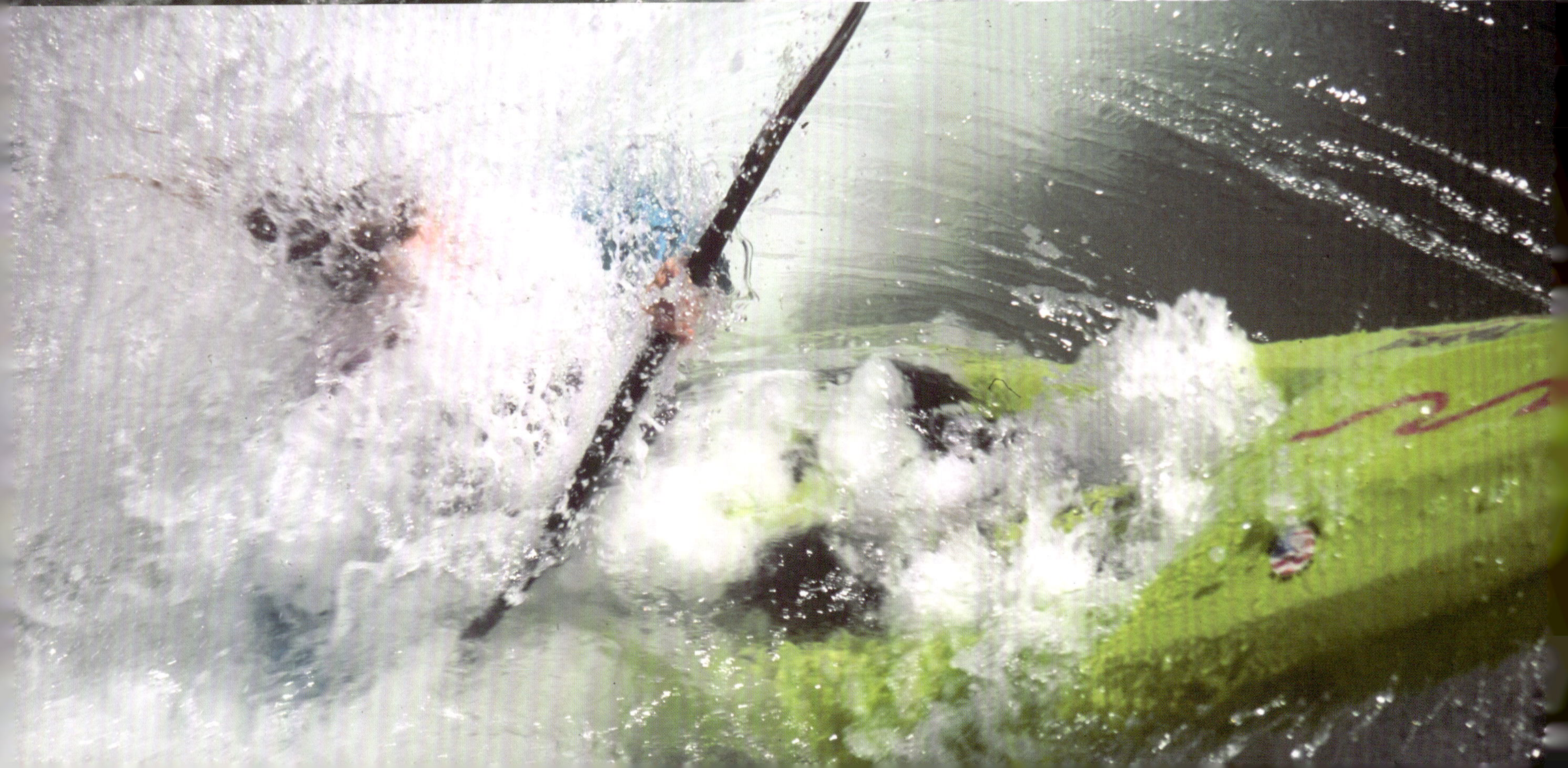

Nothing can replace courage,
a resounding motivation
and a little bit of luck.

- Sir Edmund Hillary

Tiaje was a relatively inexperienced kayaker who had never paddled in breaking surf before. Yet she was strong of spirit and embraced the challenge with passion and courage.

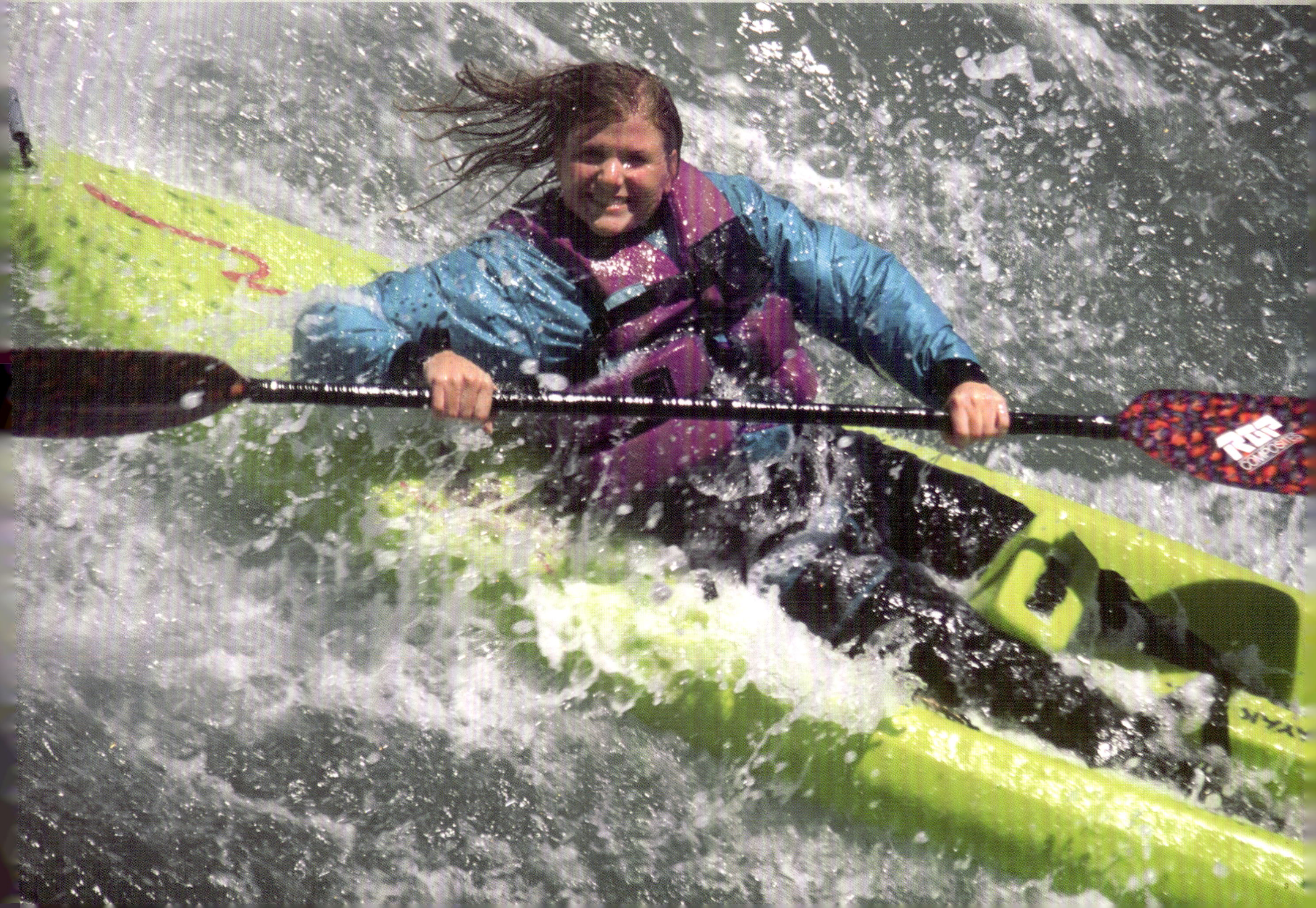

The miracle of man is not how how far he has sunk, but how magnificently he has risen. We are known among the stars by our poems, not by our corpses.

- Robert Ardrey, from African Genesis

Since ancient times sea tribes have gathered in springtime to engage in contests of skill and endurance. The winner of a kayak race at San Simeon near the south end of Big Sur, charges ashore triumphantly a split second ahead of his closest rival. The race was part of an annual event, the Traditional Arctic Kayak Symposium.

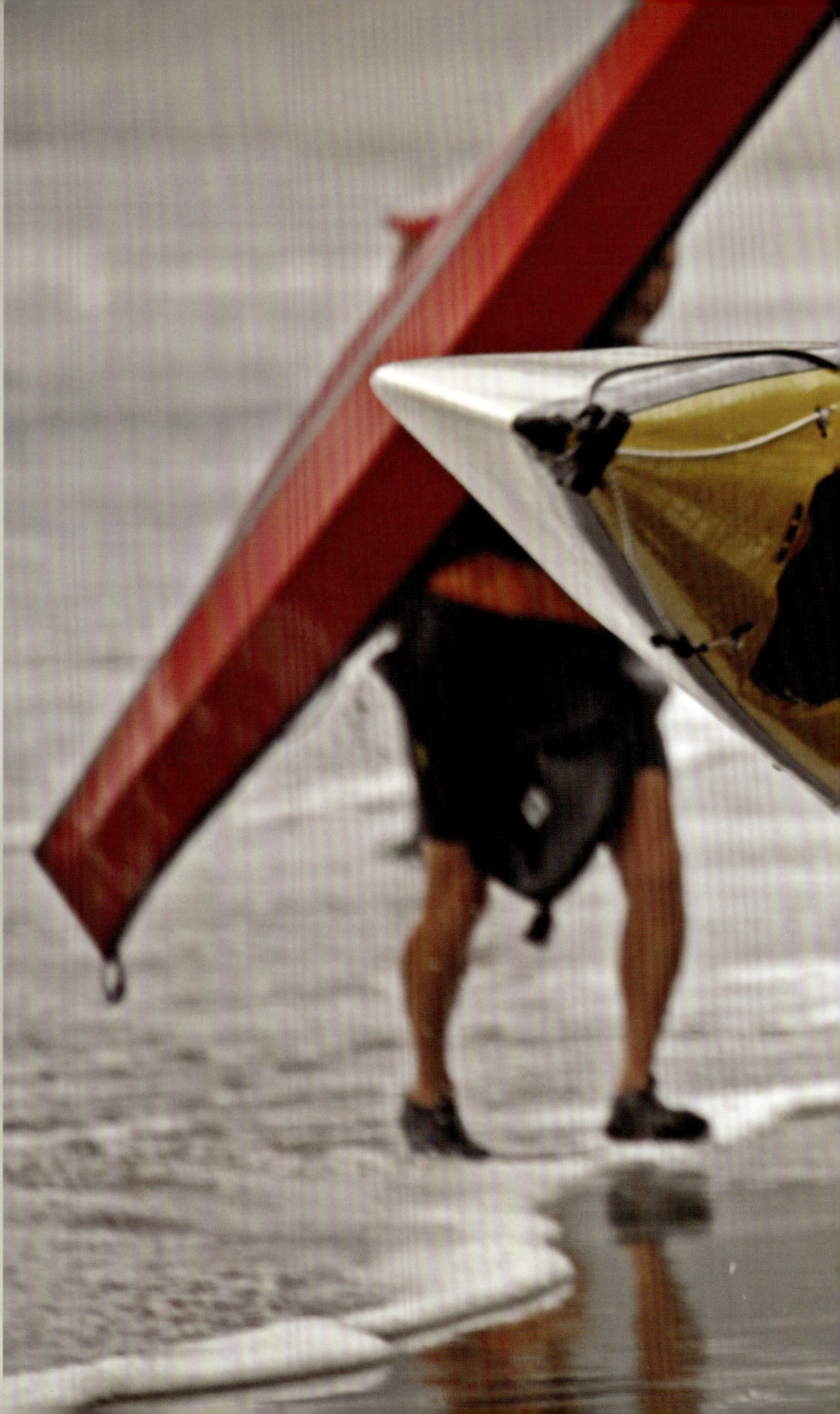

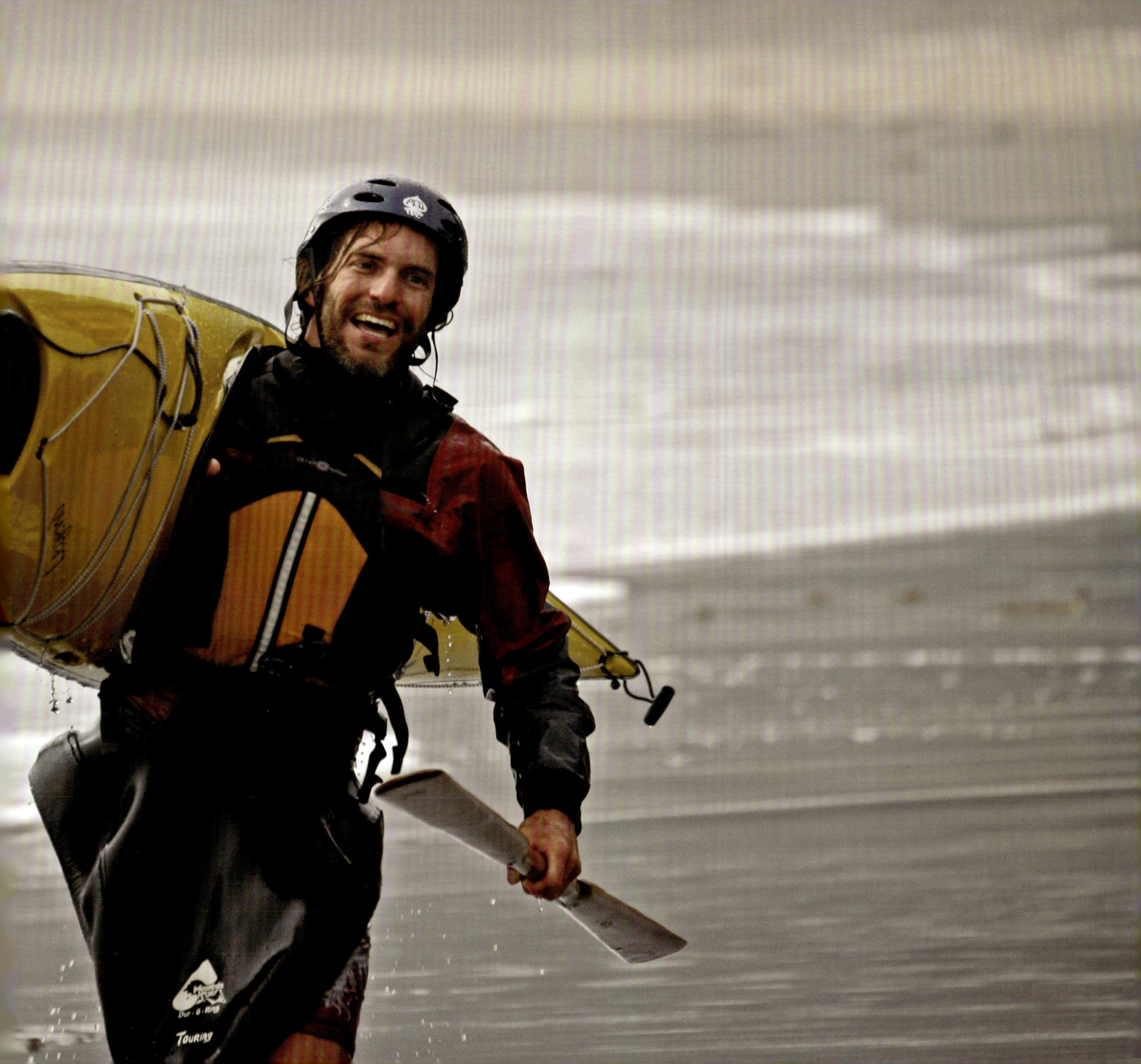
Touring

The first law of our being is that we are set in a delicate network of interdependence with our fellow human beings and with the rest of creation.

- Archbishop Desmond Tutu

September 11, 2001. Everyone remembers exactly where they were and what they were doing on the fateful day of the al-Quaeda suicide attacks in the United States. A team of 13 American climbers, their Russian trip leader Alex and native guides stopped later that morning at a Maasai village in Amboseli National Park in southern Kenya. They were en route to Mt. Kilimanjaro, where they would begin climbing the next day. For the next five days as they climbed towards the 19,341' summit, they received no additional news of the attacks. Photograph by Dr. Richard Wiseman.

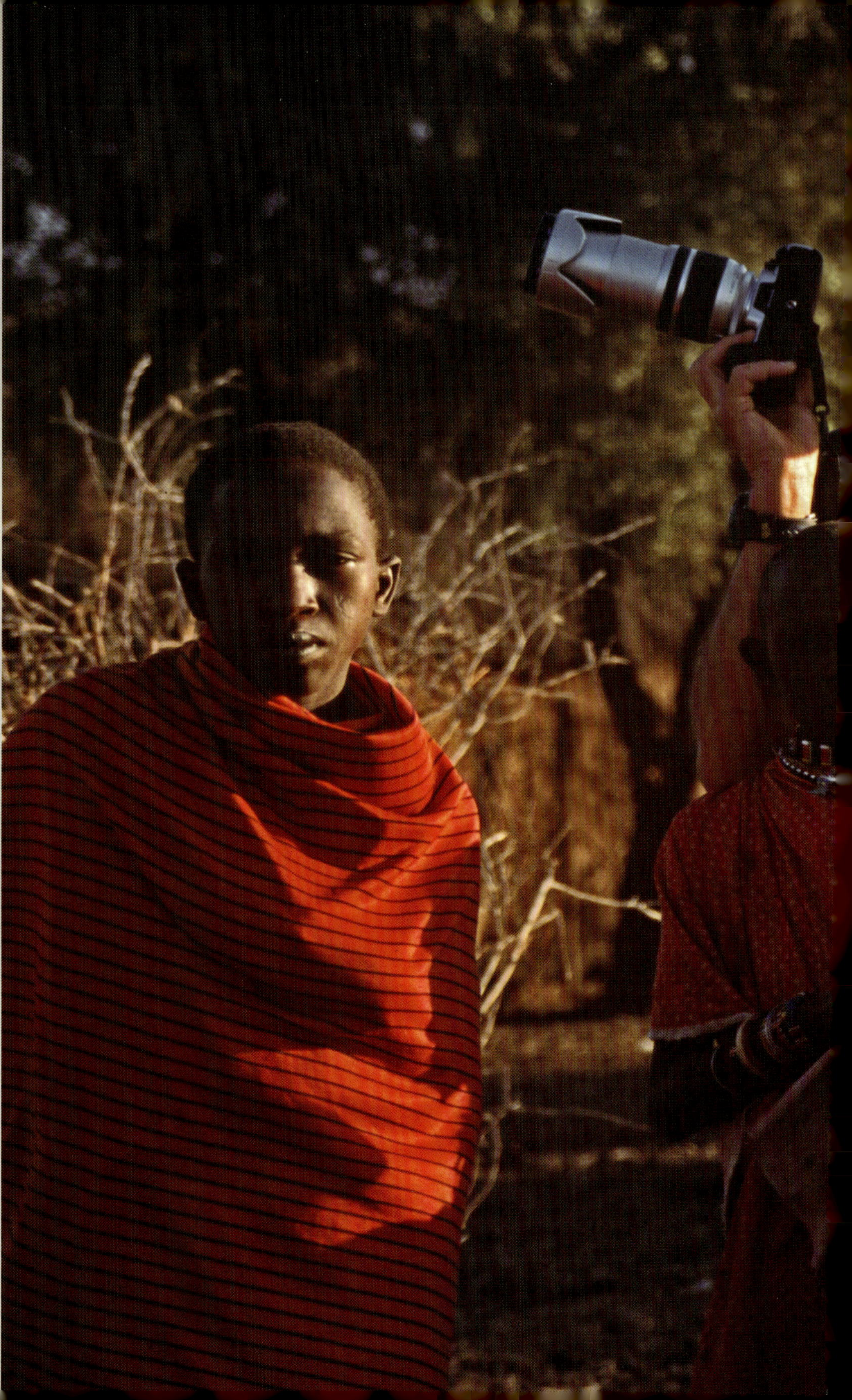

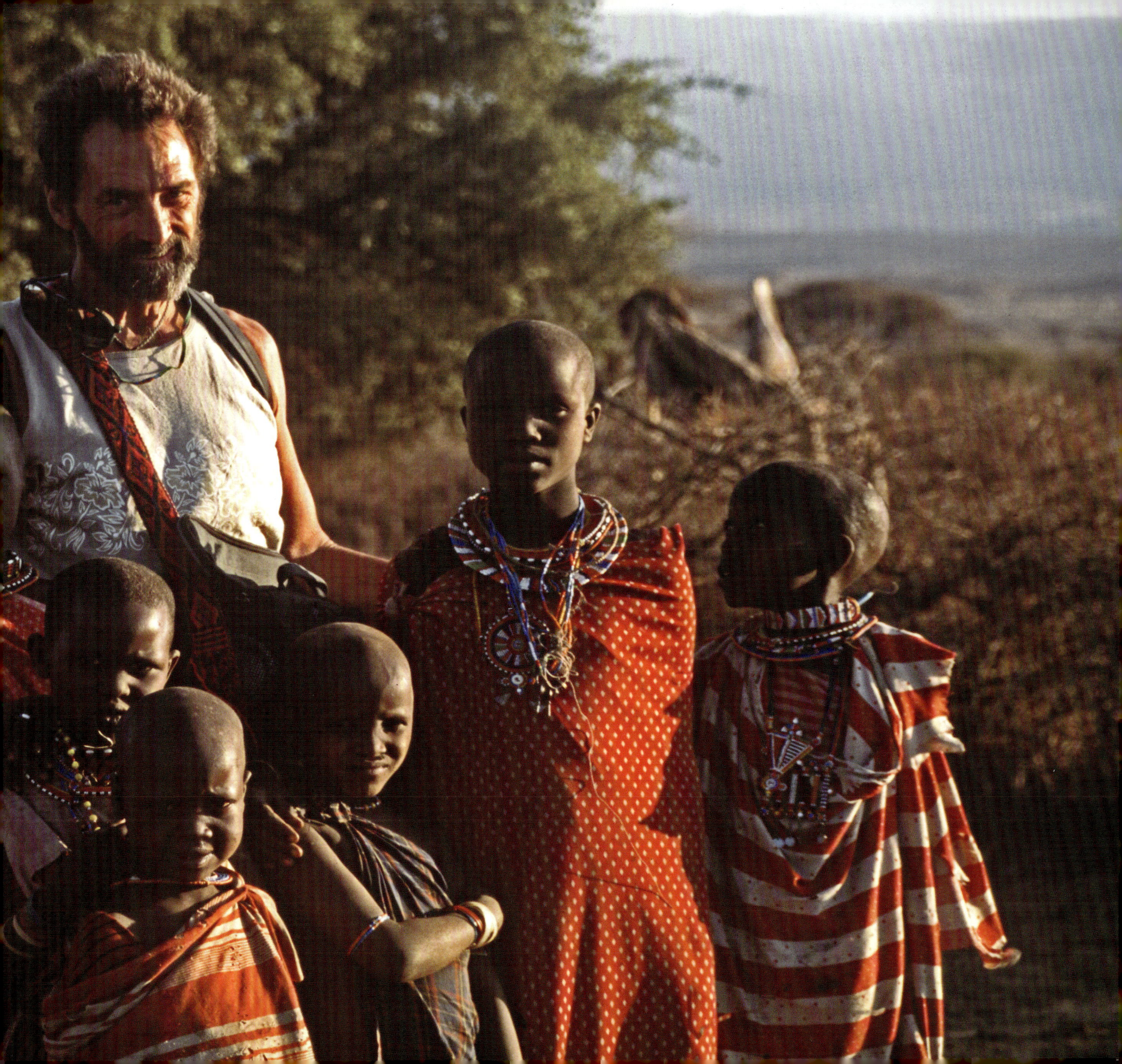

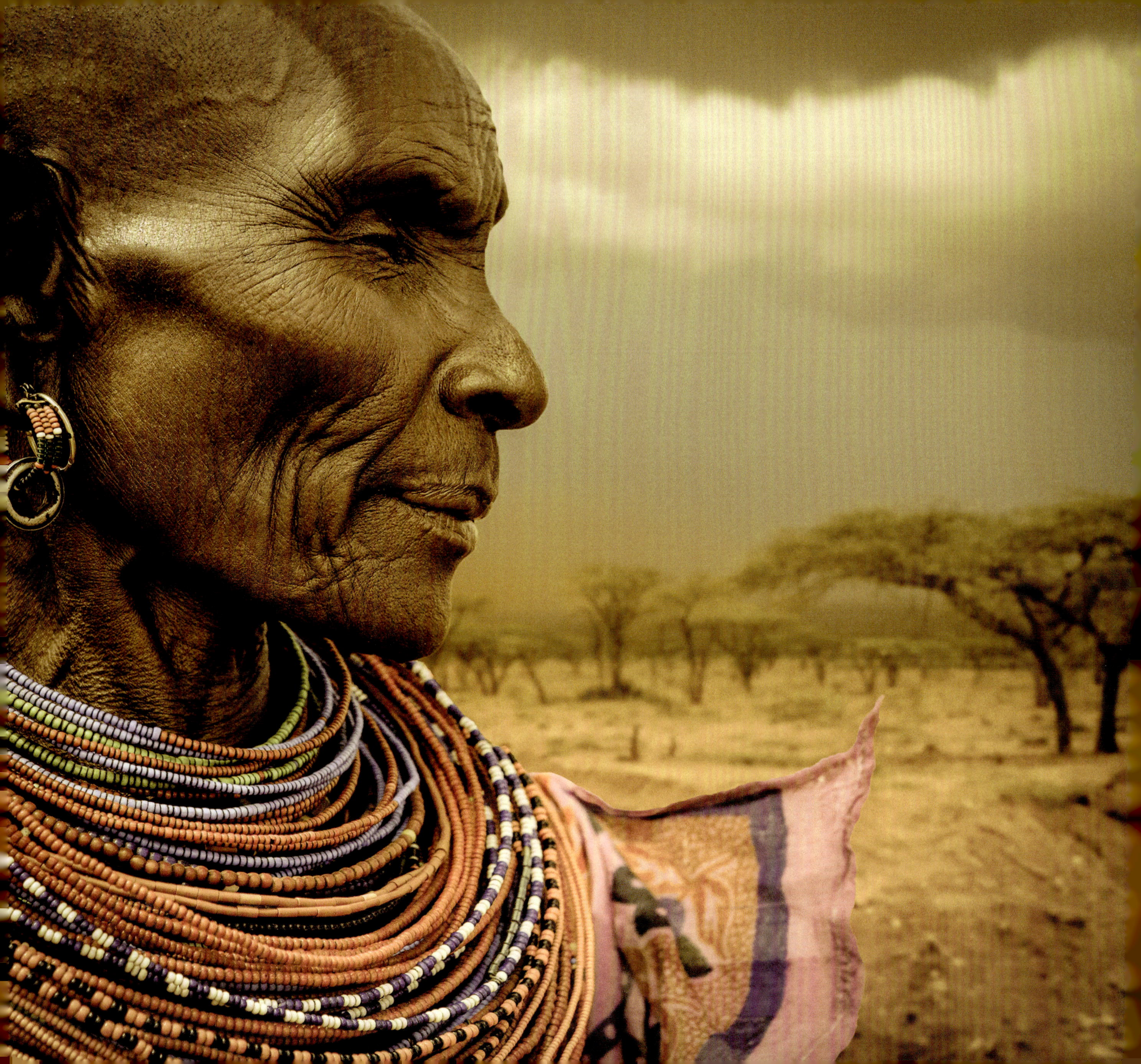

These other cultures are not failed attempts to be us; they are unique manifestations of the spirit - other options, other visions of life itself.

- Wade Davis

A Samburu elder woman, or 'mama' blends naturally into the landscape of her north-central Kenya homeland, a region of stark beauty and great diversity. Four to five centuries ago the semi-nomadic Samburu arrived here from the Horn of Africa. Today just as it has always been, Samburu women walk 5-10 km each day bearing 85-pound loads to provide water for their families.

Tom is a young Samburu warrior. Closely related to the Maasai, the Samburu are a tall, handsome people with a penchant for colorful traditional attire - and in spite of their remote location have been featured in many Hollywood movies over the years. Both photos of the Samburu by documentary photographer Rudi Dundas.

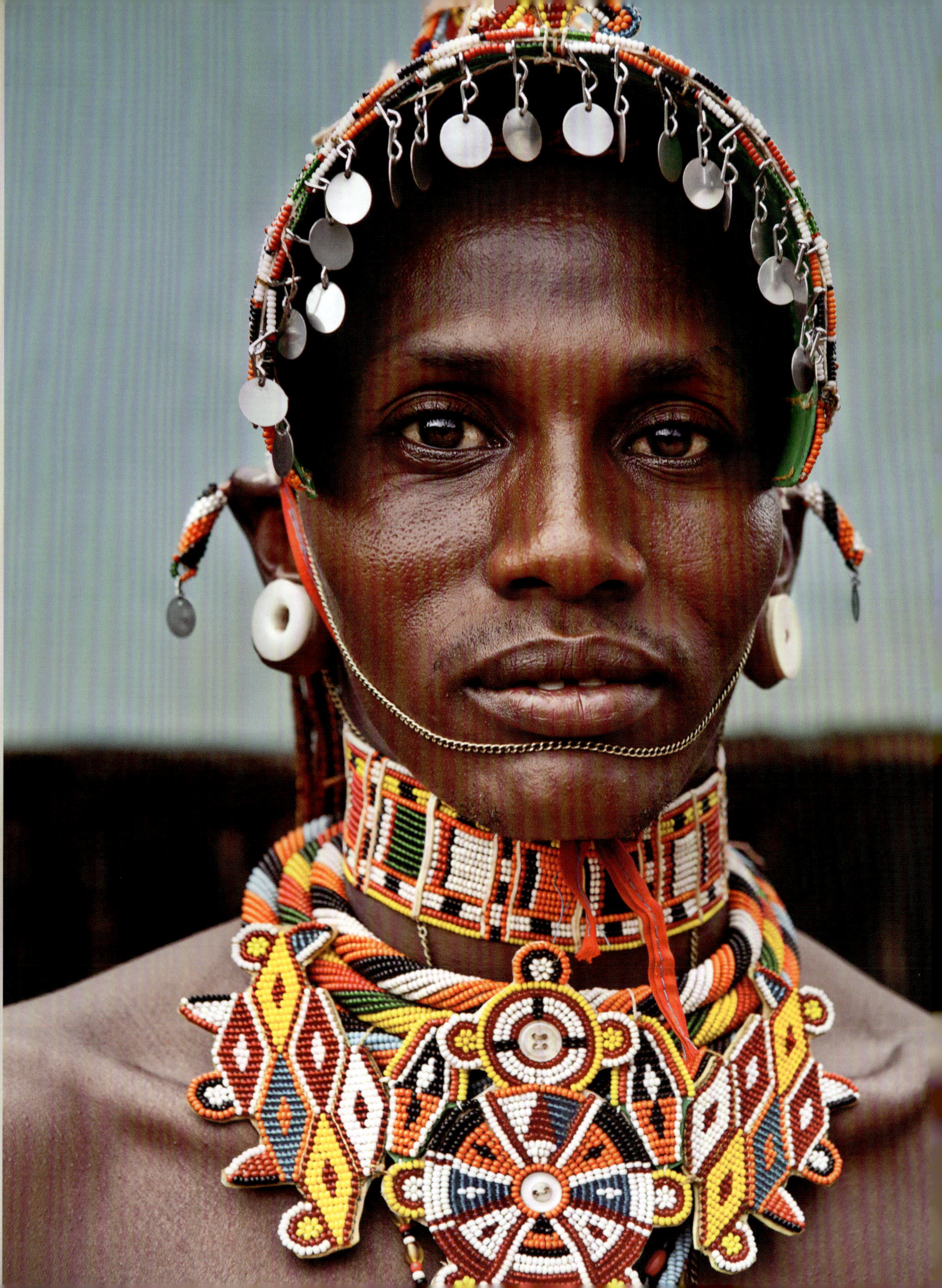

Good is when I steal another tribes's wives and cattle. Bad is when they steal mine.

- old Maasai saying

The Massai were long feared by neighboring tribes as fierce and aggresive warriors. During the 17th and 18th centuries when they reached the pinnacle of their power, many other ethnic groups in eastern Africa were forcibly displaced from their homelands by the fearsome Maasai. Today they remain strongly resistant to governmental pressure to abandon their semi-nomadic lifestle, and their reputation as cattle rustlers and wife stealers still lingers. The old tradition that required a Maasai boy to kill a lion with his spear before he could be initiated into manhood is now officially banned in Kenya. But young warriors who kill a lion today still achieve celebrity status in their community and do not face serious consequences.

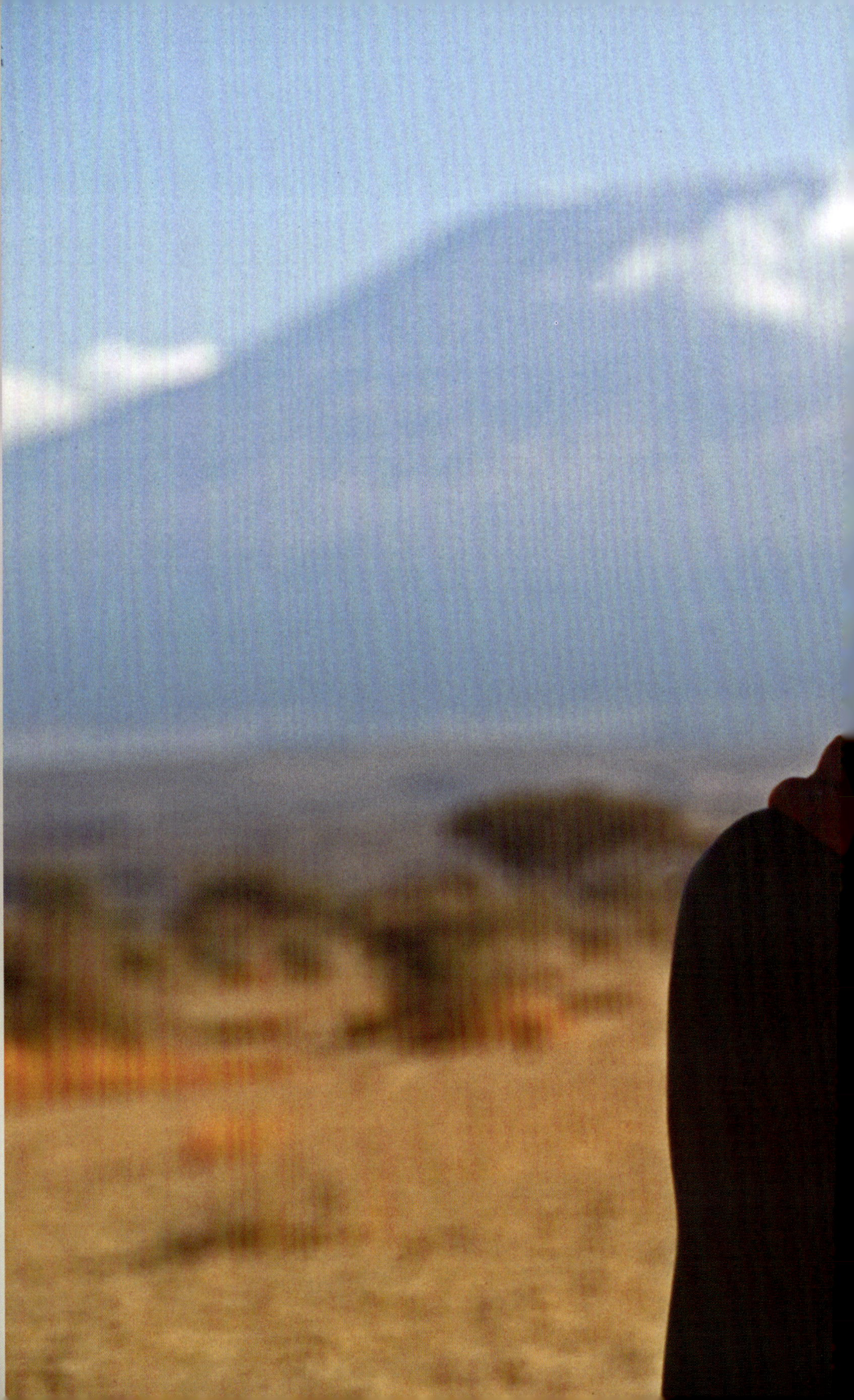

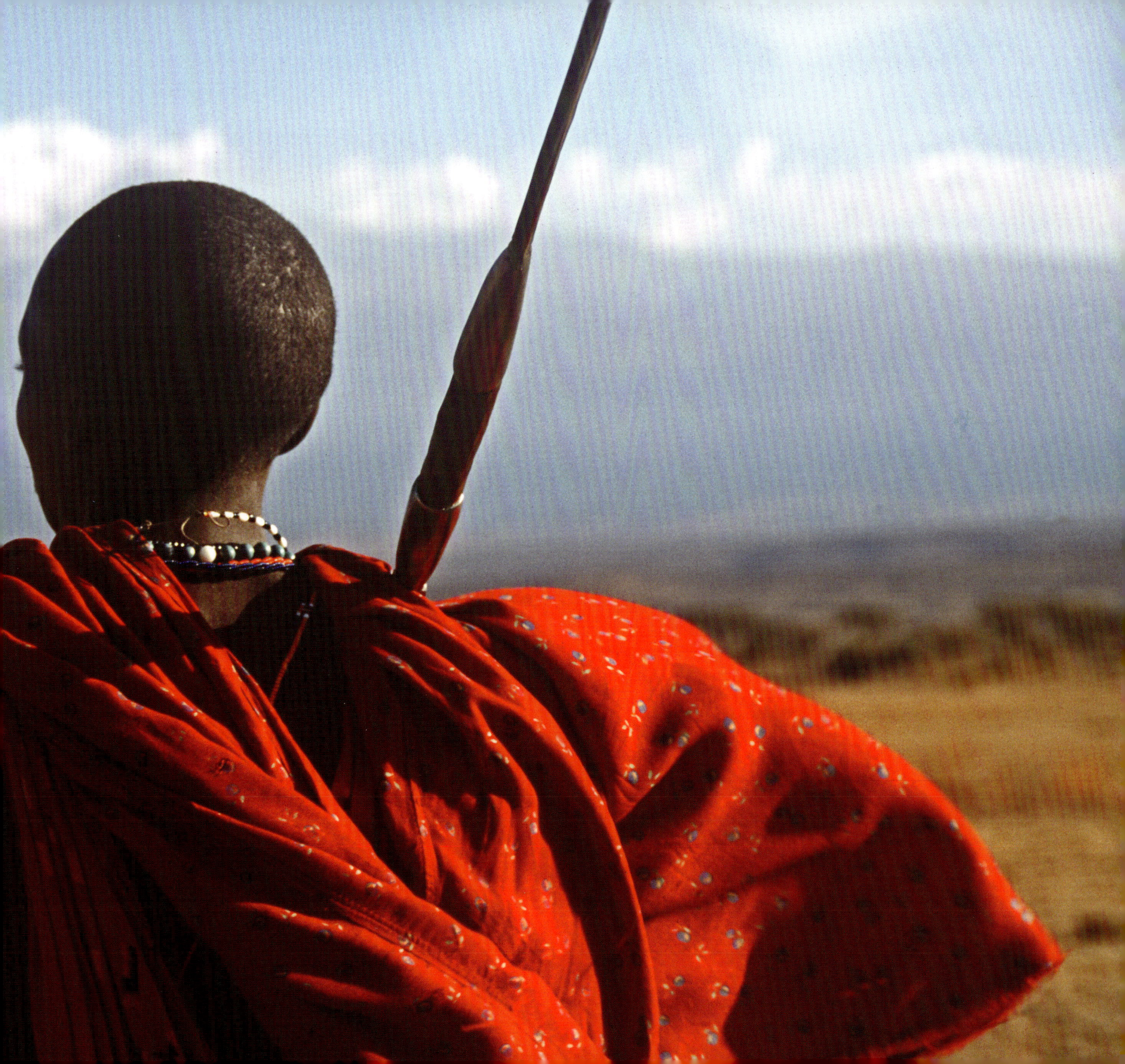

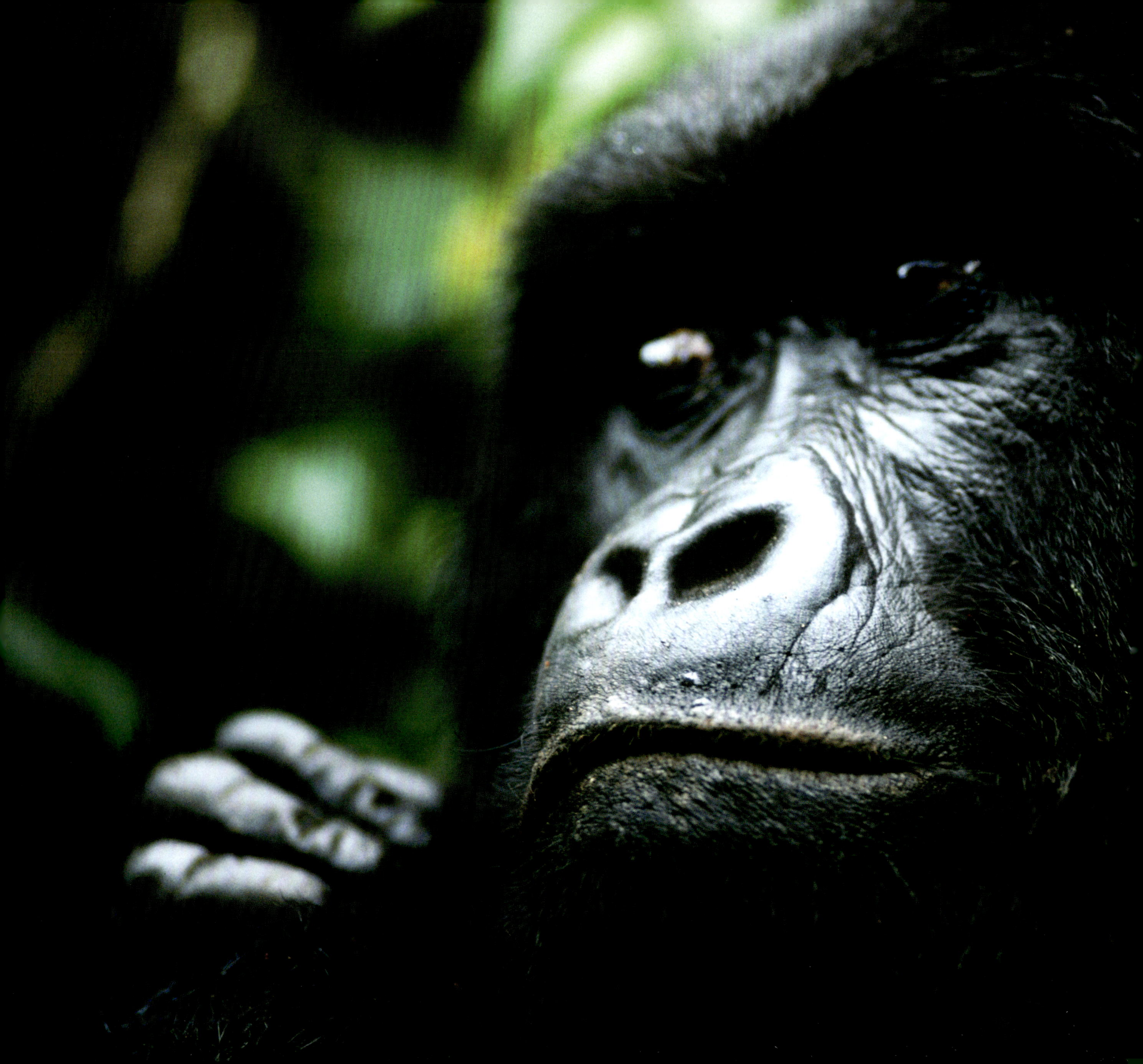

Africa is for me more than a glamourous fact - it is a historical truth. No man can know where he is going unless he knows where he has been.

- Maya Angelou

This female mountain gorilla was photographed deep in the tropical rainforest of Volcanos National Park in Rwanda, central Africa by renowned Belgian explorer Leo LeBon. Gorillas are the largest of all the primates, and their DNA is remarkably similar (95-99%) to that of human beings. Mature males, called silverbacks, head up each gorilla family and rely on their tremendous size and strength to protect females and young from predators. A big silverback and a mature leopard were reportedly once found dead together from mutually inflicted wounds.

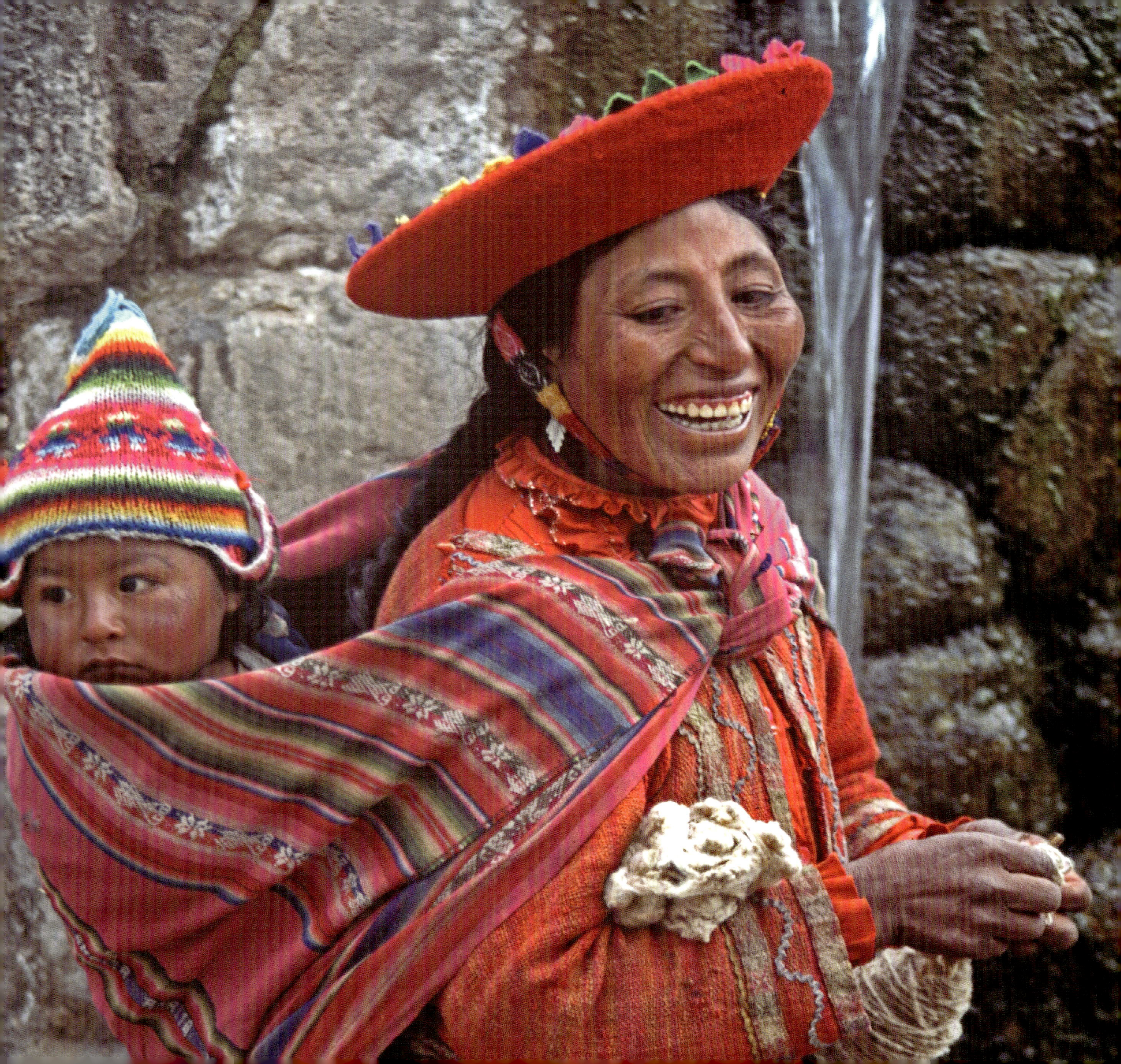

God could not be everywhere, so he made mothers.

- Rudyard Kipling, British author and Nobel laureate

Quechua mothers in the highlands of Peru are quintessential masters of multi-tasking. They simultaneously manage all the arduous tasks of survival in their demanding high-altitude Andean world - shepherding, wool spinning, firewood gathering, and tending gardens on steep terraced mountainsides - all the while bearing their small children with them everywhere, wrapped securely in their traditional *rebozos*.

A young Berber woman in a remote region of the Atlas Mountains of Morocco makes bread by hand in the age-old traditional way while her son looks on contentedly. The Berbers cling fiercely to their nomadic way of life, regarding themselves as "the free people". DNA analysis has now established commonalities between the Berbers and the Sami tribespeople of Scandinavia, dating back to 9000 years ago. Morocco photo by Maria Demarest.

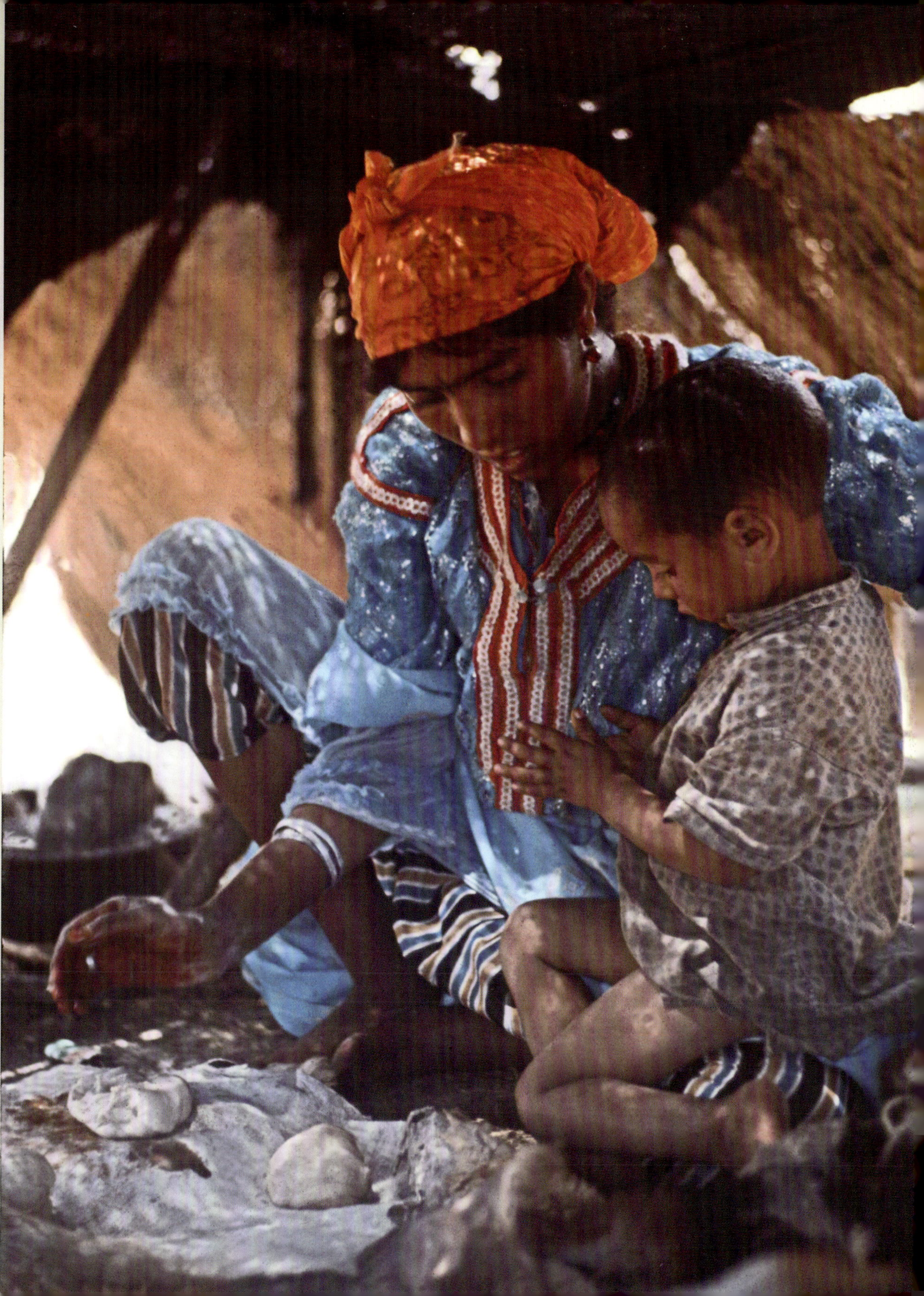

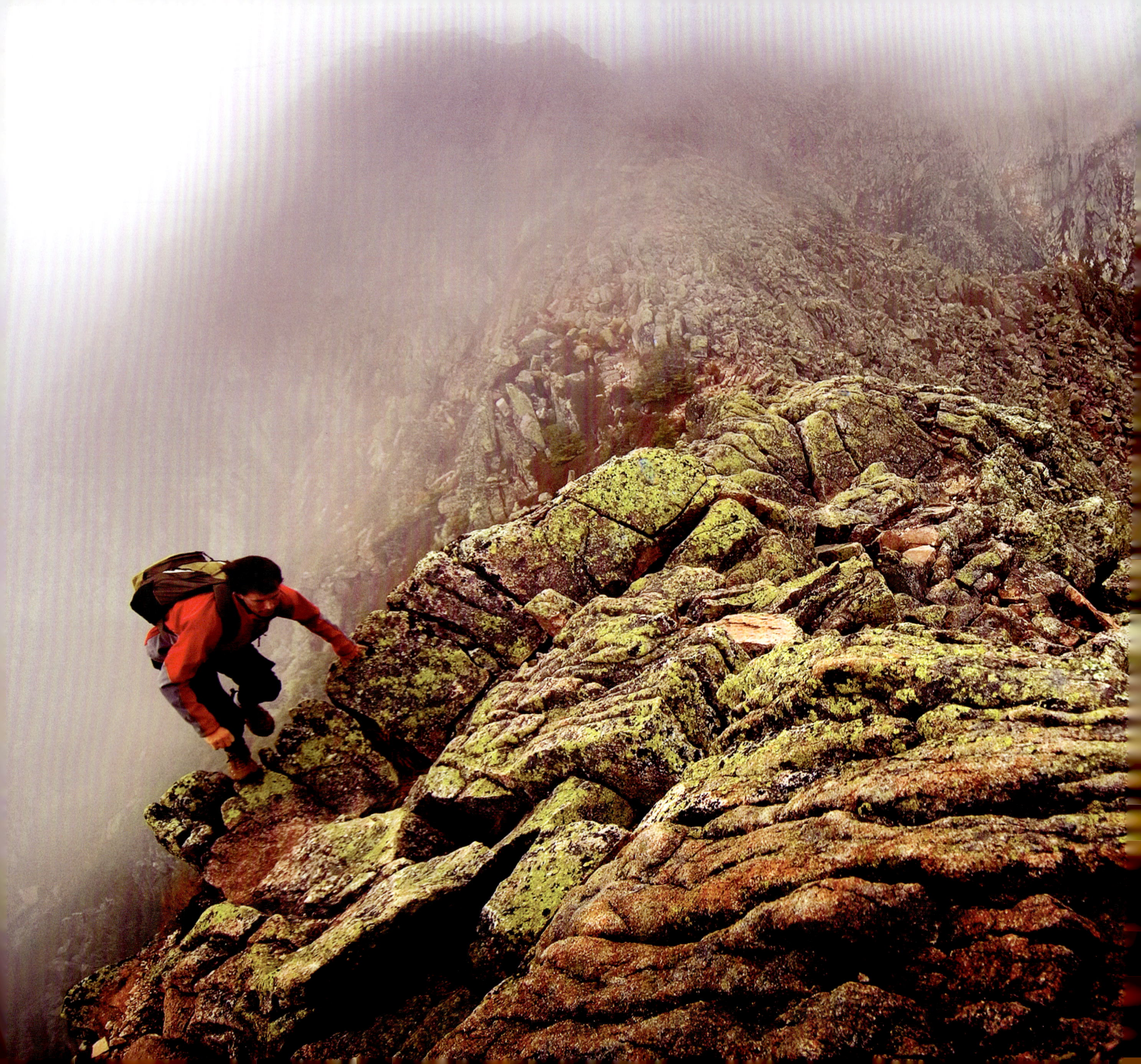

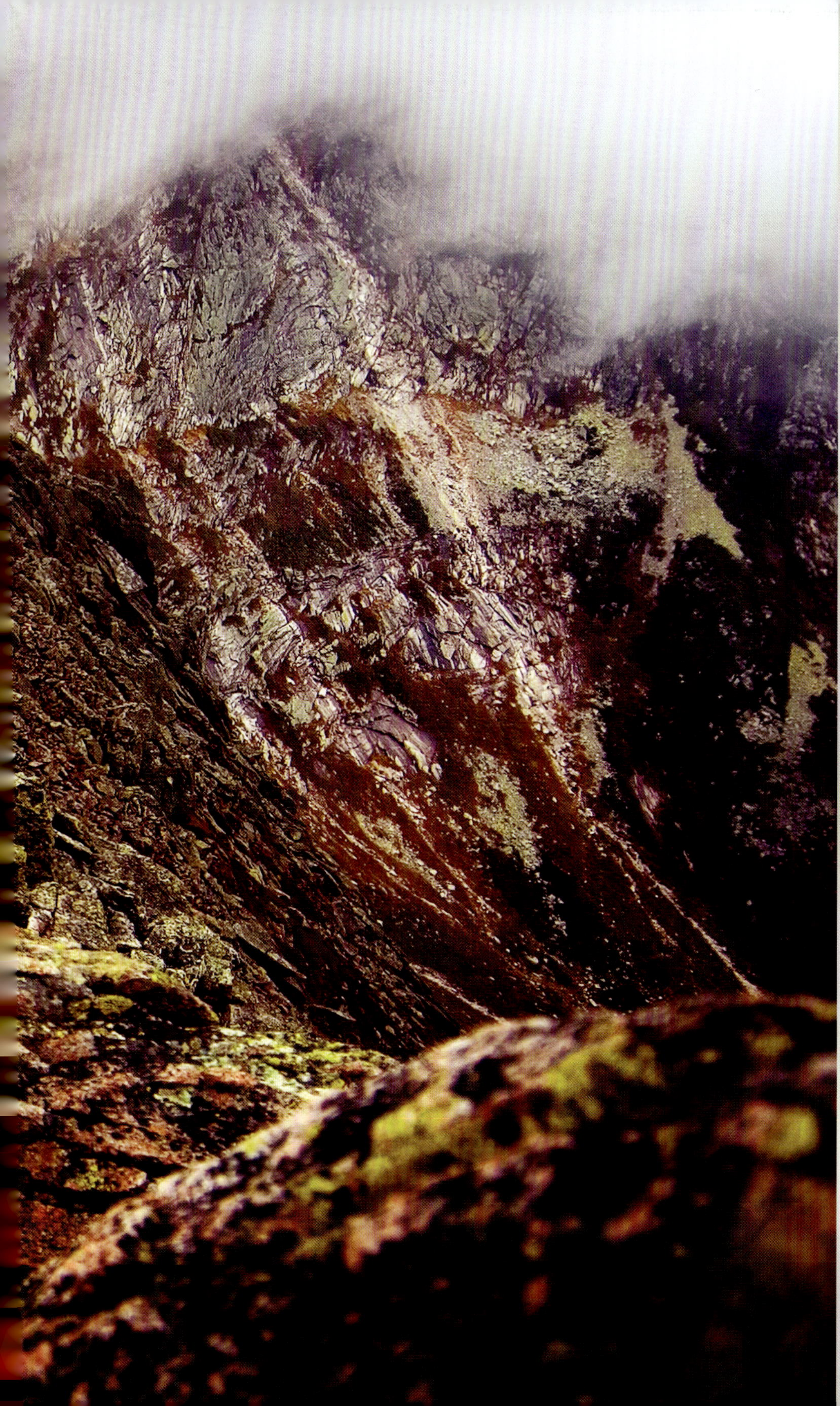

Courage is
grace under pressure.
- Earnest Hemingway

A lone climber scrambles up precipitous Knives Edge Ridge on 5,268' Mt. Katahdin, the highest mountain in Maine. Falls and violent storms that can come suddenly at any time of year have claimed many lives on the infamous Knives Edge. Some sections of the treacherous route are only 3' wide with sheer drop offs on either side. The name Katahdin, "The Greatest Mountain", originated with the Penobscot Indians, who believed that the storm god Pamola dwelled high on the summit. Today, the Penobscot continue to make annual pilgrimages to the mountain. Photograph by environmental documentarian Bridget Besaw.

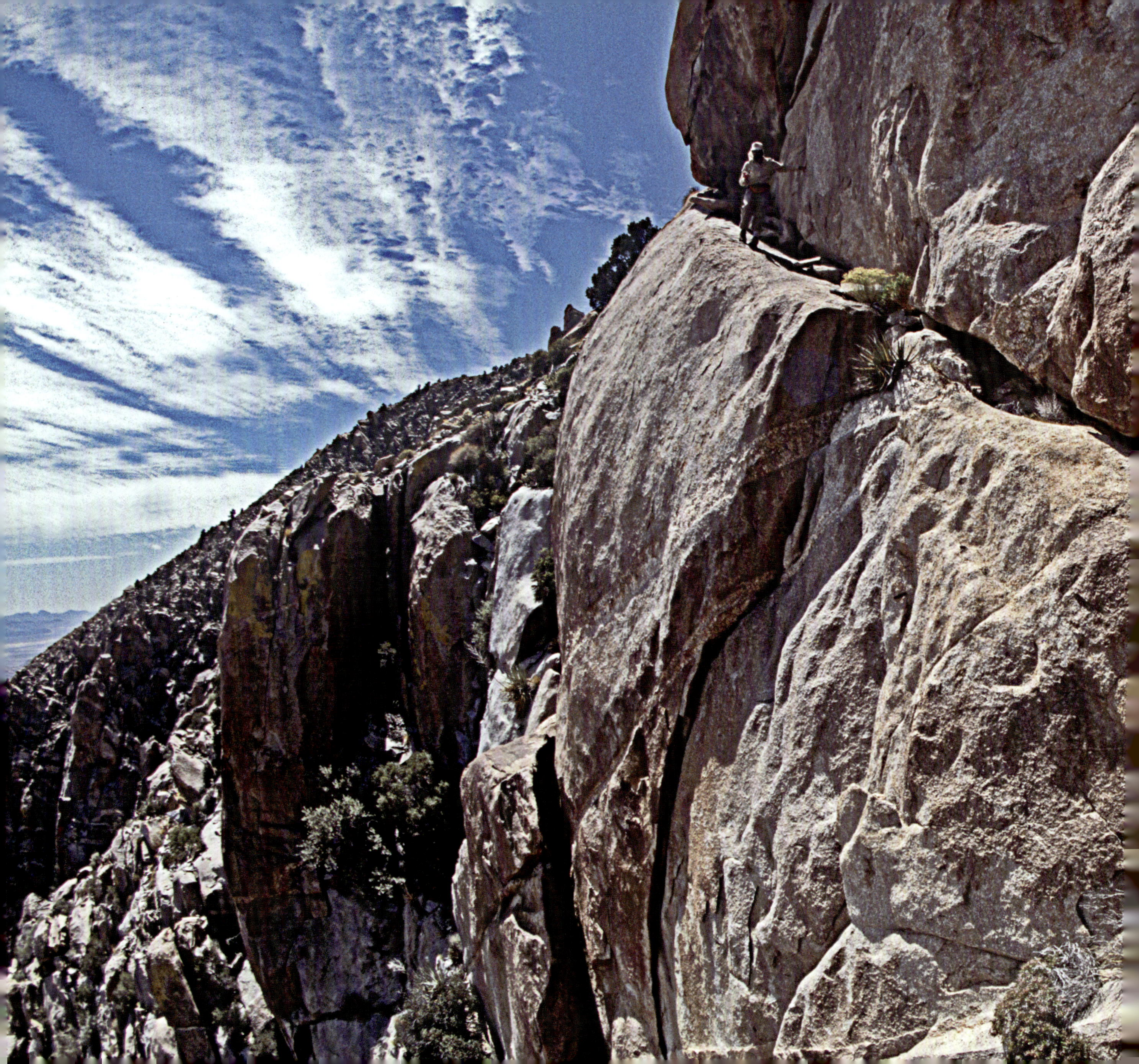

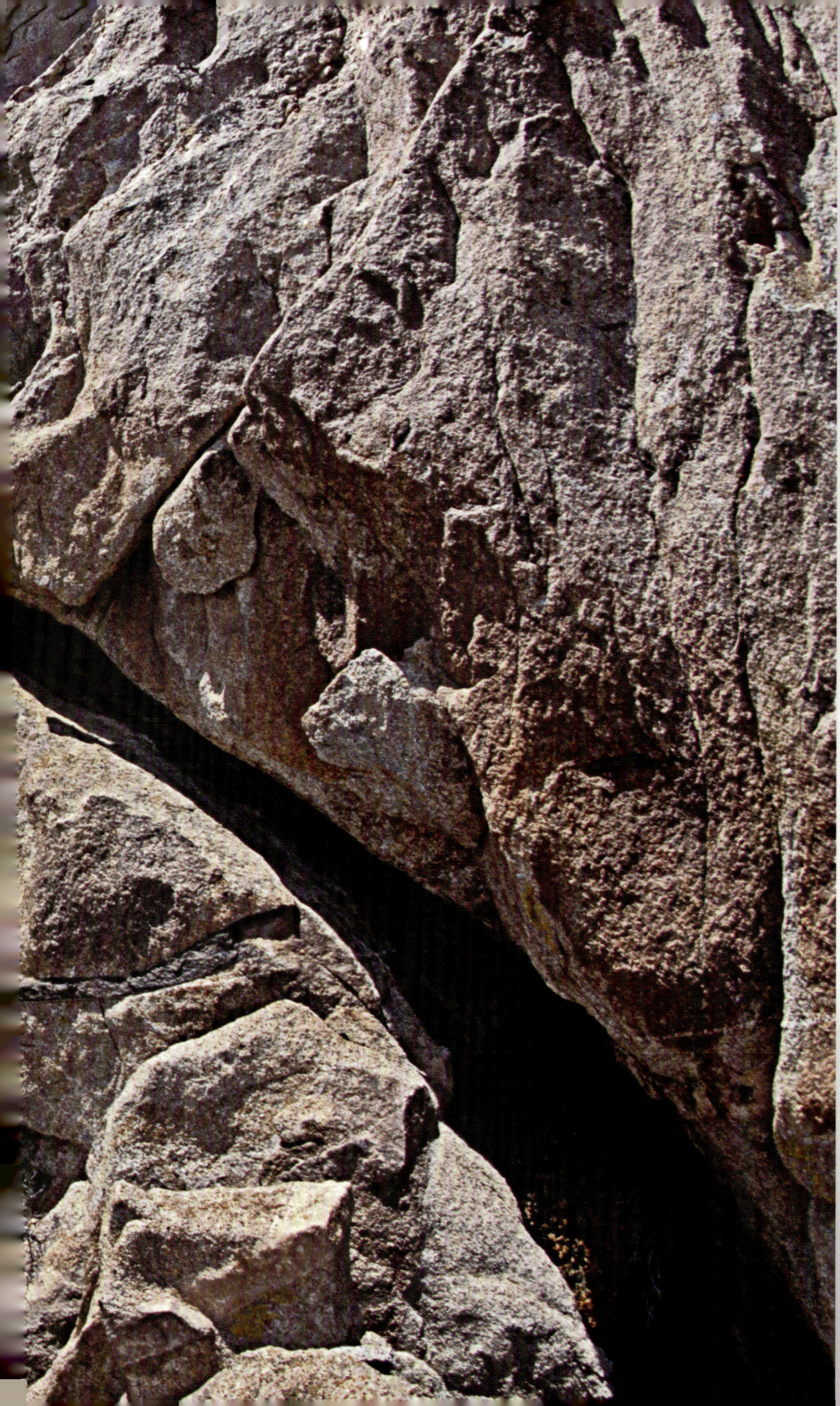

The cradle rocks above an abyss, and common sense tells us that our existence is but a brief crack of light between two eternities.

- Vladimir Nabakov

Centuries before the Spanish *conquistadores* rode north to explore the Baja Peninsula and christened the hot springs canyon they discovered in the northernmost mountains *Cañon de Guadelupe*, it was a sacred place to the the desert Indians. Ancient petroglyphs remain there today as mute testimony of the pilgrims who came to the canyon. Rising above the waterfall and palm- filled oasis is an imposing massif with a head and shoulders of solid granite that personified the Great Spirit to the early people. The pungent thermal waters flowing from the base of the sacred mountain were cherished by the Indians as they are today, for their mysterious healing power. High above the canyon floor, the dauntingly steep flanks of the mountain intimidate all but the most intrepid rock climbers.

To do all that one is able to do is to be a man; to do all that one would like to do, is to be a god.

- Napoleon Bonaparte

Adventure fimmaker Michael Brown takes a brief respite from the intensity of shooting a sports adventure show for the Expedition Earth Television series on Easter Island in 1993, to exercise his free climbing skills around the rim of long dormant *Volcán Ráno Raráku*. Brown went on to make a series of award-winning films about high-altitude climbing, including Farther Than The Eye Can See, the inspiring story of a blind climber making it to the summit of Mt. Everest. Michael has now climbed Everest five times.

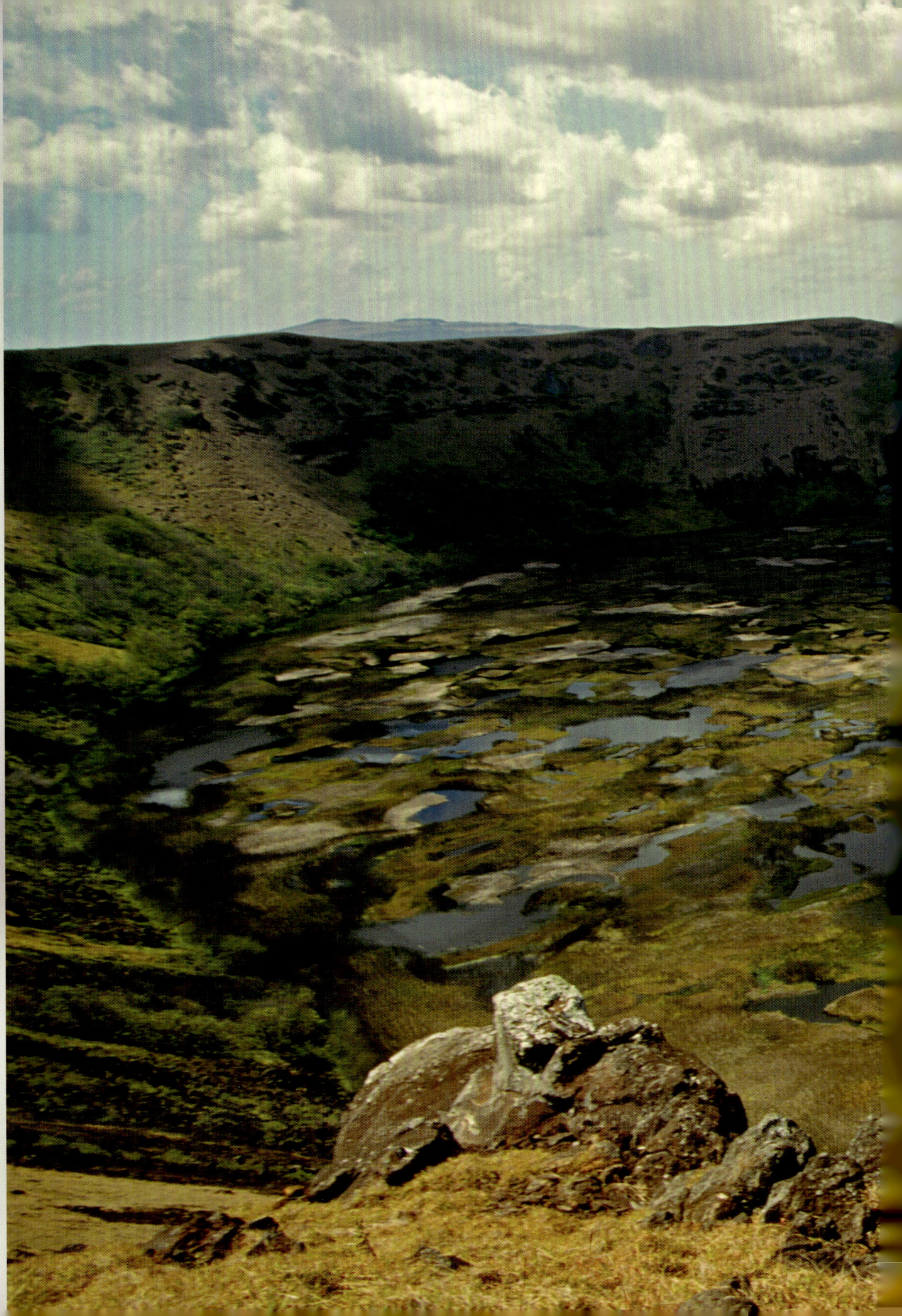

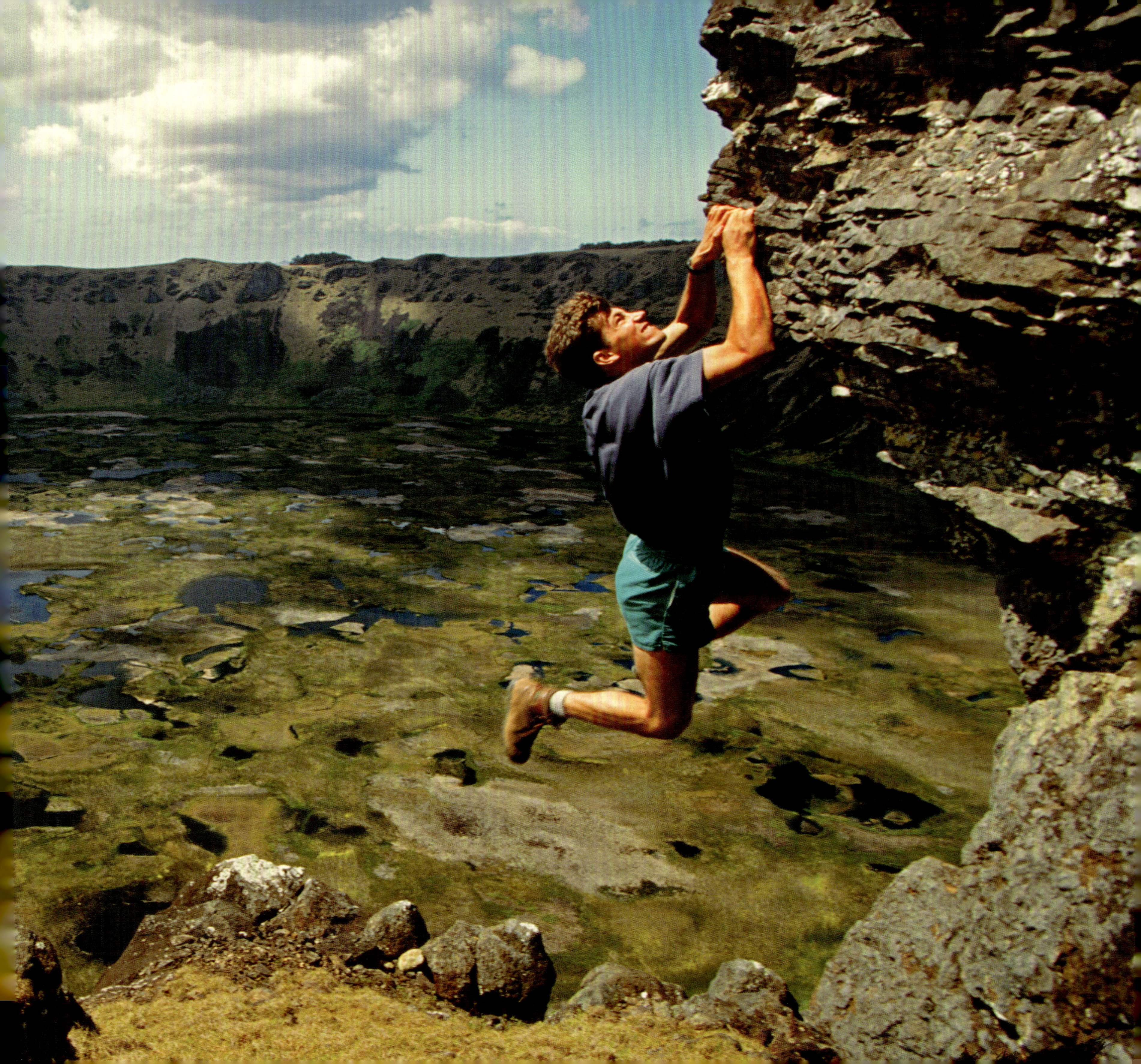

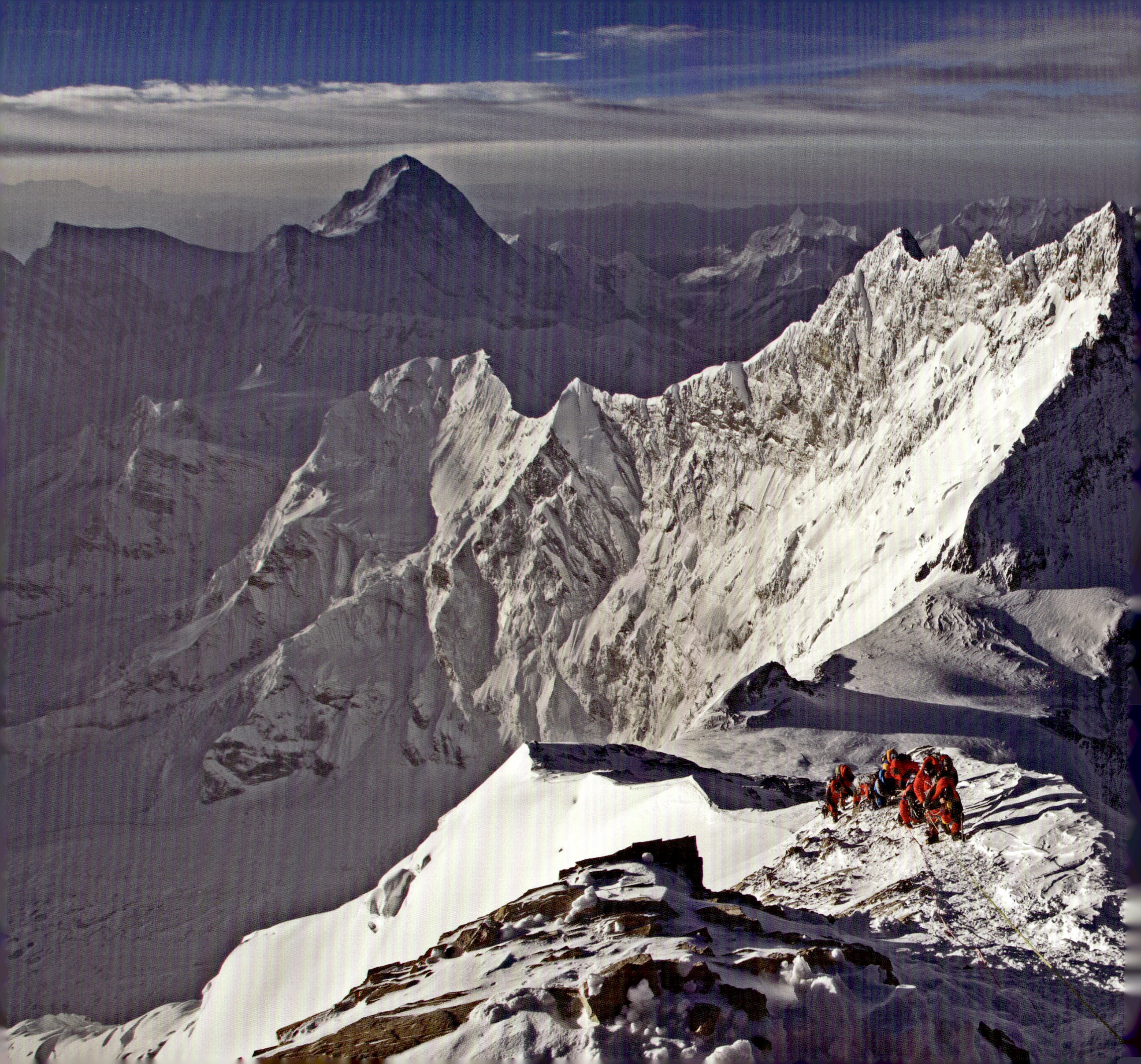

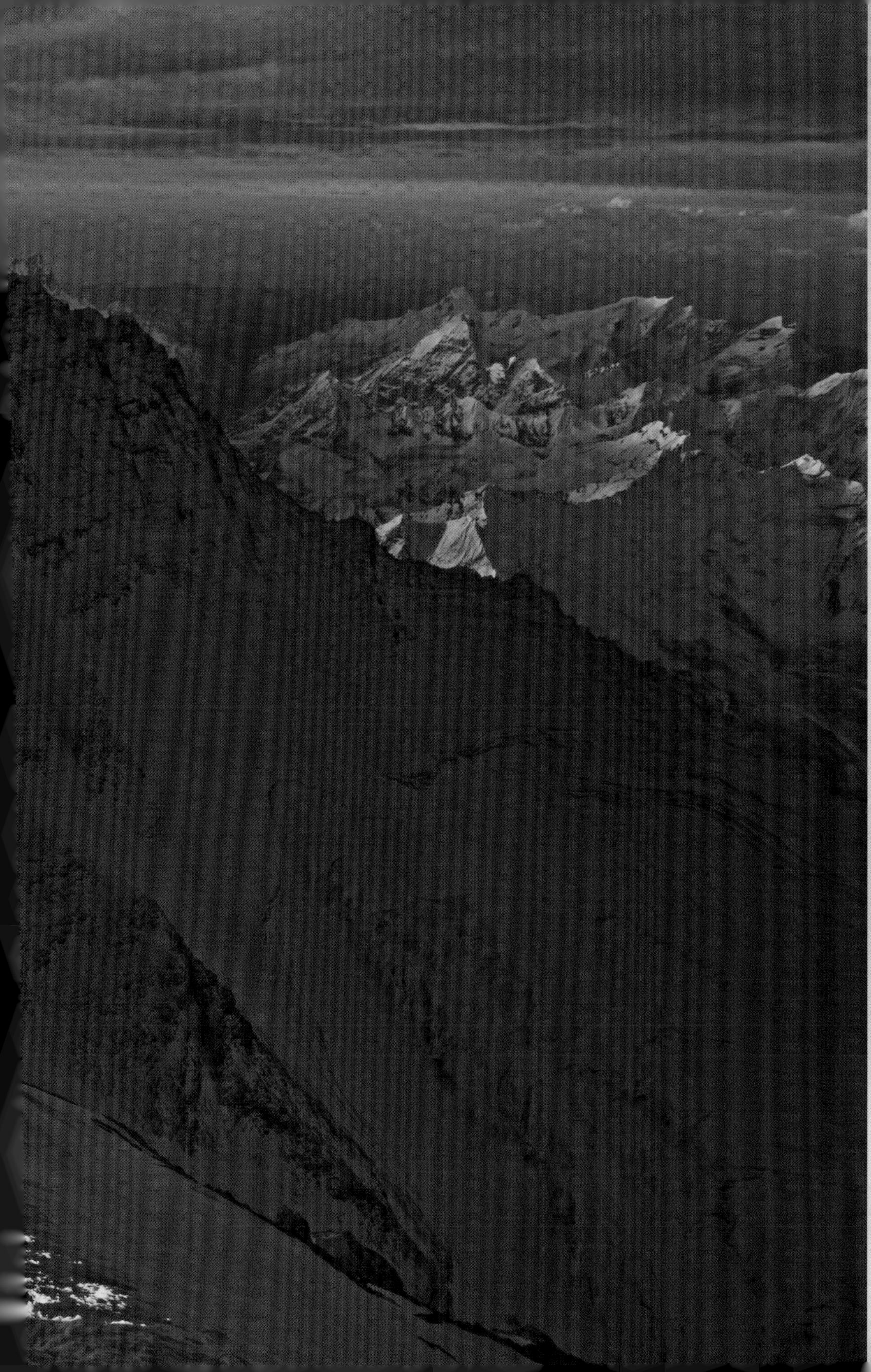

On the mountain of truth, you can never climb in vain.

- Fredrich Nietsche

208

Near the 29,029' summit of Mt. Everest, multi-award winning adventure filmmaker Michael Brown paused at the top of the NE Ridge to observe his American and Sherpa climbing companions struggling upwards a few hundred feet behind him. By now the intense cold had caused the loss of all feeling in Brown's feet below his ankles, but he pushed on for the top anyway. It was his 5th time to reach the summit of Everest. Photograph by Michael Brown.

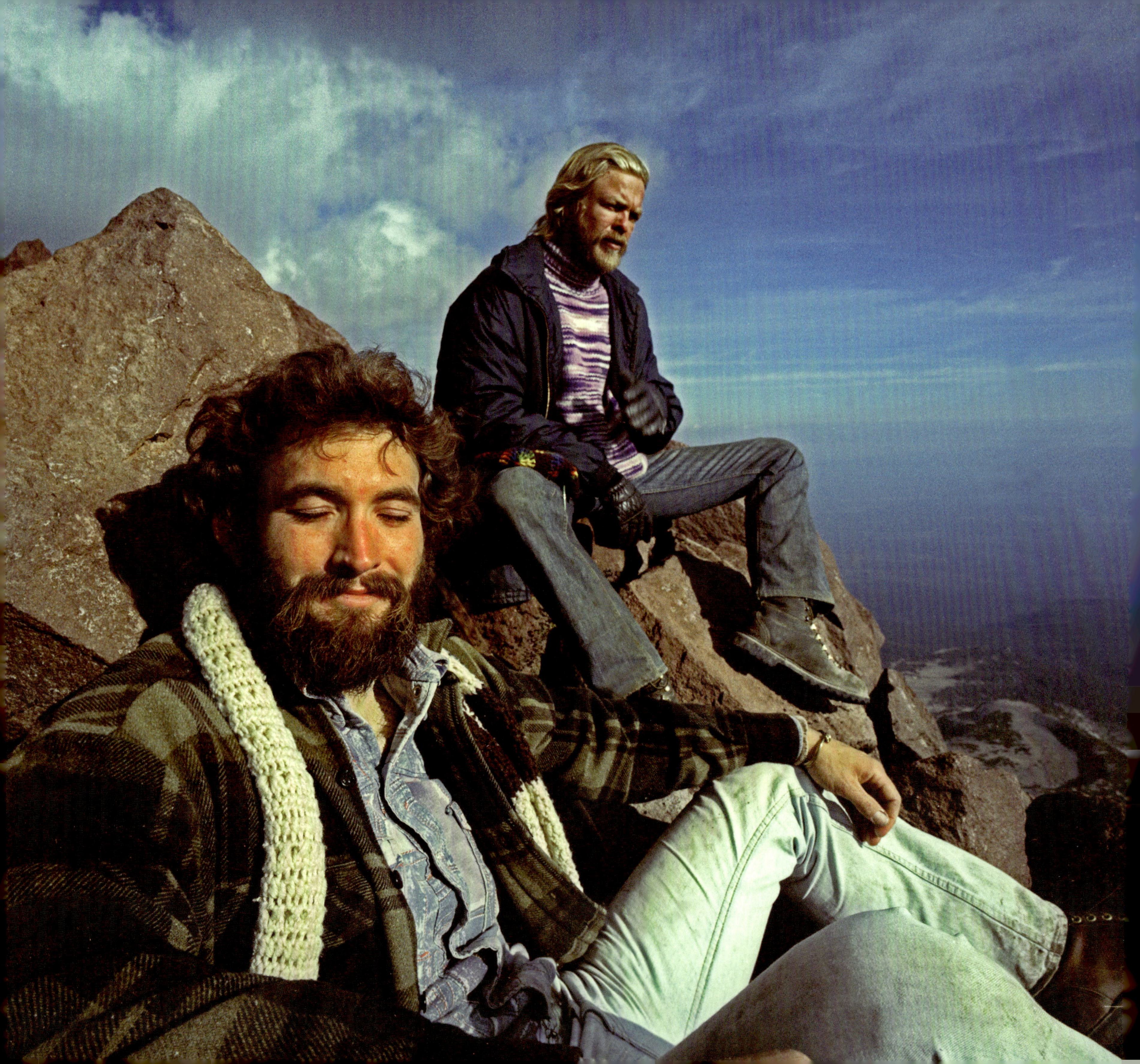

We have always been a wild, free people, free to come and go as we wished. How can we be caged?

- Victorio, Apache leader

Ascending precipitous Sargents Ridge on Mt. Shasta's southern flank, old climbing amigos Dennis and David pause at about 10,000' to rest and meditate for world peace. Shasta has always been sacred to the Native Americans, and to the early Russian explorers the magestic mountain was *Tchastal*, the "white, clean, pure one'. Strange lenticular clouds often form over the ice-crowned massif, and mysterious light is sometimes seen in the heights, further evidence to shamans and mystics who congregate around Mt. Shasta that the mountain has great power.

Like beachcombers everywhere when oceans withhdraw dramatically from shorelines around the world during extreme minus tides, another friend named Dennis heads to the sea. One of his special places is storm-weathered cove near Santa Cruz on the northern California coast.

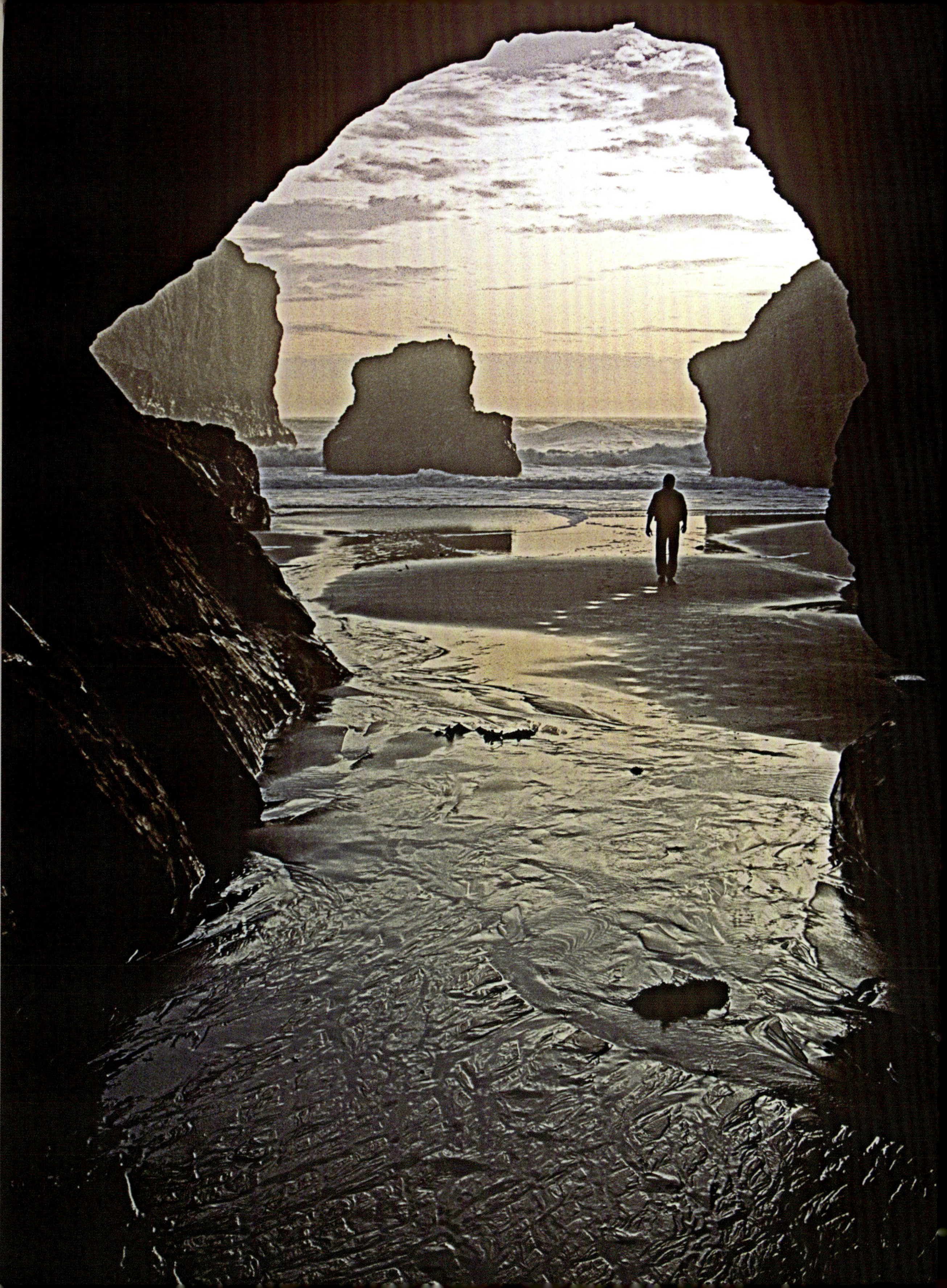

Somewhere, something incredible is waiting to be known.

- Dr. Carl Sagan

On a multi-day backpacking trip through the Yosemite high country, the photographer's daughter Marika scrambled up a glacier-polished granite ridge to scout their route ahead. Even though about 4 million visitors visit Yosemite National Park each year, pitifully few of them leave their cars behind long enough to explore the beautiful mountain country rising up magestically above the valley. So even today the Yosemite high country is blissfully uncrowded and Marika's view remains pristine and beautiful.

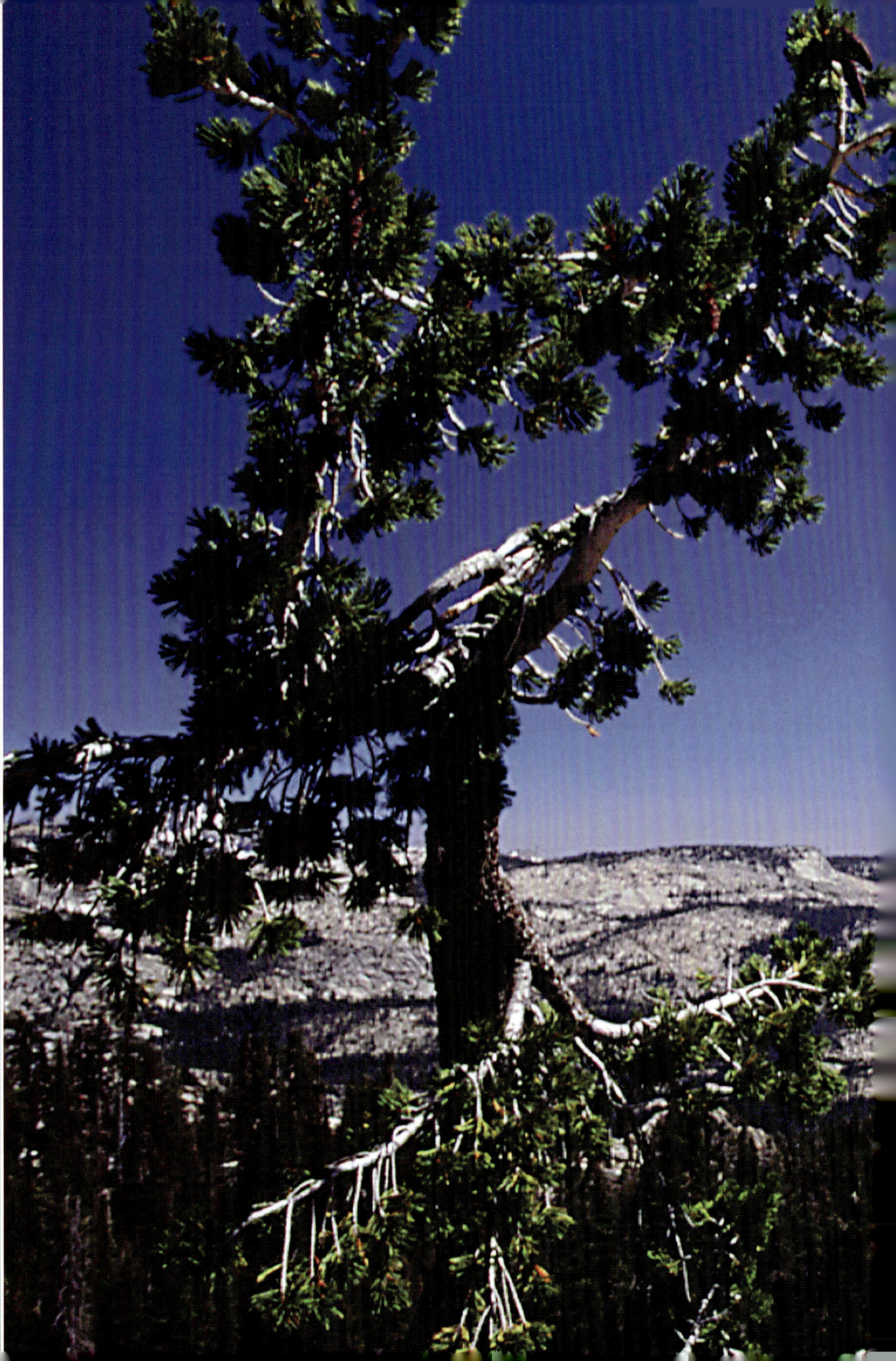

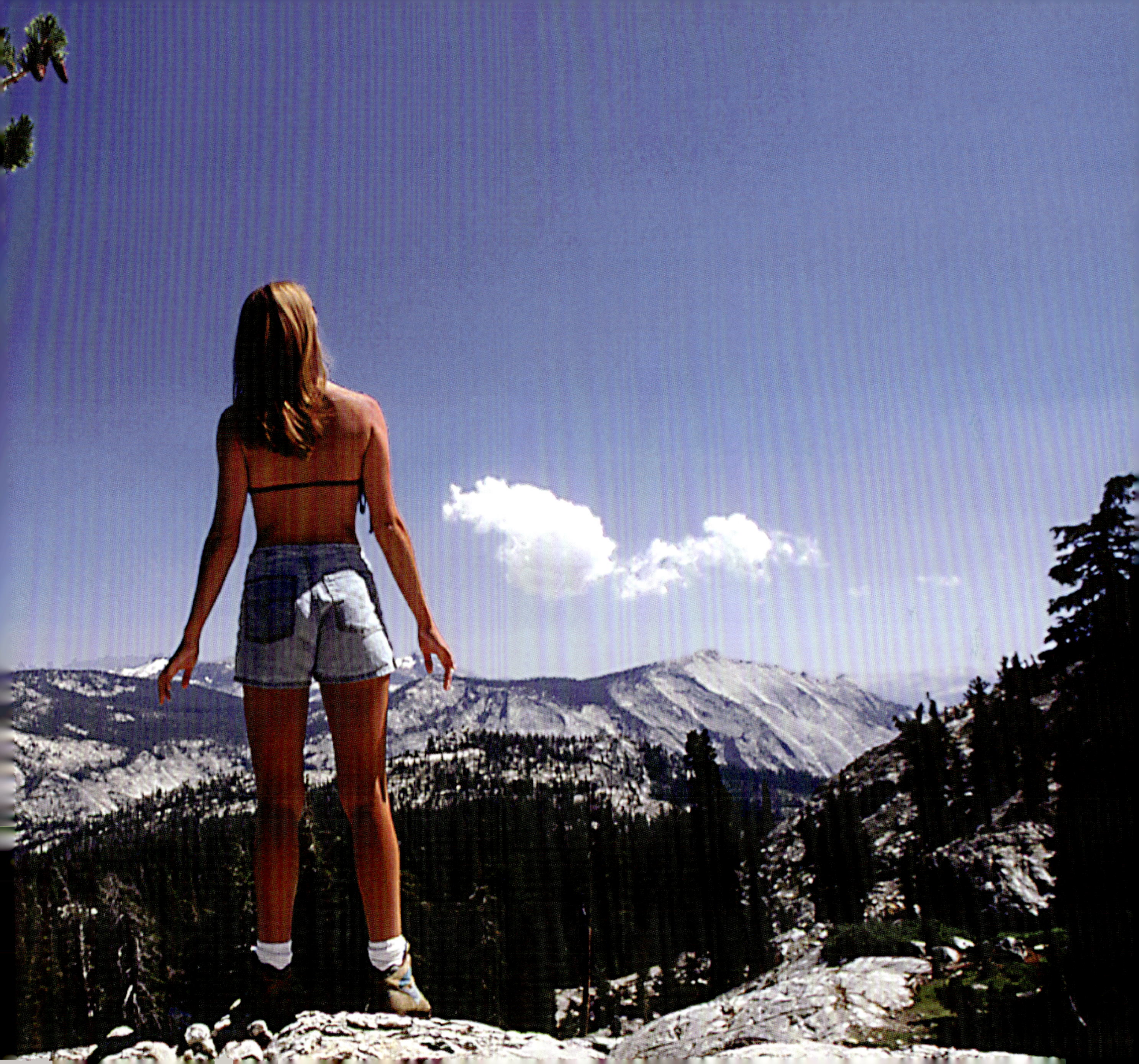

When you realize
how perfect everything is
you will tilt your head back
and kiss the sky.
- Mahatma Ghandi

Mt.Rainier is the highest mountain in the northern Cascades of Washington State, rising majestically to 14,410' above sea level. The massive stratovolcano is the most heavily glaciated peak in the contiginous U. S. and the headwaters of six major rivers. The mountain actually has a greater 'topographical prominence' (13,189') than K2 in Pakistan. For decades mountaineers have come to Rainier to train before attempts to climb to higher elevations in the Himalayas and other great mountain ranges. Even a day hike on the national park trails above 5,400' Paradise Lodge is a memorable adventure.

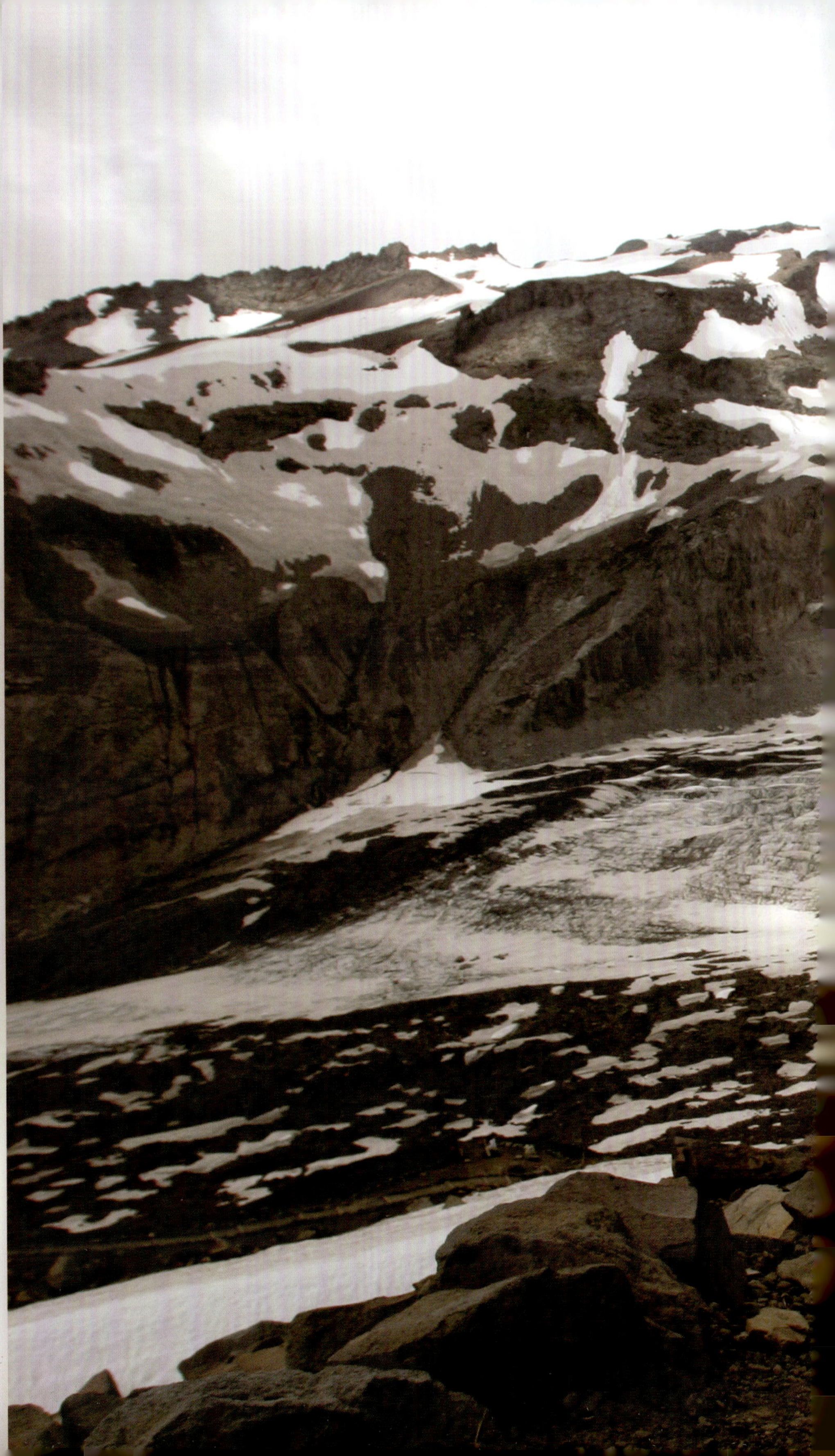

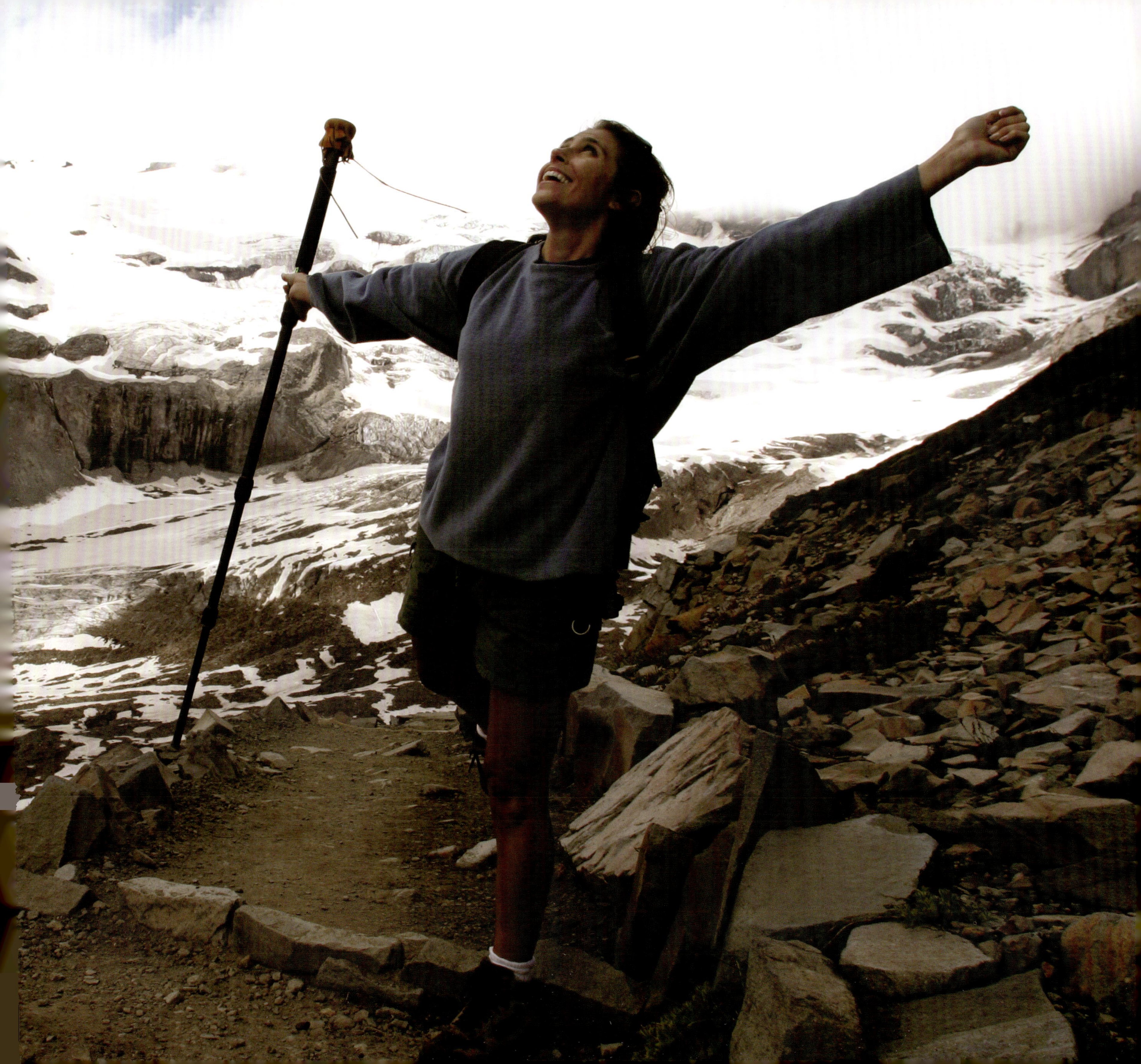

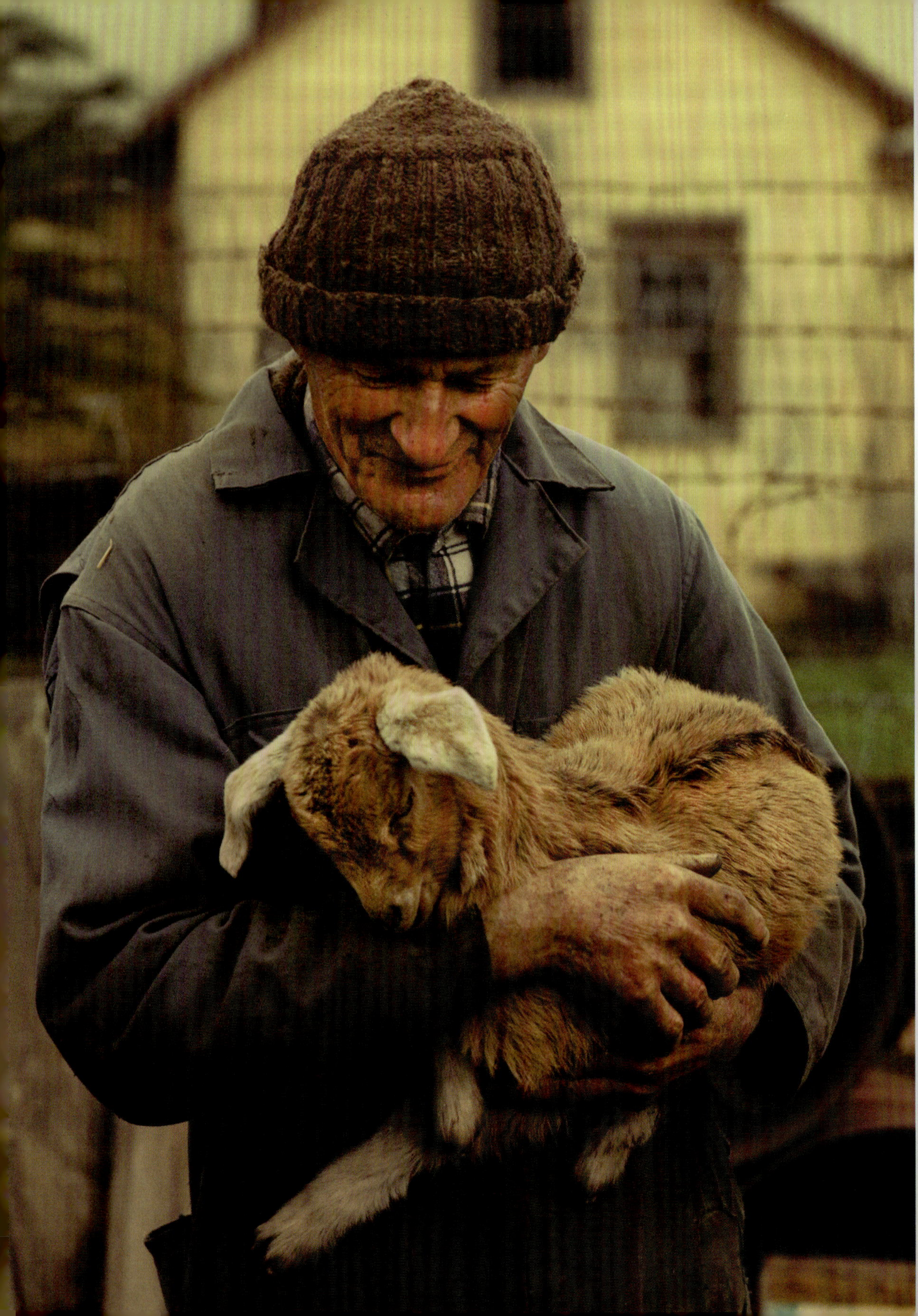

The earth is our mother and we are her children.

- timeless Hindu dictum

Angelo came from Italy as a young man and worked for many years as a farmer northern California. As he grew older family members gradually took over most of the strenuous work, but he continued doing what he loved most - caring for the baby animals.

Viviana grew up on a church farm located in a fertile valley in the south of Chile. Her great-grandparents came to Chile from the Dakota Territory in the U. S. as Methodist missionaries around the turn of the century. To reach this new land where they would spend the rest of their lives, they made the perilous journey in a sailing ship from New York around Cape Horn to Santiago.

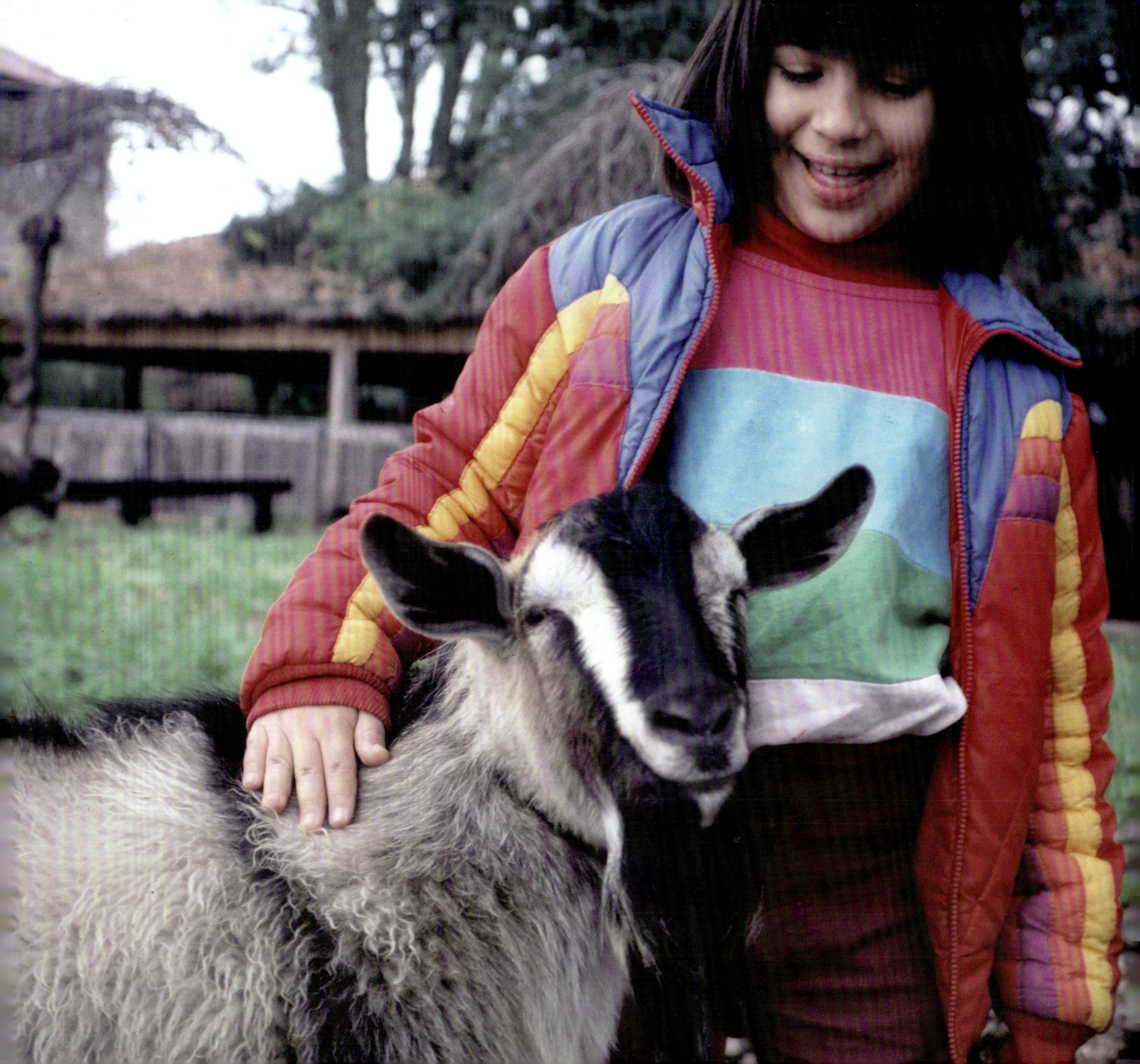

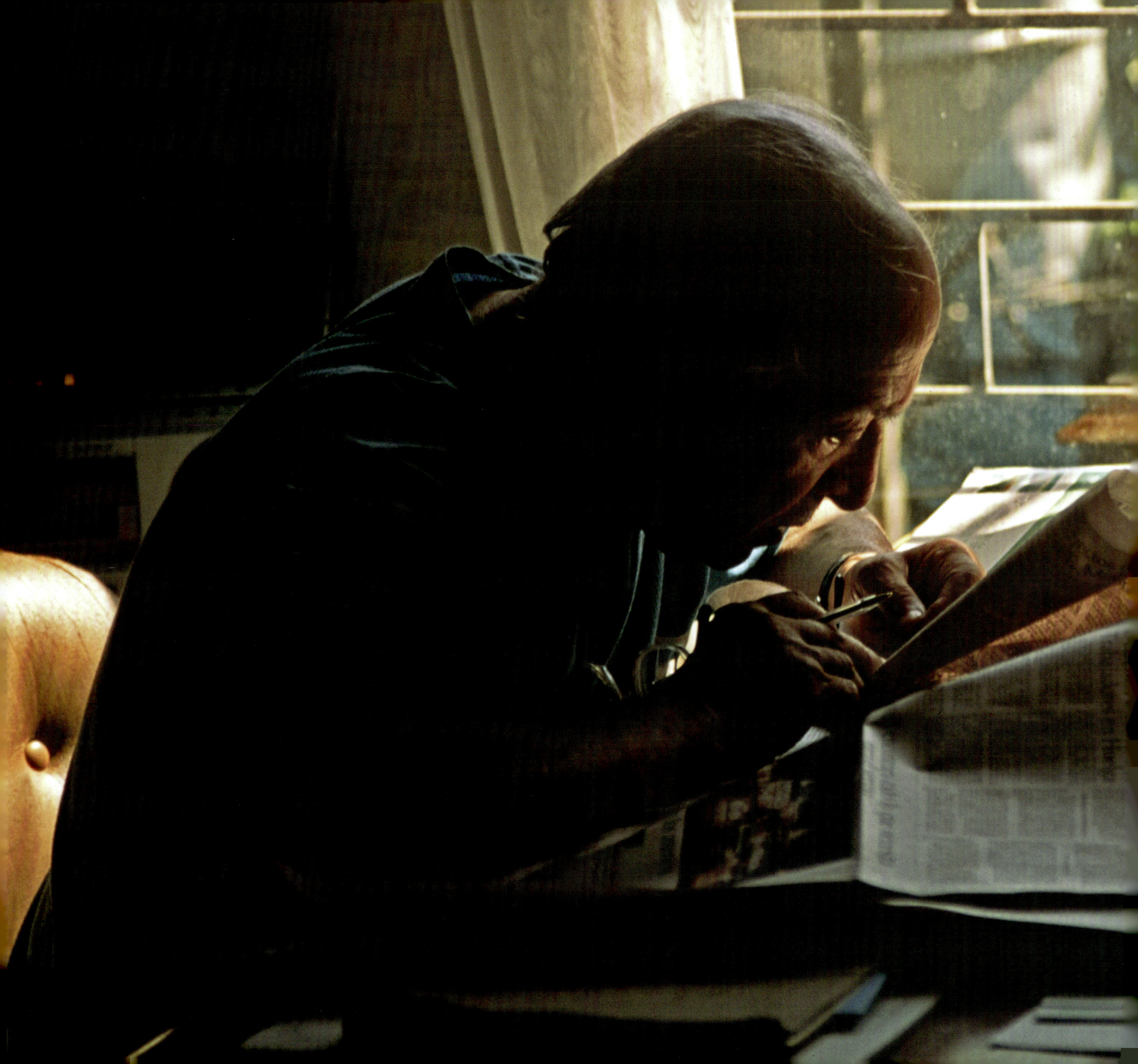

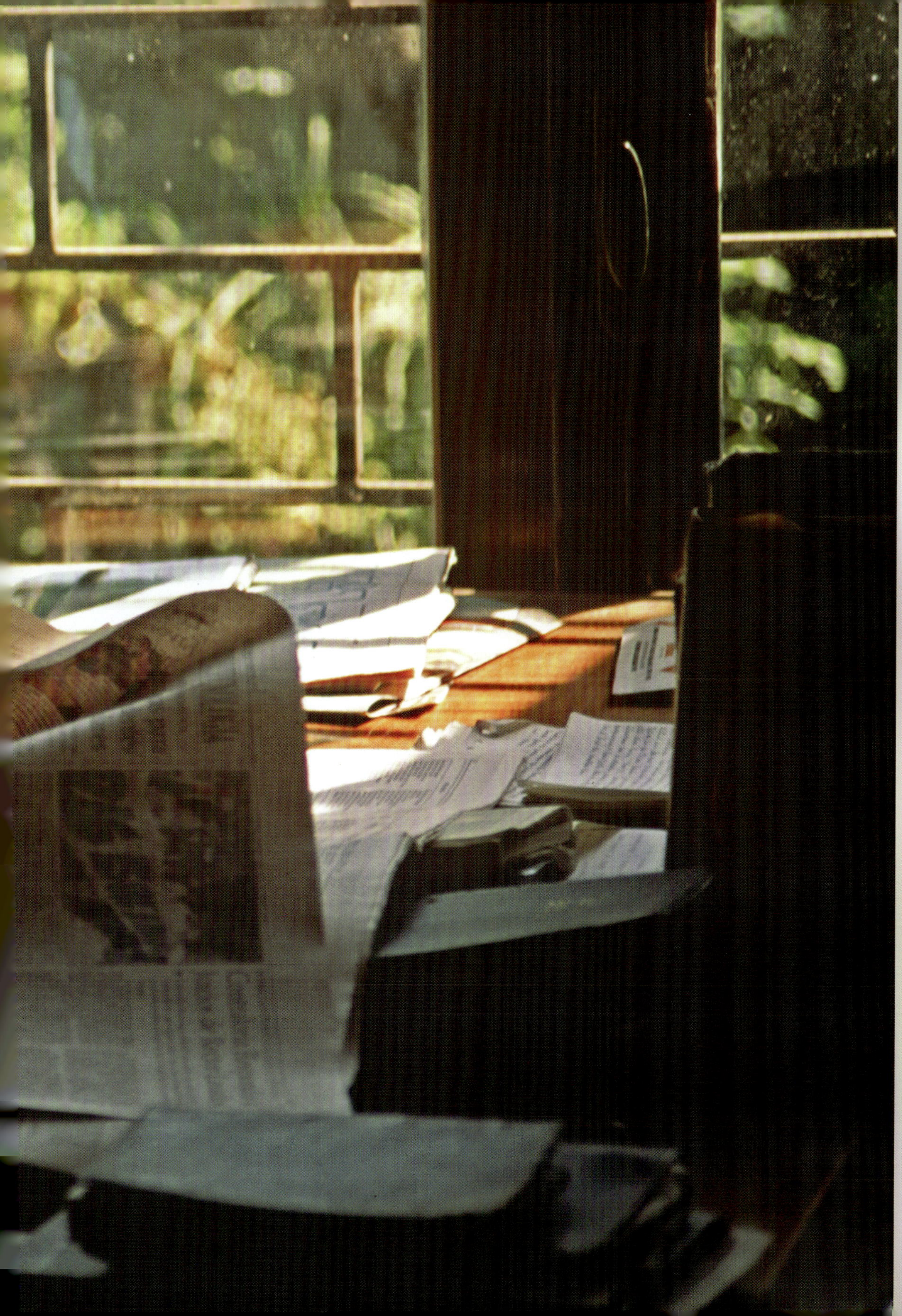

For the unlearned, old age is winter. For the learned, it is the season of harvest.

- old Hasidic saying

Arturo Venegas was a self-made man. Even though he had to quit school as a young man to support his family, he went on to complete his education and become a successful business manager and director of a popular ecumenical church choir. He was a driving force in the emerging Chilean YMCA and a skilled mountaineer, earning the prestigeous title of *andinidsta*. His wife Maurine and he once survived a tidal wave that engulfed the beach where they were camping in the north of Chile. Even in his 90s he continued to work out regularly at the YMCA and study his bible every morning in his study. Arturo remained mentally and physically vital until the day he passed away at home peacefully at nearly 93; a graceful ending to a productive and happy life.

The goal of life is to make your heartbeat match the beat of the universe, to match your nature with Nature.

- Joseph Campbell

The opportunity to embrace an old-growth redwood tree that she realized was alive and growing in a coastal canyon in northern California long before the first Spanish *conquistadores* arrived in her native land of Chile - was *muy profundo*, a deeply profound experience for Ximena, a young actress from Santiago.

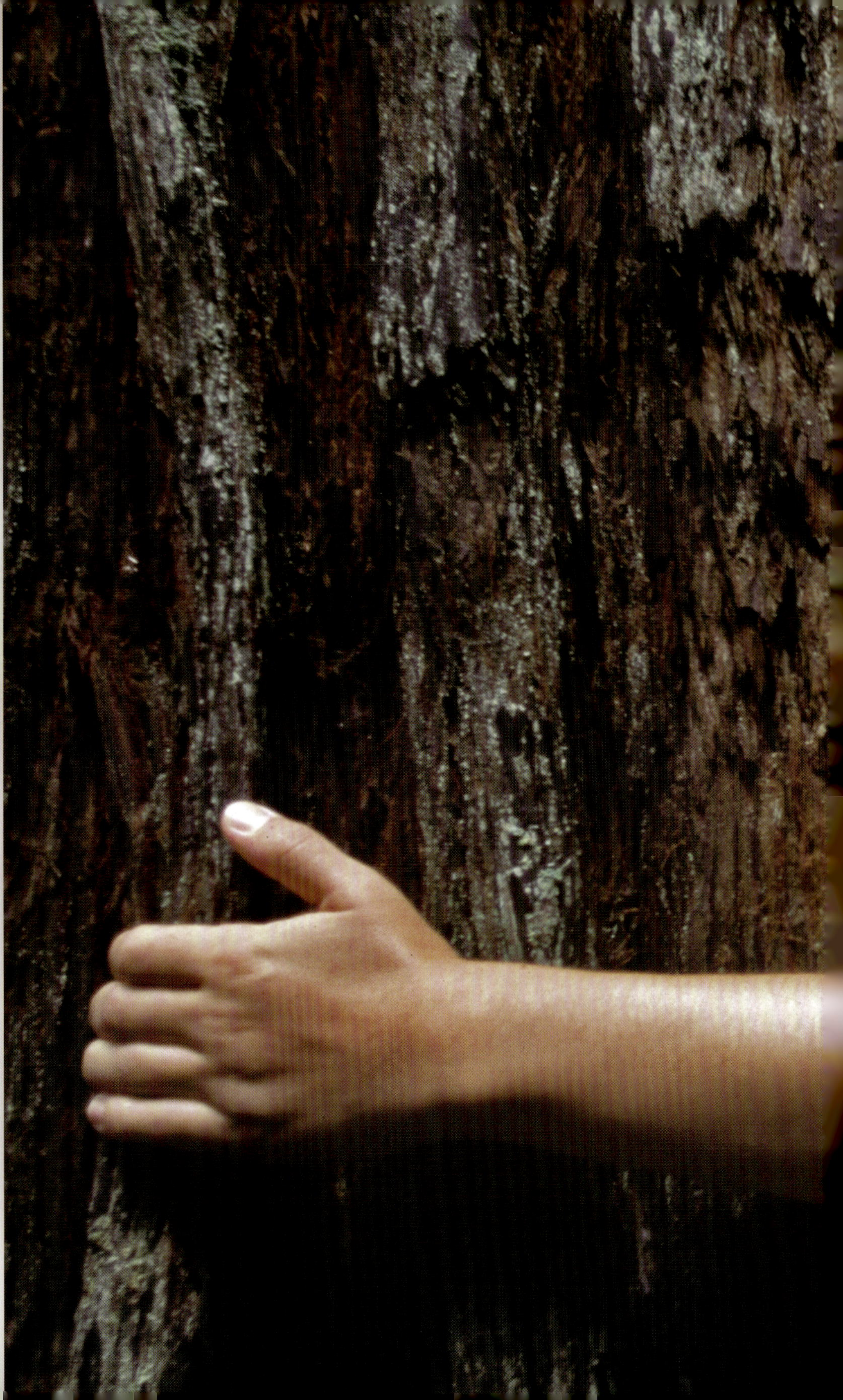

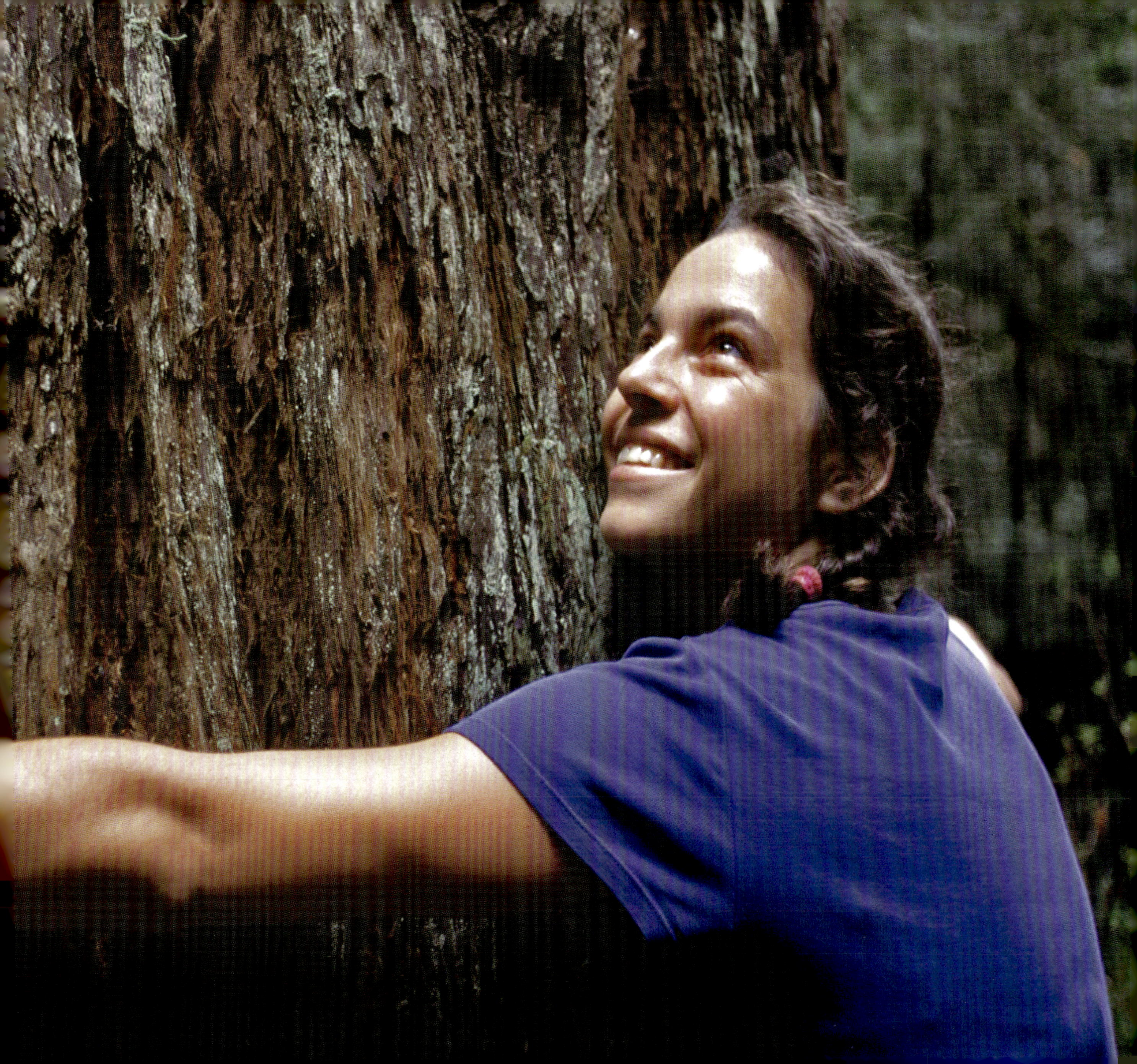

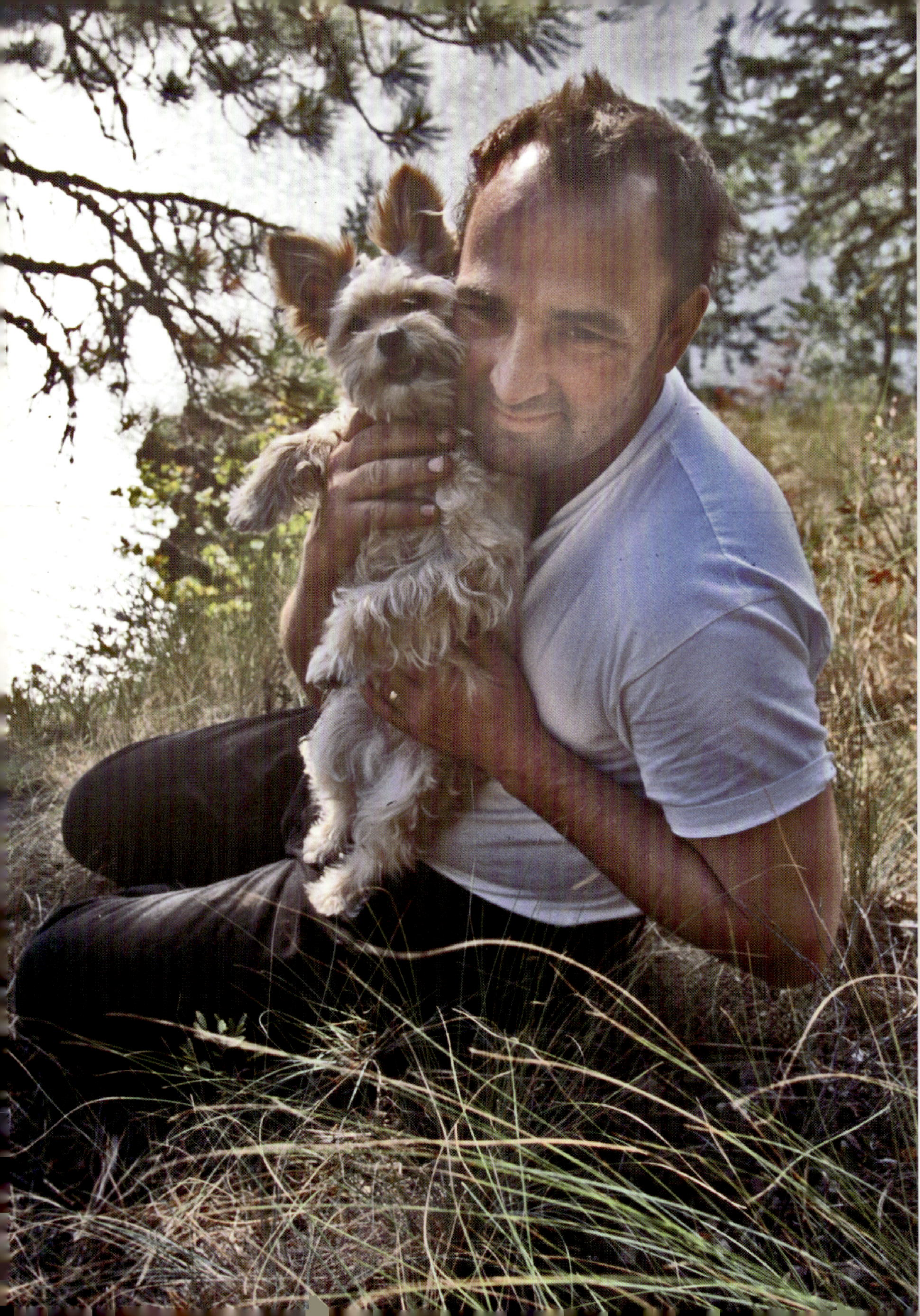

The dog is the god of frolick.

- Henry Ward Beecher

221

On a summer morning in the green mountains of northern Idaho, a logger named Randy and his little friend Milo share a tender moment.

A young girl named Giny and her dog Canuto still find good reason to be happy and play, even while the *Rio Bio Bio* flowing into the sea nearby on the coast of Chile no longer runs free.

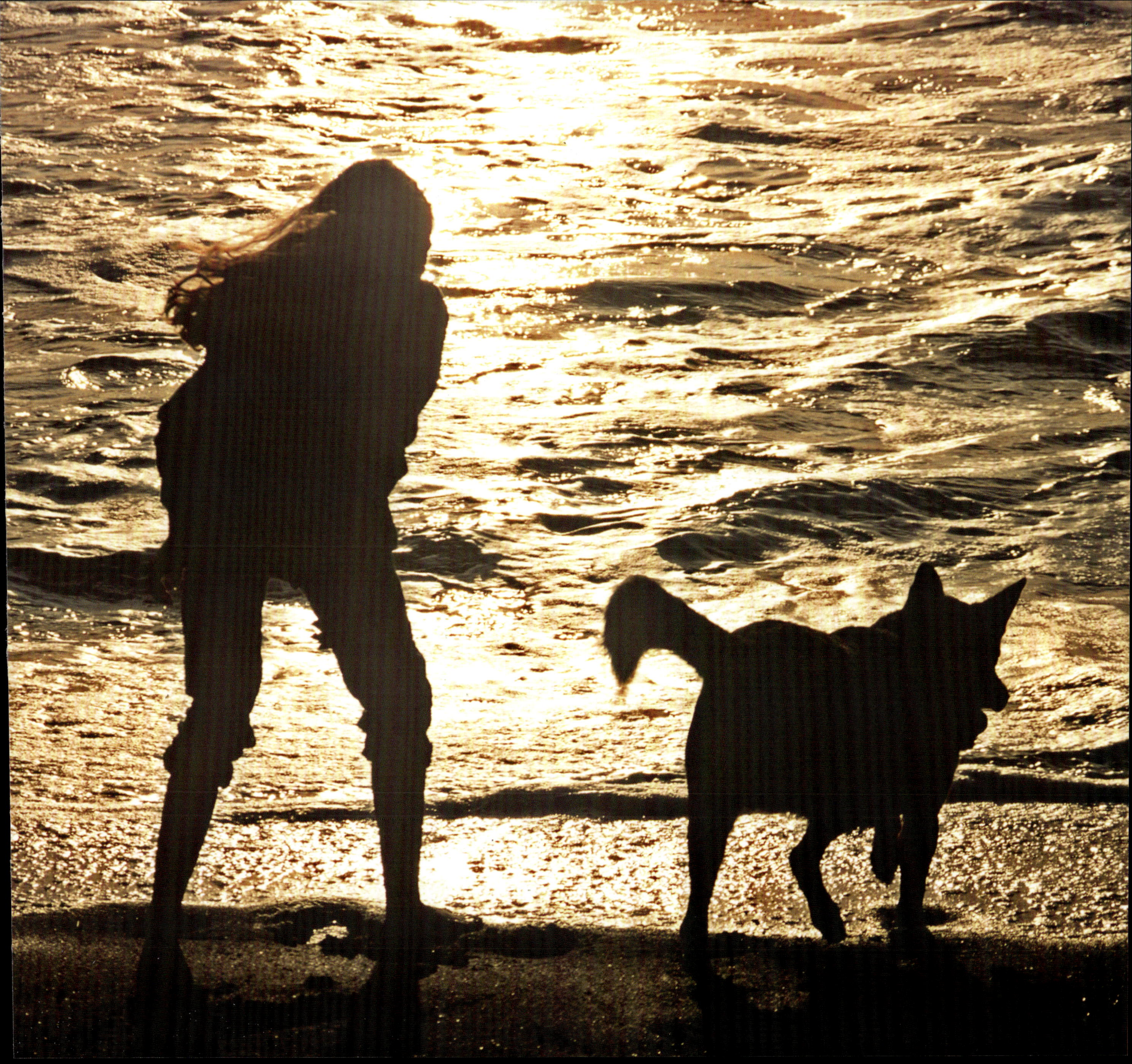

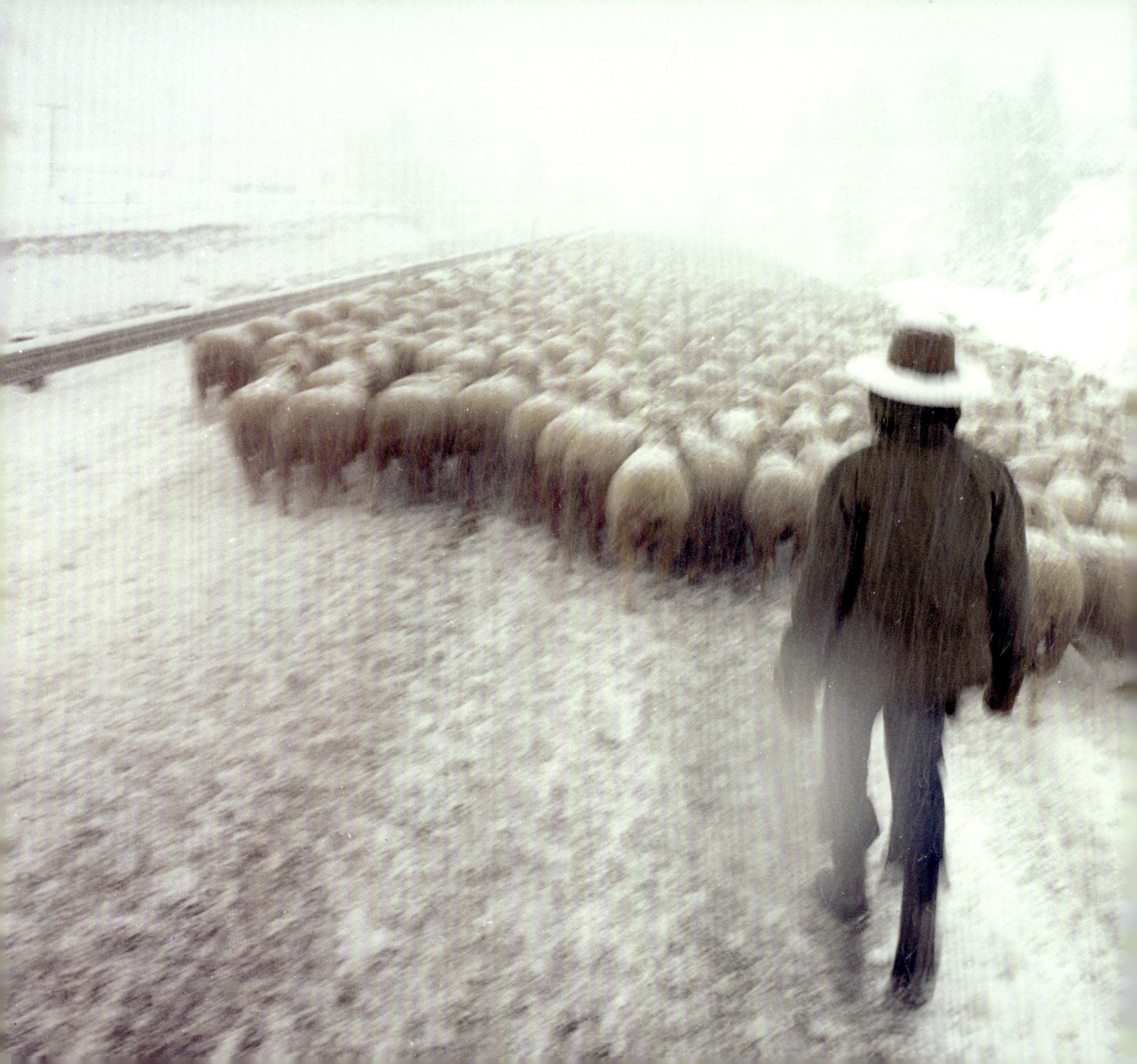

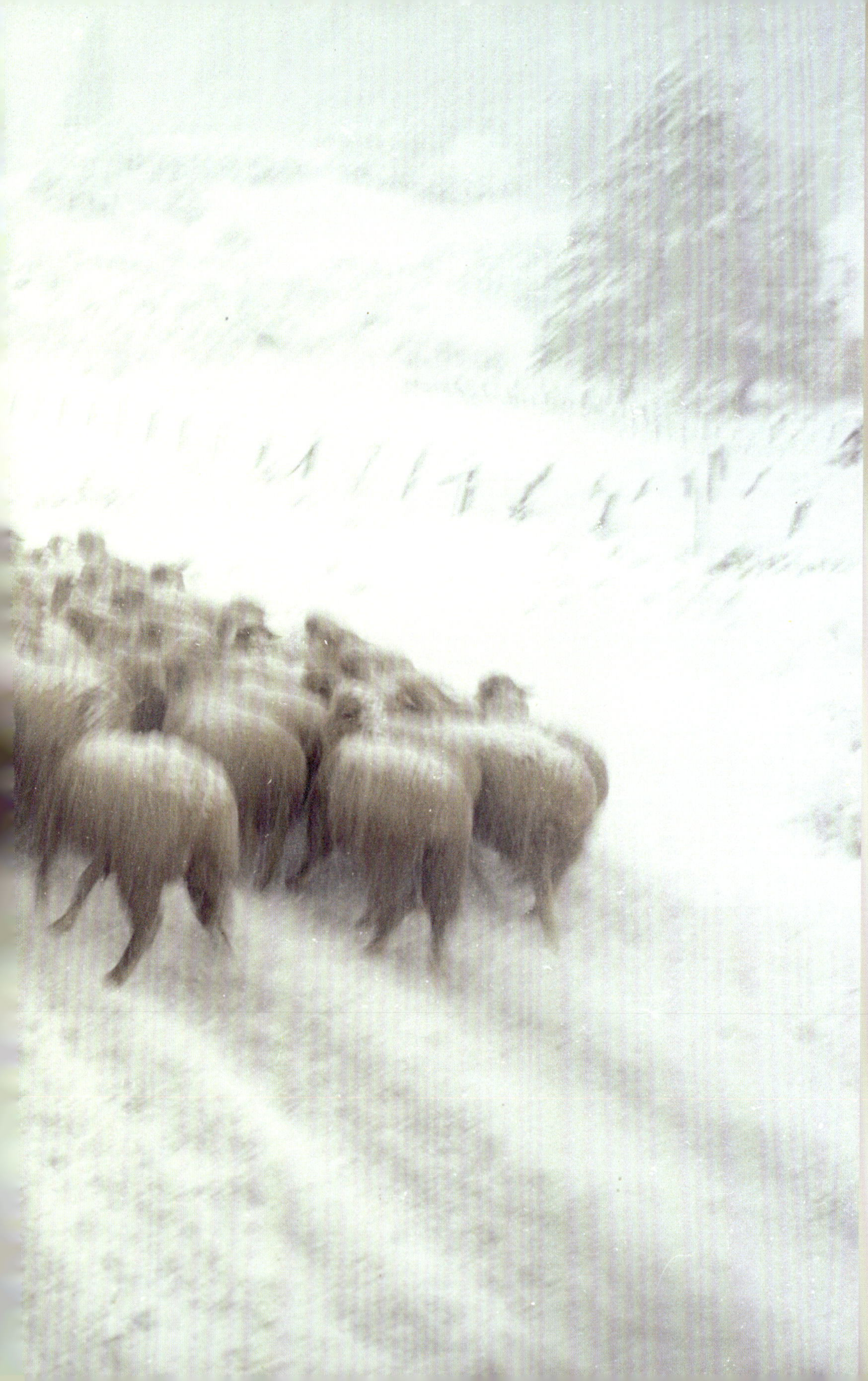

The shepherd drives the wolf from the sheep's throat, for which the sheep thanks the shepherd as his liberator, while the wolf denounces him for the same act as a destroyer of his liberty.

- Abraham Lincoln

In '97 the first winter snowstorm came early and with little warning to central Idaho. To save his flock of sheep, a shepherd had to move them down out of the mountains quickly to a more protected pasture.

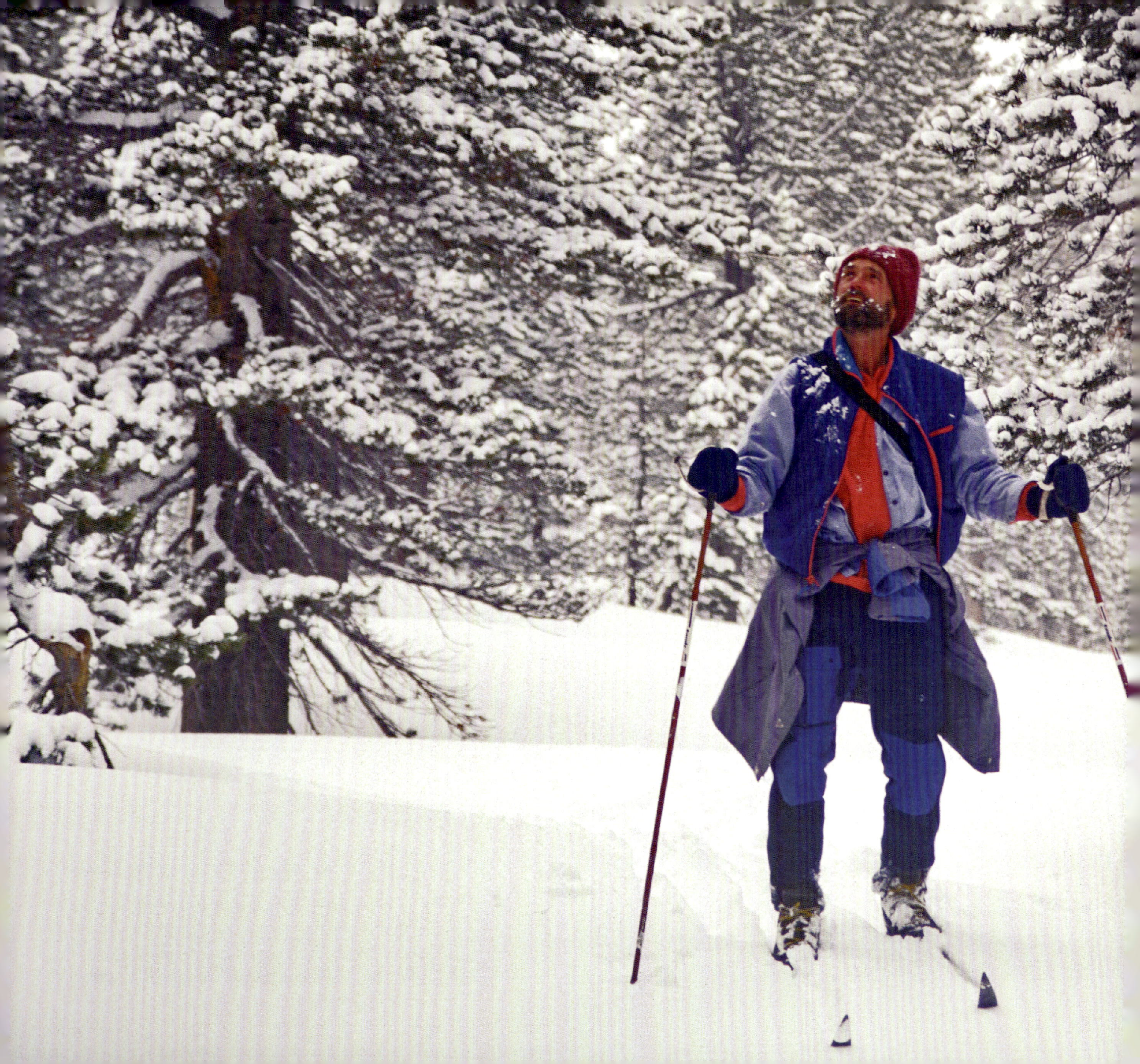

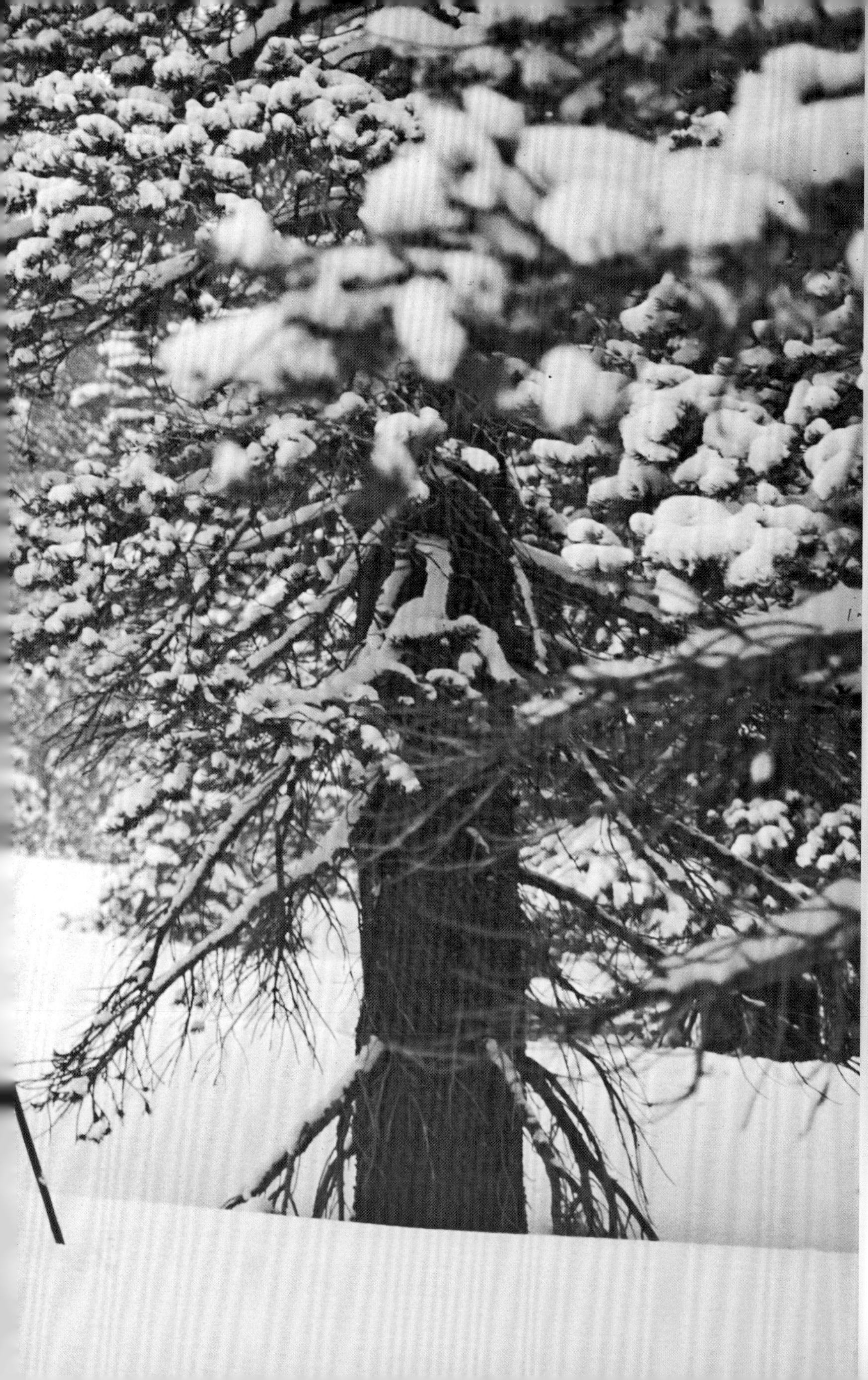

Better to go skiing and think of God than to go to church and think of sport.

- Fridtjof Nansen, Norwegian explorer and Nobel laureate

The historic Desolation Wilderness area saddles the crest of the Sierra Nevada range in northern California for a hundred square miles at altitudes between 6500 to 10,000'. During the winter months most of roads leading up to passes in the High Sierra become snowbound, and the mountains return to their original purity and silence. In 1856 nearly half of the storm-bound 87-member Donner party were reduced to cannibilism and ultimately perished when they became stranded while attemping to cross over the Desolation Wilderness too late in the fall. A few years later an Norwegian-American, John "Snowshoe" Thompson, became renowned for his crossing of the mountains twice each month on his hand-made oak skis to deliver the mail, winter and summer. Photograph by Marika Powers

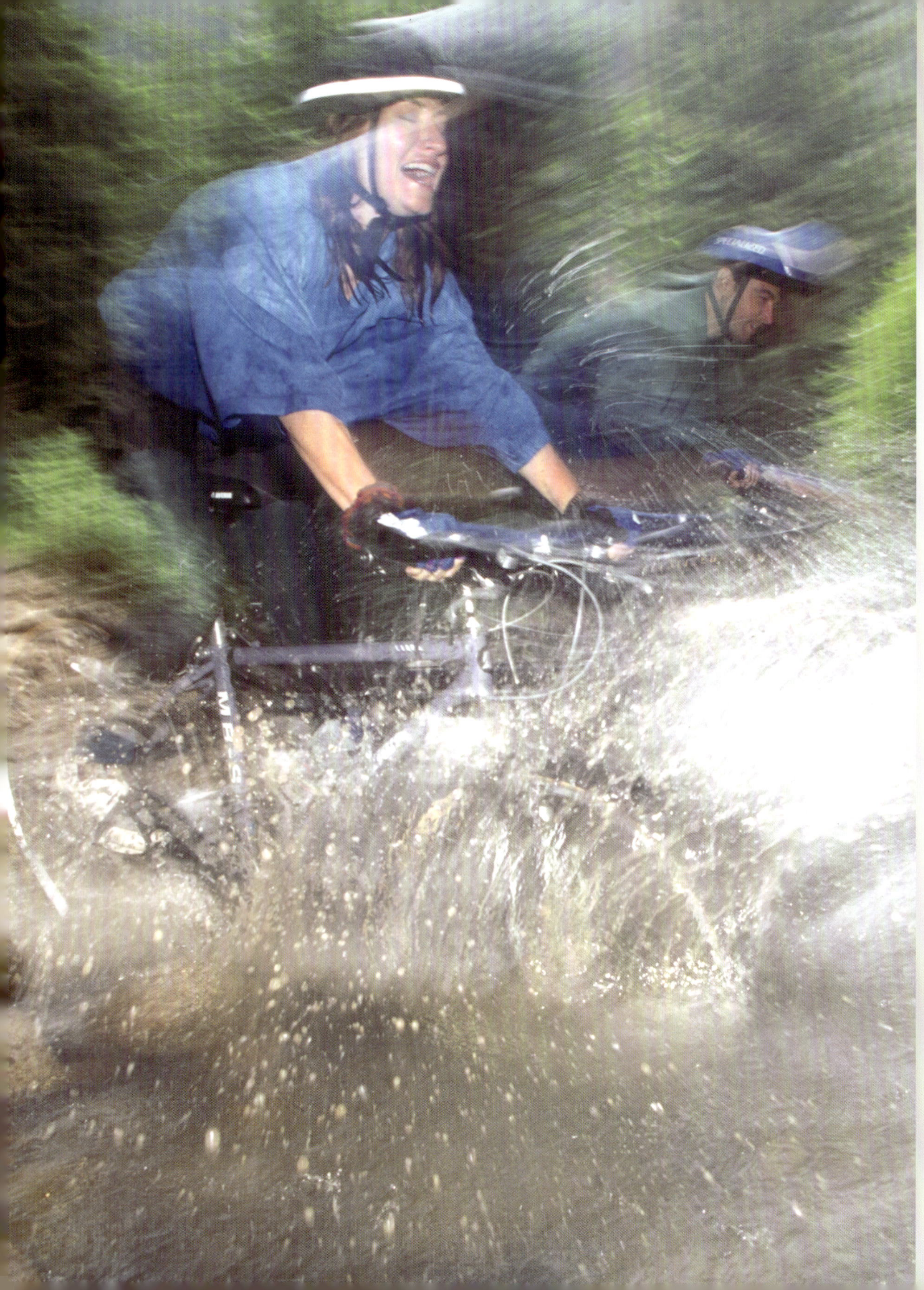

Adventure is what happens when you screw up.

- Yvon Choinard

227

Out for a training run through the Santa Cruz Mountains in northern California, multi-award winning adventure filmmakers Allison Chase and Gordon Brown attempt to power their mountain bikes across swift-moving Berry Creek during the height of the spring run-off.

Allison revels in a sublime moment of total humility after falling in the midst of the slippery, rock-filled stream. But cold and wet though she was, Allison picked up her bike and tried again - and that time she had a perfect run.

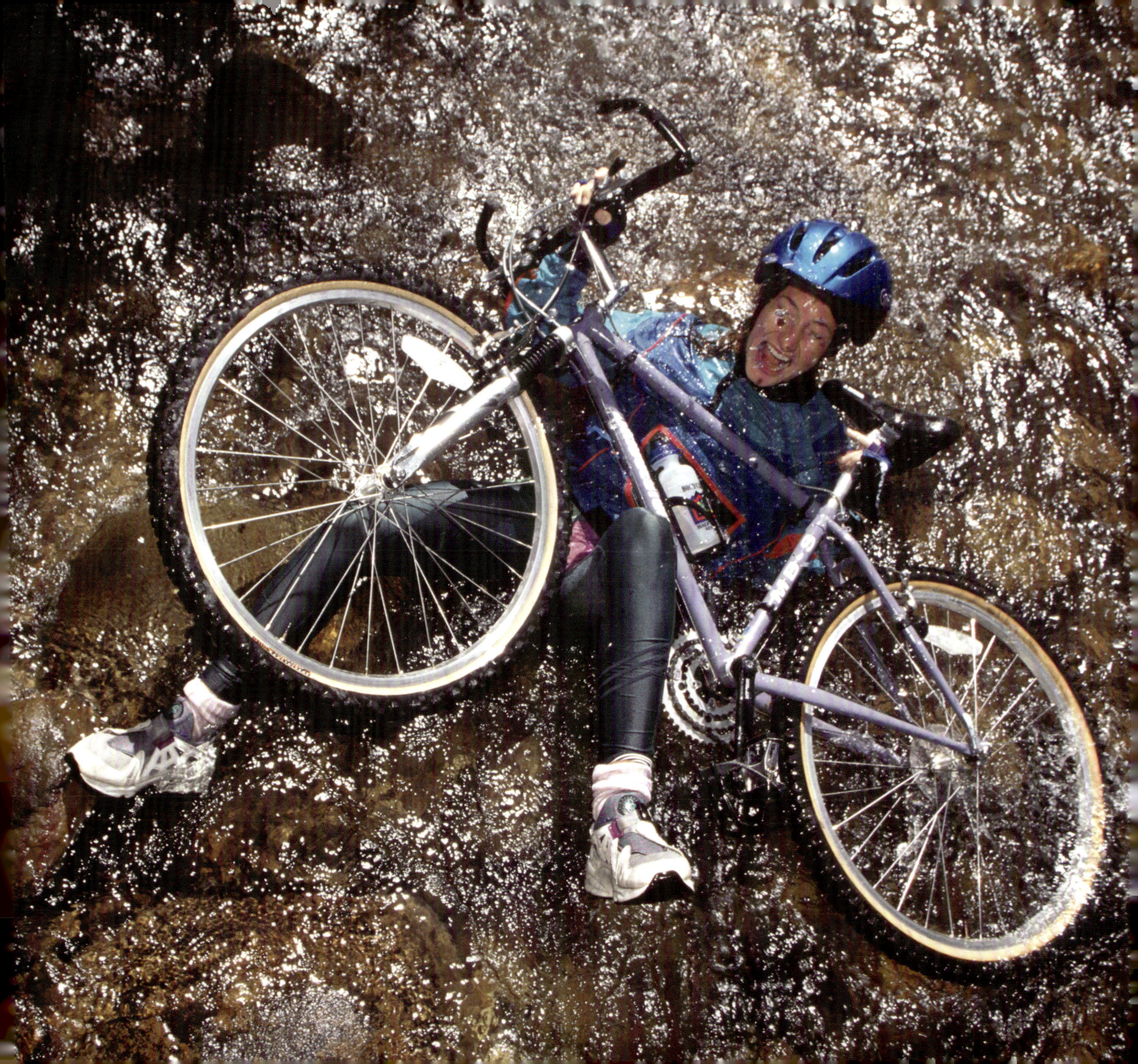

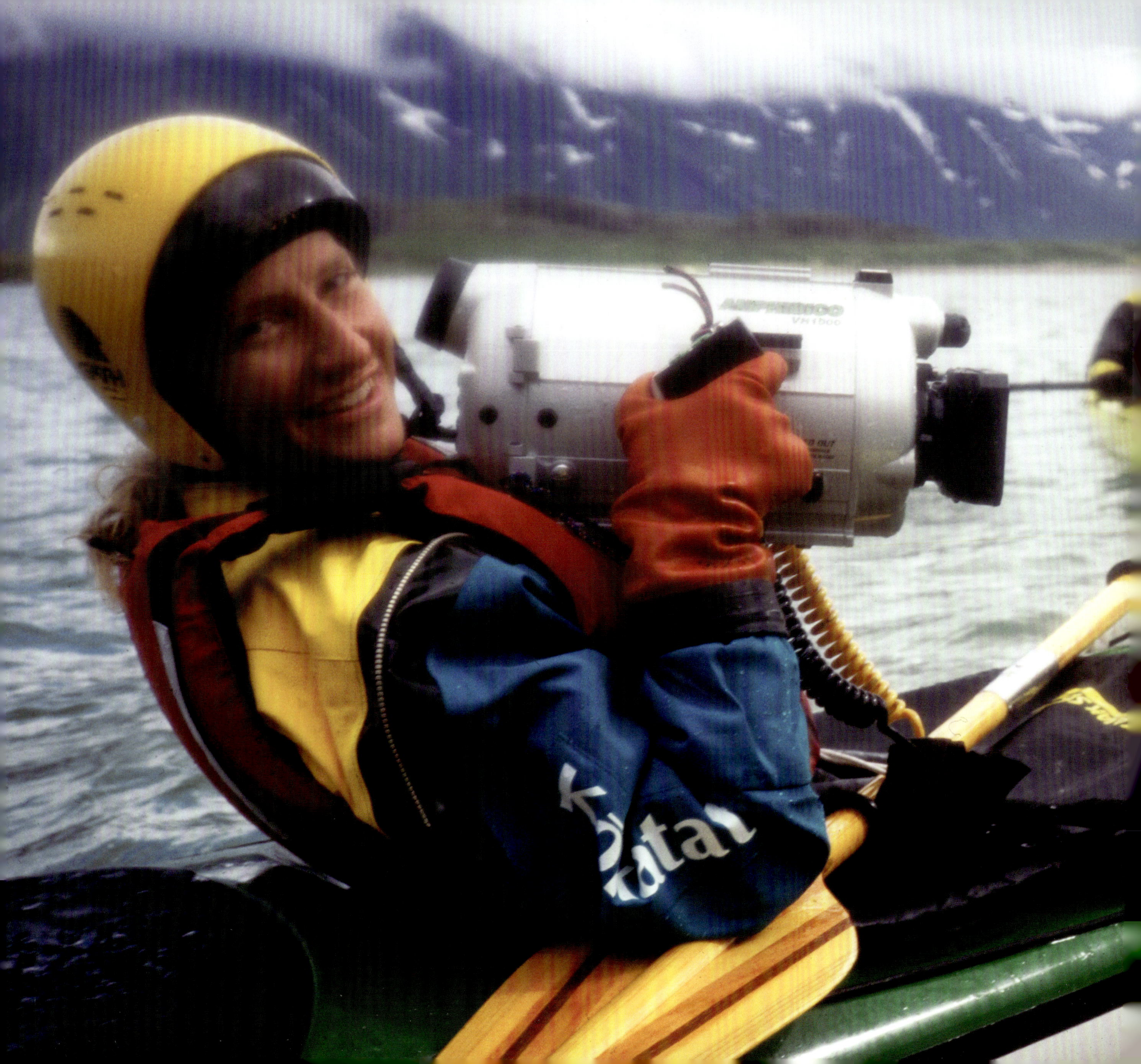

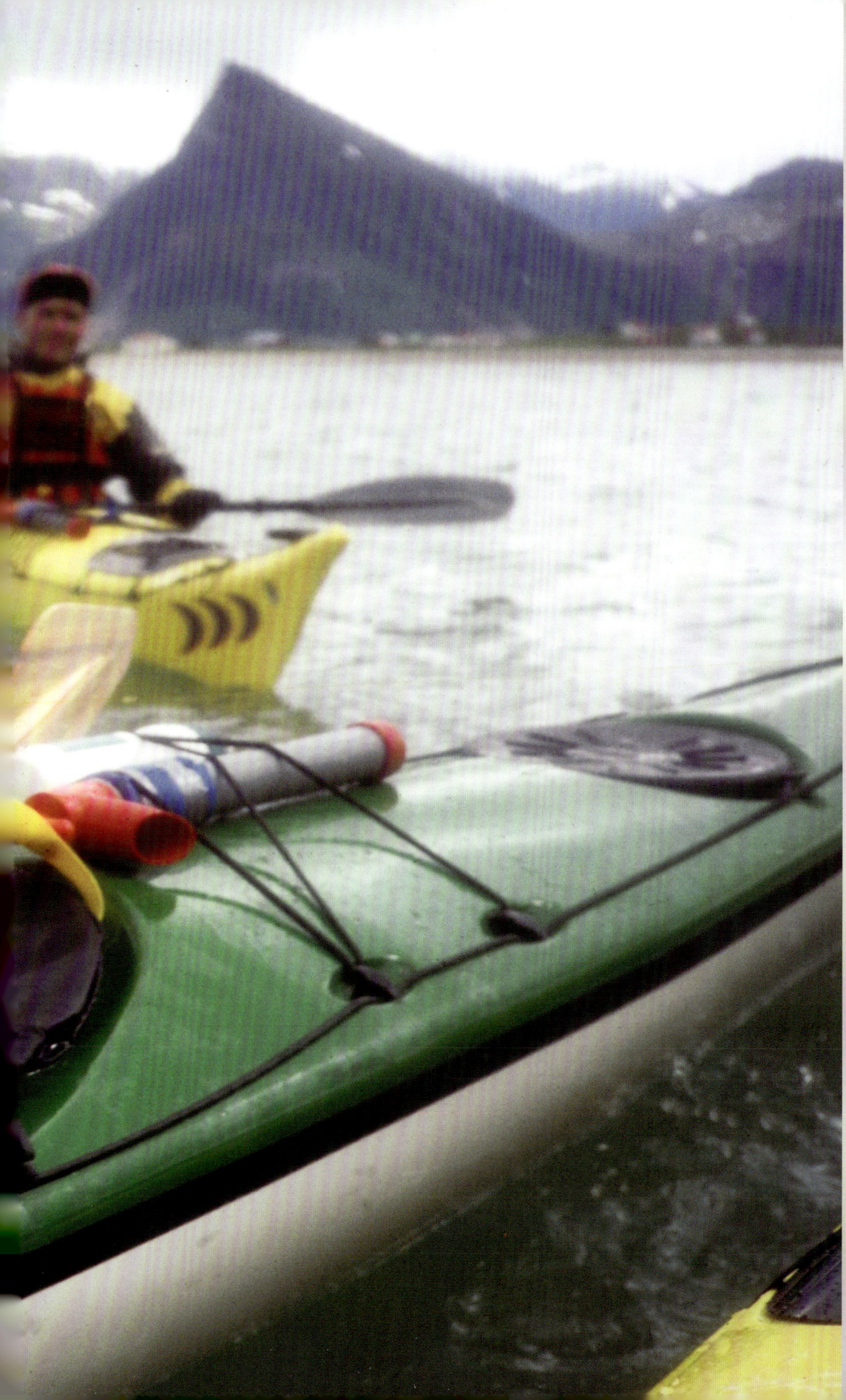

Adventure is fulfilled not in itself, but in knowledge brought back and shared with the world.

- Ian Baker, explorer and author who discovered legendary Hidden Falls on the Tsanpo River in Tibet after six attempts

Adventure filmmaker Allison Chase was a member of a team of Norwegian and Americans exploring the rugged Lofoten Islands north of the Arctic Circle off the coast of Norway with sea kayaks to make a sports adventure show for the Outdoor Life Network TV. They were careful to time their arrival at the extreme western edge of the westernmost island very precisely to coincide with the slack tide - for good reason. They knew that twice each day as the tide was changing, powerful currents would begin to surge along the shoreline in response to disequilibrium between the Arctic Ocean to the north and the Norwegian Sea to the south. This in turn would cause deadly maelstroms, composed of whirlpools and whitewater rapids, to form. Edgar Allen Poe, after viewing the fearsome spectacle from shore in 1841, wrote his terrifying account, *A Descent Into The Maestrom.*

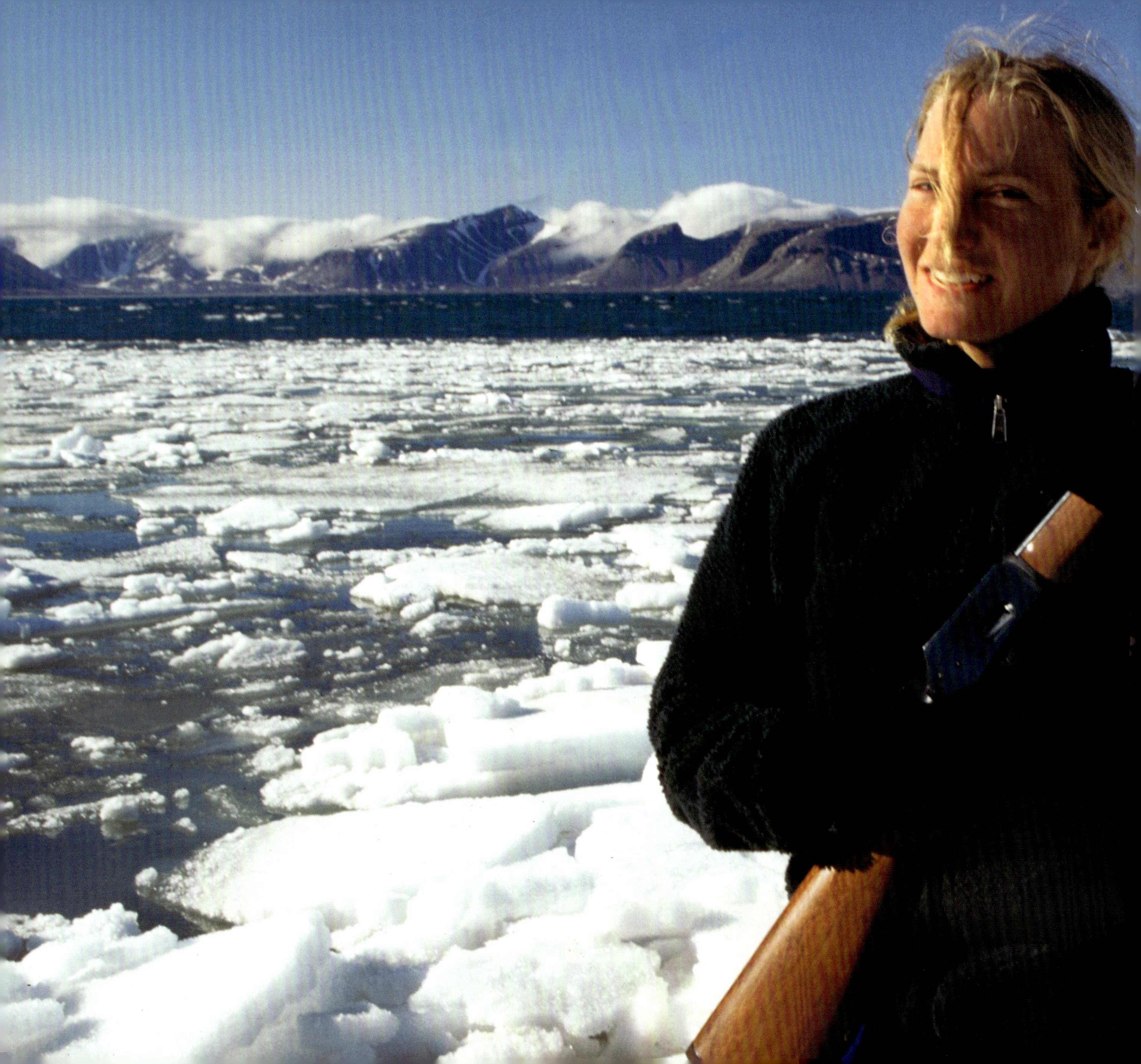

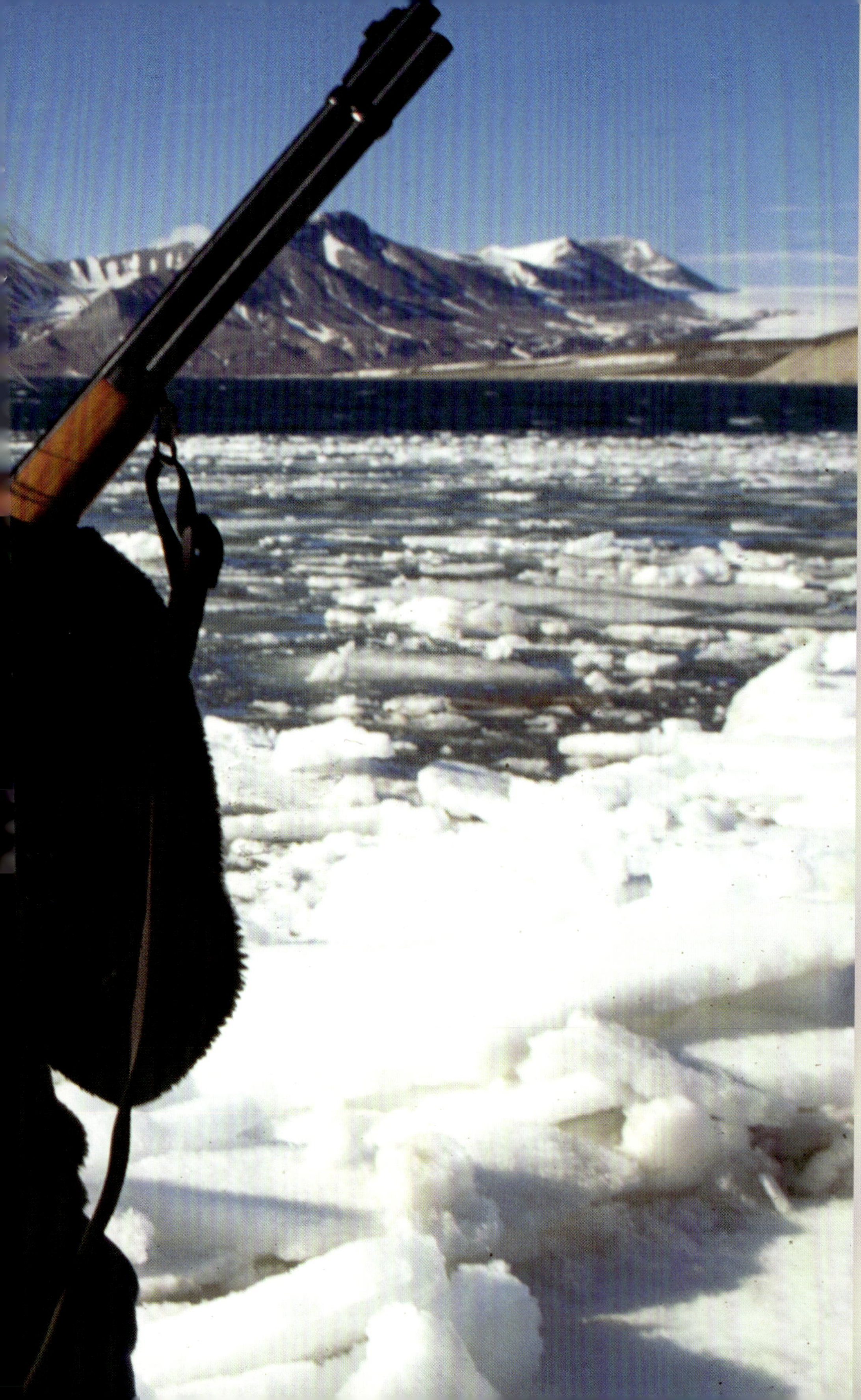

I do not believe in using women in combat, because they are too fierce.

- Margaret Mead

Adventure filmmaker Allison Chase takes her turn watching out for marauding polar bears at a camp deep in a remote ice-bound fjord in the Svalbard Islands. Chase was part of a film crew making a sports adventure show in 1997 for the Outdoor Life Television series about sea kayaking in the wild Arctic archipelago.

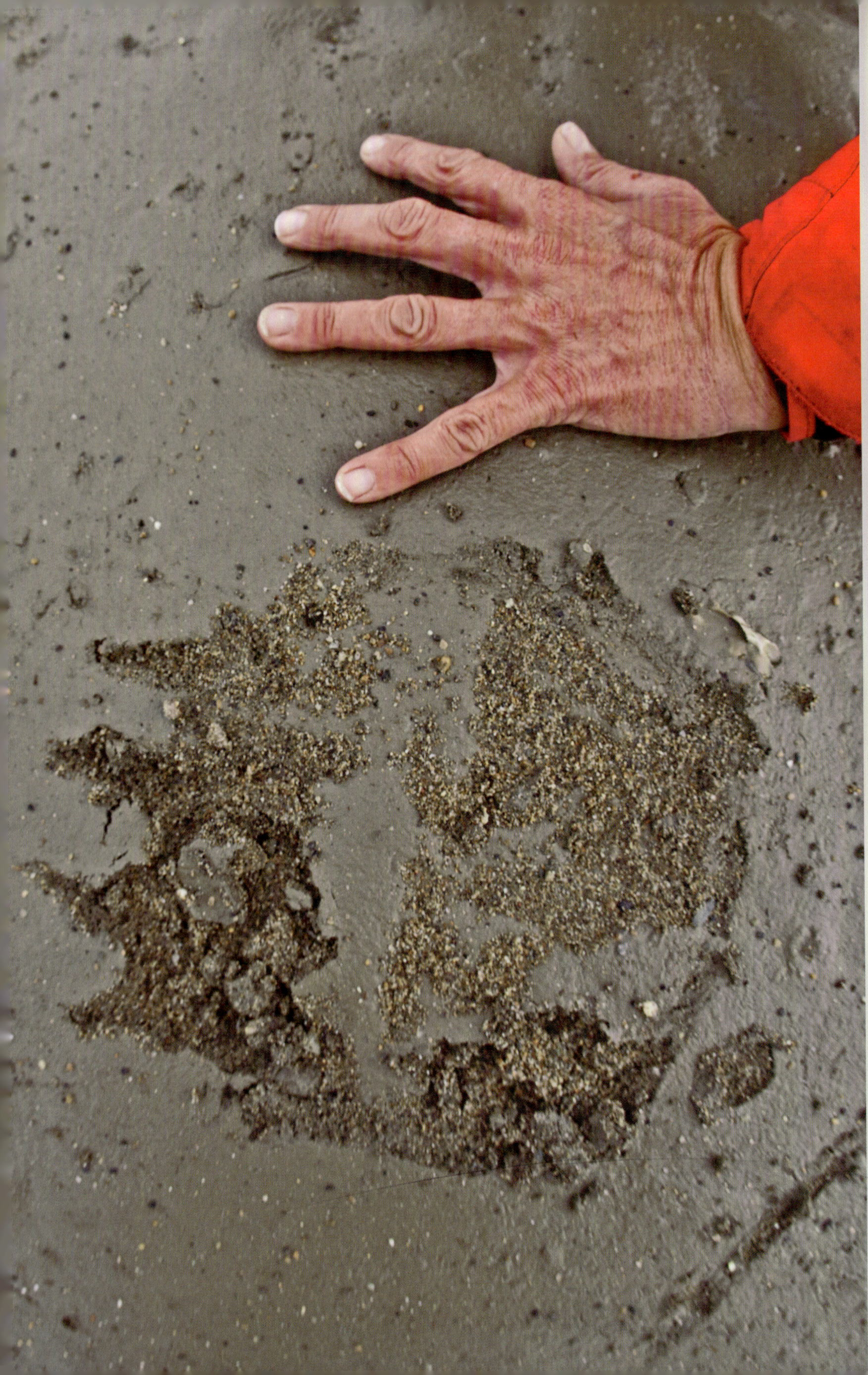

Talk low, talk slow, and don't say too much.

- John Wayne

233

In mid-summer of '08, Ocean Studio filmmaker Mark Fraser and photojournalist Michael Powers were invited to join an all-Norwegian team heading up to the Svalbard Islands for a sea kayaking expedition. Located on the edge of the polar ice pack halfway between continental Norway and the North Pole, the Svalbard archipelago remains today a wild, little changed Arctic wilderness. The Americans recognized the Norwegian endeavor as a unique opportunity to document the impact of global warming on Arctic wildlife. The first indication upon their arrival that things were changing was the government regulation, now strickly enforced, that required all persons traveling in the Svalbard wilderness to carry high-powered rifles for their protection in case of attack by polar bears. The bears' traditional food source has always been seals, who live out on the ice much of the year. Now with the advent of global warming the ice pack is melting back away from the islands to the north earlier each spring. Local hunters believe this explains the increasing frequency of polar bear attacks against humans in the Svalbard Islands in recent years. Polar bear track photo by Mark Fraser.

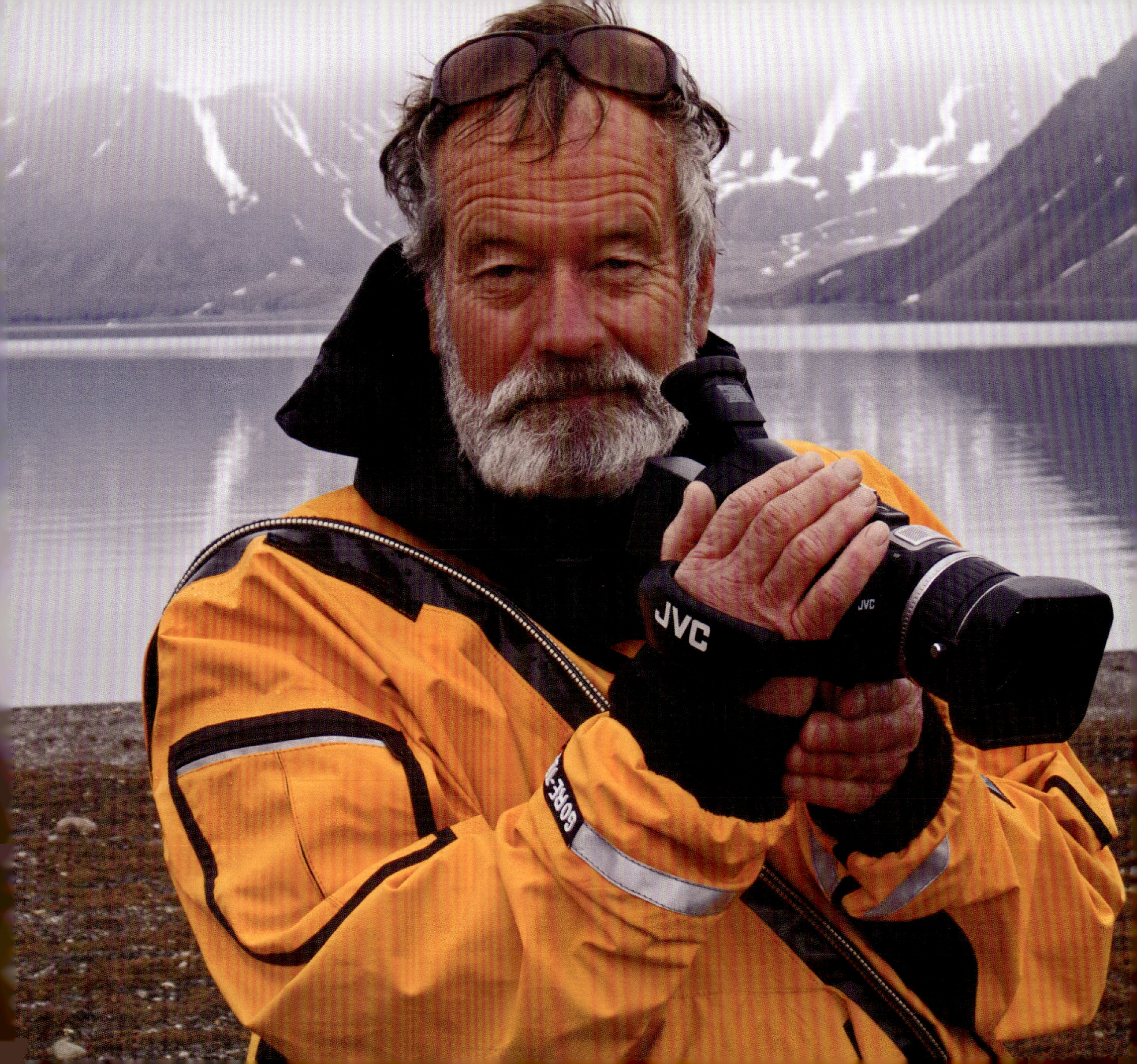
JVC
JVC

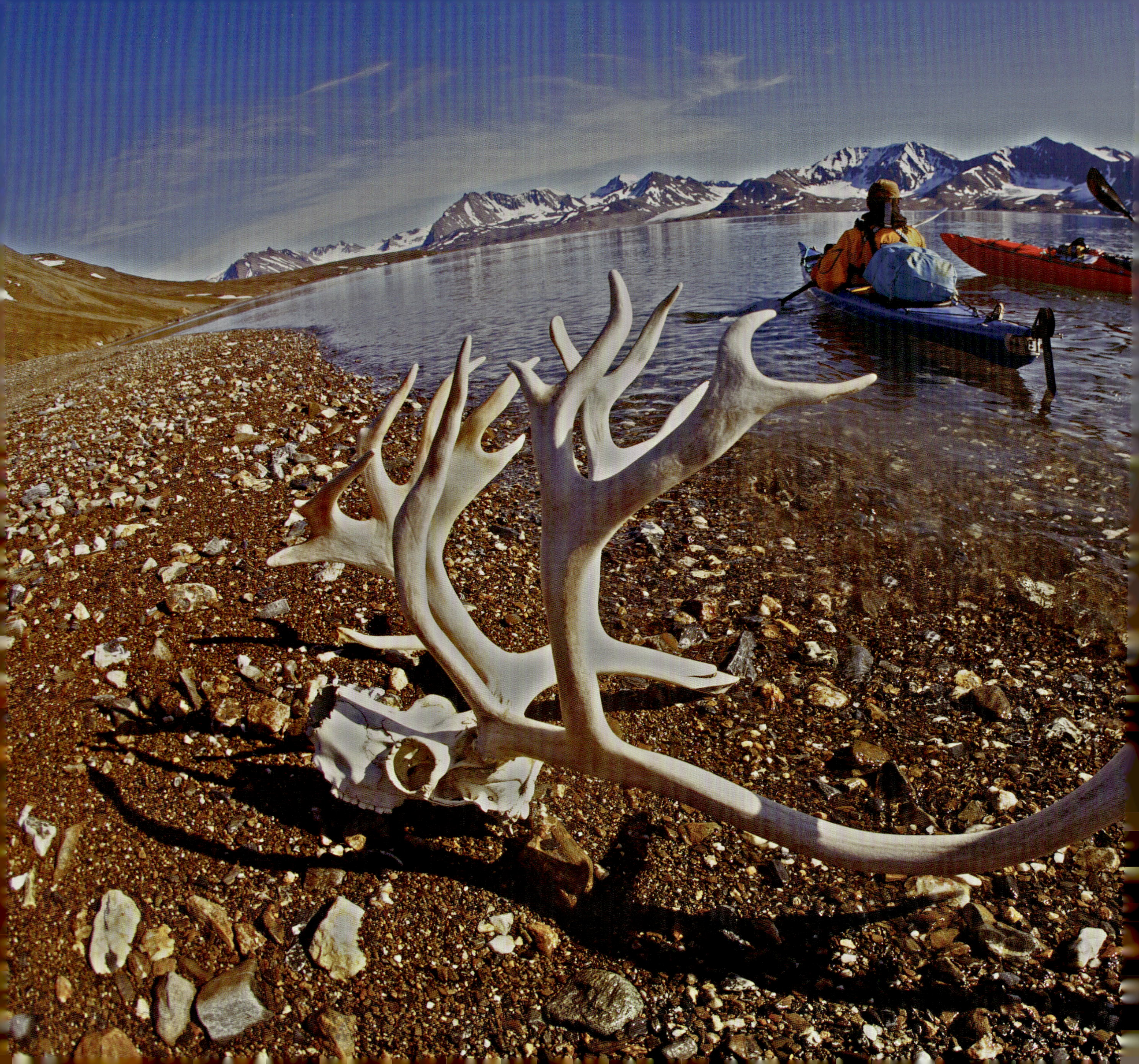

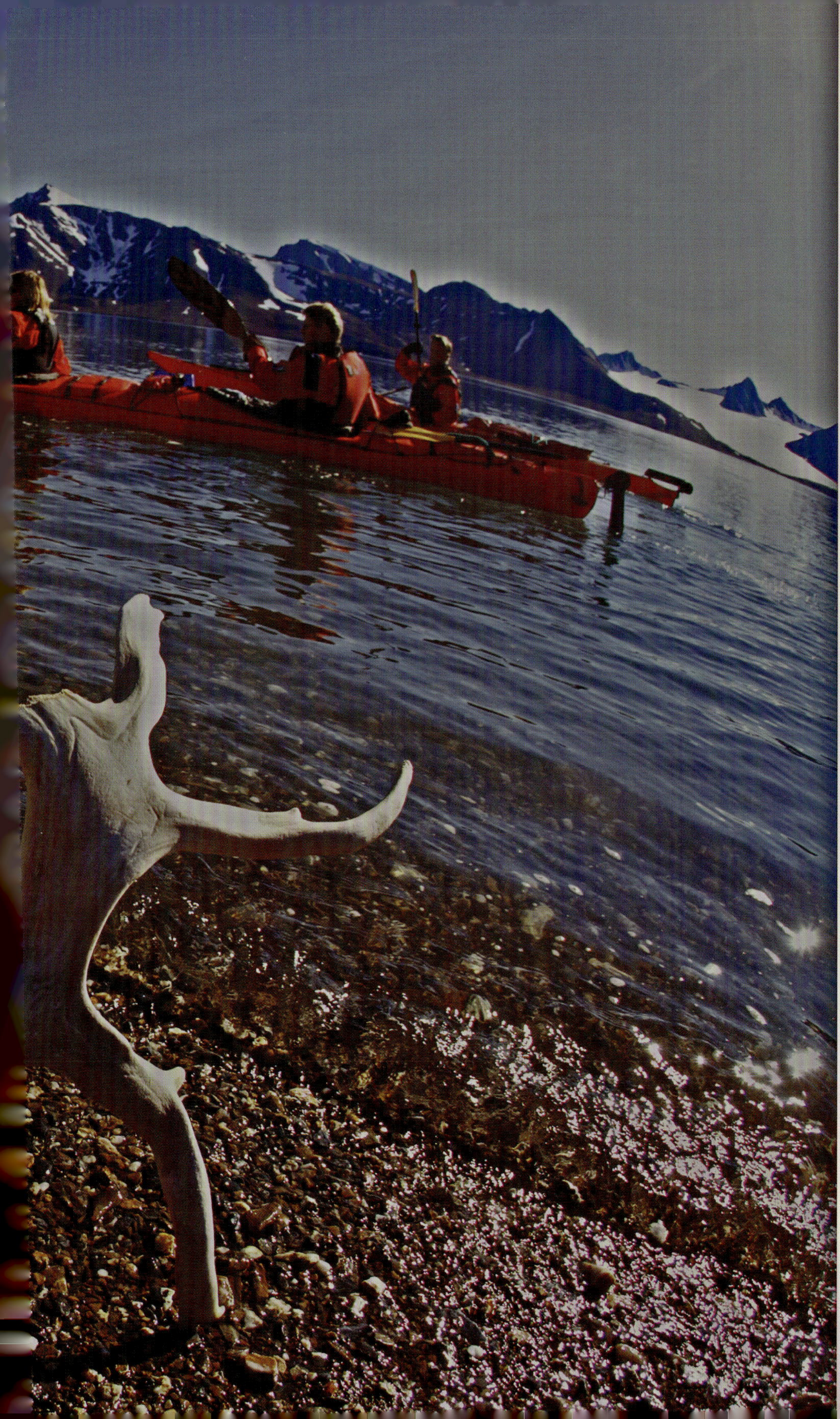

The north forgets slowly.

- Vilhjálmur Stefálmur,
18th century Arctic explorer

A team of seasoned cold-weather sea kayakers from northern Norway, whose Viking ancestors discovered the Arctic Svalbard Islands in the 12th century, return there to paddle and explore seldom-visited fjords in a remote section of the still wild archipelago in 2008. Situated on the edge of the vast polar ice pack at 74-81 degrees north latitude, the Svalbards remain today a pristine yet fragile Arctic wilderness region. The only permanent human settlements in the islands are the frontier community of Longyearbyen (a sign at the door of a pub there directed patrons to check their guns before entering), the remanents of a Russian coal mining operation on a remote island, and a few widely scattered research stations. Sixty percent of the land surface is covered by glaciers. Polar bears, seals, walrus, a few hardy reindeer and foxes - and in the summer months, millions of migratory birds, inhabit the islands. The 3000 polar bears remaining in the Svalbard archipelago are under increasing pressure as the ice pack where they hunt the seals is shrinking from the effects of global warming.

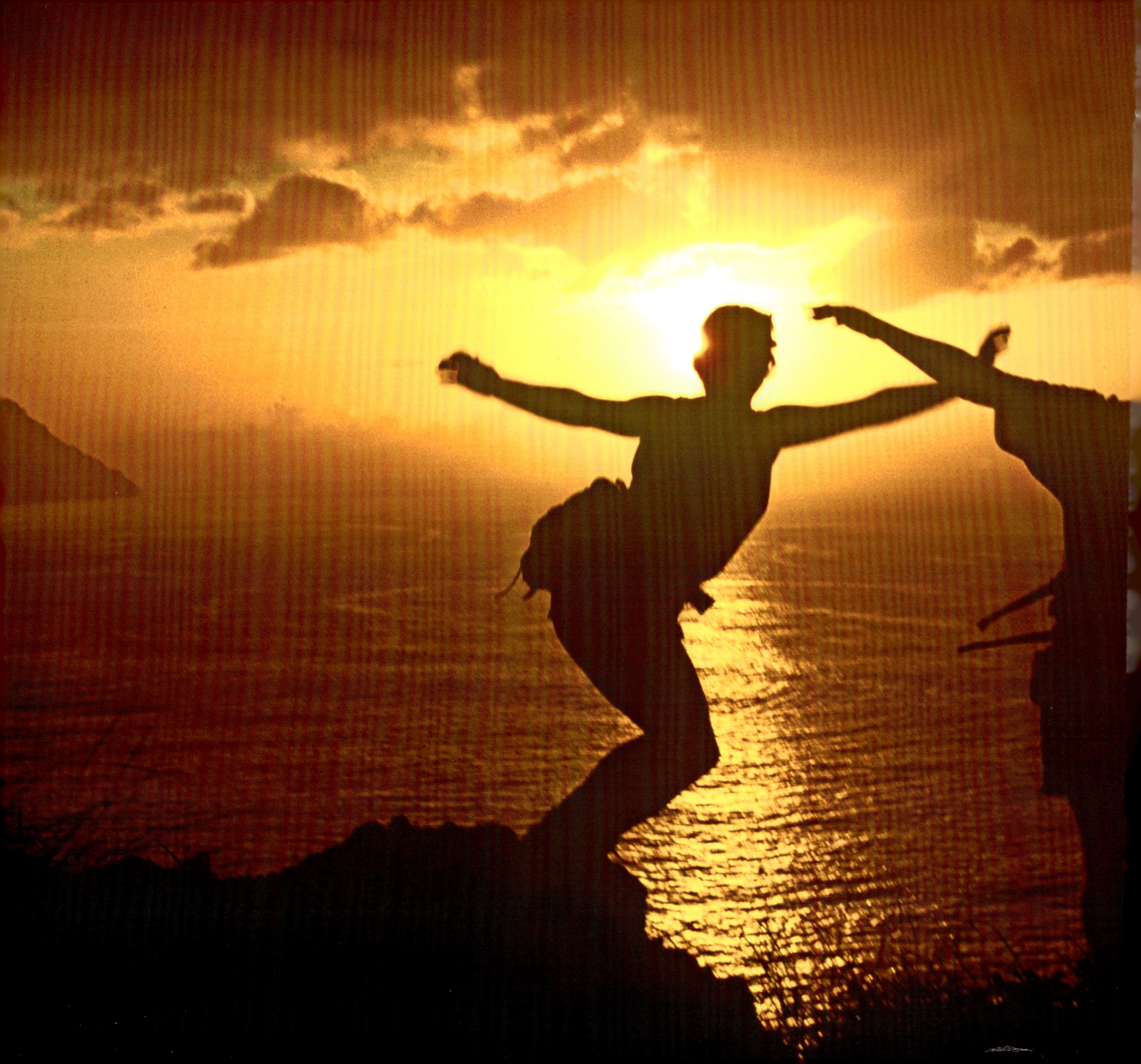

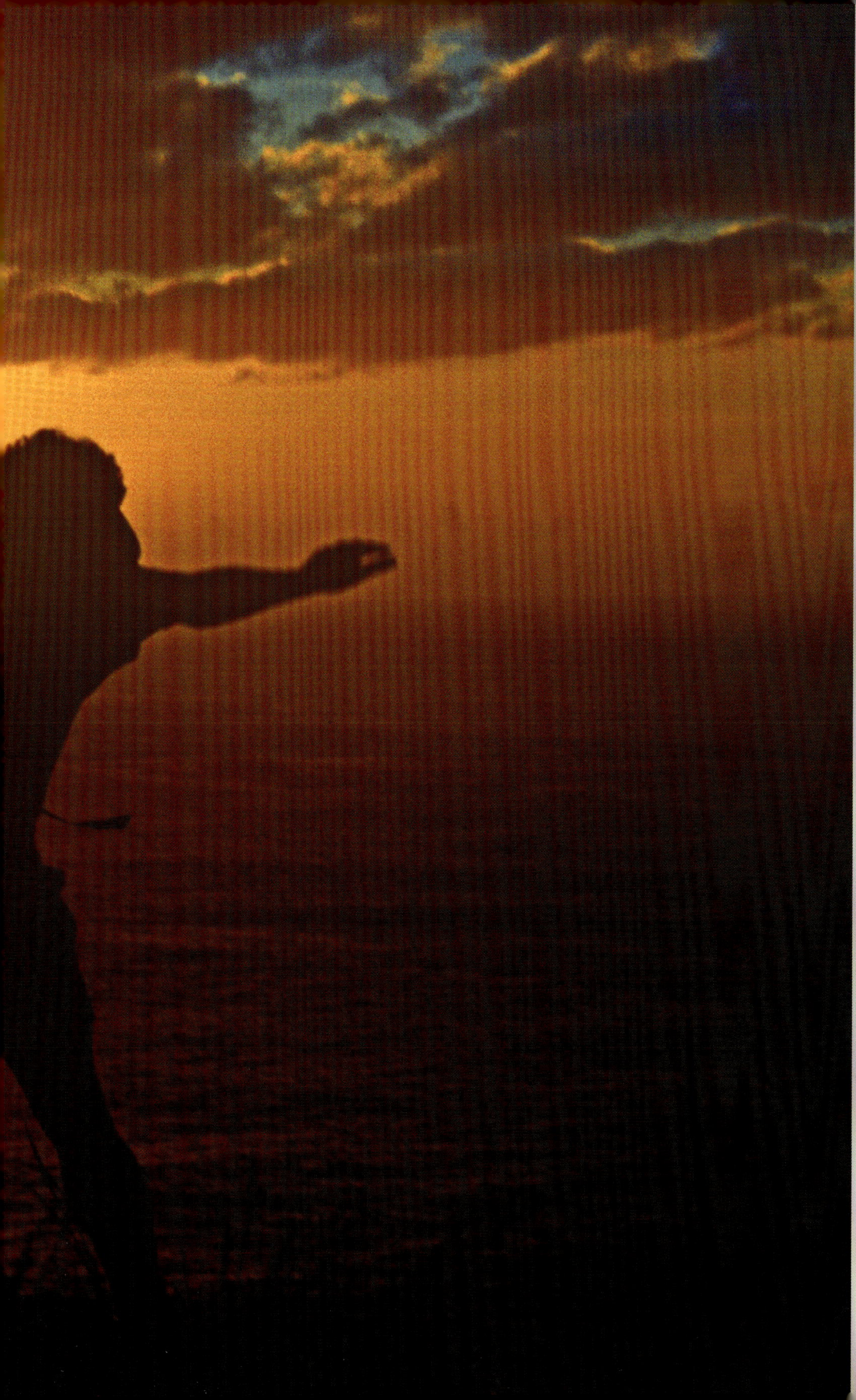

In short, all good things are wild and free.

- Henry David Thoreau

238

Along the fabled Na Pali coast of Kauai, waterfalls the color of crystaline jade tumbles down for thousands of feet through lush foilage on verdant cliff faces to the sea. Hikers and sea kayakers privileged to enter this earthly paradise are soon overcome with wonder and a sense that the old legends might indeed be true; perhaps this really was once a playground of the gods - and maybe it still is.

All right, let's go outside where God can see us better.

- Zorba the Greek

239

Deep within a centuries-old circle of stately redwood trees in Purisma Canyon on the coast of northern California, hikers gather for a few moments of profound communion with nature. The canyon and its redwoods are freely accessible to hikers to enjoy but are protected in perpetuity from logging or development on land owned by the Midpeninsula Regional Open Space District.

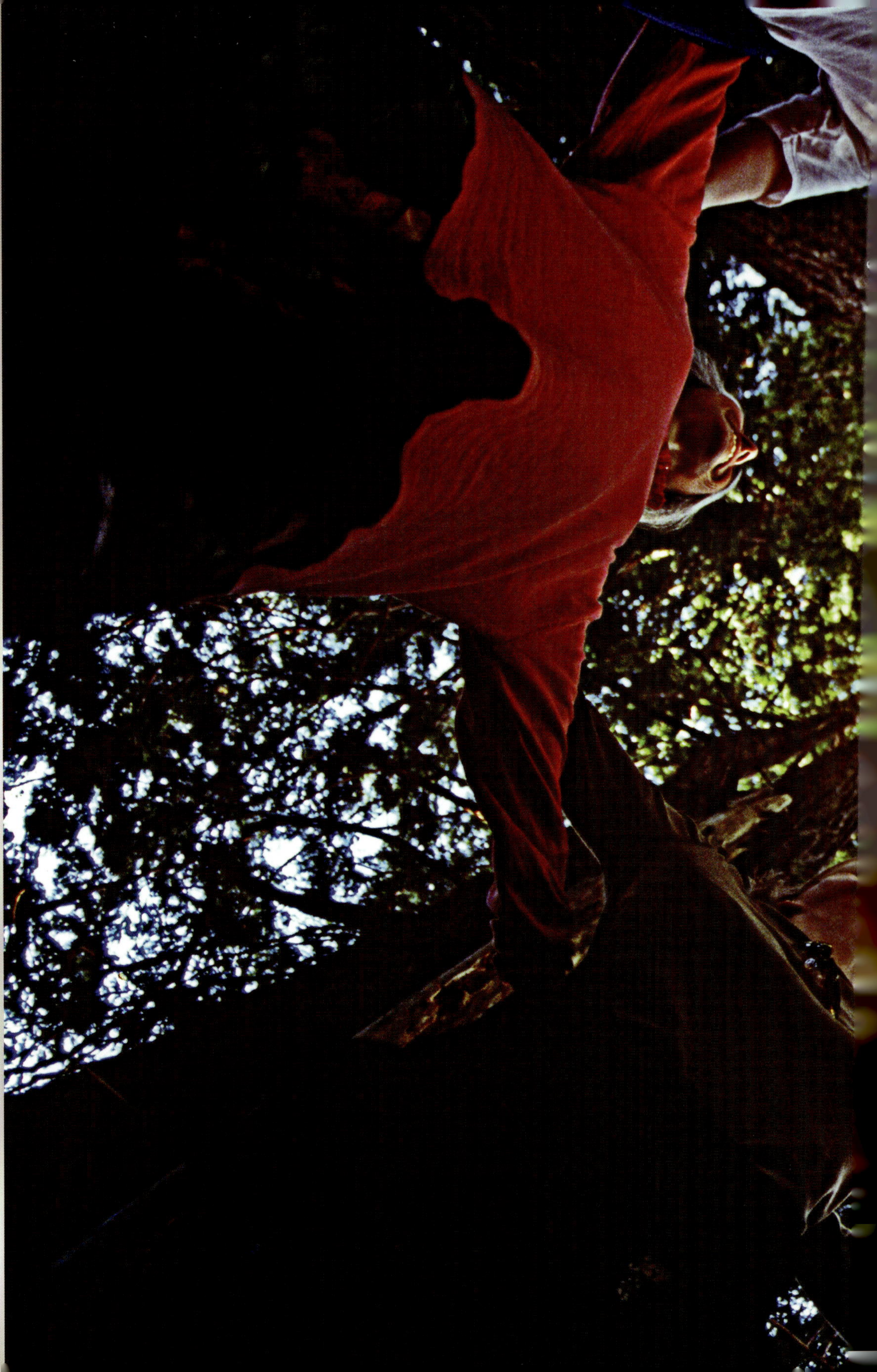

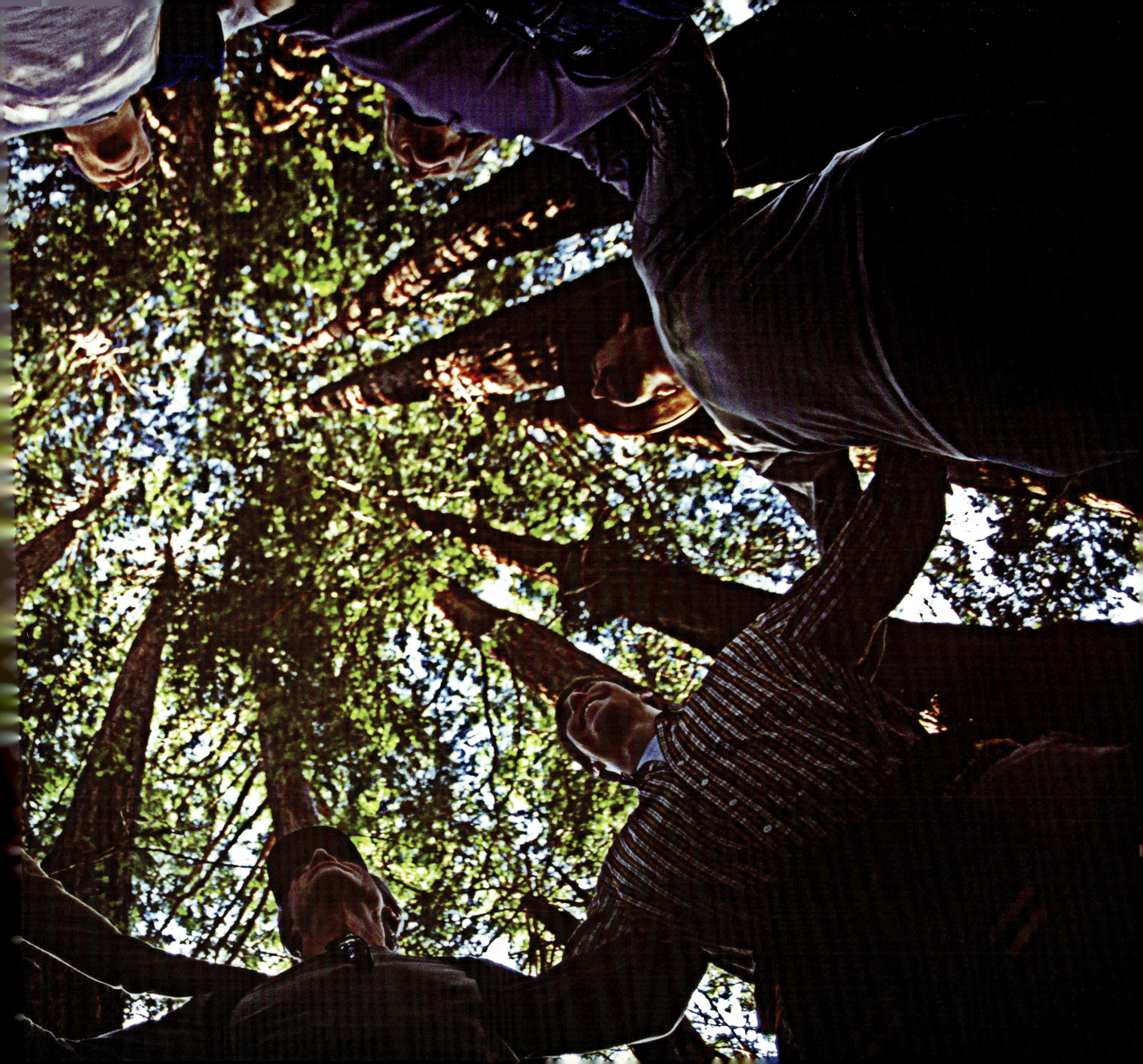

I must be a mermaid, Rango. I have no fear of depths and a great fear of shallow living.

- Anais Nin

241

Her first encounter with the tropical Pacific Ocean waters surrounding Kauai at the far western edge of the Hawaiian archipelogo was an ecstatic experience for Sidsel Jacobsen from Bodø, Norway, up north of the Arctic Circle. Yet Sidsel, a master yoga teacher back home in Bodø, found Vrksasana, the Tree Pose, to be quite challenging in the swirling sea and shifting sands along Hanalei Bay.

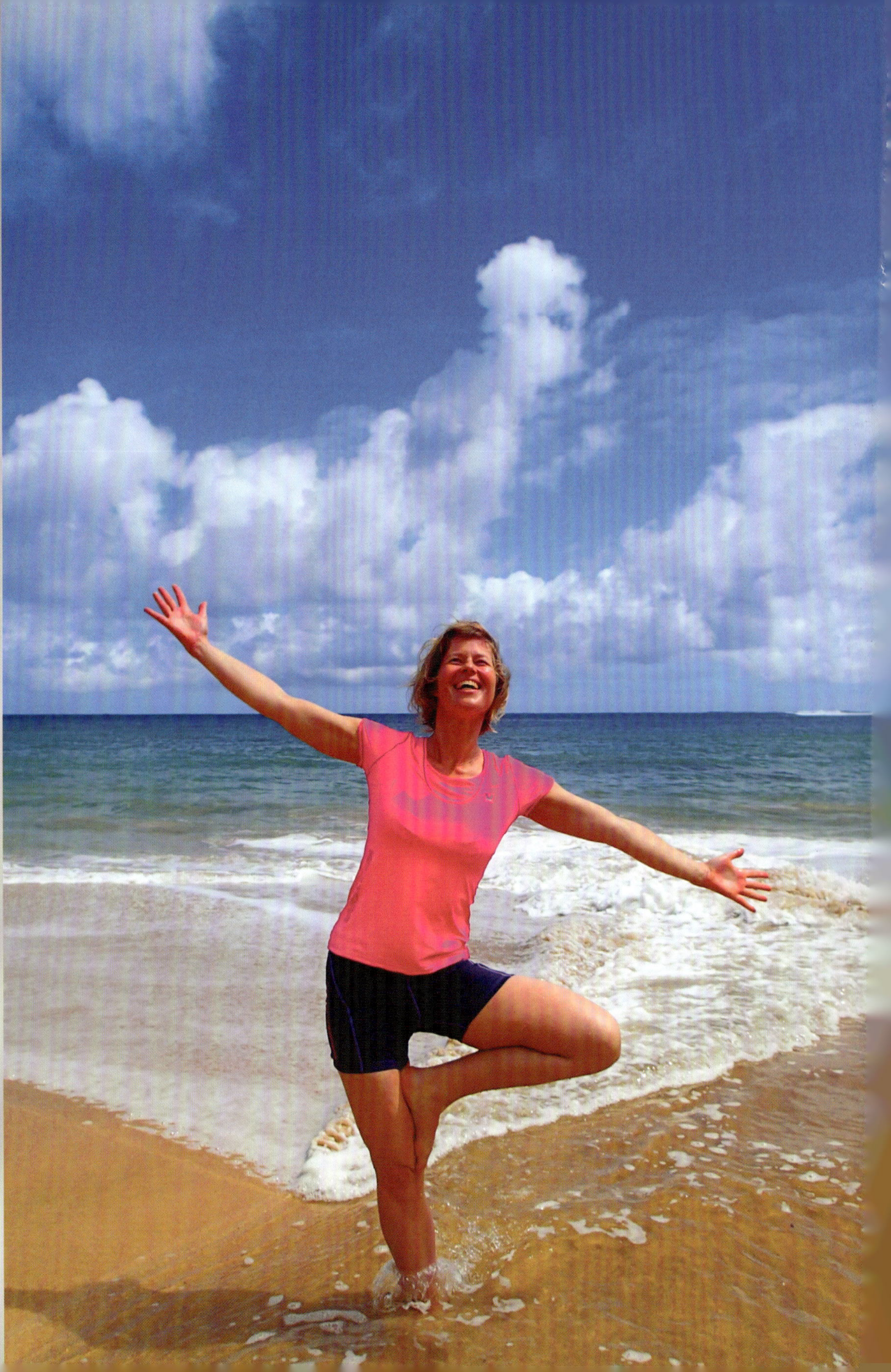

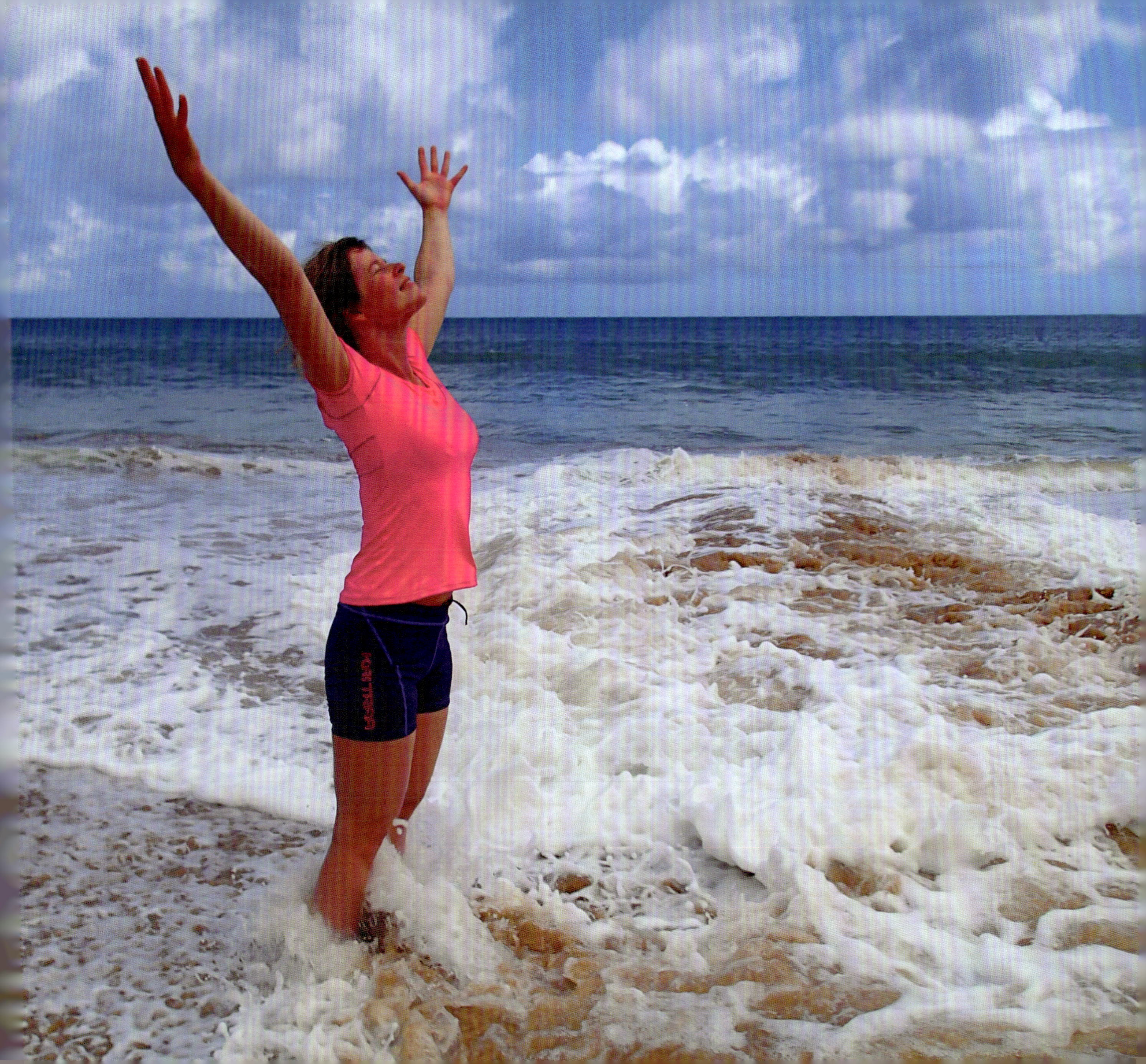

If there be righteousness in the heart
there will be beauty in the character.
If there be beauty in the character
there will be harmony in the home.
If there be harmony in the home
there will be order in the nation.
If there be order in the nation
there will be peace in the world.

- Confucius

The Jacobsens are a Norwegian family who live north of the Arctic Circle in the seacoast town of *Bodø*. They also keep a little house on an island further north in the Norwegian Sea. In the summer months they go there to kayak and hike in the rugged mountains. In the old days the fishermen returning home in their traditional wooden *Nordland* sailboats, often from great distances and many days out at sea (without the benefit of modern navigational equipment), were always relieved when they first saw the island again. They called it *Landegode* (the good land), because when they spotted it they knew they were drawing near the mainland of Norway and became assured of safe passage back to *Bodø*.

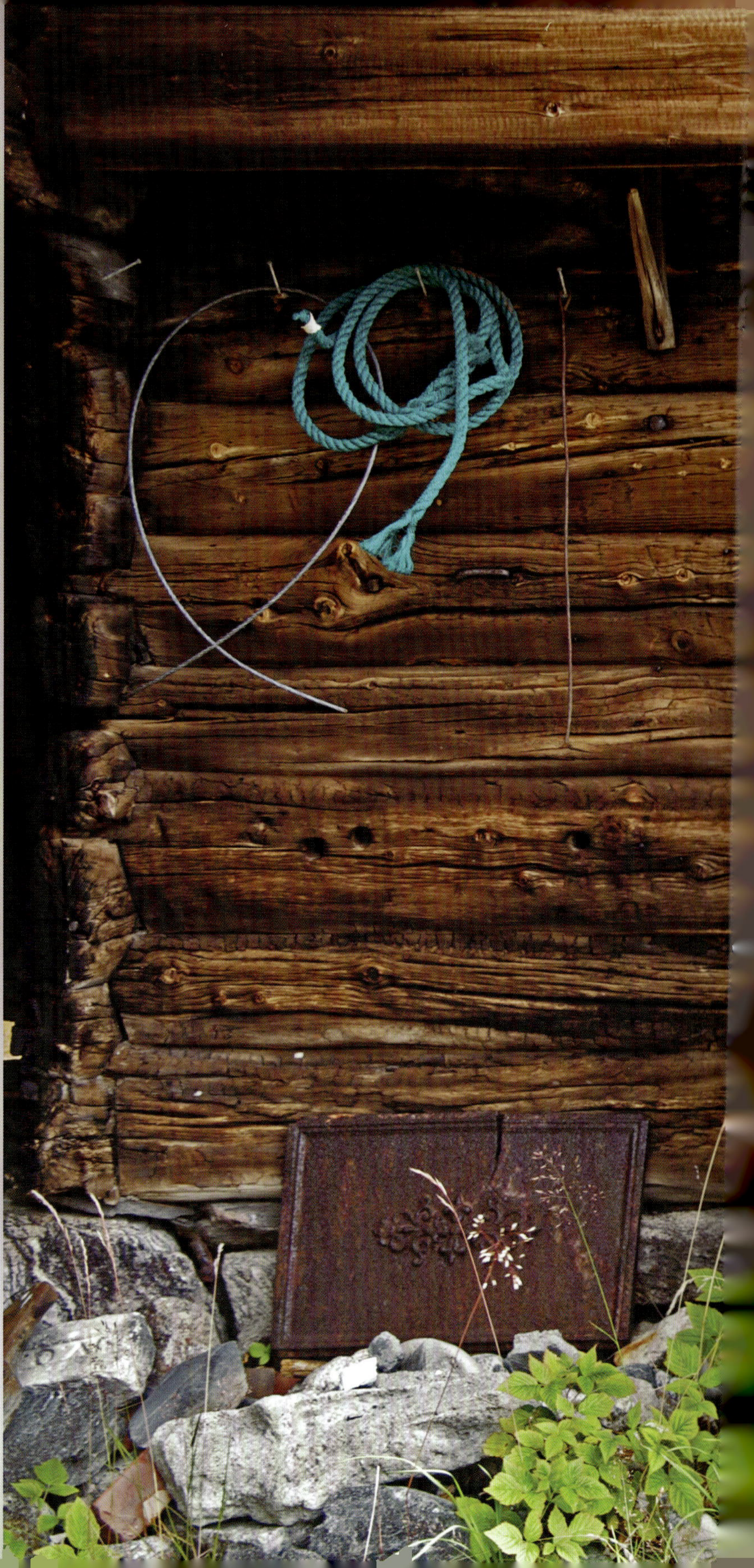

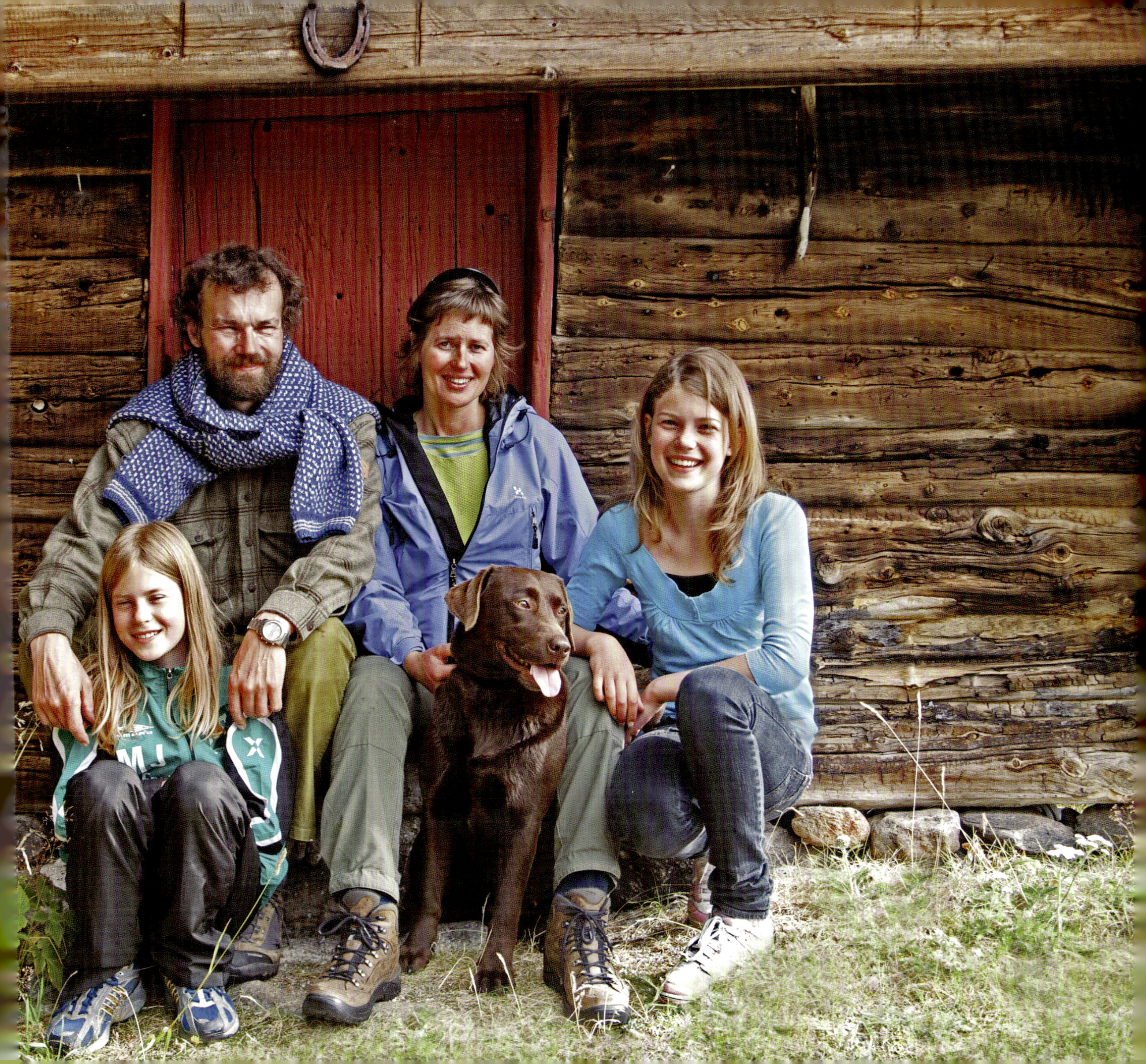

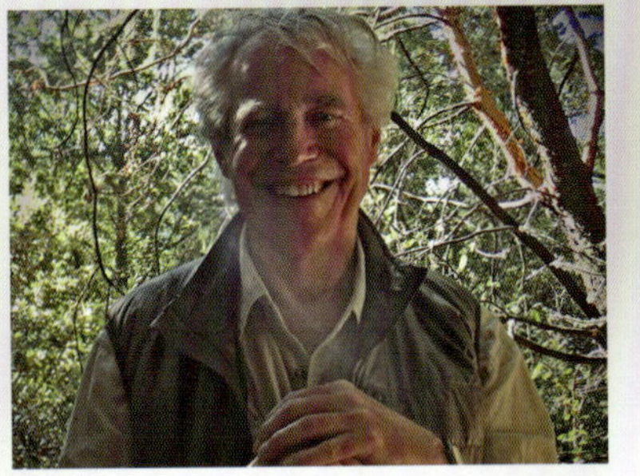

Davey Norket
Musician/Composer/Video Editor
www.norket.com

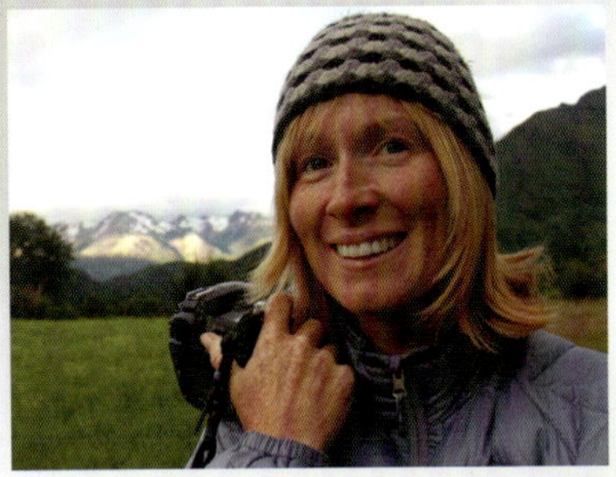

Bridget Besaw
Environmental Documentarian
www.bridgetbesaw.com

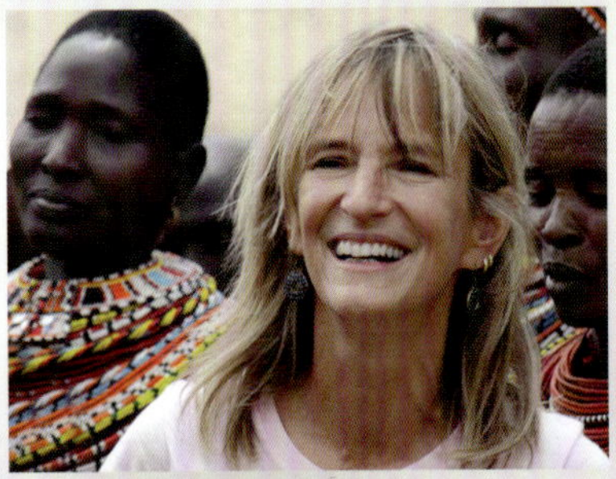

Rudi Dundas
Documentory Photographer
www.rudidundas.com

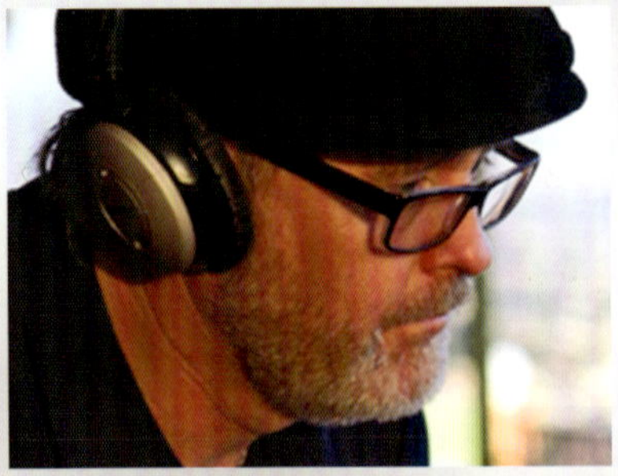

Christopher Hedge
Magnetic Poets/Composer
www.christopherhedge.com

OCEAN STUDIO

An alliance of adventure writers, photographers, filmmakers & composers working together to nurture a deeper understanding and empathy for the natural world

www.oceanstudios.net

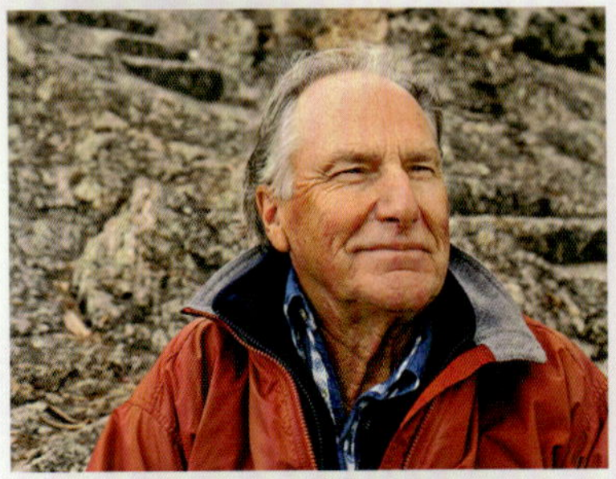

Leo LeBon
Adventure Travel Strategist
www.wanderlustconsulting.com

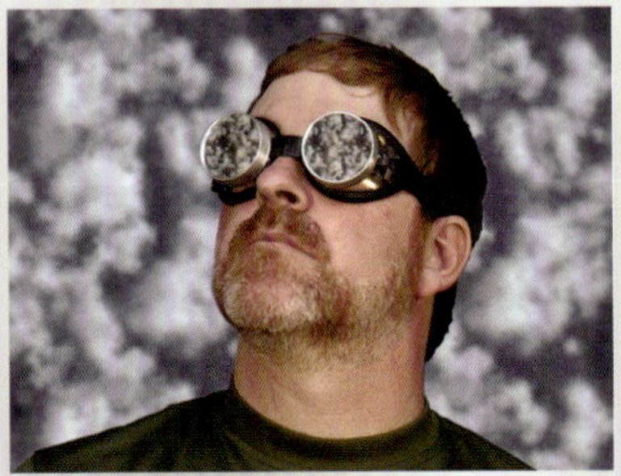

Scott Dewar
Magnetic Poets/Filmmaker
www.magneticpoets.com

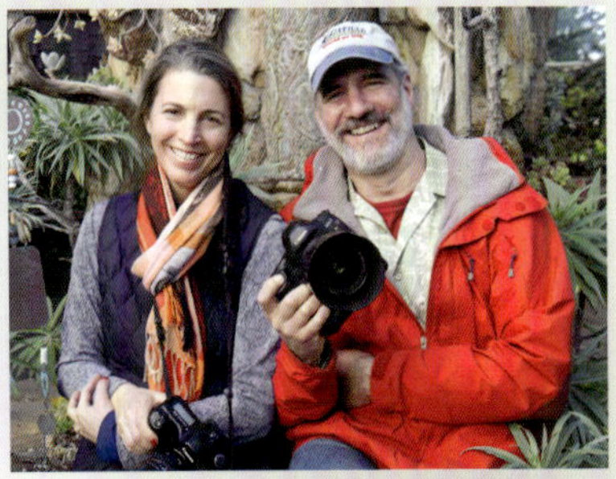

Bob & Becky Stender
Adventure Photographers
www.tibidabophotography.com

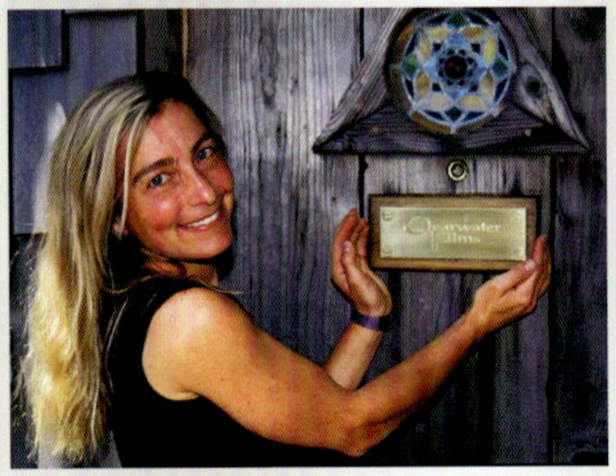

Lili Schad
Filmmaker/Artist
www.clearwaterfilms.com

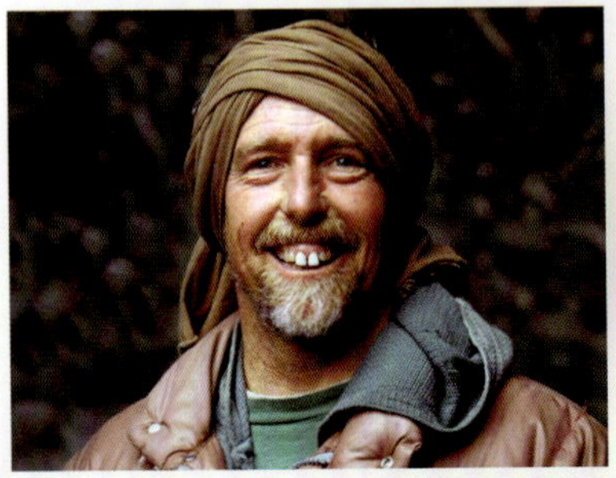

Eric Soares PhD
Author/Filmmaker
www.tsunamirangers.com

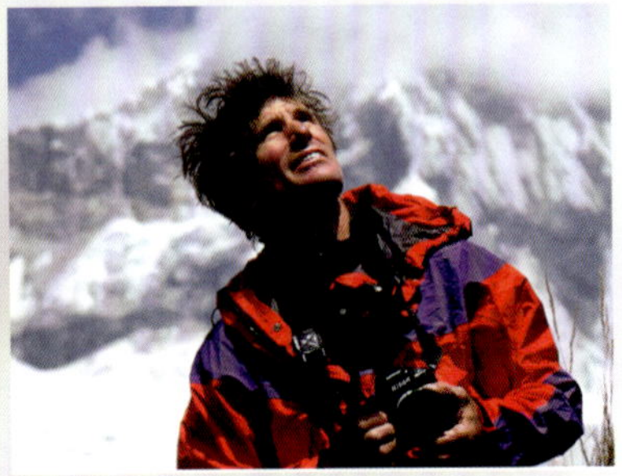

Galen Rowell
Adventure Photographer/Author
www.mountainlight.com

------------------ In Memoriam ------------------

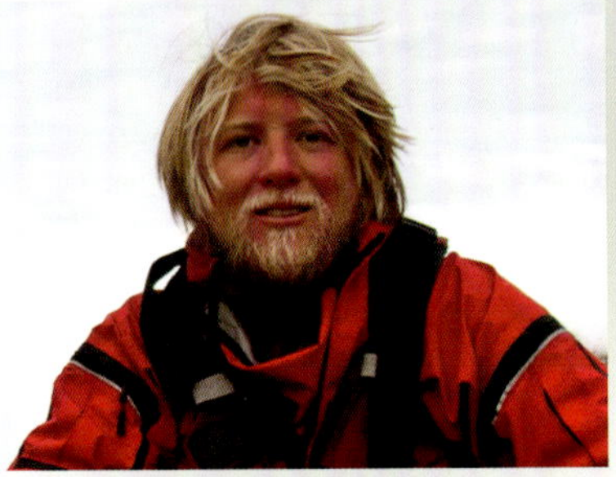

Erik Boomer
Adventure Photographer/Explorer
www.erikboomer.com

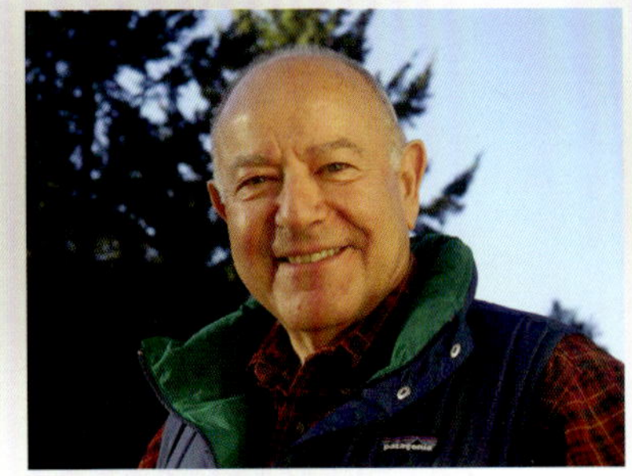

Gustavo Rabin PhD
Author/Psychologist
www.skylineg.com

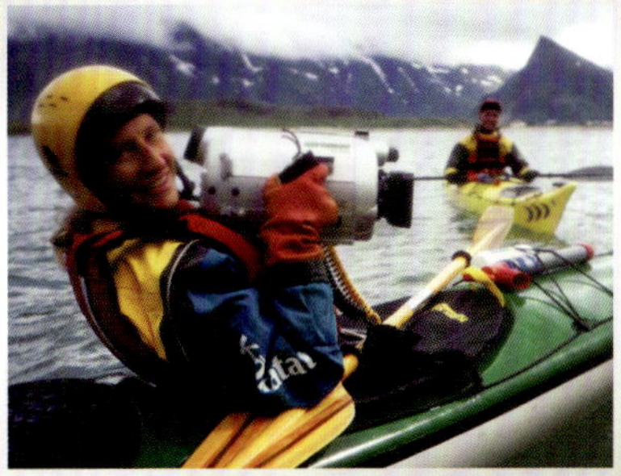

Allison Chase
Filmmaker/Producer
www.ventanapictures.com

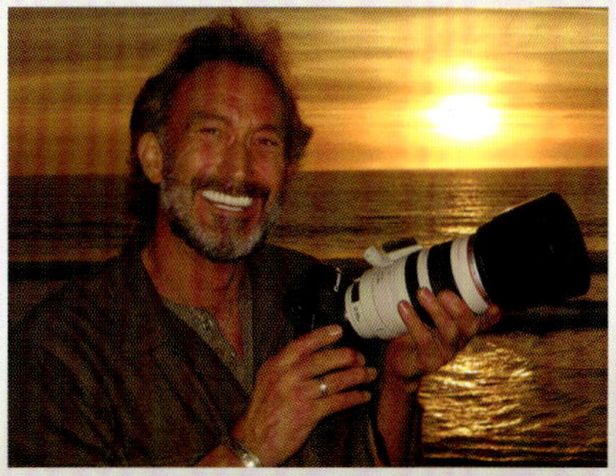

Dennis Swenson
Artist/Photographer/Counselor
www.dennisswenson.com

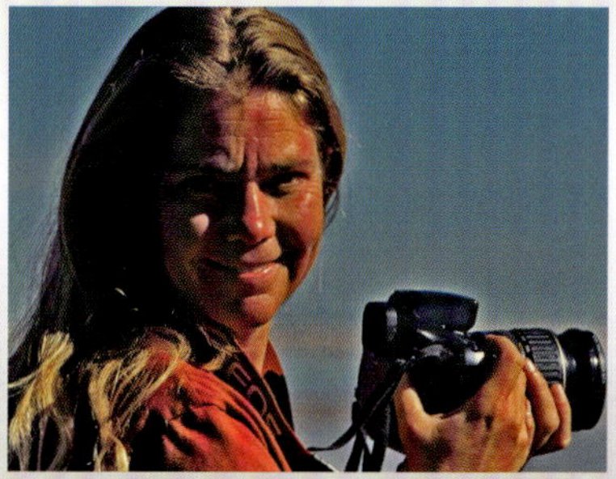

Arlene Burns
Freelance Adventurer
www.arleneburns.com

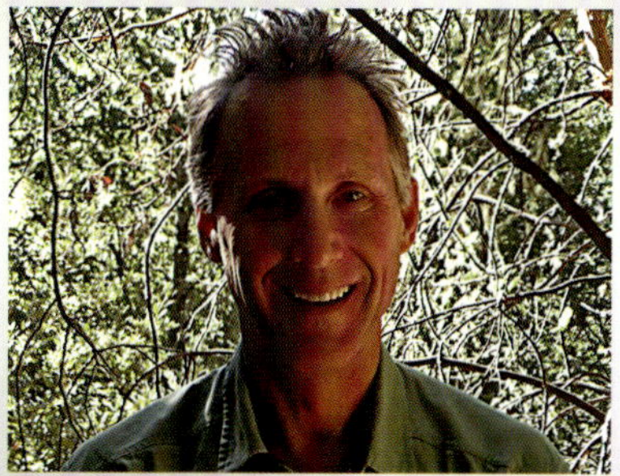

Steven King, PhD
Ethnobotanist/Author
www.napopharma.com

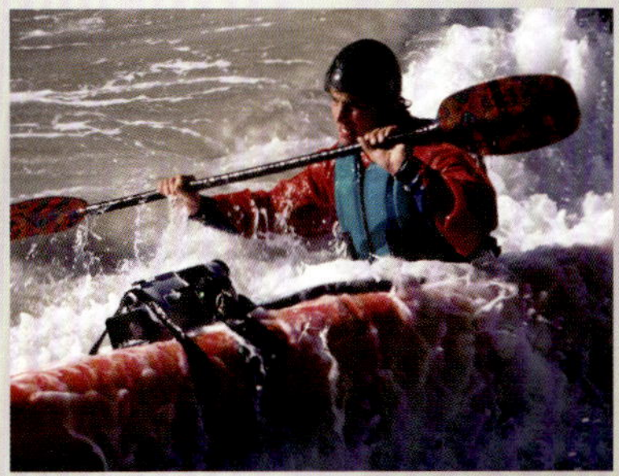

Gordon Brown
Adventure Filmmaker
www.gordonbrown.net

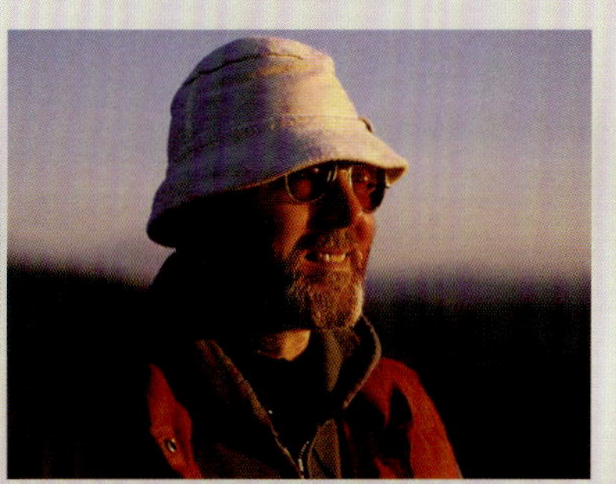

Jack Izzo, S. J.
Author/Filmmaker
www.jackizzo.com

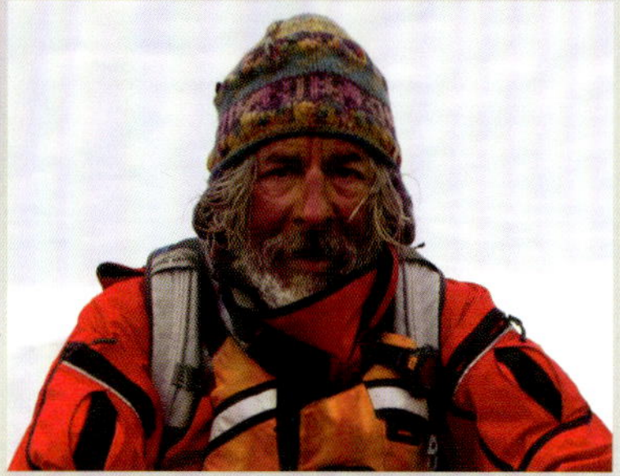

Jon Turk, PhD
Author/Explorer
www.jonturk.net

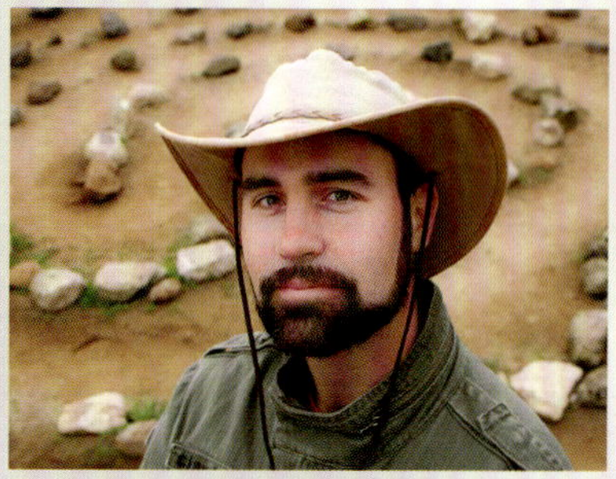

Lars Howlett
Photographer/Labyrinth Master
www.findlars.com

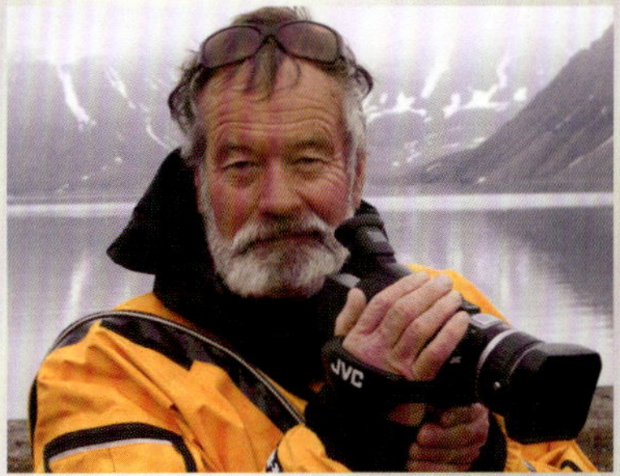

Mark Fraser
Adventure Filmmaker
www.thegoodfightthemovie.com

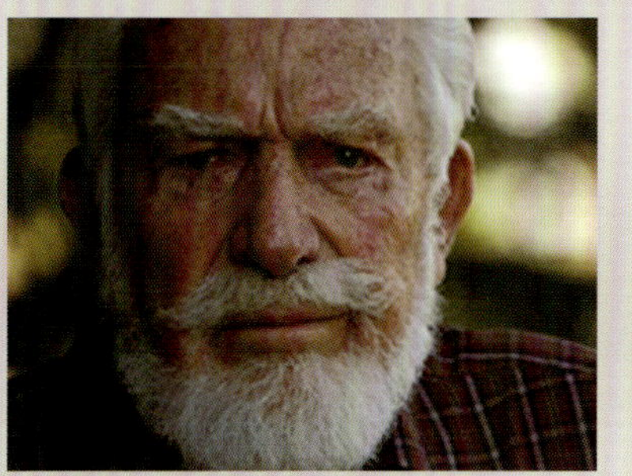

Martin Litton
Author/Conservationist
www.sequoiaforestkeeper.org

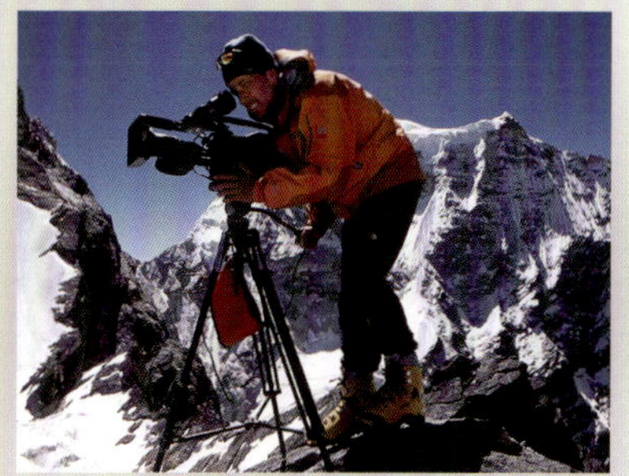

Michael Brown
Adventure Filmmaker
www.seracfilms.com.

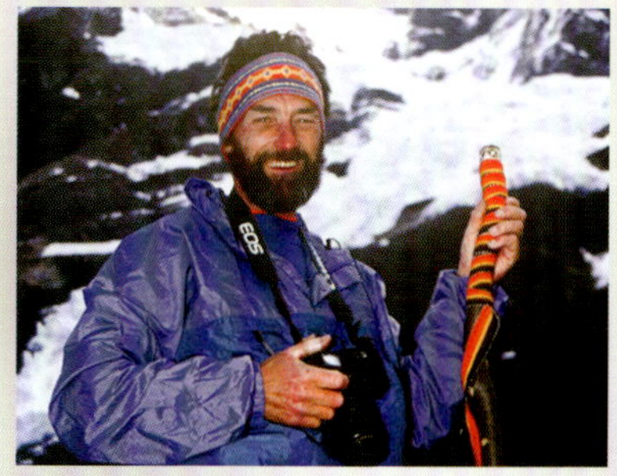

Michael Powers
Adventure Photojournalist
www.oceanstudios.net

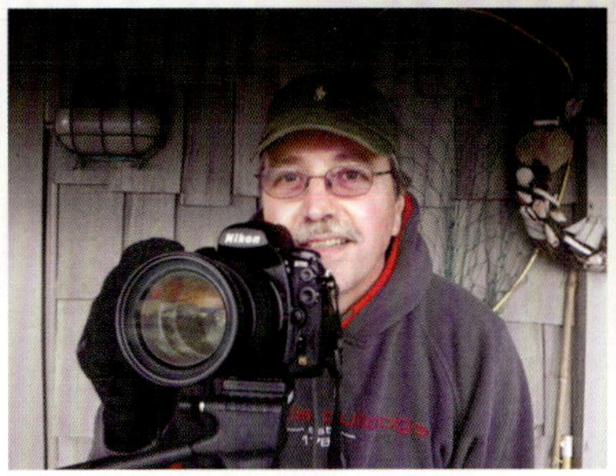

Roy Smith
Photographer/Web Strategist
www.hmbzenphoto.com

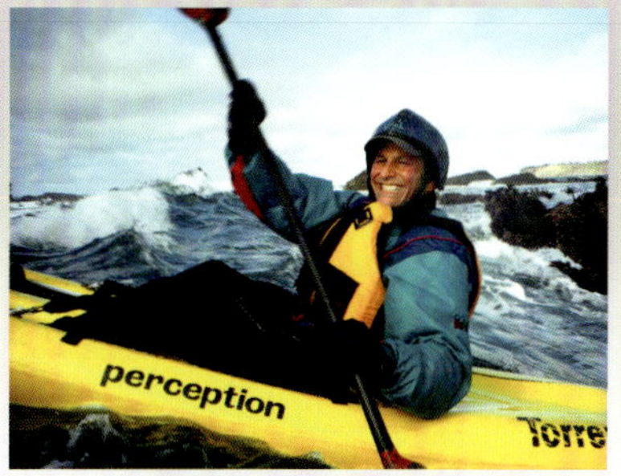

Steve Michelson
Filmmaker/Producer
www.lobitoscreekranch.com

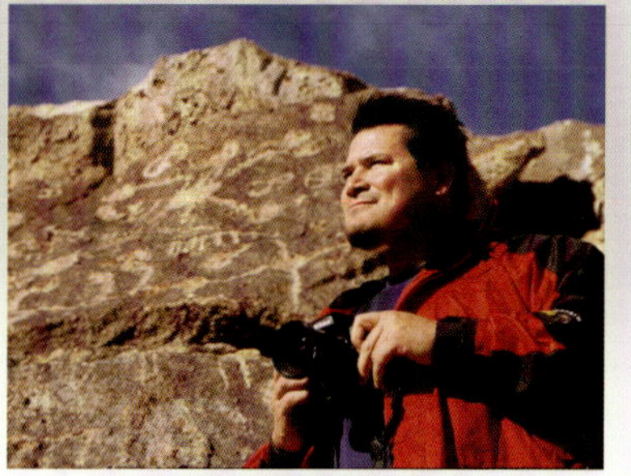

Tony Rowell
Adventure Photographer
www.tonyrowell.com

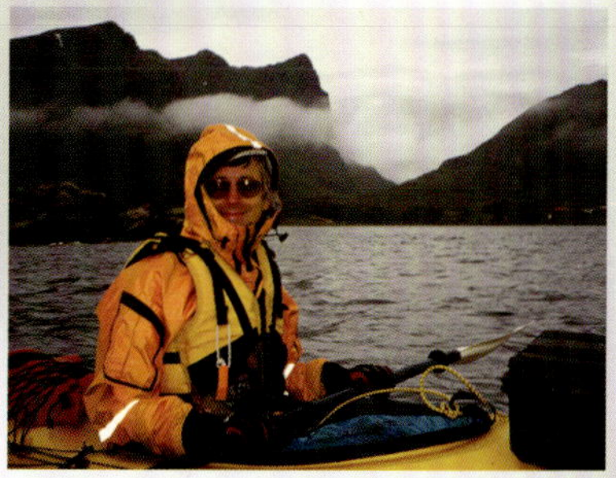

Robert Weiss, MD
Physician/Photographer
www.oceanstudios.net

RESOURCES

1-2 www.parks.ca.gov/?page_id=471
3-4 www.wildernesstravel.com www.peakfreaks.com/sherpa_culture.htm
5-6 www.wildernesstravel.com www.wavemag.com.np/issue/article324.html
7-8 www.wildernesstravel.com www.peakfreaks.com/sherpa_culture.htm
9-10 www.wildernesstravel.com www.welcomenepal.com
11-12 www.wildernesstravel.com www.peakware.com
13-14 www.wildernesstravel.com www.welcomenepal.com
14-16 www.karmaquests.com www.welcomenepal.com
17-18 www.wildernesstravel.com www.welcomenepal.com
19-20 www.wildernesstravel.com www.welcomenepal.com
21-22 www.karmaquests.com www.welcomenepal.com
23-24 www.karmaquests.com www.welcomenepal.com
25-26 ww.karmaquests.com www.welcomenepal.com
27-28 www.wildernesstravel.com www.peakfreaks.com/sherpa_culture.htm
29-30 www.karmaquests.com www.peakfreaks.com/sherpa_culture.htm
31-32 www.wildernesstravel.com ww.welcomenepal.com
33-34 www.karmaquests.com www.welcomenepal.com
35-36 www.wildernesstravel.com www.welcomenepal.com
37-38 www.karmaquests.com www.welcomenepal.com/
39-40 www.yosemitepark.com/backpacking-trips.aspx
41-42 www.norway.org/travel www.crossinglatitudes.com
43-44 www.norway.org/travel www.gonorway.com/norway/articles/87
45-46 www.norway.org/travel www.norway.org
47-48 www.visitjotunheimen.com/en/ www.norway.org/travel
49-50 www.crossinglatitudes≥com www.norway.org
51-52 www.openspacetrust.org www.openspace.org
53-54
55-56 www.mnn.net/berry.htm
57-58 www.openspace.org
59=60 www.openspace.org
61-62 www.mountaintravelsobek.com
63-64 www.mountaintravelsobek.com
65-66 www.mountaintravel.com
67-68 www.mountaintravelsobek.com
69-70 www.mountaintravelsobek.com
71-72 www.oars.com www.thegoodfightthemovie.com
73-74 www.oars.com www.thegoodfightthemovie.com
75-76 www.oars.com www.thegoodfightthemovie.com
77-78 www.wildernesstravel.com www.clearwaterfilms.com
79-80 www.clearwaterfilms.com www.openspacetrust.org
81-82 www.baynature.org
83-84 www.coastalchange.ucsd.edu
85-86 www.gordonbrown.net www.cobrakayaks.com
87-88 www.findlars.com www.hikinginbigsur.com
89-90 www.discoverlabyrinths.com www.findlars.com
91-92 www.experiencehalfmoonbay.com www.oceanstudios.net
93-94 www.ca.audubon.org/seabirds www.maverickssurfshop.com
95-96 www.findlars.com www.maverickssurfshop.com
97-98 www.tsunamirangers.com www.stormsurf.com
99-100 www.tsunamirangers.com www.stormsurf.com
101-102 www.tsunamirangers.com www.stormsurf.com
103-104 www.tsunamirangers.com www.oopskayak.org
105-106 www.tsunamirangers.com www.rumi.org.uk
107-108 www.tsunamirangers.com/books/extreme-sea-kayaking
109-110 www.tsunamirangers.com
111-112 www.tsunamirangers.com www.stormsurf.com
113-114 www.tsunamirangers.com www.tibidabophotography.com
115-116 www.gordonbrown.net www.tsunamirangers.com
117-118 www.tsunamirangers.com www.oopskayak.org
119-120 www.tsunamirangers.com www.nzkayaktours.com
121-122 www.tsunamirangers.com www.oopskayak.org
123-124 www.space.com/skywatching

125-126	www.tonyrowell.com www.mountainlight.com
127-128	www.wildernesstravel.com www.mountainlight.com
129-130	www.mountainlight.com www.everestnews.com/k2history.htm
131-132	www.summitpost.org/mount-shasta/150188
133-134	www.tsunamirangers.com www.stormsurf.com
135-136	www.tsunamirangers.com www.stormsurf.com
137-138	www.oars.com/california
139-140	www.mazatlantoday.net/mazatlan_cliff_divers.html
141-142	www.wildernesstravel.com www.seatrek.com
143-144	www.wildernesstravel.com
145-146	www.wildernesstravel.com www.travelteam.com/fiji
147-148	www.airlineamb.org www.visitguatemala.com
149-150	www.wildernesstravel.com
151-152	www.native-languages.org/quechua_culture.htm
153-154	www.conservacionpatagonica.org
155-156	www.wildernesstravel.com www.conservacionpatagonica.org
157-158	www.exchile.com www.conservacionpatagonica.org
159-160	www.conservacionpatagonica.org www.exchile.com
161-162	www.exchile.com ww.pygmyboats.com
163-164	www.adventuretravel.com www.torresdelpaine.com
165-166	www.adventuretravel.com www.torresdelpaine.com
167-168	www.exchile.com www.patagonisrising.com
169-170	www.exchile.com www.patagonisrising.com
171-172	www.exchile.com www.patagoniarising.com
173-174	www.exchile.com www.patagonisrising.com
175-176	www.conservacionpatagonica.org www.exchile.com
177-178	www.conservacionpatagonica.org www.exchile.com
179-180	www.akhistorycourse.org/articles/article.php?artID=94
181-182	www.jonturk.com www.erikboomer.com
183-184	www.wildernesstravel.com www.conservacionpatagonica.org
185-186	www.innovakayak.com www.stormsurf.com
187-188	www.oceankayak.com
189-190	www.takscalifornia.com
191-192	wwwmtsobek.com www.tanzaniaparks.com/kili.html
193-194	www.rudidundas.com www.africatravelresource.com
195-196	wwwmtsobek.com www.africatravelresource.com
197-198	www.wanderlustconsulting.com www.mtsobek.com
199-200	www.wildernesstravel.com
201-202	www.bridgetbesaw.com
203-204	www.guadalupecanyon.tripod.com
205-206	www.seracfilms.com www.gordonbrown.net
207-208	www.seracfilms.com
209-210	www.dennisswenson.com www.protides.com
211-212	www.yosemitepark.com/backpacking-trips.aspx
212-214	www.mount.rainier.national-park.com
215-216	www.gbgm-umc.org/umc-chile/
217-218	
219-220	www.nps.gov/redw www.avenueofthegiants.ne
221-222	
223-224	www.nabasque.org/NABO/sheepherding.htm
225-226	www.everytrail.com/destination/desolation-wilderness
227-228	www.ventanapictures.com www.gordonbrown.net
229-230	www.norway.org www.ventanapictures.com
231-232	www.wildlife.no www.norway.org/travel
233-234	www.oceanstudios.net www.norway.org/travel
235-236	www.ventanapictures.com www.gordonbrown.net
237-238	www.napali.org www.nzkayaktours.com
239-240	www.openspace.org www.parks.ca.gov/?page_id=24200
241-242	www.nzkayaktours.com www.napali.org
243-244	www.norway.org/travel www.norway.org

TOUCHSTONE EDITIONS
980 Lincoln Ave. Suite 200 B,
San Rafael California, 94901

T: 415.456.2934 F: 415. 456.4124

www.touchstoneeditions.com

TOUCHSTONE EDITIONS is an imprint of Channel Photographics

ISBN-13: 978-0-9910999-0-0

Text and Photos by Michael Powers unless otherwise noted
www.oceanstudios.net

www.wildinspirit.com

Printed in China by Global PSD www.globalpsd.com

TOUCHSTONE EDITIONS & Global Printing, Sourcing & Development (Global PSD), in association with American Forests and the Global ReLeaf programs, will plant two trees for each tree used in the manufacturing of this book. Global ReLeaf is an international campaign by American Forests, the nation's oldest nonprofit conservation organization and a world leader in planting trees for environmental restoration.

Replanted Paper

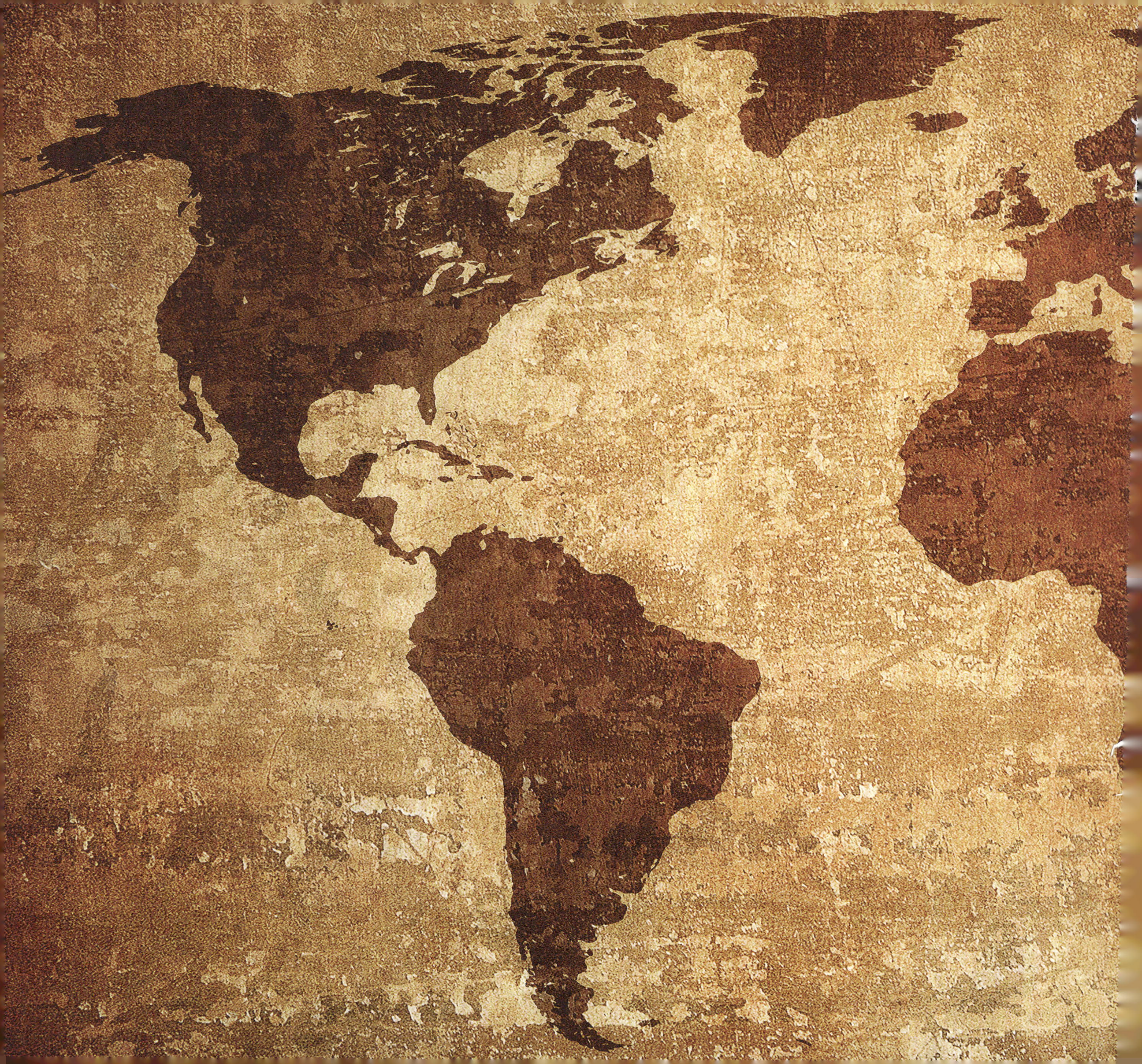